FORGOTTEN VOICES

Also available in the Forgotten Voices series:

Forgotten Voices of the Great War
Forgotten Voices of the Great War (illustrated)
Forgotten Voices of the Somme

Lest we Forget: Forgotten Voices from 1914–1945

Forgotten Voices of the Second World War
Forgotten Voices of the Second World War (illustrated)
Forgotten Voices of the Blitz and the Battle for Britain
Forgotten Voices of the Holocaust
Forgotten Voices of the Secret War
Forgotten Voices of D-Day
Forgotten Voices of Dunkirk

Forgotten Voices of the Falklands

Forgotten Voices of the Victoria Cross

FORGOTTEN VOICES OF BURMA

IN ASSOCIATION WITH
THE IMPERIAL WAR MUSEUM

JULIAN THOMPSON

EBURY
PRESS

1 3 5 7 9 10 8 6 4 2

This paperback edition published 2010
First published in 2009 by Ebury Press, an imprint of Ebury Publishing
A Random House Group Company

The Random House Group Limited Reg. No. 954009

Addresses for companies within the Random House Group can be found at
www.randomhouse.co.uk

A CIP catalogue record for this book is available from the British Library

The Random House Group Limited supports The Forest Stewardship Council (FSC),
the leading international forest certification organisation. All our titles that are
printed on Greenpeace approved FSC certified paper carry the FSC logo.
Our paper procurement policy can be found at www.rbooks.co.uk/environment

Mixed Sources
Product group from well-managed
forests and other controlled sources
www.fsc.org Cert no. TT-COC-2139
© 1996 Forest Stewardship Council

Printed in the UK by CPI Cox & Wyman, Reading, RG1 8EX

ISBN 9780091932374

To buy books by your favourite authors and register for offers visit
http://www.rbooks.co.uk

Contents

Maps

Author's Preface

The war in Burma was the largest land campaign fought by the Western Allies against the Japanese in the Second World War. For the British, it was the longest of any fought on land in that war.

Initially, the Japanese invaded southern Burma to protect the flank of their invasion of Malaya. They subsequently occupied the rest of Burma because they viewed it as the western bastion of the Greater East Asia Co-Prosperity Sphere, their name for their conquered territories. But, in addition, by holding Burma the Japanese were able to cut the only land route by which the Chinese could be supplied: the Burma Road that ran from Rangoon north-east into China. As an added bonus, Burmese oil would be a welcome addition to the Japanese economy.

The entry of Japan into the Second World War found the defence of Burma unprepared. No invasion threat from the east was anticipated; the British deemed the jungle and mountain terrain to be impassable by any invader. Although, strategically, the British colony was an outpost for the defence of India, no railways and only one underdeveloped road connected the two countries; the section from Imphal to Kalewa, some 185 miles, was a mixture of cart track and bridleway.

Since August 1940, Burma had been under command of the Commander-in-Chief Far East, based in Singapore. The Far East was, in the British Government's view, low on the priority list for all manner of warfighting equipment. Burma, as an adjunct to that theatre, was almost off the list altogether. Only on 12 December 1941, four days after the Japanese attack on Pearl Harbor, did General Sir Archibald Wavell, Commander-in-Chief India, finally persuade Winston Churchill that Burma should be part of his area of responsibility.

Once Burma had fallen to the Japanese, it took about two years for the British – in the persons of Winston Churchill and the Chiefs of Staff – to decide on strategy in the region. There were four courses open to them: one, to invade overland; two, to invade from the sea; three, a combination of the first two; four, to bypass Burma altogether and head straight to retake Malaya by seaborne assault. The British were not entirely free agents in the matter, for not only were the Americans the dominant partner in the war against Japan, but they also supplied most of the transport aircraft to the RAF and USAAF supporting the British effort in Burma. The Americans were not in the least interested in helping the British regain a lost part of their empire. Their sole motive for supporting the British was to maintain their supply route to Chiang Kai-shek's Nationalist Chinese, initially by air, but by road after north Burma was liberated.

Contrary to popular belief, the Japanese had no experience in fighting in the jungle before the invasion of Malaya in December 1941. They owed their success to the high standard of training and toughness of their soldiers. Long marches and demanding field exercises had transformed them into superb light infantry, able to cover long distances on foot over rough terrain, carrying heavy loads. Rugged, pitiless and redoubtable, they were a formidable foe. Surrender was inconceivable. Death – either at the hands of the enemy or by one's own – was the only honourable exit from the fight. Prisoners were regarded with contempt, as expendable, and treated accordingly. When the British met the Japanese in battle, their prejudiced opinions of the enemy as inferior suffered a severe shock. They found that, man for man, the Japanese were better soldiers than the Germans.

By the end of the campaign in Burma in August 1945, about 106,000 Japanese had been killed and wounded, and some 1,700 taken prisoner, of whom only four hundred were physically fit – the remainder being wounded or desperately ill. No regular officers surrendered, and none senior to major. Once captured, for the first week most prisoners tried to commit suicide, using whatever means they had to hand. A British officer reported seeing a Japanese prisoner who had cut his own throat with the jagged edge of a bully-beef tin. He was a soldier, not an officer. If prisoners survived, they cooperated with their interrogators, not through cowardice, but merely because no one had ever instructed them what to do in these circumstances, because it had never occurred to their senior commanders that any Japanese soldier would allow himself to be taken alive.

Desmond Whyte, a doctor with the Chindits, remarked:

> We underestimated the Japanese to begin with. They worshipped the Emperor as a God. They wished to die in his service. They had utter disregard of danger, and devious tactics; one could not help but admire them. In the early days they really were an invincible force until we learnt jungle craft and battle craft and realised we were superior. They were utterly ruthless and without compassion. I found a friend pinioned to a teak tree with a bayonet through both left and right wrist, and the lower limbs missing, eaten by jackals. The aim was to make us so terrified that we wouldn't wish to continue fighting. It had the opposite effect.

Until the British acquired the necessary jungle and battle craft, the Japanese were regarded as invincible. This was to change, but the process took time and cost many lives.

Burma is a large country, and if superimposed on a map of Europe, Fort Hertz in the extreme north would be in the middle of the North Sea, Mandalay near Paris, Rangoon where the Pyrenees meet the Mediterranean, and Moulmein on Marseilles. Victoria Point, at the southern end of the long isthmus of Tenassarim, would be three-quarters of the way across the Mediterranean.

The country is surrounded on three sides by mountain ranges covered in thick jungle. Four great rivers flow south into the Bay of Bengal. The Irrawaddy and its major tributary the Chindwin rise in the Himalayas to the north; to the east flow two more large rivers, the Sittang and the Salween. All have numerous tributaries, most of which are a serious obstacle to movement. The valleys in central Burma open out into thickly wooded plains, dotted with low hills. In the flatter areas rice is cultivated in paddy fields. South of Mandalay and Shwebo the country is arid with sparse vegetation.

In the cold weather, from mid-October to March, the climate is perfect, warm and dry by day and cool at night, but temperatures rise in April and May, and the heat strikes like an open oven with high humidity. The monsoon arrives in mid-May and lasts until about mid-September, enveloping the whole of Burma and Assam, except for the dry zone around Mandalay and Meiktila. During the monsoon malaria and dysentery flourish; the rivers swell; valleys and flat areas flood; thick cloud, thunderstorms and turbulence make flying extremely hazardous.

In one year, 1943–44, British and other Allied troops recorded 250,000 cases of malaria and dysentery. The rate of men falling sick in Burma equals those in earlier wars, before the introduction of modern medicine. For example, in 1943, for every man admitted to hospital with wounds, there were 120 from tropical diseases. By 1945 the rate dropped to ten men sick for one wounded, and in the last six months of the war, to six for one.

The Burmans, the indigenous Burmese, lived mainly in the centre of the country. They resented British rule, and disliked the thousands of Indians imported by the British to work on the railways and other public projects. They had no love for the Chinese, who, along with the Indians, had monopolised sections of the economy, including the rice trade, enriching themselves in the process. Before the British arrived, the Burmese had persecuted the Karens, Shans, Kachins and Chins, tribespeople living in the hills and mountains to the east, north and west of central Burma, and have continued to do so since independence in 1948.

In this book I use the term British to refer to forces from the then British Empire and Commonwealth. In Burma this included 340,000 Indians of many races: Sikhs, Rajputs, Baluchis, Punjabis and Gurkhas, to name but some. The Indians outnumbered the forces from all the other allies added together. Some 100,000 British fought in Burma, as did 90,000 Africans and about 66,000 Chinese. Around 60,000 Americans took part, most of them from the forty-seven United States Army Air Force (USAAF) squadrons (there were fifty-one British and Commonwealth squadrons). The overwhelming majority of accounts in my book are by soldiers from Britain – perfectly understandable in the archives of a national museum. It also reflects the fact that by the time the project was taken in hand by the Imperial War Museum, most soldiers of the old British Indian Army were difficult or even impossible to trace. Of those that have been interviewed, even fewer were translated, but some have now been transcribed and translated specifically for this book. The same constraint applies to the Africans and the Japanese.

The Indians who fought in Burma were part of the largest all-volunteer army in history. John Randle, whose testimony appears in this book, explains the ethos of that army:

The Indian soldier wasn't fighting for the defence of India against Hitler [or Japan]. He fought because in northern India, especially, there was a strong tradition of serving the British; and because of the culture of honour, *izzat*. Because of the land system, a small property was able to support only one son, so there was a culture of younger sons joining government service, the army or police. They got two square meals a day, pay, pensions, and were honoured and respected members of their community. Their whole history was one of service, for the Moguls and so forth, and was not anything to be ashamed of.

Following the outbreak of the Second World War in 1939, the Indian Army expanded thirteen-fold from its peacetime strength of 185,000 to nearly 2,500,000. This soon resulted in the 'milking' of experienced officers and NCOs from existing units to provide replacements in the Indian units fighting in the Middle East (from 1940 onwards), and in training centres to train the hugely expanded Indian Army. Thousands of Indian soldiers, along with their British officers, were captured by the Japanese in Malaya, and so were not available to fight in Burma. For this reason many Indian units in the early years of the campaign in Burma were not well trained or led; hence the censure levelled at these units by some of the voices in this book

Readers familiar with the 1957 film *Bridge on the River Kwai* will not find accounts of experiences on the Burma–Thailand Railway in this book, which focuses on the fighting in the Burma campaign. The 61,000 Allied prisoners of war who formed part of the workforce on the railway were captured in the earlier Malaya and Netherlands East Indies campaigns. They were hugely outnumbered by around 270,000 impressed labourers from Malaya, Thailand and the Netherlands East Indies. Prisoners of war taken by the Japanese in Burma were sent to Rangoon Jail.

What this book does capture is what it was like to fight in the demanding terrain and climate of Burma; and, from the British perspective, to be confronted by the most formidable soldiers encountered by anyone in the Second World War – the Japanese.

Julian Thompson, June 2009

Acknowledgements

Writing this book would not have been possible without the witnesses whose oral testimony was recorded by the Sound Archive of the Imperial War Museum. It is these witnesses that I must mention first. The expertise and painstaking attention to detail of the staff of the Sound Archive have ensured that the experiences of the witnesses have been recorded for posterity and assembled in such a way that researchers can access them readily. As so often in the past in my career as an author, Margaret Brooks, the Keeper of the Sound Archive, has been a great supporter, and for this I thank her, along with Terry Charman, Elizabeth Bowers, Abigail Ratcliffe and Madeleine James. I would particularly like to thank Richard McDonough, who has been a source of wise guidance and assistance.

I must also thank the Photographic Archive at the Imperial War Museum, especially Hilary Roberts and David Parry, for their help in this project. I am grateful to Barbara Levy, the Imperial War Museum's literary agent, for introducing me to the concept. I must also say thank you to my own agent, Jane Gregory, whose encouragement over many years has been invaluable.

Thanks to Liz Marvin and to Charlotte Cole, my editor at Ebury, who has been both patient and understanding in keeping me on track. I am most grateful to Hikari Nishimoto of King's College London, who translated and transcribed the Japanese interviews.

Last, but most certainly not least, my love and gratitude to Jane Thompson who has been my unwavering supporter and adviser.

Julian Thompson, June 2009

Introduction

Those who fought in Burma have never denigrated the courage of the Japanese soldier, airman or sailor. It can be argued that our nation has never fought such a tenacious, vicious and brave foe.

The 14th Army, the largest Allied Army of World War II, was built of many races and religions. It produced the leadership, spirit and courage to win and delivered the greatest defeat on land in the history of the Japanese nation.

I am a supporter of oral history as it brings the past to life and alerts the senses to the action of the moment. *Forgotten Voices of Burma* does just that. Julian Thompson, a proven battle commander himself, demonstrates in the cross section of those talking to us what it was like to fight, live and die in Burma. Duty, valour, selflessness, endurance, improvisation and above all comradeship capture the reader.

During the campaign I know my father met and spoke with many we hear from. He was so proud of these men and women of Burma. Some have since died but those who survive today, together with many from the Commonwealth and other Allies in that great army with its air forces and navies, still meet to continue their unique comradeship, and give help to those in need, through the Burma Star Association. Let us not forget there are also over 30,000 who still lie in Burma and very many more in Assam in the war cemeteries of Imphal and Kohima.

I wish Julian Thompson success with *Forgotten Voices of Burma*, and trust that our young men and women read, learn and realise that they owe much in their daily life to the generation who ensured their freedom today.

The Rt Hon The Viscount Slim
August 2009

Retreat

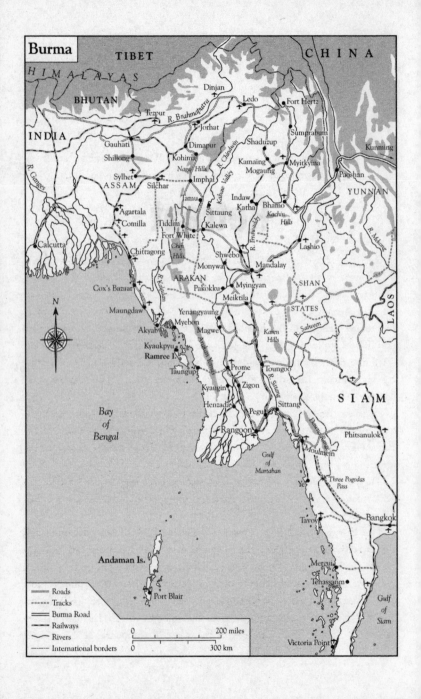

*The Japs fought with great ferocity and courage. We were arrogant about the
Japs, we regarded them as coolies. We thought of them as third rate.
My goodness me, we soon changed our tune.*

On 14 December 1941, the Japanese captured Victoria Point on the southern tip of Burma. By this time the Japanese had invaded Hong Kong and Malaya. Hong Kong fell on Christmas Day 1941, and Singapore on 15 February 1942. A month before the fall of Singapore, the Japanese had seized airfields in the Kra Isthmus of Burma, at Mergui, Victoria Point and Tavoy. Following this, the Japanese Fifteenth Army, consisting of the 33rd and 55th Divisions, deployed in Siam (now Thailand), were waiting for the moment to advance to seize Rangoon when their campaign in Malaya neared completion.

Originally the garrison of Burma had consisted of two British battalions, four locally recruited battalions of Burma Rifles, and six battalions of the Burma Frontier Force. The first priority of these troops was internal security, to contain dissent among the Burmese (or Burmans). During 1941, the troop level was increased by raising more battalions of the Burma Rifles, forming the 1st Burma Division, and shipping in two Indian infantry brigades.

The Burma Rifles had consisted exclusively of Karens, Kachins and Chins, with British officers; the Burmans were considered unfit for military service, as being neither loyal nor martial enough. Although, under political pressure, some were recruited when the Burma Rifles was expanded, most proved unreliable and even treacherous when subjected to the test of battle.

The Japanese invasion found Burma defended by the 1st Burma Division and 17th Indian Division, under the overall command of Lieutenant

General J. T. Hutton. He sent the 1st Burma Division to central Burma to cover the routes in from the east from the Mekong Valley, along the Burma–Indo–China border. Major General 'Jackie' Smyth's 17th Indian Division was ordered to hold the line of the Salween River and cover Rangoon.

The battle for Burma was lost on 23 February 1942, early in the campaign, at the disaster at the Sittang River, when the British demolished the only bridge too early, leaving half their soldiers on the wrong side. This was followed by the longest fighting retreat in the history of the British Army, 1,100 miles, ending on 10 May when the British withdrew into Assam over the Chindwin River in north-east Burma. If properly defended, the Sittang position would have provided a good chance to impose a serious delay on the Japanese, and buy time for more British reinforcements to arrive in Burma. The battle was lost by attempting to hold too far forward, and underestimating the enemy. The confusion was made worse by pitting inexperienced troops against some of the best soldiers in the world.

INVASION AND DISASTER

Major General John 'Jackie' Smyth
GOC, 17th Indian Division

Hutton was out of his element as a battlefield commander in Burma. When Alexander arrived to take over, it was too late. Had he been there earlier, the Prime Minister of Australia might not have refused to send the two Australian divisions to Burma. Also, the Sittang disaster might not have occurred.

In early December, I was told by Wavell, then C-in-C India, that two of my brigades were being sent to Singapore, which came as a great shock to me. I was to go to Burma with my one remaining brigade plus two new ones. Wavell did not give the impression that he thought there was any threat to Burma at all.

Lieutenant Anthony Dillon
1st Battalion, Gloucestershire Regiment

My battalion was stationed on Mingaladon airfield, near Rangoon. There was no threat as far as we could tell. The war was a long way away, and there was a

The Japanese enter Tavoy in southern Burma on 19 January 1942, greeted by Burmese inhabitants who saw the invasion as an opportunity to gain independence from Britiish rule.

feeling of apathy. The amount of training we did before the Japanese invaded Burma was minimal, we were an Internal Security battalion; and there was a considerable amount of unrest in Burma.

We were badly equipped, signalling by heliograph or line. We had few vehicles, our mortars and machine-guns were carried on mules. We were unfit for modern war. In the days just before the Japanese attack on Pearl Harbor, a lot of US aid came in by sea to Rangoon and was taken up to China up the Burma Road. When the Japs bombed Rangoon, the Chinese abandoned the vehicles and equipment in the docks and we helped ourselves to all this stuff.

Private Neville Hogan
2nd Battalion, Burma Rifles Armoured Car Section
I am a Karen and lived in Rangoon, where my father worked as a shipping manager. Before the war I joined the Burma Auxiliary Force, Rangoon Battalion. In order to join, I lied about my age, showing the recruiting sergeant my elder brother's birth certificate.

Most Burmese civilians were anti-British. They wanted independence. The Karens, the Chins and Shans liked the British. The Burma army pre-war was mostly Karen.

In December 1941 I was a private soldier at Mingaladon Airfield with the Armoured Car Section of the 2nd Burma Rifles. The Japanese bombed us on Christmas Day. No one was killed or wounded, but two out of four of our so-called armoured cars had shrapnel holes in them. We then witnessed Rangoon being drained of the civilian population. The people, mainly Indians, walked past Mingaladon, which was about twelve miles out of Rangoon; the City was a ghost town. My mother and sister left at this time and went to north Burma and eventually into India.

Corporal William Norman
Mortar Platoon, 2nd Battalion, Duke of Wellington's Regiment
My battalion was in Peshawar training for operations on the North-West Frontier when the Japanese invaded Malaya. I was a bandsman. I remember saying to the RSM that we ought to be training for jungle warfare to fight the Japs in Malaya. In January 1942, all sorts of equipment started to arrive; we were still equipped as the British army had been in 1918. We got Bren guns, mortars. We had never fired a mortar. I was in the mortar platoon, formed

Neville Hogan, as a lieutenant later in the war.

from the band. We got radios, which no one knew how to work.

In late January we went by train to Madras. We were all excited and glad to be getting into the war at last. We embarked on a ship, and noticed that the ship was going east so we thought we were going to Malaya. We started to train on our new weapons, we all fired two rounds from the Boyes anti-tank rifle. We arrived at Rangoon to be greeted with the news that Singapore had fallen. We were amazed to see that the Burmese were not Indian, but Asiatic. We knew nothing about the place.

Mrs Margaret ('Beth') Bootland
Wife of RSM 1st Battalion, King's Own Yorkshire Light Infantry

Alan and I, with our five-year-old son Ian, lived in the sergeant major's house at Maymyo, where the battalion was stationed. Although the war against Germany had been going on for a couple of years, to begin with we never thought the war would affect us. But one day Alan said that the Americans were getting worried about the Japanese. We listened to the news on the wireless, and when we heard about Pearl Harbor, we knew we were in for it.

One Sunday morning after an early game of tennis I was in the bath. I heard a roar of planes, stood up in the bath, peeped through the net curtains. I saw the palm trees waving, thought it's only a strong wind, and sat back in the bath. I heard Alan running up the path shouting, 'Where are you, Beth?'

I replied, 'I'm in the bath.'

He told me, 'Get out quick, it is an air raid.'

He pounded upstairs shouting, 'Get out, get out.'

I jumped out of the bath, had a quick rub with the towel and tried to pull my panties on, and the Celanese material stuck to my wet legs. Try as I could I couldn't get them on.

He asked me what I was doing, and I said, 'I can't get my panties on.'

He said, 'Come out, put on my big army greatcoat which I have got here, grab your clothes off the chair.'

As soon as I was out, he asked where Ian was, and I told him that he was away somewhere on his cycle with his friends. Alan went off to find him. The gravel hurt my bare feet as I ran down the drive in Alan's greatcoat, holding my clothes, making for the slit trench in the garden. Each slit trench in the married quarters area had an armed soldier in it. I told the one in mine to turn his back while I dressed. To my relief, Ian eventually arrived.

The quarters were full because the Gloucestershire families had been evacuated from Rangoon, which had not been captured yet, but had been bombed. I had to go round all the families to find out how many pregnant women there were, so the army knew how many would require evacuation by air.

Major Charles MacFetridge
Officer Commanding 3rd Indian Light Anti-Aircraft Battery

On arrival at Rangoon we found the docks deserted because the Japs had bombed the docks on Christmas Day. We found a good assembly area about fifteen miles outside Rangoon near Mingaladon airfield. I deployed two troops to defend the airfield, and one troop moved by rail and boat over the river Salween to Moulmein.

On the last day of January I decided to pay the troop at Moulmein a visit, as a boost to morale. I thought Japs were still well to the south in Tenassirim. While I was travelling in a Tiger Moth with the soldiers' pay in a bag, the pilot indicated that he had been recalled to base at Rangoon, telling me that the Japs had overrun Moulmein. So I had four guns on the wrong side of the mighty Salween River. In the confused fighting there I lost all four guns.

Private Neville Hogan
2nd Battalion, Burma Rifles Armoured Car Section

At the end of January, the armoured car section was ordered to go to the south of Burma on the road to Martaban and Moulmein. On 19 February 1942 (my brother's birthday, which is why I can remember the date) we were ambushed in a roadblock nine miles north of Martaban. The leading car crashed through the roadblock. I was in the second car. We came around the bend in the road to see the enemy, who had been sitting on the trees forming the roadblock, shoot to their feet in surprise. They turned out to be Thai soldiers, forced by Japs to fight us. We opened fire as did they. They were using small calibre armour-piercing bullets, which came straight through our armour. I was wounded in the right thigh. We were not expecting to be ambushed, as far as we were concerned the war was on the other side of the bay, twelve miles away. Our armoured cars were First World War vintage, and the bullets jammed the turret preventing it from training round. We backed up the road, round the bend out of sight, and the Thais did not follow up.

We then fought a rearguard action all the way to the Sittang Bridge. We were bombed three times by Blenheim bombers of the RAF, despite standing in the paddy fields waving to them.

Second Lieutenant John Randle
Officer Commanding B Company, 7th/10th Baluch Regiment

I was a newly commissioned second lieutenant commanding a company. We arrived in the middle of an air raid at Rangoon, and moved by train to lower Burma in the general area east of the Sittang and west of the Salween. The part we went to was rubber, not jungle, and we were used to the vast open plains of our training area in India. I like trees, but, in rubber plantations, with no horizon, it is a bit depressing and confining.

The Japs had barely started their offensive; we guarded bridges, then deployed on the west bank of the Salween, before pulling back to Kuzeik on the River Salween opposite Pa-an. The Salween is broader than the Rhine at this point. The brigade was dispersed. Our role was to hold the waterfront at Kuzeik, and we established company patrol bases to try to identify if and when the Japanese crossed the river, at which point the brigade reserve battalion would come up from Thaton and drive the Japanese back into the Salween. The positions had been dug by 1st/7th Gurkhas, concentrating on holding the river front and hadn't been developed as a perimeter to face an attack from the west. Because we had two companies out in bases, and one holding the front, the perimeter facing west was practically non-existent. Because the perimeter was so shallow our own mortars and the two mountain guns in support could not fire on our own front.

The 1st/7th Gurkhas had already given the 215th Regiment a bloody nose at Pa-an, before being relieved by 7th/10th Baluch, but this did not deter this very battle-experienced Japanese Regiment, experts in night attacks.

Corporal William Norman
Mortar Platoon, 2nd Battalion, Duke of Wellington's Regiment

We were deployed near the coast east of Rangoon, in case of a landing across the Gulf of Martaban. We were not there long, but did fire our mortars. A despatch rider came up and we were on the move again. The mortars and ammunition, 150 rounds per mortar, were on fifteen-hundredweight trucks, but we had to march. As we marched we got covered from head to foot in dust and were continually thirsty. Whenever I think of Burma I think of dust and thirst, not jungle, we were not in that part of Burma. Although there was some jungle, it was not continuous.

The motor transport sergeant came along and shouted 'anyone who can drive over here'. The motor transport had been issued and there weren't enough drivers. Some who volunteered couldn't even drive, they volunteered to get out of the marching and the dust. We were entrained at Pegu and went across the Sittang River and to a place called Kyaikto. From there we travelled in trucks and took up a position in the village, where the villagers greeted us and gave us tea.

Second Lieutenant John Randle
Officer Commanding B Company, 7th/10th Baluch Regiment

A Company were in a patrol base at Myainggale, seven miles south of the battalion position. I was told to take over from A Company, and my Subedar, Mehr Khan, went off with one platoon as advance party. During the night the Japanese attacked and, as we learned subsequently, wiped out my platoon with Subedar Mehr Khan, and a platoon of A Company, the remainder of the company having already left. As I was moving to Myainggale with my remaining two platoons, I ran into the middle of 215 Regiment just getting across and taking up positions on the west bank of the Salween. I had a hairy old night, lost a few chaps, but managed to get my two platoons out back to the main position. The visibility was quite good, in banana plantations, and, with the full moon you could see about fifty yards, it was so light you threw a moon shadow. The CO had not laid down routes for my company and A company to move on, in order to avoid a clash, and I was worried about having a shoot-out with them. A Company were to move, leaving one platoon under Subedar Mehr Khan of B Company as soon as he arrived. We were in single file one platoon leading, followed by Company HQ, and the other platoon, when a man charged in to our column. I thought it was one of my soldiers running away, and shouted at him. It was a Jap who ran off into the bush. A couple of Japs were shot by my men, the first dead Jap I had seen. There was quite a lot of firing, and I realised there were quite a lot of Japs about. I tried to get through on my radio, which didn't work. So I sent my runner, the company bugler, back with a message to my CO to tell him there were a lot of Japs about. They cut in behind us and we could hear the runner

11

screaming as they killed him with swords and bayonets. This was followed by an enormous lot of firing a couple of miles away from the base we were going to relieve. The Japs were running about, in a fair state of confusion too, having just come across the river. We had no idea what tactics we should adopt. I just formed a circle which, looking back, was the best thing to do: river on one side, Japs on two sides. It was pure luck, not cleverness. It was clear to me there were a considerable number of Japs to the south of me, so I decided to return to the battalion position. I only lost a couple of chaps. Luckily I picked a route where there were no Japs and got back OK.

Corporal William Norman
Mortar Platoon, 2nd Battalion, Duke of Wellington's Regiment
In the morning a lot of fire came from our right flank, and we heard that a Burma Rifle battalion had all pushed off in a panic. We were ordered to withdraw. We didn't think much of this, we had not seen the Japs yet. As we were marching through high elephant grass a lot of aircraft came over and there was an argument about which type they were. The fellows just out from England who were 'experts', said they were Hurricanes. The planes circled and started diving down. We thought they were going to give the Japs hell. They weren't Hurricanes and they started to give us hell. We withdrew into a rubber plantation. All the trees were in lines. As we heard the planes diving in, the men tried to hide behind the trees in a long line. Actually the aircraft were RAF attacking our transport on the road.

Second Lieutenant John Randle
Officer Commanding B Company, 7th/10th Baluch Regiment
The next day they dive-bombed us. We weren't far from a major airfield at Cheng Mai across the Thai border. Slit trenches saved us losing many chaps although we had no overhead cover. Morale was OK, and the chaps were not too upset.

That night at about midnight, we were attacked by 215 Regiment and pinned against the Salween. The CO had sent one of my platoons and a platoon from another company out on a patrol, God knows what for, so I was down to one platoon, and a section of two Vickers medium machine guns. At about twelve o'clock (midnight) the Japs came in and we had hand-to-hand fighting. They overran us and C Company, whose commander got an immediate DSO.

John Randle as a captain.

The Japs came in with no artillery support in what started as a silent night attack. When they got close, they screamed *banzai* and came charging in shoulder-to-shoulder. The Vickers fired across my front and caused heavy casualties to the Japs. They surged into Company HQ, I killed the chap coming for me. I was standing up firing my revolver, and missed first time. My CSM was grappling with a Jap. My batman was killed by a grenade. Just before dawn, realising if we stayed we would get taken prisoner, we charged out and then lay up about 150 yards away, and after first light heard a second assault going in, on battalion HQ. Then we had a pause, then at about seven o'clock the next morning they finished us off. We lost 289 killed, and 229 taken prisoner in our first engagement.

I had fever and a temperature of 102. It took me two days to get back to our lines. I had two soldiers with me. We had no map, no compass. A whole Jap battalion, the 111th/215th passed me as I lay up. We got back to the Donthami river, where I heard a shout, and thought oh Christ, after all this. They were waving, it was the 1st/7th Gurkhas and they sent a boat over.

I rejoined the battalion. We were staked out there like a goat for the Jap tiger and sacrificed for no reason. The CO was killed and we lost over sixty per cent of our officers. Only about fifty of the battalion got away, but we had quite a big B Echelon, who were not involved, and the two platoons sent out on patrol got away. With the exception of one officer, the Japs butchered all our wounded. News of this got back to us and this conditioned my, and the whole battalion's, attitude towards the Japs. We were not merciful to them for the rest of the war. We didn't take any prisoners.

Private Neville Hogan
2nd Battalion, Burma Rifles Armoured Car Section
On arrival at the Sittang Bridge we dug slit trenches at the foot of the bridge. The next morning all hell broke loose as the Japs attacked our position, a settlement round a pagoda. Came down the hill straight at us at first light, with a crackle of fire. Our officer Keith Laurie had gone over the bridge to get orders from HQ. Our other officer was wounded.

We had no telephone, no radios, it was chaos. A private soldier, George Hyde, took command, when we were all about to run back across the bridge. We fired at the Japs with our .45 pistols and they were effective, and drove the enemy back. We all said 'this is good', and jumped back into our trenches.

Major General John 'Jackie' Smyth
GOC, 17th Indian Division

During operations around Sittang, Wavell came to visit us and instead of congratulating us on holding off two Jap divisions with one division, he spent the whole time saying that the Japs were useless, and therefore by implication we were worse.

The Sittang disaster was the cause of the loss of Rangoon and Burma; totally unnecessarily. We had been withdrawing towards the Sittang with its single-track railway bridge. I made it clear to Hutton that we must not be caught on the enemy side of the river with this one narrow way across behind us. On 12 February, I sent Brigadier 'Punch' Cowan, my Chief of Staff, to Hutton and told him that it was the opinion of all of us that if we were to get everyone across, I must start immediately that day. Hutton was under great pressure from Wavell and the Prime Minister not to withdraw at all. At the time he was trying to get the Australian Prime Minister to allow the two Australian Divisions, who were at sea on their way to Australia, to divert to Burma. It was thought that the Australian Prime Minister would not agree if the British were retreating.

On 19 February Hutton came forward and said that saving 17 Division intact was now the most important priority. We were faced by two divisions and a superior air force; it was going to be a desperate race to get anyone back over the Sittang.

Second Lieutenant John Randle
Officer Commanding B Company, 7th/10th Baluch Regiment

We assembled, pretty demoralised after an appalling baptism of fire, then moved east of the Sittang River and got involved in the early stages of the Sittang bridge debacle. All the Punjabi Mussulmen were put into one company of two platoons, which I commanded. We were at Mokpalin on the day of the opening part of the Sittang battle and ordered to move up the railway line and cross the bridge to the west side. The Battalion was formed into two companies. The 2i/c was in command, Pat Dunn. As we were moving to the bridge still on the east side, my company was the first to come under fire from Pagoda Hill, from Jap MMG, and took casualties. One of my platoons panicked and ran back and joined the rest of the battalion. I arrived at the bridge and reported to the CO of the 4th/12th Frontier Force Regiment who were holding the bridge. He told me to go up and give Sam Manekshaw of C Company a hand.

I went up and gave Sam the best help I could. Certain amount of firing, Jap probing attacks. Then the rest of the battalion came up, and we were ordered across the bridge. We came under desultory fire as we crossed the bridge.

'Jackie' Smyth took no proper steps to defend the bridge. There was no close bridge garrison, no proper fire plan, no proper defence. This bridge was the jugular of the division. We didn't see much of the Jap attack. They were just probing at the first stage. They used to take a commanding bit of ground and sit to see what we would do about it. We would attack and take heavy casualties. By holding Pagoda Hill they had a key feature overlooking the bridge and approaches to it. Smyth lacked moral courage, he should have pushed the 1st/4th Gurkha Rifles across and dug in a proper position in depth. I didn't know all this at the time. I didn't know what the hell was going on in my own little world.

Corporal William Norman
Mortar Platoon, 2nd Battalion, Duke of Wellington's Regiment
Arriving at Mokpalin we took up positions in the paddy, wet with sweat, and dying of thirst. During the night we fired in a panic like the Burmese. Somebody would see something, fire a shot, then another and in no time all the platoon was firing at nothing. All units did this until they learned better. The Japs were there shouting out to us. Things like 'all NCOs to me', and 'all KOYLIs come here'.

During the night there had been a tremendous explosion. Everybody said the bridge had been blown up and we were cut off.

Second Lieutenant John Randle
Officer Commanding B Company, 7th/10th Baluch Regiment
After crossing the bridge we took up position in the middle of bamboo thickets, and heard a loud bang and realised the bridge was blown. My CO and I went down to the bank to see what we could do. It was chaos with Gurkha and Indian and British soldiers swimming across, some wounded. We went into the water and helped them out, and brewed up tea for some of them. When I was with Sam Manekshaw I had seen the 2nd Battalion, Duke of Wellington's Regiment moving up across the bridge, very cheerfully going

in to battle. Now some of them were swimming back. The river is wide and we could not fire back at the Japs.

Corporal William Norman
Mortar Platoon, 2nd Battalion, Duke of Wellington's Regiment
We came to the Sittang, a huge river, and we were on our own. I thought what are we going to do? Along came another fellow from the band, and he said that he had tried swimming, but had turned back. Upriver I could see the two spans of the bridge hanging in the water.

Jack found a bamboo pole. I stripped the Bren, threw it into the water, stripped to shorts and started swimming. We swam and swam, I have no idea for how long. The bamboo pole was getting waterlogged and would only support one person. There was someone swimming along behind, and I said, 'If you want to rest on this pole, you can't.' This chap said, 'I am a good swimmer, I am Anglo–Burmese.'

He swam ahead and told us that he could touch the bottom. I expected to see masses of troops on the other side, but to begin with not a soul.

Private Neville Hogan
2nd Battalion, Burma Rifles Armoured Car Section
When the bridge was blown with us still on the enemy bank, I felt devastated and lost. My first thought was where am I going to get my next meal from. Chaos reigned all that day.

On our right was a Gurkha battalion. We came under the CO's command. To get across we followed the riverbank for about two miles up the river, we met some villagers who suggested that a good swimmer would get swept down but not so far as to end up in the estuary. We started to make rafts out of bamboo and big earthenware jars, because the Gurkhas could not swim. We were organised into parties of twenty or thirty to swim the river. I had my boots round my neck, my pistol on its belt, and a pair of shorts. About three-quarters of the way across I felt a blow on my thigh, and thought I had collided with a Gurkha, but it turned out that I had been hit by shrapnel. I got to the other bank about three hundred yards from the bridge, along with about ten out of our party of about thirty.

We made our way along the railway line to Pegu. It was a long arduous walk, forty-two miles, which took two days. There we found a hospital train, where my shrapnel was removed. Ten minutes later the RAMC colonel doctor said only seriously wounded could stay on the train, remainder walk. The two nurses who had removed the shrapnel tried to hide me under a bunk, but I could not fit.

I was very stiff and in pain. I left the station and found a lot of ambulances there, which we were told we were not allowed to use; not for walking wounded again. But we were told, 'When we move off, if you stand on the step at the back you can come with us.' There were two of us on the back of each ambulance, and the drive was a nightmare, with nothing to hold on to, and the step was about nine inches wide. The driver drove at about fifty miles an hour, swerving every time a plane came over. We found out later that he had not even passed his test. After a while we got to Pyinmana and the ambulances were due to leave next morning at six am. But they left at four, and we were left without any form of transport.

Corporal William Norman
Mortar Platoon, 2nd Battalion, Duke of Wellington's Regiment
Eventually I saw a Burmese soldier who told us to go to Waw. The Anglo–Burmese said, 'Don't trust him. Come with me to Rangoon, I live there.' We fell in with another chap from the regiment with a Dogra soldier. We came to a village and the villagers all turned out with dahs and shouted at us. Nearby there was pile of bamboo poles that had been sharpened at one end, probably to make a fence. I told the chaps, 'Grab one of these, and when I say "charge", charge forward at the high port.' But this Burmese fellow ran ahead and said, 'It is all right, I speak the language. They think we are escaped convicts.' They were kind to us, and told us to cover our bodies in mud, so that we wouldn't get burned by the sun, and to wear coolie hats which they gave us, saying that if a Japanese plane came over we were to wave to it, and they would think we were Burmese. They gave us a guide to the next village. There was a penal settlement nearby, whose inmates had been let out. Our Colonel, Owen, had been killed by some people who might have been escaped convicts.

In one village, the people crowded round and shouted at us. It was frightening. They calmed down when the Anglo–Burmese officer told them that they would be rewarded if they looked after us.

Private Neville Hogan
2nd Battalion, Burma Rifles Armoured Car Section

We started walking north towards Mandalay, about five of us, all friends who had stuck together. We got a lift from a lorry, and reported to the Upper Burma Battalion who did not want to know us. We had no means of identifying ourselves, the only proof that we were soldiers were our .45-inch pistols. We persisted, they gave us shelter, food, and a few days later uniforms. They asked us if we could drive, and being armoured car chaps we said 'yes'. They sent us to a transport company, in which my brother-in-law was a lieutenant.

Corporal William Norman
Mortar Platoon, 2nd Battalion, Duke of Wellington's Regiment

We kept going, eventually meeting a brigadier who asked us why we weren't in uniform, and if we were deserters. He handed us over to some RASC soldiers making tea. They told us they were part of the 7th Armoured Brigade, which meant nothing to us. But they looked at us very suspiciously. We were handed over to a military policeman who established our identity and returned us to the battalion. We joined them at Pegu, where they were amalgamated with the King's Own Yorkshire Light Infantry. That was a wrong decision. We didn't like the KOYLIs and they didn't like us. Eventually the decision was rescinded.

We were reformed into a mortar platoon with two mortars. We set off on foot towards Hlegu, near Rangoon. I had no boots, just a pair of sandals. We had one rifle in the platoon, an Italian carbine.

Second Lieutenant John Randle
Officer Commanding B Company, 7th/10th Baluch Regiment

After leaving the Sittang, the battalion was ordered to dig in round Pegu. We lost another hundred men at Sittang, all our transport and B Echelon were on the wrong side of the river. We had about five officers. The battalion was not in good fettle. We did practically no more fighting for the rest of that part of the campaign.

Anthony Dillon, as a major after the war.

RANGOON TO MANDALAY

Trooper Robert Morris
C *Squadron, 7th Queen's Own Hussars*

The regiment was on a ship bound for Singapore when we heard that it had fallen, we could hardly believe it, the place was so strongly held and defended. This made us afraid of meeting the Jap navy and being sunk. We were told that we would be diverted to Rangoon. What would we find there and how would we cope?

All we saw were blazing fires and oil dumps set alight. Mounds of equipment such as aircraft marked 'lease lend to China from USA' lay in crates awaiting assembly. The number of lorries lined up ready for shipment to China amazed us. The port had been deserted and ransacked.

With no dockers we had to use the ship's crew to help and to show us how to use the ship's cranes to unload, and we became good at it. Unloading took two days. As soon as ships were unloaded they sailed. Occasionally Jap fighters would fly over and we imagined would strafe any troops they could see, but they did not really affect us.

I was given an American Dodge three-ton truck commandeered from the Rangoon police. I had a co-driver, Trooper Robinson. I drove stores from the docks to the regimental assembly area. Going into some of the warehouses was like walking into a large London store that had been laid waste. The gunners found cleaning material for their guns: huge rolls of beautiful white silk, destined to make clothes for the rich locals. I managed to put on my vehicle large numbers of expensive tinned cigarettes, and some beer and spirits. Eventually the remaining stores were set alight.

In Rangoon, all law and order had ceased; the prisoners of the jails had been released as had the inmates of the lunatic asylum. The zoo had released all the harmless animals and the dangerous animals were put down. Gangs of Burmese looters roamed the streets fuelled by easy access to alcohol.

We found tinned peaches, pineapples and things we had not seen for years. I got a wonderful canvas bedroll. I had misgivings about stealing this, but knew that if I didn't take it it would be destroyed. I also got a fridge, although an electrical fridge, and I had no electricity, I used it to store my food to keep it clean of dust.

From the time we docked to getting away took about three days. I took on

21

Japanese troops enter Rangoon railway station on 7 March 1942.

board some forty-gallon drums of petrol and some oil to support the regiment. We were all fully laden. My squadron was C, my brother's squadron. We kept to the main roads or mud tracks, the rest of the terrain was mainly paddy field and we could not cross them in our tanks or trucks. Our movement, especially on the dusty tracks, would draw Jap fighter-bombers, so the majority of our resupply work was done towards evening and at night.

It was quite a strain, because as well as the physical effort involved in resupply, there was always the threat of Japanese encirclement and roadblocks. We had continual fear of being cut off by the Japanese; although we slept and worked, we had a continual fear of being captured.

Lieutenant Anthony Dillon
1st Battalion, Gloucestershire Regiment

Taukkyan was a key road junction north of Rangoon, and we were told to defend it, abandoning our unnecessary kit at Mingaladon, with Rangoon burning behind us and all our families having been evacuated. The whole of 17 Division and 7 Armoured Brigade were held up on the road by a Jap division that had hooked in to attack Rangoon from the north, not realising that we would not fight at Rangoon. The Jap division set up a flank guard consisting of a battalion-size roadblock at Taukkyan. The scene at Taukkyan was chaotic. We were attacked by Zeros, the road was jammed with transport, tanks, fuel tankers, mules, ambulances etc. We were ordered to attack this roadblock to allow the army to get north towards Mandalay.

One of our carriers went up the road, the driver killed the crew of a Jap anti-tank gun with his Bren, but the next carrier was hit and destroyed. It was the first real fighting I had seen. Some way back from the block I saw some Japanese crossing the road, setting up a machine gun, and for a second thinking 'for God's sake, you'll kill someone'; stupid of me really.

The CO sent the Adjutant up the road in his jeep to report on the situation. His jeep returned with some wounded and he himself mortally wounded and he died soon afterwards. The CO turned to me and said you are the Adjutant; at the ripe old age of twenty-one.

Eventually, with help of other troops, we got through. This was partly because the Japs withdrew the roadblock.

Captain Peter Varwell
Officer Commanding A Company 1st Battalion, Gloucestershire Regiment
I was second-in-command of A Company. The Company Commander was sick and sent home, so I took over. After the Jap war started my company was sent to guard an oil refinery at Syriam across the river near Rangoon. In the middle of the night we drove up to rejoin the main body of the battalion, who had already been in action at Taukkyan. We drove up during the night from Rangoon, and when we arrived we found that the battalion had already put in one attack and it had not been successful. We were told to put in an attack at first light next morning. We did, but during the night the Japs withdrew. We discovered that a whole Jap division had been walking down the railway into Rangoon parallel to the road up which we had been driving with headlights blazing. Having arrived at Rangoon, the Japs deemed the roadblock no longer necessary.

Major Michael Calvert
Officer Commanding Bush Warfare School, Maymyo
I was head of Mission 204 based at the Bush Warfare School at Maymyo preparing people to operate in China. After the fall of Rangoon, I was given orders to take some of my instructors and keep any Jap forces on the western bank of the Irrawaddy occupied. I got hold of a paddle steamer, which had a Goanese crew and a British Army captain in charge. To support us there was one launch with a Vickers medium machine gun, manned by Major Johnson and some of his Royal Marines Force Viper people. We were ordered to raid down the Irrawaddy, destroy the railway in places, and anything that would be useful to the Japanese. We finished up at Henzada.

I went in to town leaving two layback positions behind me. In the dry season the banks of the river were forty or so feet high, so the boat was out of sight. I began to give a speech in the town square. I had three or so men with me, including Corporal Dermott, all armed with Thompson sub-machine guns. As I was talking, someone said, 'You are surrounded, lay down your arms.'

It was a party of Japanese plus Burmese dissidents. I am a slow thinker. But Corporal Dermott shouted out 'Bollocks', and opened up with his tommy gun, as we all did. We jumped off the dais, and ran down the street to my first layback position. We fought a withdrawal battle across the paddy fields. Major

Johnson told his Vickers machine gunner to give us some covering fire. As we started to cast off, we fired a few rounds from a mortar we had on the deck, but after a few rounds the recoil drove the base plate through the deck, and we had to stop firing.

I discovered that I had left a party behind, so we had to circle round, beach with the boat pointing upstream, and land again. While we were recovering the party, my batman and I climbed up the bank and saw about thirty Japs all looking down on the ground, I don't know what they were looking at; a corpse perhaps. They were about twenty yards away. We opened up with our tommy guns into this bunch, each using the full thirty-eight rounds. I think we killed most of them. We then slid down into the sticky mud of the bank, got into the boat, and with the Royal Marine fast launch giving us covering fire, we steamed upstream.

Lieutenant Anthony Dillon
1st Battalion, Gloucestershire Regiment
Our battalion provided the rearguard for 17 Division as we withdrew north. Our first set-piece battle was at one of the villages on our route. We heard that the Japanese intended taking over the village and that the Burmese would be providing a civic reception. We told the GOC, who told us that we too were to arrange a reception. It was quite a tricky operation. The plan was to attack the enemy as they arrived. They arrived late. We sent one platoon down the main road to draw attention to themselves and at the same time we sent a company, supported by mortars and machine guns in scout cars pinched from the Chinese, in on another road to attack the village from a flank. They caught the Japanese completely by surprise in houses, and as they jumped from upper windows, our soldiers caught them on their bayonets, a new way of bayonet fighting.

The Japs were routed. The CO then ordered the company to withdraw, but the other platoon got entangled with the Japs and one section was cut off and attacked by about fifty Japs who fought to the end. After the war we found out what had happened from chaps who had been taken prisoner.

Our next operation was at Paungde; the Japs were on their way to occupy the place, and the plan was similar to the previous one. This time the CO decided to take a risk and move the assaulting companies close to the objective in transport. The assault went very well, but the CO decided not to stay too long in Paungde and withdrew the two companies. We had no radios, so the withdrawal was signalled by a bugle call.

Captain Peter Varwell
Officer Commanding B Company 1st Battalion, Gloucestershire Regiment

At Paungde, I commanded B Company, having been transferred from A Company. We got into the village without any trouble, but as soon as we arrived the Japs opened fire. I and one of my subalterns climbed over a fence between two houses, and seeing some Japs in the front room of one of the houses, I threw in a grenade. The Japs rushed back through the house, but as I walked past the door, I was fired on, hitting my shoulder and taking a chunk out of my back. I thought I had had it, but managed to stagger back to the company HQ, where some stretcher-bearers took me back to the RAP. I was evacuated to Prome by ambulance, and from there by steamer up the Irrawaddy to Mandalay, then to Maymyo, and finally by train to Myitkyina, the railhead in the north of Burma. After a couple of days, the cry went up 'The Japs are coming'. All the people who could walk were sent off on foot. I had plaster all over the top half of my body, had malaria, and was not capable of walking.

There was a nasty silence about what was going to happen to those who couldn't walk. The next afternoon two American Dakotas dropped in at Myitkyina airfield on their way back from flying supplies to China from India. They took all the stretcher cases to Assam. We were incredibly lucky, if they had not taken us, the Japs would have found us when they arrived a couple of days later.

Lieutenant Anthony Dillon
1st Battalion, Gloucestershire Regiment

The divisional commander decided after the first attack to send more troops to take Paungde again. Meanwhile the Japanese outflanked us and set up a big roadblock at Shwedaung. They planned to let our armour through and then close the roadblock. Some of the armour went through, and the roadblock was closed behind them. The roads were not wide and on each side there were steep-sided, deep monsoon ditches, so the vehicles could not get off the road, and were machine-gunned by Zeros. I saw an ambulance full of wounded attacked by a Zero, killing the driver. The doors opened and chaps, some with bandages over their eyes, stumbled all over the road, and were killed soon after by another Zero.

I drove off the road in a carrier down into a monsoon ditch and was not able to drive it out. We then started taking fire from our own tanks, and only by standing up and waving to them managed to stop them.

Corporal William Norman
Mortar Platoon, 2nd Battalion, Duke of Wellington's Regiment

The operation at Paungde was very confused. Two of our companies were involved. We were cut off by a Jap roadblock at Shwedaung. One of our companies got mixed up with the Gloucesters. Our CO, Lieutenant Colonel Faithfull, gave the mortars our targets, and a sergeant said that our own troops were in the danger area. Our CO told him to obey orders, either that or our chaps would be captured. So we fired, knowing that a lot of our bombs would fall among our men. But our chaps got out.

On the way up to Shwedaung, I came across a burnt-out tank, with the men inside all roasted. I found a tin of peaches, they were still warm and made me feel a bit sick. I saw a Sikh with his bottom jaw shot off, gurgling, running about, bouncing off trees. People shouted to shoot him, and put him out of his misery. No one did, including those shouting 'shoot him'.

Eventually I joined a group of men who were going to rush the roadblock in a truck. I fired my Bren over the side. At the roadblock we came under machine-gun fire from a house, I fired long bursts back, someone else was changing magazines for me. Once through, we all got off. Next I got a lift from a gunner on a 25-pounder quad, and had to ride on the gun being towed by the quad, holding one of our chaps who had been wounded by pinning him down on the gun. After getting through, I was being taken along riding on a tank, and was thrown off when our tank hit another vehicle. I lay in the road, paralysed, and was lifted off the road by a passing refugee, just in time to prevent me from being run over by the next tank along. It crushed my pith helmet, which was lying in the road.

Major Michael Calvert
Officer Commanding Bush Warfare School, Maymyo

I got a message telling me to go back to Maymyo to hand over my mission to Colonel Musgrave, and that he would carry out some deception operations locally, which he duly did with some of the Bush Warfare School staff. I would never allow my troops to stay in one position for more than four hours. But Musgrave, who had been brought up on more rigid lines, parked his force in a village; something that I would always avoid. He gave them positions to guard at night, and went to sleep. The Japanese attacked and wiped out most of them. One lot got away under Musgrave on to his boat, but about twelve were lined up, stripped naked to be bayoneted. The Japs were taught neither to expend ammunition on killing prisoners, nor waste men guarding them. Two men ran for it: Private Williams and a sergeant major. They swam the Irrawaddy, which was about a thousand yards wide at that point, and made their way up to Prome, where, still naked, they reported. I was annoyed with Musgrave.

FROM CENTRAL BURMA TO INDIA

Mrs Margaret ('Beth') Bootland
Wife of Lieutenant, commissioned from RSM, 1st Battalion, King's Own Yorkshire Light Infantry

I got a telegram to say Alan was on the hospital train. The train came up every evening from where the fighting was. He was commissioned by then. He had malaria and looked awful, but as he had a quarter and a bed, he was not taken into hospital, which was packed, with wounded even in the corridors. I had faith in the army, I knew they would look after us. It was a blessing that Alan was in Mandalay when he was. Every day he went to the hospital for a check up.

I and my friend Lotte, the wife of an NCO who was now sharing the quarter, went to the Durzi, the tailor, and ordered two sets of khaki bush jackets and trousers which we thought would be more comfortable to travel in than dresses. He measured me and was about to measure Lotte, when Alan arrived and asked us what we were doing, and when we told him, he told us we had two hours to get out. He spoke to the tailor, cancelled the order and we returned to pack.

Alan transferred some brandy into three small bottles. Anything of use to the hospital was put out in the hall, and collected by two band boys. We had a bedroll each. We were allowed no more than sixty pounds, including blankets, mosquito nets and food for fourteen days. When I started to pack a pillow, Alan told me to get two clean pillowcases, one for me and one for Lotte, and pack the pillowcase with our clothes. We took tinned fruit, rusks, anything that would keep. It was a godsend that Alan got malaria, and organised our evacuation and organised us. On the day of the evacuation, he gave me a small revolver wrapped in a piece of flannel, saying, 'I want you to promise me that if you do fall into the hands of the Japs you'll shoot yourself. They raped the nurses in Hong Kong and Singapore, and killed them afterwards. You might as well kill yourself straight away. Shoot Ian first, then Keith, Lotte and yourself.'

I would have done. I didn't fancy being raped by the Japanese.

He took me over the road into where there was some jungle and gave me some practice with the revolver. He put a target on to a tree, and then measured out some paces, and told me to see if I could hit the target. My dad taught me to shoot when I was thirteen. I had never touched a rifle since then. Dad taught me to look at the 'bull' and fire above it because the bullet drops. When Alan went to get the target, he said, 'How the hell did you learn to shoot?'

I said, 'My dad taught me.'

He said, 'I feel a lot happier now.'

He reloaded the revolver, and he told me to keep it in my pack, and that pack came to bed with me, even in the shower that pack came with me, because things were stolen out of bedrolls.

At ten o'clock that evening the gharries came to take us to the station. The train did not pull out until six o'clock next morning, arriving at Mandalay at nine o'clock. The station was crowded, and I saw Alan go and speak to the police commissioner and two tall Sikh policemen. He then came and said goodbye to me, Ian, Lotte and Keith. It was terrible. I did not break down until he moved off, then I had a weep. That was it.

The train went over the Ava Bridge and up to Monywa where we embarked on a steamer, which took us up the Chindwin River to Sittaung, where we started walking. A lot of people got off at Kalewa and took another route, which did not turn out so well. I was a bit nervous and fluttery but it had to be done. What has to be will be, fate. Our journey was from Maymyo to Mandalay, thirty miles; Mandalay to Monywa, sixty miles; Monywa to Kalewa, one hundred and ten miles; Kalewa to Sittaung, eighty miles;

Sittaung to Tamu, forty miles; Tamu to Imphal, eighty miles; Imphal to Dimapur, one hundred miles; Dimapur to Calcutta, four hundred and fifty miles.

The bedrolls were carried by elephants as far as Tamu, and after that by coolies. For several days, having set off at six am we would be in the next camp by eleven am, children carried in doolies by coolies. Started on flat paddy ground, then started climbing the hills.

In each stopping place we normally had a bamboo hut with two beds, which we put our bedrolls on. We were woken at five-thirty to put out our bedrolls and leave them, and not to let any children out as the elephants were half-trained and might stampede. So we had to go back and shut our doors, when the bell sounded we could go to wash, and after breakfast we set off walking, the elephants went ahead. We had a guide, and in the rear there were two Sikh policemen, and Ian often walked with them because he could speak Hindi. We were a party of about sixty. There were very few men, just retired civilians, mostly women and children. We had no idea what was going on in Burma. We did hear the wireless in one camp, and heard that Rangoon had fallen.

Major Michael Calvert
Officer Commanding Bush Warfare School, Maymyo

As our forces retreated up Burma, I was told to form a battalion from my Bush Warfare School for deception and delaying operations. The only troops I had were five officers and seventeen men of the Bush Warfare School staff. I had sent the majority of the administrative people back to India. I recruited men from Maymyo, including men convalescing and people under arrest in detention. Some were fine soldiers, some with bullets still inside them. We were told to protect the Gokteik viaduct bridge. We were deployed on the viaduct, with some Gurkhas from the Burma Rifles, but without their British officers. The bridge was about one thousand feet above the water, the greatest drop of any bridge in the world. I longed to blow it up. At first the Gurkhas said we could not lay explosives, but in the end we did.

The Japanese pushed up through the Shan States, with the Chinese retreating, and their one route to China was via the Gokteik Viaduct. I kept asking Alexander's HQ for permission to blow the bridge, but kept being told, 'No, to leave it to the Chinese, hand it over, and withdraw.'

The next time I saw Alexander, he asked, 'Did you blow the bridge up?'

'No,' I said, 'I longed to blow it up, but you gave me direct orders not to do it.'

He replied, 'I chose you because I was told that you were likely to disobey orders.'

That was a sad mistake on my part, I should have disobeyed orders.

Private Neville Hogan
2nd Battalion, Burma Rifles Armoured Car Section

In the transport company in which we now found ourselves, we drove American Fords from Mandalay to Maymyo, loaded up with ammunition, petrol and vegetables, and returned to Mandalay. Here we loaded again with huge drums of aviation spirit, and drove to Meiktila. On these trips we were sometimes strafed by Jap Zeros. We had no lookout because there weren't any spare men who could do this. If we saw or heard the planes coming, or the strike of bullets on the road, we got out of the trucks and ran like hell into such cover as there was nearby, but in Central Burma there is very little jungle or thick woods.

From Meiktila we took wounded to Mandalay. The wounded were laid in blankets in the back of the truck – and then off again on our round trip, Mandalay–Maymyo–Mandalay–Meiktila–Mandalay: forty-two miles from Mandalay to Maymyo, and seventy miles from Mandalay to Meiktila.

Then we started taking Chinese troops from Mandalay to Meiktila. They were a menace. If you left your rifle or rations unattended they took them. We dared not leave the truck in case they took the truck. They had no discipline. The junior officers were just bandits. There were hundreds of them, and a handful of us. They had no rations, poor uniforms, and were totally disorganised.

The Burmese helped the Japs to find routes around us, and took advantage of stragglers and killed them. I encountered some Indian Army soldiers who robbed Indian evacuee civilians and behaved badly, there were parties of these civilians on the road all the way back to India.

Major Michael Calvert
Officer Commanding Bush Warfare School, Maymyo

The Bush Warfare Battalion, or Calvert's Commando as some people called it, was depleting all the time, because so many of the men had been sick or wounded. We fought some minor engagements near Mandalay. Here I encountered Peter Fleming, who I had met before. He had been sent to see me, to help in a deception operation, planned by Wavell. He would pretend to land at Mandalay airfield, and drive off in his staff car. It would crash, he would escape, but leave his attaché case behind, full of documents and letters to his wife. But in there were also letters to the War Office asking for more armour and aircraft to be sent to India, as well as giving fictitious numbers of our armoured vehicles, to deceive the Japs into thinking we had more equipment in India than we actually had. We took my jeep, with Private Williams my driver, and Fleming said I should drive the staff car with the Union Jack on it. We took Captain Coates, one of Wavell's ADCs, with us. There was still fighting south of Mandalay. We had to wait until the Japs were near enough to ensure that they found the vehicle. After a tense time of waiting, we set off. I was told by Fleming to drive the car in such a way that it left the road, went over the top of the embankment on which the road was built. I had to leave skid marks. I put on the brakes rather heavily, it left some skid marks, but the car did not reach the edge of the embankment. So I had to start again, and this time it toppled slowly over the edge, but without causing any damage. So Coates and Williams broke the windscreen. Coates had brought with him a supply of blood of the same group as Wavell's, and spilt it over everything.

We had to leave the area quickly, Coates and Fleming made for the bridge over the Irrawaddy, Williams and I headed for Mandalay. We found Mandalay had been bombed very heavily and there were thousands of Indians on the waterfront, bodies in the river, and many wounded. It was ghastly. We gave them some of our morphia, and some water, but as good Hindus they wouldn't let our mugs touch their lips, so we had to pour the water into their mouths.

Mrs Margaret ('Beth') Bootland
Wife of Captain commissioned from RSM, 1st Battalion, King's Own Yorkshire Light Infantry
One day, all of a sudden an army officer appeared on the path, and said, 'I am sorry to stop you but you can't go on this path any longer. They are dropping like flies with cholera in the camp you were due to go to. We daren't let you go any further. Have you got anything for the natives?'

All we had was brandy, no aspirin. We handed over the Dettol bottle that

Alan had filled with brandy back in Maymyo, to the officer. A guide came for us, it was the worst day of the whole trek, we walked on and on, the children were getting exhausted. My feet were OK, some people were wearing tennis shoes. They had no one to advise them. I was very lucky that Lotte and I had Alan to advise us. We arrived at the next camp absolutely bushed. We took the boys to a stream nearby and gave them a bath. Then Lotte and I went upstream and kept cave while we each had a bath. There was no food because we had arrived at the camp a day early, having passed the original camp we were intended for. Then it began to spit with rain, and then pour, the bashas were eight-people bashas. The heavens opened, and filled the pots in which our food was being cooked. Miss Baker, an army school teacher, poured the water out, tipped the rice out on to a plate, and from her pack took a small tin of Nestle's milk, and made a rice pudding for the children. We had nothing. The storm came back, and the rain dripped on to Ian's bed. He said, 'If Daddy knew what was happening to us, he would be awfully cross with God.'

Next morning we could not have any tea because the wood was all wet. We had to climb a big hill. Ian said he had a tummy ache, and he was flushed. I put some water in his mug and a good splash of brandy. Soon he was giggling and running around. At some time that morning we got to the top of this hill, and as we started down, we saw two big stalls dispensing bananas and hard-boiled eggs. They charged outrageous prices but we did not care. A colonel's wife said she would give a month's pay to dip her egg in some salt. About a mile further on there were some very old buses waiting, which took us to Imphal. We felt we were back in civilisation after twenty-seven days on the move.

Eventually we arrived at the railhead at Dimapur. We put the children to bed, and got some water from the railway refreshment room. It was full of soldiers and tea planters, all men. One said, 'Where in God's name have you ladies come from?'

When we told them we were refugees from Burma, they filled our bottles with clean water, and we returned to the train. We told them that there were many more refugees to follow. We were the first to be evacuated from Maymyo. The train took us to the Brahmaputra, which we crossed on a steamer. Then came the first snag. The Bengalis didn't like the British and tried to charge us for our fares. But Mrs Mansfield, an army schoolmistress who spoke Hindi, refused, and told them to get clean carriages as the ones on the train were filthy. We refused to pay and signed chits to say who we were. I was worried sick about my husband. I didn't know he had been badly wounded. The army met us on the platform at Calcutta. We went to Fort William in buses, and were interviewed. Apparently they had lost all trace of the 'walking party'.

Corporal William Norman
Mortar Platoon, 2nd Battalion, Duke of Wellington's Regiment

After falling off the tank, north of Shwedaung, my leg was broken and bruised. I was put on an ambulance, and taken to Allanmyo. Here I was robbed by an Indian soldier. I was put on a paddle steamer and taken up the Irrawaddy to Mandalay. Lying on a stretcher on deck, people would trip up over the handle of my stretcher, and this jolted me and was agony.

At Mandalay station the dogs were eating the bodies of the dead killed in an air raid. We were loaded on a train to Maymyo, a British hospital and run on army lines. I still had no treatment, but had a nice bed. There was no X-ray machine. After a while I was put on a train to Myitkyina. It was a very unpleasant trip, lots of people had dysentery and were not being cleaned up.

We were flown out by American Dakotas to Assam, dumped on the ground, and the plane left. An officer came up and said, 'Who are you, why are you so dirty?'

Someone said we had just come out of Burma and asked if we could be fed. The officer said, 'I can't feed you, you are not on our ration strength.'

He then changed his mind and did his best to help. They had no idea what we had been through. We were dumped on a train to India, and given twenty rupees. The tea planters' wives fed us at the stations at which we stopped in Assam. I ended up at Bareilly. The attitude of the army to those of us back from Burma was appalling; they blamed us for the defeat.

Trooper Robert Morris
C Squadron, 7th Queen's Own Hussars

When Mandalay was abandoned, the big beer brewery was going to be demolished. Each regiment was told to send in a lorry to collect a load of beer for their troops. It was a huge place and beer was gushing from tanks and pipes all over the place. I loaded crates of bottled beer. About twenty to thirty miles along the road, Robinson yelled, 'Planes planes, stop, stop.' There was nowhere to hide, we were on a raised road. I slammed on the brakes, and we jumped out into the recently harvested paddy field alongside the road. There was little cover, just eighteen-inch-long paddy stubble and thick black mud. The Jap planes swooped down and machine-gunned the lorry, hitting it several times. The bullets were so close that the stalks were being cut by the rounds covering us with chaff, which stuck to the ooze with which we were covered. After what seemed like ten minutes, the pilots probably thought they had killed the occupants, and flew off.

We dragged ourselves out of the paddy. Both rear tyres on the truck had been punctured, there was beer dripping over the road, but the engine and most of the beer was untouched. After recovering from the shock, we limped back about ten miles to the squadron with two flat tyres and the beer.

Major Michael Calvert
Officer Commanding Bush Warfare School, Maymyo

Having left Mandalay, I crossed the Irrawaddy, and joined up with the rest of my troops; we were still responsible for rearguard actions. I kept meeting up with Burma HQ. Alexander had no means of influencing the retreat except by his own attitude. He was very good, his uniform was always immaculate. He would visit and chat to the troops about cricket matches and army cup matches in Aldershot. He was unflappable. He didn't have any reserves so he couldn't influence the battle.

My force was depleting fast. I sent some of my lorries to evacuate some women and children, and I never saw the drivers again. I had an armed man with each driver after that. A retreat is not a pretty thing. There were masses of refugees, and people were dying of cholera by the side of the track. I was told to go to the Chindwin and to do what I could to delay the Japanese. I took an anti-tank rifle with me and a couple of the remaining men and hid in a cave.

Eventually a Gurkha company reached me in my cave, having been told they would come under my command. The Gurkha officer wanted to get back to his battalion. We set off to march to the Chindwin. On arrival we found the Japanese were in the process of landing on a large mud bank, it was dark, and they had lit fires to mark the place. I had only two men with me. I quickly went to the Gurkhas who had mortars and machine guns with them and told the officer. It was a marvellous target, the Japanese shouting and rushing about. We were about two hundred yards from them. The Gurkha officer merely said, 'My orders are to rejoin the battalion,' and he pushed off. Unfortunately he died on the way back to India. I was left with two men and no rations.

Major Charles MacFetridge
Officer Commanding 3rd Indian Light Anti-Aircraft Battery
We were ordered to move to Shwegyin on the east bank of the River Chindwin. From the jetty here river boats ran to Kalewa on the west bank and from there a track led to Assam and India. I did a recce and was so appalled at the state of the road to Shwegyin, I thought I would be very lucky to get any guns to Shwegyin. I imagined this would be the 'Dunkirk' of the Burma Army. Guns would have to be jettisoned at Shwegyin. On return from my recce, I told Brigadier Welshman at General Slim's HQ what I had seen. I was taken in to see General Slim. After listening to my description of the road, and my telling him that no guns of any kind could be got to Shwegyin, Slim summoned his CRE and G1 ops. I cannot but think that Slim took swift action, because the road was vastly improved during the next few days.

Despite the improvement, the last stretch of road was atrocious, along the edge of a chaung. I only managed to get four guns through. I was told to break all the rules for deploying AA guns and put them close together like field guns. This I did on a track leading to the jetty, about two hundred yards from the jetty.

Trooper Robert Morris
C Squadron, 7th Queen's Own Hussars
Before we got to the final stage we had to pass through Yenangyaung, the centre of the Burmese oil industry. I was carrying a load of high-octane petrol, and others with trucks full of ammo, with flames licking the sides of the vehicles as we drove through. It was keep going or remaining behind and being captured.

When we had ferried hundreds of troops back towards the Chindwin, we returned and reloaded our normal stores, and returned to the Chindwin at Shwegyin. It was hoped that ferry boats would carry the tanks across the river, but for lack of crews there weren't enough boats, so the tanks were destroyed. We took the drain plugs out of the engines and ran them until they seized. Breechblocks were taken from guns and thrown away, wirelesses blasted with tommy guns, and petrol poured on the tanks and set on fire. When Burma was

36

recovered, the tanks were found where we had left them. We destroyed our trucks, as well as throwing ammunition into the river.

We were taken to a ferry spot, where there were only enough crew for one ferry, but it was big enough to lift large numbers of troops. By then we were all mixed up with soldiers from other units on the other side. The Gurkhas were holding the enemy off.

Private Neville Hogan
2nd Battalion, Burma Rifles Armoured Car Section

After driving north to cross the Chindwin, we destroyed our trucks and crossed. At Kalewa we were grabbed by an officer who put our party to work burning money notes, and throwing cash in the river. The walk to India was in pouring rain, carrying our possessions in a bundle on a bamboo pole. No one seemed to care. It was chaos, your boots got clogged with mud, the road was unsurfaced. If a truck came along, you had to press yourself against the side of the hill. You could not ride the truck. It carried wounded or rations, as far as I could tell.

At Imphal we had no means of identification, so we had problems proving who we were. After being sent to Ranchi, we were checked out in hospital, and given ten rupees each. The first thing I bought was a huge tin of cream cracker biscuits and a tin of Australian butter. I wasn't going to share them with anyone, and ate the lot. We were not in too bad a condition, we were still schoolboys, and treated the whole thing like boy scouts.

Trooper Robert Morris
C Squadron, 7th Queen's Own Hussars

On the other side we moved along smugglers' trails, used before the war. We slithered up and down the muddy tracks, sometimes so steep we slid on our backsides. We moved all night, we were dog tired, in little groups, sometimes single file.

Mrs Margaret ('Beth') Bootland
Wife of Captain, commissioned from RSM, 1st Battalion, King's Own Yorkshire Light Infantry

After our short stop in Calcutta, we were evacuated to a hill station. I had had no news of Alan. One night I went to bed really downhearted. I dreamt it was my wedding day at Pontefract, except I was dressed in black, the flowers were withered, and Alan wasn't there. I told Lotte, 'This is a message to tell me he is gone.' That morning a telegraph boy came to the bungalow, and gave me a telegram. I asked Lotte to read it to me. It was from her husband, in Bareilly hospital. He said, 'Alan arrived in hospital this morning, badly bent but not broken, writing.'

I went to see him in hospital. He had been shot through the shoulder and the jaw. His jaw was fixed up by a man who had been the dental surgeon to the King. He made a silver splint for the broken jaw by melting down florins.

Trooper Robert Morris
C Squadron, 7th Queen's Own Hussars

At Tamu there was a reception organisation, and the sick were taken by truck, and we were sorted out into units. The worst part of the campaign was that march, by then we were exhausted, hungry, and under considerable strain.

Eventually we were moved through Imphal, to a camp we called 'dysentery hill'. Although we were there for only a few days, everybody seemed to get dysentery. To get to the cookhouse there we had to cross through a field of thick grass, and every time we ended up covered in leeches. I hated them.

Major Charles MacFetridge
Officer Commanding 3rd Indian Light Anti-Aircraft Battery

By the morning of 10 May three of my guns were deployed at Shwegyin. I realised that in the darkness that the Japs had started attacking the troops holding the hills overlooking the ferry boats evacuating the army. The surviving companies of the 1st Royal Jats were exchanging fire with the enemy. They were to be relieved by the 7th Gurkhas, an amalgamation of the 1st/7th and 3rd/7th Gurkha Rifles. I asked their CO if he had any mortars, and he did not know. The two COs agreed that the 7th Gurkhas should not relieve the Jats but reinforce them. I told the two COs that I had only three Bofors deployed that could support them, but I was a mountain gunner who had fought on the North-West Frontier, which they seemed to find reassuring. The CO of the Jats, Godley, placed his HQ by the guns and used them as match winners.

The Japs managed to get one of their mountain guns forward to shell the ferry site. My Bofors gunners picked up this gun arriving and as it was being brought into action it was destroyed by my Bofors firing over open sights. In the course of the battle the Gurkhas were committed to scale the hill overlooking the ferry site and reinforce the Jats. They wore yellow screens as they would have done on the frontier. This enabled my gunners to see where they were and to fire in their support without hitting them.

We were told to withdraw that night personally by General Cowan GOC 17 Division. As he drove off in his jeep after leaving us, his ADC was wounded by small-arms fire. When the time came to start the withdrawal, I was puzzled as to how Colonel Godley would pass his orders to his forward troops. He asked for two pairs of signallers, and he then gave both of them orders, which they were to give to the company commanders. The senior VCO told them to repeat the orders back. I doubted they would ever find the forward company commanders, but they did. The withdrawal was a model of its kind. I still had plenty of ammo, and devised a fire plan to bring down the heaviest fire possible to cover the withdrawal. At the end I ordered the detachments to withdraw. And merely said, 'Walk march to India.'

In reserve were the 1st/4th Gurkhas, under Lentaigne, he reckoned that in the chaung leading to the ferry there were at least three thousand troops awaiting evacuation, and they owed their survival to the actions of the Bofors manned by Punjabi Mussulmen gunners, and the two battalions; a fitting end to the longest withdrawal in the history of the British Army.

Major Michael Calvert
Officer Commanding Bush Warfare School, Maymyo

We arrived at Shwegyin having been chased by the Japanese and found ourselves on the enemy side of the battle. We lay in dry jungle, with tall trees interspersed with small shoots with large leaves, but no other cover. We lay in this hot, steamy jungle, on the receiving end of a British barrage, while the British and Indian soldiers fired off all their ammunition before destroying their guns and tanks.

We were going to wait till dark, but it was so hot and we were longing to have a drink. So we went to the riverside and drank and drank. We found a boat, but it was holed. We found another, and that had a hole in it. So I made a raft using empty water bottles and our packs. Private Medally could swim on his back, but my sergeant wasn't a good swimmer. I am a good swimmer, so I towed the packs and water bottles, which just floated. The Chindwin is about four hundred yards wide. There were Japs on both sides, but we cast off in a rainstorm. We got quite a long way across, when the sergeant said, 'I can't go any further.' So I said, 'Hang on to the packs,' and I let him use them while I swam free.

Medally was doing all right, but being on his back kept swimming in the wrong direction. Some Japs started to fire on us from the bank we had left, but not accurately. Finally we got to the west bank. Unfortunately the sergeant had let go of the packs and they drifted away. We had only what we stood up in. I had shorts, a revolver and a thousand rupees in coin. Medally and the sergeant had nothing other than shirts, socks and shorts.

We took a risk and followed a path: without boots we could not go through the jungle. We found some food dropped by refugees, including some sugar, which we licked up, despite the ants. We were emaciated. We huddled together at night.

We eventually came across about a hundred Indian refugees. They received us with open arms. They were from Orissa and had been employed in Burma as railway coolies. They had their complete families with them, and covered about six miles a day. They did not have cholera, thank goodness. They gave us some hot sweet tea, with marvellous jaggery sugar (Guhrr), and chapattis. We were emaciated, without weapons and bearded. They had seen the retreat of the British Army, their lords and masters, yet they behaved like that quotation in the bible: 'I was naked and you clothed me, I was hungry and you gave me food.' They gave us saris to cover up our beards. We walked along with the Indian women. We passed through a village, and there were Japanese soldiers leaning against the houses with cigarettes hanging out of their mouths, Medally saying, 'What a laugh, what a laugh. Wait until I tell my old dad.'

I told him to shut up. Our tactic would have been to scream and run off. We got through this village. When we felt stronger, I gave the Indians seven hundred of my thousand rupees, and we went ahead to find the British, still wearing Indian clothes. We eventually reached 17 Division commanded by Major General Cowan. The Divisional Intelligence Officer, whom I knew, rocked with laughter when he saw us. He made me go to see General Cowan, who said, 'I don't want to see any refugees.'

I stripped the sari off my face, and he said, 'My God, Michael, what are you doing?'

Second Lieutenant John Randle
Officer Commanding B Company, 7th/10th Baluch Regiment

The Japs fought with great ferocity and courage. We were arrogant about the Japs, we regarded them as coolies. We thought of them as third rate. My goodness me, we soon changed our tune. We had no idea about jungle fighting, no pamphlets, doctrine etc. Not only were we raw troops, we were doing something entirely new. In the early days we used to hack our way through the jungle, until we realised that this was useless, you made so much noise and it was so exhausting.

Striking Back
The Arakan Round One

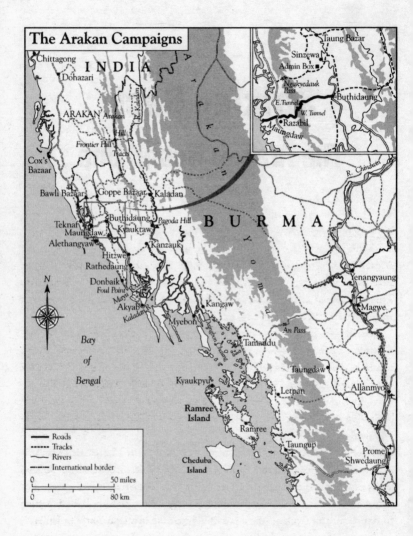

The Arakan Campaigns

INDIA

Chittagong
Dohazari

ARAKAN *Arakan*

Arakan
Hill
Frontier Hill
Tracts

Cox's
Bazaar

Bawli Bazaar
Goppe Bazaar
Kaladan

Teknaf
Buthidaung
Maungdaw
Kyauktaw
Alethangyaw
Hitzwe
Rathedaung
Donbaik
Foul Point
Mayu
Akyab
Kaladan

Bay

of

Bengal

N

R. Kaladan

BURMA

R. Chindwin

Pagoda Hill

Kanzauk

Kangaw

Myebon

Tamandu

An Pass

Yenangyaung

Magwe

Taungdaw

Kyaukpyu

**Ramree
Island**

Letpan

Allanmyo

Ramree

Taungup

**Cheduba
Island**

Prome
Shwedaung

Inset:

Taung Bazar
Sinzewa
Admin Box
Ngakyedauk
Pass
E. Tunnel
W. Tunnel
Buthidaung
Razabil
Maungdaw

——	Roads
----	Tracks
	Rivers
-·-·-	International border

0   50 miles

0   80 km

A corporal said, 'Wait, wait, sergeant major,
these Brens and rifles won't fire.'
I didn't believe him and got down behind a Bren. One round fired and
then the gun jammed. I went through all the drills, but nothing would
work. I slung it aside in disgust.

Having followed the retreating British as far as the River Chindwin, the Japanese stopped. They had no plans for an immediate invasion of Assam or the conquest of India, although they did prepare plans for an advance to seize Imphal and Akyab, and exploit to the River Brahmaputra. This was aimed at preventing the Allies using the airfields in Assam and eastern India, thereby choking off supplies to China.

The British plan for a comeback involved a thrust from Imphal into northern Burma. But so much work on logistics and communications would be required to mount both of these attacks that neither the British nor the Japanese could undertake major operations in Assam until 1944.

In the interim, the British decided on a limited offensive in the Arakan, beginning in mid-December 1942, to clear the Japanese out of the Mayu Peninsula and take Akyab Island, which controlled the mouths of the two big rivers in the Arakan, the Kaladan and the Mayu. The British saw this as a means of raising morale in their own army following defeat in Burma, and preventing the Japanese from taking the initiative in this area. For although the capture of Akyab would not open the way for a British return to Rangoon, the Arakan was a possible Japanese invasion route to India.

The British advance on both sides of the Mayu River, as a precursor to capturing Akyab Island, stalled in the face of Japanese defences at Donbaik and Rathedaung. The British 6th Infantry Brigade, part of the British 2nd

Infantry Division, which had been practising amphibious assaults in India, and was earmarked for the assault on Akyab Island, was sent to Donbaik where stalemate had set in. Meanwhile the Japanese brought up their 55th Division to mount a counter-offensive in the Arakan.

As part of the British fightback the RAF mounted sorties at an increasing rate.

Flight Sergeant Deryck Groocock
99 Squadron, RAF

I was only nineteen with three hundred hours' flying experience and was sent to deliver a Wellington to Cairo from England via Gibraltar, down to West Africa and across to the Nile. We were very heavy taking off from Gib, with extra fuel tanks, and scraped over the sea wall at the end of the runway by inches. We had to fly a long dog-leg out into the Atlantic to avoid French Vichy fighters from Dakar who, according to rumour, were paid five hundred dollars by the Germans for each British aircraft they shot down. Quite a few aircrew got lost flying over Africa on one of the legs to the Nile at Khartoum.

We expected to join a squadron in the Middle East, where aircrew were sent back to UK on completion of a six-month tour. But we were stuck in a transit camp, and when I saw a notice asking for volunteers to ferry a Wellington to India, I and my crew volunteered for lack of anything better to do. We eventually arrived at 99 Squadron in Assam. I got out and said to the CO, 'Here's your aircraft, how do we get back to Cairo?'

'Cairo! What makes you think you're going back to Cairo? You're in India now. Are you single or married?'

'Single,' says I.

'Right, a tour in India for a single man is four years. Three years for a married man.'

At the age of nineteen, four years seems like a lifetime. The squadron was just settling down to bombing ops over Burma. I had been the captain of a Wellington all the way from UK, but because of my inexperience of ops, I was made co-pilot, with the same crew, but with a more experienced captain. We bombed airfields, ports and railway marshalling yards, mainly at night for about six months in late 1942, early 1943, dropping 500-pound bombs from around ten thousand feet. Finding the target was not easy. There was not a lot of opposition. We were attacked by a night fighter once. We went low-level and corkscrewed, and lost him. We had flak over some targets, but nothing like the flak over Germany. I had taken part in one of the thousand-bomber raids over Dusseldorf. Our main worry was ditching in the jungle. We were ill-prepared for survival. We had a silk scarf map of Burma, and a little compass. We had no money, just the Burmese version of the 'goolie chit'.

Flying Officer Cecil Braithwaite
60 Squadron, RAF

I carried out numerous sorties between August 1942 and January 1943, some in support of the first Arakan offensive. We were often attacked by Jap fighters, they buzzed around but were distracted by the Hurricanes and Mohawks. We respected the Jap pilots, but their aircraft could not take damage, they were not armoured. If attacked, one ploy was to fly low, as close to the ground as possible. Some Jap fighters had telescopic sights, which required the pilot to put his eye to it to aim, unlike the gunsight in most fighters which allowed the pilot to fly 'head up'. With his eye to the sight, the pilot could not fly low and fast without risking piling into the ground.

Although the Blenheim was slow, it was well armoured. Ours were well maintained by our peacetime-trained and skilled ground crew. All the same, not many of us expected to live all that long. We were issued with rudimentary will forms, which few of us bothered to complete. At twenty or twenty-two years old you don't have much to leave anyway.

Sergeant Sidney Savin
Section Commander, B Company, 2nd Battalion, Durham Light Infantry

The whole brigade, plus the 1st Battalion the Royal Scots, moved by rail to Chittagong. Each time the train stopped, someone would rush forward to the engine with a billycan to get hot water. The journey took about a week and shortly before our arrival we were told to prepare for a seaborne landing on Akyab. We arrived at Chittagong on Christmas Day 1942. The town was deserted and many of the shops were boarded up, but in a few places you could buy a cup of tea and a handful of Burma cheroots. We were now in a highly malarial area with a very high rainfall. Fortunately the monsoon was over and the ground underfoot was quite hard. We spent the next few weeks doing landing exercises with the navy, in assault craft, in preparation for the Akyab affair.

The idea was to land on Foul Point to use this as a jumping-off point for a landing across the mouth of the Mayu River on Akyab. But we were told that things had not gone well for the 14th Division in their advance down the Mayu peninsula, and so our seaborne assault on Foul Point was called off. We were told that we would try to crack the Jap positions at Donbaik, which 14th Division had tried without success, taking quite heavy casualties.

Corporal Ernest Galley
Section Commander A Company, 2nd Battalion, Durham Light Infantry
The battalion was going into action again for the first time for two years. We left Chittagong by boat, landed at Cox's Bazaar, and from there by foot.

Sergeant Sidney Savin
Section Commander, B Company, 2nd Battalion, Durham Light Infantry
We marched the fifty or so miles to the Donbaik positions over a period of three days, marching by night and stopping at rest camps by day. The road was very dusty, it was unpleasant and we wondered why there was no transport for part of the way. Donbaik was a village on the coast some six miles from Foul Point. The Japanese occupied strong positions in well-sited deep bunkers with good fields of fire. The two main strongpoints were known as Sugar 4 and 5. They were so strong that they could withstand fire from 25-pounders and 500-pound bombs dropped from the air. There were other strong points in the vicinity to support these two positions: the Shepherd's Crook in the bed of a deep chaung which ran down from the jungle to the sea; two positions called Twin Knobs; and the Elbow. In the distance there were two other positions that gave the Japs a commanding view of the whole area. When you moved around there you were in their sights.

In the beginning of March 1943 we relieved a Punjab Battalion of the 14th Division early in the morning. Our Company faced Sugar 4 and 5, I suppose we were three hundred or four hundred yards away. From our positions we could see them, and they looked like mounds of earth. There were many dead in no-man's-land, it was impossible to get them out. When the wind blew our way there was quite a stench. These were the dead from earlier attacks. The Japs had shut themselves in their bunkers, and at the right time opened the hatches in the firing slits and picked off the attackers. We didn't have flame-throwers then. You could get on top of the bunker, but you then came under fire from other bunkers that were supporting them.

Corporal Ernest Galley
Section Commander, A Company, 2nd Battalion, Durham Light Infantry

My platoon was right on the beach. Somewhere to our left there were some Punjabis. Sometimes, when the tide came in, the sea came into our slit trenches. We had tree trunks over our trenches with soil on top. We were always told in our training, never fire at night, unless you can really see the whites of their eyes. The Japs want you to fire and give away your position. The Japs would respond with mortars.

Evening came, dusk fell, I told off the sentries, and went to sleep, to be rudely awakened by the sentry. He told me there were tram cars coming. I thought 'here we go'. He said he was a Liverpool lad and had seen some Liverpool trams. I stood with him and convinced him it wasn't tram cars. Then half an hour later, he said he could see Japanese walking about. We had a good field of fire. I could see there were no Japs, and quietened him down. No sooner had I got him quietened down, when there was rifle fire on our left, heavy fire. I stood everyone to, hundreds of rounds were being fired by people on our left. Mortar bombs going down. There was nothing happening where we were. Next day we found out it was an Indian battalion blasting off. The Japs blasted back with mortars.

One day, the Japs started shelling, the shells fell behind our position. We could see the guns firing. We asked for artillery support but couldn't get any response over the field telephone or by the Number 18 wireless set. Our platoon sergeant joked, 'I can get Henry Hall and his dance orchestra on the BBC, but not company HQ.'

So we sent the lad who kept seeing trams back to company HQ who ran out a new line to us. Meanwhile the Japs went on shelling, rounds falling all round us. Eventually the battery of 25-pounders began to fire back. The platoon sergeant gave corrections to the guns. But the Japs were pretty good at moving their guns to avoid retaliation. For four hours it all went quiet, and then shells started falling again.

We eventually sent the lad who saw trams back. He wasn't frightened, but kept on seeing things. He never came back.

We were never attacked in that position. The Japs came up as far as the wire, sometimes you could hear them shouting, 'What regiment there?' 'I've been wounded, can you help me?' They might lob a grenade. Sometimes it was difficult to hear exactly what they were shouting. You couldn't see them.

They would try to put the wind up people. They were trying to pinpoint the position. The Indians on our left fired and got the 'crap' thrown back at them. We were a disciplined battalion.

Corporal Fred Cottier
Section Commander, 2nd Battalion, Durham Light Infantry
The day was spent in the slit trench, reading or sleeping. In the day we had one man on sentry in each. At night there were fatigue duties carrying water or rations up. Stand to was at dusk and first light, waiting for the Japs to attack – often nothing happened. At night there would be twenty-five per cent on duty. If an attack came in, you spent the next day collecting casualties, reinforcing positions, digging and so forth. After stand down, the Japs would attack at say midnight, knowing perfectly well what our routine was. An attack might go on until daylight.

We had rest periods at the Arakan, we would be relieved by another battalion, and go back, not far, still within range of the enemy artillery. We could wash our clothes in a stream, and have a hot bully beef stew or curry. We could relax and write a letter, have a haircut and shave off our beards.

The Arakan campaign was the best training we ever had for fighting in Burma.

Sergeant Sidney Savin
Section Commander, B Company, 2nd Battalion, Durham Light Infantry
We learned that the brigade was to capture Donbaik. It was decided we would do what the Japs did, get round the back; not attack head on, but bypass the Jap strongpoints, set up our own company strongpoints and hold them. Then the main assault on Donbaik village, by the 2nd DLI and 1st Royal Welch Fusiliers, would go ahead. The other battalions remained in reserve.

This attack was preceded by a heavy artillery and mortar barrage. The Royal Welch Fusiliers went in first and overran some strongpoints in the area of Shepherd's Crook, but they could not get inside them, and they sustained heavy casualties from Jap mortars.

Sergeant Clifford Jones
Commanding Anti-Aircraft Platoon [Brens] under Command Battalion HQ, 1st Battalion, Royal Welch Fusiliers

At 0500 hours the attack began. All hell was let loose. Three-quarters of A Company got into the bunker but they couldn't hold it. They got into some of the trenches on the outside which were empty. I came in from the right and lost half my men trying to attack similar bunkers. I was told over the radio to move up to A Company, and take over. I wriggled forward and grabbed hold of the first man I could see and asked what was going on. He pointed to an officer doubled up down in a foxhole. The officer said, 'Are you taking over?'

'Yes,' I replied.

'Leave me here and get on with it.'

I then got the message to go back to the CO, who said, 'D Company are cut off. The Royal Scots are going to reinforce us and attack to get D Company out. I'm coming with you to A Company,' which he did.

The Japs were very astute, and shouted out in English things like, 'British soldier why are you here? Your wives are waiting for you.'

The CO shouted in Welsh through a loudspeaker to D Company to hold on. This flummoxed the Japs.

A Company and the Royal Scots' attempts to reach D Company went well for the first fifteen minutes, but then came under Jap bombardment. After two hours of fighting, we did get out about forty men of D Company. There were no officers left alive.

Sergeant Sidney Savin
Section Commander, B Company, 2nd Battalion, Durham Light Infantry

The DLI then went in and my company managed to reach its objective without any trouble. Other companies suffered casualties. We had a fairly easy ride. We moved through the scrub jungle for cover.

Company Sergeant Major Martin McLane
C Company, 2nd Battalion, Durham Light Infantry

Before the battle my company, along with the battalion, had been issued with ammunition manufactured at Kirkee in India, which proved to be defective. My company formed up in a dry nullah bed. There were a series of them every few yards. We were carrying an average of sixty pounds of kit. The artillery fire

An attack in the Arakan, Indian soldiers on the start line.

CSM Martin McLane

was going over, and everything was dusty in the early morning light. The company commander gave the order 'Bayonets on, smoke if you want to'. The men dragged on their cigarettes, and were hanging on to them for grim death, because, let's not be heroic, a man is only going to do a job if he's ordered to. He's going into an attack and the chances of him being killed is tremendous.

The order came, 'Right, get ready, over the top.'

I had the signallers and company clerk with me. We went over the top. I saw a Jap. I up with the tommy gun and the bloody thing wouldn't fire. I was disgusted, here was I a professional soldier, and I couldn't hit him. He had been throwing grenades, but scarpered.

I never heard our Brens firing, only desultory shots from rifles, which died away. I had been in attacks in France and knew what it sounded like. All there was was Japanese firing, nothing of ours at all. The CO spoke to me on the wireless set. He asked what was happening.

I said, 'This is the funniest attack I've been in. I can't hear a Bren, I can't hear a rifle. There's nothing moving, all I can see is bodies.'

He replied, 'Do something about it then.'

'What can I do?'

'Get the men in.'

Well I only had company HQ with me, the other two platoons were on their own, one was detached. I found the company commander wounded. He'd been wounded in France in the knee and his same leg had been hit again. He was bleeding badly. I dragged him back through the nullah, found A Company Commander and put my company commander on a stretcher.

I returned to my own company HQ, spoke to the CO on the wireless, and was ordered to get moving. I was leaning on the lip of a nullah when a shell burst nearby. A splinter hit the set. I could hear the CO, but could not transmit. I ordered company HQ to stay put while I went to find the two rifle platoons. I passed a stretcher on which was Lieutenant Greenwall, one of the platoon commanders. He was full of shrapnel from a Japanese plastic grenade, lying smoking a cigarette. He said, 'Well, sergeant major,' stroking his 'old man', 'they didn't hit that.' He was newly married.

I found seven of the platoon lying down. I shouted, 'Come on lads, bayonets.'

A corporal said, 'Wait, wait, sergeant major, these Brens and rifles won't fire.'

I didn't believe him and got down behind a Bren. One round fired and then the gun jammed. I went through all the drills, but nothing would work. I slung it aside in disgust.

'Give us your rifle.'

I fired it but the bolt stuck solid and I could not eject the round except by putting the butt on the ground and booting down the bolt with my foot.

I located the other platoon in a nullah bed, where they were being showered by Jap grenades. The casualties included the platoon commander. All the officers were out of action. By now my signaller had got the wireless working again, and I arranged with the CO for mortar and artillery smoke and HE to cover our withdrawal. I told the platoon to stand by to move when the fire came down, to take the wounded and leave the dead. Some were very badly wounded. They looked at me beseechingly. Although they call you what they like, the sergeant major is the kingpin of the company, and the men depend on him for so much. I went back and picked up some more wounded, but our artillery started dropping short among us. We were very lucky to have only two more casualties.

After reorganising, the defective ammunition was all dumped in a chaung and replaced by serviceable rounds.

Corporal Ernest Galley
Section Commander, A Company, 2nd Battalion, Durham Light Infantry
This was the one attack made by the battalion down there. It seemed fruitless. The enemy positions were well dug in. There had been numerous attacks on these positions, and no one had broken through.

Sergeant Sidney Savin
Section Commander, B Company, 2nd Battalion, Durham Light Infantry
As far as we were concerned things quietened down. Just the usual firecrackers at night. Then we came out of the line to rest. I got malaria, which took a toll higher than our battle casualties. I was evacuated along the beach by ambulance, and eventually put on board a hospital train at Dohazari which took me to hospital at Dacca.

With malaria you get a chilly feeling, your bones ache, you are generally lethargic and have a high temperature. You can't carry on soldiering. You don't eat and lose weight. The treatment is mepacrin and quinine. A bout would last two to three weeks. I remained in Dacca until the battalion was withdrawn from Arakan, by which time it had fought at Indin, and at Maungdaw.

Second Lieutenant Satoru Nazawa
Company Second in Command, 112th Regiment, Japanese 55th Division

The night attack on Indin was the first time that I was acting as deputy head of company. So I was nervous to the maximum point, and the soldiers, the men under my command, were mostly senior to me by age, and they had already experienced actual battles. On the other hand, I was a young lad, who just arrived from Japan. I was really nervous, but well I tried to remember all the fighting tactics that we were taught in school, on the night attacks by platoons and companies. And so I organized the system based on these fighting tactics, and went towards the enemy camp. And at first we went very slowly and quietly, and we went close to the enemy without them noticing, and I put one platoon on the north of the enemy, and two platoons from the back to the side, going around, and they went to the side, the side of the enemy. And so I wnet to guard the soldiers who were attacking the side, and from there we went into the village, and then the enemy were shooting back at us, and throwing hand grenades. They were throwing and throwing, and they exploded fiercely. I was thinking, oh this must be the end for me. then the head of the first platoon, sergeant Yamamoto, took a very bad injury to the stomach. Sergeant Abe of the second s a piece of shell in his eyes, and he can't see anymore, and I could hear many voices saying that they were being beaten, and I didn't know what was going to happen. In the end we won because it was very dark. The night wasn't the enemy's strongest point.

Corporal Ernest Galley
Section Commander, A Company, 2nd Battalion, Durham Light Infantry

Next we were told that we were surrounded. While we were watching the Japs at Donbaik, they had gone inland, and come round the back. We heard that brigade HQ had been attacked: the brigadier and staff and hospital wiped out.

If you built a defensive position they would go behind, cut the road, then attack. We were told we were going to pull out. Our CO, Lieutenant Colonel Theobalds, took over command of the brigade. This was my second evacuation, Dunkirk being the first. I had been fighting for over two years, and only taken part in evacuations.

The beach was like a parade ground, all the brigade's carriers were on the beach, the Japs were on the hill tops firing down. The carriers provided some protection. We pulled out marching in threes. We marched the full length of the beach (three or four miles), covered by the carriers. It must have taken the Japs by surprise because I don't think we had one casualty. Maybe they didn't see us. We then went inland to hill positions. We had just got in there when we heard that the Japs were on the move, to a place called Indin, a supply base for our attack on Donbaik. We stormed into Indin. The whole place was on fire. The Japs had left and destroyed it, leaving a sniper in a tree.

A lad called Bonnie killed the sniper with a Bren. He was cock-a-hoop. Confusion reigned, no one knew where the Japanese were. My good friend Jock McCleavy, a corporal in 2 Platoon, had to provide a patrol to find the Japanese. Jock went out with his section. Early in the morning, we heard they had been ambushed. Jock was badly hit. One was missing, dead or prisoner. Jock was whipped off to Cox's Bazaar. I saw him off. I was told to take out my section to find these Japs. I took with me a bloke called Ward, known as the 'Mad Mullah'. He had been in the army before, and his ambition was to win the VC. Another chap with us called Wilkinson was known as 'Brylcreem'. I was not excited by the prospect.

We set off through the forward positions. I had two scouts out front. I had a map and compass. To begin with we followed the route the other patrol was supposed to take. But I didn't like this, and took a bearing on where we thought they had been ambushed, and circled round to come in the other way. Near where we were heading we saw some Japs. They were lying around celebrating, that's what it looked like. Ward said, 'Let's get stuck in.' We had two grenades apiece. I said, 'Our instructions were to come out here, find the Japs, mark the position on a map, and go back, and not have any contact.' We had already lost half a patrol. Young Brylcreem said, 'He's in charge.' I reckoned there was nearly a company of Japs there.

I lost a friend that day. 'I can't get my medal,' Ward says. Anyway we came back. As we did so, we had to pass through C Company who had a forward listening position. They had changed its location, and hadn't told us. But we got back, and I gave the map reference to Company HQ, and the 25-pounders hit it.

SR 16730

Sergeant Frank Harrison.

Sergeant Frank Harrison
Section commander, Mortar Platoon, 2nd Battalion, Durham Light Infantry
We were in action with our mortars set up in the river bed. We could not move often enough and as soon as you opened fire, you got mortared back. I was hit by shrapnel: one in the chest and one in the top of my arm. I didn't feel it, no pain, said to my lance corporal, 'I've been hit.' I was given an injection of morphine by a stretcher-bearer. They carried me to the RAP, and then back to Maungdaw where I was in a straw basha hospital in a bamboo bed.

Corporal Ernest Galley
Section Commander, A Company, 2nd Battalion, Durham Light Infantry
We then withdrew to Chittagong. I got as far as there and started shivering and discovered that I had malaria. So I went to hospital at Dacca. Before we got back there, we were told that if anyone was wounded or sick and put in hospital, they must return to the 2nd Division because so much time had been spent on combined operations training; they must tell whoever was in charge that they were part of the 2nd Division and not to be sent anywhere else.

When some of us had recovered, a senior officer paraded us and detailed us to join some other regiment, and we refused; our hair was standing up on the backs of our necks. Someone told him that we were ordered to say that we were in the 2nd Division and would join no other. This officer walked off. So next time our names were posted on orders. We went to our huts and refused to move. We were threatened, but did not move. Some of us went to see this officer, and he damned and blasted us. We asked if he could send a signal to 2nd Division to ask.

Next morning all members of 2nd Division were ordered to parade and get on trucks and all taken to Ahmednuggur where the division was.

Sergeant Frank Harrison
Section Commander, Mortar Platoon, 2nd Battalion, Durham Light Infantry
From Maungdaw I was sent to a convalescent hospital at Comilla. I didn't like it. Some people there had no intention of leaving the place and get back to fighting. I really wanted to get back to my unit. Here there were more lads from the DLI. One night I went round to them and said, 'I am going, if you want to come with me you can. Just bring your shaving gear.'

'How are you going to get back there?'

'I will get a train at Comilla station.'

They said, 'We'll come with you but go out by road.'

Three gharry wallahs came along. Six of us got in, and we had no money so we jumped out about half a mile from the station. They were shouting, but that was that.

When we got on to the station there was red caps, and all different types of soldiers. When the train came in, they said, 'What now?'

'Bide our time,' I replied.

We got on, and got right to Chittagong where the battalion had gone out of the line. I went to our own company commander, and told him what I had done. He said you have done right. I couldn't raise my arm too far. But I was OK. I was always told to get back to your own unit.

Second Lieutenant Satoru Nazawa
Company Second in Command, 112th Regiment, Japanese 55th Division

And so we went to the line of Buthidaung. And here, we made the enemy retreat further away from this line to the north. And in Maungdaw, there was another field storage of the enemy. We saw that there were mountains of corn beef, bacon, cheese, cigarettes and rum lying around. I had never tried corn beef before that. they had water in a bottle, and we kicked it around, but when someone said it's an alocholic drink called gin, there were soldiers who were gulping down the gin, happier than ever. We had this kind of excitement, or more like comedy. We thought, my goodness, these people are fighting in such a luxurious condition. If they came and took our camp, well, they would just find a bit of dried fish and a bit of rice, nothing else.

Striking Back

The First Chindit Expedition

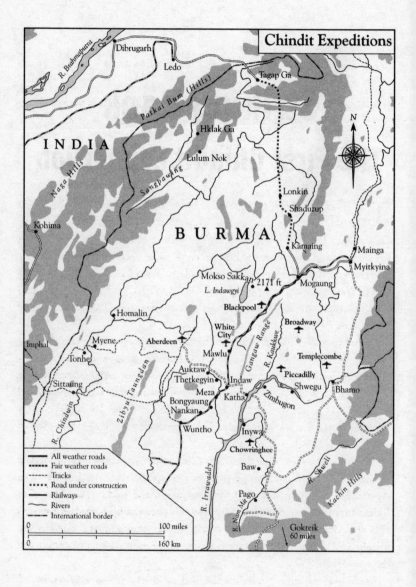

Wingate believed that you should take ordinary troops and turn them into a special force, and this would be an example to the rest of the army. 'If those people can do it so can we.'

The Chindits were the creation of a gunner officer, Major Orde Wingate. At the request of General Sir Archibald Wavell, then Commander-in-Chief India, Wingate was sent to India in early 1942, while the campaign in Burma was still in progress. Wavell had been impressed by Wingate's unorthodox soldiering methods in Palestine before the Second World War and again in Abyssinia in 1941. On each occasion Wingate had been awarded the DSO as the successful commander of guerrilla-type operations.

Wavell promoted Wingate to Colonel and sent him to the Bush Warfare School at Maymyo, in Burma, to organise long-range penetration operations against the Japanese. In the event the Japanese advanced too quickly for such an enterprise to be mounted from within Burma itself, and Wingate was posted to the staff at Wavell's HQ in Delhi. While at Maymyo, he had met that remarkable soldier, Michael Calvert, who was to play a key role in the Chindits.

Wingate persuaded Wavell to allow him to raise a special force of brigade strength to mount long-range penetration operations into Burma from Assam. He was promoted to Acting Brigadier, and told to raise the 77th Indian Infantry Brigade for this purpose. He chose as his brigade formation sign the Chinthe, the mythical beast, which stands guard outside the temples and monasteries of Burma. It was mispronounced as 'Chindit', and the name stuck.

There was nothing special about the majority of the soldiers in 77

Brigade. Most were either young and inexperienced, or overage and inexperienced. Few were well trained. The British 13th King's Regiment (Liverpool), raised for coastal defence in England, had been sent to India for internal security duties. The soldiers, whose average age was thirty-three, were mainly Scouse dockworkers, and liable to revert to their pre-war trade union habits when life got uncomfortable during training. Unable to strike, they demonstrated their disapproval of their new role by going sick in large numbers.

The 3rd/2nd Gurkha Rifles consisted in the main of under-eighteen-year-old recruits. The Gurkhas also provided leaders for the extra mules required by the brigade over and above those already with battalions.

The understrength 2nd Battalion Burma Rifles was composed of Karens, Kachins and Chins of the British Burmese Army who had been through the first campaign and fought their way to India. They were seasoned troops.

The 142nd Commando Company were far and away the best soldiers: volunteers from every regular battalion in India, augmented by men from the United Kingdom. They were the only picked men in the brigade.

Wingate broke up his brigade into columns, each of about four hundred men. His concept was that columns should march independently, be self-supporting for a week, and be supplied by air. He was aiming at mobility and security. Mobility would be achieved by not having wheeled transport, and therefore avoiding being tied to overland lines of communication; so columns could, in theory, go where they wished. Security would, again in theory, be achieved by the difficulty the enemy would experience in finding mobile columns in the jungles and teak forests of northern Burma, and on the ability of columns to disperse in smaller groups. Wingate planned to concentrate two or more columns for specific tasks. He would communicate with columns by wireless.

Wavell originally intended to use Wingate's Brigade ahead of an Allied offensive consisting of an attack across the Chindwin by IV Corps from Assam, a Chinese advance from Yunnan across the River Salween, and the American General Stilwell's Chinese–American forces pushing south from Ledo. For logistic reasons, the Allied offensive had to be postponed for many months, but Wingate was allowed to go ahead with his operation. This consisted of entering Burma in mid-February 1943, cutting the railway between Shwebo and Myitkyina, harassing the Japanese in the Shwebo area, and, if possible, crossing the Irrawaddy to cut enemy communications with the (Chinese) Salween front.

Wingate had many attributes that would have qualified him to rank as a great commander and man. Unfortunately he was also flawed. It is difficult to get a dispassionate judgement on him from anyone with whom he came in contact. He was either hated or worshipped. 'There was no middle ground with Wingate,' remarked John Masters, who took part in the Second Chindit expedition. This comes across from the voices both in this chapter and the one covering the Second Expedition.

Much of what he advocated strategically, operationally and tactically was flawed, and some of it was sheer nonsense. Yet he could inspire men to achieve things they had thought impossible. All who met him, including those who found him exasperating, such as General Slim, agree that you could not ignore him. That great fighting soldier Mike Calvert followed him unhesitatingly, whereas the young and inexperienced Dominic Neill of the Gurkhas, later to become one of the most accomplished jungle soldiers in the British Army and with vastly greater experience in that art than any Chindit, came to loathe Wingate, rightly regarded his tactics with contempt, and, given the choice, would not have followed him anywhere.

TRAINING

Major Michael Calvert
Officer Commanding Bush Warfare School, Maymyo and Chindits
When I got back from the Henzada raid, there was a man sitting at my desk. He got up and said, 'I'm Wingate.'

I replied, 'I'm Calvert, and that's my desk.'

'I'm sorry.'

I'd never heard of Wingate. He took me for walks, I found that when he talked about guerrilla warfare he was miles ahead of anybody I had met.

On arriving in India, Wingate sent for me, and George Dunlop who had also been fighting in the retreat from Burma. We were both suffering from malnutrition and disease. He said he was forming this brigade and would like us to help, and could I bring as many people from the Bush Warfare School as possible. Initially members of the staff of the School carried out the training of the brigade.

Major Walter 'Scottie' Scott
Officer Commanding 8 Column, 13th Battalion, King's Regiment (Liverpool)

I met Wingate for the first time in Central India. I was very impressed by him. He inspired us with his aims, and was completely dedicated to the end that we should be fit and trained before we crossed the Chindwin. During training up to twenty-five per cent were left out, and the numbers made up with fitter men. At the end of the training period, Wingate gave me command of Number 8 Column.

Private Charles Aves
7 Column, 13th Battalion, King's Regiment (Liverpool)

I was about twelve years younger than most of the men in my battalion. We heard about this man Wingate of Abyssinia. We thought he must be a freak who had done very well as a guerrilla in Ethiopia. He came to see us in Secunderabad and addressed us. He created a great effect on most of us. I felt I was in the presence of somebody really extraordinary, the type of person I had never come across before. He exuded an aura of power. And yet he didn't speak in that manner, he spoke quietly and convincingly, and we gradually came to the conclusion that he was talking about going to be trained to infiltrate the Japanese lines in Burma and in fact we were going to be the first troops to fight back since the debacle of the loss of Burma. He realigned our perception of what was possible for ordinary people like ourselves. He lifted us. We were left realising that our cushy life in India was coming to an end. He told us we were to be in for a very hard time training. We were going to show the Japanese we could do better. We were in awe of him. He convinced us that we could do it. He was a great man.

Lieutenant Denis Gudgeon
3 Column, 3rd/2nd Gurkha Rifles

From the time I joined the 3rd/2nd Gurkhas in March 1942, we trained to go to the Western Desert, learning the use of sun compasses, and our vehicles were painted yellow.

At end of June 1942, we were moved to Saugor to train on a secret operation, with 13th King's Regiment (Liverpool), the Burma Rifles and 142 Commando Company in 77th Indian Brigade under Brigadier Wingate. I was a bit annoyed, we had spent all this time training to go to the Western Desert and now we had to forget all that and start jungle training. We were a bit apprehensive. We had heard about Wingate and that he had been very successful in the campaign in Italy against the Italians.

We knew that he was ruthless and eccentric. I only met him when I was a young subaltern attending sand table exercises and TEWTs. Those I dreaded. Wingate would pick a hill several hundred feet high, and we would have to run up it and the last officer to get in would have to run down and up again. I was terrified of being asked some detailed military question as he would point his ruler at you, and fix you with his clear blue eyes. My mind would go a total blank.

He carried a Flit gun with him everywhere, which was a bit disconcerting when you were eating lunch and he puffed Flit about the place. He also carried an alarm clock about with him. We thought he was mad.

I did not like him. Not many of the Gurkha officers liked him. You couldn't have a rapport with him, he was aloof, never said very much. He issued reams of instructions, and we were terrified of him. We thought he was anti-Gurkha. We were split up into columns and the Gurkhas did not like being split up like that.

In the 3rd/2nd Gurkhas I was in C Company, my company commander was George Silcock. But when we became Chindits, I became administration officer of Number 3 Column. I was in charge of the RV where the mules were sent, coordinating supply drops, collecting parachutes, collecting supplies, and distributing supplies to the men.

Lieutenant Harold James
Number 3 Column, 3rd/2nd Gurkha Rifles
The Gurkhas expect very high standards from their officers: courage, to look after their interests, get to know their language, and have a good sense of humour. Out of the blue came the order that three of us were to go on a company commander's course at Jhansi. We arrived in January 1943. We were met by the adjutant, who asked, 'You know why you are here?'

'To go on a company commander's course.'

'No you are not, you are going into Burma. By the way, have you made your wills?'

We were pitchforked into Wingate's Chindits. We felt excited. I was nineteen.

I was in Number 3 Column. Originally there had been eight columns, but one had been disbanded so the force eventually consisted of seven, although we all kept our original number. The force had been training for months; it was a mistake on Wingate's part to bring in twelve hundred Gurkha troops and British officers at such short notice who had not a clue what it was all about, the various drills and so forth. As a result he went into Burma with a lot of untrained people, like me. He had suddenly decided that there should be more muleteers. Even the British column would have Gurkha muleteers, some of them recruits. Some hadn't fired a rifle, and certainly none of them had ever seen a mule. The other point was that we and other British officers were in columns with men we had never met before. Gurkhas like to know their officers. I was lucky, my column commander was Michael Calvert. An amazing man, a great leader, I have the highest regard for him. He could not speak Gurkhali, and had to rely on Captain George Silcock to translate for him. But the Gurkhas recognised in Calvert a man they could follow.

Lieutenant Denis Gudgeon
Number 3 Column, 3rd/2nd Gurkha Rifles
As we arrived at Saugor the monsoon started. It flooded and we had to climb trees. We lived up trees for several days, I tied my gramophone and records to a branch. About ten members of the force were drowned when the nearby river overflowed its banks and swept through camp very quickly. Gurkhas can't swim.

Private Charles Aves
7 Column, 13th Battalion, King's Regiment (Liverpool)
We went to Saugor, near Jhansi. The surrounding jungle was similar to the area of Burma in which we were to operate. We did long marches all through the night. We had bad and inadequate food. The monsoon started. We were never dry, night or day. There were mud holes four or five feet deep. It was an appalling month. We had our first casualties. A number of men returning in camp to their tents were drowned in what had been a small stream which had become a swollen torrent. I and plenty of soldiers went down with malaria, and lots of people went down with dysentery.

Those of us who had taken to the training and stuck it we called 'PKs', or 'pukka King's', those that opted out we called 'jossers'.

Many of the officers hated Wingate. I overheard an officer say to another officer, referring to Wingate, 'This man is mad.'

One day Wingate decided to hold a church service in the jungle. I was introduced by my column commander, Major Gilkes, to Wingate to discuss the hymns we would sing, which I would accompany on my accordion. I stood next to him as he conducted the first part of the service. I found him kind and considerate. Whenever we met on a one-to-one basis, which was not very often, he would ask how I was getting on. On one occasion he said, 'How are you finding the rations?'

I replied, 'There is not enough. We are hungry all the time.'

He just nodded his head and said, 'You will be pleased to know that we are going on general service rations. There will be more food and more variety.'

He went on his way. I felt proud to have spoken to Brigadier Wingate.

Major Michael Calvert
Commanding, 3 Column

We trained our men in the basing-up or bivouacking drills that would become a daily feature of life on Chindit operations. As the column approached the end of the day's march, the column commander would be near the front, and he would find a suitable place. You couldn't hesitate for long with four hundred or so men behind you. Some of the essentials were water and bamboo to feed the mules. Provided it was possible to combine it with water, we would try to find a place with fairly high ground so our signal sets would carry the two hundred miles back to India. We would set up a defensive position off the path, while the rearguard marched on as a deception before brushing away the footprints, and setting up an ambush to catch any Japanese following up.

Within five minutes of getting in, every unit would be lighting fires. We had been trained in this detail by Wingate who pointed out that often, just as we arrived at the bivouac area, the rain came at about four or five o'clock. He told us to collect dry sticks from the previous night's fire and put them in our packs. The wireless would be set up. The column commander would sit down and his batman would bring him a mug of hot sweet tea. Then the signals would start coming in. Our first signal out would give the position of the column to the base back in India.

The muleteers, one to each two mules, would go out and cut bamboo for their mules; you didn't need to carry fodder if there was enough bamboo nearby. The men would go to fill their water bottles. The upper piece of the stream was for water bottles, the next piece for mules, then for washing, and the lowest for defecating. We always tried to use running water for latrines, so it would be washed away and not give away our position.

We rarely stayed in a bivouac for more than one night, occasionally for two to three days. After the column commander had given orders, the column would settle down to eat and sleep. While the fires were still alight, we'd make a second quantity of tea, and put this in a spare water bottle, before burying the water bottle in leaves or earth just beside where one slept. In the mornings, before light, you drank warm tea and ate a Shakapura biscuit. The routines were carried out with few words being spoken, four hundred men and 120 animals going into their places with no fuss; the same in the morning. I would like to start the column moving just before dawn, and, if possible, get two hours' marching away from our previous bivouac before we settled down to breakfast.

Underlying all the training was Wingate's firm belief that his Long Range Penetration Force would outdo the Japanese. I don't want to be too hard on the British and Indian armies at the time, but they were to a large extent demoralised, they thought that the Jap was invincible. There were well-meaning posters up all over India showing cruel Japanese bayoneting children. Instead of making people want to fight the Japanese, it made them frightened. We had to build up the morale of the British to remember they were tough. I think this was why Wingate said that beards would be allowed. I personally would not allow mournful beards. I insisted that we should have aggressive beards, like conquistadores.

Lieutenant Dominic Neill
8 Column, 3rd/2nd Gurkha Rifles
Having been selected for a commission in the Indian Army from the 60th Rifles in the United Kingdom, I was sent as a cadet to Bangalore where the training was below standard, and all aimed at warfare on the North-West Frontier. We learned very little. Our weapon training was minimal, as was our map reading. When I joined our regimental centre our training was equally poor. My company commander was an ex-tea planter, and knew nothing about soldiering at that stage.

One day three other subalterns and I were called to the commandant's office and told that we were to join the 3rd Battalion under Brigadier Orde Wingate. Only one of the four of us was sent to command mules in a Gurkha column, the other three would go to the King's columns to command Gurkha muleteers. I had one Gurkha officer and fifty-two Gurkha Other Ranks, mostly from 10th Gurkhas and about half a dozen from other Gurkha regiments. When I joined 77 Indian Infantry Brigade I hoped I would get more training. I did not.

The 77th Infantry Brigade consisted of three rifle battalions and 142 Commando Company, which was a commando/demolition outfit. The brigade was organised into an HQ, and Numbers 1 and 2 groups. In Number 1 group were the four Gurkha columns, and in Number 2 group the three British columns, seven columns in all; around three hundred men in each column, and about ninety mules and three chargers. Each column had a headquarters; three rifle platoons; a support platoon with two Vickers medium machine guns and two 3-inch mortars; a reconnaissance platoon of Burma Riflemen and a section of 142 Commando Company. The training that the brigade had received had virtually finished by the time we joined at Saugor: mainly river crossing and tactics. On contact with the enemy a bugle would be blown, signalling dispersal. Troops would then disperse, under sub-unit commanders, and return to the former halting place. I could not believe my ears. Neither I, nor my Gurkha soldiers, received any tactical training whatsoever until we came face to face with the Japanese.

Lieutenant Denis Gudgeon
3 Column, 3rd/2nd Gurkha Rifles
We left Jhansi by train in mid-January 1943, crossed the River Brahmaputra by steamer, and by train to Dimapur railway station. We were met on the platform by Major Calvert, who was to be our column commander. We marched by night along the road through the lovely hill station of Kohima, which was to be flattened a year later, and eventually arrived at Imphal.

I was immensely impressed by Calvert, a dynamic character, he had been an army boxer, and had a flat nose and cauliflower ears. General Wavell came up and had a long conference with Wingate and finally gave his approval for us to go into Burma. He actually saluted us, and not the other way around.

Lieutenant Dominic Neill
8 Column, 3rd/2nd Gurkha Rifles

I was to join Number 8 Column, commanded by Major Walter Scott. Wingate came to visit us a day or so after the brigade farrier had branded each mule's number on their hooves. This was the first time I had met Wingate. He wandered down the mule lines with me and asked me one of the mule's number. I said that I did not know, they had only recently been branded, and haven't memorised their numbers yet. He said, 'Boy, you should know the numbers by now,' and passed on.

He looked very closely at the mules, but totally ignored the newly arrived young Gurkha soldiers, very peculiar.

After he had departed, I met Lieutenant 'Tag' Sprague, who I thought was very impressive. He was about four years my senior, had fought with 1 Commando in Norway, and was an experienced soldier. Originally the Gurkha columns were commanded by their respective company commanders, all of whom spoke flawless Gurkhali. On the eve of leaving India, two of the columns were given new commanders, neither of whom could speak a word of their language.

We had a lecture on how to handle mules, feed and water them and so forth, but had no practical training; we learned as we went along. I had never seen a mule in my life before. The Gurkhas had seen mule trains in the hills of Nepal, but never led them.

I was introduced to Major Scott, known as 'Scottie', but not to his face. He was an excellent chap. He gave my men and me a very warm welcome indeed, which was much appreciated. I was given a British sergeant, William Ormandy, an ex-17th/21st Lancer, very knowledgeable about horses, but he did not know much about mules. I also had twenty British Other Ranks (BORs) to lead the first-line mules in Number 8 Column. The mules were divided into two parties, first and second line. First-line mules carried support weapons, the heavy wireless set, ammunition, and some spare light machine guns. Second-line mules carried bedding, spare rations, and other stores. First-line mules were led by BORs, second line by Gurkhas.

The final exercise was a long hike across country of about a hundred miles. What the scheme was supposed to be about I have no idea at all, because from the start to finish in my time in Number 8 Column I was never called to one of Scottie's O Groups, even when we were in Burma. I was so inexperienced that it never occurred to me to suggest that I should attend. My orders were given to me via the sergeant major.

Lieutenant Harold James
3 Column, 3rd/2nd Gurkha Rifles

At Imphal Wingate had his HQ in the golf club, the floor was covered in maps. We went in every day in our stocking feet while Wingate held forth. He always carried a Flit gun and every now and then he would spray the room, it was dreadful. At one point Wingate asked if there were any questions and one of the doctors, a Canadian, said, 'Tell me, why do you have to use that Flit pump?'

'What do you mean?'

'It's bloody unsanitary.'

'Get him out,' said Wingate.

We were suddenly told that if anyone was wounded and could not keep up, he would be left in a village; if seriously wounded he would be helped on his way with a lethal dose of morphine. Officers were given a supply of morphine in things like miniature toothpaste tubes with a hypodermic needle on the end.

ACROSS THE CHINDWIN

Lieutenant Dominic Neill
8 Column, 3rd/2nd Gurkha Rifles

At the end of January we left Imphal for Tamu and the Chindwin. We marched through Palel and over the Shenam pass. As we approached the Burma border we marched by night. On 14 February 1943, we reached the Chindwin just north of the village of Tonhe, where there was a wide sandy beach on our side of the river, which at that point was about two hundred and fifty yards wide. Just before we started to cross, Bill Williams, the second-in-command, came and told me that a signal from Wingate had been received giving quotations from the Old Testament, which had to be interpreted by the column commander digging out his Bible. I suppose Wingate did it to try to fox the Japanese.

IND 2084

Wingate (centre) with two staff officers planning on the map on the floor of the golf club at Imphal before taking his brigade across the Chindwin.

IND 2088

General Sir Archibald Wavell, C-in-C India, inspects the Chindits before the first expedition. Nearest camera, Major Bernard Fergusson, commanding Number 5 Column, the badge on his hat has been obscured by the censor. Wingate is on the far right in the picture.

Lieutenant Harold James
3 Column, 3rd/2nd Gurkha Rifles

We had to cross the river Chindwin without the Japs finding out. The first objective was the Rangoon–Myitkyina railway, so Wingate divided the force into two groups. One group, the northern group, went with Wingate and his HQ, consisting of two Gurkha columns, including mine, Number 3, and three British columns, 5, 7 and 8; Fergusson's, Gilkes's, and Scott's.

The other group consisted of just two Gurkha columns, Numbers 1 and 2, commanded by Lieutenant Colonel Alexander, the CO of the 3rd/2nd Gurkhas. The southern group were the decoy. They crossed the Chindwin openly, and, combined with other tactical deception moves by other units not involved in the expedition, tried to attract the attention of the Japs while we went further north and crossed at Tonhe.

It worked because the Japs at that time were not all that well established on the Chindwin anyway. We were in the northern group aimed at blowing up the railway. We spent two nights marching on tracks through the jungle to the Chindwin. The river was about four hundred yards wide. None of the Gurkhas could swim. Wingate had made no attempt to teach them to swim, and indeed some British troops could not swim. Yet we were marching across the grain of the country and having to cross rivers. The British officers and commandos had to get the mules and horses across the river. It took a long time and much effort.

Lieutenant Dominic Neill
8 Column, 3rd/2nd Gurkha Rifles

When our Burma Riflemen were collecting boats from the villagers, we had another signal from Wingate in code, telling us that once we crossed the Chindwin any man wounded and unable to move would be left in a friendly village to his fate. I thought that to give an order like that on the eve of battle would cause the men's morale to dip. I know the British soldiers were not best pleased. I did not pass on the order to my Gurkhas. In those days none of them spoke English. Having received that boost to our morale we started to cross the river. We tethered the mules to the stern of the boats and swam them across; we were successful, other columns had problems. We were over by about 1700 hours or so. I remember going to sleep feeling very excited at the prospect of the operation ahead.

Swimming mules across a river.

Lieutenant Denis Gudgeon
3 Column, 3rd/2nd Gurkha Rifles

We crossed by boat, and the mules were swum across. This was very disheartening as some mules, having got almost to the other side, would panic and turn back again. Several times I got a free ride across the Chindwin by hanging on to the tail of a mule. It was broad daylight and luckily there was no sign of the Jap air force.

Lieutenant Dominic Neill
8 Column, 3rd/2nd Gurkha Rifles

That night was uneventful, as was the following day and many days thereafter. We moved north-east and received our first air drop. The dropping zone (DZ) was on an area of rice paddy. The mules were based in a bamboo forest to wait in safety during the drop.

This was the first parachute drop most of us had ever seen. While loads on parachutes were being dropped, the aircraft flew over the DZ fairly high. But the sacks of rice were free-dropped and planes came in quite low. We could see the dispatchers at the doors chucking out the sacks of rice, each weighed about 160 pounds. These came tumbling out turning over and over quite slowly, but hit the ground with a tremendous whack, and would have killed any mule or soldier had they hit.

My muleteers and I took the food back to our bivouac area. The rations were Shakapura biscuits, like square dog biscuits, rice, small tins of cheese, tinned meat and vegetables, powdered milk, tea and sugar. From this the BORs made a sort of porridge: crushed biscuits in a mess tin, with sugar and raisins sprinkled over, and either hot or cold powdered milk poured over it. It was very good indeed, but sadly my Gurkhas did not like it very much. They preferred to eat the rations straight.

Lieutenant Harold James
3 Column, 3rd/2nd Gurkha Rifles

I had a good view of our first air drop: I took a platoon to guard Bobby Thompson, our column RAF officer who was organising the drop. He later became Sir Robert Thompson of Malaya fame. The Brigade Rear HQ, a squadron of Dakotas, and supplies were located back in Agartala near Dacca. When a column wanted supplies it would radio requests and give a map reference for the DZ (at night we would light fires to guide the aircraft in over the DZ). This was all new to us, none of us had done it before, and we thought that you needed a nice open area like a paddy field for a DZ.

Squadron Leader Robert 'Bobby' Thompson
3 Column, RAF Liaison Officer

I would be sent ahead to select a place where supplies could be dropped and signal the location back to base. Sometimes we came across Japanese patrols, but usually we got plenty of warning of their approach from the local inhabitants, and we hardly ever ran into them unaware.

We got quite a lot of food in the villages. Once we paid for a meal of rice and curried fish and vegetables that was being cooked for the enemy. The main supplies were dropped to us by DC3s. We lit fires to show the dropping area. Grain was dropped in sacks, food by parachute. The ration packs consisted of paratroop rations, each pack was intended to last for two days and contained: six packets of biscuits, three packets of dates, one packet of raisins and nuts, four ounces of cheese, four ounces of chocolate, four ounces of sugar, two packets of dried milk, tea and salt, forty cigarettes, and two boxes of matches. Later on the chocolate was left out because it melted in the hot weather, but one column that wanted it particularly sent back a request for four hundred pounds of it. One of the restaurants in Calcutta took the job in hand and worked all night making the chocolate and the following day it was sent straight out to them by the officer in charge of base, whose name was Lord. One day one of the columns sent back a message 'Oh Lord send us bread'. And got the answer 'the Lord has heard thy prayer', and a full supply of bread followed. Anything you might specially need later was left behind with the supply officer and could be sent out to you. One officer had a replacement monocle sent out after he broke his. He got through several monocles during the course of the campaign.

Sergeant Douglas Williams
Wireless Operator/Gunner, 194 Squadron, RAF

Flying conditions in Burma were atrocious, there was always tremendous turbulence because of the heat. The bouncing up and down made it difficult moving supplies to the door to despatch them. We often flew through lightning. On a Hudson operation over the Chin Hills at sixteen thousand feet, we flew through a storm, the lightning flashed along the wing tips, lighting up the inside of the Hudson and the pilot's face white and tense with the strain of controlling the aircraft which bucked and dropped, thrown about like a ship in a boiling sea.. The pilot was very strong and held it while we plummeted from sixteen thousand to twelve thousand feet. But we got through, dropped our supplies, and returned to base pretty shaken.

Flight Sergeant Deryck Groocock
194 Squadron, RAF
In the monsoon you had fantastic thunder storms, towering cu-nims, air currents, low cloud bases and violent rain. We knew just about every valley in our area of Burma, so we knew which valleys we could fly up without coming to a dead end. Often there were clouds on the mountain tops, and you had to fly up a valley underneath. When trying to find a DZ, you hoped to find a hole in the cloud, find a valley leading in the right direction, drop and climb back up through the hole.

Lieutenant Harold James
3 Column, 3rd/2nd Gurkha Rifles
The rations were pitiful. Eventually, because of difficulties of getting air drops when you needed them, one day's rations had to last four days or even longer. You might get rice from villages, if you were lucky, but getting enough rice for three hundred and fifty people from a small village was not easy. When you are marching an average of ten miles a day, fighting and so forth, you got very hungry; it affected morale.

I was very fit, and coped very well with the rigours of the expedition. At first I noted in my diary what I was going to eat, and kept some reserve. Most difficult was the lack of water. When we got into the dry zone there was very little water, you had to dig for it.

Because I was so fit, Calvert made me permanent rearguard platoon commander. The worst place to march was in a long snake behind all those people and mules. There was a concertina effect with people at the back sometimes stopping for five minutes followed by running fast to catch up. Although platoons were changed over every few days, I was always rearguard commander.

We reached the railway line on 6 March without seeing the Japs. They were looking for our lines of communication, which did not exist. We marched on tracks and paths. Mike Calvert was trusted by Wingate implicitly, the only column commander who was. He allowed Calvert's column to go off on its own which is why we did better than the others.

We approached the railway at Nankan near Wuntho, between Mandalay and Myitkyina. We set off to blow up bridges. Wingate sent off one party to blow bridges north of Nankan under George Silcock and Lieutenant Geoffrey Lockett, a British commando. While Calvert and I went south to blow another bridge, an ambush was laid in the village of Nankan under the senior Gurkha officer, Kumarsing Gurung. The mules were sent to a safe RV.

My party with Calvert set off. On the way we heard firing at the station at Nankan, but continued on our way. As soon as our bridge was blown Calvert decided to go and help our party at Nankan. On our way back a Gurkha Rifleman came running up to say that the Japs had arrived in the village in lorries and that Kumarsing Gurung had ambushed them, killed a few, and was holding up the rest of the Japs. We were walking along the railway line, and had reached the path which joined the railway, when I looked up and saw a bearded face looking at me, and then a whole lot of more bearded faces; huge surprise, it was a Dane called Eric Petersen from 7 Column and his chaps. Mike Calvert, never one to lose an opportunity, said, 'How would you chaps like to join us in a little battle?'

So we all set off again along the railway. Meanwhile Kumarsing Gurung, realising they were being overwhelmed, moved away from the village towards the RV. At which point we arrived, caught the Japs napping, had quite a fight in the village, and blew up a lorry and an armoured car. The Japs withdrew, and as it was getting dark by now, Calvert decided to pull out to the RV about six miles from the station. We couldn't get to RV in time, so we based-up for the night. Calvert remarked, 'It's my birthday today, I'm thirty.'

I replied, 'If I'd known I would have bought you a present.'

Calvert laughed, 'I could not have asked for a better present than blowing up a couple of bridges and killing a lot of Japs.'

Calvert believed that boldness paid off and did not care a damn about the Japs. He lit a fire and made tea. We had just had a battle with Japs, were several hundred miles behind enemy lines, and here we were like a lot of happy campers. All the Gurkhas were asleep and contented, and not worried because they had such faith in Calvert, and had seen off the Japanese. This was our first action, and we didn't have a single casualty.

It worked well mainly because of Calvert and his 2i/c, George Silcock, a very good Gurkhali speaker, who supported him well. We reckoned we despatched fifty or sixty Japs. Mind you, you always think you have killed more people than you actually have.

To our north Fergusson had blown up the Bongyaung Bridge, but had suffered casualties and the southern group had also blown some bridges.

Lieutenant Denis Gudgeon
3 Column, 3rd/2nd Gurkha Rifles

I wasn't involved in the Nankan battle, I was in the RV with mules. The column blew up three box girder railway bridges, put charges on seventeen different places on the railway lines, ambushed a Jap lorry, and inflicted quite a lot of casualties. I could hear the bridges being blown and the lorry being ambushed.

The mules were a curse in battle. They had no 'discipline' as far as water was concerned, as soon as they smelt water they would bolt. They were very cunning and when being loaded, would blow out their stomachs so that the girth was not very tight. They loathed anything that rattled, or made a noise, and would get rid of it as soon as possible.

Lieutenant Dominic Neill
8 Column, 3rd/2nd Gurkha Rifles

After our first supply drop we marched about thirty miles due east to the Zibyu Taungdan, which we called the escarpment, and took a narrow footpath. Our mules started getting bad galls on their withers and bellies. The stench of their galls was dreadful as you marched alongside them, like a rotting corpse. If there were any heroes of the Wingate expedition it was our mules. After crossing the escarpment, 8 Column turned south-east towards the Irrawaddy. At that time I had neither map nor compass.

Up to now there had been no aggressive role for 8 Column, and I was getting bored. We marched towards the Irrawaddy, crossed in the same area as brigade HQ and 7 Column. Looking across the river I could hardly believe it was so wide, in some places up to two miles across. The villagers produced country boats paddled by villagers. We crossed satisfactorily. Some mules got loose but still got over.

Lieutenant Harold James
3 Column, 3rd/2nd Gurkha Rifles

As we approached the Irrawaddy, Wingate ordered everybody over. It was important to get across the Irrawaddy without the Japs knowing, so we marched most of that day, and all that night, traversing the Meza a couple of times to throw people off the scent. Eventually, in the early hours, we reached a jungle-covered hill where we stopped to rest. The order was that nobody was to move out of the perimeter. At daybreak there was a fusillade of fire, and the whole column got ready to move out. We discovered that a Gurkha and a Karen had very stupidly gone down to the river for water, we were very short at the time. They had been seen by a Jap patrol. We moved out very quickly leaving booby traps. We hadn't gone very far when we heard mortar fire, and shouts of Japs charging into the position, and then a couple of blasts of booby traps going off, which pleased us no end. Calvert now had to get to the Irrawaddy and throw the Japs off our track. So we had a very nasty twenty-four hours while he went one way and then the other, like a fox. Eventually in the early hours of the morning we stopped for a long time. As rearguard commander I was out of the picture. I heard mortar bombs about a mile off, so went on to the head of the column, and found the men collapsed, absolutely exhausted, in a flat area. I located Calvert, woke him up, and told him that the Japs were mortaring us. He said, 'I know,' which took the wind out of my sails. 'They don't know we're here,' he continued.

I believed him. It was probably true. He told me to stay by the chaung with my platoon and form a rearguard, and went back to sleep. The chaung was about two hundred yards wide, with thick elephant grass on both sides, and a few hundred yards away there was an open space with the whole column absolutely flat out exhausted. About two hours later I was catnapping and my havildar woke me up, saying, 'Come along sahib, come quietly.' We were in the elephant grass, which completely hid us. Peeping out I could see this Jap soldier, he was looking right across to where the column was, he couldn't see us. The havildar asked, 'Shall I kill him?'

I thought if I shoot him the Japs will open fire on the column, and also on me as my position will be compromised. So I said, 'No.' I sent a runner with a note to Calvert to tell him what was happening. The runner couldn't find Calvert. He and Lockett had gone off on horses to the other side of the island to see if they could find some boats. Luckily the runner chanced on George

Silcock, who immediately shook out the column into defensive positions. They were almost all deployed when the Japanese opened fire. With the first burst of machine-gun fire we took only five casualties. The Japs still didn't know where I was, and my Bren gunner opened up on them, putting some of them out of action. The Japs came down opposite us in the elephant grass and fired on us, badly wounding the number two on the Bren. Eventually we seemed to silence them; it went dead quiet. Just as I had got up to cross the chaung with my havildar to check if any enemy still there, Calvert appeared, and said, 'What are you doing standing in the open?'

He was always standing in the open. I didn't want to tell him I was going to cross the chaung, and said, 'I was going to get the men in the right positions.'

'Oh,' he said. 'Oh well, get in position here and keep the Japs at bay, while we cross the river.'

I had a wounded Gurkha, shot to bits in great pain, and dying. After agonising for a bit, I gave him a lethal dose of morphia. He went out very quietly, the Gurkhas were amazing, they just accepted it. We covered him with a blanket. We stayed there for some time, until a message came for me to join the main column with George Silcock. On arrival, I found only George, a section of Gurkhas and some Karens, the rest had gone off.

To my horror I found another very seriously wounded Gurkha there. I said, 'I've just had to do it.' George looked at me as if to say 'you do it again'.

I protested, 'There is no way I'm going to do it twice.'

He gave the chap a lethal dose. We were lucky: out of three hundred and fifty we had only three killed and four wounded. We moved off towards the main column where Calvert had started to organise the Irrawaddy crossing in some boats. Most of the Gurkhas were already over, and Calvert decided to put across only sufficient mules to carry essential equipment like wireless sets, MMGs and 3-inch mortars, the rest would be abandoned.

Eventually we set off into the interior, with my platoon at the rear. We passed a bullock cart loaded with straw, and on it were the four wounded Gurkhas who were going to be left in a village. The Gurkhas gazed at it; I think that this was the first time they really realised what would happen to them if they were wounded, and it went through them like being hit by a bullet. They had accepted giving a lethal dose: the chap was dying, and the officer sahib was doing the best for him. But this was quite different. This was when the seed of lowered morale was sown. It didn't appear then, but later.

We moved off. I can still see that bullock cart to this day with those four people lying there.

Major Michael Calvert
Officer Commanding 3 Column

The MO and I went the nearest village, asked them to look after the wounded we had crossing the Irrawaddy, and hand them over to the Japanese if they came along. I wrote a note to the Japanese, saying that I left the men who had been wounded, fighting for their king and country, just as they were. They have fought courageously, and I am sure that with your *bushido* you will look after them. I signed it. The Burma Rifles translated the note into Burmese. I felt that the Japanese would look after them, and they did. After they arrived in the prison camp, some of the other prisoners of war believed that they had given away secrets to earn good treatment. They had no secrets to give away.

Lieutenant Harold James
3 Column, 3rd/2nd Gurkha Rifles

Once we had crossed the Irrawaddy, we were in dead trouble for two reasons. First, which Wingate didn't realise at the time, we were in the dry zone, and at that time of year there was very little water.

Second, until then we had been spread out in jungle, so the Japs had trouble locating us. We were now in an area where columns were all within fifteen miles of each other. We were in a trap. To our east and north, the Shweli River flowed in a big curve into the Irrawaddy. A network of roads (the exact location of which we were unaware) ran to the Irrawaddy throughout the area. To our west lay the Irrawaddy, which was the lid of the trap, because the Japs took all the boats from the east bank of the river over to the west bank. So getting back over was going to be very difficult. The Japs knew where we were, realised we were supplied by air, and had gathered together a large force to smash us.

Wingate told Calvert that he would be joined by Number 5 Column, commanded by Bernard Fergusson, and that the two columns, under Calvert, were to march to the Gokteik viaduct, and destroy it. This pleased Calvert.

We set off in the direction of the viaduct, and had to cross the Nam Mit Chaung, a tributary of the Shweli River, to get there. Calvert organised a supply drop near a chaung on our route where we could dig for water, and gave everyone a good rest for three days. Up to that time officers slept with their own groups, but on this occasion, Calvert decided that all officers were to come to HQ. We started to sing popular songs, but stopped because we were not supposed to make unnecessary noise. He told us to sing on. It was a remarkable sight: eight British officers mostly bearded, very scruffy, singing songs three hundred miles inside Japanese lines. This was because Calvert was allowed to operate alone, and didn't believe in being dictated to by the enemy.

Calvert planned to cross the Nam Mit Chaung, RV with Fergusson, and go for the Gokteik viaduct. We reached the chaung at night, and first thing next morning we heard shots from where Calvert had sent a small patrol of Burma Rifles to do a recce. They had bumped some Japs, who had fired without hitting anything. So Calvert decided to set an ambush on the road near Pago, where there was known to be a Jap garrison. He selected me to set the ambush. I had a platoon of Gurkhas, a section of British commandos, and CSM Bob Blaine, a very tough character. We set up the ambush on the track, and waited. Soon a Burmese villager came along, and we grabbed him. I had a Karen with me who asked him where he was going. He said he was travelling from one village to another. We searched him and found a letter written in Japanese, which he said he had been told to take from the garrison in his village to the garrison commander in the next village.

I sent a note to Calvert on which I had rather cheekily written, 'May I suggest you come and join us for an attack on Pago?'

A little later, a Jap patrol walked into my ambush, and some of my Gurkhas, not being fully trained, fired too early and we did not kill them all; one or two escaped, and fired at us. I and my havildar decided to get rid of them. He fired a rifle grenade at the enemy while I worked my way round with a tommy gun, found one Jap there, who I put out of action, and rejoined the havildar.

At that point all hell broke loose as lots of Japs came on the scene. They struck the ambush behind us, and came round the flanks. In addition, thirty or so Japanese came rushing around to the front of my position. I had a section of Gurkhas with me. The Japs stopped for a moment, in a bunch, gazing at the enemy we had already killed; they were sitting targets. We let them have it with everything we had. Some were lying moaning, but there was no way we were going to look at them, they were treacherous even when wounded. But half a dozen or so may have escaped to my left. Then I heard a lot of firing

Chindits crossing a minor river.

from my other two sections, under the jemadar to my left, and Blaine to my right, so I told the havildar to move out. But before we could do so, we were attacked by about six Japs coming out of the jungle behind us. My Bren gunner stood firing from the hip. There was a bit of a melee, three Gurkhas were killed, one was wounded, and my havildar was killed by a bayonet. I had the satisfaction of despatching the chap who had killed him. We killed all the Japs.

Now there were just four Gurkhas, the Karen and I left unwounded. We started to move out. The place was full of Japs, and I wondered how we were going to get clear. It was thick scrub country. Suddenly our 3-inch mortar bombs started landing in among the Japs. Calvert, as soon as he realised that I had landed in something big, ordered the mortars to fire, which caused a gap in the ring of enemy through which we ran to join the main body. Sergeant Major Blaine turned up with his men saying he had had a great time, a whole lot of Japs had appeared in front of his position and he had wiped them out.

The main column remained in the position for about an hour and the Japanese never counter-attacked. But it was sad too, we lost nine people.

We moved out to go to the Gokteik, but that night received a wireless message to return to India independently. Now you could begin to tell that despite the troops fighting well at Pago, it was coming to the point where they had given practically everything they had to give. We were in tatters, stinking, hungry, thirsty. Everyone began to realise that if anything happened to them now they would be in a bad way.

DISPERSE AND RETURN TO INDIA

Major Walter 'Scottie' Scott
Officer Commanding 8 Column, 13th Battalion, King's Regiment (Liverpool)
When Wingate ordered the columns to split and return to India, I decided to cross the Shweli and hook round and cross the Irrawaddy. We had taken a supply drop at Baw but Japs closed in on us in a ring; not in great strength, but in patrols that could bring in more enemy as required.

I asked the RAF to drop me a floating rope and some rescue dinghies. I planned to cross the Shweli, using the rope and RAF dinghies. The chaps pulled themselves across with a looped rope over the grass rope, which was knotted at intervals. After getting about forty men across, one of the sergeants got his loop rope jammed on one of the knots on the grass rope. He panicked and pulled out his dah to cut the loop; instead he cut the main rope. He went sailing down the Shweli in his dinghy, on into the Irrawaddy, and was captured. I was left on one side of the Shweli, and my second-in-command with some men on the other.

The RAF dropped another rope and more boats the next night enabling me to get most of my chaps across. By then my second-in-command and forty men had been given authority to head for India. But he was killed and most of his chaps captured. I picked up four of them later.

Lieutenant Dominic Neill
8 Column, 3rd/2nd Gurkha Rifles

Just before we crossed, Scottie told us that we would shortly be returning to India. He told me to kill a mule to provide meat. I shot the mule with the worst galls with my pistol, between the eyes. Unfortunately the meat was very unpleasant and very tough. We were now only about seventy miles from the Chinese border. Return to India was very much on our minds, and when it would be. I wondered why on earth we had come to Burma, we in 8 Column had done nothing except a minor contact in Baw.

From the Shweli we marched north for two days. Tag's platoon was sent off on recce, while a platoon was left in a deep dried chaung bed, and the rest of us moved off to a forest rest house. We were marching in single file, all the men bunched as usual. No one in Wingate's brigade seemed to worry if troops bunched. If you bunch, you present a target, and if hit you take casualties. The vegetation was jungle, but not very thick. Suddenly there was rifle fire in front. It sounded like Jap fire, I saw the BORs in the leading platoon running back shouting, 'Japs!' I stood in the middle of the track, thinking would I see my first Jap? Suddenly I saw one, range twenty yards. I put my rifle up to my shoulder, had taken the first pressure, and was about to fire, when a BOR's head popped up and blotted out the target. The Jap fired, the bullet hit the sand between my feet. There was confusion in extreme up front. The remainder of the leading platoon came back with terror in their eyes, and my men in sympathy turned and ran. I shouted at them in Gurkhali, 'Don't run,' and, bless them, they slowed to a walk. As the animal transport officer I now found myself as rearguard. I thought, 'At last, I shall kill a Jap.' But not a bit of it, they didn't follow up.

We got back to the chaung bed where we had a firm base. I asked the leading platoon commander what had happened. He told me they had bumped two Japs, only two, and the leading platoon had carried out Wingate's dispersal drill to the letter. The only thing missing was a bugle call. Wingate had really opened up a Pandora's box when he told them to carry out dispersal drill on meeting the enemy. It was a shambles. There were a lot of young men in 8 Column that evening who hung their heads in shame. If a field commander teaches bad tricks in training, the chaps will react badly when they meet the enemy. It was a lesson I hoisted in then. After that incident Scottie ordered us to march to the Irrawaddy, which we reached at the beginning of April. We were, as far as I could gather, not far from Inywa; about seven hundred men were there from HQ and other columns as well as us. Some men had been sent across by Wingate to form a bridgehead. Not long after I reached the area of the river there was heavy firing from the other side, Jap 4-inch mortar and medium machine-gun fire; theirs had a much slower rate of fire than ours. It sounded just like a woodpecker.

I could not see any of the bridgehead platoon. Next I saw a group coming towards me led by Wingate like a figure in the Bible, with a huge beard and sola topi [pith helmet], his pack was bumping up and down on his back, his eyes were wide and staring, and as he passed me and my group, he shouted, 'Disperse, disperse, get back to India'. I can remember the words to this day. I thought the man had gone stark staring mad. Here we were, with a force seven-hundred strong, one platoon already across the river, and he was not prepared to carry on with the crossing. I realised we would have suffered casualties if we had persisted with the crossing, but far fewer than we eventually did by splitting up into small groups and getting back piecemeal to India.

Private Charles Aves
7 Column, 13th Battalion, King's Regiment (Liverpool)
Wingate decided to recross the Irrawaddy at the same place as he had crossed on the outward journey, counting on the Japanese not thinking that we would do this. In the early morning we approached the river, Number 7 Column was sent ahead. Some boats were found from somewhere, and some Burmese to paddle them across. I was on the third boat. As we approached the other side the Japs opened up with machine guns and mortars. My boat wasn't hit. One

behind was hit, and everybody in it killed or drowned. When our boatload got ashore, we crawled up the bank. I found one of the officers standing eating a piece of cheese from a tin, unconcerned. The firing was about four hundred yards north of where we landed.

The officer pointed to a paddy field, told me to go out there and launch some grenades towards the enemy. He produced a grenade launcher and two grenades. I had never used one before. It is difficult to cross a paddy field; it consists of mud, water, and banks called bunds. I could not walk along the bund for fear of being shot by the enemy. I crawled my way to where the officer had told me to go. I found I was the only person who had crossed who was doing anything. I could not see where the enemy were. I didn't know what to do and decided to return, which took some time. I told the officer that I hadn't fired, he told me not to worry, and that we were moving off anyway.

Here I learned that Captain Hastings, an officer I admired and respected so much, had been killed on the boat that had been hit and sunk. Sixty-five of the column landed, a captain, a lieutenant, a second lieutenant, four sergeants, a couple of corporals, and about fifty private soldiers. We went inland to a place already designated as an RV after crossing the river. We waited twenty-four hours to see if anyone else turned up. Although the opposition where we crossed was not big, I learned later that Wingate had decided to stop crossing there.

Lieutenant Dominic Neill
8 Column, 3rd/2nd Gurkha Rifles

Number 8 Column marched east away from the Irrawaddy; talk about the grand old Duke of York. That night I got a warning order from Scottie that mules and chargers were to be driven away because they might be a hindrance to us in our return to India.

I hated the idea. My charger, whom we called Rathi, the Gurkhali name for red deer, started nuzzling my face. I was glad it was dark, and no one could see me, the tears were running down my face. The following morning off we marched, leaving our mules and chargers where they had spent the night. We took one mule to carry the wireless. Many of our animals followed and we tried to shoo them off. But my beloved horse followed for hours, eventually leaving us in a big field of sugar cane. I saw his red rump disappear. I looked round at my syce, Dalbir, and he was weeping too. That night there was much talk of what orders we would receive. I asked Tag if he and his commandos would accompany me and my Gurkhas if we split up, and to my intense relief he agreed. We had a final air drop of ten days' rations and I was called to my first O group. It was a big day, all columns would split up into small groups. Wingate had played us his last ace card. He had taken us so far but he wasn't going to take us back, and for that I have never forgiven him. He took us one river too far.

The single wireless set would go with Scottie, and he told us to tell him our chosen route, so that before we split up he could issue us with maps. Tag and I said we would go north to the Irrawaddy, cross between two villages of Bhamo and Khaso, and head west to the Chindwin. We collected our set of maps and compasses.

We knew the Japs would make every effort to catch us. Tag was our salvation. Sergeant Ormandy volunteered to come with us. I was given four hundred rupees in silver coins from Scottie's treasure chest. All my equipment weighed what seemed like a ton. Never again in all my combat soldiering was I ever faced by such a test as getting my men back to India. Each group was given a section of Burma Rifles, and I had an exceptional young soldier called Tun Tin, a Karen, mission-school educated, who spoke excellent English. We took three days to reach the Irrawaddy.

Lieutenant Harold James
3 Column, 3rd/2nd Gurkha Rifles

After Calvert had been told to return to India independently, he decided to return to our earlier camp to collect the three days' worth of rations we had cached there. We then set off to cross the Shweli river and go up into the Kachin Hills where the tribes were loyal, and work our way out through China. The Shweli, although not as wide as the Irrawaddy or Chindwin, was still quite an obstacle as well as being fast flowing. There were no villages nearby for boats. So Calvert decided to make 'sapper sampans' out of groundsheets and bamboo. While we started to build these he left me to guard the rear. He sent Blaine across to the other side. Not long afterwards a Jap patrol walked into Blaine's position. Blaine exterminated the lot of them but Calvert, having decided there was no way he could linger and cross the river as the Japs would soon be upon us, ordered a quick move away at once.

When I came forward to rejoin the column, and reached the riverbank, to my horror I saw two Gurkhas on the other side. The 'sapper sampan' had been brought back ready to take another load across, when Calvert ordered the move. Calvert had left the Gurkhas, he could not wait. We marched away from the river, and had a long discussion with the other senior officers, who had suggested breaking up into small dispersal groups and making our way back to India in these groups. Calvert was against this. He felt the column had worked so well up to now that it would be wrong to break it up. In the end he agreed to what was a right opinion. He decided to break up in an ordered manner. We took an air drop, he decided on the groups and who was to command them. He ordered a good supply of maps, rations and machine guns to be dropped. Some rum was also dropped. The officers gathered and drank a toast to the king, and to Number 3 Column. Calvert said, 'Well, here we go. We will all meet again in India.' We broke up into our groups, and off we set.

Lieutenant Dominic Neill
8 Column, 3rd/2nd Gurkha Rifles

Eventually we reached the village of Zimbugon. I sent Tun Tin and some of his riflemen in, dressed in civilian clothes; they all carried civilian clothes in their packs. I told him to ask the headman if the village was friendly, and if they would hire us boats. He came back and reported that the villagers were indeed friendly, there was Jap presence in Shwegu about twelve miles upriver from Zimbugon, and the headman promised to give us early warning should the Japs approach his village. As a counter to that, we were told that it would take a day or so for the headman to collect sufficient boats for us. We spent a very tense day in a reed-covered sandbank.

We waited and waited, and early on the night of 11 April 1943, four or five large boats appeared. It took us half an hour or so to get across. I noticed that the sandbanks were not in the same position as marked on our maps. But as our maps were made in 1910 it was understandable. We disembarked on the other side at about 2100 hours. Having paid and thanked the boatmen, we moved off to some high ground about five miles off, which we picked off the map as it was shown as being jungle covered. We based up and posted sentries, and slept for the rest of the night. I felt elated at crossing that first huge barrier.

Lieutenant Denis Gudgeon
3 Column, 3rd/2nd Gurkha Rifles

I was rearguard in Calvert's party. When we got back to the Irrawaddy we discovered that the Japs had moved all the boats to the western bank. Calvert decided that we would build 'sapper sampans'. Unfortunately our groundsheets were rotten and our boat would not float. As I had a party of twelve in which the only people who could swim was the Burma Rifleman and me, I decided to march along the Irrawaddy. After several days we got to a village and hid in some thick undergrowth nearby. The Burma Rifleman went into the village, found a boatman, and after a lot of hard bargaining I arranged to pay the boatman some of my precious silver rupees with which we had been issued. He got us safely across to the other side that night. I had no maps of the area, but had a prismatic compass and if I marched on a bearing of 330 degrees it would take us more or less to where we started. I got progressively weaker as we marched, and eventually I ordered my men to go on and leave me. I was then on my own, and knew I must be near the Chindwin, and two days later on a small path I waylaid a Burmese fisherman who was selling dried fish. He said he would take me in a boat across the river, and get me to the British lines. Actually he took me to a village and handed me over to the local Burmese militia. They took me to the nearest Jap garrison and this fisherman got a reward of fifty rupees.

Lieutenant Harold James
3 Column, 3rd/2nd Gurkha Rifles

My group consisted of my platoon and Captain Taffy Griffiths, Burma Rifles: cool, brave and older than me. Half of the groups decided to head for the Irrawaddy much further south than where we had crossed. Others decided to go the way we had come.

We were now going across the dry zone, there was no water, and we were very thirsty. We had to avoid a huge forest fire. As we were going through burnt-out black scrub, suddenly a little line of green appeared in front: it was a cool clear chaung. We had a good drink, and filled our water bottles. Taffy sent a couple of Karens forward to recce the river. We knew that the Japs had removed boats. As we approached the Irrawaddy, in broad daylight, the Karens came back to say they had a boat. It was a big sampan, the home of a Burmese family. They had come to our bank to fix something in the boat. It was sheer luck. There it was at our feet, and could take about twenty people. We sent a small party across in a small boat, which the bigger boat carried, to check that there was no enemy there. We then crossed in two parties, and who should turn up but Bobby Thompson, and he used our boat too. After Bobby, Calvert turned up and used the same boat. We had sheer luck in broad daylight, but we had come a long way further south from the other crossings, and crossed the danger zone quickly before the Japs could get into position.

Private Charles Aves
7 Column, 13th Battalion, King's Regiment (Liverpool)
We needed to get some food, as we had had no air drops. Some of the men were ill and worn out. A friend of mine, Freddy, said, 'I can't go on.' I knew his mother, whom we had visited when on leave. So I said, 'It's all right for you to give up, but what about your mother? She's waiting for you to come home. She's all on her own.'

We took his rifle and his pack. You become very close in these circumstances. Even if you would have nothing in common in civilian life, a bond forms between you. Freddy did get out of Burma. We had to go to a village to get food. The officers had maps and money, so could buy food, a ball of cooked rice wrapped in a banana leaf.

The next day the officers decided to rest, and set up camp in a nullah, a dried river bed. We were spread over sixty yards, with two sentries out. I was with Corporal Hickman, near the sentries. We brewed up. We were tired. Suddenly the two sentries ran past us, saying that they had heard firing. Corporal Hickman said, 'Don't run.' We stayed for a few seconds. We didn't know if they were Japs or Burma traitors. My friend Stan Allnut said, 'Let's go.' We left our packs, and ran. On our way we picked up two packs, I didn't know whose they were at the time.

We clambered up some rocks nearby. We emptied our rifles towards the area where the Japs had been, but there was no reply. The firing stopped. There were eleven of us: one officer, one sergeant, Corporal Hickman and eight privates. The rest had disappeared. I would have been lost if it hadn't been for Stan. The lieutenant, I don't remember his name, asked how many water bottles we had. There were two. The pack I picked up had in it all the maps, all the way to the Chindwin. It was Captain Oakes's, he had left it behind. Corporal Hickman's pack belonged to the other officer Lieutenant W, my platoon officer, and in it were three hundred rupees. Both packs were left behind by people who shouldn't have left them behind.

The lieutenant said two water bottles were not enough, that we must find some more, and that we would have to go back. So bravely we went back to the area of the attack. We could hear the Japs talking. The lieutenant changed his mind saying it was too dangerous, and we would march west as soon as possible. All of the eleven of us were pretty fit. We made off into a bamboo forest, and rested.

Major Walter 'Scottie' Scott
Officer Commanding 8 Column, 13th Battalion, King's Regiment (Liverpool)

I had my CO, Lieutenant Colonel Cook, with me, who was very sick. I headed for an area of the Irrawaddy we hadn't used before, twenty miles below Bhamo where the river races through a narrow defile. The villagers said that all the boats had been taken by the Japanese. But I noted that the Burmese boats poling up the Irrawaddy were moving very slowly up through the gorge. After a while one came quite close to our side of the river, and grounded in shallow water about fifteen yards offshore. So I, and several others, waded out, and captured it. By that night, I and my party had got across the Irrawaddy. We only had one mule, the wireless mule. I gave the boatmen five hundred silver rupees, more money than they would have made in a year.

We went off into thick jungle. We still had the wireless, but the mule soon died. I sent a signal to say where we would be in four days' time, and asked the RAF to drop me fourteen days' rations. The signal went on to say that a week later I would be at such and such map reference, and take another drop. I planned these so we would have these drops all the way out of Burma.

A few nights later I walked out into the clearing we had given the RAF as a DZ, it was about fifteen hundred yards long and about four hundred yards wide. I thought right away how we might set up a rescue. If they come to supply us they could fly out the sick and wounded: fourteen men and my CO, who certainly would not have made the Chindwin.

The RAF came across as arranged and dropped our rations, but our wireless was dead. Using the first lot of parachutes we laid out a signal: PLANE LAND HERE NOW. WOUNDED.

The next aircraft circled twice, tried to land, couldn't make it, but he dropped a message on a streamer. It said, 'Hold on here.'

Lieutenant Dominic Neill
8 Column, 3rd/2nd Gurkha Rifles

After the Irrawaddy, we had one more major river to cross, the Chindwin, and many smaller rivers in between. I reckoned that as the crow flies we had about two hundred miles to reach the Chindwin. The monsoon was due to break in late May or early June, and even the minor rivers between us and the Chindwin would be tremendous barriers if flooded.

It took two days, marching to cover the twenty-five miles or so to the Kaukkwe Chaung. Where we crossed, the Chaung was about twenty-five yards wide, with steep twelve-foot-high banks, and waist-deep water. On the west bank I sent Tun Tin to recce a village about two miles to our south. We followed them closely in case they got into trouble. A short while later Tun Tin sent scouts back to say that the village was clear and we would get a warm welcome. We moved into the village and begged the headman for some rations, which he gladly said he would supply. It was now early morning on 14 April.

We got a sock full of rice per man and a few chickens. I had had a very sore toe for some time. I sat on my pack and took my boot off for the first time for days, and saw a huge abscess on my big toe. I didn't know what to do. I put on my boot and hoped for the best. I was very worried; we had no drugs or medicines to deal with such a problem.

After collecting our rations, and as we were about to leave, I saw a villager get on a bicycle and leave the village on the track we were about to take. I paid no attention, and we moved off. We were now marching north along a narrow track. I had some Gurkhas ahead of me, and Tag, plus Tun Tin and some others to my rear.

We had not gone far when an ambush exploded to my left. I shouted, 'Take cover right,' and dived into cover myself. I wasn't actually frightened but certainly shocked. Never in my training had I been taught the appropriate contact drills. I did not know what to do. A Jap machine-gunner was firing across the track from me so close I could see the smoke from his muzzle, the bullets hit the trees above my head, cutting leaves and bark, which fell on my pack and down my shirt collar. Rifle fire came in as well. Altogether I am sure that the ambush was not all that long in length along the track. I don't know how long I lay there, perhaps a minute and a half. I heard the Jap gunner change the magazine, and decided that the next time he did so we would

HU 88979

Major Scott's signal to a Dakota 'Plane land here'.

move. My heavy pack kept me pressed to the ground with my head bent down, and I could not fire my rifle easily.

I heard him change magazines again, and roared above the noise of rifle fire, 'Everybody up, follow me,' calling to my men to follow me away from the ambush into the jungle. Some of my men ran, but there was no sign of Tag or Tun Tin. I saw one of my men hit.

My men on my flanks began to close on me. I saw one of Tag's men drop his pack and thought him a fool to do so. Then I saw Tag and some more of his men. I called out again to close on my position. I suggested we lay an ambush to catch any Japs coming for us, and hope that the majority of my men still dispersed could catch up. Tag, an experienced soldier, said no, if we waited here in ambush we could get cut off. We did not know where the missing men were, we had no means of communicating with them. Our aim was to get back to India without further delay. He was right.

We took stock. We had two British officers, eleven Gurkhas, six BORs of Tag's platoon, one Burma Rifleman, a total of twenty; all the others were missing. I felt very guilty at not doing better, I had failed completely. Our first contact with the Japs after leaving 8 Column had ended in disaster. The villager must have warned the Japs so we must put the maximum distance between ourselves and the village. We must leave the others and hope that some of them joined up with other escape parties. We must head north.

That night I told Tag about my frustration at not having a tommy gun in the ambush, and Tag told his Corporal White to swap his tommy gun for my rifle. White was delighted at getting a lighter weapon. I thought now if we get hit again, I will have a better weapon.

I found that my sore toe was not hurting. I took off my sock and it was full of blood and pus. My mind was in a turmoil with utter guilt and shame. I vowed that night if I survived I would teach myself and my soldiers proper contact drills and counter-ambush drills.

Lieutenant Harold James
3 Column, 3rd/2nd Gurkha Rifles
The next danger spot on the way to the Chindwin was the railway line, but we got across that all right, followed by crossing the escarpment, a high ridge of mountains. By this time we were very short of food. We resolved not to look for trouble and attack the Japanese. We had to go into a village to get

some rice before we crossed the escarpment, as there was no food there. Then along comes Bobby Thompson and his group. We decided to join up and be double strength, which made it safer to go into a village, which we did, and got some rice. After this we went off into foothills, camped, and had a good meal. Just as we were moving off we heard machine-gun fire. I thought of the wounded Gurkhas, as did others. I saw two Gurkha sections coming along, totally ignoring the battle behind us, and taking no notice of any orders we gave them. I don't know what the firing was about.

We went up onto the escarpment. We lost touch with half a platoon, although they did get back safely. It was a most unpleasant feeling. I realised that everyone, except Calvert, would do things that they would not normally do. Hunger, tension, thirst and fear built up. Getting back became the overriding urge. This operation was quite different from the normal battle.

It was a terrible march. But Bobby was one of the world's best map readers.

Private Charles Aves
7 Column, 13th Battalion, King's Regiment (Liverpool)
We came to the railway line in the evening. The lieutenant said we would hole up and see if we could spot any Japs. He wisely decided to cross at night, having waited one night and the next day before doing so. We got across and just as we arrived on other side we heard a shout, we froze, and whoever it was didn't spot us. It was pitch black without a moon. After that we moved off and marched west day after day. We had a man with us who read us a verse from the Bible every day. We all fitted in very well with each other.

When we got to villages, the phrases I had learned back in India came in very useful. I was the only one who had any knowledge of the language at all. I went in with the lieutenant, speak to the head man, and ask if any Japs were about. We could pay for our food. We went to about six or seven villages and always looked about to see if anyone disappeared. Only one village caused any problem. Immediately we got in we knew there was something wrong. The lieutenant said, 'Let's go,' and we left immediately. We were right, because when we got out of Burma, we learned that a party ahead of us had been attacked after entering this village.

Lieutenant Dominic Neill
8 Column, 3rd/2nd Gurkha Rifles

The next two or three days were hard, over ridges rising four thousand feet. Tag's men were becoming despondent. The BORs wanted to take the British rations from the DZ where supplies had been dropped before, and then head for China. Scottie had been told and had given us the grid references of where supplies had been dropped so we could collect rations from them. Tag and I reckoned this would be suicide, the Japs had seen the supplies being dropped, would ambush the DZs. Tag explained this and strongly advised against heading off on their own. In the end his sergeant said they could not exist on rations from villages, and must have British rations. Tag eventually agreed to their plea, they already had a compass, and he gave them maps. We wished them well. They were never seen nor heard of again.

I was quite glad when Tag's men left. Their morale had gone down very much since the ambush. I think Tag made the correct decision. He still regrets it.

Apart from our physical weakness through hunger, we were only fourteen men and this was a concern. We were the quarry and the Japs were the hunters. There was little thrill in being hunted, just terror. We had about sixteen miles to go as the crow flies to reach the Myitkyina–Rangoon railway. About five miles from the railway line we came across some paddy and a small hut. The man and woman inside told us how far we were from the line. They had no uncooked rice they could sell us but gave us some cooked rice folded in banana leaves, which we ate then and there. They also gave us some tiny lumps of unrefined sugar, or ghurr.

We had to get on to beat the Japs and coming rains. I had cut my trousers to shorts and my legs got scratched and developed jungle sores. My heavy pouches caused further sores on my hips. At midday when we stopped to brew tea, we took off our shirts and had a lice hunt, killing about a hundred on each occasion. The next landmark was the Mawhan–Mawlu Road which we crossed very quickly in extended line, and brushed away our tracks in the dust with branches of leaves. Having crossed the railway and into the Mawhan Forest, we hid near a village and sent in the Burma Rifleman to buy food, while we hid nearby. He returned with some rice in a sock and a chicken. We crossed the Meza river, and it was almost dry and easy to cross. From here was the escarpment, the Zibyu Taungdan.

Major Walter 'Scottie' Scott
Officer Commanding 8 Column, 13th Battalion, King's Regiment (Liverpool)
Two days later we got another supply drop, and one plane dropped another streamer telling me to lay out a landing strip. I laid out parachutes across the area to mark the strip. He landed at the second attempt, brought in another wireless set, and took out my CO and fourteen wounded. Two hours later they were in hospital in Imphal. I got a signal saying hold there, they might try to rescue more of us. But Dakotas were in short supply and in any case the Jap garrison at Indaw close by would be bound to react soon, so I decided that we had better get out. I set out to walk to India.

Soon after leaving the strip, we came to the Kaukkwe Chaung; it was about sixteen to thirty yards wide and was lined by small parties of Japanese. We were crossing on bamboo rafts and had got practically everybody across, except for about ten men, when the Japanese opened up on us. I blew the dispersal signal, and we dispersed. I lost about twelve men there. My best colour sergeant was hit in the leg; the bullet went right through. I tried to lift him up, and he said, 'Your duty is to get the rest of these men out. You won't make it with me. Leave me.'

We had to leave him, and he was never heard of again. We linked up at an RV between the Kaukkwe Chaung and the railway.

Lieutenant Dominic Neill
8 Column, 3rd/2nd Gurkha Rifles
The men's knowledge of what we could eat in the jungle was our salvation, one of the favourite being the tips of a fern, tasty if boiled with rice. We used only game trails, for fear of bumping a Jap patrol on the wider tracks. At night we would leave the trail and bed down for the night. I had long since stopped posting sentries; the men needed all the sleep they could get.

Major Walter 'Scottie' Scott
Officer Commanding 8 Column, 13th Battalion, King's Regiment (Liverpool)
We crossed the railway, didn't meet any enemy and had a trouble-free march to the Chindwin. I chose the densest area I could to move through. We got boats from a village, and crossed in one night about thirty miles north of where we had entered Burma.

Lieutenant Dominic Neill
8 Column, 3rd/2nd Gurkha Rifles

One day we met three or four buffaloes in a deep-sided chaung. I told Tag to take one of the Gurkha soldier's rifle, knowing him to be a good shot. He fired, killing one, the rest scattered. I got the men to drag the dead buffalo out of the chaung, we knew we had to butcher and cook the buffalo as quickly as possible before a villager came to look for his missing buffalo. We cut stakes of wood and skewered buffalo meat to cook and smoke. The men knew exactly what to do. It was butchered and cooked in a very short time. As the long strips were cooked, we ate them before they were properly done. The blood ran down our chins, until our shrunken stomachs were bursting. We could hardly believe our luck. We hung strips of meat on our packs. We would occasionally chew them on the march, and cook them at halts. Unfortunately some of us kept these strips too long, they became fly-blown and stank horribly. I continued to eat mine. How I did not get stomach problems I don't know, I must have had the constitution of an ox.

We now avoided villages because of Jap garrisons, which we knew were in them. It was now mid-May, about another month before we would reach the Chindwin. Marching became slower and slower, we could manage only forty minutes' marching, followed by twenty minutes' rest, in the hour.

We thought that to use our outward route across the escarpment would be fatal, as the Japs would ambush it, and we were proved right when they ambushed other escape parties. We eventually picked a route off the map following a chaung. It was very hard going, either full of water or damp sand. Tag caught fever and was near to collapse, but he kept going; a less resolute man would not have made it. Eventually it burnt itself out. We reduced our pace to marching for half an hour and resting for half an hour.

We were so desperate that we decided to risk visiting another village, a Kachin village, it was not on our map, just a few houses. We got enough rice for one sock full per man, and some ghurr, and some cheroots in lieu of our cigarettes, which had long run out. While paying the headman, Tag and I noticed the headman's pretty daughter standing there, and I was glad that I had trimmed my beard. But she had no eyes for me, just for the silver rupees. The stinking, sore-covered scarecrows were of no interest to her at all. When we had packed the food in our packs, we thanked them and went off.

We were fearful of encountering the Burma Traitor Army. They wouldn't take on a large party of Chindits, just report it to the Japs.

Private Charles Aves
7 Column, 13th Battalion, King's Regiment (Liverpool)

The rest of the journey to the Chindwin went without incident. Suddenly we came across a patrol of Seaforth Highlanders. They were looking out for Chindits. We were in tatters. This patrol had been attacked by Japs the previous day, and were looking for the Japs to deal with them. Our lieutenant volunteered us to help. To our great relief, the officer of the Seaforths declined, saying that they were here to help us to safety not to get us killed. They took us to boats and we crossed to the other side, north of where we met the Seaforths.

We were taken to Imphal. It felt wonderful. Except that I went down with malaria. To my great pleasure, we were visited by Wingate, who smiled and said, 'I'm glad to see you here.'

I told him my story about the packs we picked up. I was disgusted at the way they were abandoned. He said, 'We won't wash our dirty linen in public, will we?'

I have not talked about it since.

I was lucky to survive.

Lieutenant Dominic Neill
8 Column, 3rd/2nd Gurkha Rifles

We hit a track leading to the Chindwin. Could we take the risk? We had to, in order to get ahead of the monsoon. We were marching along; about forty yards away there was a left-hand bend in the track. Suddenly, a Gurkha said in a low voice that an elephant was coming. Sure enough there was one approaching down the track. A mahout was sitting on the elephant's neck and standing in the howdah was a man with a white helmet and tunic. Just as I was thinking he must be a district officer, he bent down, picked up a rifle, pointed it at me or Tag, just beside me, and started to shoot. The elephant was towing a fifteen-hundredweight truck loaded with some fifteen Japs. They leapt out, took up fire positions and opened up at us. We were within a few miles of the Chindwin, we could not take on the Japs. So within half a second I roared out follow me, and we dashed off into the forest. We were all in good order. I waited for the sound of a thwack and a bullet hitting my pack. But I wasn't hit. We ran and ran, despite the fact we were exhausted, we ran and kept together. I realised the Japs had ceased fire. We ran on and didn't seem to be following up. We eventually halted in a hollow. We were all there except my orderly. A chill swept through me. There was nothing we could do for him. I told Tag.

We walked on, goodness knows how far, based up, and had something to eat. Huddled up under my damp blanket that night, I regretted the serious error of judgement in using the track, and the lack of correct reaction on my part. I was ashamed.

Next morning we set off to the Chindwin, now only thirteen strong. It took us ten more days. My havildar went down with malaria, his skin was like yellow parchment and we thought he would die. We took his rifle and pack. We wouldn't leave him. He staggered along following us, using a stick. About this time I found that the sole of my left boot had a hole in it, and I marched on my sock. The right sole was tied on by parachute cord.

Major Michael Calvert
Officer Commanding 3 Column
The Gurkha columns commanded by Gurkha officers failed. Whereas mine and George Dunlop's columns succeeded. Dunlop's column got back after most of the others, and did not get the publicity the others did. He did not disperse and carried out some excellent operations on the way back. By the time he got back the press had lost interest.

I sometimes wondered if I should have carried out the dispersal. We were told that IV Corps has patrols across the Chindwin who would meet us. Unfortunately the Corps commander withdrew his troops back across the Chindwin before we arrived near the river. When we reached the Chindwin we relaxed. I went further south than my dispersed groups, and blew the railway in order to attract the Japanese on to me so as to make it easier for the other dispersal groups to get back to the Chindwin. When we got to the Chindwin, I got on to a boat with some Burma Riflemen and drifted down the river, standing up shouting that we had arrived. I wore shorts, the Japanese didn't wear shorts.

When we eventually arrived we all marched in to the Indian Army base, to show we weren't a defeated army.

Lieutenant Harold James
3 Column, 3rd/2nd Gurkha Rifles

Our party eventually reached the Chindwin where we were met by the Sikhs who looked after us very well, with a huge curry. We should have been told not to eat too much, but even our Doctor who was with us wasn't going to hold back. At Imphal we were put into hospital, and our lice-ridden clothes were burnt.

Lieutenant Dominic Neill
8 Column, 3rd/2nd Gurkha Rifles

Early one morning we heard the noises of a village, it was Myene. Tag and I went to the headman's house. He said there had been no recent enemy movement in the area. We said our goodbyes and left. We marched to the Chindwin, about five miles from Tonhe, where we had crossed on the outward journey. We found a game trail and met a villager. The Burma Rifleman spoke to him. He said he would take us to the tiny village nearby. We asked if we could hire boats. He said that all boats had been collected by the Japs and taken to Homalin, about twenty miles away. There was nothing on our side of the Chindwin. Our spirits fell. We moved to the Chindwin, and scanned the river of our dreams. It was about two hundred and fifty yards wide and fast flowing. Tag and I could have swum across without our weapons. But this was academic. We could not leave our men. We decided to build rafts as we had done to cross the Shweli. But I tried to think of something else. I stood in an open clearing looking across, and heard a call from the other side in Nepali, 'Who is it?'

I replied, 'We are the 3rd/2nd Gurkhas. Have you got a boat that side? We have none.'

He said he had one and would get it.

The men of course had heard my conversation with what I assumed to be a V Force Levie, I knew they recruited Gurkhas, and were delighted. The Gurkha brought a dugout across, it took four men only. I put in the havildar and three men. After a while, the boat came back after what seemed like hours. We sent four more men across. It came back; there were now five of us, including Tag and me. We sent off the three and Tag and I stayed until last. We hid behind the bank, and waited. I put my safety catch to automatic. We looked towards the jungle and wondered if the Japs would get us at the eleventh hour, or would we get away with it. There was the boat coming back. We clambered in, and we crossed. I pulled out my last cheroot and lit it, as happy as a sandboy.

We came to a V Force post. There was a young captain commanding the V Force post, I can't remember his name. I asked him what date it was, he said 6 June; we had long since lost any idea of what day it was. That is one date that I will always remember.

Major Michael Calvert
Officer Commanding 3 Column

When we got back General Scoones made me write down all the points I could remember on patrolling. It was eventually published as *Notes on Patrolling* by General Scoones.

Lieutenant Dominic Neill
8 Column, 3rd/2nd Gurkha Rifles

After leaving the V Force post, we reported to the 3rd/10th Gurkhas' camp. We had a shower and were given clean clothes to wear. We were given whisky and sodas, and slept like the dead that night.

Next morning we were told that a signal had arrived from the V Force post, which, after sending a recce across the river, reported that a Jap fighting patrol of platoon strength had been tracking us for about a week. It had arrived on the eastern bank of the Chindwin about half an hour after we had crossed. It was just luck that we escaped. Had we stopped to construct rafts we would have been caught. Had I not been standing in the clearing and the Gurkha levy not seen me, likewise.

We were taken by transport to a Field Supply Depot. As we were eating a meal we saw the rain coming down like stair rods, the monsoon: we had beaten it by two days. The rain delayed our return to Imphal, but while at the Field Supply Depot, two things stick out in my memory. I calculated from the maps that the distance we had marched from Dimapur to the Shweli and back must have been about a thousand miles, give or take a hundred miles. Second, finding and stealing a four-pound tin of plum jam, which Tag and I ate in about five minutes, without any biscuits.

We went off in trucks to Imphal to IV Corps HQ and hospital. When we got off our trucks, three staff officers appeared from out of a tent, smelling of roses. One of them said, 'They must be from Longcloth,' in the same tone of voice that he might have said, 'There is the sweeper.' They must have seen the expression of fury in my eyes, as they turned and left.

We went to hospital to be checked over, and were told to shave off our beards. Wingate appeared. He looked at me and said, 'I see you are out.' Fortunately I did not reply as I thought, 'No thanks to you sir.' That was the last time I saw him.

Lieutenant Denis Gudgeon
3 Column, 3rd/2nd Gurkha Rifles

I was rather rude to the first Jap I met. I was reading a Penguin book, and went on reading. He got very angry, and when he interrogated me, although he could speak perfect English, he spoke through an interpreter and kept the point of his sword pointed at my throat. I didn't disclose that I was in the Chindits, I told him I was in a foot patrol across the Chindwin from troops guarding the other side, and he seemed to believe this.

I was questioned again and this time he tried a different tactic, giving me sake and sweets, but I wasn't taken in by that. I was put on a train, and during the journey we were strafed by a Beaufighter. I did think of trying to escape, but was rather weak and didn't. At the Ava Bridge I had to detrain because it had been blown. I ended up at Rangoon station where I was interrogated again, taken to Rangoon Jail, and spent the next two years as a POW.

Major Walter 'Scottie' Scott
Officer Commanding 8 Column, 13th Battalion, King's Regiment (Liverpool)

I didn't lose weight on the expedition. What did we achieve? We realised that the Japanese were not the supermen that we had been brought up to believe. They were very brave soldiers, and even if they were outnumbered, they would attack.

Lieutenant Dominic Neill
8 Column, 3rd/2nd Gurkha Rifles

The newspapers back in India had banner headlines about Wingate's expedition. We couldn't believe our eyes. We had achieved absolutely nothing; we had been kicked out by the Japs again. The publicity was the work of the authorities in GHQ Delhi grasping at any straws after the defeat in 1942, closely followed by the disastrous Arakan Campaign of 1942/43. Only Number 3 Column, under Mike Calvert, had achieved anything of any significance.

Ours was the very last party to escape from Burma. I had been posted missing, but fortunately no one had sent a telegram to my mother. I spent all the remaining silver rupees drinking the king's health on leave in Kashmir. The 3rd/2nd Gurkhas took heavy casualties, we lost the CO and adjutant, plus two officers, and some two hundred and ninety GORs killed in action, or died of starvation, or as prisoners.

In my opinion Wingate's concept was sound and daring, but the training was inferior. Arrangements for casevac were inadequate, as were communications. Splitting up groups was a bad decision. Columns could have called for air resupply, and posed such a potent fighting force that in the time available the Japs would not have been able to concentrate against them. In small groups we were fair game for platoon-size hunting parties. Wingate's failure to train his troops in contact drills caused frequent and unnecessary casualties. He also went too far. By crossing the Irrawaddy he overstretched himself dangerously. His achievements beyond that river were negligible, and a great number of casualties were caused by having too long a retreat. We did not have enough maps or compasses. Wingate ruled by fear. Officers feared to query his orders.

The Struggle for the Arakan
Round Two

I watched this attack by the Gurkhas, shouting 'Ayo Gurkhali', their battle cry. They had kukris in their hands, rifles slung across their shoulders and advanced throwing grenades. They threw the Japanese out. It was a beautiful sight and etched in my memory.

The monsoon of 1943 shut down all but minor operations on all fronts in Burma. With the onset of the dry season in November 1943, the British and the Japanese began to stir.

The British aimed at driving the Japanese out of Burma. To this end, Admiral Lord Louis Mountbatten, now Supreme Allied Commander South East Asia (SEAC), ordered a four-pronged offensive.

As related in the next chapter, in northern Burma a Chinese force led by the American General Stilwell would head south from Ledo, take Myitkyina, and thereby connect Ledo with the Burma Road. This would enable the Americans to supply China by road for the first time since the Japanese invasion of Burma, instead of the hair-raising air route over the 'Hump', the nickname for the eastern end of the Himalayas that lay between the air bases in Assam and China.

On the Chindwin front, IV Corps was to undertake a limited push. In support of these two operations Wingate was to lead a hugely increased force of Chindits on a second expedition aimed at disrupting the Japanese lines of communications to their troops facing Stilwell and IV Corps. Meanwhile, XV Corps was ordered to secure the Maungdaw–Buthidaung Road as a precursor to further operations to eject the Japanese from the Arakan.

The battle-experienced 70th British and 5th Indian divisions were now being shipped in from the Middle East. They were joined by the recently raised 7th Indian Division, new to battle, but commanded by the charismatic Major General F. W. Messervy, fresh from fighting in the Western Desert.

Lieutenant General A. F. P. Christison's XV Corps began the Arakan offensive by pushing down the Mayu Range with the 7th Division to the east and the 5th Division to the west. As the two divisions probed south they hit the Maungdaw–Buthidaung Road, the only lateral road fit for wheeled traffic until the Taungup–Prome Road two hundred miles further south. Along the sixteen miles of road, the Japanese had a continuous sequence of defences in steep, jungle-covered hills. They had also built three heavily fortified positions: in the two tunnels carrying the road under the Mayu hills; at Letwedet east of the tunnels; and at Razabil to the west. These were constructed in the hills with thirty-foot-deep dugouts, supported by machine-gun nests, all linked with tunnels.

The 5th Division was ordered to take Razabil, while the 7th took Buthidaung followed by hooking in to take Letwedet from the south. Thirty miles to the east, the third division in XV Corps, the 81st West African, was told to advance down the Kaladan valley, capture Kyauktaw, and cut the Kanzauk–Hitzwe Road. In so doing the division would cut the main Japanese supply route between the Kaladan and Mayu Rivers.

To support operations west of the Mayu hills, Christison ordered another road, capable of taking tanks, guns and supply trucks, to be constructed about five miles to the north of the Maungdaw–Buthidaung Road. The road, driven over the Ngakyedauk Pass, nicknamed the 'Okeydoke', was fully serviceable by the end of January 1944.

The enemy, as is their inconvenient custom, had their own ideas. In this case the Japanese, whose strategy was to remain on the defensive in Burma, decided that the best way to spoil any British offensives would be to mount limited offensives themselves. Lieutenant General Renya Mutaguchi, commanding the Japanese Fifteenth Army, planned to take Imphal and Kohima in his area of responsibility. Before this, the Japanese Twenty-Eighth Army under Lieutenant General Shozo Sakurai was to attack in the Arakan. The intention: to keep Lieutenant General 'Bill' Slim, commanding the British Fourteenth Army, looking towards the Arakan, while the main attack went in at Imphal. But, if the Arakan offensive went

Lieutenant General Sir William Slim, Commander Fourteenth Army.

well, the Japanese might exploit further and even invade India.

For the Arakan offensive, timed for 4 February 1944, and codenamed *Ha-Go*, Sakurai had the elements of three Japanese divisions, the 54th, 55th, and 2nd, and an Indian National Army (INA) force. The attack would be in a pincer movement so favoured by the Japanese. The northern pincer, a force commanded by Major General Tokutaro Sakurai (not to be confused with the commander of Twenty-Eighth Army), would seize Taung Bazaar on the Kalapanzin River (as the upper reaches of the Mayu were called), block the Ngakyedauk Pass, and hook down to attack the 7th Division. Concurrently, the 1/213 Regiment would attack the Arakan Road to cut Christison's lifeline back to India. Meanwhile the southern pincer, consisting of most of 143rd Regiment was to hit 7th Division from the south.

Although there were signs of an impending Japanese attack, Christison had no idea how big it might be, and his troops continued with their own attacks. By now the troops were starting to benefit from their training, although there was still much to learn.

Captain Alexander Wilson
Argyll & Sutherland Highlanders, attached British 2nd Division
I had fought the Japanese in Malaya. Just before the surrender of Singapore I, and my commanding officer, were ordered out, so we could pass on our experiences to the army in India. I joined the British 2nd Division and took over all jungle training.

Most British people, brought up in towns, are never in the dark. So few of our soldiers had ever been alone at night. We have lost much of our sense of hearing and smell. These are basic animal-like characteristics. The Japs smelt different to us, and you had to learn how you could smell them in a defensive position, or if they had passed down a track.

At night you are on your own. You are susceptible to noise made by the enemy, and shooting at noises and shadows, which you mustn't do. The antidote is endless training: practising movement by night, the use of pole charges to attack bunkers, and bringing down supporting fire from mortars and guns very close to us. There was a very great deal to learn.

There were problems with wirelesses in jungle and hills caused by blank areas for communicating, especially at night. You had to find the right spot for good communications, by moving around. The 6th Brigade had been detached from 2 Div in Arakan, and we learned a great deal from their experience.

We learnt about their siting of defensives and use of local materials (logs, parts of buildings etc) to build bunkers, which were shellproof, even against anti-tank guns, and marvellously well concealed. You seldom saw a Japanese move by day. They took pains to conceal their tracks because by 1944 we had superiority in the air and in artillery. They realised this and they trained to operate at night. Their positions were well sited to support each other. They tunnelled and connected firing positions with covered ways. They could call down their own gun and mortar fire on their own positions. They cleared fields of fire, but not in such a way that it gave away the location of the bunker. What you could do was try to draw their fire at night; by shooting at them, moving about etc. They did it to us. Bill Slim's adage was 'the answer to noise is silence'. It was almost a crime to shoot without having a corpse to show for it the next morning. We used the PIAT for bunker-busting, and sometimes wheeled up a 6-pounder anti-tank gun, which was very risky.

Captain Kristen Tewari
Divisional Signals 25th Indian Division, attached 51 Brigade

I didn't belong to what the British called a martial class. I joined the army because a friend of my father's, Colonel Kilroy the recruiting officer at Jullundur Cantonment, said I should because war was imminent. Some members of my family asked why join the British Army and fight for Britain, Indian independence was more important. No doubt there was conflict in my mind too. But better sense prevailed. I learned a lot during the war. I joined in a spirit of adventure. I saw Indian soldiers at drill at Jullundur and wanted to be like them. I joined the Officer Training School at Bangalore in 1942. We had British instructors for drill and PT. I admired them.

As far as the Indian National Army, the INA, was concerned, we called them JIFs. Although we knew that people had joined them, we would not break our oath. Personally I had no sympathy for those who joined the INA.

After joining the 25th Division I went on jungle training. It was very useful, I came from the plains of Punjab and had never been into a jungle. We had to build our own shelters, we learned to live in the jungle and be comfortable in it. We saw wild elephants, tiger, and snakes galore, which we learned to cope with. It was all very useful, especially as there were lots of snakes in Burma. We learned to respect and make use of the forest. We lost one or two people on that training to snake bites.

EASTERN ARAKAN

Pilot Officer Roger Cobley
20 *Squadron*, RAF

I flew the Hurricane Mk II C which was fitted with two 40-mm cannons for anti-tank work. They made the aircraft a bit unwieldy and you couldn't do aerobatics safely. We carried high explosive or armour-piercing shells. Each gun was loaded with only sixteen rounds, which you had to fire singly, not in bursts like 20-mm cannons or machine guns. You had to line up very accurately on the target, and attack one at a time.

We were supposed to have Spitfires as top cover, but didn't get it to start with. But operating very low as we did, with jungle trees below, it was difficult for Jap aircraft to see us, and in any case there weren't many about. I commanded a section, a pair of aircraft.

In the Arakan in late 1943, we started by operating from a jungle strip called 'Brighton', near the coast just behind our front line, after which we moved even nearer the front and flew from a strip on the beach, called 'Hove'. This was an agreeable place, living in bamboo huts. We swam, but had to look out for stingrays. We had a ration of drink dropped to us by parachute: four bottles of beer per month for the airmen, and one bottle of gin or whisky for the officers. We had a good mix of over half Commonwealth chaps.

Our targets were bunkers, river boats, and occasionally trucks. We lost quite a few people, shot down by flak.

Lieutenant Michael Marshall
Officer Commanding B Company, 4th/5th Royal Gurkha Rifles

The battalion's task was active patrolling. Each company took turns to send out fighting or standing patrols for three or four days at a time. As I was totally inexperienced, I went out and soon learnt what I ought to be doing. This was not easy as I had a limited knowledge of Urdu and my knowledge of Gurkhali was not much better. On one patrol I had ten men, plus Subedar Indrabir Thapa, a very experienced Gurkha officer; he always spoke to me in Gurkhali and, if I didn't understand, in Urdu. It was only when I got back to the battalion and heard him talking on the inter-company telephone system to the CO in perfectly good English that I realised that he had no intention of making my life easy, and knew I would only learn Gurkhali by speaking nothing else.

In late October 1943, I went out at night with a standing patrol, with a jemadar from my own company and about six men. Two things occurred. At about two o'clock in morning we were shot at while crossing open paddy. We all got down into the water, and stayed for about half an hour. It was probably a small Jap patrol who had moved on after hearing us. Every one of us had forty to fifty leeches hanging off us, and we spent a good half-hour removing them. Some leeches can go through lace holes in boots. The most fearsome were elephant leeches, some six to nine inches long, in flooded chaungs and rivers. We took them off with a lighted cigarette.

Having reached the patrol position, on the second morning, the jemadar pointed out to me that he had seen through his binos a small sampan containing a Jap officer, a soldier and two villagers, coming down the Ngakyedauk Chaung, about twelve hundred yards away. They were on their way from Jap positions on the ridge in front and coming to Awlinbyn Village. My instructions on leaving the battalion location were to take evading action only, unless absolutely necessary; my main task was observation. As the sampan got closer to us, I felt that we ought to do something about it. When it was seven hundred yards away, the jemadar agreed he would open fire with the LMG. The occupants of the sampan disappeared. Later we were told that a senior Jap officer and his orderly had been killed. Although not due to leave the patrol position for a further four or five hours, I decided it prudent to do so, and we left for the company base at Taung Bazaar. This took us about twelve to fifteen hours. After we left we heard mortar fire approximately on the position we had left, and a great deal of noise from the Jap positions.

When I reported to the CO his views were mixed. However, the following night a patrol from another company occupied approximately the same position I had been in; not very clever of them. During the night the Japs sent in a patrol, killing one and wounding another of our patrol. Despite my having disobeyed instructions, I think that our action established the positions of the Japs and this proved valuable for what happened thereafter.

Major Harry Smith
Officer Commanding HQ Company, 4th Battalion, Queen's Own Royal West Kent Regiment

On being moved to India from fighting in the Western Desert, we carried out jungle training near Ranchi, and at the end of December we embarked in a troop ship, the *Ethiopia*, which deposited us at Chittagong. From Chittagong we entrained and went fifty miles south to Dohazari, and then marched. In order to avoid the heat, and being spotted by enemy aircraft, we marched at night; two hundred miles at twenty miles a day for ten days. It was nice swinging along on an earthen track in the warm darkness, through clouds of fireflies. After being ferried across a chaung, we reached the forward area.

The countryside in the Arakan along the coast consisted of a lot of jungle-clad hills interspersed with paddy fields. Our brigade took over the sector from the coast inland to a range of much bigger hills, called the Mayu Range.

Private Leslie Crouch
Pioneer Platoon, 4th Battalion, Queen's Own Royal West Kent Regiment

In November 1943 we took up positions facing the Japs. We were advancing and pushing them back at Maungdaw; it was really just a village of mud huts and straw roofs. We dug in and the Japanese attacked, we came off best. They were attacking frontally. We were in trenches. We hadn't heard a lot about them, except that they were fanatical.

Captain John Anderson
HQ, 33rd Brigade, 7th Indian Division

Brigades in the Indian Army were in the main formed of three different races or castes, usually one British battalion, one Gurkha, and one Indian. It worked really well. There was a bit of rivalry and leg-pulling; but a lot of friendships.

I moved by sea to Chittagong with the brigade transport. Our division was moving to the eastern side of the Mayu range. There were no roads in this area, only a track, like a footpath. The division crossed from Bawli Bazaar by the Goppe Pass and on southwards. There was no question of getting transport by that route, so we were left behind. Eventually the call came, the division had found a better track which the engineers worked on; the

Private Leslie Crouch.

Ngakyedauk pass. It ran parallel with the Goppe pass but several miles further south. At first the engineers made a track driveable by jeeps, and I took the brigade transport and crossed the range at night, through thick jungle with steep banks on one side of the track. After a while you came out into a clearing at Sinzweya where the rear echelons of the division were located in an administrative box.

Ultimately the track was made bigger and shortly before the balloon went up, the 25th Dragoons with Lee-Grant tanks got across. Having got to Sinzweya, both sides started prodding each other to find out where weak spots were, by patrolling, artillery fire and so on.

Lieutenant Michael Marshall
Officer Commanding B Company, 4th/5th Royal Gurkha Rifles
In January 1944 the whole brigade began a general advance through the foothills of the Arakan Yomas, the intention being to cut the Japanese supply lines to the south of the Mayu river and capture Buthidaung. During all this period I was acting company commander of B Company and was joined by 2 Lieutenant Tom Briscoe who had been at school at Christ's Hospital, was captain of rugger and head boy. We became immediate friends. Two months later he was killed.

As we advanced through the foothills, among dense trees, not jungle, we had a series of brisk actions against the Japs. One I well remember was rather macabre: after an afternoon battle, where D Company and my own B Company were involved, we had killed about twenty Japs. It was very close fighting. It was the first time I had heard Gurkhas actually shouting 'Ayo Gurkhali', a fearsome noise, and it undoubtedly scared the Japs. It was the first time I had seen them using their kukris at close quarters. They mostly went for the throat, often putting down their rifles to do so. The Japs ran. We suffered considerable casualties. The Japs were not properly dug in otherwise they would not have run. They only had small one-man foxholes.

The next morning I was told to take two platoons back to this position to bury the dead. I instructed the jemadar to bury the bodies, and went off. Instead of digging graves, the Gurkhas used the foxholes dug by Japs. Because the Jap dead had rigor mortis, and would not fit, the Gurkhas cut up the bodies and stuffed them into the holes. I stopped this, but they thought I was being pernickety. The Gurkha has all the nicest characteristics of the British:

he likes games, drinking, women, gambling. However, he has little feelings for the dead, either the enemy or his comrades. Once gone, they'd gone. They had no feelings of sadness nor remorse. At the time of killing the enemy they'd get elated, and it is an interesting fact that Gurkhas going into action at close quarters get bloodshot eyes and look fearsome. They still take orders from officers. But in close-quarter fighting no one is giving orders to anyone.

The Jap was a very courageous opponent and suffered enormously. But the Gurkhas were better. I was glad I was with them, not against them. My battalion took no prisoners until well into 1945; none of our men were taken prisoner. At this time in the war the Japs were thought to be invincible by some people, including many British troops. This was not the attitude of my Gurkhas. The Gurkhas didn't like the smell of Japs, it was a very strong smell, something to do with the bad fish and bad eggs they ate.

Private Ivan Daunt
Pioneer Platoon, 4th Battalion, Queen's Own Royal West Kent Regiment
Never known a nation that wanted to die, except the Japs. We retreated, they don't. You picked up skinny Jap bodies, with their eyes popping out of their head. You would advance on a Jap lying there with a grenade waiting to blow himself up. What can you do? Shoot him?

I saw a British plane came in to pick up a wounded Jap. It landed on the road, we put him on the plane, and the pilot said, 'I'm not for this. I don't know what he is going to do.' We told him we had checked the Jap over. He was badly wounded. He was needed for interrogation.

You knew they were there at night, they gave the game away, you could hear them moving. We let them come close and opened up on them, and found them in the morning. If you were armed only with a rifle, it was not a lot of good at night-time, so you relied on grenades. But you were limited to the number you had. We used Brens as well.

The Japs dug one-man round pits. When we captured them, we would expand each to a two-man slit. Once Freddie Clinch and 'Tosh' Hill shared a slit next to mine. Both had bayonets fixed on their rifles. The time came for 'Tosh' to go to sleep; one should stay awake, while the other sleeps. But both fell asleep. A Jap crept up to them, and went to throw something into the trench, a grenade maybe. But in leaning down, he rammed his face down on

Freddie's bayonet, and let out a squeal. They jumped up and shouted, 'Somebody here.' The Jap was in a state; they took him prisoner.

Lieutenant Michael Marshall
Officer Commanding B Company, 4th/5th Royal Gurkha Rifles
On 4 February 1944 we were instructed to attack a Jap position together with C Company. The two companies set off at 0630 in the typical early morning mist that hangs over the paddy in the Arakan. We climbed up through jungle to within some four or five hundred yards of what we thought was a Jap position. C Company Commander told me to attack with my company at about 0900 hours. The attack went in. There was considerable Jap fire coming back. We used our 2-inch mortars and grenade dischargers. Eventually the position was taken by us.

We suffered one killed and thirteen wounded, one being me. I was wounded together with my orderly by a Jap grenade falling behind me, and hit in the backside, back, and left arm. We all carried morphine syringes in our kit, and my orderly, who was badly wounded in the legs, managed to extract the syringes and we both injected. Luckily my haversack contained my binoculars, compass and two grenades, which were badly dented, but took most of the blast. Without them I would probably have been killed.

I was taken back to C Company, unaware of what was happening. The Jap position was mopped up by my company. I was then taken by stretcher-bearers to battalion HQ. While I was there, my CO was informed by brigade HQ that the whole advance had been stopped, and an immediate withdrawal ordered. So the whole action and the previous month's work had to be aborted. This was because the Japs, during the night of 4 February, had sent in a task force of nine thousand men to cut the supply lines to 7 Div. This force, complete with artillery but relying on captured supplies, came through the mist in the paddy in the early hours of the morning.

Life did not become pleasant for me. I was carried on a stretcher for two days to the 114 Brigade Box at Oktaung near Kwazon. I was put in a temporary hospital with many other wounded, and after two or three days found I had gas gangrene in my left arm. Others were also suffering from gangrene. As there were no anaesthetics, limbs were being amputated without. Two large British orderlies knocked out the patient with a punch to the jaw after he had been given a large tot of whisky. This happened to my

Lieutenant Michael Marshall, taken after the war.

orderly, both his legs were amputated. He didn't survive. At this stage there was only one surgeon who had hung on to his kit. He told me I would have to have my arm off. One of my fellow officers came to see me, and said he had some of the latest sulphonamide tablets, which no one else had. He gave them to me, and I did not have to go through the unpleasant experience of amputation. On 17 February a landing strip was built at Kwazon to which the whole brigade had moved. I was lucky enough to be first to be evacuated by L-5 light aircraft.

Captain John Anderson
HQ 33rd Brigade, 7th Indian Division

Early in February 1944 Japs attacked us. The Japs were trying to open up a route northwards to Chittagong and to Calcutta.

Gunner Bert Wilkins
284 Anti-Tank Battery, 24th Light Anti-Aircraft/Anti-Tank Regiment, Royal Artillery

We acted as infantry, we were sent up the road to form a roadblock and a staff officer came up, all excited: 'No one goes back from here. You stand here.'

We had to turn all the stragglers back and put them up on the hills, but as fast as we put them up on the hill, they came down and ran off again. There were a lot of Indian non-combatants, and in the end we took their automatic weapons off them and used them ourselves. I had a tommy gun, and then a Bren. In the end we dug about three different positions, I don't think anyone knew what was happening.

In one position they told us to collect hot stew, which had been brought up to a nullah behind the position. It was raining, so by the time you go back to your trench, your mess tin was overflowing with water and stew.

Captain Peter Gadsdon
Officer Commanding A Company, 4th/14th Punjab Regiment

I had standing patrols out in the paddy fields. They heard troops coming and said, 'Halt who goes there?' Some Indian replied, 'Tikka bai, it's all right, don't bother, no problem.' and they walked straight past. The sentries came and reported this to us. There was very thick mist and we could see absolutely nothing. This column appeared to have gone through our position. We took it

Peter Gadsdon, taken after the war.

to be some of our own ration parties. In fact it was the Japs with INA pushing the sentries on one side.

Our carrier platoon commander, Jemadar Pir Gul, a Pathan, sent a carrier out into the fog to investigate, and came back with a dead Japanese on the carrier.

I am sometimes asked about the attitude of our soldiers to the INA. They would kill them, and regarded them as traitors. The INA surrendered very quickly in battle. To the Indian Army they were traitors. To the Congress they were heroes. Now in India they are heroes, and people think they were responsible for getting the British out.

Captain John Anderson
HQ 33rd Brigade, 7th Indian Division

The Japs succeeded in cutting us off completely. We were entirely surrounded, they got to the Ngakyedauk Pass, and held that. But there were two things that saved our bacon. One was air supply, the RAF were even dropping to individual companies. The other was the 25th Dragoons and their tanks. Without doubt the Japs were fine soldiers. They had gone through Malaya like a dose of salts, and as soon as they came up against opposition they split and outflanked it, which is demoralising.

I was at brigade HQ some miles south of the divisional HQ, and suddenly there was a complete collapse of communications, brigades were trying to get in touch with division and couldn't. It had been overrun and all radio sets captured. The brigade commander, Loftus Tottenham, told me to borrow a Bren gun carrier from 4/1 Gurkha Rifles and try to find out what had happened. I set off with two Gurkhas, a driver and a Bren gunner. Halfway up the track we were shot up by Jap machine guns from a small hill some way off, and the driver was shot through the mouth, and I got some grazing hits in my arm from bullet fragments or bits chipped off the carrier. I took over the driving and pushed on, having taken note of where the Japs were. My chief concern was for the driver, the Bren gunner was not touched.

Gunner Bert Wilkins
284 Anti-Tank Battery, 24th Light Anti-Aircraft/Anti-Tank Regiment, Royal Artillery

Div HQ had been overrun and our regimental HQ had been overrun.

Eventually we dug in on this hill, to begin with just thirty of us. Then two companies of Gurkhas moved in. We were there for about three days. I was young and foolish and volunteered to be a runner. This officer, a major from our unit, told me to run from trench to trench, and told everyone to watch for the flashes of Jap snipers shooting at me, and to open up on them. I thought it was quite exciting.

We were attacked by Zeros. I didn't really know what was happening. The ordinary soldier doesn't. We were shelled heavily, and the Japs dragged up 75-mm guns and fired them point-blank. We were knocked off this hill, and we had to go back in again. As we were going forward, I got hit. I rolled down the hill and a couple of blokes dragged me behind a tree. This officer crawled up to me, and said, 'I'll take your Bren gun and give you my revolver and a grenade. You'll know what to do with it if they come out for you.' The Japs used to come out and finish off the wounded if they could. So you didn't shout or make a noise. If they heard someone crying out in pain they would come out and finish you off. I was wounded by a bullet just behind the hip bone.

Lieutenant Colonel Gerald Cree
Commanding Officer, 2nd Battalion, West Yorkshire Regiment
Brigadier Evans told me to bring my whole battalion, less one company, into the 7th Division Admin Box. One company had to remain behind with the 3rd/14th Punjab Regiment still up in the hills next to our own division, the 5th. He said I must keep two companies in mobile reserve for counter-attacking, and only one company for static defence. I got in touch right away with Lieutenant Colonel Cole, the commanding officer of the 7th Division Light Ack-Ack Regiment, who had been in charge of the defence of the Admin Box up to that time, and discovered what he had done. As a result I put C Company into a static defence role, occupying a hill just above the eastern entrance to the Ngakyedauk Pass.

Colonel Cole had mustered every man he could find to defend the place, all the Indian followers, contractor wallahs, admin people and so on. They were holding their positions and acting like soldiers. We found by lending out our troops, putting one British soldier in a platoon of bakers and butchers etc, it provided moral support. My battalion headquarters was in adjoining trenches to brigade and divisional HQs.

Captain John Anderson
HQ 33rd Brigade, 7th Indian Division

Approaching Sinzweya, where the box was, the steering went, and I couldn't turn right. Then much to my delight I saw a 25th Dragoons tank, and asked him if he could give me a tow. So he passed me a bloody great chain, big enough to hold the *Queen Mary*. I hooked it on to my carrier, and he pulled me along the steep roads. We came to a right-hand bend, I couldn't turn right, and the carrier, with three of us in it, slipped off the road down a khud on the end of the chain. Suddenly to my surprise I found myself being towed up the slope. The tank commander had no idea what was going on behind him, and had just kept on going. We were pulled up on to the track, and eventually got to what became divisional HQ, because Messervy, the GOC, had escaped with several of his staff. This was when the defensive box was formed with scores of troops from different units, Gurkhas, Indians, British, engineers, signals, administrative folk.

Gunner Bert Wilkins
284 Anti-Tank Battery, 24th Light Anti-Aircraft/Anti-Tank Regiment,
Royal Artillery

My leg was dead. I tunnelled into a bush and lay up all night. Next morning, to my surprise someone grabbed my ankles and yanked me out. It was a Gurkha officer and a Gurkha. They piggybacked me down the hill, to where all the wounded and the dead were being assembled in this nullah. The road was cut so they had to take us into the box on the backs of tanks and Bren carriers. I was in a Bren carrier beside a dead man. We got to a bend in the road and the officer in command of the column said, 'The road is cut on this corner. All those who can walk beside the tanks, walk. The rest of you, duck your heads down and hope for the best.'

So all the tanks opened up on the hill overlooking the road with machine guns to keep the Japs' heads down. The tanks and carriers cut across off the road; we got through.

Captain John Anderson
HQ 33rd Brigade, 7th Indian Division

I took my driver to the Main Dressing Station (MDS). It was just getting dark, and I asked the chaps there, two or three of whom I knew, one a major, and

IND 3285

A Lee-Grant tank of the 25th Dragoons blasting a way through the Ngakydauk ('Okedoke') Pass.

asked him to attend to him. I had my arm dressed and was then told by a doctor to hand in my pistol. I didn't have an army issue revolver, I had a German 9-mm Parabellum, which fired Sten gun ammunition. I was given it by my father, who had taken it from a German artillery officer in the First World War. I said that no way was I going to hand it in. So the doctor said, 'You can't stay.'

I said, 'Fair enough.' I had my arm in a sling and walked out with my pistol. For a time I stood chatting to a Gurkha officer I knew. After I left him, I found a job in one of the defensive positions being constructed at the time.

Gunner Bert Wilkins
284 Anti-Tank Battery, 24th Light Anti-Aircraft/Anti-Tank Regiment, Royal Artillery

We had casualty labels on, and when we got to the box an MP stopped us and checked that we were casualties, not stragglers. He said, 'Dead bodies to the right, casualties to the left.' They had graves dug in rows and the dead were put down there. The seriously wounded were seen to first, naturally. An orderly said to me, 'You've got a field dressing on, we'll see to you later.'

He took me over to a ward for walking wounded: a tarpaulin on bamboo poles. We were just across the track from the ward with the seriously wounded. That night the Japanese broke in. We heard all the screaming from the ward across the track and bullets came through our tarpaulin. We all jumped up. Four of us grabbed a chap on a stretcher, he had his leg in plaster. We ran out into the river that ran at the back of the tarpaulin, and stood there, but there was still stuff flying about, whizzing into the water. So we crossed the river and hid in the bush, about two hundred yards away. We could see the Japanese bayoneting and killing, and running about. Then it all died down. Out of six doctors there was only one left alive and most of the sixty wounded were killed. They smashed the operating theatre.

Private Henry Foster
Carrier Platoon, 2nd Battalion, West Yorkshire Regiment

We were sent in the middle of the night, two or three o'clock in the morning, with a carrier to try to get to the hospital, which was at the top of a very steep rise from where the stream ran in a valley, to see what was happening. There was gunfire and screaming. We only got halfway up, got grenaded and turned back. We had never been up there before, and the track was bordered by trees and jungle.

Lieutenant Colonel Gerald Cree
Commanding Officer, 2nd Battalion, West Yorkshire Regiment
My A Company, supported by B Squadron 25th Dragoons, cleared the Japanese out of the MDS. They found that the enemy had camouflaged their machine-gun posts with stretchers in the wards and theatres. The bodies of thirty-one patients and four doctors were found, as well as seventy Japanese.

That night the Japanese pulled out after our counter-attack and started trickling down a chaung that ran up into the main dressing station. Both sides of the chaung were held by our Brigade B Echelon personnel: muleteers, orderly room staff, sanitary men, quartermasters' stores, chaps like that, nearly all old soldiers, including the Regimental Sergeant Major. They twigged what was happening and let the Japs have it. They killed an enormous number of them in the chaung, which became known as Blood Nullah. These were the chaps who had raided the dressing station, so we felt we'd avenged that one. They continued to come down this chaung, although it was a stupid thing to do. Perhaps they'd been ordered to some rendezvous.

Captain John Anderson
HQ 33rd Brigade, 7th Indian Division
Next morning there was a hell of a muddle. People were trying to get themselves into useful jobs. I can remember seeing a 5.5-inch gun firing over open sights at the Japs on the surrounding hillsides. It was all a bit hectic for a few days.

Gunner Bert Wilkins
284 Anti-Tank Battery, 24th Light Anti-Aircraft/Anti-Tank Regiment
Royal Artillery
After this I was properly dressed, a Scottish doctor looked at my leg, and said, 'No exit wound, eh laddie. Never mind, you'll cough it up one of these days.' He filled up my wound with powder using an ordinary spoon; all the equipment had been destroyed. I was there for eight days. I was glad to get out of the dressing station, because I was unarmed, and I didn't like it.

Walking wounded used to parade every day and company commanders from the various units would come along and say, 'Can I have this man?'

Gunner Bert Wilkins, in Belgium at the end of the war.

The medical officer would say, 'He's got a big hole in his back. He can't carry a pack.'

The officer would ask, 'Can he fire a rifle, that's all I'm interested in?'

Being a wireless operator, and our regimental HQ having been destroyed, I went to the Gurkhas, and they carried on dressing my wound. I could limp around.

Private Henry Foster
Carrier Platoon, 2nd Battalion, West Yorkshire Regiment
There was a clear patch of paddy which made a good dropping zone. The first time they tried they were driven off by Japanese fighter planes, but after that they had a big escort, and came in daily.

Sergeant Douglas Williams
Wireless Operator/Air Gunner, 194 Squadron, RAF
We located the DZ, but as our aircraft flew over Jap positions near it, it came under fire and was hit in the port engine. The pilot closed it down to avoid a fire, meanwhile the navigator and second wireless operator were busily despatching loads.

I noticed black smoke streaming past the door, and rushed up to tell the pilot. He told me to alert the crew to take up positions for a crash landing. By now we were down to about three hundred feet above the ground, and had lots of supplies still on board. The pilot was having a problem maintaining even that height, we threw out the supplies as fast as we could. Slowly the pilot gained height, and the navigator gave him the course for home. We managed to get over the Chin Hills, and eventually made a good landing back at base.

Private Henry Foster
Carrier Platoon, 2nd Battalion, West Yorkshire Regiment
We used to go and pick up supplies in our carriers. There were shells for the artillery and the tanks and there were big notices on the boxes, 'Dangerous Do Not Drop'. We didn't do too badly. We had plenty of water, we could go down to the stream and wash our clothes. We didn't have too bad a time. By the time we got to the Arakan, those of us who had fought in the Western Desert had got used to the way of life in action.

We lived quite well in the carrier platoon, because we had been out on a patrol and come across a ration dump left by our people in no-man's-land. We got a lot of crates of tinned milk and tinned fruit. We lived on porridge and with the tinned milk we could make really good porridge. We got bags of sugar but they'd poured paraffin or petrol over it.

We got attacked by air two or three times, they came in low over the hills and there was no warning, there was no radar. A troop of ack-ack guns were quite near where we were dug in, about forty yards away. They got attacked one day by Japanese fighter-bombers and they actually got a couple of bombs right on the target. They made a right mess. I could see the pilot, he came that low. I could see the bomb falling and it fell at the side of my carrier. Luckily only a small one. I was only two or three yards away but in a trench. It just blew the track off my carrier.

We supported the rifle companies when they were attacking the hills held by the Japanese. They used to dig themselves in these wooded hills, and dig right through so that when artillery was being fired at them, they would go through tunnels to the back of the feature. We didn't have guns that could fire in a high trajectory and get to them on the back of a hill. So a plan was devised that as the infantry attacked they were given supporting fire just over their heads. We used to do this with our Bren guns.

Captain John Anderson
HQ 33rd Brigade, 7th Indian Division

Eventually we managed to break out of the box, and I was taken back to brigade HQ in a tank. The 'Okeydoke' Pass was re-opened and we went on the offensive. We pushed further south to the road from Maungdaw to Buthidaung, which ran through the tunnels.

Second Lieutenant Satoru Nazawa
Company Second in Command, 112th Regiment, Japanese 55thDivision

But here, the men of the Tanahashi regiment, the 112th Regiment, were all like half dead, even the ones who were alive, because we were just so hungry. We didn't eat anything. We didn't have water, and our mouths were dired up. And so sometimes, a bit of chaff would be distributed, but even if they distribute chaff, we were the ones who had to polish it. So we would put it in our iron helmets, and we would use a stone to pound it. And then we would

Private Henry Foster.

blow on it, and then we would take one grain out at a time, and then put that in our mess kit, and would cook it and call it a rice gruel, but even if we cook that, we would only have a line of rice in our bowls. We would have rice gruel in the morning, rice gruel for lunch. And at night, we would finally have rice porridge.

Major Harry Smith
Officer Commanding HQ Company, 4th Battalion, Queen's Own Royal West Kent Regiment
Our first encounter with the Japs consisted of the battalion infiltrating round one of the Jap positions, while the 4th/7th Rajputs put in an attack at night, with the idea of cutting off the Japs while they withdrew. This was quite successful: we got into position behind the Jap outposts, and without being spotted. The Rajputs had quite a tough fight of it, coming up against Jap bunkers, which were very difficult to deal with. Eventually some of the Japs came back through us and were duly accounted for.

But soon after that we had a bit of a tragedy. The Japs must have spotted one of our Bren gun carriers bringing forward supplies and they fired at our positions with 105-mm guns. The Company Sergeant Major, Provost Sergeant, and the RSM all went down to unload the carrier, a shell landed beside them. The Company Sergeant Major was killed, as was the Provost Sergeant. The RSM was so badly wounded that we didn't think he would live, but in fact he did. These were our first casualties in this campaign, and very serious too. After that the war in the Arakan consisted of us eliminating the Japanese positions on these jungle-clad hill tops which rose up like pimples out of the plain; until we came up against the main Jap position at Razabil.

CSM Herbert Harwood
C Company, 4th Battalion, Queen's Own Royal West Kent Regiment
After the RSM, CSM of HQ Company and a couple of others got killed or wounded, I was promoted in the field from sergeant to CSM.

The Arakan was covered in hills running down to the sea. The Japs had been there for nearly a year and were well established. In one place we captured they had dug right through a hill from one side to the other. It was bombed by Mitchell bombers, and it made no difference. We went by night and cut them off from behind. We used cart tracks and dried-up chaungs.

These little hills delayed us. You had to send a patrol of about section strength up each to find out if they were held. Some would be held by only three or four Japs. But that was enough to hold you up. You harboured up, hit them with mortars, and the Japs might disappear during the night. But you could not be sure until you had sent a patrol to investigate. As soon as you put a patrol on top, it would be under observation, and they would mortar or shell the patrol. So as soon as you realised the hill was unoccupied, you kept going down the other side to avoid the pre-registered mortar or artillery fire. It was time-consuming to check a feature. It could take a day to travel two miles in the hilly jungle.

Major Harry Smith
Officer Commanding HQ Company, 4th Battalion, Queen's Own Royal West Kent Regiment
When we came up against Razabil, the Japs were entrenched in almost impregnable bunkers, and we were held up. So the brigade embarked on an ambitious outflanking movement round Razabil. By first light we were behind the Japanese position and encircling it. A heavy barrage from another brigade in front of Razabil heralded our actual attack from the rear. This was successful and the Japanese were ejected from the position, but many were caught in their bunkers as we fought an odd battle in which the dry jungle grass caught fire, and we made our way through blazing undergrowth to eliminate the last Japanese defenders in their bunkers.

CSM Herbert Harwood
C Company, 4th Battalion, Queen's Own Royal West Kent Regiment
On one of the round-the-back hooks, we were at the back of the column, and due to get in position in the enemy rear by dawn. We were still out in the open when light came, but we took cover in a chaung. I examined Razabil fortress after its capture; it was like an enormous underground hospital. You could exist there for months, provided you got supplied. It was all dug by hand.

Eventually we got down to within the sight of the entrance to the two tunnels. We clambered to the top of the ridge with the tunnels underneath. The Japs had used them as a supply base. B Company was in front of us. They called for artillery support from our own guns and you heard the shells coming over and exploding in front of us. I heard somebody shouting, 'Stop them bloody

The West Tunnel on the Maungdaw-Buthidaung Road, looking towards Maungdaw. In the distance the Razabil Ridge.

guns, they are shelling B Company.' We had the job of taking the place of B Company. Moving through them I have never seen anything like it, bodies, arms hanging in the trees; they lost about twenty killed and forty wounded, sixty people out of a company of about one hundred and fifty strong. It is a wonder the Japs didn't attack us. We were very confused and disorganised.

Major Harry Smith
Officer Commanding HQ Company, 4th Battalion, Queen's Own Royal West Kent Regiment
This was a tragedy, but it does happen in war. I took members of the pioneer platoon to the foot of the hill to dig a communal grave, and under very unpleasant Japanese mortar fire we buried the shell-torn victims.

When we captured positions we sometimes found Jap bodies with their right hands cut off. If they had time, the Japs cremated a dead soldier's right hand, and sent the ashes back to his relatives. We also found flags and bugles. They blew bugles and waved flags in the attack.

Private Bert Wheeler
Stretcher-Bearer, 4th Battalion, Queen's Own Royal West Kent Regiment
At the tunnels I had to bring back what I thought would be just one wounded man, but in the end it was ten. You had to pick the ones who would live to take back first, and help the walking wounded last. Being an inexperienced medical orderly, not a doctor, it was difficult to pick the worst wounded, but everybody stood by what you decided.

Most wounds were caused by shrapnel from mortars and artillery. If a man had shrapnel in his chest with maybe the heart or lungs exposed he wouldn't have much hope. Broken limbs and less serious wounded had priority. Walking wounded walked with you as you carried the stretchers, but you had to keep an eye on them. On one occasion I had shrapnel in the arm, and a broken rib, but was walking wounded.

You took the wounded to the Regimental Aid Post (RAP) where the MO worked. Conditions were primitive: he would operate on a stretcher, not a table. There was blood everywhere. He did not carry out amputations.

As a stretcher-bearer the only time you were stationed in the RAP was when you were not attached to a company. We also had to dress wounds. With fractures you put on splints, which you carried in your bag, the small

CSM Herbert Harwood as a corporal before going to Burma.

ones only, bigger splints you did not carry. On bringing the wounded in, you reported to an NCO first who prioritised everybody.

Men with flesh wounds were treated in the RAP unless there was a risk of infection, in which case the wounded man was evacuated. There was a big problem with infection. I have seen quite a lot of gangrene; this usually required an amputation.

We used acraflavine, for cleaning wounds, one of the main treatments at the time, dressed them with a cream, bandaged them up, and hoped for the best. When you picked them up you stopped the bleeding, dressed the wound; nothing more. The distance from the front line to the RAP could vary from a few hundred yards to three miles.

Ambulances came from the ambulance company in the Casualty Clearing Station. An ambulance would take two stretchers, and you piled in as many walking wounded as you could.

In addition there was malaria and dysentery. As a precaution against malaria we took mepacrin tablets daily, usually after the evening meal; it was a parade, a medical orderly put the pill in your mouth, supervised by an officer. It was an offence not to take mepacrin.

If you caught diarrhoea it caused a problem because you were excused mepacrine, and given quinine, which was not as effective against malaria. Bad attacks of dysentery, such as passing blood, were evacuated. Men with ordinary 'trots' were treated by the MO, and stayed with the battalion.

Major Harry Smith
Officer Commanding HQ Company, 4th Battalion, Queen's Own Royal West Kent Regiment
Before another attack could be mounted, the battalion was withdrawn to fight elsewhere as the whole division was moved to Assam.

Captain Kristen Tewari
Divisional Signals 25th Indian Division, attached 51 Brigade
Our Division relieved 5 Division in the area of the tunnels. The Japanese knew they had fresh troops opposing them, and the first night the Japs sent a 'jitter party' with crackers. One of the battalions opened up on their fixed lines, followed by the next company, and the next battalion, and so on. Our defence platoon guarding the brigade HQ fired away. I was sitting on the

exchange, and the brigadier spoke to the general, and immediately the divisional artillery fire was called for. After about two hours the fire died away. The next morning the general came to our HQ to check up on the ammunition state; everyone had fired all their first line.

The area between the two tunnels was dominated by Hill 551, which the previous division had failed to capture after several attempts. The hill dominated the road and the Japanese brought down shellfire on the road when they saw movement. We lost a lot of men killed by Japanese shelling the road, including two of my men.

Our division attacked the hill, using Gurkhas from another brigade. I watched this attack by the Gurkhas, shouting '*Ayo Gurkhali*', their battle cry. They had kukris in their hands, rifles slung across their shoulders and advanced throwing grenades. They threw the Japanese out. It was a beautiful sight and etched in my memory. The hill was almost bare of vegetation, just a few bushes were left.

Before advancing south we stayed in defensive positions in the tunnels area until the end of the monsoon.

THE WEST AFRICANS IN THE KALADAN VALLEY

Lieutenant John Hamilton
Platoon commander, 1st Battalion, Gambia Regiment
Some Africans may have seen jungle at home but the conditions in Africa are different from those encountered in Burma. Many Africans did not live near jungle as most of it near the coast had been cleared, especially in the Gambia. But Africans could perform well in jungle, they were used to living hard, they didn't expect sprung mattresses on their beds. They liked food but did not have fancy ideas. They could see and hear better than most Europeans. They could live as sparingly as the Japanese. They could dig trenches and cut through trees quickly. We cut a jeep track seventy miles long through the jungle using just machetes or pangas.

Patrolling along a path in the Arakanese bamboo was like taking a tank along a dyke in Holland: you couldn't get off the path easily, it is like giant grass. The bamboo grew in single stems so close together you had to turn sideways to get through it. If wearing a pack on your back, this is almost

Climbing a hill before a daylight attack in the Arakan.

impossible. Then you are faced by another, and have to zigzag to get through: exhausting. If you try this at night, even with a moon, you can't see the man in front of you.

When on top of hills, you can't see down to the bottom. The hills consist of razor ridge, the streams run in knife-slice thin chaungs. The beds of the streams are slabs of sandstone, all higgledy-piggledy – it is very difficult to walk along in a narrow stream bed.

In some places in Burma the jungle is different and you can follow the ridges, but in the Kaladan you couldn't. Because of the bamboo, any trees on the ridges don't grow branches until about twenty feet up, so climbing a tree to get a view was difficult, but not impossible for the Africans.

Sergeant Nana Kofi Genfi
Company Clerk, 7th Battalion, Gold Coast Regiment
The Burma jungle is not like the Ghana jungle. In Ghana the bamboo grows in groups, but in Burma it was like a plantation stretching for miles and very hard to pass through. There was segregation in the regiment; the white NCOs had a separate mess from black NCOs, but the whites painted their faces black in the jungle so they wouldn't stand out from their troops.

Lieutenant John Hamilton
Platoon commander, 1st Battalion, Gambia Regiment
On the march to the Kaladan in January 1944 it was very hot indeed. The nice thing about jungle paths is that you march in the shade, but on the jeep track the sun beat down full blast at midday. We had one advantage over other British troops: we Europeans did not carry our large packs, only our haversack. We had 'boys' who were 'enlisted followers'. They wore the same uniform, but weren't armed, and their job was to be a batman. They were paid the same as the soldiers: a shilling a day.

We marched in what British troops called battle order. Wingate would have 'gone spare' at officers not carrying huge packs. We lived on air supply for far longer than the Chindits did, and covered far more ground. We didn't carry as much as them, but survived better. When we arrived at a defensive position, the officers didn't dig the trenches, but went to the company O Group, supervised the administration and so forth. That is why the British Army provides an officer with a batman, so that the officer can take care of

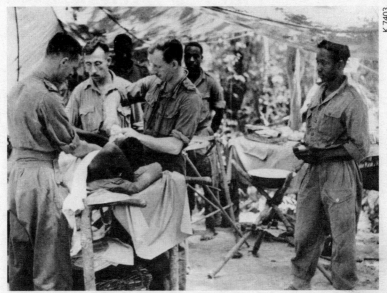

K 7403

Doctors treat a wounded soldier of the 81st West African Division in the Kaladan Valley.

everybody else, and isn't bogged down looking after himself, cooking a meal etc. Chindit columns lost lots of officers through sickness and fatigue. We had nothing like those casualties. We were the first people to be on air supply at divisional strength. Our air drops were to battalions and even to brigades. The Chindits were trying to organise air drops for half battalions, spread out all over the place; very wasteful of aircraft.

The whole division marched along the jeep track over Frontier Hill; on the other side the hills went up to two thousand feet. Then we pushed down the Kaladan. The initial opposition was light, just outposts. In the first Arakan performance the British had sent a small force into the Kaladan, not by our route, but by Taung Bazaar, a more tortuous route, more or less due east. It emerged in Kaladan village, and was called the SoutCol route after Lieutenant Colonel Souter who was commanding a Baluchi battalion.

The Jap counter-attack began in the Kaladan when two battalions of the 213 Regiment disposed of the Baluchis at Kyauktaw, while the third battalion made its way across country, attacked Kaladan village and pushed out the Indian troops defending it.

Private Ali Haji Abdul Aziz Brimah
Signaller, 5th Battalion, Gold Coast Regiment
The Japanese had been told that we were cannibals and devils with tails as a propaganda trick. We started by not taking Jap prisoners, because they were not to be trusted and we had heard stories of what *they* did to prisoners. After a while we were told to try to take prisoners. We found it was no use. We didn't let our officers see, and killed the prisoners. They would kill themselves anyway. War is not child's play.

Lieutenant John Hamilton
Platoon commander, 1st Battalion, Gambia Regiment
The Jap 55th Division was facing XV Corps in northern Arakan, initially leaving the 1/213 Japanese Battalion in the Kaladan. Eventually this battalion was ordered to join the remainder of the 55th Division for the push that resulted in the Battle of the Admin Box. They were replaced in the Kaladan valley by the cavalry, or reconnaissance regiment of the 55th Division. The first people we bumped into were outposts of 1/213 stiffened by some locally recruited people. We called them the Arakan Defence Force, or Burma Traitor Army

(BTA). They didn't put up much of a show. 4 Nigeria Regiment drove in the outposts on the Kaladan. My company drove in another, and the remainder of the battalion a day later, on a different line, drove in yet another outpost.

The Japs assumed we would have to use the river as a line of communication. Of course we didn't have to use anything as a line of communication as we were being supplied by air. There was no Jap air threat at all, as they were in the process of losing command of the air.

We advanced to Kyauktaw, but this overstretched us and at Pagoda Hill we were forced back and operations in the Kaladan valley were closed down for a time.

I and my platoon sergeant were the last to leave Pagoda Hill. The Japs were boneheaded; they had been told to capture Pagoda Hill, they did, but didn't know what to do next.

Operation Thursday
The Second Chindit Expedition

We did have our bad times; so much rain that we remained wet for weeks. Sometimes we were without water for two days at a time. We carried enormous loads, varying from seventy-two pounds just after a supply drop to fifty-seven pounds just before one.

O f some three thousand Chindits who had marched into Burma on the first expedition, 2,182 returned four months later. About 450 were battle casualties, 210 were taken prisoner, of whom forty-two survived; the remainder were missing. So little was achieved by the expedition that for a while after his return Wingate thought he would be court-martialled.

Instead, he was sent for by Winston Churchill, whom he accompanied to the Anglo/American Conference at Quebec in August 1943. Here Churchill paraded Wingate before the American President and Chiefs of Staff, as an example of how the British meant business in Burma. Meanwhile the press in India and in Britain was encouraged to trumpet the fact that the expedition had penetrated far behind the Japanese lines, which was true; other details were not passed to the press. What we would now call the 'spin doctors' busily milked the Chindit story for all it was worth. It worked. Slim remarked, 'Whatever the actual facts, to the troops in Burma it seemed the first ripple showing the turning of the tide.' Wingate's eloquence at Quebec convinced the American President, Roosevelt, and the Combined Chiefs of Staff that long-range penetration (LRP) could play a decisive part in the war in Burma. He was authorised to expand his force massively. To his original 77th Indian Infantry Brigade was added Brigadier W. D. A. 'Joe' Lentaigne's 111th Indian Infantry Brigade, which was already training for the LRP role. In addition he was given the experienced 70th British Division, fresh from the desert, which he broke up to form columns and LRP brigades. He also took under command the 3rd Brigade of the 81st West African Division.

Eventually, after many changes of plan, Wingate was tasked with supporting the American Lieutenant General Stilwell in his mission of advancing south from Ledo, to take Myitkyina, and connect Ledo with the old Burma Road into China. Wingate planned to achieve this by cutting the line of communication of the Japanese opposing Stilwell. It was not the intention that the Chindits should seize objectives in pitched battles with Japanese main force units.

Wingate returned from Quebec with a private air force assigned to him for ninety-nine days: the American Colonel Cochrane's Number 1 Air Commando USAAF, consisting of thirteen C-47 Dakotas, twelve C-46 Commando transports, twelve Mitchell B-25 medium bombers, thirty P-51 Mustang fighter-bombers, 225 Waco gliders, 100 L-1 and L-5 light aircraft and six helicopters. For major troop moves, resupply, and close air support tasks, the RAF and USAAF Troop Carrier Command would be needed to augment Number 1 Air Commando. Morale soared among the Chindits when they realised that no longer would sick and wounded have to be abandoned; the light aircraft would come and get them.

Originally Wingate's command included a three-thousand-strong US Army infantry regiment, Merrill's Marauders, named after its commander Brigadier General Frank D. Merrill. Well before the Chindits moved into Burma, Stilwell demanded Merrill's men back. Wingate's response was to tell the American officer bearing the order, 'You can tell General Stilwell he can stick his Americans up his arse.'

Wingate originally intended that his force would march into Burma. On arrival each brigade was to choose a stronghold as a base of operations, including an airstrip and a dropping zone (DZ) for supply by parachute. The enemy was to be induced to attack the stronghold, and while doing so, would be attacked in his turn by 'floater columns' operating outside.

In mid-January 1944, Wingate was told that the Japanese had closed up to the Chindwin in strength, and were keeping close watch on all crossing places south of Homalin. Although Wingate did not know it, this was in preparation for the Japanese attack into Assam (covered in the next two chapters), and was nothing to do with Japanese suspicions that Wingate planned to repeat his 1943 performance. But it caused Wingate to change his plans and fly in all his force, except for Fergusson's 16th Brigade, which would be trucked to the road head on the Ledo Road at Tagap Ga, and march to cross the Chindwin just upstream from Singaling Hkamti, well over a hundred miles north of Homalin.

Wingate chose three main objectives: Indaw, the railway from Mandalay to Myitkyina, and the road from Bhamo to Myitkyina. The fly-in brigades would be taken by glider and Dakota into four landing zones (LZs) named Piccadilly, Chowringhee, Broadway, and Templecombe. Early glider loads would carry light bulldozers and engineers to construct airstrips for Dakotas. The LZs were some distance from the objectives, and he relied on the brigades approaching their objectives under cover of the thickly wooded and rough terrain. His plan was as follows:

- Fergusson's 16th Brigade march from the Ledo Road, starting in February, and secure the two existing Japanese airfields at Indaw.
- Calvert's 77th Brigade land by glider and Dakota at Broadway and Piccadilly, and set up a block on the Mandalay–Myitkyina railway.
- Lentaigne's 111th Brigade land by glider and Dakota at Piccadilly, and head for the area south of Indaw, to protect the southern approaches of 16th Brigade's operations there. The Blaine Detachment of commando engineers (Bladet) was to operate in the same area, and demolish key railway bridges.
- Morris's 4/9th Gurkha Rifles (Morrisforce) land by glider at Chowringhee, march to the mountains east of the Bhamo–Myitkyina Road, and raid the road.
- Dahforce, consisting of Burma Rifles commanded by Lieutenant Colonel 'Fish' Herring, to land by glider at Templecombe, raise guerrilla bands from the Kachins and support Morrisforce.

The remaining brigades, 14th, 23rd and 3rd West African, were kept for a second wave, planned as a relief for the first wave in about two to three months. It was thought that ninety days was the maximum that Chindits could spend behind enemy lines. In the event the back-up brigades were flown in much earlier.

16 BRIGADE TO INDAW

Colour Sergeant Harold Atkins
21 Column, 2nd Battalion, Queen's Royal Regiment

After the Tobruk battle the battalion was due to be sent to Syria, but because of the Japanese entry into the war, we were sent to Colombo to defend Ceylon. Suddenly, out of the blue, we were told by the CO that the whole of 16 Infantry Brigade, which we had been part of for the whole war, was to join the Chindits and move to Jhansi for jungle training. We were there for three months living in jungle, as we would in Burma, and trained hard.

Wingate gave us a pep talk at the conclusion of the last major exercise at Saugor. I can't remember exactly what he said, except that we would have air support and casualty evacuation by air, so no man need worry if he was wounded; he would not be left behind. We would have supplies dropped to us. We were well trained and would show the Japs that we were better than them. I certainly wasn't inspired by Wingate. Nor were some of the other lads. Our concern was how much the press had built up the Japs as being invincible and merciless. We nursed the thought, 'What happens if you get captured?'

Private Arthur Baker
71 Column, 13 Platoon, 2nd Battalion, Leicestershire Regiment

The 2nd Leicesters were a marvellous battalion, the nucleus was all regulars. They had been all through Tobruk, fought in Syria, and were experienced. Corporal Brown commanded our section. He was a regular soldier, and had served in Crete, Syria and Tobruk.

The training was rigorous, if you weren't fit you would not survive it. Wingate visited us and spoke to us. We thought he was mad to begin with but he proved his point, he never expected anyone to do anything he couldn't do himself. But not many of the 2nd Leicesters liked him.

Lieutenant Peter Taylor
45 Column, 45th Reconnaissance Regiment

I was in the 45th Recce Regiment, part of 70 Division. We had to retrain from being a mechanised recce regiment for the desert. We were split into 45 and 54 Columns. I was in Number 45 Column commanded by the CO, 54 Column was commanded by the 2i/c. We did too much marching in training,

MH 7873

At Hailakandi airfield in Assam before the fly-in of the Chindits on the second expedition. L-R: American liaison officer, Colonel Allison USAAF, Brigadier Calvert, Captain Borrow (Wingate's ADC), Wingate, Lieutenant Colonel Scott, Chindit officer.

and exhausted ourselves before we even started operating.

Lieutenant Arthur Binnie
Blaine Detachment (Bladet)

I joined the Chindits because it had an aura of being special. We trained very hard, and the troops were proud of being trained this way, it was enormously satisfying. Wingate was about during our training, and we were impressed by his personality, with almost a manic attitude to jungle training. Although a small man, his personality came over as someone one would like to follow.

My first operation was to carry out a recce for Fergusson from the Ledo Road to the Chindwin, in February 1944. Our small party of British and West African soldiers were dressed as Americans because there were no British troops there until Fergusson's Brigade arrived. We wouldn't have fooled anybody. West Africans speak differently to American Africans, and our accents were different too. I had a packet of opium with which we bribed the village headmen.

Private Alexander Preston
22 Column, 8 Platoon, B Company, 2nd Battalion, Queen's Royal Regiment

Wingate visited us by the Ledo Road, waiting to go into Burma. We had to wait for a fortnight for extra kit to arrive. He said, 'You are going into Burma, imagine yourself climbing up one side of a house and down the other in mud, and you think it's impossible. It is not, because that is just what you are going to do.' He was right. It rained all the time while we waited. We got covered in leeches.

Colour Sergeant Harold Atkins
21 Column, 2nd Battalion, Queen's Royal Regiment

I was the Column Company Quartermaster Sergeant, equivalent to the Regimental Quartermaster Sergeant in a battalion. After our final training we moved to Assam/Burma border near the Ledo Road. We moved into a jungle clearing assembling for the march ahead. To get there we had to travel quite a distance along the Ledo Road in US trucks driven by Chinese drivers. It was an atrocious road, and was still under construction by hand by thousands of coolies – Indians, Chinese, all sorts of people, and some US giant equipment. The road, being carved out of a mountainside, consisted of masses of S bends.

The Ledo Road.

It climbed above the cloud level, and then down into ravines, crossing rivers on wooden bridges constructed out of material from the jungle. I wouldn't have trusted even a Dinky toy to cross some of them, let alone a truck. Coupled with the dangerous road, and the hair-raising way the Chinese drove their lorries, we were glad to get off the trucks after each day of a frightening journey; but at least it was a ride. The mules and muleteers walked. All the time it rained and rained and rained.

After some days we arrived in the jungle clearing. Here we got some more equipment, including some infantry flame-throwers.

Brigadier Bernard Fergusson
Commander, 16th Brigade

The brigade I commanded walked in and very tedious it was too. There were four thousand men and seven hundred animals strung out sixty-five miles from end to end, one abreast, because the paths and tracks were not wide enough to have two men walking abreast. If the leading man was in Richmond Park, the last man would be in the New Forest. Or if the leading man was on Glasgow Green, the tail-end Charlie would have been in Fort William, or Roxburgh or Carnoustie. The hills are half as high again as in the West Highlands and covered with jungle.

Colour Sergeant Harold Atkins
21 Column, 2nd Battalion, Queen's Royal Regiment

The 2nd Queens were given the lead of 16 Infantry Brigade. A battalion of six hundred men, seventy mules, twenty ponies, strung out in single file covers a huge distance. There were two columns of the Queens, two columns of the Leicesters, plus another six columns, so many people had to wait for days before setting out. Before we started the march a team of sappers went ahead to cut steps in the steep Naga hills that rise up to six thousand feet. Because we were heavily laden, as were the mules, and with all the rain, we could not have got up the hills without properly revetted steps. But within half a day, the steps were washed away by the rain.

Brigadier Bernard Fergusson
Commander, 16th Brigade

The mule leaders had the worst job of all, looking after the mule's load as well as their own, and ensuring that the mule's back did not get sore. The most important loads on the mules were wireless sets, charging engines, mortars, machine guns and ammunition. Going off the air was the thing we dreaded most.

Colour Sergeant Harold Atkins
21 Column, 2nd Battalion, Queen's Royal Regiment

The worst part of the march was from Tagap to Hklak, it took us the best part of seven days to cover thirty-five miles; it beggars description, the physical exhaustion that was inflicted on men and mules. Sometimes the mules fell over the side, down two or three hundred feet. Men had to dump their packs, climb down, unload the mule, and help it up. Strangely very few were badly injured. They loaded them up, only to have it happen again with another mule. It was as hard to go down the hills as climb up. At times you were running and felt your knee joints under strain, it was as exhausting as climbing. In some places we had to offload the mules and send them off sliding down on their haunches, and put the loads on bamboo slides to manhandle the loads down. You arrived at the bottom to see another ruddy great climb up, it seemed never ending and went on like that till we reached the Chindwin. We never met the enemy. We went through several villages. We did not have anything to do with them.

Brigadier Bernard Fergusson
Commander, 16th Brigade

The signallers and the cipher operators had to work while we brewed up and rested, sending off the signals for supplies, and receiving orders. They were all the real 'heroes'. They had to put up aerials by throwing a stone tied to the end of the aerial over a tree branch.

We did have our bad times; so much rain that we remained wet for weeks. Sometimes we were without water for two days at a time. We carried enormous loads, varying from seventy-two pounds just after a supply drop to fifty-seven pounds just before one. We saw very little of the sky. Sometimes you would come out into a clearing, perhaps around a village, and we would halt for a few minutes extra.

Lieutenant Peter Taylor
45 Column, 45th Reconnaissance Regiment
Wingate said you couldn't punish a man, for sleeping on sentry or sleeping with a local woman, by giving him twenty-eight days' detention or court-martialling him, so he would be flogged. This was accepted by the men.

Two of my men were caught stealing rations, and my CO was so bloody wet, he attempted to punish them by distributing all their chocolate around. But all their friends instantly gave them the chocolate back. Typically British.

Colour Sergeant Harold Atkins
21 Column, 2nd Battalion, Queen's Royal Regiment
When we arrived at the Chindwin the training paid dividends. Dakotas came over and dropped rubber boats, but not enough to take everyone over in one lift. If you had well-trained mules, you could swim them across in a bunch with their muleteers, although there was always the chance that one would turn round and go back. Some hung on to mules with their gear rolled up in a groundsheet like a sausage. I did this, I wasn't a good swimmer. This river crossing was part of our training.

When we reached the far bank of the Chindwin we were sitting on the bank of the river brewing up, waiting for the rest of the column to cross and two characters were walking along the banks of the river. One had a towel wrapped round him and a monocle and an enormous beard. That was our brigadier, Bernard Fergusson. The other was General Wingate looking fearsome and scruffy. I remember wondering what the top brass would think about these two senior officers.

From the other side of the Chindwin it was a matter of getting on to our objective, Indaw North. We were told that the Japs were in the vicinity of the bridgehead, but didn't see them. Eventually we arrived at the stronghold of Aberdeen. Morale was quite good. But physically we were becoming very tired.

Aberdeen was well behind Japanese lines in an area near the River Meza near a village, we constructed an airstrip big enough to take Dakotas. It nestled in a valley surrounded by hills, and if one had not been behind Jap lines it would have been a very pleasant interlude. It was subjected to Jap air raids to try to knock out the airstrip.

We were told we were getting to the meat of what we were here to do: to

Peter Taylor, taken after the war.

harass the Japs, and cut their communications and to cause chaos in the area of Indaw North. We were originally told it was planned that we should capture the Jap airfields at Indaw North and the Jap supplies for their attack on Imphal and Kohima.

Private Arthur Baker
71 Column, 13 Platoon, 2nd Battalion, Leicestershire Regiment
We built a strip at Aberdeen. The West Africans came in to provide the garrison at Aberdeen. We built it with machetes and shovels. First we flattened the banks in the paddy and then the gliders flew in carrying light bulldozers.

Lieutenant Peter Taylor
45 Column, 45th Reconnaissance Regiment
When we got to Aberdeen the other two brigades were flown in. They looked as fit as fiddles, while we were exhausted. To add to that, we had hardly got to Aberdeen when we were ordered off to carry out an attack on Indaw.

Colour Sergeant Harold Atkins
21 Column, 2nd Battalion, Queen's Royal Regiment
From now on it becomes a tale of indecision and poor results, bearing in mind the effort we put in to get there. We set off from Aberdeen, but because the columns were so stretched out behind us it was going to take three or four days before the brigade could concentrate to start the operation to take Indaw North. It was originally intended that us and the Leicesters should attack Indaw and the airfields. The other columns were to play minor roles. But because the concentration of the brigade took so long, the plan was changed. My column was sent in a long hook to attack Indaw from the south, with the Leicesters coming in from the north. But things went wrong. We tried to move south without being seen, but villagers probably reported our progress to the Japs. We arrived at the Meza Chaung, and had had a supply drop the evening before. After this we set off in a hurry, and made towards the start line for the attack on Indaw. We arrived on the day after the supply drop, towards dusk.

Lieutenant Peter Taylor
45 Column, 45th Reconnaissance Regiment

During the Indaw operation, we came to Thetkegyin. I was recce platoon commander, with two sections of British, and one section of Burmese, unfortunately in my case Burmans, that is townsmen, not hill men like Karens or Kachins. Instead of carrying out reconnaissance, my proper job, I was guarding the CO's party. We were attacked while still wearing our large packs by a bunch of lightly equipped Japs in what amounted to PT kit. The CO ordered dispersal, but at the RV there were more Japs.

The CO was over thirty-six, too old, and a great gent, he wouldn't have his pack carried on a mule or pony. As a result he was played out. He changed the RV. So he sent me with a sergeant and one Burman to find the column and tell them where the new RV was. So off I went; it was nearing dusk. I luckily found the mules of the mortar platoon and told them where to go. Then I found the rifle company under an excellent fellow called Ron Adams, and he had collected together one or two others, and I told him where to go. Then I came on what I thought were some more of our chaps, and I shouted the codeword which was Namkin. They all stopped dead. I said it again, as my mouth was rather dry, and suddenly I realised they were all Japanese. Fortunately my sergeant, a marvellous chap, shouted, 'This way sir,' and he fired away and I was able to run straight into a thicket and joined the rest of my party.

We were not in jungle, but in teak country, where there is not a lot of cover from view. I found the track of the company and followed it. We were terribly short of water; for some reason water discipline had broken down since leaving Aberdeen, mainly because we had not had any contacts with the enemy and were getting slack.

Having found the company we went to a village where the Burmans said we would get water. It was held by the Japs. The company rushed in and a lot of chaps were sprayed by Jap fire. Ron Adams was wounded, and had to be left behind; God knows what happened to him.

I found myself with about half a dozen chaps, mainly my recce platoon, and we hid up in lantana, very useful stuff, it gave us cover in this rather open area. Travelling by night we got back to Aberdeen, where remnants of the column had collected. The CO was flown out, got rid of, a Burma Rifles chap took over.

Private Arthur Baker
71 Column, 13 Platoon, 2nd Battalion, Leicestershire Regiment
At Auktaw we had a brush with the Japanese, and we charged with fixed bayonets across a river held by Japanese and Burmese. Corporal Flowers dropped dead by my side, the first man I saw killed in action, by a sniper tied to a tree. Corporal Brown shot the sniper, and he hung from the tree suspended by his ropes.

Around the perimeter of the village was a bamboo fence, and each time a man went through the gaps in it, the Japs fired at them, so I dived through it and got stuck in the fence by the pack on my back and had to be pushed out from behind. But all our platoon got through. The Japs would feign death and shoot you from behind if you did not kill them as you went by. We didn't bury the enemy dead, or our own. The CO was wounded in the arm, but stayed with us for the attack on Indaw.

Colour Sergeant Harold Atkins
21 Column, 2nd Battalion, Queen's Royal Regiment
The CO decided that we could go no further that night. Although he and some of his group had noticed tyre marks on a track they had crossed, whether they gave it sufficient importance I cannot say. But we were ordered to bivouac in that area. We were still moving in and had not completed getting the column in to all-round defence when it became completely dark, and all of a sudden we could hear the roar of engines. To start with we thought it was aircraft, but it was half a dozen lorryloads of Japs who drove slap-bang into the middle of our bivouac.

Chaos reigned. It was dark. The Japs jumped out of their lorries, there were grenades going off, there was screaming and shouting. The CO was wounded. People were milling around, people had taken off their packs, leaned their weapon against a tree, and started to brew up. Some people were close to their weapons, others weren't.

My group had not had time to get packs off. We took cover on the banks of a small wadi. The issue of orders was difficult. The night progressed. My name was called out a number of times, 'C/Sgt Atkins.' It might have been an officer trying to contact me, against all the rules of training in the jungle, under fire, that was wrong: he should not have shouted my name, indeed not shouted at all. That gave the Japs the clue where he was. I was always convinced that it was this officer, but it could have been the Japs hearing my name and continuing to shout it.

I was engaged in trying to locate my administrative officer who was with the CO to find out what to do with the mules. Nobody knew where anybody was. One chap was shooting, and crawled across and asked him what he was shooting at. He said he didn't know, but that everybody else was shooting so he thought he had better join in. I told him to stop: he might be shooting at our own people.

There was close-quarter fighting. One young soldier held a Jap while his chum bayoneted him.

The second-in-command took command and gave orders to evacuate the bivouac and move across the chaung. In a huge state of pandemonium we crossed the chaung, and several men drowned, as it was quite deep.

We went on for a mile or so leaving the Japs in possession of our bivouac area. In daylight we discovered that about seventy men were missing, nearly every mule was gone, and nearly all the wireless sets and medical stores. The mules had panicked and went in all directions; we found a few eventually. The main concern was the loss of our wirelesses. We could not communicate, coordinate the attack, take supply drops etc.

There was a system to cater for what had just happened. You were given a short RV, which would be in force for 24 hours, or a long RV three days' hence. And you made for one or the other, depending on how long had elapsed since the dispersal of the column. A lot of the blokes did turn up at the RVs. Many men lost their packs with all their rations. All the remaining rations had to be gathered in and redistributed. The CO sent for me and asked me if I had a pistol as his had been blown out of his hand by a grenade. I had just given out all the spare pistols. I took one off a soldier and gave it to the CO.

My column for the next few hours was disorientated and unnerved. Our CO addressed us later and gave us a terrific harangue and said we were a rabble and it was to stop.

Private Arthur Baker
71 Column, 13 Platoon, 2nd Battalion, Leicestershire Regiment
We captured the airfield but there were no reinforcements so we had to abandon it in the end. The Japs put in some ferocious attacks but we saw them

off. The Japs had suicide squads, one would carry a white flag, with a machine gun strapped on his back, so the man behind could fire it when the lead man threw himself down. They ended up twenty yards off crossing a dried-up chaung. We rolled grenades into it and caught them in the bottom. We had American carbines, which had been dropped to us after Auktaw.

We were in jungle green, they wore khaki. Some of the first of our chaps into Auktaw found some South African khaki uniforms that the Japs had captured in Rangoon, and put them on because their kit was so ragged. Later they were found at Thetkegyin, killed by the Japs, mutilated. A man wearing a South African bush hat had been beheaded, men with South African shirts had their arms cut off, and those with South African trousers had their legs cut off.

Colour Sergeant Harold Atkins
21 Column, 2nd Battalion, Queen's Royal Regiment

We got into contact with brigade HQ using a short-range wireless set that we still had. We were told to go to the road, find the Japs and be 'bloody', give them hell. That we started to do, but they had vanished and we did not contact them. Then we were told to get ready for the attack and to go in on a given signal and attack Indaw.

We waited at the forming-up position. All the muleteers stood by their mules so they would not make a noise. We lay up all night on the southern fringe of Indaw. Some of the men had only a machete, having lost their weapons the night before.

We waited and waited and the signal did not come. We learned that some of the other columns had come under attack. The Recce Platoon was ambushed trying to find water. The Leicesters were discovered somewhere near their forming-up position north of Indaw and were attacked. All this put paid to a coordinated attack on Indaw. The brigadier gave orders to withdraw to Aberdeen.

The journey back to Aberdeen was full of hair-raising episodes. We had halted and started searching for water. Most of us got back, but two chaps disappeared, and they were never heard of or seen again. When we were about to cross the single-track railway line from Katha to Indaw in the dark, we heard a train chugging up the line. I don't think I've seen so many men disappear into jungle so quickly. We were still very disorganised and with low morale and not about to get involved with the Japs again if we could avoid it.

One of the men sitting on a pony with a fractured thigh was yanked off the pony. He did not utter a word. He took it very well.

We lay there looking at the train loaded with Japs going off to Indaw. One Jap shouted a sort of challenge, but we did not answer it. We remained quiet and continued to Aberdeen after the train had gone.

THE OTHER BRIGADES FLY IN

Lieutenant Colonel Walter 'Scottie' Scott
Commanding Officer, 81 and 82 Columns, 1st Battalion, King's Regiment (Liverpool)

The plan was that my 81 Column would land at Piccadilly, and 82 some thirty miles to the north in another clearing known as Broadway. The role of these columns was to clear the area and hold it so that bulldozers could be flown in to construct airstrips. In the late afternoon of 5 March 1944, Colonel Cochrane had sent a photo recce flight to both strips. General Wingate, Calvert and myself were standing at the head of the glider train when a photograph of Piccadilly was shown to us. There was a silence. The clearing I had known so well from 1943 was covered in logs.

Wingate took the photograph to General Slim and after several minutes came back and handed the photograph to me and turned away with his head bent and hands clasped behind his back. He looked a forlorn and lonely figure as he walked towards the setting sun. He returned and after a brief conference returned to General Slim.

He came back and gave me fresh orders, so clear and concise that it was as if Piccadilly had never existed, I was to go to Broadway. Someone had made a bold decision. Who it was I do not know.

After I had given orders to my column commanders, he took me off and told me something that was for my ears alone and always will be. All his planning and hopes were on the line but as we shook hands not the slightest tremor betrayed what was conflicting within.

As my glider rose into the purple dusk on the hills to the east, my thoughts were not on what lay beyond, but rather of General Wingate's unforgettable display of cool, determined and inspired leadership. I believe that if ever I saw greatness in a human being I saw it in General Wingate that night.

Private John Mattinson
20 Column, Commando Platoon, 1st Battalion, Lancashire Fusiliers
Initially the Lancashire Fusiliers were the floating battalion, to patrol outside the stronghold and attack the Japanese before they could reach the block. I was in the Commando Platoon, fifty-two strong, commanded by Captain Butler of the Guides Cavalry. We were taught how to drive in case we captured Japanese vehicles. We were taught the basics of explosives. Each man was issued with condoms for underwater demolitions. You inflated it, put explosive in, with safety fuse and match inside, and tied it up. It would float and you could swim out with it to the bridge pier. Then you untied the condom, struck the match on the fuse, it burned underwater. You could use the cloth ammunition bandoliers as cutting charges by packing in explosives in every pocket, and wrapping the belt round a girder. We were told that our job was to blow a bridge near Tonlon village.

The night before the fly in, we were watching a film, and Colonel Cochrane took the mike and said, 'Now lads, the time has come; tomorrow night we shall hit the Japs in the guts. Good hunting. I know that some of you will not be coming back.' A big cheer went up.

I wasn't supposed to be going that night, but someone came up and said, 'You are going tonight, in number five glider, into Broadway.' So I flew in with Lieutenant de Witt, some American engineers and some of ours. We were to help clear the strip ready to take the C-47s the next night. I looked out of the little window in the glider and I could see the Irrawaddy and it looked like a road in the moonlight. The pilot said, 'It looks like a hell of a mess down there. But I'll see what I can do.' I thought what the hell is he doing, going straight for trees. He flew in between two trees, the wings came off, and just the body went on a bit further. But everyone got out all right.

Private William Merchant
20 Column, Commando Platoon, 1st Battalion, Lancashire Fusiliers
As we landed a Bren hit me on the side of the head, I wasn't too badly hurt. One chap had a broken ankle. But the first glider down crashed because of ruts in the paddy where teak logs had been laid out to dry, so the ground was corrugated. We got down about 10.30pm; we wondered if we would ever live to see India again.

Private John Mattinson
20 Column, Commando Platoon, 1st Battalion, Lancashire Fusiliers

There were gliders scattered all over, with quite a lot of injured; two of the American engineer officers were killed. Lieutenant de Witt went up to Colonel Allison who was sitting in a jeep, and he told him to start helping clear the strip, cutting the lantana and other trees, digging and laying out portable lights with a small generator to bring in the C-47s carrying more men and equipment the next night.

Captain Donald McCutcheon
40 Column, 3rd/4th Gurkha Rifles

We were having a party to drink the mess profits before we went into action. Brigadier Lentaigne and Jack Masters were there, both 4th Gurkhas. An officer came in with a signal saying 'Move your men now. Get to Tulihal tonight and fly tomorrow morning'. We spent the whole night packing up.

Surprise, surprise, the next morning a lot of large trucks arrived and took us to Tulihal. Then, typical army, we sat around for a couple of days.

Although we had had a certain amount of glider training, we had never actually been up in gliders. We were then told, 'You are not going by glider. You will follow in the 4/9th Gurkhas by Dakota to an airstrip called Chowringhee.' This was not the one we were originally going to, because that had been covered in logs. The snag was that Chowringhee was on the wrong side of the Irrawaddy, but all right for the 4th/9th, who were going to join up with the North Kachin Levies.

Lieutenant Richard Rhodes-James
Cipher Officer, HQ, 111 Brigade

It was extraordinary to be landing at night in a Dakota on a strip with a lit flare path in enemy territory. We had total air superiority. After landing we got into defensive positions and waited for the morning before moving to the Irrawaddy. We were to have landed at Piccadilly, north-west of the Irrawaddy, but when the plan was changed we landed east of the river at Chowringhee, so had to cross to reach our area of operations.

Warrant Officer Deryck Groocock
194 Squadron, RAF

The Dakota was a marvellous aircraft, light on the controls, with very reliable engines, and you could land it on a five-hundred-yard-long strip at night. I flew into all the Chindit strips by night and day: White City, Broadway, Blackpool and Chowringhee. Aberdeen was the worst, especially at night, it was short with hills on three sides. You had to circle at seven thousand to eight thousand feet, waiting until you were called down by the controller. You circled down, and landed one way on the five hundred- to six hundred-yard-long strip. You took off in the opposite direction. One night I came in too high, and knew I wasn't going to make it. So I opened up full throttle, found a little valley, and staggered along this at about seventy-five knots, managing to get away with it and come in for another approach.

One of our flight commanders, 'Dinger Bell', was attacked by a Jap night fighter while circling overhead Broadway. Both engines were knocked out, and four or five of the twenty or so soldiers in the back were killed. He managed to do a dead-stick landing and get away with it – fantastic.

Major Alexander Harper
94 Column, 4th/9th Gurkha Rifles

I was originally in the Deccan Horse. I was posted to the Governor of Bengal's Bodyguard, volunteered for the Chindits, and went to the 4th/9th Gurkhas. I joined them in February 1944 at Jhansi, and went into Burma a month later. The 4/9th were in two columns, 49 and 94. I was in 94, commanded by Peter Cane, of 4th/9th Gurkhas, a regular. As a cavalry officer I was supposed to be able to handle animals and so was in charge of the mules for the fly-in.

We had a ramp for loading the mules into the Dakota door which was about four feet above the ground; they couldn't jump in, but could jump out if need be. We loaded fifty planes with mules, and then got them out again, because we were told that the LZ was no good. So we loaded again the next night for a different LZ.

We flew in to an LZ on the east bank of Irrawaddy, called Chowringhee. Glider-landed troops had improved the LZ and Dakotas flew in the heavier stuff, including mules. The flight was OK. We had no trouble, although on one Dakota a mule misbehaved, and was shot. The Dakota flew back to India with a dead mule on board.

Pilot Officer James Thirlwell
194 Squadron, RAF
Even in monsoon storms when you had very little say in what happened to you, plunging down three thousand feet and up again two thousand in torrential rain and lightning, the Dakota was a wonderful aircraft. It had one snag: the cockpit leaked badly in heavy rain, and we used to put oilskins over our knees to keep the water off our laps.

Broadway was a difficult place to land at night because of mountains on either side. You approached downwind at eight thousand feet to clear the high ground, turned on to finals at eight thousand feet, and tried to pick up the light of the goose-neck flares marking the strip. There was no glide-path indicator, you went right in from eight thousand feet to touch down. My first landing there, the chap ahead of me with twenty-four soldiers on board made a nonsense, and tried to go round again; all I could see were his landing lights as he went straight into a hillside beyond the runway. I was at about six hundred feet at that stage, and just held on, all I could see was a flaming aircraft ahead. I made it OK.

Private John Mattinson
20 Column, Commando Platoon, 1st Battalion, Lancashire Fusiliers
The next night at Broadway, Captain Butler came in with the column and the rest of the platoon, and I was the guide to show them where they were to go. We worked for four days, before getting our marching orders and setting off for the Central Valley.

Major Percival Leathart
Officer Commanding D Company, 3rd/9th Gurkha Rifles
The CO and Intelligence Officer were to have gone in first. Their glider crashed soon after take off. They were all right, but the small bulldozer and horse in the glider were damaged. That was a bad start for the CO who came in with us the next day. We flew in Dakotas, each towing two gliders on long nylon ropes. They had to climb to over six thousand feet to get over the hills into Burma.

It got colder and colder as we climbed. Then we started to come down. It was a remarkable sight seeing the open space all lit up in the middle of the Burmese jungle. As we marched in the night, past the paraffin-burning lights

James Thirlwell, taken after the war.

that marked the edge of the strip there was a smell of death that accompanied us for the rest of the campaign. It came from crashed gliders; nobody had had time to remove the corpses. It was a chilling experience.

Lieutenant Arthur Binnie
Blaine Detachment (Bladet)

On the main operation, I went in as a special decoy group under Major Blaine, fifty men and five officers. Blaine had been much admired by Wingate on the first expedition. He was given an immediate DCM and promoted to officer in the field from being a CSM. Blaine was a tough Scot trained as an engineer. He was given the task of collecting a group of engineers and muleteers who would carry out whatever Wingate wanted, called Bladet, standing for Blaine Detachment.

When the main body went in our job was to disrupt the Myitkyina railway, to make the Japs aware that troops were operating further south of the main operation, which might make the Japs wonder how many troops were operating in the area.

We flew in five gliders from Imphal and landed in paddy fields near the Irrawaddy, in an LZ prepared by Gurkhas who had gone in before us. We landed in moonlight and ploughed straight into the jungle. The wings fell off, the body of the glider fell apart, and we walked out of the wreckage. My group was intact. The glider carrying the mules seemed to loop-the-loop, but landed all right. The mules walked out and started to graze.

After landing it was revealed to me that I was to take command as Blaine had been injured in the landing. This was my first time on active service, but as the senior of five lieutenants I took command. Blaine gave me my objectives before being flown out in a light plane. It was a little bit nerve-shattering.

We were told to conceal ourselves as best we could. It was likely that Burma traitors would spot us, but we were not to get seriously engaged. Our main task was to blow up the railway line. With only fifty men you were limited in the amount of damage you could cause.

Private John Mattinson
20 Column, Commando Platoon, 1st Battalion, Lancashire Fusiliers

After marching for five days we had an air drop of explosives for our task at the bridge near Tonlon, and a top-up of rations. The drop was into elephant grass, it was sharp and cut like a razor. One chap fell into a mud wallow made by elephants, and broke his leg. He was flown out the next morning by light aircraft.

For the supply drop we lit a line of fires. We saw the aircraft coming round, and Captain Butler flashed a green light twice. Six chutes came out, and a free drop of mule fodder as well. We had one chap killed with a broken neck; a bundle of fodder bounced and hit him. But morale was high, and everyone was raring to go.

The bridge was a five-pier bridge with H girders. I was in the chaung by the bridge, putting explosives in a bag, and the others were hauling it up to the bridge. We had started to lay the charge, and a shout went up, 'Jap truck coming down the road.' Captain Butler gave orders not to fire.

The truck was coming fast. It got to a level crossing and pulled up and stalled. The troops in the back sat there, they were wounded. We didn't fire, but sat looking at them. We were hidden so close, that one chap got spat at in the eye by a Jap.

Eventually the Jap truck drove on. We put a lead pencil delay fuse on the charge to give us a chance to get away. Lieutenant de Witt said to me, 'I'll give you the honour of pulling the pin out.'

Captain Donald McCutcheon
40 Column, 3rd/4th Gurkha Rifles

We, with brigade HQ, now had to cross the Irrawaddy before we could go to our objective in a north-west direction. Things started to go wrong from the beginning; it was an IMFU, or Imperial Military Fuck Up. The outboard engines we had dropped to us kept breaking down. Also, we did not cross on a wide-enough front. Came the dawn when we should have been across, we were not. Brigade HQ had got across, and half the battalion was over. We, the other half, were left on the other side.

Orders were given to 40 Column to join the 4th/9th Gurkhas as an extra column. The journey north was frustrating as the 4th/9th had been ordered to move as fast as they could to join the Levies. We were about thirty-six hours behind, and it was difficult with the Japanese stirred up. Almost level with Bhamo we ran into the Japanese and had minor engagements with them from time to time. We ambushed and destroyed the Bhamo–Myitkyina Road as we went along.

Chindits preparing a bridge on the Mandalay-Myitkyina railway for demoltion.

Private John Mattinson
20 Column, Commando Platoon, 1st Battalion, Lancashire Fusiliers

The next day the bridge blew successfully and we set off again to harass the Japs. The point men came back and told Lieutenant de Witt that there were some Japs by the road having a rest in a clearing. We approached, took up fire positions. Captain Butler said, 'When I throw grenades, you are to open fire.' He threw five grenades, shouting, 'Here, you yellow bastards, share these between you.' They screamed and fired at us, we didn't fire a round. We killed five. The rest ran off.

The man by me said, 'I've sprained my ankle.' A bullet had gone through his boot. We carried him back on a stretcher. When we got out his pack to do a brew, we found a hole where a bullet had gone through his mess tin, and through his rations. We cut an airstrip for a light plane and he was flown out.

Next day we got a message to head for White City.

Private William Merchant
20 Column, Commando Platoon, 1st Battalion, Lancashire Fusiliers

So we made our way into the White City block. Brigadier Calvert came out on a horse to meet us and rode in with us. It was the size of a city park, surrounded by wire. The Bengal Sappers and Miners had blown the bridge north of Mawlu. They had taken sleepers from the railway line to make overhead protection for slit trenches, making them into bunkers. They built a light airstrip inside the block, and a Dakota strip just outside on the far side of the railway.

Pilot Officer Joe Simpson
194 Squadron, RAF

On one occasion I flew a load of water, including a small water trailer, in to Broadway. The Chindits didn't want the trailer, they just wanted me off quickly. So I just opened the taps to drain it, before lashing it well forward in the aircraft for take-off. I must have been a bit flustered and disorientated, because I saw two lights on the runway and was opening up power, when a chap with a torch rushed out and waved and screamed, 'Those are the last two lights on the runway, you are facing the wrong way.' I turned round and took off, and in the confusion forgot to make the fifteen-degree right turn immediately after take-off. I heard trees bashing the bottom of the aircraft, did a stall turn to the right and the Dakota responded. On my return the fitter said, 'Where have you been? The engine cowling is full of twigs and leaves.'

Lieutenant Arthur Binnie
Officer Commanding Blaine Detachment (Bladet)

We had a long journey to get to the Mandalay–Myitkyina railway line, including going through the dry belt which was not a pleasant experience, surviving with very little water for two or three days when the jungle is burning with the heat and no water in sight. It was one of the few occasions in my life when I thought I would kill one of my friends, I could hear the water in his bottle sloshing around, as we were marching towards where we hoped we would find water. I thought I might kill him and drink his water; it was a passing thought.

We tried to avoid villages, as we believed that the villagers were spotting us and might give information to the Japs. At one stage one of the chaps in the rear section of the column came forward and told me that two men with rifles had been following us for half a mile or so. I said that we would have to get them, and told an officer to take some men, ambush and kill them. They killed one and the other was brought to me slightly wounded in the foot. The problem: what to do with him? I decided that he knew where we were, and our strength. I had no option but to execute him. This was my duty. The attitude of the troops under my command made this clear. So I did it. I have lived with it, but don't feel guilty. It was more important to do that than risk the lives of my men.

We did not run into the Japanese at this stage. We blew up the railway line. Then we withdrew aiming to join the main force. We had done our job. It was a long trek. We were covering about twenty miles a day. The engineers laid booby traps on our tracks and by the railway, which would blow the Japs' feet off. Food was at a minimum. My batman, Private Whiting, came to me and said he had a fever. So I told him that I would have to leave him behind. Whiting immediately got surprisingly better, and was considerably better the next morning.

Major Alexander Harper
94 Column, 4th/9th Gurkha Rifles

My column was going to operate near the Chinese border, and ambush convoys on the Bhamo–Myitkyina Road. After this it was to link up further north with a Kachin local force raised by 'Fish' Herring.

We began by ambushing a Japanese truck on the road: two Japs were killed.

One hid, was captured, and shot. We were supposed to take care of any Jap prisoner, as they were rare, and send them back as quickly as possible. We could not do that.

The next ambush, the truck had ten Japs in it. Although it went over a mine, the Japs dashed into the jungle and fought back. They moved to some paddy fields and lay down behind the bunds and returned our fire. We killed them all but it took about forty minutes. They would not surrender. We did not suffer a scratch. The Gurkhas were most impressed by the Japanese persistence and courage.

Major Percival Leathart
D Company, 3rd/9th Gurkha Rifles

The next morning at Broadway we started digging foxholes and laying wire that had been dropped to us, and after about a week we had a really strong position. The RAF based some Hurricanes there. One of our companies acted as floaters to provide warning of any approaching Japanese.

One day about twelve Japanese bombers came over and bombed us, but caused remarkably few casualties because our foxholes were quite deep. A day or two later, the floating company was attacked by Japs but they did not press their attacks.

Wingate paid us a visit early on in an American B-25. When he left, I went with him and his ADC to the plane. Two American war correspondents tried to hitch a lift, and Wingate hauled them in, although the pilot said the plane was overloaded.

We then heard that the plane was missing. His death knocked the stuffing out of the Chindit campaign.

Lieutenant Colonel Walter 'Scottie' Scott
Commanding, 81 and 82 Columns, 1st Battalion, King's Regiment (Liverpool)

The last I saw of Wingate was when I said goodbye to him at Broadway, and a cloud came over all of us in Special Force. We didn't know what was to happen to us, whether we would be disbanded or someone else would take over command. Though it was very difficult for General Lentaigne to take over after Wingate, he did a damn good job, he was a good soldier.

But to most of us there could only be one Wingate. He had a lot of things that one could get annoyed with, but overall he was one of the greatest men I have ever met. Even those who disliked him had to admit that he was an outstanding leader. He was never afraid, even in a tight corner. His leadership and his drive I shall remember always. During that second campaign we were all inspired by what we did on the first campaign.

Lieutenant Richard Rhodes-James
Cipher Officer, HQ, 111 Brigade

We wondered if the operation would come to an end when Wingate was killed. Our brigade commander, Lentaigne, was made head of Special Force, so we had to get him out by air. The Brigade Major, Jack Masters, was made commander of the brigade.

The brigade blew up roads and supplies of ammunition on the Japanese route to their operations in the north of Burma. The problem with the column organisation was that it was not suitable for conventional attacks on a strong objective, because there was no reserve, and hence no flexibility. Some COs reverted to a proper battalion organisation.

Major Desmond Whyte RAMC
Medical Officer, HQ, 111 Brigade

A doctor in the Chindits was his own surgeon, own dermatologist, own orthopaedic specialist with just your medical orderlies to help. You had one pannier carried on one side of a mule for medical supplies. It was never large enough. Of all the medicines, mepacrin to suppress malaria was the most important.

In the jungle you carried a carbine. At night the enemy could be only a few feet from you. We had no antibiotics, but sulphamine drugs had just been issued, and on my first air drop after arriving in Burma I had my first sulpha drugs dropped to me; the first time I had seen them. We did not have tents, and therefore no cover from the elements. We had no mosquito nets.

Wounded who were immobilised were dragged behind mules on a bamboo stretcher, with the front on the mule's saddle, and the back of the stretcher on the ground. Four men with ropes walked alongside to help the stretcher up over the bumps on the ground and steer the mule.

Most wounded did very well, but in the great heat it became difficult to

Giving a wounded Gurkha soldier a drink.

keep them alive. Shortage of water was a problem. We carried chaguls, canvas bags to hold water; it evaporates through the canvas to keep the water cool, but loses water in the process. The casualty would sometimes have a tube down into his mouth and into his stomach through which we poured water. Sometimes I added brandy, and occasionally hot sweet tea.

With our training we always felt we were the masters of the jungle. Our number one enemy was malaria: everybody got it. Every morning if the enemy situation would allow, everybody was lined up and the NCOs checked that everybody took his mepacrin. Your eyes went yellow. After a bit you didn't care. Word spread through the Gurkhas that this made them impotent; as the Gurkha is a very virile man, we had to scotch the rumour.

Our ration was the American K Ration. It was excellent for a short time. It was all pre-cooked. If the enemy allowed, you could heat it up. You could eat it cold. The difficulty was that although it gave you three meals a day, you soon knew what was coming up next. More serious, a day's ration gave you only four thousand calories, whereas we were burning up six thousand calories, and from the start burned up our own flesh. We had the occasional 'paradise' drop of luxuries. We didn't always get our regular drop, for example, if the enemy was near, they would mortar the DZ. If there was a ground mist the RAF and USAAF were told if you don't get the correct signal, don't drop. The signal was changed every five days.

We were running down in condition. Men died of malaria, sepsis, pneumonia, and meningitis. I always took the seriously ill or wounded from the other columns, this meant that the brigade HQ moved very slowly with a long trail of casualties. The brigadier didn't like this, but we talked him into it; an excellent person, John Masters.

We arranged for a fly-out from time to time. Several light planes would come in. The doctor with Gurkha escorts took the casualties to a place where the Gurkhas could cut a strip and hope the planes would come before the enemy came. One of the rescue planes crashed on take off, and the pilot survived, scrambled out, and said, 'Aw shit, I ought to be shot.' I said, 'You soon will be, the Japs are coming.' We got the two dead out of the plane and buried them in the jungle. I always carried a little prayer wrapped in cellophane in my pocket. I said a prayer and moved on, knowing that the shallow grave would not keep the jackals out.

We didn't have too much trouble with teeth, more with glasses. Men who

Loading a casualty on to an L-5 light aircraft.

wore glasses took in a spare pair, but if they broke the second pair they had to have another pair flown in.

Psychological cases occurred towards the end. Every man has his breaking point, and we were reaching this. You could see people going downhill. Some even died in their sleep.

The Gurkhas were the most resilient in our brigade. The Gurkha has a very tough upbringing in Nepal, and is used to hardship and disaster.

Lieutenant Arthur Binnie
Officer Commanding Blaine Detachment (Bladet)

I had one muleteer, a bit of a rapscallion, who my CSM said needed discipline. So I told the muleteer that he was impeding the progress of the operation, and that I would deduct three days' rations from him and give them to other soldiers. I added that if he did not accept my punishment or made further difficulties I would shoot him. He accepted this, and worked very well.

We were heading for the main force, very tired and hungry. All we wanted to do was find our own troops and see what happened next. We were sitting in light jungle near paddy, and I was talking to CSM Chivers who had been on the first expedition, a very good man. We had taken a supply drop but were running short. Chivers believed that because we were lost and our wireless had gone unserviceable, we should march back to Imphal across the Chindwin. He had done it before, but now the Japanese were attacking in the area. I thought it was a hopeless idea. But I said, 'If you want to take the men that will go with you, you can. But I will take the others and find our own troops'. We had got almost to the stage of doing this when we saw two Gurkhas walk out on to the open paddy a few yards away. They were part of a column that we had not seen in the jungle, despite being only about two hundred yards away. It was Colonel Brennan's Cameronians. They took us in and fed us on rations they had just taken on a supply drop. Brennan sent a wireless message to General Lentaigne who had taken over from Wingate. He told him that we were totally exhausted and useless as fighting troops, and must be evacuated. I was told to head for Aberdeen and be flown out.

Major Charles Carfrae
Officer Commanding 29 Column, 10th Battalion, Nigeria Regiment

We were split into two columns, Number 29, which I commanded, and

Number 35, commanded by Peter Vaughan, a Welsh Guardsman, who also commanded the battalion. We told the West Africans that they would find the Japanese a very different kettle of fish from the Italians, whom some of my more experienced NCOs and men had fought in Eritrea. They had little respect for the Italians. Until they met the Japs they didn't believe how formidable they were.

I flew in on 5 April with the advance party of the battalion in a Dakota, which took off just before dark and landed in a big defended position, White City, commanded by the most famous Chindit of all after Wingate, Brigadier Michael Calvert. He was a very fine commander, the finest I ever came across. He was determined, enterprising, brave and a strong magnetic personality, he has been described as flamboyant, but he wasn't, he wasn't a show-off. He talked quietly, always gave his orders in a conversational rather than a peremptory tone. He was often quite vague in his conversation. But his soldiers would do anything for him. He wasn't mad at all or impetuous, despite his nickname.

Our battalion's job was to form part of the garrison of White City. We had a platoon of Africans who were flown in to help unload artillery flown in by glider.

There was firing quite close by and in the gloom it was impossible to tell where attacks were coming from and indeed if any of the figures passing us in the dark were friendly or enemy. Eventually we bedded down under the wing of a glider on the airstrip just outside the main fortress. Next morning Calvert's RAF officer led us into the fortress itself. We were given a position to dig near a platoon of the South Staffordshire Regiment.

Major Alexander Harper
94 Column, 4th/9th Gurkha Rifles

We moved on, blew a hole in the road and ambushed it to catch the Japanese coming to mend it. In the middle of the night the Japanese arrived in a column marching down the road. We held our fire and caught them perfectly. It was pitch dark and we couldn't see what we were firing at. Some must have escaped by jumping into the ditch by the road, and crawling away. Some Japanese began to mortar us from another direction, so we pulled back. We exchanged some shots with the Japanese while we waited for the party that had been in an ambush further south. They had been surrounded but managed to break out. We then pulled back to the main body of the column overlooking the road, a bridge and a village the Japs were using. We were about two thousand feet up.

Major Charles Carfrae
Officer Commanding 29 Column, 10th Battalion, Nigeria Regiment
Our second night at White City, the first within the fortress, the Japs attacked in force and we all stood to. In daylight, before the attack started we were mortared by a huge Jap mortar known as the 'coal scuttle', firing a tremendous projectile about five feet long which went off with a huge noise – it was a 5.9-inch mortar obtained from the Germans after the First World War. At this time the British officers had not dug slit trenches, so we leapt into a hole about twelve feet by six feet, full of unsavoury tins and rubbish. The Africans had half dug their holes but with no overhead cover. Every time an orange flare went up from our mortars we looked around to see if we could spot a Jap. Our bit of the fortress was not attacked, the nearest was about two hundred yards away. But it was very noisy and went on for several hours. Next morning we were attacked by about half a dozen Zero fighters who bombed the air strip and then machine-gunned us but they were nothing like as frightening as the mortars. It was a very abrupt introduction to war, in twenty-four hours or less, from peace without a shot being fired or enemy within hundreds of miles, suddenly we were in the thick of it.

I went to Calvert's brigade major, an old friend of mine, to try to find out what had happened to the battalion, but he did not know. On the eighth day I saw our brigadier and brigade major getting out of a light plane landing on the strip within the defences. I rushed up to ask what was happening to us. He said that as well as the Jap attacks on White City, bad weather in Assam had prevented any aircraft taking off. But the battalion had flown off the day before and landed at a stronghold called Aberdeen, were marching to White City and would arrive the next day.

Private William Merchant
20 Column, Commando Platoon, 1st Battalion, Lancashire Fusiliers
The Japs used to shell the block by day and attack at night. There were hundreds of dead Japs hanging on the wire outside the block. We planted landmines and booby traps within the wire perimeter. We dug pits and put in

sharpened stakes for them to land on when they fell in. The Japanese were very brave but stupid, always attacking in the same place. I was hit in the leg by shrapnel, but the MO dug it out with a pocket knife. It was from a Jap plastic grenade.

Private John Mattinson
20 Column, Commando Platoon, 1st Battalion, Lancashire Fusiliers
Patrolling to find the place from which the big mortar was firing at us, we went out through a zigzag in the wire, which was closed up behind us. We found some weapon pits dug for the Japanese to wait in while forming up to attack. We booby-trapped them. We found tins of fish, Japanese cigarettes and photos of their wives and children. We took the fish and cigarettes, but didn't take the photos because if the Japs had taken us they would have killed us.

Private William Merchant
20 Column, Commando Platoon, 1st Battalion, Lancashire Fusiliers
Coming back into the block we saw some people, thought they were enemy and opened fire. It went on for some time until we realised they were our own people. We killed one of them, a corporal.

Private John Mattinson
20 Column, Commando Platoon, 1st Battalion, Lancashire Fusiliers
In attacks the Japs would sometimes throw themselves on the wire so others could run over them. On one occasion they got in and overran positions on OP hill. In the morning we went up and turfed them out, killed the lot of them. In the dark the jackals would come and eat the bodies on the wire. The crows would come by day.

Major Alexander Harper
94 Column, 4th/9th Gurkha Rifles
We sent one party with machine guns to attack the village the Japs were using. But they came after us with superior force. We would have had to have a pitched battle, and this was something we tried to avoid unless one held an airstrip from which to evacuate casualties. So we withdrew that night without many casualties and joined up with 49 Column.

At this stage I was told to leave and fly to Broadway, the main stronghold, and take command of the 3rd Battalion there, the stronghold garrison, because the CO had gone sick.

We had made a little airstrip just across the Chinese border on some flat fields. We flew out in American L-1s and L-5s. I went in the last one and we landed at Broadway without any problems.

Private William Merchant
20 Column, Commando Platoon, 1st Battalion, Lancashire Fusiliers

On one occasion the Japanese got in to an OP behind us. In the morning we turfed them out. We threw grenades in the weapon pits and bunkers they occupied.

Our latrine trench was about eighty feet long with just a pole over it. It was full of maggots. One of our chaps was equipped with a flame-thrower; he emptied the fuel into the latrine to get rid of the maggots, sat on the pole, and chucked a match in after lighting a cigarette. He was so badly burned he had to be flown out. We thought it a huge joke at the time.

Private John Mattinson
20 Column, Commando Platoon, 1st Battalion, Lancashire Fusiliers

The Japanese attacks on White City were massive. We had three rings of wire round the place, and machine guns. I had a 2-inch mortar and a rifle. I used to fire one illuminating then one HE, one illuminating, one HE.

We used mortar bombs or shells that had been damaged in air drops and were unfit for firing, and attached explosives to them; made them into booby traps.

The Japs would shout during their attacks. Things like 'Thik Hai Johnny', which is Urdu for 'It's all right'. We used to shout back at them.

One night I was filling a gap where two of my friends had got killed. I was sat in the slit with my Bren, and shouting, 'Come on you yellow bastards,' and a voice behind me was shouting the same. I thought it was some of the blokes in other bunkers, but it was someone standing behind me. I said, 'Get down, you stupid bastard! Are you tired of living?'

He said, 'All right, it is only me'; it was Calvert.

Private William Merchant
20 Column, Commando Platoon, 1st Battalion, Lancashire Fusiliers

The Japs would shout at us, trying to draw our fire. They attacked using Bangalore torpedoes. My job was to fire grenades from an EY rifle at the Japanese from a small slit trench at night. I used to spend all day priming grenades. One night I fired over a hundred grenades. The Japs came across the paddy banging and shouting. I was wounded in the back with shrapnel. My mate had been wounded earlier, so I was the odd one out. The sergeant used to say, 'Wait until someone is killed, and you can muck in with his mate.' The trouble was that most seemed to get killed or wounded in pairs because they shared the same slit trench.

Lieutenant Peter Taylor
45 Column, 45th Reconnaissance Regiment

Rumours were flying around that we were going to be flown out. But not a bit of it, we were loaned to 77 Brigade, Mike Calvert's block at White City. Bernard Fergusson thought we would be flown in to the White City, but Mike Calvert was under the impression to the contrary. So ourselves, the Gurkhas and the Lancashire Fusiliers were told to attack the Japs who were attacking the White City.

Major Charles Carfrae
Officer Commanding 29 Column, 10th Battalion, Nigeria Regiment

Still the battalion did not arrive. Eventually a chap called Jerry Bladen, the recce platoon commander of our sister column, came in to the block, and told us that our two columns were lying up in the jungle a couple of miles away. All the wireless sets had broken down, and although the CO had heard the noise from the White City he could not find out what was going on. As he didn't know who was in possession, he sent Jerry Bladen to find out.

Our next step was to rejoin our battalion, led by Jerry Bladen. We learned that we were no longer to be garrison battalion, but to join in attacking the Japs investing White City from the south. With the rest of the striking force we occupied a deserted village within range of the Japanese attacking White City. The Lancashire Fusiliers and Gurkhas attacked the Japanese, and Peter Vaughan with his column went off to attack Mawlu, a village occupied by the Japs south of White City. We did very little, occupied a nearby village, of no particular significance as a foot on the ground. A lot of wounded Gurkhas came in and we sent them by bullock cart to where a light plane strip had been made.

Lieutenant Peter Taylor
45 Column, 45th Reconnaissance Regiment

We were still following jungle warfare tactics, moving in single file although we weren't in jungle. I was behind the leading scouts. Suddenly we were fired on. We managed get across a chaung and then we were held up. No one else got over, so we were told to withdraw. I was told to go back to where we had dropped our packs in the charge of some Nigerians.

On the way back, with about half a dozen men, I came across a corporal giving water to a sergeant who had been shot in the head, he was blinded. This corporal had not deserted him, some people just buggered off. I was able to take him on with me.

Major Charles Carfrae
Officer Commanding 29 Column, 10th Battalion, Nigeria Regiment

At nightfall we received orders from a galloper to move. We assembled everybody and were ready to move when we received orders from another galloper to go back to our positions. We were all going back when there was a burst of automatic fire and two grenades went off very close. I was alarmed. But nothing more happened. We sat it out.

At dawn we heard a single shot, and soon a platoon commander came in and said there were two dead Japs near, and his best corporal had been killed. This corporal and a Bren gunner had blundered into the two Japs in the night. The Bren gunner had despatched them. The platoon commander took us to the spot. The single shot had been the platoon commander finishing off one of the Japs who was wounded and had tried to throw a grenade at him.

I collected a party of Africans to view the corpses so they could see what the Japs looked like. This went down well because two Japs had been killed and for the loss of only one African. The only person who was unnerved was the African sergeant major, he roared like a bull on the parade ground, but was virtually useless for the rest of the campaign.

The next day Calvert was to make another attack on the Japanese attacking the White City. Our column was to set an ambush on the road leading to White City. At four o'clock in the afternoon a truck came along. I intended to fire my Very pistol to set off the ambush when the truck was opposite me, but someone fired a PIAT before it got there. The bomb exploded on the ground, and the troops jumped off the truck and ran off into the jungle. I was furious.

The next day at dusk we heard several lorries grinding slowly towards us from the north, very slowly, with Japs walking ahead, probing the road for mines. When they were directly opposite us, within feet, this time the Very light went off at exactly the right moment. The leading vehicle was in flames, and after I had blown my whistle to stop the firing, you could hear the Japs groaning.

I sent out a couple of platoons to mop up. We lost about four or five dead, but the Japs lost forty-two. We had hit six trucks. I got my soldiers to pull the bodies out of the trucks and we laid them all beside the road. We had three prisoners – I told the Africans not to kill them. The Africans were very puzzled at this. But as I was telling them this, there were loud shouts behind me. A Jap NCO had shaken off the hands dragging him from the lorry thinking he was dead, and was brandishing a bayonet trying to shove it into the nearest African. His tunic was stiff with caked blood. One of my British sergeants shot him dead with a pistol.

Lieutenant Peter Taylor
45 Column, 45th Reconnaissance Regiment
We had one more action. We were ordered to Broadway, about two or three days' march away. We bumped into some Japanese, and everybody was very jumpy, and fled. I and three others found some Nigerians and put them on the right track to find our column.

After the first show after Thetkegyin everybody thought I was a goner, but I turned up, and then after this action, I turned up again. We arrived at Broadway and were flown out. We were emaciated, after living on K-rations. You didn't know you were exhausted until you saw someone else. Marching in was a waste of time. The chaps who flew in did lots before we even arrived. We could have flown in.

Colour Sergeant Harold Atkins
21 Column, 2nd Battalion, Queen's Royal Regiment

The brigadier and higher HQ decided that 16 Brigade had shot their bolt. We had spent February to May on operations. We were told to make our way to Broadway and be flown out to India. This took five or six days over quite mountainous terrain. We passed quite close to the Mawlu block, the White City.

Eventually we arrived at Broadway, and were given permission to use food stocks there. The column was flown out in Dakotas over the next two or three days. We were in not too good shape. We were tired, it was nerve-wracking, one very rarely spoke above a whisper. There was always uncertainty: was one going to be ambushed or not?

Lieutenant Arthur Binnie
Officer Commanding Blaine Detachment (Bladet)

We cleaned ourselves up and left for Aberdeen. We were climbing up a slope in light jungle when we were fired on. This shook us up a bit. We could see very little. John Urquhart was hit on his compass that was over his kidney, and a bullet grazed him just over his left nipple. We eventually managed to break contact. The muleteer I had punished was hit in the knee; we carried him to Aberdeen, where a plane arrived to take us out. We got in, and after about half an hour sitting on the ground the American pilot came and said, 'Say you boys, I guess we have trouble with the engine here. If you'd like to wait we can fix it in an hour or two. In the meantime there is another plane over there, would you rather go in that one?' You have never seen people scamper so quickly from one plane to another. Having survived so far the idea of flying in a plane with a doubtful engine didn't appeal at all. We very valiantly rushed to the other plane, and got taken to Shillong, a lovely hill station in Assam.

We drank a lot of booze, and had a riotous party. I went to bed and woke up thinking my God this a hangover of all hangovers. I tried to get up, but had to get back, my head was thumping as if it was being hit by hammers. I told my batman I was ill. He got me to hospital. I was unconscious for three days with cerebral malaria. One does not normally survive that, in the condition I was in. I was given intravenous quinine.

When I came to I asked about my troops. Every single one of them was in hospital with some malady or other.

March North to help Stilwell

Private William Merchant
20 Column, Commando Platoon, 1st Battalion, Lancashire Fusiliers
By now I was ill with malaria. They gave me twenty mepacrine tablets. I was delirious. They thought I might have cerebral malaria. The brigade was going to take Mogaung, but I wasn't fit to march. They took me to a slit trench by the strip to fly me out to Aberdeen, and on from there to India. Every time the pilot tried to take off, the Japs shelled the strip. So they carried me, a sergeant who had lost both legs, and a West African without an arm, back to the slit trench. Eventually they left us in the plane, and when there was a lull the American pilot who returned to the trench dashed out and took off. When we landed at Aberdeen it was attacked by Japanese bombers. They left me because I couldn't run for cover. The next day I was flown out to Sylhet. I was there for almost a week and given liquid quinine. I weighed just under eight stone.

Lieutenant Richard Rhodes-James
Cipher Officer, HQ, 111 Brigade
After carrying out demolition operations we were sent further north to attempt to replicate what 77 Brigade had done in the south of the area: set up a block to sever the Japanese communications with their forces fighting Stilwell's Chinese. We chose the wrong position. It was only able at a distance to block the railway. It was too near the enemy front line, whereas we were meant to be operating in rear areas. It was itself surrounded by country which could easily be occupied by the enemy and dominate our position.

Jack Masters recced the position. It may be he was hustled into holding there by higher command, and possibly there was nothing better. The position was on a range of hills overlooking the railway valley.

Major Desmond Whyte, RAMC
Medical Officer, HQ, 111 Brigade
We had air drops of barbed wire and began to prepare a landing strip outside the wire. The enemy attacked on the second night. When day broke the wire was littered with Japanese corpses. In the heat of the day the corpses swelled and stank, limbs putrefied, and millions of flies came in from the jungle. The

Richard Rhodes-James.

next night the Japs attacked in the same place again, broke through in one or two places, but were thrown out. They came the next night, same again. We got no sleep. Enemy planes attacked us. My dressing station began to fill up.

Then we had three days without attacks. The Dakotas came in, the strip having been levelled with a small bulldozer landed by glider. The Dakotas brought four 25-pounder guns. The enemy let us alone. We got in two AA guns. Then we heard the Jap 100-mm and 105-mm guns ranging on our position. The USAAF couldn't find the enemy gun positions. The Japs plastered our positions. We couldn't spare anyone to sortie and destroy the guns. The dressing station was hit. The monsoon broke with heavy rain. When a thunderstorm hit us, the mules stampeded. There was death and misery everywhere.

Pilot Officer Joe Simpson
194 Squadron, RAF

The technique for dealing with Japanese fighters in daylight was to stay in cloud if you were flying at height. When below cloud, fly low, right at tree-top level. If the fighter gets close, close one engine and do a steep turn. But most of the time we had RAF fighters to keep the Japs busy. Our biggest problem was the weather, particularly cu-nims stuffed into grey cloud so you couldn't see them, as well as poor maps and no navigational aids. We developed good techniques for overcoming these. You took the maximum possible fuel, and if the DZ was covered by cloud, you stooged around, until a hole appeared, and went in to drop. There were few aborted drops.

I crashed at Blackpool one night. As I was in the circuit, I could see a lot of people going round again. I thought, I won't do that. So I dragged it in at sixty-eight knots, got to the end of the runway over a huge tree and plonked the aircraft down. The undercarriage on the port side cracked and caught fire, while I belted down the runway holding it up on one wheel. At the end I swung it off to the left, clear of the runway. As we came to a stop the aircraft was getting hot. We all got out of the hatch in the roof, because the load had shifted, blocking the way to the door. I remembered we had the mail on board, right by the door, so I got a chap to give me a leg up so I could snatch the mail bags from outside.

They didn't clear the very end of the runway because the bulldozer broke down. I hit a mound of earth, which they had left unflattened.

Lieutenant Neville Hogan
Burma Rifles, attached 111 Brigade

I was flown into Blackpool. At about ten o'clock at night I was at the airstrip and a sergeant came along, called out our names and we emplaned in a Dakota. I prayed the plane wouldn't take off because of the weather. But we did take off. Watching the faces of my platoon, every one was scared of the unknown. Down we came; there were guides on the airstrip to lead us to our defensive positions round the airstrip.

The next morning a sergeant from the Cameronians gave our NCOs the fields of fire, and pointed out the water points, and where the enemy were on the other side of the airstrip.

We had one young officer straight out from England who had volunteered for the Burma Rifles, dead keen to go into action. That night the Japs attacked and he got shot through the penis, the right testicle and the bullet lodged in his right thigh; his first night of action. He was flown out.

Our job was to defend the airstrip. Not long after this the Japanese started attacking across the airfield with bayonets fixed, and the Bofors guns were firing over open sights.

Lieutenant Richard Rhodes-James
Cipher Officer, HQ, 111 Brigade

Every bombardment we had about twenty people killed. We were slowly pounded to bits. When our aircraft were overhead their artillery didn't fire in order not to reveal their positions. They then mounted infantry attacks. A fresh battalion, the 3rd/9th Gurkhas, arrived to help, under a very good CO.

Lieutenant Colonel Alexander Harper
Commanding Officer, 3rd/9th Gurkha Rifles

At Broadway I took command of 3rd/9th Gurkhas. They were not a Chindit battalion but had been commandeered by Wingate to act as garrison, and had not undergone the training. However, we were now told that Broadway was to be abandoned.

Stilwell had been complaining that we were not doing enough to help him. He had two Chinese divisions coming down the Ledo Road. So we were told to stop what we were doing and move into closer contact with his lot. We were to move further north to a new position called Blackpool, which the bulk of 111

Brigade were holding to block the railway and road north to Myitkyina.

After giving the battalion a few days' training in moving about the jungle, which they did perfectly well, we moved off to join 111 Brigade and arrived after an uneventful march. Originally we were told to split into two columns like the rest of the Chindits, but this was changed and we were told to operate as a complete battalion.

Major Percival Leathart
Officer Commanding D Company, 3rd/9th Gurkha Rifles, ex-77 Brigade, now 111 Brigade

We got to Blackpool after several days' march. We heard and saw Japanese mortars and artillery crumping down on the block. The CO decided that we would spread out and march straight in across the open paddy and hope for the best. It worked: we got in without any difficulty.

The commander was Jack Masters. The first time I saw him he was wearing nothing but a pair of shorts made from an old parachute.

We were there for several very unpleasant days. The Japanese attacks were vigorous despite heavy casualties. The block was a mess of Jap corpses outside, and inside the stench of death and latrines. I took over positions in the stronghold from a British battalion, can't remember which. When I jumped into a slit trench to check the field of fire before I put anyone in it, there was a soldier in the trench looking out. He didn't take any notice of me. I tapped him on the shoulder, and he toppled over. He had rigor mortis. I don't know how long he had been dead. Nobody seemed to know he was there.

Lieutenant Neville Hogan
Burma Rifles, attached 111 Brigade

After a day or two, I was summoned by Jack Masters. I was told to take a patrol of the King's Own across the Namkwin Chaung up the hills to meet the Nigerian Regiment of 3rd West African Brigade who were cutting steps up the steep hillside. We ran into an ambush so I didn't make contact with the Nigerians, and we were ordered back to the block. On my way I was joined by Captain Kershaw with a platoon of the King's. He took command of the two platoons. He sent my platoon back to the Namkwin Chaung to look for a crossing. I crawled through elephant grass and lantana to the Chaung, and the other side, about thirty yards away, the enemy was rustling about. We all took cover. I said, 'Don't fire until the order.' All of a sudden there was movement, followed by fire, and we fired back. A cultured English voice could be heard asking what the ammunition state was. It was a chap called Tony Gowan, a Burma Rifle officer, who we were firing at. 'Cease fire, cease fire,' I shouted, ran across the river, and embraced Tony. We sat down and counted what casualties we had. I had one chap shot in the heel of his boot. Not good, considering how much ammunition we fired.

We returned to Kershaw, and found that we were evacuating Blackpool.

Lieutenant Colonel Walter 'Scottie' Scott
Commanding Officer, 81 and 82 Columns, 1st Battalion, King's Regiment (Liverpool)

It was a poor site and eventually Jack Masters was ordered to evacuate it. My battalion formed the rearguard. It was no fault of Jack Masters, or those that served under him, that we had to hand it to the Japanese.

In the closing minutes we were fighting hand-to-hand with the Japs in the block. Colonel Thompson of the King's Own and myself had two small parties of three or four men each. Right in the middle of the block there was a tree. Although it had lots of branches blown off, it was a solid tree. Behind it stood two lieutenant colonels throwing grenades up towards where the Japanese were trying to come down the slope. But the grenades rolled back without hurting the Japanese. Colonel Thompson was firing round the left side of the tree, and I was firing round the right-hand side. All of a sudden there was a 'whumph', and Colonel Thompson went down with a wound in his left shoulder. I bent down to pull him in and I was hit. Something was gushing down my leg. I put my hand down, it wasn't blood; my water bottle had been hit.

Major Desmond Whyte RAMC
Medical Officer, 111 Brigade

We managed to cut the wire in the north, and as the barrage lifted we began to move out through the wire, with a rearguard holding the enemy off, in a series of fallback positions, we fought them back. Before we left we gave a lethal dose of morphia to those so desperately badly wounded that we could not take them with us so they would not fall into Jap hands alive. The others, some of them blinded, we walked and carried out. We had to climb a mound of at least one thousand feet in full view of the enemy. They did not follow us up. There was only one possible explanation; they had had such a mauling. Four days of nightmare followed.

Lieutenant Neville Hogan
Burma Rifles, attached 111 Brigade

We helped carry the wounded. There was a British sergeant with his boots on his hands, dragging both wounded legs behind him, but still giving orders to his men.

My Karens were marvellous, very cheerful. They knew what roots and leaves could be eaten. They brought me a mess tin of something that tasted like Bovril. I asked what it was and they told me it was boiled up roots. We took some of it to the sick and wounded.

We marched to Mokso Sakan, and set up an all-round defence perimeter.

Major Percival Leathart
Officer Commanding D Company, 3rd/9th Gurkha Rifles, ex-77 Brigade, now 111 Brigade

Halfway over the mountains we came across the West Africans, who were walking about with nothing on, a good way to keep your clothes clean in the mud. They were very helpful, but the Gurkhas were rather shocked, as they are very prudish about being naked.

We arrived at Indawgyi Lake, and had to re-equip with air drops. The casualties were all lying there under temporary shelters. But someone came up with the idea of landing Sunderland flying boats on the lake, and over a number of days the casualties were taken out by the Sunderlands.

One day I saw a herd of wild elephants when I went to the top of a hill to look at some birds. When I told my friends that I had just seen a most wonderful sight, referring to the elephants, one of them said, 'We have heard something even better, we have just heard over the radio about the D-Day landings in Normandy.'

Lieutenant Colonel Alexander Harper
Commanding Officer, 3rd/9th Gurkha Rifles

The British battalions were completely exhausted by now, and had both sick and wounded. Wingate had believed that we could not stay in for more than three months and we eventually were in for five and the rations were inadequate. This sort of operation was not intended for pitched battles because without an airstrip you could not evacuate sick or wounded. If you went sick on the march, you were left behind, so you kept going.

We marched further north of Indawgyi Lake in order to attack the road nearer Mogaung. That took some days. The ground was in a terrible state. We took twelve hours to cover a track seven miles long. Another battalion later took three days to complete the journey on that same track.

Major Percival Leathart
Officer Commanding D Company, 3rd/9th Gurkha Rifles, ex-77 Brigade, now 111 Brigade

A few days later, we were told to march north towards Mogaung. The Japs were using a stream flowing into the Indawgyi Lake as an approach route, and we were ordered to go to a village on this little stream where the Japs were supposed to have a position and we marched off and I decided to attack at dawn. We set up a base and had an evening meal, before creeping up to this village in darkness. We spent a most uncomfortable night being bitten by mosquitoes. In the morning we sent one platoon in one direction, and one in another, as stops. I, with the central platoon, went into the village. The platoon on the right came into contact with some Japs apparently coming into the village and had a bit of a battle. A section commander was hit, and I went to see if I could do anything for him. But he died. I went back into the centre of the village, with my Gurkha officer, to see what was going on. Suddenly there was a loud bang, and I was almost knocked off my feet by something hitting my left arm. I looked down and saw my forearm hanging down, with a lot of blood. My Gurkha officer said, 'I have also been hit.'

In fact he hadn't, a bit of my ulna had flown off and hit him in the chest, damaging him slightly. He then recovered and put a tourniquet on me. My orderly, who had seen where the Jap had fired from rushed into the jungle and killed the fellow with a kukri. After that I had moments of unconsciousness.

I was very weak. The Gurkhas carried me. From time to time they were engaged in skirmishes with the Japs. They could have left me but of course they didn't. Eventually we got back to the doctor. He treated me with sulpha powder. The battalion then moved on, leaving me with my orderly and a small escort. My orderly looked after me, built a hut and a bamboo bed. He gave me morphine injections, and actually made a bed pan out of a kerosene can. His service to me was exceptional and wonderful. The men with us went out into the rice paddy and constructed an airstrip. The battalion had sent a wireless message to have me picked up. One day an L-5 came in and flew me to an American base near Mogaung, where I was flown in a Dakota to Assam.

Lieutenant Colonel Alexander Harper
Commanding Officer, 3rd/9th Gurkha Rifles

We moved again and attacked a position on hill 2171 on 9 July 1944. This task was given to my battalion, which was the fittest. As CO I followed up B Company who carried out the frontal attack while C Company came in from a flank. We captured it and held it against further Japanese attacks. The commander of C Company, Major Frank Blaker, a gallant, aggressive and dashing officer, charged a machine gun and it got him and he was killed, but his example kept the momentum of the attack going. The attack was so successful we had few other casualties: twenty or thirty.

If you took up a position that threatened the Japanese, they seemed to think they had to attack it or they were 'dishonoured'. And they would throw in attacks from a tactically unsound direction, sometimes again and again. We let them do this for about a week. Although we took casualties from their mortars and artillery, we held them. We had improved their positions, we had wire dropped to us and made a very strong position.

We then marched off to Mogaung.

Lieutenant Arthur Binnie
Blaine Detachment (Bladet)

I was sent back to base and Blaine was there to receive us. I had lost three stone. When I was fit I was told to train twelve others to lead flame-thrower operators, and flown to Myitkyina, and on by light plane to Mogaung to play a part in the battle of Mogaung, where Calvert was about to take the town. We were quickly involved with what was left of a company of King's commanded by Fred Reeman, who I knew quite well. We were to go by night into a village that was holding up Calvert's advance to Mogaung. We were to spread fire here and there. The troops behind us thought it was great. We went in under our own mortar barrage to keep the Japs down, they were all in bunkers in this village. We never saw sight of them. We were told to advance in front of the company of King's, and to 'turn the f . . . . ing lights on'. They were very happy to have the flame-throwers in front of them. It was a fantastic sight, the whole village in flames. We went through the village with twenty or thirty yards of flame shooting out in front.

The Japs were in bunkers and fired along the line of the flame, so the troops behind shouted, 'Put out the f . . . . ing lights.' It seemed to have a good effect on the Japs anyway, and many of them ran off. I was blown up by a Jap grenade, and had little bits of grenade through my trousers in my legs. It did not hurt much, and I got up and carried on.

The poor CSM of the King's was shot in the head and killed, a wonderful guy who had been through the whole operation. I then realised that my right eye wasn't seeing properly. I went to the doctor, and he seemed to take my eye problem seriously. I was in a queue with Field Marshall Wavell's son, who had had a hand blown off.

Brigadier Michael Calvert
Commanding 77 Brigade

When we captured Mogaung, we heard on the BBC that the Americans and Chinese had captured Mogaung. So I sent a message saying, 'The Americans and Chinese have captured Mogaung. 77th Brigade is proceeding to take umbrage.'

When I was ordered to move to Myitkyina, still in Japanese hands, I closed down my wirelesses for fourteen days and marched out. I was summoned to Stilwell's HQ at Shaduzup to explain my insubordination. He said, 'You send very strong signals, Calvert.'

I said, 'You should see the ones my brigade major won't let me send.'

I hit the right note, because he roared with laughter. From then on we got on very well. He didn't realise we had done the glider-borne invasion, didn't realise we'd blocked the railway at White City for almost five weeks, four of them against repeated Japanese attacks. He didn't realise my brigade had not only been decimated but had had other bits taken off to help other brigades. We had no artillery; he didn't realise these things.

He kept on saying, 'Why wasn't I told? Is this true?'

His staff admitted it was.

Captain Donald McCutcheon
40 Column, 3rd/4th Gurkha Rifles

American command under Stilwell was very badly coordinated. We got the

Brigadier Calvert, talking to Lieutenant Colonel Shaw at Mogaung. Major Lumley in singlet looks on.

MH 7287

impression that American senior officers had no idea of how lightly we were equipped and therefore we were ordered to attack strongly dug-in Japanese positions with no support and not enough ammunition; the attacks failed.

On one occasion we had air support, we were told that the bombers were flown by Chinese. Instead of flying in the way we asked for, across our front, they came over us, and dropped the bombs far too close to us. It is very unnerving to see the bomb doors open and the bombs apparently coming straight for one. Luckily they missed.

Eventually we were all pretty exhausted by these fruitless attacks. A lot of chaps were flown out, and I found myself commanding about forty men that were left.

My CO was killed. We were forming up to attack a village and had moved up in four groups, the intention was that on arrival the assaulting troops would go in, all groups together. As 2i/c I was moving in the rear. We were not expecting any opposition on the move, but I heard on the radio that the CO had been shot, and I was called to take over. He had been called up to the lead when the column hit opposition. Unfortunately he was jumped by a small patrol of Japanese who shot him dead. As I suspected something like this might have happened, myself and my orderly went forward, you always moved in pairs in the jungle. My orderly had a grenade in his hand, suddenly I saw a couple of Japanese who started blazing off at us. I threw myself into a bush and started firing back. Then I heard an enormous crump close by, the orderly had thrown a grenade into the bush, fortunately it missed me but shook up the Japs. We went on forward and there was the colonel lying dead.

Then the fun started, like a cavalry charge, a horde of Japs all shouting 'Banzai', a big party of Japs who had come out from Myitkyina swept towards us. But by this time we had formed into little defensive squares so we didn't suffer much.

Towards the end we were not scared of the Japs. They never followed us into the jungle. They were not all that splendid jungle fighters, they were good fighters, but not jungle experts. They were very brave. At Myitkyina, against two Chinese divisions, they held out when most people would have given up or gone away.

My last contact with the Japanese was on a wooded hillock with an open glade leading down to a village called Maingna near Myitkyina on an island in the Irrawaddy which the Japanese used as a washing place. I was told to observe the area. We saw quite a lot of Japanese coming up, outnumbering my patrol. So I ordered a withdrawal, and I stood up, and felt a thump at the back of my head. I thought it was someone throwing stones. It was a bullet going through my hat which blew it off. Apart from a stiff neck I suffered no injury.

Lieutenant Richard Rhodes-James
Cipher Officer, HQ, 111 Brigade

We had a medical inspection at the insistence of Masters, and out of two thousand men in the brigade only one hundred and twenty-five were fit to carry on operations. Most of our casualties were sick, not battle casualties. Eventually Stilwell got the message and gave orders for us to be evacuated. We were flown out from Myitkyina, which had been captured by the Chinese under Stilwell.

Some people were never properly fit again. After being assembled after leave we were told there would be another operation, a glider-borne attack in the Rangoon area, but the powers that be saw sense, and we were disbanded. We weren't sorry.

Crisis Point
Kohima

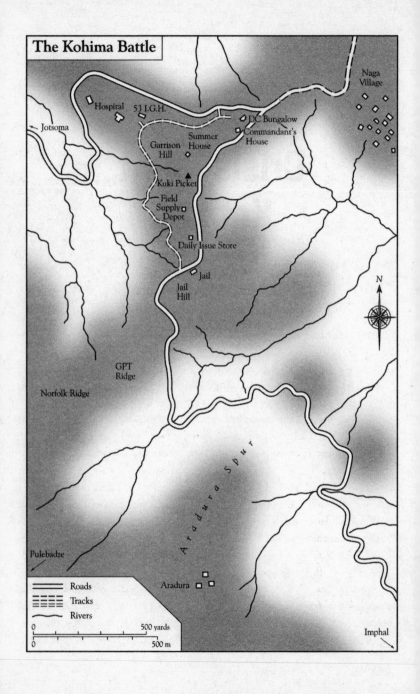

The Kohima Battle

Naga Village

Jotsoma →

Hospital

53 I.G.H.

DC Bungalow

Commandant's House

Garrison Hill

Summer House

Kuki Picket

Field Supply Depot

Daily Issue Store

Jail

Jail Hill

GPT Ridge

Norfolk Ridge

Aradura Spur

Pulebadze →

Aradura

N

| Roads |
| Tracks |
| Rivers |

0   500 yards

0   500 m

Imphal →

I couldn't imagine that I would ever see England again, or even get out of this battle. A feeling that set in with me was I couldn't care less if I get killed. I accepted it. It wasn't fear.

In February 1944, reports from patrols and OPs on the Chindwin indicated that Lieutenant General Mutaguchi's Japanese Fifteenth Army was building up for an offensive aimed at the British bases in Assam; principally at Imphal, but also at Kohima. Mutaguchi's plan was to attack across the Chindwin on nine routes between Tamanathi in the north to Kalewa in the south. In a series of pincer movements, he would cut the road from the railhead at Dimapur to Imphal in several places, and capture Kohima and Imphal, his aim, as outlined in Chapter 2, being to prevent the Allies using the airfields in Assam to supply the Chinese.

The area was the responsibility of Lieutenant General G. A. P. Scoones's British IV Corps, the bulk of which was deployed well forward of Kohima and Imphal covering the main routes west from the Chindwin. The 17th Light Division (Major General D. T. Cowan) was in the south at Tiddim; Major General D. D. Gracey's 20th Division was at Tamu and Sittaung; and Major General O. L. Roberts's 23rd Division deployed north-east of Imphal, but also responsible for Kohima.

The commander of the Fourteenth Army, Lieutenant General William Slim, decided to pull back Scoones's IV Corps to the Imphal Plain and Kohima, and fight on ground of his own choosing. He arrived at this decision because in addition to patrol reports, he had access to ULTRA, the codename for the reading of Japanese (and German) radio traffic. He was also influenced by logistical considerations. The IV Corps lines of communication on this front ran through rugged jungle-covered hills, whereas east of the Chindwin the Japanese had comparatively good supply lines. By withdrawing, IV Corps would be falling back on well-stocked bases, shortening its lines of communications, while the Japanese would be stretching theirs to near breaking point through the difficult country west of the Chindwin that the British had abandoned. If Slim could hold the Japanese for two months the onset of the monsoon would make the Japanese supply lines almost impassable.

With the Japanese held up on the Imphal Plain, Slim, reinforced with formations from the Arakan and India, could destroy the Fifteenth Army. A potentially winning card in Slim's hand was air power. By now air supremacy had been wrested away from the Japanese. By using the two good airfields at Imphal and several smaller strips in the locality, as well as air-dropping supplies, Slim could ensure that even troops cut off by the enemy could fight on. Both Imphal and Kohima were already well stocked with supplies.

Mutaguchi took a chance on capturing the British stocks within three weeks to feed his troops, and tailored his logistic plans accordingly. Until he was able to seize the British supplies, his men would have to exist and fight with whatever they could carry on their backs, or on a small number of horses and mules, supplemented by meat on the hoof in the form of cattle that accompanied their columns.

To this day there is disagreement on whether or not Mutaguchi intended to stop at Imphal. He favoured pressing on into India, and with help from uprisings by Indian nationalists in India, throwing the British out. He thought this might induce the British to abandon the war against Japan, and that the Americans might do likewise; all highly speculative, and very much in line with Mutaguchi's improvisational approach to war.

A possible indicator of Mutaguchi's aspirations for exploiting into India was the inclusion of the 1st Indian National Army (INA) Division in his plans. The INA was ineffective in battle so Mutaguchi's motive for saddling himself with seven thousand useless mouths could only have been to use them for propaganda on arrival in India.

Although the fighting at Kohima and Imphal took place concurrently, I have dealt with events at Kohima first; not least, this was the key to Slim's plan. Indeed the Japanese nearly beat him to the draw here. While the 17th Division was still fighting its way north (covered in the next chapter), it became clear that instead of just one regimental group heading for Kohima and Dimapur, the whole of the Japanese 31st Division was coming this way. Kohima had a small garrison, but Dimapur none. If the Japanese besieged Kohima, the road to Imphal would be cut: dangerous, but not disastrous. Whereas Dimapur in enemy hands would end any hope of relieving Imphal, as well as threatening the whole of the Brahmaputra Valley, its airfields and the line of communication to India.

Accordingly, Slim changed the plan for the reinforcement of Imphal by the 5th Division, ordering its 161st Indian Infantry Brigade to be flown direct from the Arakan to Dimapur. He also asked for Lieutenant General M. G. N. Stopford's XXXIII Corps Headquarters and the British 2nd Division, both training in India, to be sent in. Stopford was to take over responsibility for clearing the road from Dimapur to Imphal, while Scoones concentrated on the battle around Imphal. Slim ordered that Kohima and Dimapur were not to fall.

Kohima was both the civil administrative centre of Nagaland, and a military supply depot, hospital and staging post, about a third of the way between Dimapur and Imphal. The names of features around Kohima reflect their military or civil use at the time. The road from Dimapur climbed in a curve round the 53rd Indian General Hospital (IGH) spur, and after passing the Deputy Commissioner's (DC's) Bungalow, it turned in a sharp hairpin to the south-west whence another road ran east to the village of Kohima. From the DC's Bungalow the road ran south along the Kohima ridge past Garrison Hill, the Kuki Picket, Field Supply Depot (FSD) Hill, Daily Issue Store (DIS) Hill, Jail Hill (for civil prisoners) and General Purpose Transport (GPT) Ridge. Most of the personnel at Kohima were administrative.

THE JAPANESE ATTACK

Ursula Graham-Bower
Naga Watch and Ward Scheme and Women's Auxiliary Corps (India) (WACI)
I was educated at Roedean before the war. My parents could not afford to send me to Oxford, so instead I went to live among the Naga tribes and carried out

ethnographic work. When war broke out I joined the Women's Auxiliary Corps (India) and in August 1942 helped start a Watch and Ward scheme in Nagaland. My job was to collect information on the Japanese and send it back by runner.

But it had its problems. There was no hope I could conceal myself in the Naga village. First of all I am too tall, and light skinned, my hair was sun-bleached: I was blonde. In Burma when British officers were occasionally hidden, the Japs tortured the villagers until the officer gave himself up.

I fixed up with Namkia, the headman, that I wasn't going to be taken alive. So I would shoot myself, and he would take my head in, if the pressure on the villagers became unendurable.

Lieutenant Colonel Gerald Cree
Commanding Officer, 2nd Battalion, West Yorkshire Regiment

My battalion, having been flown to Assam from Arakan with the remainder of the 5th Division, was diverted to Dimapur instead of being sent to Imphal. I motored to Kohima, and had just completed putting together a defence plan agreed with Colonel Richards, the garrison commander, when Major General Ranking, commanding 202 Lines of Communication Area came in and ordered me back towards Dimapur to hold the road in a series of company detachments.

This was a most foolish thing to do. The road was jam-packed with refugees trying to get out of Kohima and others trying to get in. If I split the battalion into four detachments over forty miles of road, I'd have no control over them, couldn't have affected the battle at all, and would have been mopped up in detail. I disobeyed and we went back to Milestone 10 and settled there for the night.

Suddenly the general appeared. I thought, now I'm for it. However, he didn't mind at all. I explained what I felt, and he agreed, and said, 'Tomorrow go back to Kohima and help defend it.' So back we went, took up positions around the place and prepared for a long siege.

I occupied the matron's quarters in the former hospital. We found a harmonium there, which greatly pleased our padre, so we lifted it, and it accompanied us for the rest of the war. After a couple of days, orders came that the West Yorks were to move to Imphal, and transport was sent for us. Colonel Richards was rather dismayed, being left naked again without anybody to defend him, except the odds and sods of the convalescent depot. I couldn't have been more pleased.

The vehicles arrived. We piled on to them, and went off down the road to Imphal like scalded cats. We were the last people to get through. We passed some military policemen on the way, and I asked them what they were doing. They replied, 'Directing traffic.'

Major Harry Smith
Officer Commanding HQ Company, 4th Battalion, Queen's Own Royal West Kent Regiment

The whole division was moved to Assam. Two brigades of 5 Div were flown in to Imphal, and our brigade, 161, flown to Dimapur to defend Kohima. No one imagined at the time that Kohima was in any danger. We were told that only scattered Japanese forces were in the area. We thought that Kohima was unapproachable from Burma because of the huge jungles intervening. We embarked in our aeroplanes at Dohazari, in a light-hearted manner. Quite a lot of us had never flown in an aeroplane before. We loaded our Dakota with ammo and stores to the extent that he couldn't get the tail of the plane off the ground. He was an American pilot and he said, 'Sorry fellows, shift some of that junk further forward and I'll try again.' We did and he took off. After a short flight, we landed at Dimapur on a flooded airfield, and wound our way by truck up the road to Kohima. We were totally ignorant of what we were to do, but glad to get up to five thousand feet, out of the heat of the plains. We were expecting only very light Japanese forces.

CSM Herbert Harwood
C Company, 4th Battalion, Queen's Own Royal West Kent Regiment

We got to Kohima and were allocated our positions. We had no sooner got organised than we were trucked back to Dimapur.

THE SIEGE BEGINS

Ursula Graham-Bower
Naga Watch and Ward Scheme and Women's Auxiliary Corps (India) (WACI)

We were suddenly in the middle of no-man's-land, utterly bewildered, hardly armed, sharing no-man's-land with an unknown number of Japanese. We had a very dodgy three weeks, not knowing what was going on, but trying to find out and pass back intelligence.

Major Harry Smith
Officer Commanding HQ Company, 4th Battalion, Queen's Own Royal West Kent Regiment

We left the meagre garrison at Kohima and various odd bodies from the convalescent depot. No sooner were we back at Dimapur, than orders came through for the brigade to move up once more, but by this time the leading Japanese spearheads were on the outskirts of Kohima. As we wound up the road again, we met crowds of frightened non-combatants. The battalion was leading the brigade column and as it approached Kohima it came under heavy fire from machine guns and artillery. Getting out of the trucks as quickly as possible the battalion sprinted up the hlll overlooking the roads at the bottom and established itself in positions already allotted to it. The other two battalions and Brigade HQ stayed on the road because there was no room for it on Garrison Hill.

Major John Winstanley
Officer Commanding B Company, 4th Battalion, Queen's Own Royal West Kent Regiment

Garrison Hill was a pleasant pine-covered hill round which there was a 'ladies' walk'. On a spur, which ran towards the main road, cut into the side of the hill was the District Commissioner's Bungalow. The District Commissioner, the DC, was an Indian Civil servant. Behind the bungalow was a clay tennis court. On our side of the court was a small clubhouse.

Private Leslie Crouch
Pioneer Platoon, 4th Battalion, Queen's Own Royal West Kent Regiment

Some of the lorries were set on fire by shellfire. All we had was our small packs and rifles, Brens etc. We went up the hill through the District Commissioner's Bungalow, past the tennis court. It was a lovely place when we first arrived. We got to our positions and dug trenches. We were above the tennis court, about a hundred yards away, on a steep bank.

Private Ivan Daunt
Pioneer Platoon, 4th Battalion, Queen's Own Royal West Kent Regiment
We started getting out of the trucks and getting our kit out. Mortar bombs and shells began falling around us. The drivers were screaming and hollering, and didn't know what to do. We got off the road and lay down in a ditch. We crawled up the hill and stuck it out until night time. We were told to go back and get our kit out of the trucks. Some were on fire.

We then moved up above the tennis court, and started digging in. We didn't know what was going on.

Major John Winstanley
Officer Commanding B Company, 4th Battalion, Queen's Own Royal West Kent Regiment
At first B Company were only observers on Kuki Picket. After five days, we were ordered to relieve A Company on the tennis court. My second-in-command, Tom Coath, was taken to command C Company, whose commander had been wounded, so I had myself, two officer platoon commanders, Victor King and Tom Hogg, and Sergeant Williams commanding the other platoon.

Our position was on the fringe of the tennis court and included a mound above the court occupied by my right-hand platoon, my middle platoon was in the clubhouse, with my left-hand platoon holding a bank that fell away from the tennis court. The tennis court was no-man's-land. On the other side the ground fell away; that's where the Japs were, only fifty yards away.

CSM Herbert Harwood
C Company, 4th Battalion, Queen's Own Royal West Kent Regiment
We went to DIS Ridge. We dug trenches and only just got them dug in time. The road went in front of DIS Ridge, and off to Imphal. Near us was Jail Hill, a bit higher than us. Next thing I knew was one of my blokes pointing out two Japs on Jail Hill. I opened fire on them, didn't hit. But it warned people the enemy was about. Nothing happened that night. Eventually the Japs got on to Jail Hill in strength.

The Japs made a frontal attack on our company, and we let them have it with grenades and Brens. They got into the many huts in the place and some of these caught fire. In the light of the fires, lots of Japs were killed by

Sergeant Tatum with a Bren, as they ran and jumped down to the road. By the time he had finished there was a big mound of bodies on the road.

Private Bert Wheeler
Stretcher-Bearer attached C Company, 4th Battalion, Queen's Own Royal West Kent Regiment
There was a lot of rock in the soil on the hill. You dug as deep as you could, unfortunately not deep enough, so you were half exposed when standing. I shared a slit with another stretcher-bearer.

There was nowhere to evacuate the casualties to. You just had to dress and treat them as best you could. If it was a superficial wound, you dressed it and the chap carried on. If it was serious you took him to the dressing station in HQ Company. The MO decided if he should go back to his company or stay lying around the dressing station.

You had to run the gauntlet between shells arriving. It wasn't healthy but you had to do it. If a salvo came over, you knew you had a couple of minutes before the next one. But it wasn't always easy to judge. As we were in such a confined space you only had to go about one hundred and fifty yards at most to collect a casualty. Someone would shout 'stretcher-bearers', and if you didn't hear it at once, it would be shouted along the line. You crawled out, and sometimes you had to crawl back with the stretcher, dragging it with you.

Sometimes you went out with a patrol. If a man was wounded seriously you had to bring him back using a fireman's lift. If the wound was too serious you had to use your revolver.

CSM Herbert Harwood
C Company, 4th Battalion, Queen's Own Royal West Kent Regiment
We were attacked two or three nights running. They didn't manage to shift us. Sometimes during the night you would hear them shout, 'Indian National Army, come over, you are surrounded.' The Japs were across the road on Jail Hill. After a heavy shelling, one solitary Jap came out in bandages. I imagine that they were trying to entice our medical people to go in and help him. At night it was possible to shoot your own side. Our colour sergeant, while bringing up rations, was shot by our own people.

The company commander was wounded and the second-in-command. Eventually the remnants of the company was made into a platoon, I was the platoon commander, and we were attached to D Company. In the end it got so tight, we had to withdraw and leave DIS Hill as part of drawing in the perimeter.

Major John Winstanley
Officer Commanding B Company, 4th Battalion, Queen's Own Royal West Kent Regiment

The perimeter shrank and shrank until it only included the tennis court and Garrison Hill where the final stand took place. The battle took place on the tennis court – we shot them on the tennis court, we grenaded them on the tennis court. We held the tennis court against desperate attacks for five days. We held because I had constant contact by radio with the guns and the Japs never seemed to learn how to surprise us. They used to shout in English as they formed up, 'Give up.' So we knew when an attack was coming in. One would judge just the right moment to call down gun and mortar fire to catch them as they were launching the attack, and by the time they were approaching us they were decimated. They were not acting intelligently and did the same old stupid thing again and again.

We had experienced fighting the Japs in the Arakan, bayoneting the wounded and prisoners. So whereas we respected the Afrika Korps, not so the Japanese. They had renounced any right to be regarded as human, and we thought of them as vermin to be exterminated. That was important – we are pacific in our nature, but when aroused we fight quite well. Our backs were to the wall, and we were going to sell our lives as expensively as we could. Although we wondered how long we could hang on, we had no other option. We had not thought of surrender at any level; we were too-seasoned soldiers for that. We couldn't taunt the Japanese back as we couldn't speak Japanese, but there were some JIFs on the other side and we taunted them in English.

Anonymous INA corporal

I joined the INA after hearing *Netaji*. The Japanese were not cruel to anyone. They said the Asians should fight for their independence, and all Asians should be independent. We were fully confident that the Japanese would hand independence to India, as they had done to the Burmese, the Malays, the Thais; all the Asians. The Japanese remained in Burma because Nehru said on the radio that he didn't need any help from outside.

Private Bert Wheeler
Stretcher-Bearer attached C Company, 4th Battalion, Queen's Own Royal West Kent Regiment

As the days passed the casualties built up and you had to step over them in the dressing station. They had no cover: luckily it was not monsoon time. It was under shellfire. Some wounded were killed, others were wounded a second time. The MO was operating under very primitive conditions. He sometimes ran out of dressings. You couldn't clean the wounds. Gangrene developed.

The terrain changed from being covered with trees to an open space and stumps, with no cover at all. Casualties were heavy. There were some dead you couldn't reach, close to the DC's Bungalow and tennis court.

Halfway through, we were out attending casualties, we saw a flash from a gun, and dived towards a slit trench. The chap I was with, another stretcher-bearer, was hit by shrapnel in the neck and killed instantly. I was lucky and caught shrapnel in the arm which damaged the muscles. I had no grip with that hand. I walked to the dressing station, putting a dressing on myself, and saw the MO. He said, 'I'm sorry there is nothing more I can do.' He inserted ointment in the wound, and covered it with a dressing; this saved my arm.

The dressing station was under fire. I changed my dressings as and when I could when dressings were available. You just sat around, and assisted the other stretcher-bearers using one arm: feeding the wounded, giving them a drink, wetting their lips, anything you could do. We were supplied by air, on a daily basis. Dressings were dropped as well as drugs and medicines. There was enough water for cooking and drinking, but not for washing or shaving. There was rum amongst the air drops which was very acceptable. Water was dropped in metal jerrycans by parachute.

As soon as you were killed and certified dead, your comrades dug a hole, wrapped you in a blanket if one was available, and the padre buried you.

Major Harry Smith
Officer Commanding HQ Company, 4th Battalion, Queen's Own Royal West Kent Regiment

Incessant shelling was the pattern of the place. It became extremely dangerous to walk about in daylight. On one occasion a Japanese infantry gun bombarded my positions at close range, so close that the shell arrived before you heard the report of the gun, very disconcerting. The Japanese took enormous casualties from the Brens, rifles and grenades of the battalion. Their attacks went on night after night, all night. The sheer weight of the attacks threatened to overwhelm the battalion. The outer part of the defences became piled up with Japanese corpses.

Major John Winstanley
Officer Commanding B Company, 4th Battalion, Queen's Own Royal West Kent Regiment

Besides Brens, the other weapon that was so effective were grenades used by Victor King's platoon who showered them with grenades as they formed up. As Kohima was a depot, we didn't lack grenades, but we were very short of 3-inch mortar bombs. We were supplied from the air, but much of the loads went to the Japs. They had captured British 3-inch mortars, and most of the mortar bombs dropped for our use fell into enemy hands.

We had a steady toll of casualties mainly from snipers. Showing yourself in daylight resulted in being shot by a sniper. They also used their battalion guns in the direct fire role, in morning and evening 'hates'. This caused mayhem among the wounded lying in open slit trenches on Garrison Hill. We heard that 2 Div were being flown in to relieve us, and could hear the sound of firing to our north, as the division fought its way down to us.

After five days I was relieved on the tennis court by the Assam Regiment and moved to Hospital Spur. The tennis court held; the Kuki Picket changed hands several times.

Major Harry Smith
Officer Commanding HQ Company, 4th Battalion, Queen's Own Royal West Kent Regiment

We very soon ran out of water when the Japanese cut the only piped supply. Luckily a spring was discovered near my company area, and hazardous trips had to be organised every night, most of which was taken up to the casualty centre which was under continual mortar fire.

The area became festooned with parachutes as medical supplies, ammunition and water were parachuted down.

The smell of death increased as the days passed and bodies decomposed. Day after day our hopes were dashed when expected relief did not arrive. We began to walk about like zombies because we had little chance of sleep. The

The tennis court and terraces of the District Commissioner's Bungalow at Kohima.

rifle companies on the perimeter were steadily pushed back as they were forced to give ground by overwhelming numbers of enemy.

The Japs had Urdu speakers with loudhailers who would shout mainly to the Indian gunners and sappers we had with us to surrender. None of them deserted.

2nd British Div was arriving at Dimapur and clearing the road to reach us, but it seemed to take a long time. The situation got graver and graver as our numbers diminished.

Lieutenant Trevor Highett
Officer Commanding Carrier Platoon, 2nd Battalion, Dorsetshire Regiment

When we arrived at Dimapur, the Japs were only forty miles away. There were huge supplies of stores, which nobody seemed too bothered about. There are few things more unpleasant than a base in a flap. It was full of people who never expected to fight, and who couldn't wait to get out. 'Take what you like,' they said, 'just give us a signature if you've got the time.' We were pretty arrogant in 2 Div and not impressed. I acquired two armoured cars, which proved very useful. We picked up masses of stores, ammo, food, drink etc. We could carry it in the carriers. The Dorsets and 2 Div weren't short of anything.

Private Tom Cattle
17 Platoon, D Company, 2nd Battalion, Dorsetshire Regiment

Taking just a few carriers, jeeps and water bowsers, we went on to join the battalion at Zubza on the road to Kohima, where all the divisional artillery was dug in and shelling the Japs. I rejoined D Company. We were reserve battalion and guarding the Div Artillery.

We were told that the Japanese had got as far as Kohima, and the troops defending Garrison Hill were the Royal West Kents and a few Burma Rifles and were cut off as the Japs had cut the road behind them, and they were being supplied by air.

Our division was trying to push up the road from Dimapur to Kohima cut out of the hillside, with a deep ravine one side and steep hill covered in thick jungle on the other. It was difficult to advance along this narrow road.

Major Harry Smith
Officer Commanding HQ Company, 4th Battalion, Queen's Own Royal West Kent Regiment
On the night of 19 April, it was arranged that the leading troops of 2 Div with tanks would relieve the West Kents. As I was about to make my way to battalion HQ to receive orders for the relief, a mortar bomb burst on the front of my trench and a fragment entered my head just above the cheek bone. It knocked me out cold. I was treated at the RAP, given a shot of morphia and ceased to know any more until early the next morning. I came to in time to see the leading troops of the Berkshires in their nice clean uniforms making their way up to the top of the hill, covered by a very heavy barrage of 2 Div's artillery down the road. Soon I was being helped down the hill to the waiting ambulances, together with the remnants of the battalion, who were filing down ragged, bearded, looking like scarecrows. Tanks were engaging enemy positions on the road.

I never thought we would be overwhelmed as the Japs were taking enormous casualties. I was taken to the hospital at Dimapur and had a restless night listening to the cries of the wounded.

Major John Winstanley
Commanding, B Company, 4th Battalion, Queen's Own Royal West Kent Regiment
The 4th Royal West Kents, the Assam Rifles and odds and sods defended Kohima against an entire Jap division in a fourteen-day siege.

THE RELIEVING FORCE BREAKS THROUGH TO KOHIMA

Major Francis 'Frankie' Boshell
Officer Commanding B Company, 1st Battalion, Royal Berkshire Regiment
My battalion was the first into Kohima, and my company was the leading company of the battalion. We took over from the 4th Royal West Kents who had had a terrible time. To begin with, I took over the area overlooking the tennis court, although only my left forward platoon could see the court. The Dorsets were responsible for the positions closest to the court itself. The lie of

the land made it impossible to move by day because of Japanese snipers. We were in Kohima for three weeks. We were attacked every single night. On the worst night they started at 1900 hours and the last attack came in at 0400 hours the next morning. They came in waves, like a pigeon shoot. Most nights they overran part of the battalion position, so we had to mount counter-attacks. When part of my right-hand platoon was overrun, we winkled them out with the bayonet. I lost two platoon commanders, but good sergeants took over, and did better. Water was short and restricted to about one pint per man per day, so we stopped shaving. Air supply was the key, but the steep terrain and narrow ridges meant that some of the drops went to the enemy. My company went into Kohima over one hundred strong and came out at about sixty.

Warrant Officer Deryck Groocock
194 Squadron, RAF

My worst incident took place on a supply drop north of Kohima. We were flying at 8,500 feet, the mountain tops went up to seven thousand feet, but there was a layer of thick cloud between us and them. Getting near where the DZ should have been, we couldn't see anything. I thought with a bit of luck we'll find a hole and go down, so I told the two wireless operators to get the load ready to drop; it was bags of rice by free-fall that day. They started to pile the bags of rice by the door. All of a sudden, the air speed started to drop off. The natural reaction is to put on more power, but this makes the problems worse because it puts the centre of gravity back and pulls the nose up. I put on more power, and the speed dropped. Suddenly she flipped into a spin. I knew we had fifteen hundred feet to go before hitting the mountains. We dropped straight into the cloud, descending at fifteen hundred feet per minute. The altimeter unwound past seven thousand feet, and I thought any moment now. I took the correct recovery action, opposite rudder and nose down, and we came out of the spin below cloud at 4,600 feet, with two bloody great peaks on either side of us reaching up into the cloud. We collected our wits.

The aircraft had been badly loaded to start with, and by stacking the rice by the door the aircraft's centre of gravity had been put out of limits. In the spin, it all fell forward putting the centre of gravity right, so the aircraft would fly OK. Fortunately no one had bailed out, because they couldn't get their parachutes on in time. We staggered along the valley, saw a column of smoke, it was the DZ – an absolute miracle. We dropped our load, the only aircraft out of twelve who made it that day. The others all turned back.

Private William Cornell
A Company, 2nd Battalion, Durham Light Infantry

After we took over from the West Kents, we were told we were to attack the Japanese. I thought, 'I've been OK up to now, now what?', because Lieutenant Connelly said it was going to be a nasty one. We were told that at 'five o'clock in the morning we are going to move out up this track here', and he drew a little sketch, and he said, 'We expect to meet the Japs somewhere near here, in a defensive position, and we are going to clear them out.' It was the Kuki Picket.

It was just getting light, and we started to move off up this hill, it was a very narrow track. We hadn't gone very far, Corporal Breedon was leading the section, behind him a lance/corporal. I was number one rifleman. There was a tremendous racket as a Japanese machine gun opened up. There was a terrible scream, it cut Corporal Breedon right in half. We couldn't get to him where he fell down the hill.

I couldn't imagine that I would ever see England again, or even get out of this battle. A feeling that set in with me was I couldn't care less if I get killed. I accepted it. It wasn't fear. The only thought was 'will I get wounded or will I get killed'. Right round me it was chaos, shouting and screaming; stretcher-bearers running about.

The word was passed that we were going to carry on to attack the Jap position. The jungle thinned out and I saw flashes of the Japanese firing at us. I thought it's now or never, the pace quickened, and I thought, 'In we go.' We started to run forward, I was all keyed up, rifle ready, grenades ready, and the next thing I knew was a tremendous bang, which seemed right underneath me. I was blown into the air, right up the bank, and landed on the ground, it was a mortar bomb, don't know why it didn't kill me. I found myself on my own, and thought, 'What do I do?' I crawled into a little bit of cover, I wasn't in pain. Then I felt something pouring down my leg, and thought, 'Is my leg off?' I moved my toes, and no they worked all right. I started investigating and it was water from my water bottle, punctured by a piece of shrapnel. If it hadn't been for my water bottle, it would have gone through me. There was just a gash in my body. I wasn't in pain. I took out my FFD and put it on. The battle was still going on. I thought would the Japanese come, would our troops come and pick me up?

I said to myself, keep yourself under cover, and don't move until you are sure that it was your own people. I had no water, and lay there for about two hours. On one occasion, 'ping', someone shot at me, I don't know who. I had no idea what was going on. Then a faint voice shouting, 'Corny, Corny, where are you?' It was a lad from my own home town, Tommy Hunter.

'I'm glad I found you Corny.'

'So am I'.

He had a look at me, and said. 'You will be all right.'

The next feeling was immense relief, you are wounded, not serious, but it will get you out of this for a bit.

Lance Corporal Henry Bell
Signaller, 2nd Battalion, Durham Light Infantry
The night I was with D Company on Garrison Hill, they came in shouting, 'Tojo Tojo,' throwing phosphorus grenades. I was in with the signallers and dying for a smoke, so I crawled under a blanket and lit a cigarette. The company commander, 'Tanky' Waterhouse shouted, 'Who's smoking?'

'Me, sir.'

'For God's sake light me one,' he replied.

C Company ahead of us were overrun, with heavy losses.

Company Sergeant Major Martin McLane
C Company, 2nd Battalion, Durham Light Infantry
I was woken by shouts from my company commander, Major Stock. Green phosphorus was pouring into one end of the trench. I was covered with it, which causes deep penetrating burns. I was rubbing the stuff off me with earth, then the Japs came in yelling and shouting. They were in among us and just ten yards away there was a fearsome-looking man waving a sword.

The ammunition stacked on Garrison Hill exploded and parachutes from supply drops hanging in the trees caught fire. We stuck out like sore thumbs. After fierce fighting we cleared the position. My company commander, the runners and the signallers were all dead. A shell had landed right in the hole where they were located.

Henry Bell as a sergeant.

Private Tom Cattle
17 Platoon, D Company, 2nd Battalion, Dorsetshire Regiment

We were now taking heavy casualties on Garrison Hill, and the Dorsets took over the 2 DLI positions. The only way up was on the road in carriers to a place called Mortuary Corner. Anything approaching this point came under Jap mortar and artillery fire. So carriers, in relays, each took about six men up to a point out of sight of the Japs spotting for their artillery and mortars, the carrier stopped, everyone out, and back to pick up some more. From the road Garrison Hill was almost perpendicular, the monsoon had started early and every step you tried to pull yourself up, you slid back, with all your kit. At the same time being sniped at, machine-gunned and mortared and shelled. We got to the top and were given our positions, the original positions dug by the Royal West Kents. There were bodies lying around. We scrambled into a slit, three of us, me, Lance Corporal Des Walford and someone else. There was only enough room for three of us, about eight feet long, two feet wide with a roof on it. Without the roof you couldn't have stayed long.

Our position looked down on to the continuation of the road to Imphal. It was very steep. To the right of us was Kuki Picket, which the Royal Welch Fusiliers were still trying to take. The Japanese to our left were dug in on the tennis court and the DC's Bungalow beyond. We were on the top of a ridge that ran out from Pulebadze, which was about seven thousand feet high. The ridge extended down from Kuki Picket to Garrison Hill, down on to the DC's Bungalow and the tennis court, to the road leading to Kohima village.

You couldn't get out of your trench in daylight, or the Japanese snipers would have you. So many shells and mortar bombs had hit the hill that all the trees were shattered and the stumps were draped with parachutes that had come down with supplies. It was a desolate and desperate situation.

Water was dropped in two-gallon cans. We were connected trench to trench by ropes, so we could pull supplies, water cans and ammunition across from one trench to another. On one occasion we were pulling a water can to our trench and it got caught on the stump of a tree, and we couldn't move it. And Des the Lance Corporal said, 'I'll have a look and see.' He stood up, and fell back, shot dead, straight through the forehead. He had to stay in the trench with us until dark. He was such a nice chap, and we'd been together for such a long time.

Our Sergeant, 'Yorky' Seal, from Yorkshire, a regular soldier, had been with

Garrison Hill, at Kohima.

IND 3698

the battalion for a long time, in France and Dunkirk, a very brave man. He was one of those people who would volunteer for everything, including fighting patrols. So we had to go with him. You did not want to but had to. Patrols were sent to find out where the strongest and weakest Jap positions were. The only way we were going to progress was by winkling the Japs out, and the infantry were the people who were going to have to do it. To find out where they were you had to probe and poke and get them to fire so you could see exactly where the positions were.

I went on one patrol to find out where the enemy were in relation to the DC's Bungalow. We had to go down the side of a hill from our positions and try to work round the hill at the bottom towards the road because they seemed to be dug in to the ridges with their machine guns. The only way in was from the front. This night, and it is difficult moving at night, people were jittery as you moved through your own positions going out and coming back in. We got to the bottom and started to move forward and we could hear the Japs talking. It is difficult to move at night without making a noise. Suddenly all hell broke loose as they opened up with machine guns, mortars, grenades, and we had to pull back and take what cover we could as showers of grenades came over. The sergeant told us to pull out.

Major Alexander Wilson
Brigade Major, 6th Infantry Brigade, 2nd British Division, Argyll & Sutherland Highlanders

The fighting on Garrison Hill was worse than the battles at the Somme remembered by the Divisional Commander, General Grover, who had fought there in the First World War. 2 DLI had more casualties on Garrison Hill than anyone else. In A, C and D Companies there was total of four officers left. Of the original 136 men in A Company, only sixty were left. The pioneer and carrier platoons also lost many killed and wounded. The fighting was hand-to-hand. Men were kept going by training, regimental pride, and the will to survive. If you let the Japanese in you'd had it.

At night the Japs sent in fighting patrols to beat up brigade HQ, but were seen off by our defence platoon. The first morning we counted twenty dead Japs, including a young officer.

Lieutenant Gordon Graham
Platoon Commander, C Company, 1st Battalion, Queen's Own Cameron Highlanders

I was on a combined operations course when the Japanese attacked Kohima. I had met the girl of my dreams in Bombay and had just got married. I was flown in a bomber from Calcutta, which stopped at Imphal, and then on to Jorhat near Dimapur. I got there in two days, straight into the battle. I rejoined the battalion in Kohima, sad that some of my closest friends had been killed. Two sergeants of whom I was very fond had been killed by our own guns. All by accident of course.

I walked up the steep jungle-covered hillside above Kohima village, which my battalion had partly captured, but part was still held by Japs. I went over to my platoon and greeted the Jocks. The men in my platoon were a mixture of Yorkshiremen from the mining towns of south Yorkshire, and Highlanders, the original Camerons from northern Scotland, round Inverness and Skye, so you had a mixture of crofters and miners; they got on wonderfully. They were people of sterling qualities, used to the hard life, took their hardships stoically. The camaraderie between officers and men that already existed in the battalion was essential for survival in the jungle. Most of the senior NCOs were regular soldiers.

There, fifty yards away, were the Japs, also dug in. There was a curious sense of almost intimacy with the enemy in jungle warfare. In the patrols which I made in the next few days you constantly found Japanese. You were constantly intermingling with the enemy. I found it exciting.

The patrols were mainly quite long range, you went out with one NCO and five or six privates, your duty was to locate the Japanese and report back, because the command in jungle warfare is actually blind, you can't see what the hell is going on and life is full of surprises. That is one of the democratising elements of jungle warfare. The brigade command is just as vulnerable as the humblest private soldier. They were just as much exposed as anyone else, so they were always anxious for information.

The first patrol I went out on the day after I arrived, we spotted some Japanese and took a note of where they were. They didn't see us. On the way back we found the corpses of a previous British patrol that had been wiped out and I said to one of the Jocks we'd better cut off their identity discs so we can report who they are. While he was doing this a Japanese patrol opened up on

Gordon Graham, as a Lieutenant Colonel at the end of the war.

us, but we got back with only one wounded. But again that was a piece of vital information. We could say exactly where that patrol was, and also indicate where there was clear country where it might be possible to advance. In the next three or four weeks I must have led about a dozen patrols.

Prising Loose the Japanese Hold

Lieutenant Sam Horner
Signals Officer, 2nd Battalion, Royal Norfolk Regiment
The CO, Robert Scott, called an O Group. He said, 'Now the 4th Brigade – less the Lancashire Fusiliers, who are detached to 5th Brigade, so we're only a two-battalion brigade – with Brigade Tac Headquarters, we're going to do a right hook and try and come in behind the Japs, get on to the road that led from Kohima to Imphal, cut the road, shoot them up the arse.' It was as simple as that.

Sergeant Fred Hazell
D Company, 2nd Battalion, Royal Norfolk Regiment
We were issued with one hundred rounds of ammunition in addition to what we already had. This dangled round our necks in two bandoliers. Blankets were cut in half, rolled up and put on the back of our pack. Every third man was given a shovel, every third man was given a pick and the other third were given two carriers of mortar bombs.

Sergeant Albert 'Winkie' Fitt
Officer Commanding 9 Platoon, B Company, 2nd Battalion, Royal Norfolk Regiment
Around my web belt I had grenades all the way. I had five or six bandoliers, about fifty rounds in each. On top of that we had our ammunition pouches full. We didn't expect the climb and the march to be quite as fierce as it was.

Lieutenant Sam Horner
Signals Officer, 2nd Battalion, Royal Norfolk Regiment
There was a map showing where we were going. It was absolutely white

because it had never been surveyed, nobody had ever been there, the Nagas said they didn't go there, because there was a lot of superstition about it – there were witches and that sort of thing. All there was, drawn from aeroplanes, was a few little nalas, watercourses, and the rest of it was white – so it was a fat lot of use having a map.

Sergeant Fred Hazell
D Company, 2nd Battalion, Royal Norfolk Regiment

God, what a night that was. What a climb. Very steep, wooded, a lot of undergrowth. There were a lot of paths, but occasionally we had to cut our way through. I stepped on a moist tree root, lost my footing and fell flat on my back. My legs went in the air, and I unfortunately caught the chap in front on both his legs, just above the knees and he was the biggest chap in the battalion. He came down on my stomach and, God, he knocked every ounce of wind out of me. You couldn't hang about because it was pitch blooming dark, and if you lost the chap in front you could end up anywhere.

We finally arrived at this village at about two o'clock in the morning. Somebody from headquarters came up and said, 'Put your platoon in there.' I woke up, the sun was shining through the chinks in the walls of the hut, and I thought God's strewth, I never posted a sentry. I opened the door and there was a big Naga standing outside, on guard with his spear. Then somebody appeared and said, 'Have breakfast, we're moving off at ten.' Breakfast was three biscuits and a brew up.

Lieutenant Sam Horner
Signals Officer, 2nd Battalion, Royal Norfolk Regiment

We were moving across country. We had to climb up one after another of these ridges, and slide down the other side, it was very, very exhausting. We even used ropes sometimes to get up the very steep hills, which were so slippery that you went forward one pace and back half a pace. But with the Nagas' help we made it. But it was slow. Secrecy was important, we didn't want the Japs to know we were coming in behind the Jap lines – but there weren't any lines. We were well away from the actual battle going on in Kohima.

Private Dick Fiddament
2nd Battalion, Royal Norfolk Regiment

That part has the heaviest rainfall in the world. It comes down in a solid sheet. You think to yourself, if it doesn't stop soon beating against my poor skull, I'll go insane. The whole area becomes a quagmire. Combined with the rain you've got the humidity, and you're sweating – the straps of your pack, your rifle sling, and anything else you are carrying tends to chafe and rub. Your skin becomes all tender and raw. Your feet, however tough and hardened, are saturated and become sore with constant rubbing, however well your boots are fitted.

Bugler Bert May
HQ Company, 2nd Battalion, Royal Norfolk Regiment

Leeches used to get through on any part of your body that was open. We tried to keep the bottom of our trousers and sleeves closed as much as we could. If we got leeches on us we never pulled them off because the head stayed in the flesh and that made a very nasty ulcer. So you used to get a lighted cigarette, stick it on his tail, and he used to pop off.

Lieutenant Sam Horner
Signals Officer, 2nd Battalion, Royal Norfolk Regiment

The CO called his O Group for the attack on GPT Ridge. The light was failing fast so he said, 'Get your pencils out, I'm going to give you the fire plan first, it's important, you should have it written down while you can see to write.' I wrote down the fire plan in my notebook. By then it was dark. He said, 'Orders, memorise the lot, they're going to be simple.'

The doctor had dug a hole for the Regimental Aid Post. Robert Scott had strict orders from brigade that there were to be no fires lit whatsoever. He disobeyed the order, told the doctor, 'Look here, get a fire going at the bottom of that ruddy hole of yours and I want every man to have some hot sweet tea, I think it's very important for morale.' There was little or no smoke, any that filtered up, there was somebody to swish it away. Brigadier Goschen discovered this was going on and practically placed Robert Scott under arrest – but not quite. Robert talked his way out of it.

Bugler Bert May
HQ Company, 2nd Battalion, Royal Norfolk Regiment

I received some tea in my mess tin – hot tea. You don't know what a cup of tea means to you after you've been three or four days marching without having one.

Private Dick Fiddament
2nd Battalion, Royal Norfolk Regiment

Everybody's frightened. If he says he's not, then he's either a liar, or a bloody madman. Because nobody wants to die, but nobody. I certainly didn't. But you're all pals together, there's a job to do and you get on with it the best way you can.

Sergeant Albert 'Winkie' Fitt
Officer Commanding 9 Platoon, B Company, 2nd Battalion, Royal Norfolk Regiment

I was happy as a platoon commander. I was prepared for a good scrap, if there was one coming along, and I didn't fear anything or anybody. I was keen to learn and I was also keen to try and protect the men under my command. I wanted to go into battle with thirty men and come out with thirty men. That was my idea and as far as leadership was concerned, I never asked troops under me to do what I couldn't bear or wouldn't do myself. I wasn't frightened. About a couple of minutes before the attack, you'd get a sick feeling in the stomach. But immediately you moved, that sick feeling goes away altogether as far as I was concerned. Everybody, I don't care who he is, is nervous to a certain extent before a battle. But when it starts then you've got one thing in your mind, it's either you or the enemy, but somebody's going to get killed. At the back of your mind it's the enemy, not you, or your men.

Sergeant Fred Hazell
D Company, 2nd Battalion, Royal Norfolk Regiment

When we got to the top of the ridge it was almost like World War One. There were four, five or six Japs, they suddenly leapt out of their holes and raced at us with their bayonets. They didn't get very far because the lads' machine guns just went 'BZZZTTT' like that. They threw their rifles at us but it was fairly simple to side-step them. They were about twelve yards away when they hurled them at us, as they dropped.

Sergeant Albert 'Winkie' Fitt
Officer Commanding 9 Platoon, B Company, 2nd Battalion, Royal Norfolk Regiment

We went from the forming-up place, got on the start line. Poor old Captain Fulton, he had been hit through the top of his head and the scalp was laying open. You could see his brain actually moving and he had a pleading look in his eye, more or less asking you to put a bullet through him and finish him off. Well you couldn't do that. But it was obvious he hadn't got long to go.

We should have had artillery support. That was all laid on to blast GPT Ridge before we attacked it. But things got rather desperate as we lay on the start line. We were getting shot up and hadn't got a chance.

I lost my Bren gunner, a chap called Grogan. I grabbed the Bren and I had a rifle slung on my shoulder. I called out to Davis commanding the left-hand platoon. I told him I had had enough laying here and not fighting. I was going forward. Lieutenant Reeve in the centre, he had to come with us.

Lieutenant Sam Horner
Signals Officer, 2nd Battalion, Royal Norfolk Regiment

Robert Scott decided, absolutely rightly, that the momentum was being lost and he kept it going. The battery commander said, 'What about the guns?'

'No, no. Forget it, we'll just get straight on through.'

He went on as far as it was possible to get. He ran off with A Company who were then spearhead and practically led the assault.

Sergeant William Robinson
A Company, 2nd Battalion, Royal Norfolk Regiment

The CO lined us up with Bren guns. Bob Scott at that time was ill with malaria. All he had was his pistol and his khud stick. His famous words were, 'Right ho, boys let's go.' That was it. The instructions were to fire at everything, spraying some down, some up and forward because there was a bunker there. Up to that time I hadn't seen any Japanese at all. But in this semi-clearing several got up and started running away. They didn't get far because the fire power was terrific, about twelve Bren guns. The bunker was taken.

Sergeant Albert 'Winkie' Fitt
Officer Commanding 9 Platoon, B Company, 2nd Battalion, Royal Norfolk Regiment

We took the position with the bayonet. I used the Bren for the remainder of the attack, using it from the hip. The Jap positions were facing outwards, so they had to come into the open if they wanted to fight us, and that suited us. We wanted them out in the open so we could see what was going on. We tore down GPT Ridge as fast as we could. About halfway down, I saw what looked to me like a flat piece of ground, and I thought it was a bunker facing the other way. I jumped on to this, and I was looking down the muzzle of a mountain field gun. I threw a grenade in. Three Japs got out, and my runner, Swinscoe, shot the first one that was running away from us. He twizzled him like a rabbit – a marvellous shot. We'd then got two prisoners.

I left them with one man, a soldier you could trust. Colonel Scott came up and when I told him about the prisoners, he said, 'Where are they?' I told him they were being brought up by one of the chaps.

'Good,' he said.

Well, up came this fellow, no prisoners, so I asked him where they were.

'Back up the track.'

'What do you mean? They'll be gone.'

'Never,' he replied. 'Never, they won't go anywhere. Remember my brother got bayoneted in hospital. I searched them. I took these badges off them. These are Royal Norfolk's badges. Well, I bayoneted both of them.'

When I told the CO we hadn't got the prisoners, he flew at me and said, 'Bring the person who let them escape to me.'

I said, 'They didn't escape, sir. He took these badges off them.'

'So what?'

'Well, his brother was bayoneted in hospital – he bayoneted them.'

Colonel Scott said, 'That's saved me cutting their bloody throats.'

Lieutenant Sam Horner
Signals Officer, 2nd Battalion, Royal Norfolk Regiment

Robert Scott got on the wireless and said, 'Objective captured.' Divisional headquarters started coming through to the brigadier saying, 'You haven't had the fire plan yet'. Then Robert sent a message to the divisional commander, 'If you don't believe me, come and bloody well look.'

Sergeant Fred Hazell
D Company, 2nd Battalion, Royal Norfolk Regiment

Someone shouted, 'We've arrived – dig in – prepare yourselves for a counter-attack.' We didn't appreciate when we stopped there was this confounded bunker about seventy yards in front of us with umpteen machine guns inside. At that moment Major Hatch appeared and said, 'Come with me, I want to sort out the company positions for the night.' We were standing in the open with this bunker on our left, all the time there were bullets whistling past our heads.

He said, 'Let's make ourselves less conspicuous,' and dropped on his hands and knees. I dropped with him. A shot rang out, I shouted, 'They've got my bloody nose.' I put my hand up, my nose was still there. It passed right under it. The Major said, 'It missed you, but I think it's hit me.' I looked and it had got him in the leg, in an artery. I tried to put a tourniquet on him, but had nothing ready to do the job properly. I dragged him back under cover, over the ridge and handed him over to the medics. I was very upset in the morning when they told me he had died in the night.

Private Dick Fiddament
2nd Battalion, Royal Norfolk Regiment

Suddenly Robert Scott comes along. There we are crouched down in our holes. Scott says to us, 'Come on you chaps, there's no need to be afraid, you are better than those little yellow bastards.'

Sergeant Albert 'Winkie' Fitt
Officer Commanding 9 Platoon, B Company, 2nd Battalion, Royal Norfolk Regiment

When Scott got scalped by a grazing bullet, he shook his fist at the Japanese, saying, 'The biggest bloke on the damn position and you couldn't get him. If you were in my bloody battalion, I'd take away your proficiency pay.'

The plan was to attack the Norfolk Bunker from the front. It consisted of about seven or eight bunkers. My platoon was spearhead in attacking the centre, and 12 platoon on the right. Number 10 platoon was in reserve with a support platoon consisting of machine gunners and so forth under the Carrier Platoon commanded by Captain Dickie Davies.

We moved and got about halfway to the base of the hill. Captain Randle, now company commander, staggered twice before we got to the bottom, that told me that he had been hit fairly heavily in the upper part of his body. I shouted to him to go down and leave it to me, you could see that he had already lost blood. He said, 'No, you take the left-hand bunker, I'm going to take this one.'

I got mine by coming up underneath and before they could spin the gun on me I had a grenade in the bunker. After four seconds, it went up. I knew that everyone in the bunker was either dead or knocked out.

I saw Captain Randle at the bunker entrance. He had a grenade he was going to throw in. I just stood there, I couldn't do a thing. If he had held on for three minutes, I'd have got on top of the bunker, and knocked it out. But he had been hit again at point-blank range. As he was going down, he threw his grenade into the bunker and sealed the entrance with his body. So nobody could shoot from it. But he killed all the occupants. I thought, 'That's the end of Captain Randle.'

A Japanese rushed out of the back door of the next bunker, which was behind me, and fired at me. I didn't see him. He got me through the side of my face, underneath my jaw, taking my top teeth out, fracturing my maxilla, the bullet burning alongside my nose. It felt like being hit by a clenched fist. It didn't hurt as much as a good punch in a fight in the past. I just spat out a handful of teeth, spun round, and he was a few paces away, facing me. He had a rifle and bayonet. I pressed the trigger, I'd got no ammunition. As he came towards me, I felt it was either him or me. I was an instructor in unarmed combat. I let him come and threw the light machine gun in his face. Before he hit the ground I had my hand round his windpipe and I tried to tear it out. It wouldn't come – if I could have got his windpipe out, I would have twisted it round his neck. I managed to get his bayonet off his rifle and finish him with that.

I stood up and had a call from 12 Platoon telling me they were pinned down from another bunker I couldn't see. I asked them where it was. They told me. I threw a grenade. It went over the top. A chap who could see shouted a correction. I threw a second grenade. It hit the ground short, and bounced in killing the occupants. There were still more bunkers. One of my corporals spotted another bunker slightly over the crest. He started going for it. I yelled at him to stop. He continued for four or five paces and was shot down.

Captain Dickie Davies
Officer Commanding Carrier Platoon, 2nd Battalion, Royal Norfolk Regiment
There were other bunkers further down the ridge towards the road. We couldn't throw grenades at them, so you got your bayonet out and made a hole in the top and dropped a grenade in through the hole. Four Japanese ran out of one of the bunkers. I pressed the trigger, and nothing bloody well happened – my Sten gun jammed. They always jammed, a useless weapon. I threw it at them I was so annoyed.

Sergeant Albert 'Winkie' Fitt
Officer Commanding 9 Platoon, B Company, 2nd Battalion, Royal Norfolk Regiment
At the RAP I met Colonel Scott, the first words he said to me was, 'They got you then, Fitt?'

'That's right, sir.'

'Let's have a look.'

The MO removed the field dressing. Colonel Scott stood in front of me and he went, 'Ho, ho, ho! You never were any bloody oil painting.'

Captain Dickie Davies
Officer Commanding Carrier Platoon, 2nd Battalion, Royal Norfolk Regiment
I took shelter in the main bunker. It was full of dead Japs. They sent us down some bully beef and my batman said, 'Let's have it.' I said 'OK.' He got his hankie out of his pocket – it was filthy. He put it over the bare tummy of a dead Japanese. He pulled this warm bully beef out with his fingers, put it on a biscuit and said, 'Here you are, sir.' I couldn't eat it, I was sick.

Private Tom Cattle
17 Platoon, D Company, 2nd Battalion, Dorsetshire Regiment
We needed to get the Japs out of the DC's Bungalow and the tennis court. They tried to bring up a tank to provide direct fire to help take out the bunkers. The first tank found it too steep. So an armoured bulldozer was used to tow the tank, but in the end the big Lee-Grant tank pulled the bulldozer back. The next time the bulldozer cut a track and we got a tank up into the D Company position.

The next day we were to attack the tennis court positions. The difficult part was taking the tank over the perpendicular drop down on to the tennis court. We lined up, a terrific barrage from our artillery fell on the Japs, and an airstrike. We knew that the Japs were so deeply dug in that it wouldn't make any difference. But we moved forward and the tank slithered down over the ridge, a Lee-Grant with a 75-mm gun, it fired its 75-mm and machine guns into the Jap bunkers as we advanced.

Lieutenant Trevor Highett
Officer Commanding Carrier Platoon, 2nd Battalion, Dorsetshire Regiment
I rode in one of the tanks because I had a good idea of the layout of the land, having used the armoured cars I acquired at Dimapur to take ammunition to the forward companies. I was not the commander of the tank. One of the unsung heroes of Kohima was Sergeant Waterhouse, the driver. He had to go down a vertical drop of six feet on to the tennis court. If the tank had been out of action on the tennis court it would have been a disaster. We were firing point-blank at the Jap positions from about twenty to thirty yards. I was firing one of the machine guns. The longest part of the operation for me personally, which took about two hours, was waiting on the edge of the drop down to the tennis court, while the driver made up his mind if he could do it. It was probably only a few seconds. But we were aware that there were anti-tank guns around, and we were stopped.

Mopping up took time. D Company used pole charges. Richard Sharp of the BBC covered it live. Afterwards it was rather like a celebration, lots of people milling about, then the Jap artillery opened up, and the scrum of spectators dispersed rather quickly.

Sergeant William Cook
Platoon Sergeant, 18 Platoon, D Company, 2nd Battalion, Dorsetshire Regiment
My objective was a black water tank. I took one section with me, when I came under fire. I dropped off a Bren to cover the enemy, came under fire again, and dropped off another Bren. This left me with one Bren, another man and myself to take the black water tank. The tank had fired a few rounds into the black water tank, it was shot to pieces and there was no water in it. The Japs had dug trenches all round the tank, which was about twelve feet square, and

underneath it I had a pole charge, an eight-foot length of bamboo with gun-cotton tied on the end with a fuse attached. When I jumped down into the enemy trench, and looked round the corner, there were three or four Japs. There shouldn't have been any left alive – the tank was supposed to have killed the lot. So I had no option but to put the pole charge in. We had been told that if you pushed the charge in before pulling the fuse, it would be pushed out by the Japs on to you, so I pulled the fuse, counted five, and put the charge in, and it must have blown the Japs to bits. Unfortunately I forgot to close my eyes, and I was temporarily blinded by debris being blown out from the fifteen-inch gap between the bottom of the tank and the trench underneath. The explosion blew out a Japanese sword, and I could feel this thing, and said, 'There's something here.' A corporal said. 'You've got a Japanese sword there.'

The other two sections had gone round the other way and did their work winkling out the Japs. I'd done my bit, but couldn't see, so missed the mopping up. I was in the MO tent for four days, before they washed the dirt out, and I fully regained my sight after about a week.

People behave differently in action from their normal behaviour. One chap, Corporal Day, normally a mild-mannered man who wouldn't hurt a fly, had the Bren when we reached the black water tank. He stood on the top of a little trench shouting and cursing the Japanese, he was in another world.

Private Tom Cattle
17 Platoon, D Company, 2nd Battalion, Dorsetshire Regiment
Suddenly some of the Japs started running. And we knew we had done it. We mowed them down as they ran. There were bodies that had been there weeks, covered in flies and maggots, the stench was terrific.

We still had to winkle some of them out of their trenches. We pushed pole charges into the firing holes in the bunkers. Some of the Japs didn't seem to know what they were, and pulled in the bamboo pole, which was exactly what we wanted. Some were pushing them back out, so we cut the fuse to two seconds. We got on to our objective, as did other companies, and we had won the day. We still had a problem where the Japs were on Kuki Picket and Jail Hill. But we could get tanks forward now and help the rest of the division. This had all taken from mid-April to the capture of Kohima on 13 May.

Lieutenant Trevor Highett
Officer Commanding Carrier Platoon, 2nd Battalion, Dorsetshire Regiment
The Japanese were magnificent in defence. Every army in the world talks about holding positions to the last man. Virtually no other army, including the Germans, ever did, but the Japs did. Their positions were well sited and they had a good eye for the ground. They relied on rushing and shouting in the attack. We thought they were formidable fighting insects and savages. We took few prisoners, about one or two in the whole war. We wanted prisoners for information, but wounded men would have a primed grenade under them, so stretcher-bearers were very careful.

Private Tom Cattle
17 Platoon, D Company, 2nd Battalion, Dorsetshire Regiment
We could now walk about without being fired on by snipers. But we were still being shelled by Jap guns being controlled by Japs on the high hills overlooking Kohima. I was filthy, unshaven, covered in impetigo, covered in lice, with boils on my arms. My feet were in a terrible condition. We were thin, hungry, thirsty and tired.

We went back to Zubza and we were stripped. They had cut large oil drums and filled them with hot water to make baths. My face was covered in sores, it was difficult to have a shave, but it had to come off. We were covered in purple gentian violet in our armpits and crotch, put there by the medical staff.

We were taken to Dimapur and had a rest. We were visited by an ENSA party including Vera Lynn. I got so thin, I was clapping so hard, off went my wedding ring and I thought I would never find it. But afterwards, with some other chaps, among all the mud, I found it. We had new clothes and boots, and were soon on the move again.

BEGINNING THE BREAK OUT TO IMPHAL

Lieutenant Sam Horner
Signals Officer, 2nd Battalion, Royal Norfolk Regiment
We were shown the ground for the attack on the Aradura Spur. I thought this is a straightforward nonsense from start to finish. There was a very steep hill, we knew the Japs were on top, we knew they'd be in a reverse slope position,

The 1st Battalion Queen's Own Cameron Highlanders bath in half oil drums at Kohima. L-R back to camera: Captain David Murray, Captain Neil White, and Major Alan Roy.

and we were going to assault straight up the front – not a hope in hell.

CSM Walter Gilding
B Company, 2nd Battalion, Royal Norfolk Regiment

The company were lined up on the base of the hill, it was all jungle covered, no tracks leading up to it, and must have been about one in four. You couldn't walk up it, it had to be scrambled up. The Royal Scots had a company on our left flank. Solid shot was to be fired from 25-pounders to break up the Japanese bunkers on the crest of the hill. The idea was to have two platoons forward, with one platoon back and company HQ, including me and my party. With us was Colonel Scott. We were all within touching distance, there was no space to spread out. The artillery fired and this allowed us to start scrambling up the hill, bypassing a clump of bamboo, or round a tree, you couldn't go straight up. We could hear the thudding of the shot on the top of the hill. We got almost halfway up when the artillery stopped and then the fun began. Small-arms fire, machine-gun fire and grenades – we got the lot.

Second Lieutenant Maurice Franses
B Company, 2nd Battalion, Royal Norfolk Regiment

Then some Japanese grenades started coming down, so we threw our grenades up to the top. The ground was so steep, there was a great danger of our grenades rolling back on us. So I tried to land my grenades on the very top, or a little further, so they wouldn't roll back.

CSM Walter Gilding
B Company, 2nd Battalion, Royal Norfolk Regiment

The leading lads got within twenty feet of the crest. Robert Scott came up and he was with the leading troops throwing grenades, shouting, 'Get on, get on, get at 'em.' By this time I was about ten yards from him. I had a Sten gun and was firing, scrambling up, grabbing hold of a tree, firing the Sten, going a little further, encouraging the lads. You couldn't see the bunkers or slits, they were so well camouflaged. I heard the stretcher-bearers being called as people were getting hit.

Second Lieutenant Maurice Franses
B Company, 2nd Battalion, Royal Norfolk Regiment

Robert Scott had always been a keen cricketer, and when he threw his

CSM Walter Gilding.

SR 17534

grenades he reminded me of a medium bowler lobbing. He was being seen, it was a big help to us all, it certainly was a big help to me. After a few minutes of this, a Japanese grenade came down towards Robert Scott and I think he decided to kick it away. He misjudged it slightly and it went off and brought him down.

CSM Walter Gilding
B Company, 2nd Battalion, Royal Norfolk Regiment
I saw him go down and the stretcher-bearers come to try to pick him up. They cut his trousers open to put a field dressing on his wounds. This uncovered his bottom and through all the noise that was going on, Robert shouted out, 'COVER MY BLOODY ARSE UP.'

Private William Cron
Carrier Platoon, 2nd Battalion, Royal Norfolk Regiment
I had a go at the Japs with my Bren, kept their heads down while the stretcher-bearers got him out. If somebody hadn't fired at the bunkers they'd have popped him and the stretcher-bearers off. So I gave them two magazines of thirty rounds each. I got one through the arm – it didn't do much harm, it didn't stop me firing. By that time they'd got the old man on the stretcher and were getting him down to cover.

Private Tom Cattle
17 Platoon, D Company, 2nd Battalion, Dorsetshire Regiment
We were taken back up to Kohima again, the division had cleared the roads for a way. But soon we were the leading troops, and the Dorsets were to make a left flanking move instead of following the road. We started off and something went wrong and we had to come back again. By now a Field Dressing Station had been moved up into Kohima. We set off again, it was a long drag down to the paddy fields in the valley bottom. After marching all day in single file, we got to the bottom of Big Tree Hill and had to climb up to the Kohima–Imphal Road again and cut the road behind the Japs. We got to Big Tree Hill, it was getting on in the day. We were now at the bottom of Aradura Spur, it was hard climb in thick jungle. A patrol had reported that there were no Japs on Big Tree Hill.

We got so far and came under fire. It was decided that as it was getting dark we would go no further so we had to stay and dig in. Started digging, it was so hot, and we took off our equipment, we were in helmets, our battalion was not allowed to wear bush hats in the front line. I thought it was so hot and all we had to dig with was an entrenching tool. I got about a foot down. I took off my helmet, and the Japs attacked again. I felt a slap on the back of the head and I was knocked out. I fell down, and when I came round I was lying on the ground with blood pouring out of the back of my head. I shouted for a stretcher-bearer and someone bandaged me and put me on a stretcher. I was carried all the way back we had marched that day. We got back to Kohima, where the dressing station was. It was full of casualties. I wasn't all that bad. I had a bit of shrapnel in the back of my head. Others had lost legs, lost arms. People were shouting and screaming; such a lot of noise.

I was put into a bed and operated on, removing a bit of shrapnel. Three days later there was a terrific pain in the back of my head and down my neck. I told the sister and she had a look. She said it's gone bad. We hadn't got penicillin, gunshot wounds were getting gangrenous. I was a bit naive, I was only twenty. I thought that's it. I had another operation and it gradually got better.

Bugler Bert May
HQ Company, 2nd Battalion, Royal Norfolk Regiment
When it was all over you just felt 'Thank God'.

Lieutenant Gordon Graham
Platoon Commander, C Company, 1st Battalion, Queen's Own Cameron Highlanders
After the battle of Kohima, the division had to open the road from Kohima to Imphal.

Ursula Graham-Bower
Naga Watch and Ward Scheme and Women's Auxiliary Corps (India) (WACI)
There was one village that was friendly to the Japs. They took one hundred rupees to bring the Japanese my head. After the 'shouting' was more or less over, Bill Tibbetts of the Assam Rifles and I were touring the area. We came to the village, which clearly had a very bad conscience. We had our Assam Rifles with us. I think they were afraid we were going to take reprisals. There

was no point in doing that. The headman refused to appear. A very nervous young man appeared with a bottle of beer and a chicken, and sat looking at us with terror. I was tempted to point out that I was in possession of my head, and the Japanese weren't, and could I please have the hundred rupees that I felt was due to me.

The Turning Point Imphal

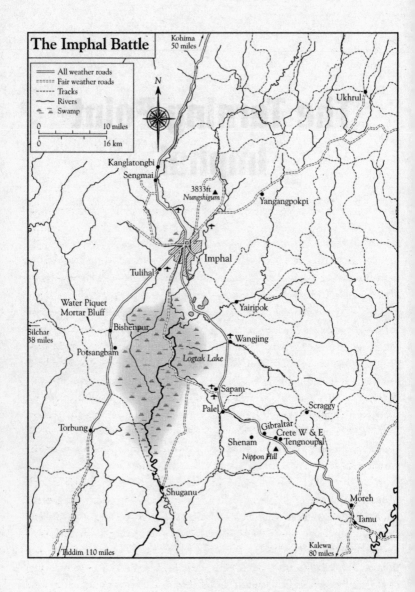

The Imphal Battle

All weather roads
Fair weather roads
Tracks
Rivers
Swamp

0   10 miles
0   16 km

N

Kohima
50 miles

Ukhrul

Kanglatongbi
Sengmai

3833ft
Nungshigum

Yangangpokpi

Imphal

Tulihal

Water Piquet
Mortar Bluff

Yairipok

Silchar
38 miles

Bishenpur

Wangjing

Potsangbam

Logtak Lake

Torbung

Sapam

Palel

Scraggy

Gibraltar
Crete W & E
Tengnoupal

Shenam

Nippon Hill

Shuganu

Moreh

Tamu

Tiddim 110 miles

Kalewa
80 miles

To my horror I saw that the barbed wire was firmly held in the ground by
big wooden stakes, it was insuperable. It seemed that every medium
machine gun in the world was opening fire on converging lines.

Imphal, the capital of Manipur State, the most eastern province of India in 1944, consisted of a small town and a group of villages on a plain about forty miles long and twenty wide, overlooked on all sides by high, jungle-clad hills. The Logtak Lake, a marshy stretch of swamp and water, lies south of the town. About twenty miles long by twelve wide, the lake's dimensions varied according to the season, wet or dry.

Beginning at the time of the retreat from Burma in 1942, Imphal became the supply base for Lieutenant General Scoones's IV Corps, and over the following two years the administrative units had mushroomed to include hospitals, fuel and ammunition dumps, workshops and airfields. Six roads radiated out from Imphal of which the three most important were: the road running for fifty miles north to Kohima; the one to Tamu and Sittaung on the River Chindwin, seventy-five miles to the south-east; and the road to Tiddim, 164 miles south of Imphal, known as the Tiddim Road, which continued beyond Tiddim for another fifty tortuous miles to Kalewa on the Chindwin.

At the start of the battle, on 15 March 1944, the most exposed British formation was the 17th Indian Light Division, which had been reorganised after the 1942 retreat with mules, ponies and jeeps replacing trucks and carriers, hence its title. Its headquarters was at Tiddim, reached by a narrow road capable of taking three-ton trucks in only one direction at a time, and winding through mountains, often with a sheer drop on one side; easily obstructed by landslides, frequently washed away by rain, and perfect for roadblocks. The 17th Division's two brigades were deployed well forward and in contact with the Japanese, as were other British formations further north along the Chindwin. The soldiers in these divisions, in fighting described at the beginning of this chapter, believed they had achieved an ascendancy over the Japanese in late 1943 and early 1944. They were, therefore, somewhat disgruntled when they learned that the plan was to withdraw to the Imphal Plain and fight the Japanese there. Slim, aware of the possible adverse effect on morale, told Scoones to withdraw only when he was satisfied beyond all reasonable doubt that a Japanese offensive was imminent.

Slim's proviso led to the withdrawal of the 17th Division being left too late. The Japanese were able to cut in behind the 17th Division and indulge in their favourite tactic of establishing roadblocks on the withdrawal route. But, whereas during the retreat in 1942, such tactics had disheartened the British and Indian soldiers, this time they fought back ferociously. They had some scores to settle with their opponents who had dealt them such a devastating blow at the Sittang Bridge two years earlier. In a series of brilliant battles the 17th Division utterly defeated the Japanese attempts to cut them off, and withdrew safely to the Imphal Plain.

The subsequent fighting at Imphal was mainly for control of the roads and tracks radiating out from the centre. Savage engagements, sometimes concurrently, sometimes following each other in succession, took place on a ninety-mile arc all round the plain; from Kanglatongbi ten miles north of Imphal Town, through the 5,833-foot twin peaks of Nungshigum, to Yainganpokpi on the Ukhrul Road, Wangjing and Tengnoupal on the Tamu–Palel Road, Shuganu south of Logtak Lake and Torbung on the Tiddim Road.

ALL QUIET ON THE CHINDWIN

Yuwaichi Fujiwara
Japanese Soldier
Wingate's Chindit first expedition changed Japanese thinking. We thought that the north Burma jungles were a defence against British advance into Burma. We now realised that they could be traversed by both sides.

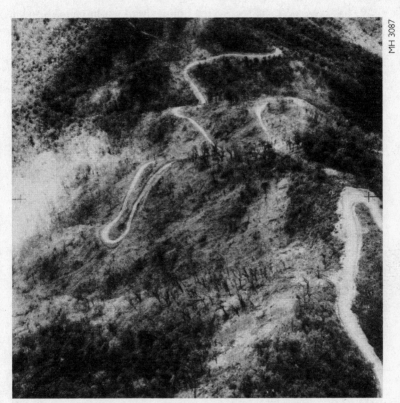

MH 3087

The Tiddim Road, possibly Milestone 109, where the Japanese attempted to cut off the 17th Indian Division during the retreat to Imphal in March 1944.

We had no intention of advancing into India, just occupy Imphal and Kohima to further the defence of Burma. But Chandra Bose and Mutaguchi wanted to invade India after occupying Imphal. There was a serious anti-British movement in India, so it was hoped that the INA would operate in Bengal to assist the rising.

We had been successful because the British always fought on roads and in motor cars. The Japanese crossed jungle and attacked the British rear. The British were not tough. The Japanese were tough.

Lieutenant Harbans Singh
Indian National Army

We were told that it was our duty to fight for India, even take our weapons from the British. We were told to say to other Indians not to fight, to come to our side. We didn't care that *Netaji* was on the side of Hitler and Mussolini. *Netaji* said, 'I have travelled the world and seen the standard of the German Army, they will win.'

Second Lieutenant Shiv Singh
Indian National Army

After being captured in Hong Kong, General Mohan Singh and Bose said you must come and fight for your own country. You are fighting for a very small sum of money indeed, now come and fight for your own country.

We volunteered without any force being used. When I heard *Netaji* in 1939, I was very impressed, and thought he was number one leader, above Gandhi.

The Japanese were cruel, but were the most nationalistic people in the world. The Japanese were not cruel to us, because Bose was our leader. There were other prominent Indians in Thailand and Japan and they influenced the Japanese to treat us well.

Lieutenant Mahesh Sharma
70th Independent Field Company, Bengal Sappers and Miners

My father was a judge in the Indian Civil Service, the ICS. My uncle had retired from ICS, and was Prime Minister of one of the independent princely states. I joined the army because all vacancies in the civil service were reserved for Indians serving in the armed services. I was a sergeant in the

University Cadet Corps, I was a science graduate, and wanted to join the Bengal Sappers and Miners.

It was not the done thing to get involved in politics, hence I was not interested in the INA. After six months of training, after two and a half years of commissioned service, two of us selected to join 70 Field Company in 1943. I was the first Indian officer in the Field Company and the only Indian officer in 48 Brigade. It was quite a shock to be holding the standard for India. I could not make a mistake. I was initially in the Sikh platoon, then in the Mussulman platoon, and finally the Hindu platoon.

One of my first experiences under fire was at the latter end of 1943; the Japanese were advancing up into the Chin Hills. One company of the 2nd/5th Royal Gurkha Rifles under Captain Crossfield was supposed to attack a feature called Basha East. I was in support, I had to blow up the bunkers after the attack so the Japanese could not use them again. So, loaded with explosives, we marched.

Unfortunately Captain Crossfield was killed instantaneously by fixed lines fire, with six of his Gurkhas. The Jemadar, the company 2i/c, was very badly wounded. So it was rather worrying. I got a 'rocket' from an officer accompanying us from brigade HQ, because brigade had ordered that a green Very light would be used to signal success in capturing the bunkers. But the Japanese must have chosen this signal for their own artillery DF.

I was also given a rocket for taking so long to blow up the bunkers. But we had not captured them. There was Captain Crossfield lying dead at my feet.

I could see the bunkers, and started towards them. The Jap mortaring started, my batman was cut in two standing beside me. Ten minutes later and the officer from Brigade HQ came running, shouting, 'Get back, get back.' So I started withdrawing. One of my sappers got hit in the tummy and died the next morning.

You can imagine what went through the mind of a young officer not experienced in war.

Anonymous INA Captain

In Singapore I was given special training by the INA in intelligence gathering, swimming and how to sketch terrain. In 1943 we were on the Chindwin River, on one side of the river were the Japanese and the INA, and on the other the British Indian Army. From January to March I was going from village to village, on the other side of the river, collecting information on the deployment of the British and Indian soldiers.

I was in a small party of about thirty people who crossed into India and we made contact with a whole company of the enemy and we had to get past this company and we decided we had the spirit to do this. We had divided into four groups, and attacked in such a way that the enemy would think that we were a large party. We attacked with bayonets and they fled leaving behind their half-cooked food. We discovered later that they were a party of engineers.

We captured thirteen prisoners and sent them back. We failed to reach the bridge, which we had been told to demolish because there were so many enemy tanks and troops. We then decided that we must discover where our troops were on the road in to India. We went to a bridge right on the border. There we were fired on. I was wounded in the head, and another behind me wounded and another killed. There was a heavy bombardment and all the bamboos caught on fire and we had to run for it.

Captain A. M. Vohra
14th/13th Frontier Force Rifles

I chose to join the army because before independence there were really few professions open to educated Indians. The ICS was top, next the army, then railways, police and so on. Most of us in university wanted to go into one of these professions. I was in the University Officer Training Corps. This did not in any way stand in the way of our desire for independence.

We came into contact with the INA. In one night harbour, I heard our telephone operator talking. He was talking to a JIF. They had got jitter parties and were putting them at the extent of the harbour defence. I talked to some JIFS who were normal soldiers who had been told by the Japs that they would be able to free India. For example I spoke to a JIF who had been a havildar clerk, and highly trained.

Lieutenant Mahesh Sharma
70th Independent Field Company, Bengal Sappers and Miners

The INA were called JIFS, I had nothing but contempt for them. The Japanese did not arm them properly, or they might have been a problem. They surrendered very quickly. The JIFs did not get involved in any fighting to speak of. Quite a lot of INA gave themselves up. They weren't popular. The Gurkhas captured one and he was sent back to brigade HQ about quarter of a mile away, and somehow he never got there. The escort said he tried to escape.

Lieutenant Peter Noakes
1st Battalion, Northamptonshire Regiment
I was put in command of the carrier platoons of Gurkha and Punjabi battalions in our brigade as brigade carrier officer based at brigade HQ. My knowledge of Urdu was primitive and of Gurkhali non-existent. But as most commands in the Indian Army, like 'Halt', or 'Fire', were in English, you could get by. The VCOs could communicate in English. In my Punjabi platoon I had three sections, one each of Sikhs, Punjabi Mussulmans and Dogras. The Gurkha platoon was all Gurkhas. Each section was commanded by a VCO.

We arrived at Dimapur in time for Christmas 1943. My battalion had gone ahead to the Kabaw Valley, with instructions to reach the Chindwin.

Shortly after Christmas Day 1943 we loaded our carriers on to trucks and we drove along the road from Dimapur to Kohima, Imphal and on to the Kabaw Valley. Eventually we got to Kabaw valley at Moreh, and were given orders, 'Put the carriers in harbour and leave a skeleton crew behind for maintenance, you and your crews will return to your units.' The Gurkhas and Punjabis returned to their battalions and I took my platoon of Northamptons on foot to the battalion near the Chindwin.

Captain George Aitchison
Officer Commanding B Company, 1st/4th Gurkha Rifles
We were in patrol contact with the Japs on the Chindwin. The 33rd Japanese Divisional HQ was at Kalewa, a really good division. But, although we shot up the Japs on tip and run raids, they were surprisingly passive. They gradually pushed out troops about thirty miles west of the Chindwin. They patrolled often dressed as Burmese. We rather stupidly thought they had no aggressive intentions.

Just twenty-two miles south of Tiddim, a small town 162 miles south of Imphal, there was a very good defensive position. Called Point 8198, because it was marked as such on the map, it was a knife-edge ridge that marked the highest point between India and Burma in this area. It was a position that everybody coveted. It broadened out sufficiently to take at least a battalion; the 1st/16th Punjabis held it.

In October 1943, I was commanding B Company at Kennedy Peak six miles from this key position. I had outlying platoons, and visiting them involved climbing up and down a total of eighteen thousand feet. One day I visited the 1st/16th Punjabis, Sikhs and Punjabi Mussulmans. They were not alert; their sentries stood about plainly in sight. Nor did they have any proper perimeter defence. An orderly called up the colonel, and he wore beautifully polished brown chaplis and a starched uniform; chaplis were totally unsuitable, he must have thought he was still on the North-West Frontier. He demanded to see my identity card. I didn't feel welcome. There was a touch of luxury about them. I was pretty scruffy, and unshaven. We had to go down thousands of feet from my position to get water. They could get it at Fort White. I looked a shaggy and undesirable chap, and trudged six miles back to Kennedy Peak.

Lieutenant Peter Noakes
1st Battalion, Northamptonshire Regiment

Orders came for an attack on a strong Japanese position at Kyaukchaw, which dominated the river Yu and its confluence with the River Chindwin. I rejoined my old rifle company, Number 4 Company, which used to be D Company; renamed on the CO's orders. The company had one too many officers. My old platoon had been taken over by Stanley Hinks. One of us had to stay behind for the attack; every company had to keep back an officer, a couple of NCOs and a few men Left Out of Battle, LOB, to provide replacements for casualties. We tossed for who should go. I won and so I was LOB in reserve with rear battalion HQ.

The attack failed. Stanley was wounded in his right shoulder, I took back command of my platoon. One day I was out patrolling the Jap position at Kyaukchaw, and came to the conclusion that the Japs had gone in the night. So I struggled ahead, and cut the wire with my wire cutters, told my men to follow me in and we found the bunkers were empty. On our left was a platoon from another company commanded by John Hopkins. There were two big bunkers and the CO called one 'Hoppy', and the other 'Noakie'. Those names stuck. We occupied the Jap position without opposition.

Captain George Aitchison
Officer Commanding B Company, 1st/4th Gurkha Rifles

Eventually the whole of my battalion joined me on Kennedy Peak and made a good defensive position.

About three am on 13 November we were woken by terrific machine-gun and mortar fire. The Japanese made a furious attack on the 1st/16th Punjabis. Next morning a bedraggled lot came through our lines, shirts hanging out of trousers, wearing what they had on when surprised in their beds: plimsolls, chaplis, some unarmed. Many of the Sikhs had lost their pugrees and their hair was all over the place. It was a dejected, defeated battalion with a deep resentment and bewilderment evident in every man. There were a lot of casualties, including the CO and four other officers killed. The entire battalion had been scattered.

Lieutenant Peter Noakes
1st Battalion, Northamptonshire Regiment

In due course we were told to withdraw from Kyaukchaw and retire to the Kabaw Valley where the 32nd Brigade was concentrating at Tamu. When we got back I was told to mobilise the carriers. I got together the Punjabis and Gurkhas and my chaps and the carriers were ready to go having been maintained, and we were detailed to go back to brigade HQ as security and guard the perimeter.

We did our patrolling in the Kabaw Valley, which has a terrible reputation for disease: typhus, malaria, dysentery, you name it. Typhus was the chief killer. We were inoculated against it. The Japs died of it in droves.

One day the brigadier said, 'I want you to go to 100 Brigade HQ commanding the 2nd Borders, the 4th/10th Gurkhas and the 4th/13th Frontier Force Rifles, you are to report to Brigadier James who feels a bit exposed on his left flank and wants protection.' So I went down there, down the one and only dirt track, and was introduced to the brigadier, sitting in his command post with maps on the wall, with a very nice bar that he had the Gurkhas build. A real old Indian Army character, he said, 'Noakes, now look here. Before we start will you pour me out a gin and French, and pour one for yourself, a decent-sized one,' which I did.

He continued, 'The Japs are advancing up the valley, I've got the Frontier Force Rifles here, the Borders are blocking the Kabaw Valley, they've had a few casualties and seem to be withdrawing. I want you to patrol down the left – east – flank here into the jungle and make sure they're not going to encircle us.'

Captain George Aitchison
Officer Commanding B Company, 1st/4th Gurkha Rifles

No counter-attack on Point 8198 took place for thirty days. It was decided that on 12 December 1943 two battalions, 1st/3rd and 1st/4th Gurkhas, would leave Kennedy Peak at 0001 hours and march the six miles to the Jap positions, the artillery would lay down a creeping barrage. Things went wrong. The barrage expended itself on nothing at all, because the Japs had contracted into a small, superbly built defensive position, which, compared with the 1st/16th Punjab treatment of the same piece of ground, was like a Fabergé egg compared with a run-of-the-mill piece of work. There was no point in a creeping barrage. The Japs were all inside this beautifully constructed position in bunkers.

The two battalions advanced side by side, the 3rd Gurkhas on the left, and the 4th on the right. The leading company of the 3rd Gurkhas found that the final fifty yards before reaching the Jap position had been cleared of jungle and ahead of them was a formidable barbed-wire obstacle five foot high and four feet across. The foliage the Japs had cleared was woven in all over it so you couldn't see the other side. The leading 3rd Gurkha company began to scramble over the wire: the company commander was killed and every man with him hit.

Our colonel said, 'We'll go right, where there's no jungle.' He shouted to me that I was to take over C Company if the company commander, Major Keeble, was hit. To my horror I saw that the barbed wire was firmly held in the ground by big wooden stakes, it was insuperable. It seemed that every medium machine gun in the world was opening fire on converging lines. Keeble was hit, but moved forward to the wire, and he was hit twice more. A couple of riflemen dragged him back, but he died of wounds.

The colonel, already wounded in the shoulder on a recce, was hit again but his binos took most of the effect. But then he too was too badly wounded to carry on. So there we were with the 3rd Gurkhas colonel dead, our colonel wounded, and up against some extremely well-sited Jap bunkers behind very strong barbed wire. Even to look at what we were attacking we had to be head and shoulders over a slight crest. That meant they could fire at us without us being able to bring a rifle to bear, let alone anything more lethal. We had wasted all our 25-pounder shells dragged nearly two hundred miles from Imphal. There seemed absolutely no answer to the Japanese bunker. Only twenty yards away ahead of me was the little hollow where the 16th Punjabis had not made me feel welcome, and now containing the strongest bunker I had ever seen, and nicknamed Gibraltar. I realised the situation was absolutely hopeless; all there was in command was me and my Jemadar. He looked at me and I looked at him. We dropped down below the crest, and from a range of not much less than twenty yards the bullets from three bunkers with interlocking machine guns cut the crest just above our heads. We lay there wondering what the hell to do next. After a while the Japs stopped firing. Two Gurkha battalions lay there and no one had any contingency plans for what to do. We lay there all day.

We waited for someone at brigade HQ to give an order. But the brigadier was miles away, standing on Kennedy Peak six miles away, unable to see quite what was going on, although there was a suggestion that came forward somehow, that the next battalion should attack at dusk. But I thought no one has been able to patrol close enough to the Jap position to see that they have got this superb position.

After about two or three hours, a Jap officer or someone started shouting. The 3rd Gurkhas thought it was instructions to mount a counter-attack. Eventually it was decided that another attack would not succeed. So we all quietly trudged back, arriving twenty-four hours later, having achieved nothing. We thought how the hell are we going to retake Burma if this is what we will face. Between the two battalions we lost about two hundred men that day.

Corporal Les Griffiths
9th Battalion, Border Regiment

Imphal was a big flat plain; from there you drove along the Tiddim Road. You could see the odd lorry down at the bottom of the ravines. The mad drivers drove with one leg under them some of the time. On the way to Tiddim you passed the Chocolate Staircase, built by bulldozers, in a series of hairpin bends. The mud was the colour of chocolate and very sticky.

I rejoined the battalion on Kennedy Peak. It was a long walk from the road.

I was shown where I was to sleep, in a hole in the ground. It was covered with tree branches covered by earth. I could see thousands of feet down and miles and miles of treetops, and in the distance the silvery sheen of the Manipur River.

Lieutenant Arthur 'Mac' McCrystal
Officer Commanding 14 Platoon, C Company, 9th Battalion, Border Regiment

When I joined the battalion it was dark. I was taken to battalion HQ and my kit was put on a jeep, and taken to C Company HQ. Officers and soldiers didn't look any different from each other. Everyone wore greatcoats because it was cold up there. The jeep stopped by the side of the road. You could see the remnants of a small fire with people sitting round. I was accosted, what was I doing here? Who was I? I recognised immediately the twang of a Prestonian. I said that I expected a better welcome from someone from Fishgate, one of the main streets of Preston. This went down quite well. I was given food and introduced to my company commander.

Many of them had been together in England and India since 1940 training and so on. Everybody knew everybody. Suddenly you arrive in the dark, in the middle of Burma. You meet a sergeant who is your platoon sergeant and you find it difficult to get to know people quickly. The best way to get to know people is to take time. There was so little time. My sergeant was Bill Stoker from Newcastle. The average age of my platoon was twenty-nine, thirty, and Sergeant Stoker was thirty-one; remarkable people, very reliable. I was only a babe of twenty. My twenty-first birthday was on Kennedy Peak; quite a gap in age.

Corporal Les Griffiths
9th Battalion, Border Regiment

We carried tins of bully beef on patrol. In that heat the fat was liquid. So you punctured the tin with your bayonet, and poured out the fat into a small hole in the ground: you didn't want to leave any signs. Having opened the top of the tin, you ate the bully beef with your spoon.

PULL BACK TO IMPHAL

Lieutenant Peter Noakes
1st Battalion, Northamptonshire Regiment

The Japs had overrun quite a number of positions of the 2nd Border, who were astride the track. We went out into the jungle and it was very close country and very difficult to manoeuvre the carriers, so I dismounted the men, left a guard on the carriers, and we patrolled on foot in various directions to see if we could find the Japs. We didn't find any, so we stayed the night out, and the next morning I said, 'Right, we are going back to brigade HQ, there are no Japs here'. We had no wireless or any other communication. I had no communication between my carrier and the others, very primitive.

When I got to brigade HQ they'd gone. They had disappeared in the night. I think the brigadier realised he was in a very vulnerable position and had withdrawn his remaining troops and the remnants of the Borders through 32 Brigade. I said, 'We're here on our own, better go home.' So we drove back to our own brigade HQ.

A patrol from the Punjabis came in. They had ambushed a party of Japs and inflicted quite a few casualties, and the Indian officer in charge of this platoon-sized patrol reported that the Japs were advancing in strength with armour, which we hadn't come across in Burma before.

One night we stood to and heard the rattle of tracks down the track. By this time the brigade box had been reinforced by a section of 6-pounder anti-tank guns, and a troop of Bofors AA Guns, ready to fire over open sights at any advancing force. The Japs advanced up a dusty track, tanks with infantry support.

The Japanese tanks arrived. The commander of the box was the CO of the 9th/14th Punjabis, Lieutenant Colonel Booth. He gave orders that when he fired a Very pistol we could open fire. When they came right up to us, we opened up with everything we had. The anti-tank guns knocked out two tanks, the Bofors did the same. The Japanese infantry were engaged by my men with Bren guns, the attack failed. At daybreak we counted the bodies and tanks, and thought we had done well.

Captain John Randle
Adjutant, 7th/10th Baluch Regiment

We had no warning of the Jap offensive. The battalion HQ was at Saizang. When we were ordered to pull out of the Chin Hills we thought why the hell have we gone to all this trouble to build these good defensive positions, the Chocolate Staircase, and the road? We were rather annoyed. We were given a couple of days' warning to withdraw to Imphal. We pulled out of Saizang and harboured up in Tiddim. The battalion was sent to Tonzang where the CO commanded an ad hoc force called Tonforce. Our task was to provide a lay-back position through which the division could retire.

Lieutenant Arthur 'Mac' McCrystal
Officer Commanding 14 Platoon, C Company, 9th Battalion, Border Regiment

When the Japs attacked they cut across the main route into Imphal. For one hundred or so miles there were attacks coming in from the crack Japanese 33 Division. There were a number of positions along the route where there were supplies. We had supply drops as we withdrew. A battalion of Japs would attack and block the road. To break it troops would probe forward; there might be only twenty Japs, there might be a whole battalion. Having got rid of the block, fresh troops would go through you to the next block. At certain points where the terrain allowed you would create a box. Into the box would come the wounded, the animals. Sometimes you might be providing a perimeter guard on the box, or with your own company form part of an operation dislodging the next roadblock.

Captain George Aitchison
Officer Commanding B Company, 1st/4th Gurkha Rifles

Starting 8 March 1944, the Japs got in behind us and dug in on high ground. We were up against the 33rd White Tiger Division who advanced up the Tiddim Road. We had retreated in the face of 33 Division, and had formed a defensive position. We had our barbed wire about ten yards out in front. My CO didn't like this and wanted a greater field of fire. I said there was no advantage in doing so because the Japs will get up close and use good field craft to get through the wire at night, and you won't see them. He was not happy.

At last light I was told to get out, take the whole company, and move up on to Tuitum Ridge about two thousand feet higher than where we were and behind us. So in pitch darkness we managed to get up and at about midnight we met the 2i/c of the 10th Gurkhas.

Lieutenant Peter Noakes
1st Battalion, Northamptonshire Regiment
Things were not going all that well elsewhere in the Chin Hills. 32 Brigade HQ was rather exposed in the Kabaw Valley. The Brigade Commander, David McKenzie, told me to take a scouting party to the east of the valley and see if there was any Jap penetration there. We came across some open, very dry paddy fields. The bunds had been knocked down and made into a landing strip. And lo and behold a flight of Hurricanes landed. I drove over in my carrier, and the flight commander jumped out and said, 'Hello old chap. Everything all right?'

'What are you doing here?' I asked.

'I'm on a recce, where are the enemy?'

'About half a mile down the road,' I replied.

'Oh my God,' he said, 'this is no good.'

'I suggest you do a bunk. We'll protect you as you go off,' I answered.

We went back to brigade HQ and had orders to withdraw to Wangjing, outside Imphal. 32 Brigade used my carriers as rearguard, and the move went without incident, except losing a Punjabi carrier that conked out under Japanese shellfire. We abandoned it, pushed it over the hillside. There was no close contact with the enemy. We halted for a few days at Palel, and the battalion sent out patrols into the Naga Hills to see if the Japs were coming that way, and we finished up at Wangjing.

Lieutenant Junichi Misana
33rd Mountain Artillery Regiment, 33rd Japanese Division
Luckily, we were able to take the territory right in front of the enemy base. So we positioned a cannon one hundred metres away in front of the enemy. We would lie low, and dug a hole all night, and put the cannon in the hole. Then at dawn, we started attacking, and we were shooting at each other.

Captain George Aitchison
Officer Commanding B Company, 1st/4th Gurkha Rifles

Major Fairgrieve, 2i/c of the 10th Gurkhas, said, 'The Japanese have taken retaken Tuitum Ridge, a beautifully-sited position: from there they can dominate the whole of the valley for five or six miles as the road snakes down and crosses the Kaphi Lui River.' He continued, 'If they can augment their men with artillery we are going to be in a very difficult position. We will attack at dawn, you will do a left hook with B Company, and reach the crest to the left of the Jap position, and I will take both the other companies frontally. The Japs are using grenade dischargers.'

He added, 'The road is only one hundred yards to your left. On it there are piles of corrugated iron sheets. Get your men to take the sheets, get them to cut some sticks with their kukris, rest the iron sheets on the sticks, and that will give you cover from the Japanese grenades.'

The Jap grenade was a poor weapon, when it exploded it hit people with tiny fragments and did little damage. We did this and nobody was hit at all; although the Japs were lobbing grenades in showers.

Next morning, when we reached the crest, we were hit by Jap artillery fire. My orderly's cousin got a shell all to himself, he looked as though he had been run over by a large lorry. The ridge was very thinly held, which astounded me because it controlled miles of road. We had no difficulty winkling out the Japs. They had some small two-man bunkers that were easily taken out with grenades. We captured and held the whole ridge with three rifle companies.

We planted some anti-tank mines. The next morning the six light Jap tanks appeared. The first one hit a mine and blew up, the rest were hit by PIATs. The whole of the brigade managed to move over the Kaphi Lui Bridge without any casualties.

Lieutenant Junichi Misana
33rd Mountain Artillery Regiment, 33rd Japanese Division

We went after them and pursued them, but I got injured. You could hear the sound 'pyoo pyoo pyoo pyoo'. So I ducked down on the ground, and then the cannonball dropped somewhere in the back, and it got my leg. My right leg was injured, and my thighs too. And my toes, and my right first toe was wounded deeply and my toes were cut off. And there was a small one in my hip too.

Captain John Randle
Adjutant, 7th/10th Baluch Regiment

The Japs attacked at Tonzang at dawn, and overran one company, the company commander was wounded and we lost two good VCOs and a lot of soldiers. Another company was attacked in a half-hearted way by the INA. Our chaps jeered at them, 'We've come here to fight proper soldiers, not a lot of yellow deserters like you.'

Major Ian Lyall-Grant
Officer Commanding 70 Independent Field Company, Bengal Sappers and Miners

The Japanese thought by blocking the road back to Imphal, we would abandon our vehicles and guns and stream back to Imphal where they would defeat us, as we would have no weapons or equipment.

At the first big block at Sakawng there was a dramatic atmosphere at brigade HQ, where I was for a time, as the brigadier liked to have a sapper officer close by. We had never so far fought our way out of a Japanese block that had been there for some time. The brigadier was cool and cheerful as a cricket, and he asked one of the officers to sing a song, which he did. And we sat round the fire as plans were made for the next day.

Lieutenant M. Martin
Officer Commanding D Company, 2nd/5th Royal Gurkha Rifles

I set off at 0230, ahead of me was the reconnaissance platoon. C Company and battalion HQ followed. The terrain was abominable. There was no track, we heaved ourselves up steep slopes tree by tree.

Eventually we hit the unmetalled road to Imphal, on the other side was an earth cliff about fifteen feet high, and above that the Japanese. We and the recce platoon dumped packs and shovels and made ready to attack. The only way up this cliff was to make a ladder with bayonets and kukris. To our astonishment we took the Japanese by surprise. Our attack roared in and the Japanese fled, leaving five dead and lots of equipment.

Major Ian Lyall-Grant
Officer Commanding 70 Independent Field Company, Bengal Sappers and Miners

At six o'clock the mountain guns in support opened up. Then the Gurkhas attacked up the hill; they discovered that there was a gap between two Jap positions. One battalion went each side, followed by the brigadier. Our job was to dig a path up the hill so the mules could get up with ammunition. This took a couple of hours. The Gurkhas attacked, it was only about two hundred and fifty yards away. There was a tremendous rattle of automatic fire.

Lieutenant M. Martin
Officer Commanding D Company, 2nd/5th Royal Gurkha Rifles

The moment we started trying to exploit our success, we were subjected to sustained and accurate fire from medium and light machine guns, and mortars. I told the men to dig in. We had left our packs and shovels and scratched and scraped with kukris and entrenching tools. Our casualties that had been light to start with, seven killed and wounded, rose in a short space of time to thirty.

C Company passed through but their attacks failed on each occasion. The company commander and two VCOs were killed, and the adjutant sent up to take command was badly wounded.

Major Ian Lyall-Grant
Officer Commanding 70 Independent Field Company, Bengal Sappers and Miners

Then Colonel Hedley came back, a rather serious officer, known as 'Deadly Hedley', commanding the 5th Gurkhas, a very fine soldier. For once he looked a little bit excited, and I thought there is a trace of emotion showing. He said, 'Can I have all the guns and all the mortars for another five minutes?' He then sent a platoon round the back of the Japanese, followed by more firing, shouting and dead silence.

I went to see what had happened. There were two circles of Japanese, about twenty-five in each circle, about thirty yards apart, every one was dead. Two of the Japanese seemed to have blown themselves open with grenades, but everyone was dead. This was a change, our infantry had outfought the Japanese for the first time in a set-piece battle.

Lieutenant M. Martin
Officer Commanding D Company, 2nd/5th Royal Gurkha Rifles
We had no food until a patrol found a lorry on the road containing tins of pilchards in tomato sauce – not my favourite food. The wounded suffered greatly, we had to keep them overnight in a collecting post. If hit in the stomach, their chances of surviving were nil. The battalion lost thirty-seven killed and sixty-seven wounded.

Captain George Aitchison
Officer Commanding B Company, 1st/4th Gurkha Rifles
We leapfrogged our brigade over the other brigade, winkling out Japs astride or dominating the road, and it took us from 8 March to 10 April to get to Imphal. We dug in at Bishenpur. Behind us was an enormous supply depot, with three dry-season airstrips and one all-weather strip. It was crucial that the Japs should not take these strips or supply dumps.

THE SIEGE

Trooper Malcolm Connolly
7 Troop, C Squadron, 3rd Carabiniers
Imphal was beautiful, lush and green and surrounded by mountains. The regiment dispersed and squadrons were deployed round Imphal. In Burma we often fought in half squadrons of eight tanks, sometimes in a troop of four, and even as individual tanks. My squadron remained north of Imphal. Each squadron formed a box with infantry. We were in Lion Box and Oyster Box. Each night you went back into the box.

My squadron had the job of patrolling the Imphal–Dimapur Road. We knew the Japs were coming, but we didn't know when. Our job was to keep this road open up to the control post operated by the military police between Dimapur and Kohima. All of a sudden there was no traffic. We realised the Japs had arrived and we returned to Imphal. As we turned round, an MP came out of the jungle, still with his red cap on. We opened the door in the side of the tank and dragged him in. We took him back to Kanglatongbi, a huge ordnance supply base, manned by Indian non-combatants and various service arms. The MP never told us what had happened. When we got back to the squadron there was big flap on. We knew the Jap was somewhere in the vicinity, but where and in what numbers we hadn't a clue.

Flight Lieutenant Owen Parry
11 *Squadron*, RAF

My first operations were flying a Hurricane Mk IIC at Imphal. The weather was always a major hazard, monsoon or no.

The Imphal Plain was 2,500 feet high surrounded by mountains rising to around seven thousand feet. Clouds developed every afternoon, and cumulus especially fast. When returning from a sortie we sometimes found it difficult to out-climb the cloud, as we did not have enough fuel left to keep climbing at full power for long enough. There was a tendency to try to find a way through the mountains below the cloud.

On one occasion we were on a squadron 'effort' south of Imphal, in two flights, not in the monsoon. The CO was leading the first flight of five aircraft, and I the second of six, spaced five minutes apart. We were returning from the strike along a narrow valley leading to Imphal. The clouds were across the top of the valley and over Imphal itself, like a lid on a basin. We were below cloud height, which was well down the slopes of the mountains on each side. Suddenly we ran into a severe rain shower, like a curtain ahead. The CO carried out the correct action, put his aircraft into line astern and climbed up through the cloud heading for the top of the cloud over Imphal, hoping to find a hole through which to descend. He gave me fair warning what he was doing over the radio. When I came to the rain barrier, I decided I wouldn't climb up through it, instead I gathered my aircraft into close formation and went through the rain below the cloud. I reckoned that it was only an isolated shower, and not very deep, and if I held my course between the two mountain walls, I would come out into a clear spot. I did after a couple of minutes. Unfortunately three of the aircraft in the CO's flight were lost, either because of excessive turbulence in the cloud, or the inexperience of the pilots. Only the CO and the most experienced pilot got through. Yet he had done the right thing, I hadn't.

Our Hurricanes were fitted with four 20-mm cannon, and our main tasks were ground strafing and escorting the Dakotas. Later the escort work diminished, and we were mainly used on strafing. At about the same time, we were fitted with bomb racks and became Hurribombers for army support, carrying two 250-pound bombs.

Owen Parry as a squadron leader after the war.

Private Peter Hazelhurst
Commando Platoon, 9th Battalion, The Border Regiment

The Commando Platoon was commanded by a lieutenant and the sergeant was an ex-gamekeeper. A lot of the platoon were poachers or employees of large landed estates. The first week we were at Imphal we were alongside 3rd Carabiniers, and they had wirelesses in their tanks. We heard Tokyo Rose, she was saying how they had wiped out the 17th Indian Division the 'Black Cats', and how they had finished what they had started in 1942.

It was a very personal war. We did it better than the Japs. They would dig a pit in the track with pangyis in the bottom. On each side would be another pit to catch you if you walked round the pit in the middle. They would smear excrement on the pangyis. So we did that too, and put them in front of our positions. They would booby trap their wounded.

Trooper Malcolm Connolly
7 Troop, C Squadron, 3rd Carabiniers

On 13 April 1944, Lion Box round the big ordnance supply base at Kanglatongbi was attacked, and held for three days and nights, defended by the non-combatants and an Indian battalion. We were sent with the 1st West Yorkshires to evacuate the Indian non-combatants. Number 7 Troop was in reserve initially, but eventually summoned forward and the place was ablaze. The Jap guns were firing down from the tops of the mountains. Jap soldiers came so close we couldn't depress the guns to engage them. We relied on the infantry lads to keep them off the tanks.

Corporal Arthur Freer
Squadron Leader's driver/operator, B Squadron, 3rd Carabiniers

We had a battle on 13 April to remove the Japs from Nunshigum, a hill about one thousand feet above the plain, with two false peaks and one main peak.

The whole of B Squadron was involved. Two troops were to mount the ridge, climbing from two different places. Half of B Squadron HQ and the squadron leader would go up as well. The squadron leader, Major Sandford, was twenty-seven years old, the 37-mm gunner was 'Sherley' Holmes, after Sherlock Holmes, the loader was Joe Nussey, I was the driver/operator, the driver was Paddy Ryan, a London bus driver, the 75-mm gunner Ginger Whitely, plus the 75-mm gun loader, whose name I can't remember.

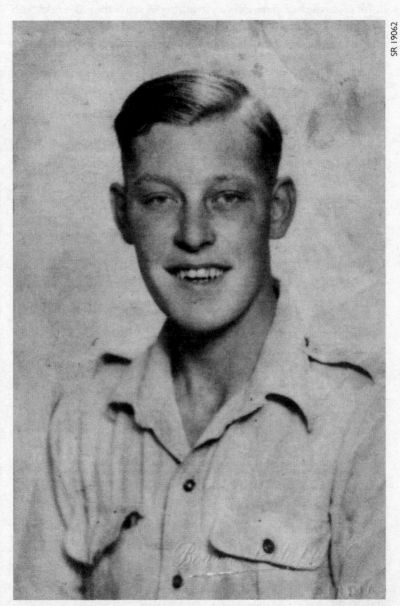
Private Peter Hazelhurst.

We got to the foot of the hill very soon, driving across the paddy fields with infantry walking on either side, two companies of the 1st Dogras: A Company up the left-hand spur and B Company up the right-hand spur, each with a troop of tanks. The squadron leader's tank and the squadron sergeant major's tank went up the left-hand spur. A sapper officer guided the tanks to the position to start climbing; it suddenly became very steep. He walked ahead of the tanks giving signals to the drivers who couldn't see very much. He walked backwards looking over his shoulder guiding the tanks till the Japs saw him and started firing. This told us where they were. We fired a few rounds and we thought they had run away.

As we got closer some of them ran out of the bunkers, and ran up to the sides of the tanks carrying sticky bombs attached to a bamboo rod, they stuck the bomb on the side of the tank and as they ran off they pulled the pin and the theory was it would blow the tank to pieces. We managed to deter them from sticking them on by firing machine guns along the side of the tank, one tank covering another. I fired the front Browning which could not traverse but only elevate or depress. If I could have traversed it I could have killed a lot more Japanese.

Over the squadron net we started hearing of people being killed, 'number nine hit in head'. They were the tank commanders with their heads out of the turret looking for the way forward. As they instructed the drivers over the intercom, they were firing their pistols and throwing grenades at the Japanese. They were exposed to rifle fire and were shot in the head. I heard a thump at the side of me, and called up to Sherley Holmes, 'What's happened?' He said, 'Dizzy's been hit in the head,' the nickname for our squadron leader. I looked into the turret, my head was on the level of the feet of anyone standing in the turret, and I could see the squadron leader lying down on the floor. I asked, 'How badly is he hurt?' Sherley Holmes said, 'It's gone into his head, and he won't survive.' I passed two morphine tubes back and Sherley injected him with both in case he was in pain.

Paddy Ryan was still driving forward and by now we were in the lead. We had left this bunker, still occupied by Japs. He was asking the gunner on his right, 'Can you see the bunker in front, have a go at it?' We had no tank commander now. I told Sherley Holmes to close the lid, we didn't want any grenades in the tank. The gunner fired a few rounds, I fired my machine gun at them. We went right over the top of the bunker.

I told them to stop: we must report what was happening, I reported to the CO on the radio that number nine was hit. He said, 'What do you mean by number nine?'

I said, 'Our number nine.'

He asked, 'Is he alive?'

I said, 'He's still got a pulse, but he's not in pain.'

He told us to try to get down. We could hear the reports over the radio of the others being killed. So Paddy Ryan went over the peak, and down to the far tip, and it was a sheer drop. So I told him to reverse. I told Sherley to turn the turret round and guide him back. He had forgotten the tank was going back and saying, 'Left a bit, left a bit,' when he meant right a bit. The tank ended up on the ridge, rocking on its tracks with a sheer drop in front and behind. Paddy Ryan, a brilliant driver, put enough power on each track to get back on the ridge, and we moved back past the other tanks. We got away and got down. By that time all the officers were killed, and four men who had replaced the tank commanders. The squadron sergeant major was left in charge.

There was a subedar major commanding the Dogras; all their officers were casualties as well. So Squadron Sergeant Major Craddock was left with the job of finishing the battle, which he did very efficiently. The tanks fired into the bunker slits, and we learned afterwards that there were about two hundred and fifty Japanese bodies found later that afternoon when the position was taken.

Trooper Malcolm Connolly
7 Troop, C Squadron, 3rd Carabiniers

We were green, and suddenly in the fray with one of the most efficient armies in the world. We were pulled on to the side of the road, and I opened my driver's hatch, and saw the infantry, who had been digging in, run like the hammers. Enemy artillery fire came down. A shell hit the right-hand sponson. Someone shouted, 'Get out of here.' I engaged reverse and backed out of it. The gunner got out to look and about six track connectors had been blown out. I knew we couldn't go very far, the troop leader had gone off somewhere, so I said to the wireless operator, 'Tell squadron we've got, to get out.'

The squadron leader, Dimsdale, didn't trust us, and came to look. He said, 'Get out of here as fast as you can.'

We laid the track out, and the LAD appeared in a scout car and we repaired the track in about twenty minutes. Meanwhile thousands of non-combatants poured out of the depot.

Corporal Arthur Freer
Squadron Leader's driver/operator, B Squadron, 3rd Carabiniers

The squadron leader was hit by a bullet under the chin, it came out of the top of his steel helmet. Under his body we found a grenade, which he had been about to throw, without a handle. We had had it in the tank with us amongst all that ammo, 120 rounds of HE, and couldn't understand why it hadn't exploded. Paddy Ryan started to unscrew the base plate to look inside. I told him to get outside the tank while he did it. So he walked off into the paddy, took the base plate off, the cap had been struck, and the fuse burnt all the way round to the detonator, and burnt out. Fortunately for us it was a dud fuse.

We left two tanks up on the mountain, one which had slipped down the ridge, and another one – both recovered. The only casualties were to tank commanders or men who took over. One tank lost three men. At the time I thought why did they stick their heads out? The reason was because the drivers couldn't see where they were going, the slope was so steep that the tank was up at an angle.

From my position in the tank I could look through a porthole on the left-hand side, about three by four inches, by raising the plate, which I didn't do. I also had a periscope to aim the Browning. The Japanese on Nunshigum were not little chaps, as we had been told, they were strapping big six-footers, formidable foes.

My first reaction on coming down was relief; instead of the rattling of rounds hitting the armour on the side of the tank, and noise of the guns going off, it was quiet. The Lee-Grant tank was a superb tank in these conditions, with tremendous fire power. The only weakness was that being a riveted tank, if a shell blew off the head of the rivet, it could fly off inside the tank and kill or wound the crew. I had friends killed in this way. We were using the tanks as mobile artillery pieces.

That night Colonel Younger came round to our tank, bubbling with the success. Although he had lost some of his bright young men, he looked upon this as one of the risks of war. I was new to it. He had fought with the 7th Hussars in North Africa and in Burma in the retreat. I wrote in my diary 'I have had my first taste of action and I don't like it'. The others felt the same. But from then on everything was better. The next day we had a lot of work cleaning up the tanks, and cleaning and oiling guns, and replenishment of ammunition. The tracks were clogged with bits of Japanese uniforms, bones and bits of meat.

Trooper Malcolm Connolly
7 Troop, C Squadron, 3rd Carabiniers

We returned to the box and were ordered to rejoin the squadron on the perimeter. Next day the RAF attacked the perimeter of the box, causing a lot of casualties to our own side. We were then moved to defensive positions at Sengmai. Our job was to hold there and ensure that the Japs did not get closer to Imphal.

On a sortie, we ran straight into three Jap 47-mm anti-tank guns. The troop sergeant in front had his tracks blown off and his gunner killed. They were a sitting target, unable to move. We came up: the troop leader, and troop corporal. The troop corporal realised that he'd better scarper, which he did, which left me in the troop leader's tank; we took the full brunt of three guns, at a hundred yards. They put out of action all our guns except one machine gun. One 47 projectile came through our 37-mm gun periscope, and lifted the scalp right off the gunner's head. You could see his brains, but it didn't kill him. A round came through and knocked the 75-mm gun's actuating shaft out, which took the back off my seat. So we had a 75-mm gun with a 47-mm AP projectile stuck in it. That gun was useless. The 37 gunner above was mortally wounded. They had hit the armour on the outside and pin-punched the two sides of armour together, jamming the 37 gun. When we got out we counted that we had been hit nine times, penetrating the tank five times. It was an act of God that we got away with it. My troop officer was in a panic. I shouted into my mike, 'For God's sake get us out of here.'

Fortunately the infantry, the West Yorks, were fighting hand-to-hand with Japs surrounding us trying to get at us. If you ever go to war, go with a Yorkshireman.

We were told to return to Oyster Box. We took out our wounded, and they were bringing out West Yorkshires by the drove. We turned round and beat it for Imphal. The battle was at its height. Tanks could not be replaced. The tanks we had had to see us through. The REME chaps said the tank was

A Lee-Grant tank of the 3rd Carabiniers supporting the 1st Battalion the West Yorkshire Regiment at Imphal.

beyond repair. She was called Clacton, because all C Squadron tanks had names beginning with C. They were bringing in tanks from other battles and there were some tanks there that had engines destroyed and not their guns, and others guns destroyed and not their engines; they cannibalised one to make another. They replaced our guns from a tank with a destroyed engine at Nungshigum. Some tanks still had dead in them. We were there for a week. They repaired the holes. Lucky the shells were AP solid shot, not AP/HE which would have penetrated and then exploded. We lived to fight another day.

Flight Lieutenant Owen Parry
11 *Squadron, RAF*

As well as being on hand to support the army, we harassed the Japanese line of communication doing low-level 'rhubarbs' by day and night. Strafing was dangerous at night. It was OK flying over the road with one's canopy open looking over the side for vehicles on the road, but once you closed the canopy to attack, and dived in at low-level head-on, the thick bullet-proof windscreen reduced visibility considerably. As soon as you fired your cannon, you were temporarily blinded by the muzzle flashes. There was a grave danger of flying straight into the ground, and we lost a number of pilots on night operations.

Night operations were very fruitful, even when we didn't destroy trucks, because the presence of aircraft slowed down the progress of Japanese road convoys. When we came overhead they would usually park. Furthermore, once you spotted a road convoy and reported its location, the chaps going out at dawn would be able to work out where it had laid up for the day – they hardly ever risked moving by day.

On one occasion, I was out on an intruder raid armed with bombs, and saw a large Jap convoy on a road crossing an open plain – a good place to attack. I dropped one bomb on the road ahead of the convoy, hoping this would be difficult to get round, and another behind them. I kept a patrol over the area, until another intruder pilot arrived. I told him where I was, and he took over the standing patrol until dawn, when more aircraft appeared and dealt with the convoy. Some Japs got away, but most were caught.

Private Peter Hazelhurst
Commando Platoon, 9th Battalion, Border Regiment

We had only been at Imphal for about two weeks when I got wounded on Black Ridge at Palel, the Commando Platoon was with the Gurkha Commando Platoon. We had to stop the Japs from getting the airfield. We went up one side and were to stop the enemy escaping, while the battalion attacked on the other side. I was in a hole with two others, and I saw a Jap, the sergeant said, 'Shoot him,' but he threw a grenade first. I threw myself sideways out of the hole as did the other lads. But the sergeant threw himself in the bottom, and the grenade landed on him; he copped it. Things went hazy after that. I got shrapnel in my back and in my leg. A kid called Fisher got a big piece in his ankle. I managed to get round to where the rest of the platoon were. I was put on a stretcher between two mules. One in the front and one behind. One was nibbling your ear hole and the other defecating over your feet. At the bottom of the hill was the American ambulance, conscientious objectors. They were fantastic, the bravest people you could wish to meet.

Private Ray Dunn
1st Battalion, Devonshire Regiment

My first experience of facing the Japs was on Crete East when Japs put in a night attack. On some features we fought on, we did not have wire or mines. The majority of Jap attacks were night attacks. The first thing you were aware of was when the Japs were almost on us, well within grenade-throwing distance.

On occasions on Crete East the fighting was hand-to-hand. On one night Japs got to within ten yards of our bunker. I woke up to shouting and firing, from another man in our bunker, followed by the Brens and tommy guns firing, and 3-inch mortars. I was the 'bomber', with a grenade-projector on my rifle. The others got out their grenades. We also used phosphorus grenades. The bunker I was in exploded. They were roofed over with timber and earth. The other two men were very badly wounded. Our rifles were on the floor, under earth. The firing stopped and I didn't know if the Japs had taken the position. But we held it. It was a long night. I wasn't sure whether to stay there or not, or get off and be bayoneted to death. I knew the Japs bayoneted the wounded, and I didn't want to leave them. My best friends were in the other side of the bunker, and one was killed, the other severely wounded. This was the first time I had been under attack. I was ill-prepared for the ferocity of the Jap attacks. We had been told to fight to the last man and last round. The OC eventually gave the order to what was left of us to evacuate the position, contrary to what we had been told. The CO was not best pleased. But if this order had not been given, I would not be here today.

Corporal Stanley May
Stretcher-Bearer, 1st Battalion, Devonshire Regiment

Nippon Hill was at right angles to the Shenam Saddle. The Japs had taken Nippon Hill. We had orders to take it. It was a tough nut to crack, with steep sides and very little cover because it was rocky.

The road was so steep that at Dead Mule Gulch there was a two-way track. Nippon Hill was in advance of that. That morning we established the RAP in Dead Mule Gulch. D company and B Company went down the valley bottom and climbed up the north face of Nippon Hill, C Company went on the other side. We had the Commando Platoon in carriers. Our mortars put smoke rounds on top of the hill, then three Hurribombers came in and dropped 250-pound bombs and raked the hill with cannon fire, meanwhile the men were advancing up the slopes. When the Hurris moved off, the artillery opened up. During the final assault, the Commando Platoon with carriers belted in, and by 1200 the battalion was on top. The Japs were in deep bunkers. The CO had carrier-loads of barbed wire rushed up and he wired the hill all round, leaving gaps where tracks were. He put a fresh company, A, up there and withdrew the others. Japs attacked and came through gaps in the wire. In the morning there were forty or so hanging on the wire.

Private William Savage
1st Battalion, Devonshire Regiment

We left our positions at 0900 hours for the march to Nippon Hill. The hill was in stark contrast to everything else around. It was brown and stripped of vegetation. We felt apprehensive, as it was pretty certain someone was going to get hurt. The attack started with three Hurricanes coming over to drop two bombs each on the hill, followed by strafing. This was the signal for us to be on our way. We were making quite good progress. Mortar bombs were dropping round us. There was a huge bang, and I was disorientated, hit by

Soldiers of the 1st Battalion the Devonshire Regiment after capturing Nippon Hill at Imphal. L-R: Private Williams, Corporal Treasure, Private Willoughby (shaving), and Lance-Corporal Willis.

shrapnel on my left leg, breaking it. Our orders were that no one was to stop to assist the wounded. Lieutenant Atkinson, my platoon commander, just stopped and asked if I was all right. I said, 'Yes.' He pushed on.

My next thought was to get back on the track where I might get some help. I had to push myself down a gully and on to the track. I was worried that our own troops following up behind us would shoot me by mistake when I put my head above the ridge. I made my way down the track using my rifle as a crutch, and got patched up at the RAP.

Corporal Stanley May
Stretcher-Bearer, 1st Battalion, Devonshire Regiment

I stayed in the gulch all night as more wounded came in. We had thirty-one killed, and eight officer casualties – four killed and four wounded – and over a hundred wounded in the gulch. We cleared the gulch by late afternoon.

They brought Sergeant Major Jimmy Garvey of D Company into us, dying, he charged in front of the men with a bayonet. He said, 'Don't waste time on me.'

We went back to the Shenam the next day, and the Frontier Force Rifles were driven off Nippon Hill. Our CO named the crests of the hills, Scraggy and Gibraltar.

Private William Palmer
6 Platoon, B Company, 1st Battalion, Devonshire Regiment

On one of the attacks on Crete East, the Japs attacked in daytime, and I could see one of them carrying a flag attached to his bayonet. Three or four of us shot at him. Every one of us claimed him. We decided that the one that got to him first would claim the flag. When the fighting died down, I went over the top and collected the flag off the Jap. I had to go about twenty yards. I got roasted by my platoon commander for going.

Major Dinesh Chandra Misra
Second-in-Command, 5th/6th Rajputana Rifles

The Japanese had outflanked and penetrated a place we called Lone Tree Hill, and there were no troops between divisional HQ and the hill. The CO sent for me and said, 'I will take two companies and you stay in the rear.' I asked him to let me take the two companies. He let me take them. I chose a frontal attack, I thought speed was of the utmost importance, as the Japs were in the middle of preparing positions. We got to within thirty yards of the objective and were grenaded back. We withdrew, took up a defensive position, and spent all night there.

Next morning, the RAF liaison officer arrived and asked what he could do to help. We were so close to the target that any shorts from artillery would drop on us. During the shelling the Japs would withdraw on to the reverse slope, and come back when the artillery stopped. I said to the RAF LO, 'You bring in strikes from north–south. When your aircraft are flying north to south, drop bombs but then don't let them go away. Turn round and attack in dummy runs while we advance.'

During the dummy runs, we got on to the top without any firing. I told the company commanders to get their LMGs out in front, facing the direction that the enemy would come from. After about ten minutes, the Japs appeared chatting away. We let them come within thirty yards and opened up with everything. They dropped like flies. The survivors withdrew. I replenished with ammunition, got everything ready.

By then it was getting dark. I told the company commanders, 'Expect a counter-attack about two hours after dark. It's 4.15 now and they will come at seven o'clock.' And sure enough it came at that time. Everything opened up. We had taken a few casualties.

I knew that in the early morning there would be a final counter-attack. It came and in the hand-to-hand fighting we had casualties. I felt detached, but hatred for the Japanese, and determined to kill them; I became a demon. I was swearing and screaming. We were shouting our battle cries, and the Japs shouting 'Banzai', the officers had swords. We fought with bayonets. I had a Sten gun. The Japs withdrew and I knew we had won. There was a tremendous feeling of joy and relief. In daylight we counted one hundred and fifty Jap dead. The hill is now known as Rajputana Hill. In battle you reach an extreme state of hatred, but it goes away. You feel sad. How insane war is, but if you don't kill the enemy, he will kill you.

Pilot Officer Roger Cobley
20 Squadron, RAF

At Palel airstrip, the Japs attacked one night, and some of them holed up around a hillock near the airfield, and come daylight the Gurkhas sorted them out. We had the RAF Regiment to defend us but they were not very effective when it came to counter-attacking.

Sergeant Douglas Williams
Wireless Operator, 194 Squadron, RAF

We flew a load of bombs into Palel for the Hurribombers. This was followed by evacuating the RAF ground crew of one of the Hurricane squadrons. Having loaded up, started a normal take-off and about to get airborne, a cross-wind gusted, the wing dipped dangerously, the pilot thumped the throttles back, but both oleo legs collapsed. Everyone got out OK, but sitting on the ground we were very shaken. Our beloved C Charlie was now a write-off – it was like losing our home. We felt insecure and lost. Having to fly other Dakotas as and when they were available was not the same.

Lieutenant Mahesh Sharma
70th Independent Field Company, Bengal Sappers and Miners

At the Torbung block, I was ordered to go as soon as it was dusk and lay some mines on the road; we had heard some Jap tanks. As soon as it became dusk we moved on to the road in a defile. We were ambushed, and lost two mules with mines on their backs. But we picked up the mines and went on. We laid the mines, were coming back about one or two o'clock in the morning, and on the way back, there was a river crossed by a bamboo trestle bridge, one bamboo wide which crossed by shuffling across. All in the day's work. Coming back I thought it prudent to stop by the riverbank to see if the Japs were about, before crossing. One of my sappers asked my permission to move away to answer a call of nature. I told him to do it here. But out of respect he wouldn't and moved about six feet away. There was a big bang and he started screaming.

You are in unknown territory. How did that mine or booby trap get there? The Japs must have been setting booby traps for us. The morphine didn't work. So I rushed back across the bridge and reported to the company commander. I had hid the man under a bush, and asked for a stretcher. I went back with four fresh men and recovered him, it was difficult to cross the single bamboo bridge. His leg was horrible, the knee was there, but his foot was held on by skin, but no bone. He died in the morning.

Flight Lieutenant Owen Parry
11 Squadron, RAF

The Japs were very good at camouflage. About an hour before dawn they would pull off the road under the trees on the sides. If there was insufficient

A Hurribomber attacking a bridge on the Tiddim Road.

cover, they would cover their vehicles with branches cut from further in. After a while we realised that the vegetation by the road was light coloured because of the covering of dust, whereas the branches brought from some way in was dark green. So we flew along the road looking for what looked like new growth, standing out fresh green against the khaki-coloured vegetation.

The Japs also took advantage of areas used by our army during the retreat of 1942, where we had set up refuelling points at intervals along the main road. Here vehicles had collected and been struck by the Japanese air force, or perhaps had been immobilised and abandoned. From time to time the Japs artfully parked some of their own vehicles among these trucks during the day. So we learned the pattern of the layout of these parks, and were able to spot when new trucks had been popped in. It used to annoy new pilots when they excitedly reported a concentration of vehicles, only to be told, 'Don't bother with those, they are our own left behind in 1942.' Then perhaps a couple of days later, we would attack one or two of these parks where we had spotted some additional trucks, and the new pilots couldn't work out how we knew.

Sometimes smoke from cooking fires would betray the position of a parked-up Jap convoy. Even so, it could be frustrating, because although you could make out the vehicles from dead overhead, when you come in on an attack heading from say half a mile out, at an angle of dive, the trees covered the target and it was hard to spot exactly where they were. Just occasionally you would catch them in the open in daylight. Once I saw a Jap staff car on a winding road in the mountains. I strafed it, and saw it go over the edge down the hillside. I assume all the occupants were killed. On another occasion my flight was returning from a 'rhubarb', when we spotted a truck on a bare hillside. Only my tail-end-charlie had any ammo left and he asked permission to break off and attack. I said, 'Yes', so in he went. I don't know whether he hit the truck or not, but the whole hillside behind it went up in an enormous ball of flame. I assume the truck was refuelling and he hit a fuel dump.

Lieutenant Junichi Misana
33rd Mountain Artillery Regiment, 33rd Japanese Division
I had to go back. Of course, my wound hadn't healed yet. I self-discharged myself from the hospital, although I wasn't scheduled to be discharged yet. The hospital was unwilling but I forcefully checked myself out. So still with crutches, I got myself a ride on several trucks. The division commander had

changed, and the new division commander became Lieutenant General Nobuo Tanaka. When the division commander changed, they said there would be a truck that would take him directly to the front line, so I asked to ride the same one. So I went in the car that took General Tanaka to his new post.

Captain John Randle
Adjutant, 7th/10th Baluch Regiment

The battalion was sent to the Silchar Track: it was rather like the Western Front, dug-in wired positions and the Japs only about fifty-sixty yards away. Everyone mixed up. For about three weeks there was very intensive fighting. Scrub thicker than in the Chin Hills, very wet. It was a very hard infantry slog. The Japs attacked, then we counter-attacked. Positions changed hands several times. I was the controller of the fire support, guns, mortars, 25-pounders, and 5.5s, also some AA guns in direct-fire role. We shared a CP with the 5th Gurkhas.

The features had names like Water Picket and Mortar Bluff, these were pimples or hills occupied by companies or platoons, and mostly mutually supporting. Subedar Netrabahudur Thapa on Water Picket called for fire through me. He spoke in Gurkhali, but switched to Urdu when realised he was not talking to a Gurkha officer. He was overrun. Got a VC.

Next day the 5th Gurkhas got another VC, Agansing Rai, only time I've seen Gurkhas go in with the kukri; an awe-inspiring sight. They were counter-attacking the position and took it back. It was the closest fighting I ever saw in Burma. There were four VCs won in a week in an area about a mile square.

Japanese attacks tended to come up and close the last few yards with bayonets. We gave enemy positions a really good pasting, then fought our way in. We cleared enemy positions with grenades, tommy guns, Gurkhas with kukris. Our chaps used a bayonet.

We had no morale problems. We had good officers, and were experienced. We thought we were winning. We had far more artillery, and the RAF were in evidence. Rations came up. Wounded were taken out by American Field Service. There were none of the uncertainties of the retreat.

IND 4157

Naik Agansing Rai of the 2nd/5th Royal Gurkha Rifles, awarded the Victoria Cross for his actions at the recapture of Water Point and Mortar Bluff on the Silchar Track at Imphal.

Lieutenant Arthur 'Mac' McCrystal
Officer Commanding 14 Platoon, C Company, 9th Battalion, Border Regiment

We were switched to finish off the 33 Div. South of Imphal was a place called Bishenpur, and the next village was Potsangbam, which was known as 'Pots and Pans'. This was one of the villages that crossed the road. On the eastern side of the road, it was held by the Japs. They had guns in the foothills a mile away. B and C Company put in an attack. We had a couple of Lee-Grant Tanks in support. It was very hot day. It was half-past one in the afternoon of Sunday 14 May.

We crossed the road with C Company on the left and B Company on the right. We moved in with two platoons up, mine and another, and one behind. We moved through sporadic bursts of fire. A soldier on my left saw a Japanese in a hole shooting out of it, and he too excitedly leapt up and fired at him and was shot by a sniper from forty yards away. All the time the tank was on the fringe, out in the open, firing in. The Jap artillery could see us, and never worried about hitting their own troops. You could hear the boom, and we lay down. At one point a shell landed near, and I was hit by shrapnel in the hand and arm. John Petty picked me up and my batman, Private Hunt from Norfolk, took me back across the road through part of the village we already held. Someone put on a first-aid dressing, and later I got a jab of morphine. I was walking wounded, and was taken to an ambulance jeep, and sat in front. We were being shelled all the time.

Corporal Les Griffiths
9th Battalion, Border Regiment

Before the battle at Potsangbam, we lay up all night on the edge of the paddy. At dawn the whole place was covered in mist. We were all tapped on the shoulder, 'Come on up.' Once up on our feet we moved forward through a line of gunners. One said, 'Good luck,' and we moved on to the paddy and lined up, on one side the Gurkhas, and further along another battalion.

We got the signal to advance, and we started to walk, just a stroll. And we had walked for quite a while and then the Jap guns began to open up. One chap fell alongside me, and the Colonel said, 'Stay by him.' So I did. He had shrapnel all over him. He was yelling, I slapped his face.

I stayed there with him as the troops moved forward. I felt very lonely.

Corporal Les Griffiths.

Eventually the stretcher-bearers came up and took him away. I was on my own. There was no one else around. Eventually I got quite close to the jungle fringes, and I jumped into a shell hole. And on the other side were two chaps who I thought at first were Japs. I threw my tommy gun forward, and they grinned and laughed, they were Gurkhas. Eventually I found the battalion.

Private Fred McCloud
12 Platoon, B Company, 9th Battalion, Border Regiment
They said this is your last 'duffy', in Potsangbam. We went across the road into a paddy field, and two Jap machine guns at each end of Potsangbam hit us. I went down on the floor. An air strike came in and hit the Japs in the wood, the road ran through it. You could hear them screaming and see them running on the road.

Corporal Arthur Freer
Squadron Leader's driver/operator, B Squadron, 3rd Carabiniers
A Squadron in Bishenpur and Potsangbam were having a rough time, so B Squadron was sent down to help. We were in action every day. It was paddy on both sides of road, on one side was the Logtak Lake. The Japs would fortify the villages with bunkers and use the bunds as defensive positions. At night, having half-cleared a village, we would remain guarded by the Bombay Grenadiers.

There were three of us with the 'runs' at the time and I was the worst. To sleep in the tank you sit in your sleep. To crap, the 75-mm gunner, who was standing on the escape hatch in the floor of the tank on the other side of the tank, moved to your seat, and you lifted the hatch, and crapped on the ground a few feet below. You then got the driver to move the tank a bit away from the stench, and put the lid back again. Nobody slept. We all stank to high heaven, we were all unwashed and sick. There was always a revolting stench in the tank. At dawn you stood to, the infantry tank guard would move away, and we would go into action again. It could go on for three days and nights at a time.

Private Fred McCloud
12 Platoon, B Company, 9th Battalion, Border Regiment
We were marched down the road and there were marquees, and we went in

there and went through a delousing centre, where they looked in our crotches for crabs. We had a bath, were shaved by barbers and given a haircut. Our rifles and ammunition were taken off us, and new rifles and bayonets, and brand-new uniforms, were given to us, everything new. We went in like rag men and came out like bloody princes. We couldn't recognise each other.

When we came out we fell in, and were ordered to slope arms. Somebody in the middle started singing 'D'ye ken John Peel', the regimental march.

BREAKING OUT AND BACK TO BURMA

Yuwaichi Fujiwara
Japanese Soldier
By the end of May the monsoon had started and our campaign had already failed. But GHQ Burma Area Army and Southern Area Army did not give orders to withdraw until July. Almost all Japanese soldiers were suffering from malaria and starvation. Many soldiers died on the retreat to the Chindwin, we called the road to Sittaung the 'death road'.

Lieutenant Junichi Misana
33rd Mountain Artillery Regiment, 33rd Japanese Division
They called it battlefront realignment. Yes, that's how it was. And we went all the way down that mountain, the same way we came up. By then we were hurt everywhere. We only had one cannon each.

Lieutenant Mahesh Sharma
70th Independent Field Company, Bengal Sappers and Miners
The Japanese were very tough. They stored their rice in old socks tied to their belts. I have seen a Japanese officer with part of his arm missing and maggots crawling over him still fighting. They are very brave. They had no idea of preserving human life. They lived off the land a lot of the time, which was hard on the villagers. They had few medical facilities.

Private Jim Wilks
11 Platoon, B Company, 2nd Battalion, West Yorkshire Regiment
On the Imphal–Kohima Road we broke out, each side of the road was jungle

and steep khuds. Every now and then there was a roadblock, where the Japs had felled massive trees across the road. You had to go round it or through it. We got to this roadblock on the Imphal–Kohima Road and our colonel, Colonel Cree, could see we couldn't get past this roadblock, the Japs were dug in both sides. So Colonel Cree sent D Company round the left of the roadblock to go right round and come in on the rear of the Japs. B Company, my company, went round the right-hand side to come in behind the Japs. Unfortunately D Company didn't go far enough to get behind the Japs, ran smack into them, and lost twenty-six men, including all the officers. We heard the fighting going on. The roadblock was plastered by artillery and the next day we went in. We were lucky and by the time we got there the Japs had scarpered.

We found the bodies of the D Company chaps who were killed. We buried them there.

Major Alexander Wilson
Brigade Major, 6th Brigade

Coming south from Kohima, we were clearing roadblocks quicker than the Japs thought we could. The Japs would blow the little culverts between two ridges, and sit on the other side, they could be anything up to battalion strength. There were no bunkers, but foxholes, and they fought hard. The technique was to fix them in the front and climb above them, and outflank them. The Japs were getting short of men, their artillery was very sparse, they were an army in disarray, but that didn't mean they didn't fight.

We went through and met the Imphal garrison coming north.

Trooper Malcolm Connolly
7 Troop, C Squadron, 3rd Carabiniers

During the clearing of the Imphal Road we were sent to bury the crew of a tank that had been hit, caught fire, and exploded a few days earlier. There was only one complete body: 'Chick' Henderson had managed to get out of the side door, and crawled to the back, possibly to cover the retreat of his crew. But the Japs must have killed him. He was pretty badly burned by the exploding tank. We had the job of bringing him down and finding the pieces of the crew. The inside was derelict; we crawled inside and managed to find a foot here and a hand there. Then the job was getting them down. Chick's body was rotting, we rolled him into a blanket and put it on a stretcher. As for the bits and pieces of the others, nobody had an idea of which bit belonged to who.

Private William Palmer
6 Platoon, B Company, 1st Battalion, Devonshire Regiment

During the monsoon we went to the Ukhrul Valley to ambush Japs retreating from Imphal. On one ambush in the early morning, the Japs were using bullocks to carry their equipment. First of all came troops, then the bullocks, then more troops, about sixty of them. The signal to open fire was a grenade thrown at the far end of the ambush, at which we threw grenades, and fired using Sten guns and Brens. We had two wounded. Most of the Japs ran off into the jungle. We counted eighteen dead Japs, and buried them.

Lieutenant Junichi Misana
33rd Mountain Artillery Regiment, 33rd Japanese Division

They came and came and came. So we would do it little by little. Every five mile or maybe a few mile, or ten mile or so, we would take a good mountain that we can use to our benefit, and we would do this for a few days. That's how we proceeded.

The plane was the enemy. I thought that by the time we reach the Manipur River we would get caught. If they pursued us in the way that the Japanese army would have done it, they would have already caught up with us. Yes, so I thought to myself, that we would probably get caught before we reach Manipur. But I would never say this out loud.

But we were able to gradually retreat, and managed to reach the Manipur without getting caught.

Private Jim Wilks
11 Platoon, B Company, 2nd Battalion, West Yorkshire Regiment

We started going along the Tiddim Road, crossed the Manipur River – there was a dead elephant in the water – up the Chocolate Staircase, to Tiddim, then Kennedy Peak and on to the Chindwin.

Trooper Malcolm Connolly
7 Troop, C Squadron, 3rd Carabiniers
The Tiddim Road was like a shooting gallery in a fun fair, as the tanks drove along one behind each other they were targets for the Japs. If you panicked you risked driving over the edge and falling hundreds of feet.

Captain Peter Noakes
Number 4 Company, 1st Battalion, Northamptonshire Regiment
I was now second-in-command of Number 4 company to Mike Hazelhurst. We got ready to go back to Burma, assembled and marched along the Mombi Track. The Mombi Track is a well-known track between Burma and India, only fit for mule or horse transport, across the Naga Hills. It rises to six thousand feet and when you get to Mombi you overlook Burma and the Kabaw Valley. Some Nagas came to meet us. They hated the Japanese.

We got to the Kabaw Valley, crossed it and there our problems started. On the maps it said 'Path follows the chaung'. We followed the chaung and struggled for days, in water. It was forty-five miles long, and took us five or six days to get to where the chaung finished. Every night you were wet, you put a clean pair of socks on, you had kept in your pack, and left the others out to dry. Eventually we came to the end, it was a hard slog with mules.

We sent out patrols, found the enemy had decamped and made our way towards Monywa.

Trooper Malcolm Connolly
7 Troop, C Squadron, 3rd Carabiniers
My troop had to take out a 105-mm gun that was holding up the division. That might seem strange that one gun could hold up a division. The infantry they sent out to find and destroy it couldn't find it; the Jap camouflage was so good. But they did locate approximately where it might possibly be. They used us as 'stooges', making us go forward hoping the Jap would open up.

We were able to leave the road, which was unusual. The first tank, the troop corporal's, was mined just after leaving the road. I was driving the troop officer and we climbed past the tank which had had its track blown off, nobody hurt. We headed for the top of the mountain where we had been ordered to sit, hoping the gun would fire at us. The troop sergeant coming up behind us had difficulty climbing. As soon as we got on to the skyline, this gun opened up and plastered all round us. We couldn't go back and had to continue on up, the firing went on. The troop officer's face was bleeding, but he was OK.

Eventually it was decided to back out the way we had come, and the 'Nips' let us go. We went back down the hill, and harboured in a nullah with the troop sergeant. After my troop officer and I had crawled up on to the ridge with binos to see if we could spot this gun, we got the order to leave. A matter of minutes later the troop sergeant reported that he had thrown a track. The troop officer got out to see if he could help. He was standing in front of the troop sergeant's tank when a shell burst killed him: blew his belly open. A lump of shrapnel went straight through the visor. It took the driver's head off, the arm muscle off the 37 gunner, and stunned the troop sergeant. The young operator was out of his head as he had all the driver's brains all over him, and we had a hell of a job to persuade them to open up. Eventually over the wireless we persuaded them to open up. I got in touch with the squadron by wireless and asked, 'What do we do?'

We were told that a Jap counter-attack was imminent, we were to leave the tanks, and go. All fit members of my crew helped all unfit members of the other crew, and they scarpered. I decided I wouldn't go, and I stayed. Nobody knew I was there. I decided they weren't going to have my tank. I was there, two dead men, two tanks and me.

I don't know what made me do it. Late in the afternoon, Captain Law, a Canadian officer attached to the regiment, was sent to find me. He asked me what I was going to do, and I said that I would take the tank down. He left to tell the squadron what was happening.

I brought the tank down and the squadron met me on the road.

Corporal Arthur Freer
Squadron Leader's driver/operator, B Squadron, 3rd Carabiniers

In the autumn of 1944, we headed down the Kabaw valley. It was typical wet jungle. Disease was rife: tick typhus, dengue fever, and malaria. B Squadron was allocated to supporting the leading battalion whoever it was. Whichever troop was leading, the squadron leader was up with them. This was a bit of a strain. We arrived at the southern end of Kabaw Valley at Kalewa, where the Bailey bridge across the Chindwin had just been completed. Mountbatten came to inspect it, and I was walking down the track to check up on some of the other wireless operators in the squadron. I had my Sten without a butt, and no hat. My trousers were torn at the knee. Coming towards me I saw an immaculate admiral's uniform covered with medals, and six red-tabbed officers behind him. I didn't know what to do, I couldn't salute him, but at that moment a Jap Zero flew over, spotted this target, and came down machine-gunning. I threw myself into the ditch by the road, but Mountbatten beat me to it. I landed about two yards from him. I looked at him thinking I had an excuse for looking scruffy now. He laughed and walked off.

Trooper Malcolm Connolly
7 Troop, C Squadron, 3rd Carabiniers
That evening Major Morgan said, 'Have you seen Captain Law?'

'No,' I replied.

So they said they wanted me to go up with some of them and find him. I went to the cookhouse to get a cup of tea before we set off, and lo and behold, Captain Law was there. He had been found by a patrol of the West Kents who had found him hiding in the jungle.

He had gone off and a matter of fifty to a hundred yards away from us, two Japs took him prisoner. They were marching him away and our artillery started to shell the area. One shell landed close and the Jap in front of Captain Law scarpered, and slipped running down the hill. Law turned and hit the Jap behind him and dived down the bank and down the hill.

He said he had enough and wanted to go back to his own army.

Captain Peter Noakes
Number 4 Company, 1st Battalion, Northamptonshire Regiment
Before Monywa we had a battle, at Budalin, quite a battle. I commanded the company as Mike had been repatriated. We were on the right flank, and by the time we got there we had marched about two hundred and fifty miles from Wangjing, and had to put in an attack. Here there was a railway, the first we'd seen for a long time; it ran from Rangoon to Mandalay. The line was built on an embankment, which we had to cross in full view of the enemy. The idea was to rush the Japanese positions, and secure the main road between Monywa and Shwebo. We never got there. We were met by heavy machine gun and mortar fire, and my company had to withdraw. We dug in that night.

Corporal Arthur Freer
Squadron Leader's driver/operator, B Squadron, 3rd Carabiniers

We crossed the Chindwin on Bailey pontoon sections towed by DUKWs. There were no Japs on the other side. The advance to Shwebo was through teak forest and jungle. Travelled for about three days like this. Nothing happened until we started to get into thicker jungle. When there were signs that we were catching up on the Japs, such as food left behind, I told Major Huntley-Wright, the squadron leader, and asked, 'Shouldn't we net in on the sets to talk to the infantry?' He didn't do anything about it. On 23 December 1944, we came upon a Jap roadblock, and came under small-arms fire. He couldn't speak to the infantry CO on the wireless, and got out of the tank to do so.

About an hour later there was no sign of him. A troop leader, Captain Swann, called us eventually, telling us that the squadron leader was badly wounded and dying. I was sitting next to the driver, I took off my headset, and climbed into the turret to take command of the tank. I put my head out, and I felt a heavy bang on my head, and woke up on the floor of the turret. My head was hurting, no blood, but there was a lump the size of an egg. The sniper's bullet had hit the turret outside chipping off something, which hit me, but I got away with it.

I ordered the turret gunner to spray the trees above us and around. Captain Swann came on the air and said he was taking command of the squadron, and asked why I was firing. I told him I was trying to spray the sniper. He told me to leave him alone, the infantry would sort him out. We were told to bypass the Japs and press on.

The next day we burst through a Jap cookhouse, smashing a huge pot of boiling rice, which burst all over the tank. We were hungry and the rice smelt delicious, but we couldn't stop. By now we were out of the jungle and smashed through the Jap roadblocks. Each day another battalion from 2 Div took over the lead.

Captain Peter Noakes
Number 4 Company, 1st Battalion, Northamptonshire Regiment

B Company on the left flank of the battalion commanded by Peter Cherrington managed after a couple of days to get the Japs out of Budalin. It had a railway station and police HQ. Peter was awarded an immediate DSO.

SE 3173

A Lee-Grant tank of the 3rd Carabiniers on a pontoon constructed from a Bailey Bridge section crossing the Chindwin.

SE 1883

Soldiers of the 9th Battalion, Border Regiment cross the Chindwin at Kalewa.

Flight Lieutenant Owen Parry
11 Squadron, RAF

We had very little opposition from enemy fighters, the Spitfires dealt with them pretty easily. The majority of sorties by Jap fighters seemed to be sneak raids on airfields or ground targets, and they were a nuisance only. Flak was more of a problem for us. They would defend key points like bridges with Bofors-type guns. Impossible to spot were their heavy machine guns, you just saw the bullet holes when you returned, or an aircraft shot down.

You were always conscious that you might have to walk back if you were unlucky enough to be shot down. In our squadron we flew in long trousers and long-sleeved shirts, wearing army boots and short puttees, so we were well equipped to walk if we had to. You tried not to think too much about what would happen if you fell into Jap hands, but concentrated on how you would get away into the jungle and survive.

Ursula Graham-Bower
Naga Watch and Ward and Women's Auxiliary Corps (India) (WACI)

After the Imphal Plain had been clear for some time, it was arranged for a team of Nagas and me to train RAF personnel in jungle survival. They were faintly surprised at my teaching them survival and ambush techniques. The clearing where the camp was was right on top of an elephant trail. We used to take the men out into the jungle and practise stalking and hunting techniques. One day we found a large bull elephant in the middle of our class. We tiptoed away.

At the end of the course the air crew were taken out by jeep and dropped off in the jungle about twenty miles away with a compass and emergency rations. They were taught that if you happen to meet a tiger he is probably not hostile. He wants to be left alone. If you hear a deep growl in a thicket, turn round and creep away. He won't interfere with you. One of a party of two walked in on a tiger, there was a growl in the thicket, and they did creep away. It worked. After that the reputation of the instruction went up a lot.

Corporal Arthur Freer
Squadron Leader's driver/operator, B Squadron, 3rd Carabiniers

Two days after Huntley-Wright was killed we got a new squadron leader, Major E.S.P. Dorman. He was an Irishman. We had an Irish driver and they used to curse each other with Irish curses, nothing serious, just fun.

To get to Shwebo we had to cross the Mu River. It was shallow, and slow flowing. We crossed using a ford. We encountered continual sniping, and mines on the road, covered by machine guns. The few Japs we saw were dead or dying and emaciated. I didn't feel sorry for them in those days.

We entered Shwebo from the north. We took a war correspondent in our tank. We came to the gateway where there was a dry moat crossed by a bridge. There was no sign of life, but there were Jap bunkers on the other side of the moat. The leading tank crossed and others behind him noticed wires from the bridge over the moat to bunkers. Everybody was told to halt, and our sapper officer went forward and found some 500-kg bombs set for setting off by men in bunkers, but they had been abandoned because we had sprayed the bunkers first. We went into the town, it was dead, with a few chickens running around: no Burmese or Japs.

The war correspondent produced a report, which he showed me, and the only thing I could recognise was the names and addresses of the tank crew. The rest of the report was his imagination.

Captain Peter Noakes
Number 4 Company, 1st Battalion, Northamptonshire Regiment
When we came to Monywa I was still commanding Number 4 Company, but then it was taken over by Major Donald Eales-White who had been wounded in action some months before. I became 2i/c again.

We attacked through a mango grove, the Japs were up in the trees and in foxholes. Poor old Donald got wounded again, and I took over. We cleared the area. The rest of the battalion cleared an area known as the rifle butts, used by police. The Japs retired post haste to defend the passages over the Irrawaddy. Peter Cherrington was killed in this battle.

Corporal Arthur Freer
Squadron Leader's driver/operator, B Squadron, 3rd Carabiniers
After Shwebo, we had a few more actions in villages in the area between the Irrawaddy and Chindwin. The tanks were wearing out. New tracks were dropped to us by parachute and we fitted them within hours. Food was also dropped by air. In mid-January 1945 it was announced on squadron orders that Christmas Day 1944 would be on 15 January 1945. The cooks produced some chickens and we had Christmas pudding.

After that it was back to sorting out roadblocks again.

Captain Peter Noakes
Number 4 Company, 1st Battalion, Northamptonshire Regiment
We advanced over open country. It was very strange at first, advancing in extended line; two platoons up, one back. We saw Japanese running out of a village, and I sent in patrols. They reported Japs there. I said, 'Dig in.' The next day they had gone.

Corporal Arthur Freer
Squadron Leader's driver/operator, B Squadron, 3rd Carabiniers
We were clearing a village with a company of the Royal Scots, with tanks in the lead. The squadron leader was to the rear with the infantry. I saw two Japs jump into a slit trench just ahead. The squadron leader told me to guide the driver to it. I opened my little port, and a grenade landed beside the trench, about five feet away from my port. It was the squadron leader who had thrown the grenade. It killed the Japanese. Splinter from the grenade had cut wires under the tank wing leading to the aerial. The set wouldn't work, so the squadron leader ordered me out to repair it. I asked him to turn the tank sideways to give me cover. I climbed out with a pair of pliers and jack knife. I looked under, found the two wires, repaired them, but not before I got a tremendous shock: the squadron leader was transmitting, using me as an aerial. Fighting continued and we had tiffin on the move, eating cold baked beans out of the tin.

We then went back to the slit we had attacked earlier. We lifted up the Jap bodies and took the papers out of their pockets. Just then machine guns opened up and rounds cut up the ground around us. I recognised the sound of a tank Browning. We all threw ourselves to the ground. I said, 'It's one of our tanks, sir.'

He said, 'Well, go and stop it.'

That's when the hundred-yard record was broken for the first time. I jumped into our tank, picked up my headset to hear a troop leader say, 'I still think there's some movement there, give them another burst or two.'

I said over the radio, 'Able 5, were you firing your Maggie?'

He said, 'Yes, I'm engaging some Japanese, over.'

I said, 'Cease firing.'

303

'Why, over?'

'You are firing on number 9 and his crew, over.'

There was a horrible hush, then, 'Wilco out.'

Next day followed the same routine. During that second day, one of our troop leaders wirelessed back to the squadron leader, 'There are some boats crossing the Irrawaddy.'

He replied, 'Sink them then.'

They were laden with troops, and they were sunk.

That was the end of that phase. We relaxed, swam, fished with grenades to improve our diet. Then we were told we were going to cross the Irrawaddy, and go to Mandalay.

On to Rangoon

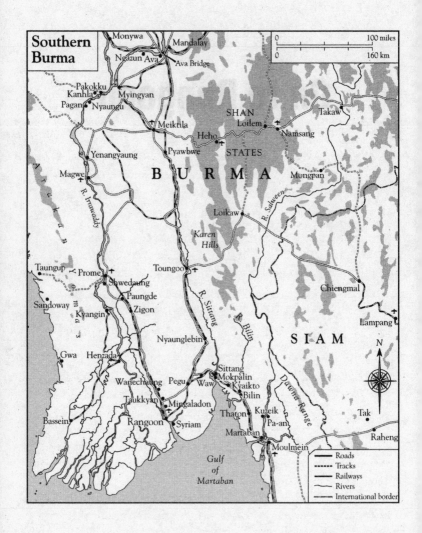

Southern Burma

0   100 miles

0   160 km

Monywa
Mandalay
Ngazun   Ava
Ava Bridge
Pakokku
Kanhla
Pagan   Nyaungu
Myingyan
Meiktila
SHAN
Loilem   Takaw
Heho   Namsang
STATES
Pyawbwe
Yenangyaung
B U R M A
Mongpan
Magwe
R. Irrawaddy
Loikaw
Karen
Hills
R. Salween
Taungup   Prome
Toungoo
Shwedaung
Paungde
Chiengmai
Zigon
Sandoway
Kyangin
R. Sittang
R. Bilin
Lampang
Gwa   Henzada
Nyaunglebin
S I A M
Wanechaung
Sittang
Pegu   Mokpalin
Taukkyan   Waw   Kyaikto
Bilin
Bassein   Mingaladon
Rangoon   Syriam
Thaton   Kuzeik
Pa-an
Martaban
N
Tak
Raheng
Dawna Range
Moulmein
Gulf
of
Martaban

	Roads
	Tracks
	Railways
	Rivers
	International border

We were moving about twenty to thirty miles per day. We had to get to
Rangoon if only to get proper rations. The monsoon was not far away,
air supply would be unreliable in monsoon.
The whip was out.

After the defeat of the Japanese in Assam and before the subsequent advance by the British, Slim was told by Mountbatten to limit his objective to securing Mandalay. Rangoon, he was informed, was to be captured by Operation Dracula, an airborne and amphibious force consisting of formations released from the Arakan after that area had been cleared of the enemy. Mountbatten considered that it was pointless to push further south into central Burma, and was concerned that by driving the Japanese closer to Rangoon, they would be in a better position to oppose Operation Dracula.

Slim, believing that his great victory should be fully exploited, ordered that the Fourteenth Army would take Rangoon overland. In order to do so, he aimed to bring the Japanese army to battle as early as possible, in a place where his superiority in armour and in the air could be employed to best advantage. To begin with, he thought that this would be on the Shwebo Plain on the approach to the Irrawaddy. But he discovered that the Japanese had changed their plans.

Lieutenant General Kawabe, commanding Burma Area Army, had aimed to hold the area between the Chindwin and the Irrawaddy in strength. However, he was replaced by Lieutenant General Hyotaro Kimura, who changed the plan to one which involved allowing Slim to start crossing the Irrawaddy, and, as he was committed, finishing him off.

Slim, therefore, also changed his plan, to destroying the Japanese east of the Irrawaddy instead of west of it, by getting across their line of communication to Mandalay in the region of Meiktila. In essence, he would cross the Irrawaddy north of Mandalay, which is where he identified that Kimura expected him to cross, but his main effort would be well south of the city. Having smashed the Japanese army, Slim would head for Rangoon.

Concurrent with operations in central Burma, the efforts of Christison's XV Corps in Arakan were aimed at helping the Fourteenth Army by holding down the maximum number of Japanese in the Arakan. In addition, if the XV Corps captured air bases on the Arakan littoral at Akyab, Cheduba and Ramree, this would hugely reduce the range that aircraft flying to support Fourteenth Army would have to cover.

Although Christison had pulled back to easily defended localities in the Arakan in mid-1944, British troops were kept busy with local attacks, aggressive patrolling and intelligence gathering. Even while the great battles in Assam were underway, the British, with their command of the sea, were able to raid down the Arakan coast. Later, more amphibious operations were mounted, and these, combined with a series of limited offensives, kept the Japanese from reinforcing their troops facing the main effort in Assam and the advance to the Irrawaddy, Mandalay and Meiktila, and eventually to Rangoon.

The Japanese, on their part, fought hard to prevent the British breaking into the Irrawaddy Valley through the Arakan Yomas.

In early 1945 the pro-Japanese Burmese National Army of around nine battalions, led by Aung San, decided to change sides. The Burmese people, in contrast to the Karens, Chins, and Shans, had initially welcomed the Japanese as liberators from British rule. Eventually they became thoroughly disillusioned by their new masters' conduct, culminating in systematic looting of Burmese towns and villages as the Japanese retreated. From the end of the British retreat in May 1942 until they advanced across the Chindwin at the end of 1944, the Burmese in the central plains were hardly touched by the war. But they suffered casualties and extensive damage to their homes as the fighting moved out of the Assamese and Arakan hills and jungles into the more heavily populated terrain in the Irrawaddy valley.

THE ARAKAN

Lieutenant Richard Acton
Support Troop, 44 (Royal Marine) Commando

We embarked in Z lighters, and went down the Naf River to a small village on the west side of the Naf River, to carry out an operation at Alethangyaw. The idea was to interrupt the Japanese communications leading up to where 25 Div were fighting. We were told that Alethangyaw was very lightly defended and wouldn't cause much problem. Unfortunately the information was out of date. There was a battalion of Japs at Alethangyaw, so we landed at night into a bit more than we anticipated from LCP(L)s. These were funny craft with gangways let down each side of the bow, manned by RIN people. They were keen we got off the craft quickly, and dumped us in deep water. My chaps were carrying about a hundred pounds on their backs, parts of Vickers machine guns or mortars, and ammunition. We were reluctant to jump into deep water as our lifejackets would not keep us afloat with all that weight. So there was a little bit of a palaver. The Rifle troops had gone in before us.

Sergeant John Webber
B Troop, 44 (Royal Marine) Commando

B Troop was the reserve troop at Alethangyaw. With a heavy surf running, the crews were reluctant to push the boats in; we kept going in and being washed back out again. Finally when we got in again I said to Lieutenant Ryder, 'For God's sake jump,' gave him a push, and jumped in after him. I landed in water up to my chest. We staggered ashore where there was a state of complete confusion. C Troop were tangled up in a battle in Alethangyaw, and eventually we finished up among a collection of huts. By morning we had dug ourselves in near a bamboo fence looking towards Alethangyaw. There was sniping coming from there. I was with our sniper, George Deacon.

Eventually, I said to George Deacon, 'I'm sure that's the sniper up in that tree.' He raised his sniper rifle, with a telescopic sight, and fired a round at the tree. There was no more sniping from that tree.

Colour Sergeant 'Dinger' Bell
B Troop, 44 (Royal Marine) Commando

We went into the foothills and could look back and see the village. I had a sniper in my section with a telescopic sight on his rifle, and from a hill, we saw six Japanese washing in a water hole, about six hundred yards away. He got one, and wounded another in the leg. After half an hour they sent out a patrol. Our TSM was sent out to capture these blokes. They laid an ambush for them. The TSM went forward to take them prisoner, and his tommy gun jammed so the Bren gunners opened up and killed all the Japs.

Sergeant John Webber
B Troop, 44 (Royal Marine) Commando
The next night we were given orders to withdraw down a chaung. My section was due to go first, followed by Sergeant Grant's; somehow he got in front of us. He never made it, and was missing presumed killed, in the darkness. We went to the West African base at Nahkaungdo, we called it 'No can do'.

We then went back for Operation Screwdriver Two, where troops were based on villages. We patrolled at night, by day the Japs could spot our movements. Captain Sturges would always take me with him, because I was the only single sergeant; a dubious honour.

On one patrol, which we did from 'No can do', we had quite a scrap with the Japanese in a village. We got into the village and could look through and see the Japanese in their pits. Sturges wouldn't let us fire on them, but as we were withdrawing, the Japs opened fire on us from another position; our machine gunners were firing back to cover our withdrawal.

We had a marine with us, the bane of my life, who was always doing things wrong. He got up from a depression in the ground to run, and as he ran the Japanese machine-gun bullets were nearly catching him up. Suddenly his trousers fell down, he went headlong into a dip, and the bullets went over his head.

Lieutenant Dominic Neill
Intelligence Officer, 3rd/2nd Gurkha Rifles
I would often go out with patrols. On one occasion we were tasked with seizing a prisoner from behind Japanese lines. The plan was to board a small coastal steamer at Maungdaw, steam down the Naf River by night, towing three large country boats to a point about five miles south of the river entrance, where we were to get into the country boats, and row ashore. Having left a section to hold the beach, with the heavy radio to brigade HQ,

we were to advance about a thousand yards to set up an advance patrol base.

At about midnight, in an ominous swell, we climbed, heavily laden, into the country boats, which were about the size of a fairly large rowing boat. The mens' faces in the moonlight were studies – if I was afraid, how much more must the men have been, in fear of their lives as not a single one could swim. After a nightmare five-hundred-yard journey in the boats, we all landed safely and spent the rest of the night on the beach.

We were taking up a position overlooking a strip of paddy between the two halves of a village, when three Japs stood up from behind a small mound about three-quarters of the way between us and the far side of the paddy. After a few minutes, perhaps they were suspicious, they took up fire positions behind the mound, but still clearly in sight. We watched fascinated for another minute, as they lay exposed about seventy-five yards away.

We had never had the chance in 1943 to study Japs at leisure, at short range. We made the most of this opportunity and then killed them. I fired first with my Thompson SMG, and my Bren gunner shot the other two.

The next day while ambushing a track, a Japanese patrol approached. We watched like cats watching mice, but these mice were dangerous. A long burst of Bren shattered the silence.

The Japs took cover behind a bund like lightning. A Jap tried to crawl away, I fired quickly two or three times, seeing hits on the wet shirt on his back. A wet rump poked up for a moment, and I fired three quick shots, one hit and flung the Jap back into the flooded paddy. As I hit him with another shot, I remembered that our mission was to take a prisoner, and if I didn't act soon, all candidates for the POW cage would be dead. I screamed above the din to the left-hand section to give me covering fire, ordered the section with me to cease fire, fix swords, draw kukris and charge.

Two enemy broke cover and tried to make a dash for it. One stopped and flung up his hands in surrender. I was not gaining on the other man, my chest was heaving, my tommy gun muzzle was going up and down, my eyes full of sweat. I fired three bursts and could see the rounds hitting the man's back, flicking away pieces of shirt and flesh. I had not realised the hitting power of a .45 bullet before. The Jap shot forward like a rag doll hit with a sledge hammer.

I walked back to where the prisoner was standing among the dead and the reddening rice water. We had shot them to ribbons. I told my men to check the remaining seven bodies for signs of life, and search each for documents. Our prisoner was a JIF.

Lieutenant James Sherwood
C Group, 2 SBS

Shortly after I arrived at Teknaf with my group, I took the place of a sick chap in A Group on an operation. We were taken in an MGB run by the Indian Navy, a tremendous bunch of blokes running those things. We motored down the Naf River into the Bay of Bengal. By nightfall we were some miles from where we were supposed to land. There was only a slight swell, which can be very big by the time it reaches the beach. We got our canoes over the side, there was no moon, and set off to the beach.

By this time A group had developed a technique for dealing with surf on a beach, which no one had thought of before. Not to plane into the beach, but turn and face the swell, watch for the moment when the horizon went black, which it did when the wave built up, and paddle like hell into it; bash through it before it broke, or as it was breaking, and you had enough speed on to go straight through it, shipping the minimum amount of water, and remain upright. Once that had passed, you paddled astern as fast as you could, waited until the same thing happened. With successive waves you got on to the beach dry-shod and upright. This we did.

We pulled the canoes up just above the water line. A bloke was left to guard the canoes; we could hear drums inland. We crept inland, the object being to glean information, not stir up a hornet's nest. We heard whistling and spotted a figure ambling along the beach. We lay in the sand. I had alongside me a great big hulking bloke who had been a member of the Manchester City Police before the war. I said to him, 'You grab him.'

He did. He was no Jap, only a young Burmese, a coast watcher appointed by the Japanese to look out for people like us. He was terrified and thought he would be killed. He spoke a little English. We reassured him we would not kill him, and asked him to lead us to the nearest village. He agreed to do so. He said there was a Japanese sergeant living in a basha. He would take us there, but only if we took him with us. You could always stuff a passenger in the bow section of the canoe, with his head in the lap of the front paddler.

He led us up the beach along a track and we could see flames from a fire. The officer in charge, Holden Wright, allocated people to tasks, covering

James Sherwood as a captain in the Royal Ulster rifles after the war.

approaches and so forth. As we approached we could see light through the split bamboo of the basha. The local would go to the door and tap on it to get the Jap to come out at which point he would be grabbed or shot, whichever seemed appropriate.

There must have been about eight of us, all armed with tommy guns or pistols. The chap knocked, the door opened, a figure appeared and came outside, and must have realised that something wasn't quite right or something, because he took to his heels pursued by a fusillade of shots, none of which got him. He escaped, astonishing, but that sort of thing happens in war. But the hut was full of all sorts of valuable intelligence information.

The coast watcher told us that there was a Jap platoon just down the track who must have heard the firing, so we returned to our canoes, tucked the coast watcher into the bows of one of them, and got back to the MGB without further problems. The intelligence was of value to the corps commander, we subsequently learned. But it was typical of so many SBS operations: somehow they went off half-cock very often. I don't think we thought far enough ahead.

Pilot Officer Roger Cobley
20 Squadron, RAF
We had been sent to attack Akyab, where a Japanese general was supposed to be visiting. There was no aircraft there. I was leading, and was hit by flak. The others peeled off. My engine kept stopping then picking up, and glycol smoke was coming out. I had eighty miles to go, and wasn't going to make it. I told the others to go home. I headed for the Kaladan Valley where I knew there were some relatively bare hillsides, and the West Africans were still about. I landed wheels up on a barer patch, and it was right by a West African forward patrol. The West Africans arranged for an L-5 to come into a strip they had prepared and fly me out. I was back in the squadron before nightfall that day. I was very lucky, I didn't get a scratch.

Lieutenant Stamford Weatherall
C Group, 2 SBS
We penetrated the chaungs in our canoes. We went as far as the Kaladan River and were able to watch the Jap sentries on a jetty. We had with us two Burmese interpreters. Major Livingstone and Lieutenant Sherwood went across in two canoes at night with the two interpreters to see a village

headman. While they were gone, a rowboat pulled up not far from us, and out of it got a woman, a man and three children. We grabbed them, the man was escaping from the Japanese and returning home. He could speak English and read a map, so I took a lot of notes off him. I captured a young Burmese fishing and hauled him into our den. He was the first man's brother-in-law, and was suffering from horrible sores, and we bandaged him up. When Livingstone came back he got him to come with him with a map and pinpoint all the Japanese positions. We took him and his brother-in-law to Chittagong for interrogation. They were taken to Calcutta from there, were feted and given money.

Havildar Umrao Singh
33 Mountain Battery

I volunteered to attack a hill near the sea in the Arakan, this hill was proving very difficult to take, so I took my troop down a path which we had made. Unfortunately the Japanese had discovered that we had made this path and we ran into a party of them. It was very difficult terrain, the bamboo was so thick you couldn't see anyone. All the main troops who were accompanying me ran away or were killed. But my troop stayed with me. I was with one troop and I had two howitzers with me and we started firing on the Japanese, and eventually we ran out of ammunition for our howitzers. We suddenly found ourselves surrounded. So I told my troop to withdraw. They said they would not go without me, so I started to withdraw with them. Suddenly I thought to myself a gunner never leaves his gun, so I went back again, and started firing at them with my Bren gun, which was all I had. This went on for five hours, firing when someone came within five yards of me. Eventually I ran out of ammunition, so I picked up a hammer from my howitzer and attacked the Japanese with this, and I managed to kill quite a few of them. Until some aeroplanes flew overhead, this frightened the Japanese, and they ran away. I collapsed senseless because I had several wounds.

When I was eventually rescued I was told that there were thirty to thirty-five Japanese dead in the small area near where we had been fighting. Of course I did not kill them all, many of them were killed by my colleagues in my troop.

Lieutenant Richard Acton
Support Troop, 44 (Royal Marine) Commando
Soon after Christmas 1944 we mounted an operation on Akyab, but had an unopposed landing, just a few Japanese booby traps. Bit of a damp squib.

Sergeant John Webber
B Troop, 44 (Royal Marine) Commando
After the unopposed landing at Akyab, we were bombed by Zeros. A Dakota came to land at the airfield and the Indian AA gunners opened up on it. They stopped when it fired a red Very light.

Havildar Umrao Singh
33 Mountain Battery
When I got back after hospital, it was announced that I had the VC. I did not know what it was. I thought that it meant I was going to get a Viceroy's Commission. So I was taken to the commandant who told me that I was Bahadur, a brave man, and I was being rewarded for bravery. I thought to myself I don't know what bravery is. I joined the artillery to fight, and I fought, that was my job.

Sergeant Frank Allison
A Troop, 42 (Royal Marine) Commando
After Akyab we landed at Myebon. The air strikes had gone in. We landed in deep mud. As we were getting off, the chap sitting four rows in front of me had his head taken off by a shell. Jed Allen, just to my left, put his hand to his head and said, 'I've been hit.' Blood was coming from between his fingers. But he hadn't been hit, this chap who'd had his head blown off had sprayed him with blood.

We charged ashore. I took my section just off the beach, in front of us was a Jap bunker. I took my section round the back. I charged in, it was all in darkness, you couldn't see a thing. I pressed the trigger of my tommy gun. Nothing happened. I rushed out. The magazine was jammed with mud. I put on a fresh magazine, and this time threw a grenade before I went into the bunker.

From there my section had to go up to establish a radio on a hill. Before we set off an officer came up and asked, 'Who cleared the bunker?'

'Me and my section.'

'Anything to declare?' says he.

'No, if there was there wouldn't be anything left of them.'

He said, 'There was a 2-pounder gun in there.'

'Well, I couldn't see because it was dark.'

We went on about two hundred yards. My first thought was to make a cup of tea. But my water bottle was full of salt water.

Sergeant John Webber
B Troop, 44 (Royal Marine) Commando

Landing at Myebon, we were the reserve commando. It was late afternoon and we were put ashore on a receding tide on a mangrove swamp, mud up to our midriffs. The longer the landing lasted, the more the tide went out. Once we got ashore we weren't fit to fight – weapons and equipment covered in mud. I took off all my clothes in a shell hole full of water, washed my clothes and myself, and the sun dried it all out. Luckily the other commandos had landed ahead and pushed the Japanese back. There was some Japanese mortar fire, but the bombs exploded in the mud and didn't do any damage. We spent the night in some old Japanese defensive positions, cleaning all our clips of ammunition.

Private Victor Ralph
4 Troop, 1 Commando

Having cleared the Myebon peninsula it was decided that the next landing should be at Kangaw. The Japs were pulling out down through the Arakan and had used the Daingbon Chaung and Myebon river as an escape route. We had virtually cut them off by taking Myebon, but there was a road that led over the mountains. Kangaw was a key point that overlooked the road; they would have to use it to complete their withdrawal. It was not far from Myebon, but impossible to get to overland, so another landing was needed, by sailing up the Daingbon Chaung in landing craft.

We were first ashore, having negotiated the mangrove swamp, which wasn't easy, we got to the paddy, and we could see Hill 170 in front of us. The Japs opened up on us. But we took the hill fairly easily. About halfway up the hill there was a young Burmese girl, about seventeen or eighteen, and her baby a few months old, lying in a pool of blood, her stomach torn open.

Sergeant John Webber.

I thought, was it our shelling of the hill that did that or was it when we were attacking, when the Japs mortared us? And it occurred to me that it didn't matter very much, she was in her homeland and here were two foreign powers fighting each other and she and her baby had died because of that.

Sergeant Jack Salter
4 Troop, 1 Commando
We dug in around the hill top, with firing positions all within a few yards of each other. I was the demolition man for laying booby traps at night. I went out and laid Bangalore torpedoes and grenades in tins with trip wires. Every morning I would go out and disarm them.

Sergeant John Webber
B Troop, 44 (Royal Marine) Commando
We landed on the beach and moved up behind Hill 170 which had already been taken, and moved on to take the next hill called Milford, and on again to Pinner, the hill nearest the track which led into central Burma. We started to dig in on Pinner. We hit rock not far down. We were told to stop digging because we were due to move on to the next hill called Duns that night. We stood to and waited for orders to move. It was a beautiful moonlit night. The Japs had a gun dug in on the hill opposite us and no sooner did you hear the gunfire than the shell exploded in amongst us.

The hill was heavily tree-covered, and some of the shells exploded in the trees and shredded the trees into sharp bits of wood, and these showered down on us. Then they put in attacks, one after another supported by mortar fire; it was a very long night. I never saw them, but heard them. Corporal Fleming was killed close to me. 'Ack-Ack' Marshall, another of my corporals, was hit. We carried him down the hill, getting hold of his shoulders was like catching hold of pulp, because he had been hit by showers of wood. He kept on shouting, 'Come on Number 1 Section, at 'em,' which was bad, because it pinpointed the position. But he died during the night.

Acting RSM 'Dinger' Bell
44 (Royal Marine) Commando
Pinner was right up alongside the track the Japs were using to withdraw down the Kaladan Valley. I was standing in for the RSM, and had a lance corporal

with me as an orderly. The signals officer had his back blown off by a tree burst. He was dying. My orderly had a big hole in his back from a tree burst. Why he got out of the trench I'll never know.

Japs came in with sandbags with corners pushed out over their heads as camouflage. They crawled up and tried to throw grenades into our trenches, but most of our casualties were from tree bursts. We ran out of HE grenades, and instead threw phosphorus grenades, which burnt them, especially their eyes.

My job as RSM was to organise the burials, get the discs off them, and make a note of where they were buried. I went to get the details off a chap who had been a BBC pianist before the war. He was so badly blown to bits, I had to leave everything in his trench, and put a wooden cross on it. I burnt his name on it with a blackened nail. The rest were buried down below the hill.

We lost twenty-seven killed and nearly one hundred wounded, some badly, that night. We went into action well below strength at about 320 and when I did my muster the next morning there were about 180 left to fight, out of a commando that should have been 450. Behind us we had fourteen Indian stretcher-bearers. The Japs got in behind us, we heard screaming, it was the Japs kicking their heads in. We found them the next morning.

I thought the Japanese were very brave. Once the Japanese started attacking in a place and they were failing, they went on without any sort of manoeuvre, or looking for another place. You knew that once they started attacking in one place they went on doing so in that place.

Captain Richard Acton
Officer Commanding Support Troop, 44 (Royal Marine) Commando

I was dug in between commando HQ and C Troop. When darkness came the Japs started to attack. Their method was always to try and make us reveal ourselves, by coming close and trying to taunt you. The response was to throw grenades. They retaliated with grenades. One chap in a slit trench near me got a foot blown off by a grenade. The TSM went to him, and I went to commando HQ to get the doctor, a marvellous chap. Eventually we managed to evacuate him.

All night we were shelled by the Japanese, and we directed return fire from the RIN sloops *Nerbudda* and *Jumna*.

Sergeant John Webber
B Troop, 44 (Royal Marine) Commando
Brigadier Hardy came up the next morning, and I think was surprised that we held it. Later in the day we were relieved by the Hyderabad Regiment, and withdrew behind Hill 170 to defend the beach, codename Hove.

Sergeant Frank Allison
A Troop, 42 (Royal Marine) Commando
In the night on Hill 170, reinforcing Number 1 Commando, the Japs were shouting, 'Come out and fight, you marines.' They knew we were there. You couldn't shout back. Except one chap did shout back and told the Japs where to go, using an obscene word. He was put on a charge.

A Troop was on the end of the hill. We were relieved by another troop. But the Japs took that part of the hill. A Troop was about to go in to take it back, but being under strength, two other troops were put in. They took it back with heavy casualties. One troop was wiped out completely. We had to go in and dig the bodies out of the trenches and bury them at the bottom of the hill. As we were burying them the Japanese were sniping at us.

Sergeant Jack Salter
4 Troop, 1 Commando
I was given orders not to put the booby traps out because Indian troops were relieving us the next day and they wouldn't know where they were. The next morning, at about four o'clock, a terrific barrage of artillery and mortar fire hit us. They blew up the three tanks we had at the foot of the hill with pole charges and the attacks lasted all day. The OP for the artillery was knocked out in the early stages, so messages were passed back by shouting to troop HQ.

I lost a lot of friends there. One of them, 'Snipe' Lander, I had known for years. He came up to rejoin us as a reinforcement wearing a bush hat instead of his beret. I said, 'Hey Snipe, take that off. They'll think you're the brigadier.'

Next minute he was shot through the head.

Private Victor Ralph
4 Troop, 1 Commando
Hand-to-hand fighting took place all day. The Bren gunners in the Bren pit were being wiped out one after the other. One of our officers, Lieutenant

Nolan, I don't know if he was mad, or very brave, but he was walking about in the open with a 2-inch mortar which he fired from the hip, with a Bren gun, a tommy gun, a rifle, anything he could lay his hands on. He took out an awful lot of Japanese. Eventually he was killed.

Number 4 Troop took the brunt of the attacks, but as we lost a lot of men, various sections of other troops, troops of Number 5 Commando came and troops of 42 Commando as the day went on. Parts of the whole brigade were involved all day. It was like Rorke's Drift. The hill was quite overgrown and this was a problem, you couldn't see people approaching until they were quite close. One, a Japanese warrant officer, came charging waving his sword. Everyone on the hill seemed to fire at him, and he went down. Some idiot ran out to grab his sword, and waved it over his head, shouting, 'I've got it. I've got it.' He went down, shot by the Japanese. But he had only leg wounds and was dragged back in.

A Japanese left by himself by an abortive attack and likely to be taken prisoner pulled out one of his grenades and, lying face down, put it under his stomach and blew himself to pieces.

Sergeant Jack Salter
4 Troop, 1 Commando
When the evening came the attack had been pushed back. We counted about four hundred dead Japanese. We had fighter planes in support, and gunfire from ships, and from artillery on pontoons off the beach.

Private Victor Ralph
4 Troop, 1 Commando
I was too busy to be frightened at the time. I don't think any of us expected to come out of it. It was not a question of bravery, but you had too much to do to think about it. After the battle was over and we were relieved, the next day, the thought of what might have happened overtook you.

Lieutenant James Sherwood
C Group, 2 SBS
Before the landing on Ramree we did a recce, involving eight Folboats. We embarked in an MGB and put our canoes over the side, not far from Ramree Island at the entrance to Kyaukpyau Harbour, which is a huge bay,

25-pounder guns on a Z-lighter pontoon supporting the landings and battle at Kangaw.

there is no harbour. It is dotted with tree-clad islands. We paddled to the RV on one of these islands to establish a small base from which we would carry out recces of the surrounding area, of Kyaukpyau Harbour and Ramree Island generally.

It was dark when we landed on a rocky little beach there, established our base and waited for daylight. No sooner had it come than we saw a group of Burmese come along the beach, they were living on the island. They were wholly cooperative and were delighted to see the British coming back.

Livingstone decided to lead the first recce of Ramree, and one of the Burmese volunteered to go with him. He saw a Japanese patrol on a road running south out of the town, without being spotted, and returned to the island but did not discover anything.

The next night we all went back, guided by a Burmese who said he would take us to a village about a mile inland. This was quite a long way. We landed, and crossed dried-out paddy fields. Our chief fear was being caught by Japs. We arrived in the village and while we waited outside, the Burmese went to the headman of the village, and discovered that there were no Japs there. We spoke to the headman. We got all the information we wanted and where the Japs were. He got one of his chaps to go back with us to the island, the aim being to take him to Div HQ at Chittagong so he could be debriefed there.

Livingstone was staying on a day or two longer. He said, 'You take three canoes, take this bloke back, and RV with the MGB.'

It was a long paddle of about six miles to the prearranged RV. I had this chap in my bow with his head in my lap. The bow was low in the water and it was a hell of an effort paddling. The MGB got us back to Teknaf by daybreak next morning. I took the Burmese up to Chittagong for debriefing with General Lomax, 26th Indian Division. The Burmese was taken home with the invasion fleet a few days later.

Major Dominic Neill
Officer Commanding B Company, 3rd/2nd Gurkha Rifles
At first light, the CO passed through my position and warned me to take Snowdon East. He reminded me that the position was to be taken regardless of cost. Rumours that 25 Div was about to be pulled out for retraining and refitting, were among the thousand and one thoughts that range through an

infantryman's mind as he prepares himself to cross a start line, glancing so frequently at the minute hand of his watch as it moves towards H-Hour. There were many of us in B Company that hot afternoon that wondered if this was to be our last attack, and which of us would remain behind forever on the hill that rose in front of us. At 1428 the troop of 25-pounders and medium guns boomed out from behind us, and the shells whistled over our heads to burst on Snowdon East. For a moment we forgot our own thoughts as we watched the shells burst. Then the bombardment ceased: it was H-Hour. At 1430 both assault platoons fixed swords and advanced.

The leading sections came through the bamboo and into the primary jungle. The trees had been splintered and shattered by our artillery fire, many felled in a criss-cross fashion making an obstacle to us that no Jap working party could have equalled had they toiled for days. On the right flank, in the path of 5 Platoon the dry jungle had started to burn. It was while the assault platoons were struggling through this tangle of broken trees that the Japs first hit us with every weapon they possessed. Then they rolled grenades taped to mines down on us. The leading soldiers started to fall, tumbling over like shot rabbits. So far the assault did not falter, individual soldiers gave covering fire to others as groups leapfrogged up the hill.

Then they hit us again, from Whistle, where Japs had a rifle company dug in. They hit us with MMGs on fixed lines. The stream of bullets came at hip height, mowing like scythes through the timber. As the Jap fire started from our left flank so it intensified from the dug-in position ahead. With numbers of soldiers going down, we began to waver and finally halted, cover was sought, and the long fire-fight, which was to use up so much of our precious ammunition, started.

The guns on Whistle never ceased firing until the very end of the battle. The momentum of our attack was failing. I wondered then if the rumours about the division coming out of the line were having a subconscious effect on our actions.

Content to remain where we were, I was doing no leading. I went forward and as the platoon commander was badly wounded, told the havildar to take command. I crawled to 5 Platoon, then asked for artillery fire on to Whistle. But, because the gunner was further back and couldn't see the target, all the ranging rounds for Whistle fell among my forward platoons, causing casualties, and effecting morale. A rifleman just in front of me was hit in the face by a large piece of shrapnel, reducing it to pulp and showering everybody in the vicinity with blood. If the FOO had been beside me at that moment I would probably have killed him. I crawled back and shouted at the gunner in Anglo-Saxon and told him the result of his ranging. He shouted back his apologies and said the guns could not clear the crest and hit Whistle. There was nothing for it but to accept that the Jap machine-gunners on Whistle would continue to fire at us for as long as they pleased, or ran out of ammo. Our prospects looked bleak.

Then the unexpected happened. Lance Naik Chamar Singh Gurung rose to his feet and, yelling obscenities to the Japs above him, started clambering through the broken tree trunks and up the hill. In the face of showers of grenades and heavy rifle and machine-gun fire, and urged on by the screams of encouragement from the men of his platoon, he ran on up the hill spraying the hill with his tommy gun. He was hit by goodness knows how many enemy bullets as he reached the first enemy trench. But he stumbled on, squeezing the trigger of his tommy gun, falling dead across the lip of the Jap trench. Chamar Singh Gurung was the first man on Snowdon East that afternoon. His gallant conduct and inspiration turned what might have been defeat into victory. His action triggered off a series of other actions, which resulted in the Japs being flung off Snowdon.

Rifleman Bhanbhagta Gurung stood up and, inspired by Chamar Singh's bravery, yelled to those near him to follow, and started to run towards the top of the hill. Others rose and charged with a tremendous roar. The Japs met this attack with showers of grenades and rapid fire. The MMGs on Whistle cut down soldiers, and once again they wavered in the face of this murderous fire, and went to ground this time only twenty yards from Jap forward trenches. This, however, was no repeat of the first time. Without waiting for orders, Bhanbhagta Gurung dashed forward alone, attacked the nearest enemy foxhole just above him, and throwing two grenades he killed the two occupants. Without hesitation, he rushed to the next trench and bayoneted the Jap in it to death.

The leading platoons rose and fell upon the Jap defenders of Snowdon East, and the battle lasted until the last Jap soldier had been killed or run off. Bhanbhagta Gurung then attacked a lone machine gun in a bunker. Now, out of HE grenades, he flung in two white phosphorus grenades, two Jap soldiers came out with their clothes on fire, to be cut down by him with his kukri. A remaining Jap, despite grievous wounds from burning phosphorus, continued to fire, whereupon Bhanbhagta Gurung crawled inside the bunker, where he beat out the Jap gunner's brains with a rock, capturing the machine gun.

Seven Japs with fixed bayonets counter-attacked, and were repulsed by a naik with grenades and a bayonet charge, killing two and putting the rest to flight. Enemy positions bypassed started firing and holding up the reserve section and were taken out by the section commander.

There were eleven men left in the right-hand platoon. The left-hand platoon was still under fire when the platoon commander, screaming with rage, killed Japanese with his bayonet red with blood. He had six men left. One NCO attacked the enemy using his TG as a club when out of ammo. Then, drawing his kukri, charged the position, hacking to death one enemy: two others fled.

The reserve platoon now came up as the assault platoons were pitching in to the enemy, and I told the platoon commander to take over the ground from the assault platoons. As they advanced they came under fire from the guns on Whistle, killing and wounding soldiers. As they reached the top the machine-gun fire from Whistle stopped momentarily, and twelve Japs appeared with fixed bayonets and attacked the rear of 4 Platoon. Seeing them, the reserve platoon left-hand section killed them. They then beat off a counter-attack from Whistle.

It was chaos on the top of the objective. The first of the organised counter-attack Banzai charges was beaten off with heavy losses. Snowdon East was now ours. My two assault platoons were smaller than one weak platoon. The part of Snowdon East held by enemy was eighty yards long by thirty yards wide, the whole area pockmarked by trenches. All over the objective lay bodies.

After three further Japanese counter-attacks there was silence. More than sixty per cent of B Company had gone. I was very proud of them. They had captured Snowdon East, regardless of cost.

Corporal Jim Dunning
15 Platoon, C Company, 2nd Battalion, Green Howards
We were the first company wave ashore at Letpan. There was very little opposition. Going up the narrow chaungs in landing craft I thought how vulnerable we were. On our way in we passed a hospital ship and the nurses

Corporal Jim Dunning.

waved to us. I thought how nice it would be to be on board with all those nurses.

We were supposed to advance down the road to Taungup, the roadhead for the Japanese route from Prome in Central Burma. It took us quite a long time to get to Taungup. Along the road there were lots of small hills, covered in secondary jungle, bushy and small trees. All places where the Japs could defend and delay us. All the time we leapfrogged companies taking these hills. You were advancing up very narrow tracks and had quite a few casualties taking these hills. It was so enclosed you couldn't see very far.

Fifteen or twenty people could put up a lot of opposition. Our battalion never took a prisoner. Each engagement happened so quickly. You would bump into the Japanese on the hill, there would be a fire-fight, and they would melt away, usually taking their wounded with them. It was nerve-wracking, fighting in constricted spaces.

I was a section commander until our platoon sergeant went sick and I took over. We were on top of a hill, you had the sea on one side and hills on the other, and through our binoculars we could see a warship with sailors on the deck sunbathing. I thought I'd swap places with you any day. A few minutes after that the platoon commander was killed. He was a lovely chap. I started the morning as a section commander and ended up as the platoon commander.

Then the two battalions we were with were pulled out of the brigade to take part in the capture of Rangoon. We got to the outskirts of Taungup, and the Japs just melted away.

ACROSS THE IRRAWADDY

Major Frederick Rowley
Officer Commanding A Company, 5th/10th Baluch Regiment
Crossing the Irrawaddy was the longest swim I ever had. I was charged by my divisional commander to take my company across the river, four miles higher than where the main crossing was to be, and we had to swim it. I had some Indian Sappers who helped us build bamboo rafts to carry our weapons and kit. We also took our eighteen mules. The Irrawaddy is quite a fast-flowing river, so we had to work out how far we had to start upstream to hit the bank

on the other side where we wanted to be. I took one platoon to start with, and I got across reasonably all right. I was able to signal the rest of the company to come over plus the mules. Mules are very good swimmers, we crossed dressed, except for our boots. All mules got across. I was very relieved; a mule swept away down the Irrawaddy would have given away the fact that we were there to the Japs. In fact they did not know we were there for several hours. I moved downstream to where the main crossing was to be, and we joined the main bridgehead.

Gunner James Baker
134 Medium Regiment, Royal Artillery

We were firing on a Japanese division on the other side of the Irrawaddy with our 6-inch howitzers. Guarding our guns were Sikhs. I was told to report to an officer with my Bren gun, to lay line from guns to where the Gurkhas were being held up in a village. I didn't have a wireless. That night the Japs came charging in to within about fifteen yards. The Jap mortars set the village huts alight. I had to call fire from the guns, but the Japs had cut the wire. I couldn't see the Japs but could hear them. I was firing my Bren gun into the dark. Then everything was lit up by village huts on fire. The Japs sniped at us. The Gurkhas got rid of the snipers, we traced the wire back, found it booby-trapped, but got back to the regiment.

Major Frederick Rowley
Officer Commanding A Company, 5th/10th Baluch Regiment

The Japs still had occupation of a hill called Pear Hill. They were bombarding our crossing. The crossing had to stop. I was having a few hours' rest, having rejoined the battalion, when I was summoned to divisional HQ, to our magnificent commander Pete Rees, who said to me, 'I want you to get Pear Hill, and hold it.' When you are told by your general that's what you've got to do, you say, 'OK sir, I'll do it.'

I went back, sorted out my company, and we left the bridgehead. This was quite risky because the Japs had surrounded us and were potting at us; I didn't want to get too close to where they were. We went out in single file along the riverbank. Several hundred yards along, we got to the bottom of Pear Hill. I left my company at the bottom, and climbed with my subedar major, my orderly and my signaller. I wanted to recce and see what was up there. It was very rugged, and I was trying to keep as quiet as possible. It was quite lightly wooded. I got on top, and there was no sign of the enemy. I turned to my subedar major and told him to bring the rest of the company up. Like an idiot I had taken my equipment off with my revolver; to my horror I found myself looking straight at a Jap OP close by. I turned to shout at my men, the subedar shouted 'Sahib'. There was a Japanese officer rushing towards me with sword raised to knock my head off. He got to within three yards of me. My subedar major shot him. We killed the OP party, all of them.

We could hear the gun position calling up the OP on the telephone. We didn't know what they were saying, but we could hear them calling up. I told the subedar major to get the company up as fast as possible, and I laid them out ready for an onslaught, which we knew would come without question.

As I sat on a rock I felt the most appalling anguish. I was not religious at that time. But I sat saying, 'Lord Jesus, what is wrong?' And I listened, the most important thing when you pray is to listen, and this is what staggered me. I got a message, not a voice, but a message, and it said, 'You're not on the top of the hill.'

I thought oh my God. I walked forward. We were short of the top by about eighty yards, and the Jap emplacements were totally empty. I shouted to my chaps, 'Get up, advance at once.' We secured that place. And in due course the Japs belted us. But it would have been a massacre if we had been in the original place. We held the hill. In the OP there were maps of the Jap positions. I asked for a gunner to be sent up. The following morning a captain and subedar of Indian gunners came up. As I was explaining the position to this captain, he was hit by a huge piece of shrapnel.

Another company joined us the following day. I was up there for four nights, the rest of the battalion for more. But the battle of Pear Hill was fundamentally the opening of the big drive for Mandalay.

Pilot Officer Harry Morrell
211 Squadron, RAF

I did my first op sortie as one of a pair attacking river craft on the Irrawaddy. We lost touch with the other aircraft in cloud, but got there OK. I had done lots of navigation using rivers, roads, railways etc. Pagodas were especially useful, you could see the Shwe Dagon's gold dome forty miles off in daytime.

We were highwaymen, anything that moved we hit. The big prize was a train. If there were no trains about, we attacked the stations, or the engine sheds. The Beaufighter was a formidable aircraft and had four 20-mm cannon, six machine guns, eight 60-pounder HE rockets or eight 25-pounder AP rounds. We always used HE on river craft.

Captain Peter Noakes
Officer Commanding 4 Company, 1st Battalion, Northamptonshire Regiment

We eventually found ourselves on the banks of the Irrawaddy. It was hot. A couple of nights before we crossed a young officer called Thomas was sent out with two or three signallers in a rubber dinghy to cross the river and set up an Aldis lamp on the far bank as a guide to us. He was told to put a red filter in the lamp, and it would be a beacon for us to home on. The Irrawaddy flows very fast. You have to head well upstream in order to land up where you want to finish up. This red lamp was a brilliant idea. The RAF were asked to fly their loudest planes to fly up and down to mask the noise of our outboard motors.

My company was reserve for the crossing. The crossing, at night, was to be carried out by 1 and 3 Companies. When 3 Company got in their boats to go, their boats promptly sank. Major Norman Vita, the company commander, ordered his men out of the boats and on shore. The CO was fed up about it because it meant our plans were awry. He ordered me to take over from 3 Company and get my boys into other boats that were available and we set forth in a crocodile of rubber dinghies, with an outboard on the one in front, which kept on conking out. As we crossed the river we were met with rather inaccurate machine-gun and mortar fire from the Japs who didn't know where we were and fired at random.

We landed after some mishaps and alarms. When we got out of our craft, we found ourselves in four feet of water; the sand banks had shifted, but it didn't matter, we were on the other side. We immediately dug in. The other companies got across. The next morning battalion HQ got across with supplies. The Japs shelled the far bank, and our side, using their infantry guns, we called whiz-bangs. They were quite small calibre, and were manhandled up into the front line, with a very flat trajectory. You heard the gunfire as the shell was exploding. They caused quite a few casualties.

Captain William Rhodes-James
Officer Commanding B Company, 1st/6th Gurkha Rifles

Having crossed, we advanced south following up the Japs as they withdrew. We had Grants in support. We formed up on the start line and were shelled by Japs, which was disconcerting. I rode on the tank until the bullets started to bounce off the armour. We found the Japs dug in, the tanks seemed to hypnotise and cow them. My men sorted them out, while the tanks stopped. My left platoon found two battalion guns dug in ahead. My right-hand platoon commander rushed forward and captured both.

There were a lot of Jap bullets flying about. A Jap grenade landed in the road, the shrapnel hit my forehead, and filled my eyes with blood. It was not serious.

Private Tom Cattle
17 Platoon, D Company, 2nd Battalion, Dorsetshire Regiment

The next obstacle was the Irrawaddy. On the way towards the river, we bumped the Japs at a place called 'Gun Copse', a very arid area with bits of jungle and villages, and we couldn't move as we were caught in the open. All we could do was bury our noses in the ground and hope for the best. They called in an air strike to help us. Instead of dive-bombing the village they dive-bombed us. We could see the bombs falling and exploding, the earth opening up in front of us. Luckily it was just in front of us. After a while they realised they were bombing the wrong place, and started bombing the village. We put in a flanking movement and got the Japs out of it. The Japs were dug in, in foxholes, letting us go past and shooting people in the back. We had quite a few casualties shot in the back.

The Irrawaddy is a mile wide. I was a bit apprehensive: I couldn't swim. We could see the Japs on the other side and knew it would not be an easy crossing. We were at a village on the west bank and dug in. We were patrolling across the river and so were they. One night the Japs managed to get in amongst us. It was hand-to-hand fighting, and hope for the best. We were so close to each other you couldn't even use grenades, just bayonets. Eventually they left. There were not many of them.

Some fold-up canvas boats operated by Royal Engineers with an outboard engine were produced by the division and brought up. These boats weren't very stable and the engines were not reliable. Some people had to paddle to get across or back to where they started. It was a steep bank on the other side, and immediately we were into high elephant grass. We were being shelled and machine-gunned, but managed to enlarge the bridgehead.

Captain Peter Noakes
Officer Commanding 4 Company, 1st Battalion, Northamptonshire Regiment

After a few days it was decided to extend the bridgehead and my company was sent to occupy the North Chaung, a big chaung running from the Irrawaddy leading eastwards inland. It was used as an OP for Japanese artillery. When we advanced into it there were two or three Japs lurking around, we got rid of those. We occupied it, dug ourselves in, and we got shelled. It was an impossible defensive position because the area round was elephant grass, about eight to ten feet high. The Japs attacked us one night, not through the elephant grass, which crackles and gives you away, but up the chaung. Fortunately we heard them; the Japs are great chatterers, they talk a lot. I put up parachute flares from our 2-inch mortars, and we beat off the attack.

Then some barbed wire came up for us. We had plenty of trees round our perimeter; we managed to erect a two-strand fence of wire round our position, which was a godsend. We also had a section of Vickers MMG from the 9th Jats, a machine-gun battalion. We had a very big attack two nights later. The Japs got fed up with our parachute flares, because they illuminated them and we could pick them off. So they employed smoke with smoke canisters. For a while we thought it was gas; our anti-gas respirators were back in India. But it was smoke.

Our Royal Artillery 4.2-inch mortars and the MMGs put down defensive fire in our support, this curtailed the Jap advance to the wire. The Japs brought up Bangalore torpedoes, but we never allowed them to get close enough to put the Bangalores through the wire and blow gaps. The Japs eventually withdrew. We found a lot of Japs on our wire, and nearby in the morning. I can't remember how many dead, but there was certainly one officer, whose sword I took. His name was Second Lieutenant Yamamoto. He was dead and beautifully dressed.

Lieutenant Michael Marshall
Officer Commanding Mortar Platoon, 4th/5th Royal Gurkha Rifles
Our objective on the way to the Irrawaddy was the town of Pakokku. Within four or five miles of Pakokku our patrols found a heavily defended position at Kanhla. Here we had the biggest battle the battalion had experienced so far. The battle took all day. We overran the position at about 1600. Many Japs were finished off in their holes as they refused to surrender. During the morning of the battle, our new CO, Lieutenant Colonel John Turner, was giving his orders in middle morning, and was hit by sniper in the stomach. I was one of those taking orders from him and was about three feet away from him. He died that evening.

Lieutenant Colonel Hugh Pettigrew
GSO 1, HQ, 17th Indian Division
I flew with 'Punch' Cowan, the divisional commander to Slim's headquarters, to plan our part in the campaign. 7 Div had already got to Pakokku on the Irrawaddy and was in contact with the Japanese. We had to advance secretly to Pakokku; 7 Div would seize the bridgehead, then the whole of our division, less one brigade, would cross, and make for Meiktila. We would block the Japs in Mandalay from getting out.

Lieutenant Michael Marshall
Officer Commanding Mortar Platoon, 4th/5th Royal Gurkha Rifles
Shortly after, we crossed the Irrawaddy. Our crossing was relatively straightforward. We landed at Nyaungu and had a battalion position close to Pagan.

Sergeant Stanley Wood
Platoon Commander, 2nd Battalion, Durham Light Infantry
We got across with very little trouble, and dug in ready to advance. When we moved out, we were moving up a dried up riverbank with tanks. In the middle of the riverbed we saw a pile of fresh straw. I contacted the tank commander through the tank telephone, and suggested he gave the heap a short burst with his machine gun. Luckily, because no sooner had he blasted away the straw, than a little Japanese jumped out of the hole. I don't know what he was going to do, but was caught by another burst of fire. When we got there, he was

A Japanese soldier shot sitting in a hole with a shell between his knees waiting to detonate it when a tank passes over him.

sitting, dead, cross-legged in the hole, with a huge shell between his legs, and with a stone to hit the detonator, waiting for a tank to go over.

After moving up the riverbed we were held up by fire, by now it was getting dark, so we laagered up with the tank. We were in a crescent shape round the tank. The tank commander fired the gun without checking his barrel clearance for branches: the shell burst, and wounded three of my men.

Private Tom Cattle
17 Platoon, D Company, 2nd Battalion, Dorsetshire Regiment
Our objective now was Mandalay. We were in open ground and from Ngazun we headed for Ava. At one place we found ourselves in a huge area of tomatoes. And as we were walking along, we were picking them and eating them. I had never come across anything like it. The CO, Colonel White, behind us, thought we were taking casualties as people were bending down to pick tomatoes and asked what was going on.

We reached Ava Bridge without much opposition. It started getting dark. The Worcesters were in front, and we were on both sides of the road. At this point it was rocky and hilly, and the Worcesters halted, for some reason. The Dorsets took the lead and advanced at night on to a hilly position. Why I don't know. We went through the Worcesters, they were in a nullah. It was a pitch-black night. We got to a bit of a hill with a black pagoda on it. There was no one there and we advanced through and C Company went over the top to the other side of the hill. We went to the top and to the left. Battalion HQ were in the area of the pagoda, and the other companies at the back of the hill. We got to our positions without any opposition, and started to dig in. It was quiet, but the clanking of our entrenching tools hitting hard rock made a noise you could hear for miles. I thought my God, this is a bit precarious.

A patrol came back and said there were no Japs. We couldn't dig down far and had to build up to get protection. At daybreak, all of a sudden a hell of a machine-gun barrage started to sweep the hill, and from where C Company was we could hear shrieks and screams and shouts; we knew they were taking casualties. Bullets were sweeping over the hill and our positions and we were taking casualties, as was everyone else. Jimmy Wells, our platoon commander, was badly shot in the legs. There were about two Japanese machine guns doing the damage. They seemed to know exactly where we were going to be.

We had to pull back, we couldn't sustain the casualties we were taking.

SE 3153

Soldiers of the 2nd Battalion The Dorsetshire Regiment about to cross the Irrawaddy at Ngazun.

There was no cover. My friend I joined up with was killed. After causing all the casualties the Japs withdrew. It was a stupid attack that we had to do.

Lieutenant Harpratab Singh
A Squadron, 7th Light Cavalry

On the Mandalay bridge we shot them where they were on the bridge structure, sniping. We shot them, but admired them; one man could hold up a company, and he would not give in. One Japanese attacked my tank on his own with an explosive charge, and for a moment I wondered if I should shoot him, but had to in order to stop him.

Lieutenant Colonel Hugh Pettigrew
GSO 1, HQ, 17th Indian Division

Next day, started to move. 'Punch' Cowan had a real rush of blood to the head, because he cut straight across country with the whole of Divisional HQ. It was highly exhilarating, the whole lot in jeeps, signalling trucks etc, over fields, leaping over the bunds. Flat and dry, went all right, across the short side of the triangle.

Major John Randle
Officer Commanding B (Pathan) Company, 7th/10th Baluch Regiment

At Meiktila we surprised the Japs by our advance, and caught them. I came across a Jap field hospital on fire. It was like a scene from hell. There were wounded, there were sick, it smelt ghastly, chaps were screaming. It had been about one hundred miles behind the Japanese lines.

I pushed on at dawn next morning on a company sweep, with one tank and a FOO. We ran into a main Jap position. The leading platoon commander was killed. The FOO was killed. The enemy was widely deployed. I couldn't get on. I stayed where I was, and another company put in an attack with a whole squadron of tanks, very successfully. The tanks just fired point-blank into the slits of the bunkers.

Lieutenant Colonel Hugh Pettigrew
GSO 1, HQ, 17th Indian Division

One bit of shrapnel took the toes off a gunner officer alongside me and hit the general's caravan. We captured Meiktila, but it took a long time to root out the Japs. Every night there was a battle as brigades sortied to catch Japs on the move. We were on air supply. We were stuck there quite a long time.

Gunner James Baker
134 Medium Regiment, Royal Artillery
Then we had a headlong rush to the outskirts of Mandalay and could see Mandalay Hill right in front and sighted our guns and fired on Mandalay Hill. The infantry could not get the Japs out of the caves, so they drilled holes and poured in oil and set fire to it. Most Japs stayed in the caves; others, in full view of us, jumped from the caves all alight. I saw about eight or nine. We had captured the hill but the Japs were still inside.

Major Frank Brodrick
Second-in-Command, 9th Battalion, Border Regiment
We crossed the Irrawaddy at Pakokku and on the way across from there the armour came with us. They were very efficient and made the move to Meiktila so much easier. There were quite a number of Japanese there, hidden behind trees. The chap doing the attack was a friend of mine and I thought he could do with help, so I went forward, and heard somebody groaning. I got two people to cover me to see if I could see this wounded person, in an old paddy field without water, so I went and stood behind a palm tree and looked to see where the noise was coming from. A Jap fired at me with a rifle, which hit me on the lip. It felt like being hit by a sledge-hammer. I dropped down behind the bund, and these two I had brought to cover me, they dealt with the Japanese who had fired at me.

I went back to report, I picked up a Japanese flag on the way. Often the Jap would keep a flag folded inside his tin helmet, which is where I found it. I met my CO on the way back, I explained what I had done, gave him the flag and went off to the RAP to be treated. They stitched me up and I waited there to be flown out next day.

Corporal Les Griffiths
Battalion HQ, 9th Battalion, Border Regiment
The battle for Meiktila was fierce, each village had to be fought for. We went for three days without water supply. We had tanks with us; some of us were on the tanks and some walking alongside. The Japs were firing at us, I was

alongside the CO, waiting to go in, and out came 'Smudge' being carried out, grimacing and holding his stomach, and just as I looked at him, a figure ran across in my vision, running like the clappers. Chaps started shouting, and I ran too, shouldn't have done, I was supposed to be looking after the CO. We ran on a converging course. I was going like the clappers, then he appeared to fall over. I caught him up and pointed my tommy gun at him. I didn't know what to do. I hadn't the heart to shoot him. An officer came up and said, 'Shoot him, corporal.' I still couldn't shoot him. The officer went off, and another officer came up, a tank officer, and he stood there, and said, 'Shoot him, corporal, now!'

I did. I went off, didn't bother to look round, I knew I'd shot him. I went back to the CO and where 'Smudge' was waiting for a small aeroplane to come in, and he had all his fingers blown off. The butt of his rifle was smashed, and his fingers with it, he had a little finger and thumb on each hand. I felt justified in shooting the Jap.

Private Jim Wilks
11 Platoon, B Company, 2nd Battalion, West Yorkshire Regiment
They decided to fly our battalion in Dakotas into an airstrip at Meiktila, some troops had taken it, but it was still under Jap attack. The snag was, as we were landing, the Japs were shelling the strip. So the American crew said, 'We are not stopping, as we taxi along you lot jump out. And as soon as you lot jump out, we are taking off at the other end.'

This is what happened. The plane landed, taxied, it was a bit of a shambles: men and packs all over the airstrip.

Private Peter Hazelhurst
B Company, 9th Battalion, Border Regiment
The fighting on the plains was different. I rejoined B Company. The commando platoon had been disbanded. Our company commander was 'Long John' Petty, he was a classic soldier, a good fighting man.

The advance was great: we had trucks to ride in. At Meiktila a couple of companies of us were sent out to liven up the Japs. We were in trucks and drove straight into the attack of a Jap camp, 'Long John' Petty bayoneted a Jap. The bayonet went straight through, bent when it hit the ground, and he couldn't get the bayonet out.

Private Jim Wilks.

Private Jim Wilks
11 Platoon, B Company, 2nd Battalion, West Yorkshire Regiment

When we got sorted out we went into a defensive box. The Japs shelled the airstrip and shelled us. Then it quietened down. I've been frightened before, but this was one of the worst. Our job was to go out and clear that airstrip before the next lot of planes could land. The Japs were in the jungle on each side of the airstrip; up in the trees sniping at us. You never knew who was going to get hit next. That was our job for about eight or nine days.

They used to tie themselves in the trees. We could not see them. We advanced down the airstrip, about five yards apart, spread out. We walked along spraying the trees with bursts. Eventually we got them. Of course we lost one or two of ours at the same time. After we cleared the strip, the planes came in.

When we shot a Jap we had to search them for diaries and letters etc, to hand in for intelligence. We kept things like watches. I have a Jap silk flag. The Jap was a brave man. We only ever took one prisoner. He didn't know what day it was, he was wandering about in a coma. We gave him a cigarette, and bandaged him up. If it had been one of us they would have used us for bayonet practice. Another we went to pick up, when he saw us coming, he took the pin out of his grenade and blew himself up.

Private Peter Hazelhurst
B Company, 9th Battalion, Border Regiment

The next action was south of Meiktila. That was one of the hardest fights we had. We went in on tanks. The Kittyhawk fighter-bombers came in and strafed and bombed the village, but only half the bombs went off. When they fired their cannons people were hit by the empty shell cases falling out of the planes. We went to the edge of the village and the snipers were having a go at us, some lads were knocked over.

We got to the edge of the trees and things were getting really warm, and I was tired and thirsty. I was sitting on an unexploded bomb, I was that exhausted – if it goes up, it goes up. There was a great big bunker in the centre of the village, a tank came up and put a 75-mm shell in it. Sam Wilson was the wireless operator with the company commander. He was sitting on a tree trunk with a wireless on his back when a Jap shot out of the bunker with a sword in one hand and a grenade in the other shouting, 'Banzai!' He set out

SE 3287

Soldiers of the 9th Battalion the Border Regiment clearing a village on the outskirts of Meiktila.

SE 3102

A Bren gun team of the 1st Battalion the West Yorkshire Regiment clearing Japanese positions at Meiktila.

for Sam who jumped up off the log, and vaulted over another log. The Jap threw the grenade at him, which did not explode, and then turned and ran back, waving his sword. Of course everybody started shooting at him. He went down. An officer jumped up and finished him off.

Major Frederick Rowley
Officer Commanding A Company, 5th/10th Baluch Regiment
We surrounded Fort Dufferin in the centre of Mandalay. My battalion, with the 2nd Worcesters, were charged with attacking across the moat. As we were preparing ourselves to go, our aircraft bombed in support, but unfortunately killed twenty-seven of the Worcesters by mistake.

Gunner James Baker
134 Medium Regiment, Royal Artillery
At Fort Dufferin, we had to fire the guns over open sights to breach the wall. We fired at the bottom but didn't make any difference – no breach. Then we fired at the top of the wall, and slowly made a breach with our 120-pound shells. US bombers came over and bombed.

Major Frederick Rowley
Officer Commanding A Company, 5th/10th Baluch Regiment
The Japanese departed: we were told by people coming out with white flags that the Japs had left. We went in all ready because we didn't trust the Japs. We crossed the moat, climbed up over the rubble, and into what had been the prison courtyard. We knew there was a prison in there, but not that the doors were locked from outside so we could not get out. I had to use machine guns to blow the locks off. The fort was deserted except for one person. We were gingerly going along, when we heard and saw a figure about fifty yards away. As it got closer it didn't look like a Japanese. I shouted out at him, and challenged him. He turned out to be an American from Shwebo, who had just driven in to look for souvenirs in his jeep. He said, 'The gates were open. I'm on holiday, on leave.'

Gunner James Baker
134 Medium Regiment, Royal Artillery
A Signal Sergeant Williams decided to climb and look in. Inside there were

Fort Dufferin Mandalay under air attack before the British take the city.

A 6-in howitzer of 134 Medium Regiment Royal Artillery firing point-blank to breach the walls at Fort Dufferin.

some Indian civilians with white flags who told him the Japs had left. This Sergeant kicked a bag which he thought was rice, and he got peppered: it was a booby trap. So don't touch anything, not a single thing. Not even a flag, especially flags.

Private Tom Cattle
17 Platoon, D Company, 2nd Battalion, Dorsetshire Regiment

By the time we got into Mandalay the 19th Division had taken the place. We saw General Rees hauling up the British flag in the centre of town.

Corporal Arthur Freer
Squadron Leader's Driver/Operator, B Squadron, 3rd Carabiniers

B Squadron commander was told that his squadron was not required for the attack on Mandalay, it would be A Squadron. He lost his temper and said it was only right for B Squadron to go to Mandalay. The Brigadier told him to calm down. We couldn't care less. We wanted to get home to England.

However, he was told that one tank of B Squadron could enter Mandalay. He chose his own tank, so we set off for Mandalay next morning. We had no infantry with us. No one wanted to know us. We drove in alone, until we reached the Jap detention centre, mostly women, detained there for two or so years. The Japs were not willing to open the gates when demanded by the infantry who had appeared, but the squadron leader volunteered to charge the gate with the tank. The Japs opened the gates, and internees wandered out, mostly young women, some with babies.

Captain Peter Noakes
Officer Commanding 4 Company, 1st Battalion, Northamptonshire Regiment

Eventually we got behind Mandalay, astride the road. The Japs were evacuating Mandalay; we ambushed a party that walked into one of my positions. One turned out to be a Jap warrant officer who was the head clerk of the Japanese Army HQ at Mandalay; we shot him, and as we heard him moaning, I said to one of my platoon commanders, 'Put him out of his misery,' but before he could, this warrant officer shot himself. He carried a briefcase full of documents, which were immediately sent back to division. They were translated, and they were very important intelligence.

Major General 'Pete' Rees GOC 19th Indian Division entering Fort Dufferin on 19 March 1945.

SE 3459

Major Harry Smith
4th Battalion, Queen's Own Royal West Kent Regiment

We went up the road to 7 Division's bridgehead and cleared the road to Meiktila as the Japs had taken the road between the town and the Irrawaddy. I was sent to occupy a hill top which was under heavy fire. The next day we advanced again like a partridge drive against scattered Jap forces. Our jovial colonel, together with the signals corporal and the OC HQ Company, were blown up in a jeep by a mine. The CO and OC HQ Company were grievously wounded and the signals corporal killed. So the 2i/c became acting CO and I was dug out from a rifle company to become battalion 2i/c.

I commanded the advance down the road to Meiktila where we met odd Japanese positions. We had tanks with us and tanks could operate in the open country in the Burmese plain. We also had two Typhoons circling overhead, and an RAF officer in a jeep behind me to contact the Typhoons to attack the Japanese positions with rockets. With tanks and Typhoons in support we made splendid progress, and covered forty miles in a day and linked up with the 17 Div who were already in occupation of Meiktila. Japanese dead were everywhere.

Major John Randle
Officer Commanding B (Pathan) Company, 7th/10th Baluch Regiment

I was nearly put under close arrest after a para drop. I was putting a parachute in my jeep, when a major from the military police said he was going to put me under close arrest. I said, 'Look around at my one hundred and twenty Pathans, they won't take it kindly if you manhandle me.'

He looked round, and said, 'You'll hear more of this.'

I heard nothing more for a bit, then had a note from the assistant adjutant general of the division, saying, 'John don't be a bloody fool, if you're going to nick things don't do it with the assistant provost marshal around.'

Major Harry Smith
4th Battalion, Queen's Own Royal West Kent Regiment

Very soon after this, our two divisions 17th and 5th started the advance down the road and railway to capture Rangoon before the monsoon broke. The orders were to go as quickly as possible and not be held up by Jap positions on the flanks. We began our drive to Rangoon, three hundred and twenty miles away.

THE RANGOON ROAD

Captain Michael Marshall
Officer Commanding A Company, 4th/5th Royal Gurkha Rifles

In March I took over A Company as a captain. The general advance started and we were told to capture the oilfields at Yenangyaung and Minbu. At all these places we came across telltale signs of the 1942 retreat: old British vehicles, burnt-out light tanks, and oil wells demolished and set alight.

The Japs fought a rearguard action throughout. We were supported by the Carabiniers tanks. They were excellent. I saw a young tank commander receive a direct hit while we were advancing at Minbu. At the moment he was hit, he was standing up giving instructions, the whole tank burning in front of our eyes.

Trooper Malcolm Connolly
7 Troop, C Squadron, 3rd Carabiniers

We crossed the Irrawaddy at Magwe to Minbu. Our job was to cut the Japanese off and stop their retreat from the Arakan. We had plenty of crews, but were running out of tanks. The infantry was held up by a Japanese gun, and they said the tanks could take them out. They'd lost two or three tanks the previous days. The tank advanced, the gun fired, and the tank went up with the loss of seven men. When the infantry overran the gun it was a British 25-pounder which we didn't have a hope against; one of the finest tank busters in the world. The Japanese had a lot of these which they had taken on the retreat.

Captain Peter Gadsdon
Officer Commanding A Company, 4th/14th Punjabis

In one village we came under machine-gun fire. We took cover quickly. There were Jap wounded all over the place. One in particular I hoped to capture. I shouted at him, 'Hands up,' in English, putting mine up to show what I wanted. All he held up was a grenade, so I hastily backed off and told my troops to lie down. Nothing happened, so I advanced again. The same thing happened, and the third time he banged the grenade to set the fuse, put it down his shirt front and blew himself up. No prisoner.

Major John Randle
Officer Commanding B (Pathan) Company, 7th/10th Baluch Regiment

We had heavy fighting down the main axis south to Pyawbwe, which was held strongly by Japs. Our brigade did a right flanking movement, and a squadron of tanks reported a strong force of Japs on Point 900 were in the mood to surrender, so they said. The CO deployed the battalion in attack formation, my company on the left. It was a bare hill. We were engaged by Jap MMGs on the left. We dealt with that, got to the top, and all the Japs were up there. The tanks had pushed off, they seemed to have a habit of doing this. Then, as we went over a little crest, a soldier just in front of me was shot by a Jap. On that my soldiers went mad, and we killed 124 Japs with bayonet, grenades and tommy guns, the men were screaming and had a wolfish look with bare teeth. I tried to take a few prisoners, but my subedar said, 'It's no good, you're wasting your breath.' It was unusual, we saw the Jap company commander running away, my boys put a burst in him. They gave me his sword. We were on a high, adrenalin running, all steamed up. My chaps were in a bloodlust.

Private Peter Hazelhurst
B Company, 9th Battalion, Border Regiment

At Pyawbwe, we lined up on the paddy fields and were told we were going to have to move on foot, there was a big railway embankment about a mile in front of us. We were told we had to take the railway station. They were shelling us. We fought our way to the embankment and lost a few lads crossing the paddy fields, and we killed about four hundred or five hundred Japs that day. There were big railway sidings in the town. The Japs retreated out of the town and left it to us. That was our last big battle.

Lieutenant James Sherwood
C Group, 2 SBS

By now the monsoon was approaching. We then heard that an amphibious operation was to be mounted against Rangoon from Kyaukpyau. We were to accompany this force. This fleet ambled out of Kyaukpyau harbour just as we heard news about the war with Germany coming to an end. This cheered everybody enormously.

Private Peter Hazelhurst
B Company, 9th Battalion, Border Regiment
We got to Pegu and were all lined up ready to go in and the word came that the war in Europe was over. And we shouted, 'What the bloody hell use is that to us? When's our war going to be over?'

Sergeant Stanley Wood
Platoon Commander, 2nd Battalion, Durham Light Infantry
We were then pulled out and told that we were being taken out of Burma by air to Chittagong, by train to Calcutta, and then assault Rangoon from the sea. We had a very pleasant two weeks' rest on convalescent rations and had beer etc. As we were going down the Arakan coast in a trooper, tank landing craft and LCAs were launched to allow us to go ashore at Cheduba to swim. At that time we learned that the war in Europe had finished. The general remark was 'the lucky sods'. The pleasure of the good news was tempered by the prospect of an assault landing at Rangoon.

Lieutenant Colonel Hugh Pettigrew
GSO 1, HQ, 17th Indian Division
A sergeant despatch rider came up and handed me a message, which read, 'The war in Europe is over.' I called out to the sergeant, 'I've got a message here. The war in Europe is over.' He said, 'Very good, sir,' saluted, turned to some men nearby, and said, 'The war in Europe is over. Five-minute break.'

Major John Randle
Officer Commanding B (Pathan) Company, 7th/10th Baluch Regiment
We were moving about twenty to thirty miles per day. We had to get to Rangoon, if only to get proper rations. The monsoon was not far away, air supply would be unreliable in monsoon. The whip was out.

We ran into quite stiff opposition at Pegu. We put in an attack with A Company on my right. I had a bad day there. We got on to the hill, in pretty thick stuff, but couldn't get on through, because the Japs had a MMG and a 75-mm dug in, in defilade. They also had quite a few mortars. My leading platoon commander was badly wounded. We had a stupid order that morphine could be held only by company commanders, so I had to administer the stuff instead of getting on with my own job.

We were mortared badly in company HQ, the FOO was killed. It was so steep, the 25-pounders couldn't get crest clearance and hit the Japs. The battalion mortars did quite a good job. I just couldn't get forward at all, it was a semi-reverse slope position, and I couldn't get tanks up, it was too thick. Every time we moved we got fired on from flank. Just over the crest the foliage was cleared so there was no cover. When we captured the position we found that the MMG was dug in with logs overhead with a small slit allowing a critical arc of fire.

At nightfall the Japs counter-attacked with a few tanks. I had the whole of the corps artillery firing on my company front, about four field regiments, a medium regiment, and a troop of 9.2-inch heavies, on a front of about two hundred yards. My God, it didn't half make a crump. It broke up the Japs' counter-attack. This convinced the Japs that they would never take the position back. The plan was that another company would push through me the next morning, and take the rest of the position. But at first light, my leading platoon patrolled forward and reported that the Japs had pushed off. That was that.

Major Harry Smith
4th Battalion, Queen's Own Royal West Kent Regiment
Just as we were about to continue our triumphant march, the monsoon broke overnight. All the ground became a lake.

Corporal Les Griffiths
Battalion HQ, 9th Battalion, Border Regiment
At Pegu the monsoon had just started and the bridge collapsed, the river rose so high. We were stuck on the north side of the bridge. The CO, Major Brodrick, and a jeep driver called 'Blackie' Blackett, and I went to have a look at the state of the river.

The driver took us to the bridge and parked on a hump, and we decided we would just walk along the bank and look at the river. It was very hot, so we took our weapons off and left them with 'Blackie' in the jeep, and walked along in the pouring rain. The river was coming round the bend, and a Burman came out of the grass and pointed at a hut and said, 'Japani Sahib.'

Major Frank Brodrick
Second-in-Command, 9th Battalion, Border Regiment
We had stupidly left our rifles in the jeep, and had no weapons. I was faced with a CO who I didn't want shot, I could not send an NCO, so I walked to this house, it had outside stairs, I walked up, nothing happened. I opened the door at the top of the stairs and as I did so I heard a loud creaking of a door opening on the other side of the house. I thought you silly so-and-so. Out from this door came a miserable little Japanese about five feet high, knees knocking, he came downstairs with me.

The Japanese signed that he would like a drink. The CO was a blood and thunder man who used to tell everybody what he would do if he came across a Jap. He got his water bottle out and gave it to the Jap. We looked on with our mouths open.

Corporal Les Griffiths
Battalion HQ, 9th Battalion, Border Regiment
I tied his hands behind his back and took his knife off him. I gave him a cigarette. When we took him back everyone thought it was very funny, the CO and us two getting a prisoner, very rare.

Pilot Officer Henry Morrell
211 Squadron, RAF
Our Beaufighter squadron was operating from a tarmac strip in the Chittagong area, when the monsoon arrived early. We had to take off in the rain, sheets of spray flew up. As you flew across the paddy fields, flocks of birds would fly up and hit the aircraft, hitting the windscreen and engines. The blood and feathers would soon blow off.

We covered the landings at Rangoon. Wing Commander Montague Brown, our CO, flew over Rangoon Jail and took the photo 'Japs Gone'.

Lieutenant James Sherwood
C Group, 2 SBS
We joined the convoy, rounded the mouth of the Irrawaddy, and sailed up the mouth of the river in a landing craft, and were told that the Japs had gone, and withdrawn eastwards to Siam.

Sergeant Stanley Wood
Platoon Commander, 2nd Battalion, Durham Light Infantry
So we were able to sail upriver and land in the docks. We landed at Pyongi Street Docks. We had very detailed maps showing every Jap position. There was not much damage in Rangoon.

ROUNDUP

Major Harry Smith
4th Battalion, Queen's Own Royal West Kent Regiment
The Japs still had divisions cut off in the Arakan, and they tried to fight their way into Siam. We found ourselves positioned along the road and railway and as the Japanese emerged from the Pegu Yomas they were met by tanks and artillery and were massacred.

Private Peter Hazelhurst
B Company, 9th Battalion, Border Regiment
We were thirty-eight miles from Rangoon, but never got in because of the landings that took place. So we went north again to the Sittang river. We were lined up on the roads to stop the Japs from getting to Thailand. We took about three prisoners in over two years of fighting. We started taking more towards the end. But they fought back on the Sittang. They were in a bad state. I saw one with his kneecap gone and he was on a crutch. He begged us to shoot him.

Major John Randle
Officer Commanding B (Pathan) Company, 7th/10th Baluch Regiment
We stayed in Pegu for a while, then we went to Nyaunglebin. The division was strung along from Nyaunglebin to the north like guns in a partridge shoot, the whole of Jap 28 Army stuck in Arakan and west of Pegu trying to break out. We were well dug in, with massive artillery support. I had a platoon of six MMGs supporting my company. We killed countless Japs, but they did start to surrender then. I had taken a prisoner in Pegu, who just walked in. He seemed quite well nourished.

In the battle of the breakthrough the Japs were in appalling conditions, their attacks were pretty half-hearted; it was a pretty uneven contest. Their attacks were not to capture our positions but to divert our attention and get men across to the Sittang and across to Jap-held Burma. Some did get through in small parties. They had heavy casualties from disease. On one patrol we found a dying Jap, we gave him the *coup de grâce* with the bayonet. By this time the Burmese had changed sides again, and Aung San's chaps were harrying the Japanese.

Private Peter Hazelhurst
B Company, 9th Battalion, Border Regiment
We did a fourteen-day patrol by the Sittang River and counted the Japanese bodies floating down, dozens and dozens of them. George MacDonald Fraser was my section commander. I shot a vulture out of a tree there, because I was bored stiff. I looked at the vulture and thought, 'I bet you think you are going to eat me later. You're not, mate.' Fraser said, 'You could have alerted the Japanese for miles around.'

Major John Randle
Officer Commanding B (Pathan) Company, 7th/10th Baluch Regiment
We thought we would go on and on. We were wearing a bit thin by then. I had been in Burma from the beginning. If my CO had said, 'You have earned a rest,' even before we went back in early '45, I would have taken it. But I would never have asked for it; couldn't put your hand up and say. 'I've had enough.' One other officer had been in the battalion for the same period of time, but he had missed Imphal. We had a very aggressive brigade commander, from Probyn's Horse, who wanted aggressive patrolling. Neither our brigadier nor our CO ever came to see the companies, so we ignored this. The prospect of fighting on across the rest of Burma, Siam and China didn't appeal.

Major Harry Smith
4th Battalion, Queen's Own Royal West Kent Regiment
The battalion suffered ten men killed in one last effort, against Japanese marines of whom we killed forty. That was our last battle. I was told that I would be flown home and missed VJ Day.

Corporal Les Griffiths
Battalion HQ, 9th Battalion, Border Regiment
Then the bomb was dropped; nobody would believe it. Most chaps said, 'What's an atom bomb?' We'd never heard of it. The Japs didn't believe it either, there were lots of Japs killed after the bomb was dropped. They fought on.

Major John Randle
Officer Commanding B (Pathan) Company, 7th/10th Baluch Regiment
I heard of the bomb while my company was defending a gun box. I went into the gunner officers' mess, and heard about it there. The full significance did not sink in at once. All we heard was that the Japs were thinking of surrendering. About a week later, the division moved south, we were dug in and patrolling. We began to take a bit of a 'couldn't care less' attitude.

When the Japs surrendered, we were in line on the banks of the Sittang, the rain was pissing down. We put up a terrific *feu de joie*, with some captured Jap MGs. The gunners were firing star shell. Brigade HQ asked, 'What are you firing at?'

Major Frank Brodrick
Second-in-Command, 9th Battalion, Border Regiment
At the surrender I was given the job of meeting the Japs between Pegu and Bilin. I had to wait to meet this Jap officer with a jeep to take him back to our lines to arrange the surrender. He appeared, he was a major, in a beautiful uniform; I was scruffy.

Major John Randle
Officer Commanding B (Pathan) Company, 7th/10th Baluch Regiment
We were ordered to cross the Sittang by ferry, by the bridge, which we had been about the last unit to cross in 1942; a poignant moment. Then to Kyaikyto, where we were ordered to arrange the surrender of 18 Jap Division, and disarm them. The CO was on leave, I was acting 2i/c. When we arrived a whole crowd of Japs with fixed bayonets rushed up, and I thought we were going to be killed. It turned out to be a quarter guard. There was only one chap who could speak English, an oily Chicago University-trained chap.

We took a view that this was not a time for arrogant behaviour, and we would teach the Japs how to treat defeated people. We told them to hand in all weapons in Kyaikyto railway station. Then they asked about their swords. They wanted to hand them in personally and not have them dumped with the rest of the weapons. We decided that to treat them in a civilised fashion over their swords would mean they might cooperate over other weapons. So we told them that, provided all the other equipment was handed in, at the end each officer of the division was to hand in his sword individually to officers and the divisional commander to hand his to the brigade commander. Each Jap officer came up and saluted, unsheathed his sword, and handed it over.

Final Words

Final Words

On 6 August 1945 the first atomic bomb was dropped on the city of Hiroshima, and three days later Nagasaki suffered the same fate. On 14 August the Japanese surrendered unconditionally. Three years and eight months after the beginning of the Burma Campaign the Japanese signed the preliminary surrender arrangements at Rangoon, thus ending the longest campaign fought by the Commonwealth army on any front.

We will never know how many lost their lives in this bloody campaign. No two sources agree, even approximately, on the precise numbers of killed, wounded and missing on either side. The best estimate we have of casualties to the 530,000 British, Empire and Commonwealth troops in the Fourteenth Army is 9,400 killed in action, and 61,800 wounded, taken prisoner or missing. Despite the well-tried British casualty procedures, and partly due to the nature of this campaign, doubts still remain as to the exact numbers.

Japanese figures are even more problematic. Their Burma Area Army records were lost or destroyed during the final days of the fighting. The very lowest estimate of Japanese casualties is 106,100 of which it is thought that 46,700 were killed in action, out of a total strength of approximately 400,000; a figure which itself has never been confirmed. It is impossible to guess how many of their soldiers died unseen in the hills and jungles of Assam and the Arakan, or how many bodies floated down the monsoon-swelled rivers of Lower Burma during the Japanese attempts to reach Thailand in the final months of desperate and confused fighting.

The terrain and climate in Burma challenged both sides, particularly in the monsoon when the rain sheeted down almost incessantly: clothing, webbing equipment and boots rotted and fell apart and the men could be soaked for days on end. In Assam and western Burma, men and animals were tormented constantly by sand flies, ticks, mosquitoes and leeches. Dengue, typhus, malaria, cholera, scabies, yaws, sprue and dysentery were endemic. Soldiers in the Arakan encountered all these, but with mangrove swamps and muddy chaungs thrown in for good measure. It is not surprising that soldiers were glad to emerge on to the plains of central Burma after crossing the Chindwin, and to fight there during the dry season.

Nobody knows who coined the phrase 'Forgotten Army', but its soldiers were calling themselves that long before it was picked up by the press. But as Slim himself said, 'The people of Britain had perils and excitements enough on their own doorsteps and Burma was far away. Its place in the general strategy was not clear, nor did what happened there seem vital. Much more stirring news was coming out of Africa.' Although victories followed the initial setbacks, progress in this remote campaign was intially slow, and the courage and hardships of the Fourteenth Army I went largely unreported.

To this day many people know about the Chindits, but the rest of the Fourteenth Army remains forgotten. This was the outcome of a deliberate campaign to publicise the first Wingate expedition to demonstrate that an enemy who had seemed terrifyingly invincible could be beaten. In the end, the publicity about the Chindits endowed them with an aura out of all proportion to their actual importance in the scheme of things.

There were many reasons for the lack of a clear strategy for Burma, not least because it was seen by the western Allies as a distraction from the main Eastern conflict in the Pacific. For after the USA's entry into the war, the British could not decide the strategy to be followed anywhere without consulting their major American partner, who did not necessarily share the same views on how and where the main offensives should be carried out. Because Burma was always a low priority for equipment compared with other theatres of war, plans for seizing Rangoon – the planned base for the British amphibious assault on Malaya – by sea had to be postponed time and again for lack of landing craft. Not until December 1944 did Slim lose patience waiting for Rangoon to be captured by assault from the sea, and extended his scheme for taking just Mandalay to advancing to Rangoon.

When the war against Japan ended so unexpectedly, plans for Indian and Burmese independence were still undecided. The end of colonial rule was seen as inevitable, but no one knew when, or how. No date had been fixed for the British to relinquish sovereignty, and the ultimate composition of an independent India had not been decided; including the vexed question of partition. Still economically crippled from the fierce fighting within its borders, Burma became the Independent Union of Burma on 4 January 1948. By this time Aung San was dead, having been assassinated. In 1962 a military oligarchy took control of Burma. Under international pressure an election was allowed in 1968. Aung San's daughter Aung San Suu Kyi won an unexpected landslide victory, which the military dictatorship immediately annulled, arresting and imprisoning Aung San Suu Kyi. At the time of writing she remains in house arrest. The Karens, Chins and Kachin hill tribes, who have no wish to be ruled by the Burmese, have been engaged in a guerrilla war ever since 1948.

As for the soldiers who returned home from Burma, many suffered after-effects for the rest of their lives. As with all conflicts, we will never know how many were mentally scarred by their experiences. Our ignorance especially applies to the Indian and African soldiers. Some of the Indian soldiers subsequently found themselves faced with the added trauma of fighting old comrades when the British Indian Army was divided up between the independent nations of Pakistan and India, who were soon at each other's throats over the disputed territory of Kashmir. Most old soldiers will talk only to one of their own, because they feel that anyone who has not been through the extremes of war could not possibly understand. This makes the Imperial War Museum's oral history records even more important. Fortunately, perhaps because of the official nature of the project, a number of survivors agreed to sharing their stories and we have on record experiences that might otherwise have been lost.

Private Henry Foster
Carrier Platoon, 2nd Battalion, West Yorkshire Regiment
I think it's good to talk about these things, although it affects me a bit. I talk to Burma Star people, that is when I talk. I never mentioned the war until about twelve years ago, aged 65. Since demob, I often wished I had stayed in, although at the time I was glad to get away.

Major Dominic Neill
Officer Commanding B Company, 3rd/2nd Gurkha Rifles
As for the Japanese, their soldiers were some of the bravest and most effective fighting men in history.

Lieutenant Colonel Gordon Graham
1st Battalion, Queen's Own Cameron Highlanders
I immediately formed a very high opinion of the Japanese as soldiers, as it seemed they were enormously self-contained. They had this mythical reputation of invincibility because we didn't know what to expect. But they also intrigued me, because they didn't react as we did. They didn't seem to be afraid of dying. Others didn't seem interested in psychoanalysing them, but I thought it would help to understand the enemy. It was important to understand that their whole thought process and motivation was so different from ours, that we should recognise this if we were going to defeat them. We were not schooled at all in what the Japanese mores were; they were entirely based on subjective observation.

Some of the troops shot the Japanese as they lay sick on the ground, until I stopped them. There was one incident when one of the Jocks was knocking a Japanese prisoner about, and a medical officer said, 'Stop that. We've got to live with these people after the war.' So there were interludes of humanity. Mostly it was just hate and destruction. There was no chivalry involved in this war. There was a clarity about it. No one had any doubts. The Japanese had a terrible reputation of cruelty to prisoners. It sharpened the hatred and determination of those fighting against them. It became counter-productive and, in the campaign in the early months of 1945, the Japanese were ruthlessly exterminated by thousands and tens of thousands, and nobody gave it a second thought.

Trooper Malcolm Connolly
7 Troop, C Squadron, 3rd Carabiniers
There was no compassion between British, Indian, Gurkha and Japanese. Even if he put his hands up, you didn't trust him. Vast numbers of Japanese were killed in the last stages. They were just like targets in a fun fair. If you saw a dead Japanese lying there, you drove the tank over him, because you didn't trust him.

When I watched the infantry lads advancing, Indian and British, if they came across a Jap lying there, everyone stuck a bayonet in him. And the tanks coming behind would roll over him. If he had been given the opportunity he would have taken someone with him, so we didn't give him the opportunity. But in the British Army if you had done half of the things the Japanese did you would have got a VC. They wouldn't give up.

Lieutenant Colonel Gordon Graham
1st Battalion, Queen's Own Cameron Highlanders

And yet there was this thrill, that sense of reality, that here you are facing death in conditions of extreme risk and it was not all a negative experience. I guess that each person engaged in the sharp end of warfare is brought to confront himself, either consciously or subconsciously; you get almost in touch with a sense of reality which can be gained in no other way. One's senses become sharpened. And even if there is nothing pleasant or constructive about it, it still is a trial of the human spirit which has got a positive outcome for those who are ready to acknowledge it.

I don't regret any part of fighting in the war with the Cameron Highlanders. When one considers one's experiences against the background of the history of these times I felt that was the right place to be. I said to myself, aged nineteen, if there is to be a war the place to be is in the infantry, in the front, that is what wars are about. That may have been an innocent, misguided attitude, but looking back on it I think I was right. There is a sense of satisfaction of having been at the sharp end. There is also a sense of conscience about having survived. You feel very bad about your contemporaries who have not survived. Why were they killed and why was I not? These are questions that lead one into all kinds of philosophical and quasi-spiritual reflections which I think become an asset in one's subsequent life when one is no longer dedicated to destruction. I was not wounded. My batman was wounded next to me, twice.

Trooper Malcolm Connolly
7 Troop, C Squadron, 3rd Carabiniers

On the Tiddim Road, during shelling, I jumped into a slit trench by the road, and in it was an Indian IEME soldier. He was attached to us. He spoke English. I said, 'You have no need to be here.'

He replied, 'Sahib, you share my house. It is only right in time of trouble we help you. But when this is all over we are going to kick your butts out of India.'

Captain Kristen Tewari
Divisional Signals, 25th Indian Division, attached 51st Brigade

We had three battalions in our brigade, all different castes and races: Kumaonis, Punjabis, and Baluch. Kumaonis are very conservative hill people. The Baluch regiment consisted of Muslims and Hindus combined. Punjabis are Mussulmans. In Akyab, after the battle of Kangaw, we had a party with the commandos before setting sail for India. It was amazing: with our conservative Indian troops in a huge tent all together, sitting one commando, one Kumaoni, one Baluchi, one Punjabi, being given rum to drink and drinking rum from the same mug. These troops, who normally wouldn't touch anything touched by someone of a different caste or race, were doing this, there was such comradeship. As for the commandos, we had seen their gallantry and their toughness and were amazed that they could be so friendly.

Private Victor Ralph
4 Troop, 1 Commando

Lieutenant Nolan, who was awarded the VC, was a very recent member of our unit; he had joined us at Myebon as a reinforcement. We knew nothing about him. He seemed a good, keen, young Lieutenant. He was from the Norfolk Regiment. Men behave in that fashion for two reasons, either they are very stupid or very brave. I assume in his case it was the latter. To put that into perspective, there was a private who, previous to us going into action, bragged that he was going to win the VC, but when the action started he hid behind a tree all the time. A lot of bravery is done knowingly, for example when one sets out to rescue a wounded comrade. We had a medic and he went out on several occasions to bring men in and treat them. He got killed; he got nothing. War is a peculiar thing.

Captain Kristen Tewari
Divisional Signals 25th Indian Division, attached 51st Brigade

Have my war experiences changed me? Yes, you must surrender truly to your destiny.

Squadron Leader Arjun Singh
Commanding Officer, Number 1 Squadron, Royal Indian Air Force

You mature very fast in war. If a man takes ten years to mature in peace it will take only a few weeks in war.

Major Ian Lyall-Grant
Officer Commanding 70 Independent Field Company, Bengal Sappers and Miners

I don't think the Chindits achieved much. They were brave, but from a military point of view they were a very big diversion of effort. Although they blocked the road to where Stilwell was fighting, he was fighting only one Jap division. They made no difference to Kohima and Imphal. Wingate's head was in the air. He had never fought against any real opposition in his life.

Captain A. M. Vohra
14th/13th Frontier Force Rifles

The Chindits did good things for morale after so few battle successes. It was very good going behind enemy lines, but no follow-up or link-up was possible; strategically, the Chindits were a failure, as any airborne operation that does not end in a link-up is a failure.

Major John Randle
Officer Commanding B (Pathan) Company, 7th/10th Baluch Regiment

The Chindit Operation? It was an epic of human courage, but strategically it was a waste of time. It was a case of a very strange and mentally unbalanced man getting the ear of important people and being allowed to prove his own strategic visions. I don't think it achieved anything. At Imphal so much air effort was diverted to the Chindits. The battles of Kohima and Imphal won the war.

Lieutenant Richard Rhodes-James
Cypher Officer, HQ 111 Brigade

Now people ask, 'Were you in Burma, were you in the Chindits?' It continues to attract an enormous amount of interest. It was imaginative and romantic. When somebody said that they turned the tide in the campaign, I said, 'No, they didn't turn the tide.' The tide was turned when the Fourteenth Army held the Japanese at Imphal and Kohima.

Brigadier Bernard Fergusson
Commander, 16th Brigade, Chindits
Wingate had the ability to make us believe in ourselves and be confident that we could achieve what we had set out to do. One day he wanted to send a patrol into an area of jungle, which I knew was impenetrable and I said so. He rolled a contemptuous eye on me and added to his orders, 'No patrol will report any jungle impenetrable until it has penetrated it.'

Havildar Umrao Singh VC
33 Mountain Battery
When I went to London to receive my VC, I had a wonderful moustache in those days. And a lot of women came up and kissed me on my moustache, I didn't know what on earth was happening. So I went and looked in a mirror and saw I was covered in lipstick. So I washed it off quickly.

At first I was a bit afraid, but got to like it very much.

Glossary

2i/c – Second-in-Command

AA – anti-aircraft

Ack-Ack – slang for anti-aircraft, from the phonetic alphabet in which 'Ack' stood for 'A'. By 1943 replaced by 'Able', and now 'Alpha'

ADC – aide-de-camp, a general officer's personal assistant. Nearest civilian equivalent is a PA.

Adjutant – the CO's personal staff officer in a battalion or regiment in the British and Indian Armies. In the Second World War, and for several years thereafter, there was no operations officer at this level, so the adjutant was responsible for all operational staff work as well as discipline and all other personnel matters

Aldis Lamp – a hand-held lamp used for flashing Morse signals.

AP – armour piercing (ammunition) – see HE

Aung San – leader of the pro-Japanese Burma National Army (BNA). Aung San, along with the BNA, changed sides in March 1945, when they saw that Allied victory was inevitable. His daughter, Aung San Suu Kyi, is still, in 2009, kept under house arrest in Burma (Myanmar) by the regime there

Ayo Gurkhali – 'the Gurkhas are coming', battle cry of Gurkha troops

Bangalore torpedo – a length of piping filled with explosive, used for blowing a gap in barbed wire entanglements

Basha – the correct definition is: 'a wooden hut made from bamboo and roofed with jungle foliage.

Beaufighter Mk VI – British long-range fighter with crew of two. Armed with four 20-mm cannon, six .303-inch guns, and eight rockets

Bhisti – water carrier, like Kipling's Gunga Din

Bofors – a quick-firing 40-mm anti-aircraft gun of Swedish design

BORs – British Other Ranks, collective term for all British soldiers other than officers

Bose – Subhas Chandra, President of the Indian National Congress in 1939, who saw the Second World War as an opportunity to throw off British rule. Fled to Germany, and sought the assistance of Hitler. He was sent to Japan in 1943, where his government in exile was recognised by Germany, Italy, and the Irish Free State, whose President, Eamon de Valera, sent him a personal telegram of congratulations. He was in Singapore when the war with Japan ended, and was killed in an aircraft crash in Tawain while fleeing to Russia (See INA and *Netaji*)

Bren – the British light machine gun of the Second World War and until the late 1950s. Fired a standard .303-inch round from a thirty-round magazine (usually loaded with twenty-eight rounds)

Brigade – a formation of two or more infantry battalions or armoured regiments, commanded by a brigadier

Brigade Major (BM) – the senior operations officer of a brigade, *de facto* chief of staff

BTA – Burma Traitor Army, British name for Burmese who elected to join the Japanese side in the naïve expectation that the Japanese would grant Burma independence

Buffaloes – domesticated water buffalo

Bunds – earth banks built to contain paddy fields, or to hold back thecourse of a river to prevent flooding

Bushido – Japanese for the way of a warrior, a military code of honour

Carrier – a lightly armoured tracked vehicle, often called a Bren-gun carrier, although it was also used to carry the Vickers medium machine gun, and for many other tasks

Casevac – Casualty Evacuation

C-47 Dakota – the great workhorse aircraft of the Second World War and for years afterwards. Had one door, and could carry twenty paratroops or a few more troops in the air-landing role, and had a radius of action of 450 miles

(350 miles towing the US WACO glider). The C-46 Commando had two doors, carried forty paratroops, and had a radius of action of 500 miles. Twenty C-46s carried a lift equivalent to thirty C-47s

Chagul – a canvas water bag. Keeps water marvellously cool in hot weather through condensation

Chaplis – stout leather open-toed metal-studded sandals, worn by many troops of the Indian army on the North-West Frontier. Pronounced chupply

Chaung – Burmese for watercourse or minor river, could be as narrow as a ditch, or wide enough for small craft, particularly near the coast

C-in-C – Commander-in-Chief

CO – Commanding Officer

Commando – can refer to the individual commando soldier or marine, or to the unit. A commando unit was around 450 strong, divided into five rifle troops each of about sixty men, a support troop of Vickers medium machine guns and 3-inch mortars, and a headquarters troop. The 3rd Commando Brigade, which served in Burma, consisted of two Army Commandos, numbers 1 and 5 Commandos, and two Royal Marine Commandos, 42 (RM) and 44 (RM) Commando

Coolies – manual labourers.

Corps – a formation of at least two divisions commanded by a lieutenant general. Also a generic term for arms and services except armour, artillery and infantry, hence Corps of Royal Engineers, Royal Signals, Royal Army Service Corps, Indian Army Service Corps, Royal Army Medical Corps, Indian Army Medical Corps and so on

CP – Command Post

CRE – Chief Royal Engineer, the senior Royal Engineer in a Division

CSM – Company Sergeant Major

Cu-nim – cumulo-nimbus cloud, very dangerous cloud formation consisting of towering thunderheads containing very powerful up draughts and down draughts. Aircraft entering such cloud often crash after being borne up faster than an express lift, followed by hurtling earthwards, while the men inside are thrown around like peas in a pod. The aircraft might be completely inverted after having its wings torn off. Modern aircraft have weather avoidance radar to warn them to avoid such cloud. This was not available in the Second World War, and it was easy to fly into cu-nim by mistake, either in bad visibility or at night

Dah — Burmese equivalent of a machete

DC3 – the airliner on which the C-47 Dakota military transport aircraft was based (see C-47), but the name was still used by some to refer to the C-47

DCM – Distinguished Conduct Medal, a highly regarded decoration, instituted in 1854, the equivalent of the original DSO for Warrant Officers, NCOs and soldiers of the army (and Royal Marines when under army command). Awarded for gallantry in action. Now discontinued

Deccan Horse – an Indian cavalry regiment

DF – defensive fire, mortar, artillery, or machine-gun fire by troops in defensive positions against attacking troops or patrols. Usually pre-registered on a number of key places, and numbered, so a particular DF can be called down quickly by reference to its number. Guns and mortars will be laid on the DF SOS when not engaged on other tasks. As its name implies, the DF SOS is the target deemed to be the most dangerous to the defenders

Dhobi wallah – man who does the washing, literally the washing fellow

Direct fire – weapons that have to be aimed directly at the target as opposed to indirect fire weapons such as mortars and artillery

Division – a formation of two or more brigades, commanded by a major general

Doolies – hammock-like pieces of canvas suspended from two poles, carried by two or four people on their shoulders. Used for carrying wounded or sick

DSO – Distinguished Service Order, instituted in 1886, and until the awards system was changed in 1994, it was a dual-role decoration, recognising gallantry at a level just below that qualifying for the VC by junior officers, and exceptional leadership in battle by senior officers

DUKW – American six-wheeled amphibious truck. Initials from maker's code, pronounced 'duck'

DZ – dropping zone, the area chosen for landing by parachute troops, or on which supplies are to be dropped

EY rifle – a rifle fitted with a discharger cup on the muzzle for launching grenades

FFD – first field dressing, a packet containing a bandage impregnated with antiseptic, carried by every officer and soldier on active service

Flak – German slang for anti-aircraft fire, from the German for anti-aircraft gun *fliegerabwehrkanone*

Flit gun/Flit pump – a small hand-pumped device for spraying insecticide, known by its commercial name: Flit

Folboat – originally a two-man, collapsible canoe built for recreational purposes by the Folboat company. During the course of the Second World War, some eight marques of canoe were designed and built by the British to improve on the original design

FOO – Forward Observation Officer, an artillery officer who directs artillery fire. Normally one with each forward rifle company and provided by artillery battery supporting the infantry battalion

G1 ops – short for GSO 1 (Operations), see GSO

Galloper – a messenger on horseback

Gharry wallahs – a gharry is a horse-drawn carriage, or cab; see Wallah

GOC – General Officer Commanding

Goolie chit – was, and still is, airman's slang for a document carried for use by downed aircrew to show local tribespeople, guaranteeing a financial reward in return for the airman being handed over unharmed. Tribesmen on the North-West Frontier of India, where the practice of issuing goolie chits originated, commonly castrated the enemy, either before or after killing them

GSO – General Staff Officer, a staff officer who dealt with General (G) Staff matters (operations, intelligence, planning and staff duties), as opposed to personnel (A short for Adjutant General's Staff), or logistic matters (Q short for Quartermaster General's Staff). The grades were GSO 1 (Lieutenant Colonel), GSO 2 (Major), and GSO 3 (Captain). The GSO 1 in a division was the senior operations staff officer, effectively the chief of staff. The AAG, or Assistant Adjutant General in a division was the senior personnel staff officer, and the AQMG, or Assistant Quartermaster General, in a division was the senior logistics staff officer

Gun Box – an artillery gun position defended by infantry, and possibly armour

H-Hour – the time an attacking force crosses the start line

Havildar – see ranks

HE – high explosive

High Port – carrying a rifle across the body at an angle with the muzzle upwards

Howdah – a box-like arrangement on an elephant's back in which people sit

Howitzer 3.7 inch – a mountain gun, designed for operating in country impassable for wheeled vehicles, primarily the North-West Frontier of India. Dismantled into nine parts: breech, chase, cradle, split trail, carriage and two hard-rimmed wheels. Could be carried by eight mules. The gun could be modified to be towed by a jeep, by fitting pneumatic tyres and a smaller shield. The shell weighed twenty pounds, and the gun had a maximum range of seven thousand yards. (Compare with the 25-pounder which had a maximum range of 12,500 yards with a 25-pound shell)

Hurribomber – the fighter-bomber version of the Hurricane Mk II

Hurricane Mk II – single-engined monoplane, of Battle of Britain fame. Various sub marques, equipped with either twelve .303-inch machine guns, four 20-mm cannon, or two 40-mm cannon. Below ten thousand feet was less manoeuvrable than the Japanese Zero, but above twenty thousand feet proved superior. Also developed as a highly successful fighter-bomber (see Hurribomber)

IEME – Indian Electrical and Mechanical Engineer, see LAD

INA – Indian National Army, formed from Indian soldiers taken prisoner after the fall of Malaya and Hong Kong, who were persuaded to fight for the Japanese by a Japanese officer, Major Fujiwara, assisted by Captain Mohan Singh of the 14th Punjabis. Around twenty thousand out of the total of sixty thousand Indian soldiers taken prisoner joined the INA initially. When Subhas Chandra Bose arrived in Singapore about a year afterwards (see Bose) the INA was increased several thousandfold by recruiting civilian Indians living in Malaya, Hong Kong, Singapore, Thailand and Burma. Very few Gurkhas joined

Jemadar – see Ranks

JIF – Japanese Indian Forces (see INA)

Jitter Party – a party of soldiers sent to create noises near enemy positions at night in order to give them 'the jitters' and get them to fire their weapons thus revealing their positions. The Fourteenth Army was trained not to respond, the watchword was 'the answer to noise is silence'

Jocks – slang for soldiers in Scottish regiments

Khud – khud is Urdu for hillside, and a khud stick is a stick with a metal point to assist one when climbing or descending the khud

KOYLI —King's Own Yorkshire Light Infantry

LAD – light aid detachment, a small sub-unit of fitters and mechanics from the Royal Electrical and Mechanical Engineers (REME) or Indian Electrical and Mechanical Engineers (IEME), to provide immediate battlefield repairs to vehicles and equipment

Lance Naik – see Ranks

Lantana – a particularly thick scrub resembling raspberry canes. It is almost impossible to advance through without cutting, and offers good concealment to the defender. The Japanese made skilful use of it

LCA – landing craft assault, maximum load an infantry platoon. Designed to be carried at a ship's lifeboat davits, and to land infantry in a beach assault

LCP(L) – fast landing craft of American design and originally bought by the British for Commando raids. They had no ramp, and a spoon bow over which troops landed either by gangplank or jumped straight into the sea, the latter leading to a very wet landing

Lead pencil delay fuse – a metal tube containing a strong spring pulled out to its full extent. When the retaining pin was removed, the spring was held in tension by a lead wire. A combination of the thickness of the wire and the outside temperature determined how long it took for the lead wire to snap, thus allowing the spring to drive a firing pin on to the detonator which set off the primer and the explosive. The warmer the temperature the more malleable the lead wire, and the quicker it would break. Provided one could accurately forecast the temperature at the target, one could select the timer with the necessary thickness of lead wire to achieve the delay required

Lee-Grant – American-built, M3 tank. Had a 37-mm gun in the turret, and a 75-mm (main armament) gun in a sponson in the hull

Liberator Mk II – American B-24 four-engined heavy bomber with crew of eight

Lightning P.38 – twin-engined American fighter. Crew of one. Four .50-inch and one 20-mm cannon. Very effective low-level attack aircraft

LMG – light machine gun

LO – Liaison Officer

Longcloth – the codeword for Wingate's first expedition behind enemy lines

LZ – landing zone, in the Second World War an area chosen for glider landings

Martial Class – the British Indian Army was mainly recruited from what were known as the martial classes (sometimes known as Martial Races), such as Sikhs, Jats, Rajputs, Gurkhas, Garwhalis, Dogras, Kumaonis, Punjabi-Mussulmans (Punjabi Muslims) and Pathans

MC – Military Cross, instituted in 1914, and awarded to army officers of the rank of Major and below, and Warrant Officers, for gallantry in action. Now all ranks are eligible

MGB – motor gun boat, a small, fast vessel armed with small-calibre guns

Mitchell – B-25, twin-engined American medium bomber with crew of five. Good at attacking ground targets in support of ground troops

MM – Military Medal, instituted in 1916, and awarded to army NCOs and soldiers for gallantry in action. Now discontinued, see MC

MMG – medium machine gun (see Vickers)

MO – medical officer

Mahout – elephant driver, sits astride the elephant's neck.

MDS – Main Dressing Station, located in a rear area. the place to which casualties are taken from the RAP (see RAP), and where, if necessary, surgery can be undertaken to stabilize the casualty before further evacuation further back

MG – machine gun

Mohawk – single-engined American fighter, earlier version of the Tomahawk. Obsolete by 1941, but retained by RAF for use in India/Burma. Six .303-inch guns

Mosquito Mk IV – twin-engined light bomber, or high-level reconnaissance aircraft. Crew of two. Almost as fast as a Spitfire, and much faster than any other aircraft, Allied or enemy

MTB – motor torpedo boat, a small, fast vessel mainly armed with torpedoes

Naik – see Ranks

NCO – non-commissioned officer; lance corporal to colour sergeant

Netaji – Hindi for leader, equivalent of the German term *führer*. Subhas Chandra Bose, the figurehead of the INA, decreed that he was to be addressed by the title *Netaji*. He wore uniform although he had never been a soldier. See INA

Nullah or nala – a small watercourse, ditch or depression in the ground

OC – Officer Commanding, applicable to commander of sub-units below battalion/ regimental level: companies, batteries, squadrons, platoons etc

O Group – short for Orders Group, the group to which orders are given at any level of command from platoon to army. For example at platoon level the platoon commander briefing his section commanders, the battalion CO briefing his company commanders, and at brigade level, the brigade commander briefing his battalion and supporting arms COs, and other people who need to know the plan

OP – observation post

Panga(s) – the African equivalent to a machete or dah

Pangyi – a sharpened stake usually made out of bamboo and pronounced punji. The point can be hardened by scorching in a fire. Excellent for use in booby traps, or obstacle belts, and can be concealed in pits, covered with twigs and grass or leaves, and planted in the undergrowth. Once impaled on a bamboo stake, it is difficult to pull oneself off, because the bamboo fibres act like a barb

PIAT – Projector Infantry Anti-Tank. The hand-held anti-tank weapon of the British Second World War infantryman from about mid-1942 on. Consisted of a powerful spring mounted in a tube which threw a hollow-charge projectile. Effective up to one hundred yards

Pugree, puggaree – turban

RA – Royal Artillery

Radius of action – the distance an aircraft or ship carrying out a sortie can cover from base to target and back without stopping to refuel

RAF – Royal Air Force

RAP – Regimental Aid Post, the place where the Medical Officer (MO) of a battalion or equivalent-size unit sets up his aid post. Usually the requirement is to administer 'sophisticated first aid' to stabilize the casualty sufficiently to enable him to survive the next stage of evacuation; in 'conventional' warfare usually within hours. In Chindit columns casualties might spend days in the RAP before evacuation was possible, and the MO had to do far more

Range – the distance to a target, or the total distance an aircraft can fly or a ship can steam. See Radius of action

Ranks – Indian Army Ranks below 2nd Lieutenant were as follows:

Indian Army	Typical Job	British Army Equivalent
Subedar Major	Senior VCO (see VCO)	None
Subedar	Company 2i/c or platoon commander	None
Jemadar	Platoon commander	None
Havildar Major	Company Sergeant Major (CSM)	CSM
Havildar	Platoon Sergeant	Sergeant
Naik	Section commander	Corporal
Lance Naik	Section 2i/c	Lance Corporal
Sepoy/Rifleman		Private/Rifleman

The word Sepoy is an eighteenth-century British misspelling of the Persian word *Sipāhi* from the Persian word, *Sipāh* meaning army

RASC – Royal Army Service Corps

Regiment (British and Indian Army) – originally of horse, dragoons or foot, raised by command of monarch, and later Parliament, and named after its colonel, originally a royal appointee. The regiment became the basic organisation of the British Army and Indian Army, for armour, artillery, engineers, signals, and logistic units equivalent to battalions of those arms in other armies. In the case of the infantry, the British or Indian Army battalion belongs to a regiment, of which there may be one or more battalions and who may not serve together in the same area, or even in the same theatre of operations.

The Indian Army reorganisation of 1922 formed infantry regiments of up to six battalions each, and, on the outbreak of war, many more battalions. There were several regiments with the same title, depending on the origins of their soldiers, and these were numbered. Often an Indian Army battalion would contain mixed classes of soldiers (see Martial Class) divided into companies. Hence the 7th/10th Baluch Regiment is the 7th battalion of the 10th Baluch Regiment whose soldiers are Dogras, Punjabi Mussulmans (Muslims) and Pathans. The 3rd/2nd Gurkha Rifles, is the 3rd battalion of the 2nd Gurkha Rifles

Regiment (Japanese) – a formation of three infantry battalions, usually stronger than a British brigade

Regimental Sergeant Major (RSM) – it is one of the idiosyncrasies of the British Army that infantry battalions and regiments (artillery and armoured) all have a Warrant Officer Class 1 called the Regimental Sergeant Major. He is the commanding officer's right-hand man and adviser on many aspects of battalion/regiment daily life, especially matters involving the soldiers and NCOs. The CO and the RSM have very likely known each other since the former was a second lieutenant and the latter a young private or equivalent. There was no equivalent in the Indian Army of the time, the nearest being the Subedar Major (see VCO and Ranks)

'Rhubarb' – an RAF slang phrase for opportunistic strafing

RIN – Royal Indian Navy

RM – Royal Marines

RV – rendezvous

Sapper – the equivalent of private in the Royal Engineers, or a name for all engineers

SBS – there were two organisations with the acronym SBS in the Second World War. The first was founded as a Folboat Section in 1940 and was known as the Special Boat Section (SBS). The sections were numbered, and 2 SBS appears in this book. This was entirely separate from the Special Boat Squadron (also SBS) formed from a squadron of the Special Air Service in the Middle East, which did not serve in Burma

SEAC – South East Asia Command. The Supreme Allied Commander SEAC, Admiral Mountbatten, was responsible direct to the British Chiefs of Staff in London, and through them to the Combined British and US Chiefs of Staff for all operations by land, sea and air in Burma, Malaya, and

Sumatra, and for clandestine operations in Thailand and French Indo-China

SMG – Sub-machine gun, a short weapon, capable of firing automatic. (See Sten gun)

SpitfireMk VIII – single-engined fighter of Battle of Britain fame. Proved superior to Japanese Zero and Oscar fighters

Start Line – a line in the ground, usually a natural feature, stream, bank, or fence, preferably at ninety degrees to the axis of advance, which marks the start line for the attack and is crossed at H-Hour in attack formation. Can be marked by tape if there is no natural feature which lends itself to being used as a start line

Sten gun – a cheap, mass-produced sub-machine gun of British design. It fired 9-mm ammunition, and had a thirty-two-round magazine. Ineffective except at close quarters; it was inaccurate and the round had poor penetrating power. Because of its propensity to fire by mistake, it was sometimes more dangerous to its owner and those standing around, than to the enemy

Subedar, Subedar Major – see ranks

Syce — groom

Tac HQ – Tactical Headquarters, a small group including the CO, or brigade commander forward of the main HQ

TEWTS – Tactical Exercises Without Troops, theoretical exercises conducted on suitable terrain to test officers and non-commissioned officers in tactical problems, map reading, and giving orders, but not involving troops

Thursday – the codeword for Wingate's second expedition behind enemy lines

TG – short for Tommy Gun, or Thompson Sub-machine gun, favoured by American gangsters in the 1920s and 1930s

Tiffin – lunch

Tiger Moth — a light aircraft of pre-1939 design

Tokyo Rose – the name given to Iva Toguri D'Aquino, an American–Japanese citizen with an especially beguiling voice who broadcast propaganda in English to the Allies

TSM – Troop Sergeant Major

ULTRA – originally the British codeword for intelligence gained by decrypting German and Italian codes. When the war against Japan began, the British and Americans used this codeword to include all Japanese military communications broken by cryptoanalysis. (Neither the Soviets, the Chinese nor any other Allies were privy to the secret)

USAAF – United States Army Air Force; until 1947 the air force was part of the US Army

VC – Victoria Cross, the highest British award for bravery in the face of the enemy. To date, in the 145 years since its inception by Queen Victoria during the Crimean War of 1854–56, only 1,358 VCs have been awarded, including a handful of double VCs, and the one presented to the American Unknown Warrior at Arlington. This figure includes the many awarded to Imperial, Commonwealth and Dominion servicemen

VCO – Viceroy's Commissioned Officer. There were three kinds of commissioned officer in the Indian Army of the time. British and Indian officers with the King's Commission who, in peacetime, or when not in battle or on operations in wartime, lived in the Officer's Mess. VCOs were commissioned from the ranks of the regiment or battalion, had a Viceroy's Commission as the name implies, and were junior to all King's Commissioned officers of any rank. Their nearest equivalent in the British Army was Warrant Officer, but VCOs had much higher status, commanded platoons, were second-in-command of companies, and lived in their own mess. They were addressed as Subedar Sahib, or Jemadar Sahib, by all ranks including by King's Commissioned officers. The Subedar Major was the senior VCO in an Indian Army Battalion, and had probably joined as a young sepoy or rifleman at about the same time as the CO joined as a subaltern. He was the CO's right-hand man and adviser on all regimental matters such as customs, promotions, recruiting, religion, and how well, or otherwise, the British officers (especially the younger ones) were relating to their Indian soldiers

Very Pistol – a smooth-bore pistol for firing green, white or red Very signal cartridges. Hence Very lights

Vickers medium machine gun – First World War vintage, belt-fed, water-cooled machine gun, rate of fire five hundred rounds per minute. Maximum range with Mark VIIIZ ammunition, 4,500 yards. Last fired in action in 1962

Waco glider – so called because it was made by the Waco Aircraft Co, USA, a fifteen-seater, troop- and cargo-carrying high-wing monoplane glider; payload 1.7 tons. The nose of the glider, including the pilot's cockpit, could be raised up and locked into position, which allowed jeeps and small bulldozers to be loaded, and driven out, through the nose

Wadi – Arabic for valley, a term much used by British troops in the Middle East at the time, and by the British Army to this day

Wallah – an Anglo-Indian civilian and army slang expression meaning 'chap' of 'fellow' as in, 'tell that Wallah to go away.' Often associated with a profession, or someone in charge of a particular activity. For example, the 'amen Wallah' is the chaplain, the 'gharry Wallah' is the driver, and the 'box Wallah' is a businessmen

Watch and Ward scheme – set up by an ex-Assam Rifles officer to use local tribespeople as intelligence scouts against the Japanese

Zero(s) – Mitsubishi A6M Zero-Sen, the most famous of all Japanese combat aircraft, fast, highly manoeuvrable, and with a long radius of action. To begin with it ruled the skies, but it was eventually outclassed as the Allies produced better fighter aircraft

Z-Lighters – flat-bottomed vessels, usually without engines, and towed by tugs, used for unloading cargos from merchant ships, or for transporting vehicles and stores to a beach. Can be beached and used as a pontoon or jetty

PRONUNCIATION OF BURMESE NAMES

The more unusual names are as follows:

Spelt	Pronounced
Buthidaung	Buthidong ('u' as in 'book')
Chaung	Chong
Daingbon Chaung	Danebonchong
Indawgyi Lake	Indoorji Lake
Kabaw	Korebore
Kyaukchaw	Chalkchore
Kyaukpyu	Chalkpew
Kyaukse	Chalksi
Kyauktaw	Chalktore
Maymyo	Maymeeoh
Meiktila	Miketiller or sometimes Mecktiller
Moulmein	Moolmain
Myebon	My-ee-bon
Myitkyina	Michina
Tuitum	Tweetum

Index of Contributors

Number in brackets denotes IWM Sound Archive catalogue number. Page numbers in **bold** refer to photographs.

General Index

Page numbers in **bold** refer to photographs.

Michael Gregorio are Michael G. Jacob and Daniela De Gregorio. She teaches philosophy. He is interested in the history of photography in the nineteenth century. They have been married for twenty-six years and live in Spoleto, a small town in central Italy. *Critique of Criminal Reason* is their first novel.

Praise for *Critique of Criminal Reason*

'A vivid evocation of the dirty, everyday life in an 18th-century mid-Europe threatened by an imminent invasion by Napoleon. The outcome is a tremendous shock, but all the more impressive because this sleuth seems to have been selected in the expectation that his inquiries will fail.' Gerald Kaufman, *The Scotsman*

'A sweeping and brilliantly detailed read . . . Gregorio threads philosophical underpinnings through his dark narrative with genuine assurance.' Barry Forshaw, *Crime Time*

'The setting is brilliantly portrayed and the harsh, superstitious, masculine world springs to life, making one very glad not be there and then . . . a well-written and intellectually demanding novel.' *Literary Review*

'Michael Gregorio's *Critique of Criminal Reason* is a solid, atmospheric example of the burgeoning historical-figure-turned-detective genre . . . Great fun.' Daneet Steffens, *Time Out*

'Quite the best element in Michael Gregorio's novel is its setting: a luridly tinted version of Konigsberg, where everything is freezing, sinister or decaying . . . Gregorio gives us an unusual perspective on history and has a gift for melodrama. This novel is the first of a series, and it will be interesting to discover where Siffeniis goes from here.' Andrew Taylor, *Independent*

'This novel is an absorbing read . . . and if the sequel is as entertaining as this slow-burner, he has longevity. The many twists guarantee you are guessing until the end. Delicious use of the English language throughout ensures you are captivated, educated and entertained throughout.' Ian Clarkson, *Birmingham Post*

Critique of Criminal Reason

MICHAEL GREGORIO

faber and faber

First published in 2006
by Faber and Faber Limited
3 Queen Square London WC1N 3AU
This paperback edition first published in 2007

Printed in England by Mackays of Chatham plc, Chatham, Kent

A CIP record for this book
is available from the British Library

ISBN 978–0–571–22928–4

2 4 6 8 10 9 7 5 3 1

A False Start

'*Observe, Stiffeniis. It slid in like a hot knife cutting lard.*'

Like Logic slicing through the fog of Ignorance, thought I, fully conscious of the illustrious company I was keeping. Even so, my stomach revolted at the sight. I had to force myself to look, and might have turned away, had not duty obliged me to examine the evidence with all the zeal that I was capable of mustering.

'*Yet, it was not a knife . . .*'

Inside the ample glass jar, the severed head lolled in a swirling sea of cloudy preserving alcohol. Tangled grey-red sinews, clots of blood and gore shifted gently in the straw-coloured liquid like the trailing tendrils of a jellyfish. The grey eyes had rolled upwards in their sockets, the mouth twisted in an expression that seemed to signify surprise more than pain. I could not help but ask myself whether the immediacy of death had stopped the electrical flow of thought as quickly as it had blocked the animal reactions. I ached to know what the victim's final impression might have been, put out by the fact that there was no known method of filtering distilled wine for the precious ideas that might be suspended there to help me understand how death had been inflicted. I had read De viribus electricitatis in motu musculari, *but this physical examination went far beyond anything that the great Galvani had ever contemplated.*

The head rolled slowly like a large conch-shell in the swelling sea, and my mentor stretched forth his spindly finger to indicate the exact spot. '*Here at the very base of the cranium. Do you see it?*'

'*What caused the wound, sir?*' *I asked cautiously.*

'*The Devil did it. His claws are sharp,*' *he replied with penetrating calm.*

He might have been demonstrating an elementary principle in the discipline of material deduction to the class of university students which I had attended once myself, only seven years before . . .

Almost three years have flown since that conversation took place and I decided to set my quill to paper. My hope was to inform the world of a working method that would be of practical use to any magistrate called upon to solve a murder. In short, I set out to write a treatise for which the greatest son of Eastern Prussia had already supplied a tentative, if ironic title.

But this noble plan was abruptly terminated after those few introductory lines had been inscribed on paper. And not by the dramatic twists of history alone. My mind and my soul were pitched down into a bottomless black pit by what I discovered in the course of that investigation, and I was hard put to find my way out of it. Indeed, the simpleton who wrote those lines, and the man writing these, are two such alien creatures – despite the claims of common sense and the evidence I see in my shaving-mirror – that I feel called to question whether they are the self-same person. The sights I saw in Königsberg will haunt me for the remainder of my days on earth . . .

Chapter 1

Whalers returning from the Arctic seas in the summer of 1803 reported an *aurora borealis* of an intensity never observed before. Professor Wollaston had described the phenomenon of polar refraction to the satisfaction of the scientific community some years before. Of course, that fact did not diminish the awe of the folk who dwelt along the Baltic seaboard. All those who lived in Lotingen, myself included, not eight miles from the coast, stared up at the night sky. We could not fail to be stupefied by what we saw. The massive clouds were painted as darkly crimson as fresh blood, the Northern Lights flashed like a lady's fan of mother-of-pearl held up to the mid-day sun. Little Lotte Havaars, the nursemaid who had been with us since the day that Immanuel was born, told us that the neighbours in her village had noted unnatural behaviour in their animals, and autumn brought news of hideous plants and monstrous births which seemed to defy the laws of Nature. Two-headed piglets, calves with six legs, a turnip as large as a wheelbarrow. The coming winter, Lotte muttered darkly, would be like no other in the history of Man.

My wife's dark eyes glittered with amusement as Lotte prattled on. Helena glanced at me, inviting me to share her mirth, and I was forced to return her smile, though it went against my nature, for I was born and bred in the country. My heart seemed to knot itself in a tight ball, I felt a heavy sense of oppression, suffocation almost, the sort of unsettling sensation that a distant thunder-headed cloud provokes on a broiling summer's day. And when it came, it *was* a terrible winter. Lotte's intuition had been proved correct. Lashing rain by day, biting frost by night. And then, snow. More snow than I had ever seen before.

Indeed, the seventh day of February, 1804, was the coldest in living memory. That morning, I was busy in my office at the Court House in Lotingen, writing out the sentence of a wrangle which had required the better part of a week to decide. Herman Bertholt had taken it upon himself to improve the landscape. He had lopped two branches off a valuable apple tree belonging to his neighbour, Farmer Dürchtner. That tree spoiled the view from his kitchen window, the offender argued. The rights and wrongs of the case had divided the town, of course, it was a matter of vital importance. If a precedent were allowed, we could expect an epidemic to follow. I was in the very act of writing up my conclusion – *I therefore sentence Herman Bertholt to pay thirteen thalers, and pass six hours in the village stocks* – when a knock sounded at the door and my secretary entered.

'There's a man outside,' Knutzen slurred.

I glanced with distaste at my aged secretary. His grubby shirt was still unchanged, the collar stained a grimy brown, his heavy boots unpolished. He had been working in his duck-run again. I had lost that battle and had long grown tired of complaining. Gudjøn Knutzen was one of a handful of men in the village who were able to write their own names. On that strength alone, he had escaped the destiny of his father, and all the male ancestors of his family. But the Royal purse was empty. The King had chosen armed neutrality, while the other great states of Europe took their chances against the French. Civic expenses had been cut to pay for military necessities as a consequence. Soldiers had to be re-equipped, generals better paid, horses pampered and fed, fit and ready for the war which everyone knew was bound to come. Heavy cannon had been purchased from Bessarabia. All this brought hardship, even misery to Prussia. The lower ranks of the judicial administration, myself included, had been hard hit by the latest economies. But Knutzen had been thrust back into the Dark Ages. His wages had been halved. Consequently, he worked as little as possible, and spent as much time as he could filch from me with his ducks. He had become a peasant again. Like every man in Europe, he was paying for the French Revolution and for the fright that Napoleon was spreading throughout the continent of Europe.

Helena had promised to give him one of my cast-off shirts next time the pedlar came to town. I glanced out of the window, reflecting that the pedlar's wagon would not be coming through for quite some time. Snow had begun to fall again, the flakes as large as laurel leaves. It had fallen all day the day before, and had been threatening all the morning. What – I wondered idly – could drive a man abroad on such a day? My curiosity was piqued, I admit. Even so, I decided, the minute the visitor has finished his business, I shall close the office and take myself home for the rest of the day.

'Show him in,' I said.

Knutzen wiped his nose on his sleeve. Whenever he happened to take his one-and-only jacket off, which was rarely, I was inclined to believe that it stood up of its own accord.

'Aye,' he said, withdrawing slowly from the room.

He left the door wide open, and I could hear him mumbling out in the hall.

Some moments later, a heavily built man in dark travelling clothes and high riding-boots clumped determinedly into the room, leaving a trail of scattered drips and melting slush in his wake. The ghostly pallor of his face, and the unhealthy tremor which shook his body as he stood before me, led me to believe that he had mistaken his destination. He seemed to require the care of a physician, rather than the services of a magistrate.

'What can I do for you, sir?' I asked, waving him to the visitor's chair, sitting myself down again behind my desk.

The stranger pulled his copious black cloak more tightly around his shivering frame and loudly cleared his throat. 'You are Magistrate Stiffeniis, are you not?' he said gruffly.

'Indeed, I am,' I nodded. 'But where are you from, sir? You are not from Lotingen.'

The visitor's large, grey eyes flashed defiantly.

'Weren't you expecting me?' he asked with evident surprise.

I shook my head. 'Given the sudden turn in the weather,' I said, glancing out of the broad bay-window at the snow, which fell even thicker than before, 'I was expecting nobody this morning. What can I do for you, sir?'

He was silent for a moment. 'Didn't the Königsberg coach arrive?' he asked suddenly.

'I have no idea,' I replied, wondering what this was leading up to.

'You received no news from Procurator Rhunken?' he insisted.

'I received no post at all this morning,' I replied. 'Nor do I know Herr Procurator Rhunken. Except by reputation.'

'No post?' the stranger muttered, slapping the palm of his right hand down hard on his knee. 'Well, that throws a stick in the wheel!'

'Does it?' I asked, perplexed.

He did not reply, but opened his leather shoulder-bag and started to rummage around inside it. Any hope I had that he might produce something to explain his presence in my office was dashed as he pulled out a large white linen handkerchief and loudly blew his nose.

'Am I to presume that *you* are Procurator Rhunken?' I probed.

'Oh no, sir!' he spluttered behind the white square. 'With all respect, he's the very last person I'd wish to be at this moment. My name is Amadeus Koch, Sergeant-of-Police in the city of Königsberg. I work as the administrative clerk in Procurator Rhunken's office.' He pressed the linen cloth to his mouth to stifle a cough. 'In the absence of the post, sir, the best thing I can do is to tell you why I have come.'

'Please *do*, Herr Sergeant Koch,' I encouraged, hoping to make some sense of this puzzling interview.

A weak smile appeared on the man's white lips. 'I won't waste any more precious time, sir. In my own defence, and given the present state of my health, I will only say that the journey from Königsberg has done little to assist my powers of reasoning. To be brief, I have instructions to take you back with me.'

I stared at him. 'To Königsberg?'

'I only pray the snow will not prevent us . . .'

'Instructions, Herr Koch? Tell me exactly what brings you here!'

Sergeant Koch began to search about in his bag again. At length, he pulled out a large white envelope. 'The official communiqué regarding your appointment was sent yesterday by the post. For reasons unknown, it has not arrived. But your commission was entrusted to me. This is for you, sir.'

I tore the packet from his outstretched hand, read my name on the cover, then turned it over. A large red Hohenzollern seal closed the flap, and I hesitated an instant before daring to break it and examine the contents.

Most honourable Procurator Stiffeniis,

Your talents have been brought to Our attention by a gentleman of eminence, who believes that you alone are capable of resolving a situation which holds Our beloved Königsberg in a grip of terror. All Our faith and consideration are due to the notable personage who suggested your name, and that same faith and consideration now resides in you. We have no reason to doubt that you will accept this Royal Commission, and act accordingly with all haste. The fate of the city lies in your hands.

The note was signed with a flourish by King Frederick Wilhelm III.

'There have been murders in Königsberg, Procurator Stiffeniis,' Sergeant Koch pressed on, his voice hushed as if fearing that we might be overheard. 'This morning I was ordered to inform you of the matter.'

Confusion clouded my mind.

'I am at a loss, Herr Koch,' I murmured, staring hard at the paper in my hand, reading one particular phrase over and over again. What were the 'talents' that I was supposed to possess? And who was the 'eminent gentleman' who had brought them to the attention of His Majesty, the King? 'Are you certain that someone hasn't made a mistake?'

'There's no mistake,' the sergeant replied, pointing to the envelope with a smile. 'This *is* Prussia, sir. That envelope's got your name on it.'

'Isn't Procurator Rhunken investigating the case?' I asked. 'He is the senior magistrate on the Königsberg circuit.'

'Herr Rhunken has suffered a stroke,' Sergeant Koch explained.

'He has lost the use of his lower limbs. It would appear that you have been chosen to carry on his work, sir.'

I considered this proposition for a moment. 'But *why*, Sergeant Koch? I have never met Herr Rhunken. Why should he recommend me in such glowing terms to King Frederick Wilhelm?'

'I cannot help you on that point, sir,' he said. 'All will be made clear in Königsberg, no doubt.'

I had no alternative but to accept this assurance. 'You mentioned murders, Sergeant. How many are we talking about?'

'Four, sir.'

I caught my breath.

I had never had to deal with a serious crime in my career as an arbiter of the law, and had always considered the fact a matter of good fortune. The sentence I had been writing not ten minutes before was the most important to come my way in the three years that I had been employed in Lotingen.

'The first victim was found a year ago,' Koch ploughed on, 'though the police made no progress on the case and they forgot about it quick enough. But three months ago, another corpse was found, and a third person died last month. Just yesterday another body came to light. The evidence would seem to suggest that they all died by the same . . .'

A knock at the door froze the words on Koch's lips.

Knutzen came shuffling in again and dropped a letter on my desk. 'This has just been delivered, Herr Procurator. The post-coach lost a wheel on the outskirts of Rykiel and was four hours late getting in.'

'I took the coast road, fortunately,' Koch murmured as Knutzen left us alone once more. He gestured to the unopened letter in my hand. 'You'll find confirmation there of what I've just told you, sir.'

I opened the envelope, and found an order signed by Procurator Rhunken in a spidery, uncertain hand, which seemed to confirm what Sergeant Koch had said about the magistrate's poor health. It provided formal notification of the fact that the murder case had been handed over to me, but added nothing more. I set the letter down, swept by waves of conflicting emotion. Obviously, I was gratified that my professional talents had been recognised. And by Procurator Rhunken, whose name was foremost among magistrates in Prussia by reason of his rigour and his determination. What surprised me more, however, was the fact that he had even heard my name. And that he had passed it on to the King. What had I done to attract their notice? Why should such powerful people place their trust in me? I was not so vain as to imagine that nowhere in the whole of Prussia was there any man better suited to the task. Except, of course, for the unresolved question of my mysterious 'talents'. The concluding words of Herr Rhunken's communiqué did nothing to set my doubts at rest:

> . . . there are particular aspects of this case which should not be committed to paper. You will be informed of them in due course.

'Are you ready, sir?' asked Sergeant Koch, gathering his shoulder-bag and standing up. 'I am yours to serve in any way which will expedite our departure.'

I remained seated in mute protest against this driving sense of urgency. The contents of another letter that I had received from Königsberg seven years before echoed in my mind like a taunt. On that occasion, I had been compelled to make a promise which the simple act of accompanying Sergeant Koch to the city would force me to break.

'How long will I be required to stay?' I asked him, as if it were, above all, a practical question.

'Until the case is solved, Herr Stiffeniis,' he answered flatly.

I sat back in my chair, wondering what to do for the best. If it were a matter of passing a few short days in the city, closing a case which Procurator Rhunken had been preventing from completing by ill health, no harm would come of it. If I proved unequal to the task, I would simply be ordered to return to the oblivion from which I had come. But then, I thought with a spurt of mounting ambition, what would be the limits to my future career if I were to succeed?

'I must take leave of my wife,' I said, jumping to my feet, the choice made.

Sergeant Koch pulled his cloak more tightly around him. 'There's not much time if we're to reach Königsberg before nightfall, sir,' he said.

'I need but a few minutes to wish my wife farewell and kiss my little ones,' I protested on the strength of my new authority. 'Neither Procurator Rhunken nor the King would deny me that small luxury, I think!'

Out in the street, a large coach bearing the Royal coat-of-arms stood waiting in the snow. As I climbed aboard, I could not avoid reflecting on the incongruity of my situation. There I was in a state coach, holding a letter signed by the King imploring me to solve a case that not one of the great magistrates in his service had been able to resolve. It should have been the crowning moment in my short career, the day the dark clouds parted and the sun shone brightly on one of her own, my abilities not only recognised, but usefully employed for the good of the nation. But then the words of that old letter came echoing back once again:

Do not return. Your presence has done more than enough damage. For his sake show yourself no more in Magisterstrasse!

The coachman cracked his whip, and the vehicle leapt forward. I took it as a sign of destiny. I should leave the past behind, and look towards a brighter and more prosperous future. What more could I possibly want? It was, when all was said and done, a glorious opportunity for professional advancement.

Helena must have been sitting at the window as the splendid vehicle pulled up outside the small, draughty house on the edge of the town which was tied to the prebend of Lotingen. As I climbed down, she ran out to meet me with neither hat nor coat, ignoring the biting north wind and the driving snow. She stopped before me, looking uncertainly up into my face.

'What has happened, Hanno?' she gasped, stepping close and slipping her arm through mine.

She listened as I told her all that had come to pass, slowly drawing away from me, clasping her hands protectively across her breasts. It was a gesture that I knew only too well when she was disturbed or upset by something I had said or done.

'I thought that you had chosen Lotingen precisely to avoid such things, Hanno,' she murmured. 'I truly believed that here you had found what you were seeking.'

'I did, my dear,' I told her instantly. 'I mean, of course, I have.'

'I do not understand you, then,' she replied. She hesitated for a moment, then went on: 'If you are doing this for your father's sake, nothing can change what happened, Hanno. Nothing will ever change *him*.'

'I hoped you would be proud to see me getting on,' I said, perhaps a trifle more harshly than I intended. 'What ails you, wife? I have no choice. I must go when the King commands it.'

She looked down at the ground for some moments.

'But *murder*, Hanno?' she challenged suddenly, glancing up. 'You have never dealt with such a heinous crime before.'

She spoke with fierce passion. I had never seen her in such a nervous state before. She threw herself upon my chest at last to hide the evidence of her weeping, and I glanced quickly in the direction of Sergeant Koch. He was standing stiffly by the carriage door, his expression blank and unchanging, as if he had heard nothing of what my wife had just said. I felt a flash of resentment for the embarrassment she had caused me.

'Wait there, will you, Sergeant?' I called back. 'I'll not be long.'

Koch bobbed his head, a tight-lipped smile traced faintly on his thin lips.

I led Helena quickly into the hall. Her manner was restrained and watchful. I cannot say what reaction I had expected from her. Pride, perhaps? Joy at my rapid promotion? She had shown no sign of either.

'The King has called me to Him,' I argued. 'A senior magistrate in Königsberg has given His Majesty my name. What would you have me do?'

Helena looked at me, puzzlement traced upon her face, as if she failed to understand what I had just told her. 'I . . . I do not know. How long will you be gone?' she asked at last.

'I cannot tell,' I said. 'Not very long, I hope.'

'Run upstairs, Lotte. Fetch your master's things,' Helena cried suddenly, turning to the maid. 'His carriage is waiting at the door. Be quick! He'll be gone some days.'

As we stood in the hall alone, I knew not what to say. Helena and I had been wed four years, and had never spent a single night apart. A special bond of shared suffering tied us, one to the other.

'I am not going off to fight the French!' I declared with a nervous laugh, reaching out and drawing my darling close, kissing her gently on the forehead, cheek and lips, until the return of Lotte interrupted those brief, welcome moments of intimacy.

'I'll write every day, my love, and tell you of my doings. The minute we arrive, you'll have word of me,' I said with all the bluff sanguinity that I could muster to brighten the melancholy of parting. 'Kiss Manni and Süsi for me.'

As I took the travelling-bag from Lotte, Helena threw herself upon me once again and let forth her emotions with a force and intensity I had never known in her before that moment. I thought it was on account of the children: Immanuel was not yet one, Süsanne barely two.

'Forgive me, I am so troubled, Hanno,' she cooed, her soft voice almost lost in the deep folds of my woollen cloak. 'What do they want from *you*?'

Unable to reply, unwilling to speculate, I drew back from her embrace, straightened my mantle, threw my bag over my shoulder and walked quickly down the path towards the waiting coach and Sergeant Koch, my head bent low against the blizzard. I skipped aboard the coach with a light foot and a heavy heart.

As the vehicle slowly pulled away, the wheels crunching on the thick carpet of snow, I looked behind, watching until the dear, slender figure in the white dress was entirely swallowed up by the snowstorm.

The question that had perplexed Helena now returned to vex and puzzle me. Why *had* the King chosen me?

Chapter 2

The coach jolted onwards for more than an hour, and barely a word was said. Sergeant Koch sat in his corner, I sat in mine, both as melancholy as the world through which we journeyed. I stared out at the passing countryside. Bleak villages and isolated farms dotted the landscape here and there, marking out the hilltops and the highway. Peasants toiled in the fields, up to their knees in the snow, to save their stranded cows and sheep. The world was all a massive grey blur, the distant hills blending into the horizon with no precise point at which the earth ended and the heavens began.

We had just passed through a little village called Endernffords when our coach was forced to stop on the ramp approaching a swing-bridge over a narrow river. Screams of suffering rent the peace. Such wild, blood-curdling howls, at first I thought that they were human. I leapt up from my seat, pulled hard on the sash, dropped the window, and leaned out of the carriage to see what was going on.

'A farmer's cart has skidded on the ice,' I reported over my shoulder to Koch. The horse had slipped its traces, and it lay on its back in the middle of the road, one of its fore-legs dangling broken in the air. A man stood over the animal, howling drunken curses and lashing out viciously at the fallen beast with his whip. My first impulse was to get down, though whether to help the doomed horse, or to berate the senseless cruelty of the driver, I cannot say. What followed happened so quickly and in a manner so well-ordered, I was convinced that such things were a common occurrence at that isolated crossing, and I remained where I was.

Every man present at the scene – there were four of them sitting on the wooden beam of the bridge – seemed to know exactly what was going on. Three of these idlers rushed out suddenly, one brandishing a long curved knife, the other two with raised axes in their fists. The knife-blade flashed, then sliced through the horse's straining neck. The keening wail of the beast's distress died in a whistle of spouting blood and froth which turned the snow beneath the murderer's feet into a gory, reddish mash. The driver froze, the whip raised high above his head, then, in a flash, without a word, he dropped his whip, turned, and ran away, slithering and lurching across the bridge to safety. In silence, the butchers fell upon the carcass with their axes. It was the work of a minute. Steam rose all about them in a swirling cloud as they furiously hacked and chopped the fallen animal into a dozen pieces, then quickly loaded the meat up onto the cart. The fourth man hurried forward, helping the brigands load the cart, then push it out of the way, signalling to our coach to pass across the swing-bridge.

My legs gave way and I sat down. But I jumped up quickly again to close the window. As we passed by the cart with its disgusting load of offal, flesh and guts, the stench of fresh blood filled our coach in a warm, engulfing haze. It was sweet, nauseating, corrosive, painful to my sensibility.

'Hard times breed hard men,' said Sergeant Koch quietly. 'What are we to do about that, sir?'

I closed my eyes and leaned back against the leather bench.

'They're probably starving,' I murmured. 'Hunger has driven many a good man to shame.'

'Let's hope they're ready to butcher Frenchmen with the same enthusiasm,' Koch said dryly. 'If Bonaparte turns up in Prussia, there won't be anything left to eat, let alone horses. Then we'll see what sort of men they really are.'

'Pray God, we are never put to the test!' I replied, more sharply than I meant.

Another hour passed with very little said on either side.

'Whoever saw such a sky!' exclaimed Koch suddenly, shaking me from my lethargy. 'It looks as if the whole lot's going to come crashing down about our ears, sir. Foul weather's fit punishment for our sins, the proverb says.'

There was something almost comical about the seriousness of the man. The lurching of the coach had shifted his tricorn hat on his head, stark black strands of hair peeping out from beneath the stiff white curls of his periwig like shy maidens. I gave a nod and smiled, making the decision to pass the remainder of the journey in a more sociable manner. And yet, I hardly knew how. From a professional point of view, Koch was my inferior, little better than a servant.

'This would be a good moment for you to examine these papers, Herr Stiffeniis,' Sergeant Koch announced, reaching for his bag before I had the opportunity to speak.

The good humour I had decided on dissolved in an instant.

'Do you mean to tell me that you have kept something from my sight, Herr Koch?'

'I'm only doing as I was instructed, sir,' he said as he pulled a sheaf of papers from his leather bag.' I was told to hand these documents to you once we'd reached the Königsberg highway.'

As if in response to his words, the coach swung left at the Elbing crossroads.

So, *that's* your game, I thought. I have been flattered into accepting an unpleasant commission and now that it's too late to pull out, I'm to be told all the nasty details that would have convinced me to refuse it.

'The authorities must guarantee the peace,' Koch continued blithely. 'All those involved in the investigation have been sworn to secrecy.'

'Does that include you?' I asked sharply. 'You must have given your wife some reason for leaving her alone so early this morning.'

I felt mounting anger at the thought of this graceless messenger concealing information from me. 'You hold back facts, Koch, unveiling them whenever the need arises, or it suits your mood.'

The suspicion was growing on me that Sergeant Koch was not simply taking me anywhere; he was observing me, judging me, mentally preparing critical notes to be written up for the eyes of his superiors. That was the normal procedure in the Prussian civil service. To spy on others was the surest way to step up a rung on the uncertain bureaucratic ladder.

'I have nothing to hide from you, sir,' Sergeant Koch replied through clenched teeth, his handkerchief out again. 'I am a clerk. I have played no active part in the investigation. This morning, like any other, I took myself to work at five-thirty and I was instructed to do what I have done. I had no need to tell my wife, or anyone else, of my doings. I live alone.'

Koch and I had got off to a bad start.

'You claim to know so little of this affair, Herr Koch. I find it odd that you should be charged to illuminate a person who knows absolutely nothing. A case of the blind leading the blind, is it?'

'Those documents should answer your questions, sir. Obviously, I was told not to let you see them until you had accepted the task.'

'Do you mean to say that I could have refused?' I said, and snatched the papers from his hand.

He looked out of the window, but he did not reply.

With a bad grace I turned my attention to the documents. The first murder had been committed more than a year before. Jan Konnen, a middle-aged blacksmith, had been found dead in Mer-restrasse on the morning of 3 January 1803. Police enquiries revealed that he had spent the previous evening at a dockside tavern not far from the spot where his corpse was found. The innkeeper did not recall ever having seen Herr Konnen before and denied that he had seen him gaming in the company of foreign sailors. He believed that the man was a foreigner, he said. A Lithua-nian sailing ship had docked that day and the tavern had been particularly crowded until the early hours of the morning. Konnen had left the tavern shortly after ten o'clock that evening, but no one had noticed him outside. It was very cold that night and the streets were empty of casual passers-by. His corpse had been found at dawn by a midwife on her way to assist at a birth. Hurrying through the fog, which was exceptionally thick that morning, she had almost fallen over Konnen, who was kneeling up against a wall. The midwife thought that he was ill, but on drawing closer she saw that he was dead. The report had been signed by two officers of His Royal Majesty's night-watch, Anton Lublinsky and Rudolph Kopka. Penned in passable German, it was dated six months after the murder. I glanced up, noting that heavy sleet had now begun to lash the windows of the coach, determined to ask Koch for an explanation. He was a bureaucrat, he was from Königsberg: he must know what the standard procedure was in such matters. But Koch's head had fallen forward on his chest, his face half-hidden in the folds of his cloak, and he let out a rattling snore. For a moment, I toyed with the idea of waking him up. Instead, I turned to the second fascicle.

First, I glanced at the date written at the foot of the fourth page. This report had also been compiled recently, on 23 January 1804, to be exact, a week before, and almost four months after the murder, which did not say much for the efficiency of the local authorities. Had the second killing prompted them to review the first? It seemed a most irregular way of going about things. The name of the second victim was Paula-Anne Brunner. And there went my first hypothesis! I had formed the notion that there must be something banal at the heart of the matter, something so simple that it had been overlooked. After all, there was nothing startling about gambling debts and violent litigation in a low tavern between men who diced and drank more than was good for them. But Prussian women, as a rule, don't drink in public or play at dice. Especially in Königsberg, which is renowned for its moral Pietism.

'On 22 September 1803,' I read, 'the corpse of Paula-Anne Brunner (née Schobart) was found in the public gardens in Neumannstrasse.'

An Austrian cavalry officer, Herr Colonel Viktor Rodiansky, a registered mercenary in the Prussian army, was strolling there while awaiting a lady whom he refuses to name. He arrived in the public gardens at four o'clock when he knew that a large part of the citizenry would be attending the funeral ceremony of the late-departed and much-lamented Superintendent Brunswig in the Cathedral. Colonel Rodiansky reports that the evening was neither excessively cold nor wet, but there was a sea mist which reduced visibility to a maximum of six or seven yards. The inclement weather exactly suited his purposes, he said. Strolling up and down, smoking a cigar as the appointed hour approached, Colonel Rodiansky spotted a woman kneeling beside a wooden bench, and was not a little put out by her unwelcome presence in that place. At that moment, the lady for whom he had been waiting arrived, and Colonel Rodiansky's attention was distracted from the kneeling woman. He thought little of the fact that she was kneeling in a public park, attributing her position to the fact that she was praying for the soul of Superintendent Brunswig, like many another of her townswomen, though, for some reason, prevented from adding her voice to the others in the Cathedral.

Colonel Rodiansky's lady friend was more perturbed at finding a third party present at the meeting, and looked often in the direction of the kneeling woman, hoping that she would finish her prayer and remove her person from the park. At last, wondering if the woman had been taken ill or had had a mishap, the pair drew close. They realised that the praying woman was actually a kneeling corpse, and the police were called by Colonel Rodiansky, who had first taken measures to protect the anonymity of his mistress by sending her home.

The report was signed by the same two officers who had written up the report of the first murder, Lublinsky and Kopka.

I sat back against the leather seat. The second account was rich in detail, almost literary, but as with the first, there were missing elements far too obvious to escape my attention. No mention was made of how the victim had been killed. Nor of the weapon that had been used.

I turned again to Koch. He was still asleep, his head jolting uncomfortably up and down with the unpredictable lurching of the carriage on the muddy, potholed road. His hat had fallen onto his knees and his wig had now slipped down over his right ear. I closed my own eyes and let myself be rocked by the motion of the vehicle, trying to get the picture clear in my mind. How had these people died? What purpose had been served by killing them? And why had two officers with considerable investigative experience (as I presumed from the fact that Lublinsky and Kopka had been present on both occasions) failed to confront these vital questions?

A deafening crash of thunder followed by a blinding flash of lightning put an end to my meditations, and to Koch's dozing. He sat up as if he'd been struck by a bullet, his first impulse to reach for his wig with one hand, his second to make the sign of the cross with the other.

'Good God, sir!' he grumbled loudly. 'Nature was created to plague the affairs of men.'

'It is only water vapour, Sergeant,' I smiled. 'Electrical discharges in the heavens. That is all. An eminent fellow citizen of yours once wrote a pamphlet on the subject. Nothing exists, he said, which the laws of Science cannot explain.'

Koch turned to me, his grey eyes flashing with unmistakable indulgence. 'Do you believe that, Herr Stiffeniis?'

'Indeed, I do,' I replied.

'I envy you your certainty,' he murmured, bending to pick his hat up from the carriage floor where it had fallen. He brushed the brown velvet, and set it on the crown of his head with care. 'No mysteries exist for you, then, sir?'

I could not ignore the vein of incredulity with which he expressed his doubts.

'I have always tried to follow the pathways of rationality to their logical conclusions, Herr Koch,' I answered.

'You do not admit the possibility of the Unknown, the Unthinkable?' He had a trick of sounding capital letters where there ought to have been none. 'May I ask what you do, sir, when you find yourself face to face with the Inexplicable?'

'I do not mean to suggest that human reason can explain and justify every human action,' I said with barely contained annoyance. 'There are limits to our understanding. What is unknown, as you call it, remains so for the simple reason that no one has chosen to explain it for the moment. I would call this qualified ignorance, not a defeat for Enlightened Science.'

Lightning flashed again and his pale flesh turned silvery blue against the rushing backdrop of dark trees and fleeting drops of rain, framed by the window pane.

'I hope the honour falls to me of taking you home when this affair has been successfully resolved,' he said, leaning close. 'I pray sincerely that I am wrong and you are right, Herr Stiffeniis. If not, God spare us all!'

'You seem to doubt my capacity to plumb these murders,' I returned with acid irritation.

'I would not dare so far, Herr Procurator. Indeed, I think I begin to understand why so much hope has been placed in you,' he said, and looked away.

I rubbed my nose, and took the plunge. 'My concerns are practical ones, Sergeant Koch. No mention is made in these reports of the cause of death. What am I supposed to do? Divine the nature of the weapon with which the victims were killed? The passage from life to death is not merely a religious question. It is a hard and fast fact, and there are very few facts here,' I said, holding up the papers in my hand and shaking them. 'I don't know how you go about your business in Königsberg, but we in Lotingen believe that if an egg has disappeared, someone has stolen it.'

Sergeant Koch ignored this barb.

'I've no idea what you may have read in those reports,' he said.

'Have you seen the bodies, Koch? Do you know how they died?'

'No, sir.'

'So, even you, a trusted employee of the police, have no idea how these people were killed? Doesn't the population talk of such things? Were the victims stabbed, strangled, beaten to death?'

'You mean to say no mention is made of the weapon used?' He looked genuinely surprised. 'I can understand the need for discretion, but the fact that even you have not been let in on the secret's hard to credit, sir. The town's full of rumours, as you can imagine.'

'What sort of rumours, Koch?'

'I hardly dare speak of such things to a rational thinker like yourself, sir,' Koch replied with an archness which seemed affected.

'Do not humour me!'

'I did not mean to offend, sir.' The sergeant took off his hat and looked penitent. 'The folk in Königsberg say that the Devil did it. Word's out that death came quick and mighty cruel.'

'What else?'

'This is wagging tongues and nothing more,' he said with sudden seriousness. 'What good will gossip do you, sir?'

'Wag your tongue, Sergeant Koch. Let me be the judge.'

He sat back against the seat and considered for a moment before he spoke.

'They say the woman who found the body of Jan Konnen saw the weapon.'

'She did?'

'They *say* she did,' Koch corrected me.

'What do they say she saw? What was this weapon that the Devil used?'

Herr Sergeant Koch looked at me and an embarrassed smile graced his lips.

'His claws, sir.'

'Claws, Koch. And what is *that* supposed to mean?'

Again, he seemed reluctant to speak his mind. 'I think you'd better talk to Procurator Rhunken, sir. I'm hardly qualified to say.'

'I want to know what *you* think, Herr Koch. I will ask Procurator Rhunken for his opinion of the matter when the opportunity presents itself.'

'I can only tell you what I've heard, Herr Stiffeniis.' Koch shifted uneasily in his seat and replaced his hat. 'These murders have been committed in a strange fashion. Everything points to it. All the facts . . .'

'Which *facts*, Koch?' I interrupted. 'I have not lighted upon one, single *fact* in all that I have read!'

He regarded me coolly for a moment.

'That's just the point, Herr Stiffeniis. Is it not? It's mystery which opens the gate to wild speculation. The word going the rounds didn't say that Konnen was stabbed, throttled, or beaten to death. Just that he was murdered by the Devil. And that the Devil used his claws to do the deed.'

'Claws, indeed! I say again, this is superstitious nonsense!'

'But if the authorities won't even tell *you* what caused the deaths, sir,' he hissed, pointing at the sheaf of official papers I held in my hands, 'it only leaves two alternatives. *They* don't know, or they don't want *us* to know! In either case, it leaves the door wide open to superstitious nonsense, as you call it.'

Koch fell back against the seat, his eyes clenched shut, clearly disturbed by what he had told me. I returned to my reading, making more pretence of work than progress, disconcerted by the sergeant's suggestion that the authorities were less than willing to reveal precise details of the murders even to myself, the magistrate appointed to direct the investigations. I was almost as much in the dark as I had been the day before when I knew nothing of the case.

I decided to skip the third report for the moment and look at the evidence that might have surfaced the previous day, hoping that the local police had established some method in their working and that the latest affair would be more illuminating than the first two.

> On the 31st January, in the year of Our Lord, 1804, the body of Jeronimus Tifferch, notary, was found before dawn by Hilde Gnute, wife of Farmer Abel Gnute. The witness reports that it was a cold morning, snow having fallen most of the night, her eyes were watering and she could not see very well. As she walked along Jungmannenstrasse in the direction of the grocery shop belonging to Herr Bendt Frodke, to whom she intended selling eggs, she came upon the body of Herr Tifferch kneeling up against a wall. He had been murdered by a person, or persons, unknown.

The account was so short as to be ludicrous. The name affixed to the report was that of Anton Lublinsky alone. Could the officer find no more to say about how or why the man had been butchered? I rested my forehead against the cold window-glass and closed my eyes, which burned and ached from reading in the failing light. When I opened them again, we had entered a wood. Still, the rain poured down. A group of peasants had taken shelter beneath the trees waiting for the storm to end. The coach splattered them with mud as we passed. Silently, I prayed to the Lord our God, asking Him to protect both those poor people and myself. I realised that I would need to humble myself, I would need to pay the most careful attention and listen with a new ear to what the people in Königsberg might say. I would have to try to comprehend what they were truly thinking and interpret their beliefs, no matter how extravagant or superstitious their thoughts might strike me as being. I bent close to the window again, using the little light that remained to read a note which had been pinned to the report: '*Asked if she had seen any persons near the place of the murder, Hilde Gnute replied that only the Devil could do such a deed.*'

There it was, written in black on white, the possible identity of the murderer. Satan himself. That was to be my starting point. I could only wonder where such a beginning might lead. Was it simply a matter of faith? Perhaps, after all, the name of the murderer *was* truly known, and all that was lacking was my own willingness to suspend disbelief.

I cannot say how long I sat staring out of the window at the bleak landscape. The rain had ceased and snow began to fall heavily again. Slowly, the fields transformed themselves before my eyes from turgid grey to sparkling white, the moon a pale, shallow disc on the black horizon, and wolves began to howl in a chorus somewhere in the woods. I cannot recall what thoughts crossed my mind, but I must have fallen asleep at some point. Whether in pleasant dreams or foulest nightmares, the journey passed.

Suddenly, I felt a light tap on my shoulder.

'Our destination, sir,' Sergeant Koch announced. 'Königsberg.'

Chapter 3

The sky above our heads was an immense, dark sheet, furled, rippled and corrugated by the driving wind. Shards and shooting splinters of the Northern Lights shimmered low along a silver-edged horizon that I knew to be the Baltic Sea. The snow had ceased to fall. It lay on the ground in a sparkling carpet as we approached the city.

'The weather seems to be easing,' I began to say, as the coach drew up before a massive Gothic arch which marked the western entrance to Königsberg.

Sergeant Koch made no reply as a troop of heavily armed soldiers came running out of the gate and quickly surrounded the vehicle. Opening the window, he leaned out to face them. 'I am an employee of the Court. This gentleman is the new Procurator of Königsberg,' he stated boldly to the guards, inviting me to show my face at the window.

The soldiers looked at us, then at each other, their muskets at the ready, while one man ran back in through the gate. Not a word was said until he returned a few moments later in the company of an officer.

'Which one of you's supposed to be the magistrate?' he asked sharply.

The dark blue of his cape, his leather kepi and tall purple plume, the impressive array of silver decorations criss-crossing his uniform jacket lent little dignity to the man as he scrutinised my face. His eyes were bagged and bovine, his waxed moustache sagged heavily, his expression a disconcerting compound of mocking incredulity and alert tension. His podgy right hand, formed by Nature for the purpose of turning heavy clods in some secluded village out in the wilds of Bory Tucholskjie, pointed a percussion pistol in my face. Clearly, he would not hesitate to unload it.

'I am Procurator Hanno Stiffeniis,' I said, holding up my bag for him to see. 'I have a letter here which is signed by the King himself . . .'

'You are obstructing the Procurator in his duties,' Koch said suddenly, an unexpected authoritative tone in his voice.

'I'm sorry, sir, but I must see your *laissez-passer*,' the officer insisted. 'I have got my own instructions to follow. General Katowice's order-of-the-day. No one is to enter Königsberg by land without authority. Haven't you heard? There was a murder . . .'

'That is why I am here!' I snapped, handing him the commission which Sergeant Koch had delivered to me that morning.

The officer read it over, looked at me again, then handed the document back.

'Don't lose that paper, sir,' he warned, waving the guards back. He saluted, then called to the driver to proceed.

'What was that all about, Sergeant?' I asked as the coach rumbled over the cobblestones in the direction of the centre of the town. It was not yet four o' the clock, but all the shops were closed and shuttered, the streets empty, except for squads of soldiers marching through the town or standing guard with bayonets fixed at almost every corner. 'Has martial law been declared?'

'I've no idea, sir,' Koch replied. Indeed, he said nothing more for quite some time, until the vehicle came to a stop in a tree-lined square before a large, green, barn-like building.

'Ostmarktplatz,' he announced, skipping down from the carriage with surprising agility and pulling out the folding step for me. 'Herr Rhunken is expecting you, sir.'

I ought to have guessed that Herr Procurator Rhunken would wish to speak to me immediately. But why had Sergeant Koch not told me beforehand? I took a deep breath, and did my best to smooth my ruffled plumage, telling myself that all would soon be revealed. After all, Rhunken was the person best placed to instruct me in my duties. I hoped to obtain from him by word of mouth the essential facts which were missing in the documents I had been reading during the journey.

'You said that he was in no fit state to speak, Koch.'

The sergeant did not reply, but busied himself giving orders to the driver, whose oilskin and leather gauntlets glistened with crystals of hoar-frost in the gathering gloom. I had to repeat myself twice before I could manage to catch Koch's attention.

'Procurator Rhunken has suffered an apoplexy of the brain, has he not?'

'Indeed, he has, sir,' Koch replied. 'Herr Rhunken was an excellent magistrate to work for.'

I chose to ignore the implications of this compliment. 'Has he been ill for long?'

'Always in the best of health 'til yesterday, sir. Herr Rhunken collapsed in his office, and the physician diagnosed an apoplexy as the cause.'

Koch pointed beyond the ugly green building to a pretty pink villa with a tiny snow-covered garden set back from the road. 'That's his house, sir. It stands opposite the Fortress on the other side of the square, as you can see. The Court House is in there. Work was everything to him.'

My eyes followed the direction indicated by Koch's stubby forefinger, as it swept the vast, snow-strewn space and ran the length of an enormous building in soaring grey stone. Battlements, keep and watchtowers in bewildering display. A massive central doorway with a steel portcullis bore a marked resemblance to the rat-traps used throughout Prussia. Narrow pill-boxes on either side of the doorway were occupied by sentries wearing grey winter capes and black fur busbies. They stared fixedly ahead, long muskets frozen to their broad shoulders.

'I suppose I'll be spending much of my time over there,' I said warily. The building was an architectural horror. At the same time, I recollected, it represented the limitless power and authority that I would be free to wield in my new position.

'I'll take you over at the appointed hour, sir,' Koch said shortly, striding away along the pathway towards the villa, slipping and almost falling in the knee-deep snow in his haste. As I reached the door, the sergeant gave three short raps on a large brass knocker to

26

announce our arrival. The door did not open for quite some time, and not before Koch had been obliged to knock again.

'Herr Stiffeniis to see His Excellency,' Koch announced to the pale young chambermaid who opened the door.

The serving-girl raised her watery blue eyes to mine for just an instant, then quickly looked down again. 'Doctor Plucker is with my master,' she murmured.

'How is Herr Rhunken today?' Sergeant Koch enquired, a note of genuine concern in his voice.

The girl shook her head. 'He's in a sorry state, Herr Koch. He was always such a fine, proud, handsome man . . .'

'Take Herr Stiffeniis through. I'll wait with the driver,' Koch said to me, rudely cutting in on the girl, whose words dissolved in sobs.

Closing the door, the maid looked uncertainly at me, as if she knew not what to do with me.

'Your master is expecting me,' I said, too sharply perhaps, taking my cue from Koch.

'This way, sir,' the girl mumbled timidly into her handkerchief, before leading me through a series of small connecting rooms, the walls of which were lined with glass-fronted bookcases full of leather-bound volumes. All the tables were piled high with books and papers, sofas and armchairs forced to do the camel's work of accommodating on their backs what would not fit on the crowded shelves. Procurator Rhunken seemed to have transformed his house into a private library. With the exception of the maid, there was no other indication of a female presence, no suggestion of the tempering influence of a mother, wife or daughter.

The girl stopped short before a door which stood ajar. A low voice could be heard murmuring inside, and suddenly a drawn-out whimper shook the air. I laid my hand on the wench's arm before she could knock.

'Can the Procurator speak?' I asked.

'Doctor purged him twice this morning. He's going to do it again . . .' She stopped to wipe her nose and dab her eyes. 'Sent me down the port this morning, he did, sir. To fetch those . . . creatures.' Her shoulders shook with fear or revulsion, or just possibly with the cold. The temperature inside the house was lower than the air in the street.

'A ship came in last night. The sailors laughed and told me to carry the bucket with care. If I touched one, it would suck my life out, they said.' She looked up at me with fear in her eyes. 'I did not know such creatures existed, sir. I did it for my master,' she whispered, sniffling into her handkerchief again.

I had no idea what she was muttering about. The sailors? The creatures, whatever they might be?

'If he has truly seen the Devil,' she added, 'all the physicking in the world won't save him.'

I did not shift myself to reassure her, reflecting only that the Devil's name enjoyed great popularity in Königsberg. Just then, the door was thrown open and a tall, gaunt man stepped out into the dimly lit passage. He was wigless, his head recently shaved. A tight, dark suit made him seem even taller and thinner than he really was. He saw the maid and his face lit up with some private satisfaction. But then he saw me, and his manner changed.

'Who are you, sir?' he barked in an uncouth manner. Without waiting for my reply, he turned on the girl and hissed, 'His Excellency is in no condition to receive visitors. I told you that before!'

'I am the new Procurator,' I announced. 'I have business with your patient, sir. Urgent business, which cannot wait.'

The doctor drew himself up like a hooded serpent preparing to strike. His eyes gleamed like points of light in the dim corridor.

'So, *you* are the person who is the cause of this distress!' he snapped in a blunt and accusing fashion. 'Herr Rhunken has been in a state of nervous anxiety all the day regarding you. I confess my surprise,' he continued, staring rudely at me. 'I was expecting someone altogether . . . *different*. An older man, let's say. A more . . . experienced magistrate.'

'I will not keep him long,' I said.

'I should think *not*!' he replied. 'I have work to do.'

If the doctor was rude, I put it down to strain. I was on edge myself as I followed him into the sick-room. Procurator Rhunken was not confined to bed, as I had expected, but lay on a leather chaise longue close to the far wall, his legs naked and raised on pillows towards an open window. This ice-cold chamber was more cluttered than the rest of the house put together. Three thin candle-tapers wedged together in a single candle-holder lit up books and papers scattered everywhere, great piles of them tottering like drunkards against the walls on either side of a four-poster bed which stood in the darkest corner.

If Doctor Plucker had been expecting someone older, His Excellency, Herr Procurator Wolfgang Rhunken, was far younger than I had anticipated. He could hardly have been forty-five years of age. I recalled the chambermaid's description of him as fine and handsome, but I could find no evidence of those attributes. He was propped up in a sitting position, large cushions at his back, a dark woollen shawl draped around his shoulders, his careworn face hollow with suffering, his naked legs raised to the freezing night air. Drawing nearer, I observed the sickly colour of his face, his mouth drawn tightly into a thin black slit, eyes half-closed like a man looking into the next world. Large beads of sweat stood out on his pale brow like condensation on a warm glass, his hair drenched, despite the glacial cold. He turned like a blind man as my boots clattered on the stone pavement.

I looked uncertainly at the doctor.

'Closer, sir. Go closer,' he urged. 'Let's get it over with, and quickly!'

As I approached the patient, I heard the doctor out in the passage, calling to the maid. 'Bring a stool for the *new* Procurator! And bring in that bucket!'

Rhunken's feverish eyes flashed open at the rude note of irony in the doctor's voice. He glared at me, though he did not speak. The stool arrived and was placed beside the couch. I hesitated for an instant as the sick man raised his quivering right hand with what seemed to be a superhuman effort, then let it fall with a heavy thump on the stool.

I took a deep breath and sat down, as the maid placed a large oak bucket covered with a linen cloth on the floor beside her ailing master. The sharp odour which I had at first taken to be the musty smell of a little-used room intensified. A heady compound of sweat, faeces and urine dosed with camphor and other medicines, it was the ethereal vapour of the magistrate's volatilising decay.

'I hope you'll soon recover your health, sir,' I began, uncertain what else to say, my voice lower than I might have wished.

Procurator Rhunken's mouth fell open, his lower lip trembled, the left side of his face twitched frantically. He struggled against the rebellious muscles, grasped my arm and pulled me close to that vile stench. Then, gasping desperately for air, he fell back against the cushions without having managed to say a word. For one moment, I thought that he was going to expire before my eyes. A violent tremor shook his body as he attempted to raise his head again.

'Do not exhaust yourself, sir!' Doctor Plucker exhorted. 'This gentleman has excellent young ears and patience aplenty. Now, stay still, sir, while I apply the remedy,' the doctor muttered. 'A ship came in last night from Rio del Plata. I had to fight for these with Surgeon Franzich from the Fortress infirmary. You'd baulk, Herr Rhunken, if you knew how much they cost. *Haementaria ghilianii*,' he announced, whipping the cloth cover from the bucket and raising it to his nose. 'Hmmm! The primal stench of the Amazon forests! You can almost see the dark, musky swamps where it creeps and crawls. These will do you the world of good, sir. They're a hundred times more effective than the hiruda worms that Monsieur Broussais brought back from Egypt. Military authorities throughout Europe are stocking up before the outbreak of war.'

I watched in awe as the physician extracted a massive black worm from his bucket with a pair of callipers. The creature squirmed and wriggled, trying to wrap itself around the doctor's arm. The instant it touched his patient's naked flesh, all the fight went out of it. Doctor Plucker stretched the massive leech out along Herr Rhunken's calf from the knee to the ankle, and left it there to feed.

'If I can help in any way,' I offered weakly, my gaze horridly attracted by the massive Amazonian slug. It was twelve inches long, at the very least. As it began to siphon off the invalid's blood, it seemed to surge and swell. 'I am . . .'

A yellow hand shot out from beneath Rhunken's shawl and came to rest before my face with such rapidity that the words froze on my tongue. 'You have come, then,' Rhunken gasped. 'From Berlin, I suppose?'

'Berlin, sir?' I repeated, uncertain what he meant. I darted a glance at the physician, but found no comfort there. He was busily engaged, laying out another giant leech upon the sick man's other leg. 'I have come this day from Lotingen, Your Excellency.'

Herr Rhunken frowned. A chasm seemed to split his brow.

'*Where?*'

'Lotingen. On the western circuit,' I said. 'I am the presiding magistrate there.'

'*Lotingen?*' Rhunken cried, the distress on his face painful to see. 'What are you doing here?'

The last thing I expected was to be quizzed about my identity by the man who had recommended me.

'I was ordered by His Majesty to relieve you of the case. I have your own note here in my pocket!'

Rhunken shook his head, disbelief writ large on his face.

'Surely you nominated me?' I pressed.

Procurator Rhunken turned his face to the wall as Plucker applied two more famished bloodsuckers to his naked thighs.

'I nominated no man,' the patient muttered angrily. 'This is *his* doing! That serpent does it to torture me!'

I chose to ignore his raving. Herr Rhunken was ill, after all. I could understand his situation. When a man is ill, he knows not who to blame, and so blames every man whose health is better than his own.

'I expected a special emissary,' he went on. 'From Berlin. From the secret police. Not you . . .'

'He's never heard of you,' Doctor Plucker hissed angrily in my ear, as he draped a smaller black worm across his patient's sweating brow, and another on his right temple. 'Any fool can see that. You are inflaming his brain, sir! You'll kill him! He was removed from the case. Sacked! Forced to cede. To an expert, he believed. Have you no grain of pity, sir?'

Suddenly, the magistrate gasped for air. Phlegm bubbled in his throat, and he coughed violently, spitting into a bowl which the doctor held up for him. 'Do not exert yourself, sir,' the physician implored. Looking over his shoulder at me, his expression tense, he cried, 'I beg you, sir!'

'I am not to blame if he is sick,' I replied stubbornly, then stopped short, uncertain how to continue. I had no wish to worsen his condition. 'I have been empowered to act by the King. Herr Rhunken knows more about these murders than any other living soul. I need his help.'

Doctor Plucker turned on me with anger.

'Herr Rhunken needs *rest*. You have robbed him of peace enough, I think, for one day. Leave him be!'

If the physician was determined to end the interview, the patient seemed intent on prolonging it. His hand clenched at my sleeve, dragging me down, and I was forced to my knees on the floor at his side. The leech at his temple throbbed and buckled, gorged with blood, sliding onto his cheek until the doctor picked it off with haste.

'Go to the Court House,' the magistrate said weakly. 'See if you . . . can do what I have failed to do.'

He fell back against the cushion, eyes closed, panting desperately for air.

'This will be the end of him,' Doctor Plucker protested, pushing me away from the stool without ceremony and sitting down himself, his hand on the pulse of his patient.

I stood back, my brain in a whirl, and watched the doctor administer to him.

'But you must know what weapon killed them!' I shouted, confusion giving place to frustration, as Procurator Rhunken closed his eyes and seemed to fall into a dead faint, those worms on his face and temples wriggling and twisting like the portrait of the Medusa I had seen in Florence.

'Can't you see the state he's in?' Doctor Plucker shouted, taking hold of my arm, pushing and pulling me to the door. 'I must order you to quit this room!'

Throwing open the door with great energy, the doctor surprised me by his strength as he thrust me out into the corridor, where the maid was waiting.

'Show Herr Stiffeniis out!' he thundered.

I must have looked like a lost child, for the girl began to coax me gently along the corridor in the direction of the front door.

'Come along now, sir,' she said, retracing our path through the book-lined rooms and darkened corridors. 'Just follow me.'

As the front door closed behind me, I stood stock-still in the cold light of the low moon. Beyond the garden fence, Sergeant Koch was waiting. He turned at the sound of the door closing and began to advance towards me, his face mottled like veined marble in a church. The temperature had dropped while I had been inside, and fresh-fallen snow had settled on the crown of his hat.

'Is everything in order, Herr Stiffeniis?'

I ignored his solicitude. 'Who instructed you to come to Lotingen today, Sergeant Koch?' I was quivering with humiliation and with rage.

'Procurator Rhunken, sir,' he replied without a moment's hesitation.

'He had no idea who I was,' I said with a coolness which surprised me.

Koch opened his mouth to speak, then closed it again. Finally, he said, 'I *presumed* it was Herr Rhunken. I was handed a despatch by a messenger.'

'Who signed this despatch?'

'It was not signed, sir. I am an employee of the Procurator. The messenger said that the note had come from upstairs. Herr Rhunken does not need to sign his orders to me,' he said. 'That order told me what to do, and where to go. The same messenger handed me that letter with the Royal seal and those documents I was to consign to you while travelling to Königsberg. If I've done any wrong, I am most heartily sorry for it, sir.'

'You did not see Herr Rhunken at all?'

Koch shook his head. 'No, sir, I did not.'

'I must go at once to the Court House,' I said, turning on my heel, setting off in the direction of the massive Fortress on the far side of the square. I had gone some way before I realised that Koch had made no move to follow me.

'The Court House, sir?' he called after me. 'Don't you want to see your lodgings first?'

I turned on him. There was something ludicrous in what he had suggested. 'Do you think I am here on holiday? I have come to Königsberg to investigate murders, Sergeant!'

Koch took a step forward and removed his hat. 'The moon is not yet high enough, sir,' he said. For a moment I thought I had misheard him, but then he went on: 'We have time enough to . . .'

'Has the cold afflicted your brain, Koch?' I interrupted. 'What in the name of heaven has the *moon* to do with it?'

'I was instructed to take you to the Fortress after the moon had reached its peak, sir. Not a minute before.'

I strode back through the snow, resisting the urge to grab him by the throat.

'Is this the way that time is generally measured in Königsberg, Koch? By the phases of the moon? Or is this just one more instance of your superstitious nonsense?'

'There's to be a meeting over there, sir. When the moon is at its height. That's all I know,' Koch stated flatly.

'You made no mention of this before, Sergeant,' I observed. 'It is not the first time that you have tricked me.'

Koch looked at me with measured coolness. 'Mine is not to question why, sir. A person has been appointed to help you, that's all that I have been told,' he said.

'People have names, Koch,' I replied.

Snow began to fall again in drifting, wispy flakes, and Koch glanced up at the sky before deigning to answer. 'The person's name is Doctor Vigilantius.'

I opened my mouth to protest, but words would not come. Snowdrops settled cold on my lips and melted on my tongue.

'A *necromancer*?' I managed at last. 'What is *he* doing here?'

'I have heard,' Koch replied hesitantly, 'that the doctor will be conducting experiments of a scientific nature, sir.'

'Which *science* are you talking of, Koch?'

Sarcasm appeared to be lost on my stolid companion.

'I've been told that he is an expert regarding the flux of electrical currents in the brain,' he replied.

'Exactly, Koch. What is Vigilantius doing *here*?'

'I have just told you, sir. Experiments.'

'Let us try another tack, Sergeant Koch,' I persisted. 'Who called Augustus Vigilantius here to Königsberg?'

Koch stood to attention. 'I really am most terribly sorry, Herr Procurator Stiffeniis,' he apologised. 'I cannot answer that question.'

'Cannot, or will not? That seems to be your personal motto,' I muttered through clenched teeth, though Koch did not move a muscle or make any attempt to explain himself.

'You've time to spare before the appointed hour,' he said instead. 'I'm to take you to your lodging first, sir. The coach is waiting.'

I pointed to the Fortress on the far side of the square. 'Am I not staying over there?'

'Oh no, sir,' he returned quickly. 'I have been instructed to take you to another place.'

Suddenly, I felt drained of energy, as if I had just been leeched myself. Was there any point in arguing or complaining further with this intransigent man? I followed him to the coach as meekly as a ceremonial lamb being led to the slaughter.

Chapter 4

The coach pulled away slowly. The fresh snow on the cobbles made the horses nervous, the driver hesitant. The rattling wheels echoed off the towering walls of the dark stone buildings lining the narrow streets through which we drove, but I paid no heed to my surroundings. My thoughts were taken up with Procurator Rhunken. He had not been expecting me. He had no idea who I was, nor why I had come. In which case, why had I been sent to see *him*? If he had not given my name to the King, *who* had? Rhunken had admitted himself that he was expecting a magistrate from Berlin. The Royal capital was home to the Secret Police. Was that who he had been waiting for, a Procurator from the Secret Police, a specialist in politics and murder? These new uncertainties, together with the host of unanswered questions lurking in the sparse official documents that I had been permitted to read on my way to the city, threw me into something approaching despair. And to make my situation even worse, I was bereft of reliable assistance. Herr Sergeant Koch was a minor official, an uninformed messenger following orders, as rigorous as he was unhelpful.

The raucous screeching of seagulls broke in on my thoughts. My nose began to twitch with the stink of stale fish and the nauseous tang of seaweed as I raised the blind and looked out of the coach. The listless grey sea stretched northwards beyond a narrow sand bar to infinity. The tide was out, and a small fleet of fishing-smacks lay awkwardly on their keels, the masts and rigging a forest of icicles. The shallow beach was a sheet of solid ice, except for a narrow channel of fast-flowing water in the centre of the estuary. A black stone pier projected out like an arm into the stream. Tall three-masters lining the sea wall were moored in line like dead whales waiting to be hauled on shore. Navvies carrying sacks and bales went running up and down the gangplanks, while ancient derricks creaked and groaned under the weight of the cargoes being loaded and discharged. Apart from the ubiquitous presence of the soldiers on the streets, this was the first sign of life that I had witnessed since arriving in Königsberg. The city was renowned for the industry of its inhabitants, the canny tight-fistedness of its merchants. It was, after all, the most extensive port on the Baltic coast. Hamburg and Danzig were rivals to some extent, but neither place could boast a tonnage equal to that of Königsberg. In a normal day, Koch reported, a dozen ships from the farthest reaches of the earth hove to along that pier, while another dozen weighed their anchors and plotted their route in the opposite direction. The labourers came and went, each one following an identical path to the dock-side warehouses, hard on his neighbour's heel, then running back to the vessels, like ants carrying a grain of seed to their communal store. One of those ships, I thought, had journeyed all the way from the tropical jungles of South America with its cargo of leeches for the army.

'Where are you taking me, Herr Koch?' I asked.

'To your inn, sir. It's down on the quayside. It's out of the way, I admit, but the coach will always be . . .'

'An inn?' I snapped. 'Like a travelling salesman?'

Was this a further attempt to humiliate me? I had suffered knocks enough that day. First, Rhunken had denied all knowledge of who I was. Then, a meeting by moonlight had been arranged for me with a notorious alchemist, and now I was to be lodged in a low tavern in the company of smugglers and pirates, far from the Fortress and the Court where I ought to have been by rights.

'I am not in Königsberg for my pleasure, Sergeant,' I reminded him.

'My instructions were to bring you here, sir,' Koch answered bluntly.

Even at that early stage, I began to feel that a precise scheme had been laid out for me. My introduction to Königsberg had all the appearance of an elaborate courtly dance. I was being led deliberately from step to step by Koch, my taciturn dancing-master. But who had called the tune? And for what purpose?

'I only hope this place is comfortable,' I muttered to myself as the coach skidded to a stop in front of an ancient red-brick building with a ribbed, uneven roof. A weather-vane of a seagoing ship with her sails puffed by the wind spun furiously above the central chimney. In the gloom, the frosted glass of the bow window flickered with a lively amber glow, which suggested that a large fire was blazing inside. It was the first heartening thing I had seen that day. A wooden sign above the door was so plastered with driven snow that it was impossible to read the name of the inn.

'The Baltic Whaler, Herr Procurator,' Koch confided. 'The food here is excellent. Far better than the Fortress barracks, I believe.'

I ignored this attempt to smooth my temper, the icy cold penetrating my bones as we made for the entrance. Inside, a wave of muggy heat hit me in the face, and I glanced around the room while Sergeant Koch went to speak to a man who was busy stoking the fire. The fireplace itself was so wide as to take up almost the entire wall at the far end of the room. Tables had been laid for dinner. Fresh white linen tablecloths and gleaming silver made a favourable impression. The place seemed clean and inviting enough.

Sergeant Koch returned in the company of a tall, thickset man with an untidy mass of curly grey locks cascading over his forehead, and a brass ring in each ear, who nodded in welcome, then ducked behind the bar-counter. A waxed ponytail tied up with a bright red ribbon added to the impression that he had once been a whaling man. He returned with a large bunch of keys, smiling at me in a manner that was respectful without being obsequious.

'I am Ulrich Totz, owner of the inn. We've been expecting you all day, sir,' he said in a deep, strong voice which made him sound younger than his grey hair suggested. 'I've sent the groom upstairs to fuel the fire in your room. Now, let me get your bags from the coach.'

I thanked him and glanced around the room again, while Koch stood warming his hands before the blazing fire. There were few other people present at that early hour of the evening. Near to the fireplace, a knot of customers sat on high-backed wooden settles and regarded Koch and myself with undisguised curiosity. Having satisfied themselves that we were nothing more or less than two travelling gentlemen seeking refuge from the snowstorm, they turned back to their beer and pipes and resumed their conversations. Three of the drinkers wore Prussian naval uniforms, while another sported the garb of a Russian hussar with a short green cape and festoons of gold braid stitched like skeletal ribs across the breast of his uniform. The man seated nearest to the fireplace was dark-skinned, and stroked a huge handlebar moustache, a bright red fez sitting lopsidedly on his small head. I guessed him to be a Moroccan or a Turk, most probably a naval officer from a merchant ship. Mediterranean novelties had been arriving in Europe, and even Prussia, for some years now. Indeed, it was widely agreed that if the Egyptians had had the good sense to keep their exotic secrets to themselves, Bonaparte would have left them in peace. But the Emperor loved the fruits of the date-palm tree to distraction, and so he . . .

Before I had the opportunity to notice more, the innkeeper entered with my luggage. 'Yours is the second room on the left, first floor. Come up whenever you are ready, sir.'

I joined Koch in front of the fire and warmed my hands.

'This is a welcome sight,' I conceded.

Koch murmured agreement, without lifting his eyes from the crackling logs; we remained standing there together in silence for some time, as if bewitched by the dancing flames.

'We have an hour or so before your appointment with Doctor Vigilantius, Herr Procurator,' he reminded me.

'Ah yes, the moon!' I joked. 'You'll keep me company, I hope?'

Koch turned to me, a show of surprise on his face. 'Sir?'

'Do you have any other plans tonight?'

'Oh no, Herr Procurator,' he enthused. 'My orders were to make myself useful in any way you might think fit. I wasn't sure . . .'

'That's settled, then,' I said with decision. The thought of entering the bleak fortress in Ostmarktplatz and having to do so alone was daunting. Up to that point, my relationship with Sergeant Koch had been neither cordial nor easy, but he was the only person in the city to whom I could turn for aid.

'As I have had good reason to note today, Koch, you are both efficient and discreet,' I said, pausing for a moment. 'Discreet' was the most tactful word I could find to describe behaviour which had touched a raw nerve more than once. 'I was wondering . . . that is, I'd be grateful to benefit from your knowledge of the city. Will you assist me during my stay in Königsberg?'

'Procurator Rhunken has no need of me at the moment,' Koch considered, his eyes fixed upon the fire. 'If I can be of use to you, sir.'

Beneath the detached, austere attitude of Koch I thought I read a hint of willingness to help me in my task.

'I am Herr Rhunken's successor,' I said with relief, making a bluff attempt at humour, 'so I suppose I inherit you. Now, if you'll excuse me, I must write a letter. Can it be delivered this evening?'

'I'll take it myself, sir,' Koch replied promptly.

'Thank you, Sergeant. Order two large glasses of hot toddy, will you? I won't be long.'

Upstairs, I found my room without any difficulty. The door was ajar, so I walked straight in. Herr Totz, the innkeeper, was standing next to a boy who was down on his knees working a wooden bellows which caused the fire to roar. Their backs were turned to the door, so neither of them was immediately aware that I had entered the room. I laid my hat on the bed, conscious of the delicious warmth and general neatness of the apartment, noting the low, sagging ceiling with dark, tarred oak beams, the whitewashed plaster, and a carpet that was only slightly worn at the centre. A small desk was placed beneath the window, an oil lamp glowed brightly, while along the opposite wall a large trunk and a matching dresser of walnut stood on either side of a bed hung with curtains which appeared to be fresh and clean. A large blue Dresden ewer and washbowl on the dresser completed the furnishings.

Content with what I had seen, I glanced back in the direction of the innkeeper and his boy to announce my presence. But something in the *tableau vivant* stopped me. The red-faced boy was still crouching down before the fire, the tall innkeeper hovering over him, hands on his hips. I could see only Totz's profile, but there was no mistaking the menacing expression on his face. With the roaring of the bellows, the swoosh of flames and the crackling of wood, I could make little sense of what they were saying. Totz was speaking earnestly to the boy, the veins standing out boldly on his neck as if he suppressed a desire to shout.

'Play with flames, Morik, you'll burn your fingers!' he sneered.

'He certainly does know how to start a fire, Herr Totz,' I said out loud, taking off my travelling-cloak, and dropping it on the bed. When I turned back to the fireplace once more, I was astonished by the sudden transformation of the scene, the expressions frozen on their faces. Fear was written on the boy's pinched features like a cornered fox as the hounds close in for the kill, despite his attempt at a welcoming smile. Ulrich Totz, who had been so angry only a moment ago, was now all accommodating smiles and seasoned humility. His left hand rested with a heavy, proprietorial air on the skinny shoulder of his young charge. For all the world, innkeeper Totz looked like a village beadle who had just taken the lad up for thieving.

'Here's your room, sir,' the landlord said with a conspiratorial wink in my direction. 'Whatever you need, my wife'll be back from her sister's this evening. I'm downstairs in the tavern as a rule. This here's Morik, my nephew.'

The hand on the boy's shoulder gave a quick, hard nip, and the hollow smile on the boy's face was shattered by a grimace of pain.

'That fire is to my liking, Morik,' I said, measuring my enthusiasm to avoid increasing the animosity of the master in the boy's regard.

The innkeeper smiled again broadly, though I had the impression that his good humour cost him a great deal of effort when I told him to go, but ordered the boy to remain behind to unpack my bag. The mere fact that the master had been dismissed from the room seemed to put the young servant at his ease. He was a sprightly little lad, bright of eye, his round face as rough and shiny as a golden russet apple, no more than twelve years old. He fell on my valise like a quick little monkey, pulling out the contents, laying out my shirts, stockings and linen on the bed, positioning my combs and hairbrushes with excessive care beside the washbasin, opening and closing drawers. He seemed to take some pleasure in feeling the cut and the quality and the weight of everything he touched. In a word, he was slow.

'That will do, Morik!' I stopped him, my patience running short. 'Just pour some warm water into that bowl, will you? I need to wash before going out again. A gentleman is waiting for me downstairs.'

'The policeman, sir?' Morik asked quickly. 'Is the inn being watched?'

'All of Königsberg is under strict surveillance,' I replied vaguely, smiling at this impetuous show of childish curiosity. Then, I sat myself down at the table near the window, laid out my writing *nécessaire* and began to pen a letter that I had never believed I should need to write.

Herr Jachmann,

Circumstances beyond my personal control bring me once more to Königsberg. I have been assigned a Royal Commission of extreme gravity and exceptional importance which I wish to explain to you in person at your earliest convenience. I will call on you at 12 a.m. tomorrow. I hasten to repeat my word as a gentleman that I will avoid any form of contact with Magister-strasse until I have spoken to you. RSVP. Obsequiously,

Hanno Stiffeniis, Magistrate.

'Shall I run to the post for you, sir?'

I turned around with a start. The boy was looking over my shoulder. I had been so involved in what I was doing, I had forgotten that he was still in the room.

'The post? At this time of night? Aren't you afraid to go out after dark?' I asked.

'Oh no, sir!' the boy replied with vigour. 'I'll do anything your Excellency may ask of me.'

'You're a brave little fellow,' I said, pulling a coin from my waist-coat pocket, 'but a foolish one. There's murder on the streets of Königsberg at night. You'll be safer indoors.'

He cast a furtive glance towards the door, then picked the coin from my hand like a thieving magpie. 'I wouldn't be so sure of that, sir,' he whispered. 'There's more danger in this here tavern than on the streets. The water's ready for you.'

I hardly gave a thought to what the boy had said, dismissing it as infantile braggadocio, as I slipped off my jacket and waistcoat, rolling up my shirtsleeves with a smile.

'Don't you believe me, sir?' he said, stepping closer.

'Why should I *not* believe you, Morik?' I replied, paying little attention to the conversation, my mind on the evening that lay ahead.

'There are strange things going on in this house, sir,' he whispered in an even lower voice than before. 'That's why you're here, is it not?'

'Of course,' I joked, splashing my face with warm water. 'What sort of things are you talking about?'

'A man who was murdered passed his last night here. Jan Konnen . . .'

A sharp knock at the door interrupted him.

Without waiting to be called, Herr Totz walked in, as I was drying my face.

'If you've finished with the lad, sir,' the innkeeper said with an air of tight-lipped anger, 'I need him down in the kitchen. Now!'

Before I could say a word, the boy had skipped around his master, and ducked artfully out of the door.

'That lad!' Totz said with a roll of his eyes and a shake of his head. 'He's a lying little scamp. An' workshy with it. With your permission, sir?'

'He was telling me that Jan Konnen was in your inn the night he was murdered, Totz,' I said. 'Is it true?'

Ulrich Totz did not respond immediately. Then, a thin smile appeared, and the reply flowed like warm milk and melted honey. 'That's right, sir,' he said. 'I have already told the police everything

I know. Under oath. Konnen was here one minute, gone the next. I cannot tell you more than that, sir. May I be excused now? We're very busy downstairs at the moment.'

I nodded, and out he went, closing the door quietly behind him. Had I been drawn into some sort of bizarre labyrinth, or was it mere coincidence that I had been roomed in the inn where the first victim of the murderer had spent his last hours? I decided to search out Ulrich Totz's statement to the police at the first opportunity. Clearly, there was more documentation regarding the murders than the scant evidence that I had been shown by Koch in the coach.

Down in the saloon Sergeant Koch was seated before the fire, two tall glasses of rum toddy set out on a small table beside him. The inn was busier than before, all animated – two women in loose, red skirts and low-cut blouses were the centre of attention – except for the Russian officer in his extravagant uniform who had fallen sound asleep at his table, his head propped up against the wall, a glass of grog upturned and dripping onto the floor.

'Koch,' I said, tapping him on the shoulder.

The sergeant jumped to his feet and slammed his hat on his head, as if I had caught him in a desperate state of undress. 'The coach is . . .'

'Jan Konnen was murdered here,' I interrupted. 'Did you know that?'

Koch paused long enough for me to wonder whether he was prevaricating once again. 'I had no idea, sir. None at all,' he answered.

'Is that so?' I queried. 'That is strange. All the town must know.'

Koch took a deep breath before he answered. 'As I told you, sir, the details have been kept a very close secret. I knew, of course, that the man had been killed somewhere near the sea, but *not* in this very inn.'

'*Outside* the inn,' I corrected him mechanically. 'You may not know it, but whoever decided to lodge me here most certainly did, Sergeant.'

We stood there for a few moments, face to face in silence, while I felt the cold frost of misunderstanding fall between us once again. I held up the envelope I had been holding. 'This is the letter I mentioned before,' I said. 'It is meant for a gentleman in town. His name is Reinhold Jachmann.'

If Koch had ever heard the name, he gave no sign of it.

'I'll deliver it after we've been to the Fortress, sir,' he said with a dutiful nod. 'I'll take it there on my way home.'

This generous proposal cast a new light on Koch. I had done little all day, I suddenly realised, but blame him for mounting a conspiracy that I was quite unable to explain to myself. What I had taken to be interference and heavy-handed manipulation on his part might prove to be nothing more than excessive zeal in the execution of a tiresome duty.

'First thing tomorrow morning will do, Koch,' I said, relenting a trifle. 'Herr Jachmann's house is in Klopstrasse.'

'Do you require anything else, sir?' he asked.

'Transport, Koch. The moon should be in its mansion by now, don't you think?' I added in an attempt to be more jovial.

A barely perceptible shadow of a smile traced itself out on the sergeant's lips as we walked towards the door. 'Indeed, sir. I think it should.'

Outside on the quay, snow lay on the rough cobblestones in swirling piles and massive drifts, though it fell no longer. The wind gusted more fiercely than ever, a biting, hissing whistle of a gale whipping off the sea, which made the teeth chatter and the spirit rebel.

'God preserve us!' Koch muttered as he followed me into the coach.

As he shouted to the driver to pull away, I remembered the hot rum toddies we had left untouched on the table in the inn. That night we would both regret the omission.

Chapter 5

Darkness had fallen in Ostmarktplatz. There was not a living soul abroad. Even the sentry-boxes outside the Fortress and the Court House stood empty, the gendarmes having been recalled inside for the night. On either side of the main entrance, flickering firebrands cast weak pools of light and etched deep shadows into the sombre stone facade. As Koch and I stepped down from the coach and approached the gate, the massive building loomed high above us. In the pale light of the rising moon, its towering pinnacles, central keep and watchtowers cast an ominous gloom over the glistening carpet of snow.

Sergeant Koch raised a large iron ring and let it drop against a small lych-gate set into the gigantic defensive wooden door. A heavy bolt was drawn noisily, a Judas-window slid back, and a pair of needle-point eyes scrutinised us from within.

'Procurator Stiffeniis to see Doctor Vigilantius,' Koch announced.

The peephole closed with a metal clang, the door was thrown open, and we stepped into a small inner courtyard.

'Wait here,' the guard announced, and we were left to dally in the cold for some minutes. In the centre of the courtyard, two tall soldiers in shirtsleeves were labouring with spades beside a long wooden box. With such an abundance of fresh snow covering the city, I asked myself, what was the point of storing it in boxes?

'General Katowice!' Koch hissed suddenly, and I turned to see a cluster of officers in blue serge striding purposefully in our direction. 'He's the commander of the garrison,' Koch added in a whisper.

With some trepidation I braced myself to meet the general, and found myself confronted by a person of less than average height and wider than average girth. He also had abominably black teeth, and a huge white moustache which swept over his upper lip and red cheeks. Crossing his short arms over his massive chest, he formed his wrinkled forehead into a frown, then flashed his head to the left in a singular gesture which brought a long white braid of hair whipping through the air to rest along his arm like a snake on a branch. High-ranking officers have never ceased to wear their hair in the style made fashionable by Frederick the Great.

'Stiffeniis?' the general barked, offering his tubby hand.

I had to smile with relief. Here, it seemed, I *was* expected.

'I will not waste your time, except to say I am glad you've come,' he began, his beefy hand playing with the hilt of his sword. 'The city is in turmoil, as you know. These murders! The King wants to tidy the matter up without delay. It is clear to *me* what's going on.' He leaned too close for comfort, reeking of garlic and other nameless half-digested things. 'Jacobins!' he said. 'There, that's your answer.'

'Spies, sir?' I asked.

General Katowice placed his hand on my arm. 'Exactly! I want to know where they are hiding!' he said with some agitation, the white tress now dangling wildly on his chest. He looked more like a barbarian chieftain than a Prussian general. 'Never trust a Frenchman! They're cunning devils led by Satan himself! Napoleon would give his left arm and leg to seize the fortress of Königsberg. I have my forces strategically placed in and out of the city. They'll strike without mercy. A word from you, a word from me. That's all it takes.'

He placed his right hand on my left shoulder, looked straight into my eyes, then tightened his hold. 'If you find anything that *looks* French, *smells* French, I want to know of it. Rhunken suspected a foreign plot against the nation, but proof was lacking. Which tied my hands, of course. If you can track them down with more solid arguments, I'll persuade the King to take the initiative. We will strike before they do. All may depend on you. Any questions?'

The first that came to mind was more than sufficient to start a flood. *What was I doing there?* But I did not ask it. Nor did General Katowice wait.

'None? Good man! Now, they're expecting you, I believe.'

The general and his staff marched off to the left, while a corporal stepped up before us from the right and saluted. 'Follow me, gentlemen,' he said, spinning on his heel and marching away.

Was that the motive for the murders, a Jacobin plot to undermine the peace in Königsberg and in Prussia? I followed in a daze. We thundered along a dark corridor, through a large empty hall which echoed to the noise of our steps, passing beneath a low arch which led into a maze of gloomy corridors until we reached a narrow door cut into a damp grey wall.

'This way,' the corporal said, as he took a flaming torch from a ring on the wall and skipped lightly down a stairwell which spiralled into the bowels of the earth. The smell of mildew was sickening. Our guide's torch fought a guttering battle with the pitch darkness.

'Aren't the offices above ground?' I asked Koch.

'So they are,' he replied.

'Why are we going underground, then?'

'I've no idea, sir.'

We might have been descending into a crypt.

'This is a strange place for a meeting,' I said, my anxiety mounting. 'Where are you taking us, Corporal?'

The corporal stopped, glanced at Koch, then at me, his brutish face topped by a battered tricorn hat and framed by a tattered wig which had not seen powder in a month. 'To see the doctor, sir,' he replied brusquely.

Just then, a heavy clumping and clattering of steel-tipped boots sounded loudly on the staircase above us. Our guide raised his torch, lighting up the two soldiers I had noticed working in the courtyard above. They came hurtling down the stairs, manhandling a large box between them. The weight of it seemed to drag them downstairs faster than they wished to go, and we had to push ourselves up hard against the wall to escape being crushed.

'Has he come yet?' our guide called after them.

As the labourers stumbled past, I saw how very tall they were. Frederick the Great had set the fashion, visiting every corner of the continent in the search for new pieces to add to his collection of giant soldiers. Now, they flocked to Prussia. Those two were excellent specimens. Even so, they groaned beneath the weight.

'Dunno,' the soldier at the front cried back over his shoulder. 'Get a move on, Walter!'

'Are they being punished?' I asked the corporal as the darkness gobbled them up.

'They're just obeying orders, sir,' he replied, and cantered on down the stairway.

At the bottom of the shaft, a square skylight shone above our heads. The corporal looked up, an expression of bemused terror on his face. The full moon was perfectly framed by the window high above.

'Strike me blind!' he cursed. 'Right on bloody time!'

'What *are* you talking about?' I asked.

The corporal looked at me, his expression tense. 'That doctor's very keen on details, sir,' he murmured. 'He said the moon would appear from the clouds, and there it is!' The fear written on his face was childishly comical. 'Better not keep him waiting, sir,' he said, proceeding quickly on his way towards a door at the far end of the corridor, which opened into a large, empty store-room. It was cold in there, extremely cold. The other two soldiers were hard at work shovelling snow from the box onto a black tarpaulin cover.

'Well, Koch . . .' I began to say, vapour forming an ectoplasm in front of my face as I spoke.

'You are just in time, sir,' a haughty voice accused at my back.

I turned and gaped. I seemed to have been addressed by one of the age-encrusted ancestral portraits hanging from the walls of my father's country house. It was the style of his wig that impressed me. Grey curls cascaded from the crown of his head in undulating waves on either side of a long, gaunt face. Large, snow-white hands held a huge cloak of shimmering black velveteen clasped tightly to his body.

'My name is Vigilantius,' he announced rather stiffly. 'Doctor Vigilantius.'

He did not offer his hand or make any sign of welcome, but swept past me, his black cloak billowing and rippling out as he

49

drew close to the waiting soldiers. There was only a hand-span of difference in height between him and the lesser of the two giants.

'I hope you have followed my instructions to the letter.'

It was not a question, though one of the men stood forward. Wiping his forehead on his sleeve, he said: 'All as you ordered, sir.'

'Let us begin in that case,' he said, his attention directed at the labourers, who were sweating despite the cold.

'Begin *what*?' I demanded in a loud voice, stepping forward to assert my authority before Koch and the soldiers.

Vigilantius arched his bushy eyebrow and stared back defiantly at me, but he did not answer my question.

'What are we doing in this dungeon?' I insisted.

'I am here to enter the Spirit World,' he said quite plainly, as if the place truly existed and might be found by any sharp-eyed person on the *mappamondo*. Before I could speak, he turned on Koch as if he meant to eat him.

'Who are you, sir?' he said, like a lizard snapping up flies.

'Sergeant Koch is my assistant,' I shot back.

The doctor made a face, but no objection. 'He'll remain, then. These two men are needed for the first part of the operation. Corporal,' he said, throwing out his forefinger like a dart, 'be gone!'

Our guide hurried out of the room without a backward glance.

'Bring our guest over here,' Vigilantius ordered sharply.

Instinctively, I took a step backwards, thinking that they meant to lay hands on me. From the other side of the room, with a tortured shriek like a hunting horn in the hands of a novice, the labourers began to push the snow-covered tarpaulin towards where we were standing.

A wave of anger swept over me. Was he trying to make a fool of me? Did my authority mean nothing to this vulgar showman? I had been designated by the King to take charge of the case. If anything were to be done, *I* would decide.

'Stop where you are!' I shouted, advancing on the soldiers.

'Are you not . . . curious to know what lies beneath this cover, Herr Procurator?' Vigilantius asked, a mincing smile on his face. 'You will obtain no greater help in Königsberg, I promise you.'

'What are you hiding here?' I demanded.

'Sweep it away,' he said to the soldiers without answering me.

As the men removed the snow with their bare hands, I stood simmering with rage. Was this why I had been placed in charge of such a delicate investigation? To be guided, manipulated, frustrated? Had I no effective power?

'Shift him here,' Vigilantius instructed, and the workmen revealed what had been referred to so obliquely. 'Now, get out!'

The soldiers obeyed him willingly, leaving us alone with Vigilantius.

I drew close and looked down.

'Who was he?' I asked.

'*Was?*' the grating voice challenged. 'This *is* Jeronimus Tifferch, fourth victim of the killer terrorising Königsberg.'

I had seen corpses in France. I knew what the slicing blade of a freshly oiled guillotine could do. But that did not prepare me for the sight of Lawyer Tifferch. He lay on his back in a wholly unnatural position. Trunk curved upwards, knees bent to form a high pointed arch above the table, arms stretched out and reaching downwards. The life seemed to have been ripped out of him. His skin was glassy, unnatural, the ivory-yellow colour of mummified Italian saints. Cheeks sucked inwards, his mouth gaped wide open. He was the picture of puzzled innocence. His hair had frozen stiff, and was so very white I thought it to be ice. A long straight nose led down to a thin pair of twisted black moustaches which Tifferch appeared to have cultivated with more than usual care. His suit was olive green and well cut with narrow gold piping around the collar, hem and buttonholes. Biscuit-coloured stockings hung limply away from slim calves which had contracted with the cold. Both kneecaps were heavy with caked mud. There was no evident mark of death on him. Nothing to explain what had brought Lawyer Tifferch to such an end.

'How did he die?' I asked, more to myself that to anyone else.

'We will soon discover *that*,' Vigilantius replied darkly, as he began to go about his work. It was like a Roman Catholic ritual. I had attended the mass in Rome some years before and been fascinated by the pagan ceremonial that the priests employed there. Placing a hand on either side of the dead man's face, the doctor closed his eyes and touched his forehead to that of the corpse like a priest consecrating bread and wine at the Offertory. He remained like this for some time, silent and stiff like the dead man beneath him. Suddenly, he began to sniff noisily, wildly at the nose and mouth of the corpse. Sweat rolled down off his brow in a torrent. He quivered violently, all his limbs shook, he seemed to be possessed of a frenetic energy that he could not control.

'Jeronimus Tifferch,' he intoned in a loud voice. 'Jeronimus Tifferch. Return from the shadows. I, Augustus Vigilantius, command you . . .'

A rattling growl rang to the stony vaults and ran skittering around the room, dissolving in a long agonised howl.

'Someone else is hiding here,' I said aside to Koch.

Koch stared back at me. His teeth were clenched, eyes aflame with the firelight from the torch. 'There's nobody, sir,' he said. 'Just him, us, and the body.'

Vigilantius swayed wildly back on his heels.

'*Let me be. Let me rest in darkness,*' he hissed. His mouth was huge, twisted, formless, the strange disembodied voice sharp, clear. There was an infinite sadness in it which I would not have imagined Vigilantius capable of evoking. His breathing became troubled, laboured, and – my God, I wish to deny it! – his voluminous cloak began to rise up of its own accord like a malignant black cloud which threatened to engulf him whole. Everything happened so fast. We were like men adrift in the middle of a raging torrent or a howling storm.

'Take energy from me!' screamed Vigilantius, as if an unseen hand were ripping the heart from his body. 'Who *are* you?'

'*I am no longer I,*' the voice replied in a shrieking howl, and I felt Koch's hand grasping at my sleeve for comfort. There was silence for some time, then the wind began to moan and wail again. '*I am . . . I . . . no more . . . no more . . .*'

'Who took you into the darkness?' Vigilantius asked calmly, as if it were the most natural question in the world.

'*Murder . . . murder . . . murder . . .*' the wind raged back a dozen times, like a hammer blow repeated over and over again. It echoed and resounded in my brain. In the flickering light, I seemed to see the stiff frozen mouth of the corpse open and close in speech. Vigilantius quivered from head to toe. Mangled words and rent phrases rushed from his lips in an incomprehensible avalanche.

Then, there was a sharp cry of pain.

'Who did this, Spirit?' Vigilantius stormed. 'Who murdered you?'

I heard the hoot of an owl, the sound of pigeons cooing, the howl of a cat, the wild babbling of a tuneless song, then that wind-like rush again.

'*A tongue of flame. A fire at the back of my sku . . .*' The speech slurred suddenly, then picked up more clearly with a snatching, nasal sibilance which was quite distinct. Was this the true voice of Lawyer Tifferch? '*Dark . . . dark . . . a voice . . .*'

'Which voice?' Vigilantius shouted against a babble of disconnected sounds like the tuneless mangling of a hurdy-gurdy when the handle is turned the wrong way. 'Who spoke to you? Describe him, I command you!'

I saw, or thought I saw, the lips of the dead man move in answer. '*The Devil's . . . is a face . . . no more,*' the corpse said, and silence fell as if a tomb-slab had been dropped in place. Time stood still, but questions rattled in a swirling vortex through my brain. What had I just seen? What jiggery-pokery had I just witnessed? Sweat ran cold along my spine. The performance had certainly been impressive, my heart was still heaving like a bellows. I gasped for air, and had to clear my throat for fear of choking. In that instant, I realised, Doctor Vigilantius was watching me. The *real* Vigilantius, if anything could be called real in that dark place. Suddenly, his upper lip curled, his black eyes sparkled, and he grinned fiendishly from ear to ear.

'You heard it, did you not?' he said. 'The human corpse is the receptacle of vital sensations. My *magister*, Emanuel Swedenborg, taught me how to tap them long ago. Open your blinkered mind to mystery, Herr Procurator. More illustrious men than you have learnt to see without using their eyes.'

He took a step towards me, blocking the body from my sight. His sense of his own powers was absurd, unquestioning. Arrogance oozed from his person, sweat rained from his brow, rivulets ran down his face and his neck. 'Make the most of what you have just been privileged to witness,' he said, waiting for my reaction, the smile slowly fading from his lips.

I took a step forward.

'Impressive, sir,' I said, my pulse thumping rapidly. 'You've missed your calling. You should have been an actor. But what remains of the play when the curtain falls?'

I stared into his eyes for some moments, but he did not reply.

'You have told me nothing useful,' I went on, my anger mounting. 'How did this man die? What weapon killed him? And why could he not describe the face of his murderer? You are a ventriloquist, sir, a conjuror. I have heard not a single word of truth from the dead man's lips. Nor from yours. You are wasting my time, obstructing my investigation. The King will have a report of what is happening here.'

The necromancer's coal-black eyes stared defiantly into mine, and that annoying, self-satisfied smile twisted his thin lips once more. 'What has the King to do with this, Herr Stiffeniis?'

'Surely, you remember him?' I replied sarcastically. 'Our monarch? King Frederick Wilhelm III? The person who entrusted this case into my hands? I have his letter of authority here in my . . .'

'You couldn't be more wrong,' Vigilantius interrupted, waving his hand in the air as if to dismiss a bothersome fly. 'King Frederick Wilhelm knows nothing of you, or me. A person of eminence whom His Majesty trusts has promised to solve these mysteries for him. With your help, and with mine. Your letter of authority isn't worth the paper it's written on. It was signed and sealed by some faceless secretary in Berlin, I'd wager. A pretext to bring you here.'

My hands began to shake with rage, and I thrust them deep inside my cloak, trying to keep my voice cool and sharp when I spoke. 'An eminent person? A person whom the King trusts? And this great man has promised the King to solve these murders by means of sleight-of-hand and conjuring tricks. How remarkable! I am eager to meet this Professor of Chicanery. The city of Königsberg could not be in better hands.'

Vigilantius stared at me in silence, that mocking smile fading into a stiff and brooding glare. 'You are insulting a great man, Herr Procurator. I hope that I am present when you meet him.'

'In this world, or the next?' I muttered, staring down at the corpse, before turning to Koch. 'Help me. I wish to examine the empty shell of this man now that the *spirit* has departed!'

We bent over Jeronimus Tifferch. There was not a drop of blood on his clothes, nor any bruising of the skin, no evidence of a blow or strangling. The tip of his tongue protruding between his yellow teeth was a clear pink, neither black nor swollen. I put both hands flat on his chest and pushed against the ribcage. All was sound. I opened his shirt and found no sign of stabbing or assault. What kind of murder was this? Which closed door had the robber, Death, unlatched to enter Lawyer Tifferch's body?

'Help me turn him over, Koch.'

I forced myself to lay my hands on the stiff, cold corpse again, and together we levered the dead man onto his left flank. His clothes crackled as we shifted him, the skin hard to the touch like wet stone. In times past, doctors of medical science must have felt as I did then, while they practised the forbidden art of anatomical dissection. The place was fitting enough, a secret room in the stinking bowels of the earth. Outside, it was night. Inside, it was night too, but of a far darker hue. Was it possible to imagine doing what we were engaged in beneath the unforgiving light of day? There was something desecrating in the action.

'Do you have a knife, Sergeant Koch?'

'What do you intend to do with it?' Vigilantius objected.

I ignored him, taking the pocket-knife from Koch's hand, and scoring a line from the collar of the dead man's jacket down to the hem. With a rent I tore the stiff cloth away and repeated the cut through his linen shirt. We both stared in amazement at what was revealed.

'Good God!' Koch exclaimed in a whisper.

I replaced my gloves to avoid contamination. The dead man's

upper back was a mass of ancient weals and recent cuts. Had Tifferch been a living-room carpet, one might have thought he had been recently beaten and combed with an iron brush. Slowly, carefully, with the tip of my finger, I rubbed away the crust of congealed blood to reveal the frozen flesh beneath.

'Whipped,' Koch murmured.

'There can be little doubt of that,' I said, my eyes racing over the flayed skin as if it were an ancient scroll written in a mysterious language that I had still to decipher.

'Could this have caused his death, sir?' Koch asked, gesturing uncertainly at the man's tormented flesh.

'He told you himself!' Doctor Vigilantius erupted. 'He spoke of flames. Of fire in his brain. That must be your starting point.'

'I'll decide where I will start!' I snapped back.

'Those wounds are *not* the cause, Herr Stiffeniis,' the necromancer insisted. 'Your stubborn incredulity is the poisoned fruit of dogmatism. Logic is only one of many systems of understanding. Can you not see? There are a hundred paths to Truth.'

'This man has been beaten,' I replied forcefully. 'I know that the beating did not kill him. But it may explain why he was killed. I cannot ignore that fact. The investigation must begin with this.'

Augustus Vigilantius smiled broadly. Facts, apparently, did not diminish him. 'Tifferch himself has just told us a different story. You would not be wise to ignore his words.'

'If they *were* his words,' I countered.

'My information is not the result of physical examination of the body,' he replied stiffly. 'My concern is with the vital energies imprisoned inside the fragile human shell. I am merely the drum, the sounding-board.'

'Hocus-pocus!' I sneered. 'I'm surprised that you haven't produced a rabbit from the dead man's hat!'

The arrow bit home.

'When the moon is at its height,' the necromancer spat back, 'the flux of the human spirit waxes to its fullest power. Then, it may be tapped by any scholar learned in the art of divination. His body was preserved here for that purpose. But the vital moment has passed, it will come no more. You intoxicate yourself with external appearances, Herr Stiffeniis.'

'Help me turn him back, Sergeant Koch,' I said, pointedly ignoring the mountebank.

'You should be grateful to me, Herr Procurator,' Vigilantius insisted at my shoulder. 'Do not disdain the help I can offer you.'

I did not answer, but in the silence which followed, I heard the same disgusting noise that had given me the shivers only minutes before. As I turned, I met the necromancer's mocking eyes. His nostrils twitched open, then closed, sucking at the air with greedy energy. His head was close to mine, and he was sniffing me.

'Are you a dog, sir?' I snarled, standing back. 'This trick may work with the dead. But I am alive.'

He drew further off, but nothing could wipe the smirk from his face.

'Only on the surface, Herr Stiffeniis. Beneath, I smell the death you carry with you everywhere.' He tapped the side of his nose. 'It stinks. There is a dark, stagnant pool where a carcass lies rotting. A dead thing is poisoning your mind and your life. Am I wrong, Herr Procurator? What stalks you in your nightmares? What secrets do those murky waters hide? You are afraid of what might float to the surface at any moment.'

His words resonated and echoed beneath the vault.

'Thank you for your invaluable opinions,' I murmured. 'There's nothing more to keep us here, Koch.'

Vigilantius's eyebrows arched with surprise. 'But I have one thing left to show you. Something even more important may be got from this corpse.'

'I've had my fill of corpses and their keepers,' I snapped.

'But, sir!' he opposed, and there was something two-faced in his way of doing so which contrasted sharply with the honeyed entreaty which followed. 'There is another aspect of my *art* which may be of use to you.'

'Your arts do not interest me,' I sneered.

'As you wish, then, Herr Procurator,' he said with a bow of exaggerated courtesy. 'I cannot force you to stay against your will.'

I strode out of the room with Sergeant Koch hard on my heels, and we retraced the dark and musty passages through which we had come. We climbed the staircase to the surface without exchanging a word, our matching footsteps ringing along the narrow corridors and across the claustrophobic courtyards.

'What an impertinence! Talking to you like that, sir?' said Koch with feeling as we emerged into the central courtyard. 'What do you think he's up to?'

'That's anybody's guess,' I said dismissively. I felt no desire to imagine what Vigilantius might be doing down there with the dead body. A stiff wind had swept away the clouds, and I raised my eyes to gaze at the stars which dotted the dark sky like precious grains of sugar accidentally scattered across a table, drawing the fresh air deep into my lungs. 'Did you have any idea that some other person than Procurator Rhunken was involved in this investigation, Koch?'

The Sergeant did not reply at once.

'No, sir,' he said at last. 'None at all. But can you wonder that the city fathers would appeal to any person that they thought might be able to help them out in their trouble?'

If there was one irrefutable good quality to be found in Koch, it was his sound common sense. I took comfort in it and had to smile.

'The coach is waiting,' he reminded me.

'Let it wait,' I said. 'Take me to Herr Rhunken's office. We have wasted time enough this evening. The investigation must begin in earnest. Sniffing dead men's bones will get us nowhere fast.'

Chapter 6

If the basement cellars of the Fortress of Königsberg had reminded me uncomfortably of the lower reaches of Hades, the upper floors were as confusing as the maze of Crete. Gloomy, ill-lit passages shot off left and right of the main corridor, no feature distinguishing one way from any of the others.

'The building was erected in the twelfth century by the Teutonic Knights, sir, as a stronghold during their long struggle to capture Prussia from the pagans,' Sergeant Koch explained with obvious pride as we trod the labyrinthine corridors. 'It has been enlarged in recent times, of course. Now it is an impregnable fortress. Bonaparte himself could not hope to storm it successfully.'

'How many men are stationed in the garrison?' I asked.

'Three thousand soldiers, as a rule,' the sergeant reported, though we met not a single one that night.

'So, where are they all?'

'General Katowice has sent them out on defensive manoeuvres.'

At that point, we were obliged to pass across a wooden walkway laid over iron gratings which had been let into the stone floor. Rough voices snarled curses beneath our feet as we clattered across this makeshift bridge, while others cried out for food and water. The clinging vapour of sweat and stifled breath rose all around us in drifting clouds, like steam from a kettle on the hob. We might have been crossing a marsh. The air was rank, fetid, the noise little short of demonic – Alighieri's harrowing vision of Hell came unwillingly to my mind. Had the Italian poet, I asked myself, been to visit the prisons of his native Florence in his search for inspiration?

'What's happening down there, Sergeant?'

'Prisoners awaiting transportation,' Koch informed me.

He paused for a moment and inclined his ear towards the grating as a fine female voice rose high above the hubbub, wailing a keening lament. I knew the ballad well enough. It was one that my own grandfather often crooned. He had learnt it, he said, during the Seven Years War, and it was the only song that he ever sang. When he had no voice for singing, he whistled the tune beneath his breath. There was a pining, nostalgic note in the woman's voice which added a new, tragic dimension to the soldier's tale: *The snow will feed me, the snow will sate my thirst, the snow will warm my bones when I am dead.*

'Mezzo-soprano,' said Koch with a smile and a shake of his head.

We moved on, and shortly after, having climbed a newel staircase to the floor above, stopped before a heavy wooden door no different from a hundred others that we had passed along the way.

'Here we are, sir,' Koch informed me. 'This is Herr Rhunken's office.'

I was too stunned to speak. There was no nameplate on the door, no symbol of the authority that Herr Procurator must surely have enjoyed, nothing to indicate that the owner of the capable hands to which the peace and safety of the city had been entrusted was to be found inside that room.

'So close to the squalor down below?'

'Procurator Rhunken was in charge of Section D, sir. If you'd rather be somewhere else . . .'

'I wouldn't think of it,' I replied quickly. 'If this room was good enough for him, I will make the best of it.'

'The felons destined for Siberia are kept in those cages. Herr Rhunken was still working on the list. There are places left on board the ship. Once the ice-pack begins to break up . . .'

There had been a raging debate about deportation over the last three or four years. King Frederick Wilhelm III had decided to rid the nation once and for all of recidivist criminals, despatching them to some remote penal colony for life, under sentence of death if they should ever dare to return. His Majesty's overtures to many distant foreign powers with colonies or unpopulated territories, including the United States and Great Britain, had been rejected, but finally, the Russian Tsar had declared his willingness to take them for a substantial fee. There was still a great deal of lingering controversy among liberal thinkers concerning the Royal decision. Criminals do not occasion much sympathy in Prussia, or anywhere else, but the notion of selling them into Russian slavery had met with much opposition in Enlightened circles. The Noble Savage was still a popular catchphrase, and the French government, and the Americans before them, had declared all men to be equal. Still, on 28 February 1801, an agreement had been signed. Prison governors throughout the land had been ordered to select the most serious and incorrigible offenders in the land for banishment.

'Herr Rhunken chose this room himself, sir,' Koch reported. 'This is where he carried out interrogations. Those cries and screams down below had a certain effect on the person being questioned.'

'I can picture the scene,' I said with an involuntary shudder.

'Herr Procurator was held in great respect for the severity of his methods,' Koch concluded, drawing a large key from his pocket, and opening the door.

He stood aside to let me pass, and I waited in the darkness with growing impatience while he struck a damp flint again and again, eventually managing to light a candle. The apartment was large with a high ceiling and grubby grey walls which needed a fresh coat of paint. A large rust-stained iron stove filled the far corner, though it had not been lit. Narrow window-slits looked out over the prison-gratings on the floor below. Four lanterns had been hung on the walls to provide illumination, and Koch hurried to light them all, but the flames of a dozen more would not have done the trick.

'Two smaller rooms adjoin this one, sir. One is the Procurator's archive. In the other one, there's a cot where Herr Rhunken sometimes took his rest when he was obliged to work late.'

This is where I should have been put up in the first place, I reflected. Not in a quayside inn, comfortable as The Baltic Whaler undoubtedly was. In the austere and inhospitable Fortress of

Königsberg, my newly gained authority as the magistrate-in-charge of the investigation would be clear for all to see. I made myself comfortable at a heavy, elaborately carved desk which stood in splendid isolation in the centre of the room. This piece of furniture alone spoke of power and status. A wine carafe and cut-glass goblet had been provided for refreshment during the hard hours of labour. Now the decanter stood empty, its stopper thick with dust, and a large, dead spider lay imprisoned beneath the upturned wine glass.

'I want to see Procurator Rhunken's reports and files concerning the murders. They should be here somewhere, Koch. The ones you showed me in the coach are incomplete. Ulrich Totz told me he had been interrogated personally by Procurator Rhunken soon after the murder of Jan Konnen. I wish to read what he had to say for himself.'

Koch glanced around uncertainly.

'I've no idea where they are kept, sir. Papers the Procurator gave me are locked up in my own desk. The rest are stored in the archive, I suppose. But my master would allow no one to enter there.'

'You have *my* permission to enter, Sergeant.'

I stood up and walked to the window to cut short any objection he might have made. Wiping the dust away from the filthy pane of glass with the hem of my cloak, I gazed down onto the floor below with its iron gratings and the hum of imprisoned misery. In the darkest corner, one of the guards, the first I had seen, was squatting in the gloom, his white trousers down around his ankles, defecating. The memory of my own pleasant office in Lotingen returned to me in a blinding flash of light and warmth. With its cheerful flower beds and clipped green lawns, mothers and nursemaids brought their charges to play beneath my windows in the spring and summer. The soldier finished his business, hauled up his pantaloons, then adroitly covered the mess with his boot before going on his way.

I turned back to the room once more, but I felt little in the way of comfort. The dismal rumbling of the prisoners down below was inescapable. I hoped to go at least one step further than Rhunken had gone. Despite his vast experience, Herr Procurator Rhunken had been as helpless to stop the murders as any of those who had died directly at the hands of the killer. Could I dare to hope for success where he had failed?

I paced out the length and the breadth of my predecessor's professional tomb, preparing myself for the work that lay ahead, until Sergeant Koch returned some minutes later.

'I found this lot, sir,' he reported, the papers in his hands pitifully few. 'They were stacked on one of the shelves.'

'Nothing more?' I asked incredulously.

Koch shook his head. 'Nothing, Herr Stiffeniis. Except for this letter, which I placed on top. I thought that you would wish to examine it.'

'A letter? From whom?'

'It is addressed to Procurator Rhunken,' he said, placing the papers on the desk. 'I would not presume to open it. You did tell me to bring everything, sir.'

I sat down again, and took up the thin sheaf of papers. Despite the lack of more substantial documentation, I felt a deal of satisfaction. At last, I thought, I am sitting in Herr Rhunken's chair, resting my elbows on his desk. His papers and his reports are in *my* hands. His sergeant is now *my* assistant. For the very first time since arriving in the city, I began to feel at ease. I began to enjoy the sense of power that attached to my new position. It was my first taste of real executive power, and it made a mockery of the shallow civic authority I had been permitted to exercise in Lotingen. I would, I realised, be responsible for the lives of the inhabitants of Königsberg. Whether they lived or died would depend on myself and General Katowice. Or on Napoleon Bonaparte and the Army of the Revolution, should he decide to invade Prussia.

Picking up the first document, I began to glance through the long list of names of condemned men who were destined for transportation to the distant borders of Siberia and Manchuria.

Sergeant Koch noisily cleared his throat. 'I could not help noticing, sir,' he said, pointing with his finger, 'that letter is from Berlin.'

I snatched up the missive and looked it over, noting the presence of the same large Hohenzollern seal which had turned my own ordered life upside-down.

'Sir', I read,

In view of the imminent danger which the country faces, vis-à-vis, the upstart, Bonaparte, and the growing risk of French invasion, this spate of murders in the city of Königsberg has been allowed to go unchecked too long. To remedy this deplorable situation, a highly qualified person of the most particular talents has been recommended to Our attention. His task will be to conclude the investigation which you began – with all possible haste. You are commanded to resign your commission and surrender all relevant documents to the magistrate in whom Our hope now resides, and return to your former duties. As of this moment.

The edict was signed with a flourish by King Frederick Wilhelm III, and it was, I noted, a distinctly different flourish from the letter which had been sent to me.

Was Doctor Vigilantius right?

Was my summons to Königsberg a fake?

This letter had been sent from the Royal capital three days previously, so Rhunken had received it two days before. And that very day, his health had taken a turn for the worse. What I had mistaken for a natural illness – the trembling face, quivering limbs and stench of physical decay – had been provoked by the shock of receiving that letter. Rhunken had suffered a crippling apoplexy as a direct result of the humiliation that the announcement of my arrival had occasioned.

I recalled the shattered wreck of a man I had confronted in his bedchamber only hours before. How that curt letter must have soured his opinion of me! I had no illusions now about how he viewed me. The magistrate appointed to replace him – 'a highly qualified person of the most particular talents' – the man who had ousted him and won the patronage of the King, was not only young, he was also totally inexperienced. And he came from Lotingen, a tiny *village* on the extreme border of the western circuit. Rhunken had been expecting a serious rival, a senior magistrate, a member of the secret police, or the Security Council, some gifted doyen from Berlin. What he had got was me!

'The statements of the witnesses should be there, sir,' Koch prompted, his voice intruding on my thoughts.

I shuffled through the miserable bundle of papers and found with ease the declaration that the innkeeper of The Baltic Whaler had made to the police. It was short, and added nothing to what Ulrich Totz had told me in person. Jan Konnen had been drinking in the saloon bar that night, though not excessively. He was in the company of a group of foreign sailors, who may, or may not, have been playing cards for money, but Totz refused to be drawn on that subject. In the past, it seemed, there had been fierce objections to the renewal of his liquor licence after fierce fighting between gamblers over allegations of cheating. The sums involved had been quite substantial, and one man had lost two fingers in a knife fight. 'But no one had been gambling that night,' Totz claimed. I skipped down the page and read:

Herr Totz declared that he had made no immediate connection between the man seen in his tavern that night, and the body found further down the quayside the following morning. When first approached by police, he denied all knowledge of the victim.

No mention was made of the strange goings-on at The Baltic Whaler, which the prying serving-boy had mentioned so particularly to me that very afternoon. Indeed, the name of Morik did not appear in the report at all. Evidently the boy had made no claim to superior knowledge when the opportunity presented itself. I was surprised that he had said nothing to excite the interest of the gendarmes who must have filled the tavern that morning with their conversation about the dead man. Morik had, after all, made such a fuss of my own presence at the inn. He had risked a flogging from his master in doing so. Had he been absent that day? Or might the Totzes have prevented him from speaking? Did they have something to hide? Why else would Morik fail to approach Procurator

Rhunken when he interviewed the landlord and his wife?

The wife . . .

Three lines at the bottom of the affidavit confirmed that Frau Totz had served short beer and hot sausages to Jan Konnen. She declared that she had never seen the man before, and that he had made no particular impression on her. She thought he had left the inn alone at ten o'clock, or thereabouts, though she could not be certain. In her opinion, the murdered man had visited their inn in search of wholesome food and good ale, and for no other reason.

A single sheet of paper, the next in the sheaf, drew a verbal portrait of the first victim. The information, such as it was, could have been chiselled with ease onto his tombstone. Jan Konnen, blacksmith, fifty-one years old, lived alone. He had never wed, and had no known living relatives. A taciturn and secretive man, Konnen was a complete enigma even to his closest neighbours. On this account, Rhunken had ordered the police to make extensive enquiries into his private life, but nothing untoward had been discovered. Konnen had no debts, no friends, he did not mix with women of low repute, nor belong to a political faction. He held no known grudge against any man, had never committed a crime, never been arrested. To all appearances, he was a blameless innocent who had been in the wrong place at the wrong time, and he had paid with his life for that mistake. At the bottom of the page, Rhunken had written a note: 'Enquiries made regarding possibility that victim might have had foreign political connections – no evidence found.' The last words Procurator Rhunken had written made me gasp: 'victim – category C – protocol 2779 – June 1800, I. M. O., Berlin'.

Like any other young magistrate just setting out on his career in the very first year of a new century, so soon after the revolution in France, and the rise of Napoleon, I had read that particular protocol. It warned of the possible infiltration of spies and revolutionaries who aimed to undermine the stability of the Nation and introduce Republicanism. Rhunken appeared to have convinced himself that the investigation should proceed in that direction, and he had given Konnen a low, but significant grading, as a potential danger.

I turned the page in search of more, but the following sheet referred to the case of Paula-Anne Brunner, second victim of the murderer. A statement taken from her husband related that his 'poor missis' had done more or less the same thing the day she was murdered as she always did, which amounted to feeding her hens, collecting their eggs, and selling them to her neighbours and to one or two shops in town. 'The only new thing she did,' the bereaved spouse complained, 'she went and got herself killed!' Frau Brunner was a sociable woman who went to the Pietist Temple twice a day, three times on a Sunday. She was renowned for honesty, moral rectitude and good works, and she was immensely popular with all the neighbours. She had no known enemies. Indeed, it was believed that she had never argued with any single person in her entire life. Clearly, Rhunken had suspected the husband of the crime. Heinz-Carl Brunner had been held in prison for two days and subjected to 'severe interrogation'. In short, they had beaten him until he screamed for mercy, then let him go when he said nothing incriminating. At the exact time of the murder, as several rival farmers had noted, Brunner had been working in his field with two of his helpers, and this alibi could not be shaken. So, *he* was in the clear. Once again, Rhunken had added a note which seemed to sum up the direction which his enquiry was taking: 'No political ties or radical affiliations reported or found. Prot. 2779?'

I suppose I must have let out a groan.

'Is everything all right, Herr Stiffeniis?' Koch enquired.

'Was Procurator Rhunken collaborating with any other magistrate? I mean, might someone else have been helping him to collect evidence or take statements from these witnesses?'

'Oh no, sir,' Koch replied at once. 'Herr Procurator always worked by himself. I know that for a fact. He trusted no one.'

I nodded and turned my attention to the next sheet of paper, a report concerning the third murder in the series. As I read the name of the victim, a jolt of electricity raced through my veins. *Johann Gottfried Haase*? How I cursed myself for my ineptitude! While travelling towards Königsberg in the coach that day, I had purposely skipped the name of the most important man to die at the hand of the assassin. Johann Gottfried Haase was a scholar of wide international fame, and a frequently published author. Some years before, I had read a pamphlet he had written. A Professor of Oriental Languages and Theology at the University of Königsberg, Haase had caused a sensation when he asserted that the Garden of Eden was by no means fictional. Adam and Eve had, indeed, been tempted by the Serpent, the scholar claimed, more or less on the very spot where we were standing. According to Haase, the city of Königsberg had been built on the original site of the Biblical garden. Who would dare to kill such an eminent man?

Looking down the page, eager for details, I had to laugh. Indeed, I laughed out loud, while Sergeant Koch regarded me with an expression of serious concern.

'What an idiot I've been!' I said.

'Sir?'

The victim's name was Johann Gottfried Haase, but he was not the person I had been thinking of. It was a simple case of two men sharing exactly the same name! The Johann Gottfried Hasse who had been murdered was a destitute halfwit. He eked out a miserable existence begging crumbs of stale bread and cake from the city bakeries, and asking for money on the streets from casual passersby. Everyone in the city knew him by sight, but no one knew him well. Procurator Rhunken remarked that no written record had been found regarding his birth – he was not so much as related to the scholar. No one could say whether he had ever been to school, passed a night in a poorhouse, a month in an orphanage, or a year in jail, though enquiries had been made by the police on all of those questions. Herr Haase was, to all effects, an utter nobody. 'NOT OPENLY POLITICAL', Rhunken had noted. He had not even made the obvious connection with the unknown victim's eminent namesake. Still, the perplexing question that I had asked myself before returned to my mind, and even more forcibly this time. Why kill such a poor and apparently useless creature? An Oriental linguist-theologian might provoke animosity in some quarters, but a penniless beggar? Again, the protocol number '2779' appeared at the foot of the page.

It was a recurrent theme. I could only ask myself what had prompted Procurator Rhunken to decide that the murders were politically motivated. The only common factor that I could find was the absence of anything even remotely political in the victims' lives. Had their apparent indifference to politics seemed to him to be a blind? He had made a note to the effect that Konnen might be a secret agent. Did he believe the same of the others, too? And if so, which foreign power did he suspect them of spying for? Perplexed in my own mind, I turned slowly to the next sheet of paper.

Though not in sequential order, I found it to be the deposition of the midwife who had discovered the body of Jan Konnen. In all that I had read before, this witness had been referred to only in terms of her trade and but never by name, which was very odd. I glanced quickly through the information. Again, no name was given. Early that morning, this mysterious midwife declared, while on her way to minister to a fisherman's wife who lived on the quayside, she came across the body of a man who appeared to have slumped against a wall. The only detail which added to the scant account that I had read in the coach was of some importance. 'I knew that there was evil in it,' she declared. 'Satan used his claws.'

I paused. Sergeant Koch had used the same expression when first he told me of the crimes, but what exactly was *she* referring to? This superstitious woman had seen the dead body with her own eyes. Why use those particular words to describe what she had observed? The Devil's name, I realised, was never far away in Königsberg. I had heard Satan invoked already with great familiarity by Koch, by the maid of Herr Rhunken, by Doctor Vigilantius, and by the soldiers remaining in the Fortress. Was it nothing more than a superficial reflection of the fierce religious sectarianism for which the city was renowned throughout Prussia? The Pietists were a dominating influence in Königsberg; the University was packed with members of the sect. Their reading of the Bible led the Pietists to believe that eternal salvation could only be achieved by personally wrestling with the Devil and his temptations. They had even invented a specific term for it. *Busskampf*, they preached, was a necessary battle that every true believer must fight and win if he hoped to enter the kingdom of Heaven.

I shook my head, and read on to the end. Lublinsky and Kopka, the two officers who had countersigned the woman's statement and based their own report on it, had not pressed her for precise details. Indeed, they had not asked her much at all. Not even her name! Then again, neither had that most excellent magistrate, my predecessor, Procurator Rhunken . . .

'Your master kept few notes, Koch,' I said, as I replaced the sheet.

'True, sir, very true. Kept it all in his head, he did.'

I made no comment, reflecting only that Procurator Rhunken's way of going about the investigation left much to be desired. A degree of professional jealousy might explain his determination to tell me nothing more at our interview than the scant information which his papers contained, but it did not speak well for him, and it made my task all the more difficult.

Finally, there was a brief note about the latest victim, Jeronimus Tifferch, the notary, whose body I had examined in the cellar not an hour before. In his case there was a notable and remarkable difference. Regarding his personal history and habits, there was absolutely nothing. Merely a statement of his death. No other word had been consigned to paper. No person had been questioned, no detailed examination had been made of the corpse. So far as I could tell, no doctor had even been called to verify that he was actually dead, nor to sign a certificate to that effect. As a result, no possible cause of death had been hazarded. As in the notes I had read in the coach the day before – I was getting used to the omission by now – no mention was made of the nature of the weapon which might have been used to kill him, nor of the sort of wound it had inflicted. Indeed, the normal process of legal investigation seemed to have been suspended in Tifferch's case. In anticipation of my coming, perhaps?

There was a knock at the door. Without lifting my head from my work, I heard Koch murmuring with someone on the threshold.

Above all, I reasoned, there was one glaring omission in all that

I had read so far. The name of the 'eminent person' who had called Vigilantius and myself to investigate the string of murders in the city. I could find no reference to it in what Rhunken had chosen to record. Did he not realise that some rival authority was conducting a parallel investigation?

'Herr Stiffeniis, sir?'

Koch's voice interrupted my considerations. I looked up and found him standing stiffly in front of the desk, his linen handkerchief close to his mouth, his glaring eyes red and puffy.

'What is it, Koch?'

'His Excellency, Herr Procurator Rhunken, sir. A guard just brought the news. My master is dead.'

I have rarely seen such naked sorrow on a human face. Instinctively, I looked down at the pile of papers scattered on the desk.

'When will the funeral take place?' I asked.

'He's been entombed already, sir,' he said, slowly passing a hand over his eyes. 'An hour ago, apparently.'

'But that's impossible!' I protested. 'Herr Rhunken was an authority. The city will want to pay its tribute to . . .'

'It was his final wish, sir. He wanted no one present at his burial.'

I looked away to the farthest, darkest corner of the room. Koch had been greatly attached to the magistrate who had died. Still, he could hardly reproach me for Rhunken's death. And yet, I sensed a hidden vein of condemnation in his voice. I could not help myself, a feeling of discomfort crept up on me. Half an hour before I had been congratulating myself on the fact that I was sitting at Herr Rhunken's desk, that his assistant was standing stiffly to attention in front of me, that the Procurator's personal archives were at my complete disposal, that his own sparse accounts of his investigative methods were in my hands to be rifled through, criticised and challenged. But now, suddenly, he was dead.

In some indefinable manner, I felt as if I had been the cause.

Chapter 7

It was past ten o'clock when Sergeant Koch left me at The Baltic Whaler that night. The tavern was busy when I entered, so I sat myself down at a table in the quietest corner, that is, the one furthest removed from the fire, to pen a note to my wife before calling for my dinner. But what should have been a simple task proved far harder than I had anticipated. What should I tell Helena about what was happening in Königsberg? What could I say of the investigation that could reassure her, and what, instead, was better kept to myself? I mused for a moment, took up the quill once more, dipped it in the inkpot and went on:

> *Believe me, my love, when I tell you that I am not doing this in the vain hope of winning back my father's affection. What has happened will never – ever – be erased from his mind, no matter what I try to do, or fail to do. I have lived under that shadow far too long, and have forced you to share the seclusion of Lotingen with me. It is time to forge a better life – for ourselves, and for our little ones. Lotingen has been a safe haven, but now the storm is over. I refuse to hide away any longer. This investigation opens a doorway . . .*

I stopped, uncertain how to go on. I had no desire to tell my wife of the difficulties that I had been obliged to face that day, nor of the horrors that I had seen. What could she do to help me? I swirled the point of the duck-quill in the ink, and turned my thoughts to brighter matters.

> *Herr Koch and I arrived safe and well in Königsberg this after-*

noon. I am writing from my lodging near the port. The air is
fresh here, I can tell you! But my bedroom is warm, clean and
welcoming. It is almost a home from home, indeed . . .

'Sir?' a honey-sweet voice recalled me to my immediate surroundings. A buxom woman in her mid-forties with a moonlike
face and large, bright, green eyes stood before me, holding an
empty tray in what seemed to me to be a parody of servitude.

'I am Gerta Totz, sir,' she announced with a hideous, mincing
smile, 'wife of the landlord. Are you ready for your dinner? Would
you care to try something in particular?'

'Anything at all will do,' I said, quickly folding up the letter to
my wife. I had not eaten since my arrival in Königsberg six hours
before, and the smell of fine cooking which filled the room was sufficiently enticing to whet my appetite.

'I'll bring the best we have, then,' she said, bobbing and removing herself in the direction of the kitchen. As she moved away, I
noticed that she stopped to say a quiet word to three prosperous-
looking gentlemen who were sitting in a tight huddle at a table
quite near to my own.

Something in her manner of addressing them caught my attention, and I followed her progress across the room, wondering
whether she would be equally deferential to all the other customers
in the place, but she disappeared into the kitchen without saying a
single word to anyone. My interest awakened, I looked around at
the assembled company. Beyond those gentlemen with whom Frau
Totz had just spoken, closest to the fire, sat the same plump, dark-
skinned man wearing the red fez and bright oriental naval garb
that I had noticed in the afternoon. He sat peering intently into the
darting flames, as if to evoke the warmer lands of his home. In the
far corner of the room, a knot of fishermen were drinking strong
ale and singing sea shanties. Other less notable customers were
scattered around the room in groups of two or three. A couple of
women with brightly painted lips and rouged faces sat with a
group of foreign navy officials whose uniforms I could not place.
The men were drinking and playing cards, the women watching

the movement of money around the table with sparkling eyes and animated smiles. There could be little doubt where their interest lay, nor of the means they would employ to procure it. In short, it was the sort of scene one might find anywhere along the Baltic seaboard on a cold, winter night, and I soon grew bored of looking.

I had just unfolded my letter again and primed my pen, when a shadow fell over the page. Surprised at such remarkable alacrity, I glanced up, expecting to find Frau Totz with my dinner. Instead, Morik, the serving-boy, was standing over me, his hands firmly clasped behind his back like a common footsoldier waiting to address a confidence to a superior officer.

'What can I do for you?' I asked him.

'Those men at the next table,' the youngster hissed out of the side of his mouth. Leaning closer, eyes wide and staring, he added, 'They meet in the cellar at dead of night, sir. Pretend to order something, or they'll catch on.'

I attempted to look past him, but the boy was standing hard up against my table, blocking out the prospect. 'Now, listen here, my lad,' I began sternly.

'Please, sir!' he whispered urgently. 'Do it loud, or my goose'll be cooked.'

I sat back, perplexed. Then, in a voice that was calculated to wake the dead, I announced to the inn at large: 'Bring me another quill, boy. And be quick about it! The point of this one's ruined, I am unable to finish my letter.'

Morik leapt to attention.

'Right away, sir,' he shouted.

He was gone in a flash.

I looked more attentively at the three men seated close by. Each one smoking a long clay pipe and quaffing ale from an ample *stein*, they were the picture of respectability.

The landlady appeared again from the kitchen, and came bustling across to my table, though there was still no sign of my dinner arriving.

'Is everything in order, Herr Stiffeniis?' she enquired, smiling still. 'Has our Morik been bothering you?'

'I needed a quill,' I said. 'The boy is seeing to it for me.'

'Oh, you should have asked *me*, sir,' she said, wiping the back of her hand across her face. I got the impression that she seemed relieved by what I had just told her. 'He is such a nuisance, that lad! Can't be trusted to do a thing! Be sure and tell me if he gets up to any mischief, won't you, sir?'

'I most certainly will,' I assured her.

'I'll be a-getting back to the kitchen, then,' Frau Totz announced, trotting off and nodding silently to the men at the next table as she went.

I put aside my letter, my attention now engaged by the three strangers, my curiosity heightened by this odd exchange with the landlady. Could Morik be telling the truth? There was something decidedly staid and measured in the behaviour of the three guests that was out of place in a quayside tavern. They did not joke, or laugh, and they seemed to speak to each other in unnecessarily hushed tones.

On impulse, I rose from the table and moved towards the blazing fire, as if to warm my hands. As I passed close by their table, I caught a phrase in French. Was that what had tickled the serving-boy's fancy, the fact that those men spoke the language of Napoleon Bonaparte?

'Your quills, sir!' Morik called loudly from my table, holding them up for me and everyone else in the room to see. I returned to the table, recalling what both the landlady and her husband had said of the lad's untrustworthy nature.

'I've sharpened them to your satisfaction I hope, sir?' he said out loud. In a whisper he added: 'Those men are French. They arrived three days ago.'

'So? What of it?' I said quietly, taking up one of the quills and trying the point against the paper, playing my part in the charade.

Morik raised his voice again. 'Right, sir! A sharp knife in case they split again.'

But he made no move to leave me in peace as the landlady passed by, taking four more pints of frothing ale to the fishermen who were merrymaking in the far corner. As soon as she had gone, Morik lowered his voice again. 'Stop them, sir! Before they strike again.'

I stared hard at the boy. He stood looking around the room, a stiff smile engraved on his lips. I could see quite clearly that he was afraid.

'Stop *who*?' I asked.

'Those Frenchmen, sir! Two nights ago that man was killed. They've been here before, they'll murder again.'

'Why should they wish to kill anybody?' I asked quietly, holding a pen up to the light and examining the point, playing my part with more care now.

'Let *me* try, sir,' Morik said aloud, grabbing the pen from my hand and a scrap of paper from the pile I had placed on the table. He wrote something, his hand shaking as he did so, then glanced up to gauge my reaction.

'Napoleon intends to invade Prussia,' I read.

Before I could speak, he picked up the paper, rolled it into a tight ball, strode across to the fire and thrust it deep into the flames. He did not return to my table. Instead, Frau Totz appeared at my side. Morik must have seen her coming.

'Here's your dinner, sir,' she said, laying a large, full plate on the table. 'I hope I have not made you wait too long?'

Her sharp eyes followed Morik as he moved away from the fire and through a door that led into the kitchen.

'Did Morik serve you as he ought?' she asked.

'He seems a most accommodating fellow.'

'He always makes a fuss of new guests,' she explained. 'But he's far too nosy for his own good, that lad! Drive my poor sister to her grave, he will. He's all she's got. Working here in the inn, with all these sailors passing through, has turned his silly head. He's interested in everybody's business but his own. Enjoy your meal, sir.'

Was that the true explanation of the boy's behaviour? The coincidental fact that the first victim of the unidentified murderer had spent his last night on earth in the bar of The Baltic Whaler might be at the root of the boy's gossip. But then another aspect of the situation struck me forcibly. If the mysterious person who had had me called to Königsberg had been behind all that had happened so far, had he also decided that I should be lodged at The

Baltic Whaler? Did he suspect that something illegal was going on there? And if so, what was I supposed to do about it?

I determined to do two things. I would speak privately to Morik about his absurd accusations. Then, I would question Innkeeper Totz more closely with regard to the statement he had made to Procurator Rhunken. But first of all, I had my empty stomach to care for. I took up my fork and spoon and set to with a will, dining on a rich vegetable broth, roasted chicken and an abundant helping of those tiny turnips that are stored under ice through the winter. The wine was white, a fruity vintage imported from the Nahe region, and it was surprisingly good.

As I ate my dinner, however, I did not lose sight of the three men who had aroused Morik's suspicions. One of them in particular caught my attention. He was taller, older, more heavily built than his companions. Detached and watchful, seemingly aloof from the general conversation, he appeared to be more alert than the other two concerning what was going on in the inn. Every now and then, he would lower his head and say a quiet word to them in confidence.

French spies conspiring against Prussia? Murdering innocent people in the streets? It took an incredibly wild stretch of the imagination to credit what Morik had said of them. What military objective could such a devilish strategy serve? The victims were men and women of no civic importance. Their deaths would not affect the city and its defences, except, perhaps, by spreading panic. But would the spread of panic help Bonaparte invade Prussia if it was happening in Königsberg alone?

I did not realise until too late that the three foreign gentlemen were looking in my direction. While I had been mentally analysing them, they had been paying more careful physical attention to me. Suddenly, the tallest one – the leader, as I described him in my own mind – rose from his seat and came across to my table.

'Good evening, sir,' he began with a polite bow. 'My name is Guntar Stoltzen. I hope I'm not disturbing you?'

'Not at all. I have finished my meal, Herr Stoltzen,' I said, sitting back in my chair and looking up at him. 'What can I do for you, sir?'

'My friends and I are jewellers,' he began, nodding over his shoulder in the direction of his companions. 'The serving-boy told us yesterday that there have been a number of murders in the city, sir. He said that you are here to investigate them.'

So, Morik had been at work with them as well.

'Forgive me, sir,' he continued, 'I would not have you believe that I am more interested in the affairs of other men than of my own, but we are concerned for our safety. We've still a long way to go and . . . well, you understand, of course. We're carrying precious gems to Tallinn. What we heard alarmed us. Being robbed is one thing. Being robbed *and* murdered is quite another!'

I sipped a little wine and gathered my thoughts. Clearly, this Morik was a scandalmonger. He had frightened these innocent travellers, and awakened my own suspicions with ease. Frau Totz was right about him. The boy was definitely a troublemaker.

'You are French, are you not?' I asked.

'German, sir, my companions are French. We have travelled through East Prussia many times before and nothing unpleasant has ever befallen us. But this news is alarming. If these murders were committed by robbers, we might easily be in danger. Do you not agree?'

'Where did you hear that these crimes had been committed by thieves?' I enquired, expecting Morik's name to be raised again.

'What other reason could there be for killing innocent people?'

'Why kill, if not for gain? Is that what you mean, sir?'

Herr Stoltzen smiled and nodded his head.

'Would you be happier to believe that the murders had been committed for political reasons?' I probed.

'Politics?' He frowned, evidently surprised by the suggestion. 'Is that why these people have been murdered, sir?'

I shook my head. 'You have formed one opinion, I offer an alternative which would guarantee the safety of you, your companions, and the valuables you are carrying.'

'A political plot?' he mused. 'For what purpose, sir?'

I shrugged my shoulders and put a piece of bread in my mouth, chewing slowly for some moments before I replied.

'Imagine that someone wished, for reasons still to be determined, to spread terror here in Königsberg. A spate of apparently random murders would do the trick, don't you think?'

'If your investigation points that way, I wish you all success. But now, sir, I will leave you to digest your meal in peace,' he said with a warm smile and a bright twinkle in his eye, as if meaning to return to his own table.

'A political coup does not worry you, then?' I said, unwilling to end the conversation.

He stared at me intently. 'Of course it does, sir, but such an explanation would mean that commercial travellers like myself and my friends could go about our business undeterred. One government is very much like another where trade is concerned.'

'I am glad if I have set your mind at rest,' I replied with a smile.

Herr Stoltzen bowed his head and smiled back. 'My friends and I will toast your good health. With your permission, sir?'

He clicked his heels lightly, returned to his companions and spoke to them quietly. All raised their beer mugs and smiled at me convivially.

I raised my glass to return the courtesy.

I have just interrogated my first suspect, I thought.

I drank my wine to the lees. Then, wishing good night to the three men with a nod of my head, I rose from the table and retired upstairs to my bedroom. The fire had been banked up for the night, a copper jug of water was warming on the hearth. Despite feeling deathly tired, I sat down at the desk to finish the letter to my wife.

Reading over what I have written thus far, my dear, I find that I have failed to report the progress of my investigations. I may have found a trail to follow, and hope that I will not be staying very much longer here in Königsberg. And so, my darling wife, with this good news I wish you a fond farewell.

I added a few tender words of love for the children, then sealed the envelope and set it to one side. Leaving the candle on the table by the window while I put on my night-clothes, I glanced casually out of the window to see if it were still snowing. The sky was a mass of heavy swirling clouds, the moon barely visible. I was just about to turn away and take myself to bed, when a sudden movement in a window on the far side of the courtyard caught my eye. Peering through the misty glass, I observed a dark figure in the far room holding a hooded candle, his head turned to one side as if he were eavesdropping. In the flickering candlelight, the face was grotesque, the eyes two dark, gaping, black holes, the forehead and nose monstrously distorted by the shadows. The figure placed the candleholder on the window ledge, and in that moment, I recognised him. It was Morik.

What was the boy playing at?

He looked up and waved his hand. The lad knew the room in which I was lodging and he appeared to be trying to attract my attention. My thoughts flew to the three travelling merchants. Was he daring to spy on them? The serving-boy truly was a pest. I decided that I had better speak to him about his behaviour the very next morning. Sooner or later, the boy was going to get himself into serious trouble.

I snapped the curtains shut and blotted his figure out, determined to have no more to do with Morik and his foolishness. It had been a long, hard day and I was thoroughly exhausted. Quickly, I washed my face and hands, then I retired to my bed. The crispness of the fresh linen sheets, their heady perfume of blubber soap and starched cleanliness, induced a strong sense of well-being as I nestled down beneath the heavy eiderdown coverlet. Soon, I knew, I would be sound asleep. But in those delicious moments before gentle Morpheus had fully narcotised my senses, I suddenly tensed with fright. Had I dreamt it, or had I actually seen a moving shadow lurking at Morik's back? A pale apparition glimpsed so fleetingly that my conscious mind had not fully registered it?

I sat up with a start, jumped out of bed, and darted over to the window. Throwing back the curtains, I looked out across the yard. All was dark on the other side of the court. There was nothing left to see.

No candle. No Morik. No sign of man, or ghost.

Chapter 8

The first pallid intimation of the dawn caressed the curtains around my bed, but I had been wide-eyed and awake for an hour already. The ritual nightmare had brought me choking from my sleep, hair plastered to my forehead, limbs rigid, my heart in my mouth. And yet, somehow, the frightful dream had been less painful, less vivid in its gruesomeness than usual. The rock had barely penetrated his skull. The grass had not been red with blood. His glassy eyes had seemed to be less fixed, less accusing than they had been on previous occasions. For the first time, in those dreams that had plagued my sleep for seven years, I had not been frozen with fright. I had *moved*. I had tried to reach him, skipping down from the towering height of the rock, holding his salvation clasped in my hand. I could not be blamed for neglect this time. I had taken the vial from my pocket, the glass cold against my fingers, a flash of sunlight making the contents gleam and glisten like melted amber . . .

I dismissed the memory as I jumped up from my bed, shivering in the cold as I agitated the grey embers of the fire, adding wood shavings and some larger chips of wood which Morik had left behind for that purpose the previous evening. The first flame crackled into life, and I swung the copper pot over the fire to reheat the water I had used to wash myself the night before. Crossing over to the window, I looked out on the day. There had been more snow during the night, but the pearl-grey sky was free of further threatening clouds. A freezing day to come, I thought, noting the extraordinary length of the icicles that dangled from the guttering of the roof above my room. The window on the far side of the yard where I had seen Morik the night before was dark, reflecting only the gleam from my candle. What had the boy been doing there? Had somebody been watching him, an accomplice, perhaps, or had I imagined the entire scene?

I wrapped the top coverlet from the bed around my shoulders, and sat down at the desk to make a list of all the things I would need to do that day. The name of Lawyer Tifferch was at the top. He had been dead three days already, so the trail was already growing cold. Today my work would start in earnest. I had wasted time enough with the necromancer, Vigilantius, the night before. I had not been long at my task, however, when I heard someone clumping about in the hall outside my door.

'Morik!' I thought, rising quickly and striding to the door, intent on catching the little sneak off his guard. The boy was spying again. On me, this time.

With a sudden wrench, I threw the door wide open.

Frau Totz was on her knees in the hallway, staring hard where the keyhole had been but a moment before. She fell backwards onto her large bottom, her legs seesawed into the air, and she let out a yelp of surprise. A second later, raising herself to her normal height again as if nothing untoward had happened, she fixed me with that mincing smile she habitually wore. It appeared to have been painted on her face.

'Good morning, Herr Procurator,' she chimed brightly. 'I hope I haven't disturbed you? I thought I saw a glimmer of light beneath your door, and did not know whether to knock. I was wondering if you would care for something special for your breakfast.'

'I told you last night what I want, Frau Totz,' I answered sharply. 'Bread, honey, hot tea.'

That smile did not fade or flicker, despite my rudeness. It was fixed, immovable, dreadful in its intensity, especially so early in the morning.

'We have fresh cheese and some choice cuts of ham in the cold-room,' she went on smoothly. 'I was wondering whether you might like to try . . .'

'Another time,' I said, cutting her insistence short. The landlady had been spying on me. Morik had been spying on the other guests

82

the night before. And someone else had been spying on Morik. Was spying a contagious disease in the Totz household? I could not suppress a note of sarcasm when I added, 'Your great concern for my well-being is most reassuring, ma'am. Send Morik up at once, if you please.'

Her head was covered with a linen bonnet a size too small from which her reddish-brown curls seemed stiffly intent on fighting their way out. The bonnet drooped towards her right shoulder and that grotesque smile slowly faded away until it was a poor, pale shadow of its former self.

'Morik?' she murmured. 'That boy should have been busy down in the kitchen an hour since, but I haven't heard a peep out of him. I thought that he might have come up here to wake you, sir.'

'Morik, here?' Was that her true motive for peeping through the keyhole? I hesitated, wondering what sort of a vile bawdy-house I had been lodged in. 'His bedroom stands on the far side of the courtyard from mine, does it not?'

A frown flitted across her brow. 'Oh no, sir, no,' she said. 'Morik sleeps down in the kitchen behind the stove.' She let out a sigh. 'I'd better go and see what's got into him. With your permission . . .'

'Who *is* staying in that room over the way, then?'

'That room, sir?' she said with a puzzled expression, glancing across the yard. 'No one, sir. It's been vacant since two business gentlemen from Hanover left last Thursday.'

'But I saw someone in there last night. I'd have sworn that it was Morik.'

'You must be mistaken, sir,' she replied quickly, and the smile reappeared like a carnival mask, but it was tense and rigid, ever more patently false. 'If you'll excuse me, I'm needed downstairs in the kitchen.'

'When you find him, Frau Totz, send Morik along with my breakfast, will you?'

The woman's lips pursed like those of an insolent child suppressing a remark for which she knew she must be scolded. Whatever she might have been intending to say, however, she simply said: 'As you wish, Herr Stiffeniis.'

I returned to my desk and added a few more items to the list of things I had to do, then I washed and shaved with care, dressed myself in a clean linen shirt and my best brown suit and took out my periwig from its travelling-box. Lotte had remembered to pack it for me, despite the fret of my departure. I disliked wearing the wig – it made my scalp hot and itchy – and generally I avoided doing so, but in the present circumstances I was not a private citizen: the people of Königsberg would expect formality of the man who had been entrusted with the salvation of the city. That mass of silver curls would, I hoped, lend an air of authority to my person which my youth might seem to deny. It would also, I reflected, protect my ears from the cold . . .

There was a knock at the door, and Frau Totz appeared again, carrying my breakfast on a tray.

'He's nowhere to be seen, sir,' she announced grimly. This time she did not attempt to smile. Her green eyes glanced away from mine and darted swiftly around the room, almost as if she thought the boy might be playing hide-and-seek, almost as if *I* were a party to the game.

'Do you think he's hiding under my bed?' I asked her.

'Oh, no, sir. What an idea!'

Nevertheless, she did glance towards the four-poster again. 'He ought to be down in the kitchen getting breakfast ready,' she murmured slowly.

'He has probably gone out on an errand,' I said to put an end to the subject. 'Now, can I have my breakfast?'

Frau Totz blushed bright red and cried: 'Oh, dearie me! Forgive me, sir!'

I took the tray from her hands and looked her squarely in the eye. Tiny beads of sweat had begun to break out on her forehead along the line of her ginger hair.

'What, precisely, are you afraid of, Frau Totz?' I asked.

'Well, sir, I'm not . . . not afraid exactly,' she muttered uncertainly. 'But Morik's such a hothead. His noddle's full of strange ideas.'

I found her manner of speaking allusive and annoying at the same time.

'Strange ideas about *what*, Frau Totz?'

'I did tell you, sir. An' I tried to warn you last night, too. He invents things.' She fixed her eyes on her meaty hands; they seemed to be engaged in a nervous tug-of-war over which she had no control. 'Always up to no good, that lad,' she went on. 'My Ulrich was saying just last night that my nephew's been acting odd since you arrived, sir. Asking questions about who you are, why you're here, that sort of thing. Morik seems to think that if you're staying here, instead of in town, it's because you are watching the inn.'

She looked nervously around the room again, then back at me, and I had the distinct impression that my arrival at The Baltic Whaler had whetted the curiosity not merely of Morik the serving-boy.

'There is no reason for you to worry, Frau Totz,' I said, intent on being rid of her. 'Your house is far more comfortable than the Fortress. Now, if you'd be so kind, I would like to enjoy your excellent breakfast while the tea is still hot.'

She jumped as if she had been jabbed from behind with a sharp needle. 'Oh, pardon me, sir!' she exclaimed. 'Wasting your time like this when you have more important things to do! If you need anything, just ring the bell. You're right about Morik, sir. He'll be back in his own good time, no doubt.'

She bowed herself out as if I were the King. Ten minutes later, my breakfast done, my toilet completed, I went down to the lounge where Amadeus Koch was standing before the fire.

'Good morning, Koch,' I said with energy. 'I am glad to see you.'

And indeed I was. I could not have imagined the day before that I would be so happy to see his severe, pale face again.

Koch bowed deferentially. 'I hope you slept well, sir? I delivered your note to Herr Jachmann's house half an hour ago,' he reported at once.

'Did he send a written reply?'

'No, sir.'

I was surprised.

'A message by word of mouth?'

'Nothing, sir. I'd have told you if he had. His servant took the note, then closed the door. I waited five minutes or more, but without result.'

'Of course, I . . . Thank you, Sergeant.'

I stared at the fire and asked myself what this silence on Jachmann's part might signify. I had stated my intention to call at his home at twelve o' the clock that morning. Was I to conclude that the absence of any message implied consent?

'The coach is waiting,' said Koch, breaking in on my thoughts. 'D'you wish to go to the Fortress, sir?'

'Is Kliesterstrasse far from here?' I asked.

Koch looked at me curiously. 'A mile, sir, no more. It's in the business part of town.'

'The weather is better this morning, is it not?'

'It ain't snowing, if that's what you mean, sir.'

'Let's go on foot then, Koch. A walk will do us both good, and I need to learn my way about town,' I said.

Frau Totz was hovering near the kitchen door, her eyes fixed on me with an intensity that I could not fathom.

'I'm sure that Morik will turn up soon,' I called across the room.

The rigid smile materialised once more like the horrid grimace on the face of an Etruscan figurine. 'He certainly will, Herr Stiffeniis,' she replied, and instantly bowed her head. For a moment, I thought that she was about to cry. But with a shrug, she turned and disappeared through the door to the kitchen.

Out in the street, we turned away from the ice-bound port and set off up the long rise of Königstrasse hill, Sergeant Koch walking in dutiful silence at my side. Shops here and there on either side of the thoroughfare were beginning to open their shutters for the day's business, though there was no one in the street apart from ourselves, and a boy with ringlets and a white skullcap whom we met halfway up the hill. He was kneeling with a bucket and cloth, attempting to scrape the paint off a wall, where some night-creeper had daubed the Star of David and a slogan in large letters using whitewash: *Blame the sons of Israel!*

I looked away, not daring to think what might happen if bigoted hotheads chose to take that accusation seriously, as had happened in Bremen three years before. Twenty-seven Jews had lost their lives there, and thousands more had been forced to flee.

'Since these murders began, sir,' Koch confided, 'there's been no lack of threats against the Hebrews. Hostile pastors openly blame the Jews for murdering Our Saviour. The killing of a churchgoer in Königsberg might provoke a bloodbath . . .'

He fell silent as we approached a tobacco shop.

The owner, a tall, thin man wearing a soiled brown apron and black skullcap, was idling against the door-post, smoking what must have been his first pipe of the morning, studying us attentively, nodding in an inviting sort of manner. He let out an audible growl of contempt as we walked on past his emporium without so much as stopping. Glancing in at the dusty window, the sort of trade that he attracted was evident. Twists of dusty, rough, black tobacco-shag dangled from hooks; short cob-pipes, and even shorter ones of white clay, yellow with age, lay scattered in a heap beside a pile of mouldy cheese roundels. Situated so close to the port, I chose to speculate, the sort of customer who frequented the area was rough and ready, neither choosy nor particularly extravagant in his tastes. They would be sailors for the most part, or soldiers from the garrison, men in search of cheap, strong smoke and the sort of pipe that would suffer any number of hard knocks.

Jackets made of stiff canvas hung suspended on rails outside the next shop. They were ugly garments stained with sea-salt and clearly second-hand. Koch's pea-coat, I noted, was of heavy grey wool, and it was almost new, while my own black mantle of imported English wool – fashioned by Helena on the occasion of an invitation two months earlier to a Christmas dinner at the home of Baron von Stiwalski, whose estate of Süchingern was less than a mile from Lotingen – was a trifle light for the season, perhaps, but no one could possibly doubt the quality of the material. Even so, the owner came running out onto the pavement, bowing and inviting us to step inside and try on waterproofs 'guaranteed to resist the rigour of the very coldest seas,' as he proclaimed with a certain pomp. We might have been the only customers he had seen in a month or more.

I smiled, and said: 'Thank you, no.'

'Half-price to you, sirs!' the man called after us.

'Business does not seem to be booming,' I said to Sergeant Koch, as we continued on our way, our progress continually monitored by the shopkeepers all along the street.

'It's a problem, sir. Not just here, almost everywhere in town. The shops open first thing in the morning,' he replied, 'then close by three o'clock, most of them. No one goes out after dark. The vegetable market near the cathedral has a bit of a crowd around midday, the fish market down in Sturtenstrasse is still pretty busy, depending on the state of the tides, but not the way it used to be. Just look, sir!' Sergeant Koch observed with a sweep of his hand as we turned the corner into a broad cobbled street marked 'Baltijskstrasse'.

I noted two well-dressed gentleman fifty yards ahead, walking in the same direction as ourselves. On the other side of the street, a maid in a linen cap and a red-and-white striped apron was furiously sweeping the snow from the steps of an elegant town-house. Another maid in a similar garb, carrying a covered basket under her arm, hurried into a house further down the row, slamming the door at her back. Otherwise, the street was empty. No horses, carts or carriages disturbed the peace. There was nothing remarkable to be seen.

'What do you mean?' I asked.

'Baltijskstrasse was the busiest street in Königsberg, sir,' he said excitedly. 'A year ago, you couldn't take here a step without bumping into someone.'

'Where have all the people gone?'

'They're barricaded in their homes, sir,' Koch replied. 'Waiting for the killer to be caught.'

'You may be right,' I allowed with a sigh of discomfort. I had never imagined that accepting the investigation would require me to re-establish normal life in Königsberg, and safeguard the lives of potential sacrificial goats.

'What news is there this morning, Koch?' I asked, suddenly aware how silent, how aloof, I must have appeared to my assistant.

'All men under the age of thirty-five with military experience have been recalled to active service by General Katowice, Herr Stiffeniis,' Koch replied with his usual vigour. 'That's another reason why the town's so empty. The general wants a close watch to be kept on all known agitators, foreign residents and other aliens.'

'Is there a list, Koch?'

'I suppose there must be, sir.'

'Can you get a copy of the names for me?'

'I'll try, sir. God knows how complete it will be. The hotels will be easy enough to check' – Koch panted with the pace I was setting, letting out little puffs of steam as he spoke – 'but the dock area is another matter. You'll have noticed that yourself, sir. There's much coming and going, but if they made you sign the visitors' book at The Baltic Whaler, it's only because they know who you are.'

'I want the names of all visitors who have slept in the city in the past two weeks, Sergeant,' I returned with force. 'And The Baltic Whaler would make an excellent place to start the hunt for the killer. There are two Frenchmen and their German companion – travelling salesmen, they call themselves. I would like to know more about them.'

Koch said nothing for some moments.

'Do you want them interrogated, sir?' he asked gravely, as if he thought he might be putting into words what I had lacked the courage to say.

'For God's sake, no!' I exclaimed. 'I share General Katowice's fear of the mob. We must exercise control without being heavy-handed. If these crimes are politically motivated, the important thing is to lull the terrorists into a false sense of security. Interrogate anyone and the whole city will know what we are about. When I say check on them, I mean by talking to the hotel owners in a confidential manner. Sound out their suspicions, ask them if anything out of the ordinary has happened. The police are capable of that sort of strategy, are they not?'

'Is that the line you mean to take in these investigations, sir?'

'What do you mean, Koch?'

'Politics, Herr Stiffeniis. The mere thought of invasion by French cut-throats is enough to frighten the life out of anyone living here in Königsberg. If such a possibility exists, General Katowice should be informed at once. The King too . . .'

I pulled up short and turned to him. 'What can we tell them, Koch? We have nothing to communicate. Bonaparte has not chosen to show himself as yet. Local agents may be at work to undermine the government, using the tactics of terrorism to scare the populace, but this hypothesis needs to be verified. There may well be other alternatives.'

Koch blew into his handkerchief. 'May I ask what other alternatives, sir?'

The question caught me off guard. What alternatives, indeed?

'Well, Sergeant,' I began, walking on, 'you voiced one yourself just yesterday in the coach.'

'Did I really, sir?'

'You mentioned the Devil.'

'And you, sir, laughed at the suggestion,' Koch objected, scrutinising my face as if uncertain whether I might be joking.

'I cannot afford to exclude any avenue, Koch,' I smiled. 'No matter how abhorrent the idea may be to me personally.'

We walked on in silence, Koch occasionally indicating the geography of the place as we went along. 'This is Kliesterstrasse,' he announced at last. 'Which house are we looking for, sir?'

I did not reply, but began to walk along the dark, narrow alley of uneven cobblestones. Dwellings of different shapes and heights were clustered on either side of a shallow sewage ditch which ran stinking down the centre of the street. Some of the houses were fashioned out of faded wood-and-wattle daub, while others dotted here and there among the leaning terraces were of ancient wind-worn sandstone. They might have been put there to hold the frailer buildings steady in their places. The upper floors on either side seemed almost to touch, closing out the grey sky. Leaded windows, like a honeycomb of stacked wine bottles, gave light, but prevented the curious from looking into the ground-floor rooms. There was a listing, drifting, slanting air about the place, as if a violent puff of wind might bring the whole lot crashing down.

'Procurator Rhunken left his work unfinished at this point, Sergeant,' I explained. 'Let us see if we are able to discover what the man we examined last night on that anatomical table has left behind to help us solve his murder.'

A bronze plate was fixed to the door:

JERONIMUS TIFFERCH, NOTARY AT LAW & RECORDER OF OATHS.

Chapter 9

The door swung open framing a diminutive stunted figure in the entrance. Her face and hair were hidden by a lace cloth of the same sombre hue as her plain black gown. 'Office closed,' the woman chimed in a high-pitched, sing-song voice. 'Herr Tifferch is no more.'

'Frau Tifferch?' I asked, jamming the door with my foot as it began to close again in our faces.

Suddenly, the door flew back, the veil began to nod from side to side, then jerked as a cackling whoop escaped from the woman's lips. 'Ooh, no! Do you wish to see my lady? Expression of sympathy, is it?' Throwing the shroud back over her head as she spoke, the ancient exposed a lantern jaw of singular extension as she glared up at Koch and myself. Two yellow fangs protruded from the centre of her shrunken gums like the ravaged teeth of an aged buck-rabbit.

'This is not a social visit, ma'am,' I corrected her. 'My name is Hanno Stiffeniis. I am an investigating magistrate and I wish to speak to your mistress about her late husband.'

The woman cackled again, and said quite plainly, 'You won't have much luck there!'

She did not seem put out by the fact that her master had been murdered, her mistress widowed. Despite the mourning weeds, her attitude was most irreverent in the circumstances. 'What d'you want to see her for?' she asked.

'I need to look through Herr Tifferch's things,' I said.

'Help yourself,' she shrugged. 'What's stopping you?'

'I wish to ask permission of your mistress *first*.'

The maid stepped back, and waved us in, nodding towards a closed door on the right of the entrance hall. 'Her ladyship's in there. In all her glory! Ask her all you want.'

I was puzzled by this cryptic description. Her Ladyship? Was Frau Tifferch a member of the *Junker* aristocracy? Certainly, the surname she had acquired by marriage had nothing noble-sounding about it. Before I had the chance to ask, however, the maid had slammed the door to the street, and taken herself off along a dark corridor to the left without another word, her pattens clacking noisily on the floor tiles as she went away.

'Not the sort of maid I'd have in *my* house,' I muttered, remembering my father's terrified domestics and our own compliant Lotte, as I tapped my knuckles gently on the sitting-room door.

'Go on in!' the maid screeched from the end of the corridor. 'She'll not answer, though you wait all bloomin' day.'

Koch pushed the door open, and I followed him into the room. It was dark and gloomy, more like a funeral parlour than a suburban sitting room. Wide black swathes of ribbon had been tied to all the candlestick holders, and the tapers were lit. Black shrouds glistened everywhere, hiding the furniture, the fittings, and even the pictures on the walls, though a plaster statue standing almost three feet high on a table in the far corner had not been covered from view. It represented Jesus Christ. A sort of shrine reigned over there. Red votive lamps burned beside His pierced and naked feet, and Our Saviour held His vestments open wide in a most unseemly fashion, His heart exposed for the careless world to see. This organ was crowned with golden tongues of flame, bright red, pulsing with blood. I looked at Sergeant Koch. And Koch held my gaze. We had entered Roman territory. In the centre of the room sat a woman in a high-backed chair. Dressed like the maid in black from head to toe, her finery was of an earlier generation, richer by far, costly silk with trimmed flounces and ribbed fustian. She wore a magnificent jet necklace which covered her breast, while matching jet bracelets weighed down her slender wrists. Death seemed to have figured prominently in this woman's history.

'Frau Tifferch?' I asked, advancing across the room. 'May I offer my most sincere condolences on your unfortunate loss?'

The woman looked at me. That is, she lifted her face at the sound of my voice. Bright pinpoints seemed to glint at me from beneath the veil, but no word of greeting or gratitude issued from her lips.

'Your husband, ma'am,' I hinted, pausing to hear the sound of her voice.

Frau Tifferch did not move. She appeared not to breathe.

'I am leading the enquiry into the circumstances regarding his murder,' I was obliged to continue. 'I must ask you some questions about your husband. I'm interested in any business he might have been engaged upon when he was killed. He was out of doors after dark, it seems . . .'

The woman reached out a hand. Her bracelets tinkled as she took a black handkerchief from a small table at her side, carried it beneath her veil, and began to sob.

'Frau Tifferch?' I pressed gently.

Silence answered.

'Frau Tifferch?' I repeated.

Koch crossed the room on tiptoe and stood behind the lady's chair. Leaning forward, he whispered in her ear, 'Frau Tifferch?'

Standing to his full height at the woman's back, he raised his forefinger, touched himself twice on the temple, then shook his head.

'Call the maid back in,' I said, waiting in silence until the servant traipsed noisily into the room a minute later, followed by Sergeant Koch.

'What do you want?' she muttered. Her ill disposition had not softened in the least in the interval.

'Is your mistress feeling unwell?' I asked.

'You could call it that,' she said. 'Out of her wits. That's what *I* would say. Frau Tifferch's in a world of her own. Never says nowt, she don't.'

'What's wrong with her?'

She shrugged. 'I've no idea. No one told me, did they? I'm just the nursemaid. It happened four or five years ago, I believe. I wasn't working in this house then. But this I *was* told by the neighbours. It happened out of the blue. She was strong and active before.' She pointed at her charge and shook her head. 'It must have been something fearful, that's all I can say.'

I frowned. 'What do you mean?'

She shrugged again. 'You don't become a turnip for no good reason, do you?'

I stiffened, fighting off the sudden overlapping of images in my mind. I saw my own mother sitting there before me in the place of that heavily veiled widow, her eyes fixing themselves on mine while she asked a question for which there was no simple answer: 'How could you do it, Hanno?' That was the last coherent sentence she had ever uttered. A spasm had wracked her body and she collapsed apparently lifeless at my feet. Her tomblike silence endured for days. The doctors were called, but no remedy could be found. The pastor came to pray, and stayed to read the Last Rites. And all that time, my father said not a single word to me. But in his gaze I saw my mother's question. 'How could you, Hanno? Why did you do it?'

I closed my eyes to free myself from those painful memories, and opened them again on the gaping lantern jaw of the housemaid.

'What is your name?' I asked.

'Agneta Süsterich.'

'How long have you been working here, Agneta?'

'Too long.'

There was nothing subservient about the old woman. Words like 'sir', phrases such as 'by your leave', did not figure in her already limited vocabulary. She was brusque to the point of rudeness. Had Lawyer Tifferch never taken the surly drudge to task for her foul manners?

'Be more precise!' I insisted.

'Two years,' she replied in a forced fashion. 'An' curse the day I came! Once this lot's over, I'll be on my way. I should have left him to it . . .'

'Does your mistress have anyone else? Sons or daughters?' I pressed on.

'No one,' the woman replied. 'No relatives. I never seen a soul all the time I been a-staying here. No one visits this house. No one . . .'

She paused significantly, as if inviting me to complete the sentence.

'Except for *whom*?' I said.

'Priests!' she flared. 'Catholic priests! Blasphemous vermin! An' now, the police messing around . . .'

'You are not of that religion, I take it?'

The maid's eyes narrowed, as if I had just accused her of the most heinous crime under the sun. 'I am a Pietist!' she protested. 'Everyone in Königsberg's a Pietist. I goes to my Bible reading every night to cleanse my Christian lungs of the foul Catholic air I am forced to breathe in this house. I told the master. Told him straight, I did. I goes to Bible meetings, Herr Tifferch, I said, or else. But now there's no one to look after her. What am I going to do?'

'Did you light all those candles?' I intervened, trying to stop the angry flow before it became a raging flood.

'I had to, didn't I?' the woman muttered. 'Only way to keep her quiet. She likes her candles. All them Catholics do. Heathen rubbish, I say!'

'What are your duties here?' I asked with all the patience I could muster.

'Everything.' She started ticking items off on her fingers as she spoke. 'Wash her, clean her, dress her, comb her, feed her. I decked her out in black in case one of them bloodsuckers came.'

'Has a "leech" been called?' I asked.

'Papists!' she spat. 'Stayed clear so far, they have.'

'Your master was murdered three days ago,' I ploughed on. 'Late in the evening. Did he tell you where he was going when he left the house?'

The woman lifted her eyes, stretched her jaw, and grinned. 'Master allus kep' his counsel to hisself. Never knew what was going on in *his* mind. He was a dark horse, all right.'

'He carried on his business from this house,' I persisted. 'Which clients came to visit him that day?'

'I've no idea. None at all. That front door was allus open. Seven 'til five, Monday to Sat'day. They come, they go.'

I tried another tack. 'Did you hear anyone shouting, or quarrelling with Herr Tifferch?'

'I keeps meself to the kitchen,' she replied. 'It's warm out there.'

'Do you know if your master had any enemies?' I asked.

Agneta Süsterich thought this question over for some moments. Then she looked at me with a smile, and my expectations rose.

'Only the missis,' she declared. 'Used to scream every time she saw his face. Does that answer you?'

It most certainly did not. Whoever had produced those livid cuts and scars on Lawyer Tifferch's body, it had undoubtedly not been his wife. 'Did anything out of the ordinary happen the day he died?' I pressed on.

Agneta Süsterich sighed aloud, her annoyance growing more visible with each new question.

'He worked in the morning. As usual. Had lunch with his wife. As usual. Sat in his office 'til five. As usual, I went to Grüsterstrassehaus . . .'

'What's that?'

'The Pietist Temple. I left a cold supper out for them. As allus. I was back at half past seven to put the mistress into bed. As usual. I never seen *him* at all, but that was nothing new. He went out every night . . .'

'And where did he go?' I interrupted.

The woman's ugly face twisted with disgust. 'I can only imagine,' she said. 'I seen him staggering down them stairs that many times of a morning. Pain was writ all over his face. As if he just been kicked in the bollocks by an 'orse. Can't hardly stand on his own two feet some days! Them Catholics like to sin, all right. The priest absolves 'em quick enough for a thaler or two.'

'Do you hear him return at night as a rule?' I asked, coughing to stifle a laugh at this lurid description of the rival faith.

'I says my prayers and I goes to sleep. Ain't no use waiting up for the Devil. More so that night, 'cos he never come home, did he? Night Watch knocked us up afore the first crow of the cock.'

'So, where is his office?'

'There are four doors out in that hallway,' the woman said.

'One's mine, one's hers, one's his. The other goes upstairs to the sleeping quarters.'

'Show me to your master's workroom,' I said.

Before leaving the sitting room, I turned to the widow again. She was as still and silent as the plaster idol in the corner. She had given no sign of life since we entered the room, and she showed no sign as we left it.

Agneta Süsterich pointed to a closed door on the other side of the hall.

'That's where he worked,' she said. 'It's locked.'

'Do you have the key?'

'Master kept it,' she replied.

'But surely you cleaned the room for Herr Tifferch?'

'He cleans it hisself. Herr Tifferch let no one in, except when he was here. Customers, an' that. Go on, break it down,' she challenged. 'You're the police, ain't you?'

Koch stepped forward with his clasp-knife. 'Shall I try my luck, sir?'

I nodded and the sergeant dropped on one knee, thrusting the blade into the ancient lock. He prodded away and twisted, while the maid stood watching him, as if he were a thief, shaking her head with the disgust she seemed to reserve for the world at large. With a sudden crack, the door swung back on its hinges.

'You have a talent for the work, Koch!' I exclaimed.

'I just hope he can close it again,' the maid muttered, as if Herr Tifferch might come back and berate her for the ruined lock.

Larger than the sitting room we had left, there was only one desk in the centre of the room. Two straight-backed chairs were set out in front of it. The notary kept no clerk, the maid reported, but handled all his business for himself. Glass-fronted bookcases lining the walls held tight scrolls of documents bound up with ribbons of diverse colours. Laid out in alphabetical order, they gave an impression of industriousness.

'Mistress needs a-changing,' the maid announced from the doorway, gazing into the office as if it were a forbidden land. She disappeared without waiting for permission, and shortly after, we heard her shouting in the room across the hall. In answer, the lady of the house began to scream. The high-pitched keening went on for quite some time.

'Herr Tifferch's situation was not a comfortable one,' Koch observed.

'Light some candles, Koch,' I said. 'I hope to know a great deal more about his life before we've done.'

For the next two hours, we sifted through the dusty documents in that room, rolling them up again and putting away what was useless or irrelevant. Some were thirty years old, the paper yellow and brittle with age, legal transactions of every imaginable sort: marriage contracts, bills of purchase, receipts of sale and lading, inheritances resolved and claims disputed. Anything in those papers might have been important, I suppose, but nothing came to light that could be directly linked with the lawyer's death, no indication that might serve to connect his murder with any of the other recent killings.

The last case on which Tifferch had been working was laid out neatly on his desk. Arnolph von Rooysters, a rich burgher, had left all his moveable property to his butler, a man named Ludwig Frontissen. Apparently, the relatives had tried to reverse this decision, but Tifferch had a sworn testament in the hand of the dead man in favour of the servant which settled the argument. I had sat myself down at Tifferch's desk to read these papers; Koch was busy on the other side of the room with the last of the scrolls.

'Herr Stiffeniis,' Koch said, 'there's a cupboard here that's locked.'

Having noticed a large bunch of keys in one of the desk-drawers, I took them out and tossed them across to him. 'See if one of those will fit,' I said.

I heard him jangling the keys uselessly against the lock while I continued reading a sequence of letters and declarations relating to the quarrel between von Rooysters' relatives and the butler. The descendants of the deceased had appealed to a certain Minister in Berlin who had written to Tifferch to know exactly how things stood in the case. Tifferch maintained that the law was undeniably on the side of the fortunate butler. Minister Aschenbrenner, who was a distant relative of the von Rooysters, agreed with Tifferch, but proposed a compromise to put an end to the squabble. Accordingly, Tifferch had offered the family members one half of the inheritance, which, it seemed, the butler was well disposed to share with them. The dates on some of these documents went back a couple of years, and Tifferch had most recently concluded the dispute to the advantage and the satisfaction of all parties. There was absolutely nothing that might suggest a possible reason for his murder.

'It's no good, sir,' Koch's voice broke in upon my thoughts. 'None of the keys fits.'

'Well, then,' I replied, 'do as the housemaid suggests.'

'Sir?'

'Force the lock, Sergeant. If he hid the key, he probably kept money and valuables in there.'

With a nod Koch set to work on the lock. Some minutes later, he let out a grunt of triumphant satisfaction. Then, silence followed.

'Well, Koch?' I asked impatiently, dragging myself away from the paper I was reading. 'What have you found?'

'You'd better come and see for yourself, sir,' he replied.

I clapped my hands to remove the dust, then joined him on the far side of the room. Koch had placed a candle on one of the chairs to light the cupboard, which was deep and dark. On the top shelf stood a grinning porcelain bust of Napoleon Bonaparte. I stretched out my hand to pick the statue up, and almost dropped it as my fingers closed upon the base. The pressure of my thumb had triggered a hair-spring: the Emperor's hat flipped up and two satanic horns popped out of the flat hair on his head.

'What a remarkable toy!' I exclaimed with a laugh. 'What else is there?'

On the shelf below was a stack of pamphlets and broadsheets, which Koch and I examined with mounting curiosity. They were ribald and even erotic in their contents, and referred in the most scabrous terms to the Emperor of France. If the anonymous cartoonists were to be believed, Bonaparte showed a marked sexual preference for the animal world. Donkeys he particularly favoured, though in one instance, he was portrayed in amorous coupling with a female elephant. As Koch was quick to point out, the satirical comments beneath these drawings were in the German language, and the obscenities appeared to have been printed on a hand-press using wooden print-blocks, a system long out of commercial fashion.

'I wonder where he bought these,' I said, glancing through the pages.

'Do you think he might belong to a political group, sir?' Koch asked.

'A scurrilous circulating library, more like! You could be right, though. It seems as if Herr Tifferch led a busy secret life.'

Were these seditious materials, I asked myself, the cause of his domestic problems? Had his wife chanced upon those disgusting images, the shock proving too great for her health to withstand? The sudden knowledge that one's apparently respectable husband was, instead, a radical pervert might quite easily transmute a woman of over-strong religious ideals into a living statue.

A living statue . . .

My mother's image rose to my mind once more. Sweat broke out on my forehead, and a nervous tic in my throat brought on a coughing fit.

'It is dusty in here, isn't it, sir?' Koch responded diligently. 'Would you like me to get you a glass of water?'

'That won't be necessary,' I replied, and really it was not. The maternal ghost with her desolate air of constant accusation had fled at the sound of his voice.

'Do we need to go through all of these pamphlets, Herr Procurator?' Koch asked, his dislike for the task quite evident.

'I am afraid we must, Koch,' I said. 'We cannot afford to leave any avenue unexplored.'

'I see, sir,' Koch replied, and made haste to do what he had so hastily wished to abandon not a moment before.

Still, I tried to make it easier for him. We examined the leaflets front and back, looking for names. None was found, of course, except for *noms-de-plume* of an evidently fantastical and franco-phobic origin: *Cul de Monsieur*, *Seigneur Duc de Porc*, *Milord*

Mont de Merde, and so on. We returned this material to its shelf, then moved on down the cupboard. A large, brown velvet box on the next shelf was closed by a small padlock. Applying himself to the key-ring again, and finding no help there, Koch removed the padlock with his knife on my orders. The box opened up to reveal a domestic tableau in wax and wood: Bonaparte and his paramour, Josephine Beauharnais. The Emperor was standing, the Empress sitting on a stool, and they were facing one another. There was an odd expression on the woman's pretty face, her mouth open, her eyes gaping wide, as if she were in a state of shock or terror. At the jerk of a rod on the base of the model, Napoleon's trousers slid down around his ankles, his third leg rose stiffly into the air – it was as long as the other two – and hovered close to the mouth of the lady. A lever on the other side of the automaton caused the woman's head to lean forward and do perverse and beastly things that no self-respecting French Empress ought to do in public.

'A most . . . unusual sense of humour,' Koch murmured uncertainly.

Without looking at his face, I knew that he was blushing.

Could Herr Tifferch have been murdered by Napoleonic sympathisers in Königsberg? A man might keep such toys a secret from his wife and maid, but surely he would share them with his friends. And friends in times as dangerous as ours need to be handled with care. Since the revolution in France, not every man in Prussia is as patriotic as he ought to be.

'How strong are sympathies for France in the city, Sergeant?'

Koch stroked his chin before he answered. 'Prussia has been isolated by the political events of the past few months, sir. We have so few allies, and Bonaparte intends that we shall have none. Then, he will attack. But he *does* have followers in Königsberg. He has supporters all over Europe . . .' He stopped, and looked at me. 'But do you really think that some fanatic killed Herr Tifferch for his ribald attitude towards the French Emperor, sir? What about those scars on his body? How do they fit in?'

'I don't know,' I said with a sigh. 'I can't see any link. Rhunken's reports make no mention of whip marks on the other bodies, but he seemed to believe that the connection between the murders was political. He suspected that there was a conspiracy of some sort behind all of these deaths, although he could not say what *sort* of plot it was. This,' I said, indicating the collection of items in the cupboard, 'appears to lead us in the same general direction.'

Just then, a ray of sunlight entered the room. Like a beam piercing the dark interior of a *camera obscura*, the light settled for an instant on a rolled-up bundle of dark purple silk pushed to the back of the bottom shelf. Uncertain what Herr Tifferch's next posthumous trick might be, I retrieved the bundle carefully and held it up in both hands for Koch to see. It was as long and thick as a spicy Danish dried sausage.

Setting this object down on the top of the notary's desk, I carefully rolled it open. Koch and I looked at the contents in silent disbelief for some moments.

'This may explain the pained expression on Tifferch's face when he came down to breakfast,' I said.

'I've never seen such a thing,' said Koch in a hushed voice.

I took up the dark leather stick, and shook it in the air. Three long tails with knotted tips waved free in a sinister cascade. 'At least we know what made those lacerations on Tifferch's body, Koch. Old scars, new wounds . . .'

Koch struggled to find his voice. 'Do you think he did it to *himself*, sir?'

'There can be little doubt,' I said. 'But whether to punish himself for his sins, or as a source of sexual pleasure, we cannot even begin to guess. Perhaps both?'

'That such a thing could exist in Königsberg!' It was clear from the expression of shock on Koch's plain, honest face that he found himself in a new and disturbing dimension. 'In France they do such things, I've heard. In Paris. But here in Prussia?'

'Put everything back where you found it,' I said quietly, watching as he returned each object to its allotted place in the cupboard. He handled them as if they might corrode his fingertips, closing the door again with gusto.

As we took our leave, Agneta Süsterich was preparing to feed her mistress. Frau Tifferch was seated in a stiff-backed chair without her veil, a white linen cloth spread protectively over her finery. Her round face was puffy, white, expressionless, her pale blue eyes two empty blanks fixed on the bowl of gruel on the table before her.

'I hope you've found what you need to catch Herr Tifferch's murderer,' the maid huffed sharply over her shoulder, the only note of sympathy she had offered for her master since we stepped into the house. 'You know where the front door is. Her pap's the only blessed thing the lady's interested in. She won't be kept a-waiting.'

Outside in the street I felt a grey blanket of depression fall upon my spirits. What sort of life would Frau Tifferch lead without her husband? What future did she have, a helpless woman in the company of a bitter maid in an empty house? Then again, I thought, what was Agneta Süsterich's lot? A Pietist forced to live in a Catholic shrine she hated, she was bound to discover the secrets of her master's cupboard sooner or later. Would the stark revelation make her less caring of her mistress, more resentful of her sinful master? Would she continue to nurse Frau Tifferch? And if she did not, who would? The person, or persons, who had killed Jeronimus Tifferch had brought distress into that household. How much havoc had been caused, and how much more had been swept away forever, with the deaths of Jan Konnen, Paula-Anne Brunner and Johann Gottfried Haase? I knew from my own personal experience the immense distress that a single thoughtless action could unleash on the lives of the people close to a family tragedy.

'Sir?'

I looked up, and took stock of my surroundings. The winter sun shone weakly above the almost-touching roofs in a narrow strip of blue sky. Packed ice flashed as blue as steel on the cobblestones. The cold wind cut deeper than a sharp knife as it whistled in from the sea.

'What are your conclusions, Herr Stiffeniis?' Koch asked cautiously as we made our way to the end of the street.

'We have found a whip in a cupboard,' I said. 'But we still do not know exactly how or why Herr Tifferch died. And neither have we been able to find any connection between him and the others who were murdered. I hardly have room in my head for conclusions.'

I lapsed into a dejected silence as we emerged from the street into a small snow-filled square with a huddle of leafless trees in the centre. I had hoped to discover a great deal more.

'Do you think that a war with France is inevitable, sir?' Koch asked suddenly.

'I certainly hope not,' I returned promptly, 'but there isn't much we can do about it. Russia hovering on our right flank; France on the other, and all this idle chatter about Bonaparte! Who's for him, who's against him. And whether King Frederick Wilhelm can keep Prussia out of it. And will the Frenchman let him? The argument never seems to end. In such a climate of mounting suspicion and intrigue, these murders aren't helping things one little bit.'

General Katowice had warned me that whether the country went to war, or not, might depend on how I managed the criminal investigation. The memory of his alarm set my head spinning once again. Nervously, I unhooked my fob-watch and glanced at the face. It was almost ten to twelve.

'Is Klopstrasse far from here?' I asked briskly.

I had no wish to be late. Herr Jachmann was a stickler for watching the clock. He was very like his oldest and dearest friend in that respect.

'It's just across the square, sir.'

'Good!' I exclaimed.

Before Koch could say a word, I struck out across the snow-filled square.

Chapter 10

The house in Klopstrasse stood out from its brightly coloured neighbours like a rotten tooth. The once-green paint was peeling and grey. A dead ivy vine grasped the facade like a skeletal hand intent on throttling the life out of the building. A rusty balcony running the length of the upper floor seemed likely to collapse with the next winter storm. The shutters, half-closed and broken, hung sadly from their hinges. It was not a pretty sight. Herr Reinhold Jachmann's days of gracious and fashionable living seemed to be long past.

'Shall I go in with you, sir?' Koch asked.

'No, Sergeant,' I said quickly. I wanted no witness to the conversation I was about to have. 'Go to the Court House, and see about that list of aliens I mentioned. Send the gendarmes out to check it.'

Koch bowed stiffly. Was it my impression, or did a look of disappointment flash across his face? I watched him march away with all the haste that the fresh-fallen snow would permit, then I turned towards the house. The wrought-iron gate protested loudly when I pushed to open it. A loud shriek gave way to a long painful groan as I forced back rusty hinges which had not tasted whale-oil in many a month. Apart from the crusted footprints that Koch himself had left there earlier that morning as he came to deliver my message, no other impression had been made in the snow. No visitor or tradesman had called before or since.

I let the iron knocker fall against the door, and the sound seemed to echo and rebound on the icy air as if the house and garden were enclosed within a vacuum. A lone blackbird flew away, twittering angrily. That sudden noise shattered the silence which reigned supreme in the garden. The motionless shrubs and bushes hidden beneath the deep coverlet of snow might have been forgotten tombstones in an abandoned graveyard. I was looking around forlornly as the door opened silently at my back.

'You have come then, Stiffeniis.'

I recognised the deep, resonating boom of Reinhold Jachmann's voice, though I did not recognise the man as I turned to face him. A cold, unearthly winter had blown over him, too. His thin hair was as white as bleached bed linen, his eyebrows large snowdrifts above piercing, coal-black eyes. His stiff seriousness alarmed me. I remembered a warm friendly man during our first and only meeting seven years before, but the suspicious stranger glaring down at me from the top of the steps was the very opposite. For one moment, I thought he would refuse to allow me to enter his house. We stared at each other in silence.

'This way,' he said at last, and led me through the hall and into a sparsely furnished sitting room on the ground floor. Pointing to a sofa before a cast-iron fireplace where a single log smoked and smouldered, he asked me to be seated. It was more an order than an invitation. He watched me sit without a word, then he walked to the window and looked out over the garden.

'What brings you here?' he enquired without turning around.

'A matter of the greatest urgency, Herr Jachmann,' I replied. 'A Royal commission.'

'So you mentioned in your note,' he said. 'Can I know its nature?'

I had hoped he would not need to ask.

'I have been appointed to investigate the recent spate of murders in the town,' I said quietly.

With a sudden movement, he turned to look at me, some of his former energy returning. 'You, Stiffeniis? Investigating murder?'

He appeared to be stunned by what I had just told him. 'I thought that Procurator Rhunken was in charge of the case?' he said.

'He died, Herr Jachmann.'

He shook his head and looked confused. 'I have heard nothing of his death, nor of his burial.'

'It happened just yesterday evening,' I explained. 'Herr Rhunken was buried immediately. There was no funeral. It was his final wish.'

'Gracious me! What has become of Königsberg?' he whispered, turning again to the window. He remained there for quite some time, peering out at the snow.

'I warned you, I *told* you, never to come here again,' he growled over his shoulder, his face livid with anger, as if I had brought these new disasters along with me from Lotingen.

Another brooding silence followed his outburst.

'I was very surprised to be assigned the case,' I ventured to say at last. 'I accepted the commission with trepidation, sir. For the sake of . . .'

'Have you seen him yet?' Jachmann interrupted gruffly, his eyes still fixed on the garden and the street.

'Oh no, sir,' I replied. 'I would never dream of doing so without consulting you.' I paused for a moment, then blurted out, 'Your letter came as a great shock to me, Herr Jachmann. I have not gone back on my word, sir. His peace of mind is as precious to me as it is to yourself. I've not forgotten your warning.'

He turned to face me. 'But you intend to visit him now, do you not?' His voice had risen again, the blood rushed to his cheeks, and he stared at me with evident distaste.

I shifted uncomfortably in my seat. 'Not if I can help it,' I said, 'though there is the possibility that we might meet by accident. I thought I ought to warn you, sir. That is why I am here.' I stopped for some moments, but then curiosity got the better of me. 'How is he, sir?' I dared to ask.

'He is well enough,' Jachmann returned brusquely. 'His valet reports to me on a regular weekly basis.'

'His servant?' Now it was my turn to be surprised.

'His servant,' he confirmed sharply without adding anything more.

'But you are his closest friend, Herr Jachmann . . .'

'I *was* his closest friend,' he interrupted, his voice cracked, broken. 'I am still his domestic administrator, but I have not seen him in the past twelve months, or more. He has become secretive, almost a recluse. I go to his house no longer. All essential communication passes through his valet.'

'How can this be, sir?'

He waved his hand dismissively. 'There was no quarrel, no argument, if that is what you mean. The professor has no time for old friends. His door is closed to all and sundry. His servant is instructed to say that he is busy, and does not wish to be disturbed. Work and study, as you know, have always been the mainsprings of his existence.'

He twirled away and paced up and down the room in silence, then came to rest once more in front of the sofa. He bent close, the deep lines of age in his long face etching themselves even more sharply with the effort to control his emotions or his temper.

'Why would any responsible person want *you* to conduct this investigation, Stiffeniis?' he enquired.

I know what I would have liked to reply. That the King had recognised my qualities, knowing that I would succeed where all other investigators, including Procurator Rhunken, had failed. But I was obliged to concede the truth.

'I do not know, Herr Jachmann.'

'I expected an angry reply to that harsh letter of mine,' he said suddenly. 'I knew that you would return to Königsberg unless I managed to stop you. Had you answered telling me to mind my own affairs, or asking me to explain the motives that obliged me to write to you in such a manner, I would not have been in the least surprised. But when your answer came, stating meekly that you would comply with my wishes, I was more than surprised, I can tell you. I was alarmed.'

'I took you at your word,' I began to say, but he was not listening.

'You knew *why* I did not wish to see you ever again,' he continued angrily. He paused, drew a deep breath, then added: 'I have tried many a time to fathom what passed between you both that day in the fog.'

I stared into his accusing eyes and held my breath, recalling the day seven years before when I had been privileged to speak in private with the most famous man in Königsberg, Jachmann's friend and colleague at the University, Professor of Philosophy, Immanuel Kant.

'You ordered me to avoid the city for the good of Professor Kant,' I whispered. 'I had no idea why, but I saw no reason to question your integrity. You were his dearest friend. You knew what was good or bad for him, and . . .'

'*You* were bad for him!' His white face suddenly blazed with resentment. 'That is the point. Don't you see? Why should there have been any need for me to forbid you to see Kant? What other reason could there be to make me fear for the mental stability of the most rational man on Earth?'

'You are unjust, sir,' I protested, but Jachmann rode over me.

'I realised that something was amiss whenever your name was mentioned afterwards,' he continued with great intensity. 'It had such a marked effect on him. There was agitation in his manner, wild distraction in his eyes. It was out of character, totally unlike him. This madness began the day that he invited you to lunch. In itself, *that* was an event without precedent.'

'Why do you say so, sir?' I asked.

'He had never invited a stranger to his home before. Not once!' He looked at me inquisitively. 'Something in you triggered his interest. Something that you had done, or something that you had said to him.'

'But you know why he invited me,' I replied with passion. 'I had just come back from Paris, Professor Kant was interested in what I had seen there.'

Jachmann nodded grimly.

'I recall your speech about what you saw the day the Jacobins executed their legitimate ruler . . .'

I closed my eyes to block out the memory. Would the image of that moment never leave me in peace? How long would it haunt me? The sight of human blood on the ground. The stench of it in the air.

' . . . Paris, January 2nd, 1793,' Herr Jachmann intoned pedantically.

The scene flashed before my mind's eye. The bubbling gaiety of the crowd. The condemned man in his soiled finery proudly climbing the steps to the block. The oiled blue triangle of steel shimmering in the early morning light. The sound of grating metal as the blade fell. Then, blood! Oceans of crimson blood, spurting out of that severed neck like water from one of the ornamental fountains that the King had built for himself at Versailles, drenching the faces of the onlookers. Falling like rain on my own face, on my mouth and my tongue . . .

'They murdered the King that day.'

A king? A man had been butchered before my eyes. A flick of a lever, and a shadow had been cast upon my soul. A hidden part of myself had risen up with the mob and taken possession of my confused mind.

'Kant had met others who had been in France,' Herr Jachmann continued. 'Others who were involved in those tragic events. He was not upset by what they had to say. But you, Stiffeniis! *You* brought a malignant plague to his house that day.'

He stared fixedly at me.

'Whatever happened between the two of you, Stiffeniis, it changed him. It changed him totally. And it all began with that conversation about the effect of electrical storms on human behaviour.'

'It was not *I* who raised the subject,' I spluttered in my own defence. '*You* started it, sir.'

'But it was you,' Jachmann replied, his finger pointing accusingly, '*you*, Stiffeniis, who led the discussion in such an unsavoury direction. You froze the blood in my veins!'

He turned his gaze to the fire. 'How many times have I regretted that odious conversation! Kant was studying the effects of electricity on the nervous system in that period, he was interested in little else. And the night before, there had been a terrible storm.'

Every single detail was still vivid in my mind.

'Looking out of your window,' I murmured, 'you found a stranger in your garden. Careless of the lashing rain, the thunder and lightning, he was staring up at the sky in a trance. You'd been disconcerted by his behaviour, and you asked Kant if static electricity might provide an explanation for it.'

'And he replied by saying it was not the electrical discharge, it was the unbounded energy of Nature which had fascinated the man,' Jachmann went on. 'The destructive power of the elements had mesmerised him. Kant referred to the *incantamento horribilis*. Human Kind, he said, is fatally attracted by Sublime Terror.'

He sat down heavily in an armchair, his forehead couched in his hand. 'I was shocked. Unable to believe my ears. Immanuel Kant? The Father of Rationality celebrating the powers of the Unknown? The dark side of the human soul?'

'I remember, sir. You objected that such power belongs to God alone. That Man is bound by moral ties which he should never question . . .'

'Then *you* spoke up,' Jachmann interposed, still shading his eyes, avoiding my sight, 'and suddenly the pleasant young student who had won our respect with his good manners and his sound reasoning appeared in a different light.'

'I just said . . .'

He held up his hand for silence. 'Your words are indelibly printed on my memory. "There is one human experience which may be equal to the unbridled power of Nature," you said. "The most diabolical of all. Cold-blooded murder. Murder without a motive."'

Jachmann stared at me, his eyes narrowed and resentful. I felt as if my body had been stripped away, my soul exposed to view.

'When Professor Kant shifted the discussion elsewhere,' he went on, 'I felt grateful to him. But the ghost that you evoked that day had not been laid to rest. He insisted on taking a turn around the Castle Walk alone with you, though he had not been out of doors all winter, except to go to the university. The fog was dreadful, you remember. But I knew that he would wish to talk with you again.'

'You are curious to know if we talked further of the same subject. Are you not?' I asked, on the defensive.

'You are wrong, Stiffeniis,' he replied. 'Totally wrong! I do not wish to know what was said. But let me tell you what happened as a consequence. When Kant returned to the house, I was waiting for him. Long before I saw him through the fog, I heard his footsteps. And what I heard was enough to convince me that something was wrong. Very wrong. Kant was running. Running! But from whom?

From what? I rushed out to meet him, and the expression on his face was frightful to behold. Rather, I was frightened by what I saw. His eyes sparkled with nervous energy. I thought he had taken a fever. I expressed my concern, but he announced that he had work to do which could not wait an instant. In short, he sent me about my business! And the very next day, he told me that he had begun to compose a new philosophical treatise.'

I frowned. 'I have not heard of any new book,' I said.

Jachmann shook his head dismissively. 'It has not been published. That is why you've never heard of it. No one has read a single line. Indeed, I am inclined to believe that the work does not exist. At that time, he was under great mental strain. Some younger philosophers accused him of ignoring the deeper resources of the soul. Emotion, they suggested, was more powerful than Logic, and Kant was ruined by the bitter controversy. His classes were empty in the last years of his tenure. The young did not want to pay to listen to him.'

'So I heard,' I said.

'It was very sad. He was all but forgotten. "Old-fashioned" is the new-fangled term, I believe. Things had got to such a state that one of his former protégés, a bright young fellow named Fichte – you've heard of him, I'm sure – described Kant as the "philosopher of spiritual idleness" in a book which sold very well throughout Europe.'

'That must have been humiliating.'

'Remember his legendary timekeeping?' Jachmann reminisced. He seemed calmer as he recalled the distant past. 'How the people in Königsberg used to set their clocks by Kant's coming and going? Well, the new generation of students thought it such a clever joke to interrupt his lessons, coming in one after another, watch in hand, saying, "Late, sir? Me, sir? Your timepiece must have stopped, sir." It drove Kant to a premature retirement.'

'I can imagine his distress.'

'I doubt it!' Jachmann snapped. He was rambling now with the frantic energy of an old man for a lost cause. 'But the person who was most distressed was Martin Lampe.'

'His valet?' I asked in surprise.

'I had to dismiss him. After thirty years of faithful service! He'd been the perfect servant. Mental order and discipline may produce fine thoughts, but they do not make for the efficient running of a household. Kant has trouble putting on his own stockings! Lampe looked after him, while the master concentrated on his books.'

'So why did you send him away?'

'For Kant's own good, Stiffeniis!' He looked at me intently, as if searching for the correct tone of voice with which to say what followed. 'I no longer trusted Lampe. More to the point, I was afraid of him.'

'Afraid, sir? What do you mean?'

'Strange ideas had found their way into Lampe's mind,' Herr Jachmann went on. 'He had begun to behave as if he were Professor Kant. Why, he told me once that there would be *no* Kantian philosophy if not for him! The new book on which Kant was working, he claimed, was his, not his master's. When the students started deserting Kant's lessons, it was Lampe who had the most violent reactions. He became quite vehement, shouting, saying that Kant must show the world what he could do.'

'He had to go,' I agreed. 'But who is looking after the Professor now?'

Jachmann cleared his throat noisily. 'A young man named Johannes Odum manages the house and he seems to be doing it well enough.'

He fell silent. Indeed, there seemed to be little left to say, and I stood up, reaching for my hat, preparing to take my leave, having said what I had come to say.

'Why in the name of heaven did you choose the law of all subjects?' he asked me quietly.

I paused before replying. I ought to have been insulted, I suppose, but there was a measure of satisfaction in what I was about to tell him. 'That day I came to Königsberg, Professor Kant himself advised me to become a magistrate.'

'Did he really?' Jachmann frowned, evidently puzzled. 'Given the wild opinions you expressed, I can only wonder at the soundness of his judgement!'

'It was during our walk around the Fortress after lunch,' I hurried on, ignoring the sarcastic jibe.

Herr Jachmann shook his head sadly. 'That walk! Everything seems to have started out there in the . . .'

There was a sharp rap at the door, and a man in dowdy brown serving-livery poked his head inside without stepping into the room.

'That person's here again, sir,' he announced, surprise writ large on his face, as if his master were unused to receiving visitors, and my own visit had been more than enough for one morning. 'To speak with Procurator Stiffeniis, he says.'

Koch was waiting out in the hallway, his face ash-white, his expression drawn and tense. 'I'm sorry to disturb you, sir, but it's a question of necessity.'

'What is it?'

'The boy at the inn, sir.'

'Morik?' I said sharply. 'What about him?'

'He's been found, sir.'

I glared at him for a moment. 'I am glad of that, Sergeant, but I do not see the urgency . . .'

'I'm sorry, sir,' Koch interrupted forcefully. 'Perhaps I didn't make myself clear. The boy is dead, sir. Foul play's suspected.'

Chapter 11

Wild, angry shouts exploded suddenly all around us.

'The King! Where's the King?'

'Napoleon will slay us, no one seems to care!'

'Down with the King! To the scaffold! *Vive la revolution!*'

Our coach rumbled onto the long wooden bridge that spanned the River Pregel, scattering a furious crowd of cat-calling men and screeching women who jostled towards the scene of the crime. In that barrage of noise and derision it was impossible to isolate the individuals who were fomenting the protest. Perhaps there were no leaders in that rabble. I had the unpleasant impression that the coach was a fragile boat forced to run between converging reefs, which threatened to sink us at any moment.

'They blame the authorities for what is happening,' I said, as we trundled on and left the raving mob behind us.

'Their fears feed on each new corpse,' Koch replied. 'It's just as General Katowice feared, sir. Rumour, unruly gatherings, riots. These murders will lead to trouble. Rebellions have a way of spreading.'

'Terror is what they aim at,' I said, feeling the enormous burden of the delicate task with which I had been entrusted. 'But what were you saying before we were interrupted?'

'About the eel-fisherman, sir. He found the corpse while setting his traps. The troops brought him to the Court House, then they called me. I spoke to him, but he had nothing much to add, beyond the macabre discovery. If you wish to interrogate him, sir, I made a note of his name and address . . .'

'We'll see him later, Koch. How far is The Baltic Whaler from here?'

'Half a mile, sir. No more.'

I thought back to what Morik had told me the previous night, and to the scene that I had witnessed later from my bedroom window. What further proof did I need that the boy and all the others had been murdered by terrorist infiltrators?

'Were the landlord and his wife taken into custody?'

'They were, sir.'

'As soon as we've seen the body,' I said, 'I will interrogate them. Then, perhaps, I'll be in a better position to report my findings to General Katowice.'

The coach slewed and skidded suddenly, rolling and jerking to an uncertain stop at an angle to the bridge-rail.

'Get back there! Go on, get on with you!' Soldiers were blocking the way, their muskets pointed in a menacing fashion at our driver. Sergeant Koch jumped down and some minutes later the coach was allowed to pass through the road-block on my authority. For once in my life, I must admit, I felt reassured by the bullying behaviour of the troops.

Having crossed the bridge and turned to the left along the far bank, the vehicle pulled up a hundred yards further on beside a long, slippery flight of slime-covered stone stairs, by means of which we reached the rutted, muddy bank of the river. It was a vile, salt-smelling sort of place. The river was low, the weeds dank and black, flattened by the force of the retreating tidal waters. We hurried on beside the stream to where a knot of soldiers stood braced in a tight circle, facing outwards, firearms at the ready. They waved us away with bayonets fixed to the muzzles of their guns.

'I am the new Procurator. Make sure that no one else approaches,' I ordered sharply, glancing across the river as the troops fell back. The far bank was packed with idle onlookers. Half the town had gathered there, as if to see some gruesome public spectacle or welcome a travelling circus. With a feeling of disgust for Mankind in my heart, I turned to my task, but I pulled up suddenly. A figure was down on his knees in the mud, his trademark wig glistening with damp, the corpse of Morik visible only as a shapeless, twisted heap of mud-stained clothes and pale flesh beneath him. Like a wild beast poised to feast on fresh blood and warm flesh, Doctor Vigilantius was sniffing and slobbering over the body.

'In the name of Heaven!' I cried.

Vigilantius did not look up. The blasphemous ritual continued unchecked.

'This is an outrage!' I erupted. 'Who called him here?'

'I did, Stiffeniis.'

The voice at my back was feeble, but I recognised it even before I turned.

'*I* sent for Doctor Vigilantius.'

A three-cornered hat sat low on Immanuel Kant's head, his face almost hidden beneath it. He wore no wig. A fine mesh of silvery-white hair graced his deformed left shoulder. Wrapped up against the weather in a shimmering, waterproof cloak of dark brown material, he held on tightly to the arm of a young man so tall, robust and protective that they might have been a father and his son, age reversing the roles that Nature had assigned them.

His unexpected arrival there on the banks of the river robbed me of the power of speech. Of course, I realised, it was inevitable that I would meet him sooner or later in Königsberg. But not in that place, nor in such doleful circumstances. Who had told him of the finding of the body of Morik? Had Jachmann informed him of my presence in the city, and of the reason for my being there? Herr Jachmann had warned me of the changes advancing age had inflicted on the philosopher, but I could only compare what I saw with what I recalled as we parted that afternoon seven years before, and Kant made his way home alone, limping painfully as the swirling fog swallowed him up. He did not seem a day older.

'My dear Hanno, how happy I am to see you!' he said warmly.

My first impulse was to take his hand and press it to my lips, but natural reserve stopped me. 'I did not expect you, sir,' I said, attempting to hide my confusion and embarrassment.

'I expected nothing less of you,' he returned with a welcoming smile. 'You made the acquaintance of Doctor Vigilantius last night, did you not?'

He did not wait for me to reply, but shuffled forward, still clutching the arm of his servant, and cast his eyes on the horrid spectacle. 'He has not wholly finished his examination, I see.'

Vigilantius was on his knees beside the dead boy, grunting like a pig over a mountain of offal. At the sound of his name he looked up quickly, acknowledged Kant with no more than a nod, then returned to his business. The scene was vile, nauseating, revolting, but Professor Kant did not appear to be in the least disturbed by what he saw.

'I hope the doctor will be able to tell us something useful,' he confided quietly, looking over his shoulder at me. His passionate concern spoke all the louder for a lack of violent animation. The keen intelligence shining from his eyes seemed to suggest that he had lost none of his renowned intellectual powers. 'You are wondering what he is doing here, are you not?'

Kant remained silent, waiting for me to reply.

'He is a follower of Swedenborg,' I said, carefully measuring my criticism. 'He claims to speak with the dead, sir. You condemned his master as a fake and a cozener.'

'Oh, that!' Kant returned with a tinkling laugh. '*Dreams of a Spirit Seer* is the only book of mine for which I have ever apologised. Do you disapprove of my having called on Swedenborg's spiritual heir in my search for the murderer?'

'*Your* search, sir? Indeed, I am puzzled,' I admitted.

'Were you not impressed by what he had to show you at the Fortress?' he asked, a thin smile tracing itself on his pale lips.

I hardly knew how to respond. 'The séance, sir?'

Kant frowned. 'Séance? Is that all you saw last night?'

'What else should I call it, sir? A man asking questions of a dead body, the corpse supposedly speaking back. I left Vigilantius knowing nothing that my own eyes did not tell me when I examined the body.'

'Ah!' Kant exclaimed with a smile. 'You ran out of patience and did not stay until the end. I should have foreseen that possibility,' he murmured. Then he looked at me attentively. 'So, you *are* surprised to see Vigilantius here, but you are *not* surprised to have been nominated in the place of Rhunken. Am I correct?'

His open irony regarding my appointment struck me like a slap in the face.

'It seems that I have you to thank for the honour, sir,' I began, but a louder voice than mine cut in.

'This death is not like the others, Herr Professor.'

Vigilantius was towering over Morik's body. 'This is the work of another killer,' he said.

'Another killer?' I repeated, appealing to Professor Kant. 'In God's name, sir, what is he talking about?'

Kant ignored me. Turning to Vigilantius, he said: 'Explain yourself.'

The doctor smiled triumphantly in my direction before he spoke. 'This corpse does not confirm what we know from the other bodies, Herr Professor. The scent here is . . . entirely different. The energy with which the soul left this body is distinct from what I have divined in other instances. They were taken unawares; this boy was not. He realised what was about to happen. He saw the blow before it fell, and he was terrified.'

Kant was silent, absorbed in his own thoughts.

'I see,' he said at last. 'And does this corpse tell you anything more?'

I was lost for words. What devilry could induce him to speak in such a deferential manner to an infamous necromancer? Kant had formulated a code of social ethics and rational analysis which had dragged Mankind out of the Dark and into the Light. And was he now inviting a smooth-tongued quack to reveal what a dead body had told him during a vulgar spirit-raising?

'Professor Kant!' I burst out, unable to contain myself. 'Herr Tifferch's corpse revealed what was obvious to any man with two eyes in his head. His back was covered with wounds, old and new . . .'

'I told you how he was murdered,' Doctor Vigilantius sneered. 'He did not die of those wounds. You would have had the proof if you had had the courtesy to wait last night.'

Kant turned and fixed me with a stare.

'Indeed, Herr Procurator, what did you make of those wounds?' he queried, like a falcon that has spotted a limping hare.

'I know they did not kill him,' I muttered. 'They were self-inflicted.'

'Self-inflicted?' Kant interrupted me. 'What do you mean?'

'I searched his house first thing this morning,' I began, 'and there I found evidence of how he had procured those wounds . . .'

I stopped, embarrassed to speak to Kant about such things.

'Well?' he insisted.

'A goad was carefully hidden in a cupboard, sir,' I murmured. 'Herr Tifferch had quite an eccentric private life.'

'How interesting!' Kant exclaimed. 'Rip the mask from any man's life, and what do we find? A black heart behind a smiling face, the bent wood of Humanity. Do you think that this is the motive behind his murder?'

'Not at all, sir,' I replied. 'There is another element which may indicate a common factor in all of the other killings, too.'

I took a deep breath before continuing. Immanuel Kant was the person that I admired above all the intellectual authorities in the Enlightened world. His learned meditations upon the topsy-turvy broomstick that was Man had marked out the path of Rational analysis and Enlightened behaviour. He had summoned me to Königsberg to assist in solving a mystery, and I did not intend to disappoint him.

'Herr Tifferch had a secret hoard of anti-Napoleonic trash hidden away in a cupboard,' I announced. 'He may have been assassinated by the political enemies of the State. Procurator Rhunken held the same opinion. I've read his reports . . .'

'But *how* did he die?' Kant spat out the question like an angry adder. 'That is the question which interests us, Stiffeniis.'

'I . . . I do not know yet,' I admitted hesitantly. 'He might . . .'

Kant was no longer listening. Curtly, he turned to Vigilantius.

'Is there any trace of the claw on the child's body?' he asked.

I was stunned. Professor Kant had used the term employed by the woman who had found the body of Jan Konnen. *The Devil's claw.*

'No sign, sir. Not this time,' Vigilantius replied gravely.

'What are you talking of?' I cried in frustration, excluded from their conversation by the cryptic intimacy of this exchange. Had

Jachmann been right to express concern for Kant's mental health?

'No trace of *what*?'

'I'll show you later,' Kant replied with a flash of impatience. 'If there are two murderers, we don't need paranormal powers to see the problem that it poses for the authorities. Come, Stiffeniis, let us take a closer look at the physical evidence.'

Laying his slender hand on my arm, pulling me forward, we took a step towards the body. Vigilantius moved aside with a sweep of his cloak like an actor who has successfully recited his lines and I forced myself to look down. I did not see the dead boy from The Baltic Whaler. I saw another body lying there on the wet ground, the skull crushed, bone splinters white and stark against the mess of blood and brain, eyes staring at me through a glassy veil. I fought to cancel out the unwanted vision, struggling to concentrate all my attention on what was, in that moment, before my eyes.

'This is him,' I mumbled. 'Morik.'

Signs of terrible violence were written on his face, or what was left of it. The left side of his skull had been crushed like a fragile eggshell. Slivers of brain and spots of congealed blood were splattered on his hair, temple, forehead and cheeks. His left eye stared up at the cloudy heavens from the corner of his mouth, as if it had crawled there of its own accord like some hideous slug.

Kant might almost have read my mind.

'Does this sight disturb you?' he asked, looking intently at me, studying my face, rather than the disfigured face of the dead child on the ground. 'Of course, it must. Your brother suffered similar wounds to the cranium, I suppose?'

I swallowed hard. Kant's concern had quite unmanned me.

'It . . . the crushing . . . was on the other . . . the right lobe,' I managed to reply.

'Were you obliged to examine his body?' Kant asked, scrutinising me closely. 'I don't remember having heard of a criminal investigation afterwards.'

'No, sir,' I murmured. 'There was no investigation.'

He hesitated a fraction. 'Let's get on with the business, then.'

'It . . . This, I mean, was a fearful blow,' I said, struggling to direct my attention to the dreadful sight before me. 'Death must have been instantaneous.'

'And the boy saw it coming,' Kant added. 'His fists will be clenched, I'd wager. Move his clothes away, will you?'

Before I could react, Koch had dropped to his knees and pulled the sodden clothes away from the boy's hands to reveal the accuracy of Kant's intuition.

'Sergeant Koch is my assistant,' I explained quickly, having completely forgotten his presence just a few steps behind me. 'He used to work for Procurator Rhunken.'

'His name is not new to me,' Kant replied, eyeing Koch curiously. He drew closer and followed every movement, his hand still on my arm, the other gripping his silent manservant for support.

'Note the look on the boy's face, Stiffeniis,' he said, his voice quavering with emotion. 'Physiognomy teaches us much regarding that expression, does it not?'

I could only stare at the dead boy's face, unable to frame a single thought.

'Can't you see?' Vigilantius snapped. 'Everything is different here.'

'Note the position of the legs,' Professor Kant continued, ignoring both of us, completely absorbed in what he was doing. 'The others were kneeling when they were murdered. This boy was not. You saw the position of the body of Herr Tifferch last night. Now you have room for comparison. I instructed the soldiers to conserve his corpse under the snow for you and the doctor to examine.'

So, there it was. The answer to the question with which I had been plaguing Koch. Professor Kant had been behind it all. He had arranged and orchestrated every move that I had made since reaching Königsberg. He had sent me to see Herr Rhunken, who was not expecting me. Then, I had been directed to the horror chamber of Vigilantius. Kant had decided that I ought to lodge at The Baltic Whaler. The police had had no say in the matter. Nor had the King. Immanuel Kant knew more about those murders than any man in Königsberg.

'Let's see if Vigilantius is right,' he said. 'Turn the boy on his stomach, Herr Koch. If you would be so kind?'

Koch lay Morik gently face-down in the mud. The boy's hair and neck were caked with blood and mud. 'Bring water, Sergeant,' Kant urged, and Koch sped off towards the bridge, returning with a metal water bottle he had taken from one of the soldiers.

'Douse his head,' Kant instructed. 'Pull back the hair. Remove that mud.'

He directed Koch's attentions with the firmness he might have used to guide the hand of his laboratory assistant at the University. 'More water. Clean the neck. Yes, there, there!' Kant pointed with impatience.

As the blood and the dirt drained away, white flesh emerged. Kant leaned forward and stared intently at the bumpy vertebrae of the boy's neck. 'There is no wound here. No sign of it at all. The injury to the skull was done with a hammer, or a heavy object. It ought to have bled copiously, and yet I see no sign of blood here on the ground.'

'The cold might have staunched the bleeding,' I suggested.

'The temperature cannot explain the absence,' Kant snapped with a flash of irritation.

'What would you suggest then, sir?' I asked.

'He was not killed here. Nor by the person that we are seeking. The evidence is quite plain,' he replied. 'This boy was killed for a different motive, whatever it may have been.'

I was bewildered. Kant had reached the same conclusion as Vigilantius.

'But there *cannot* be two murderers in Königsberg!' I protested. 'Morik was killed at the inn. I saw him there. His body was left here to throw me off the trail. I have every good reason to believe that he knew something about the other murders. Why, I spoke to him last night!'

Kant's eyes sparkled with excitement. 'You spoke to the boy? Do you mean to tell me that you arrived at the inn and immediately won his confidence? Well, that is truly remarkable! I was right to choose you, and correct again in sending you to The Baltic Whaler.'

For a moment, I believed he was teasing me. Then, I thought, perhaps he *was* genuinely impressed. He had placed me there for no other purpose, after all. 'That tavern is a hotbed of spying and sedition,' I said. 'But you knew that already, sir, didn't you?'

Kant looked at me, and I'd swear there was a mischievous twinkle in his eye.

'Your arrival must have caused some tension,' he observed quietly.

The events of the previous evening at the inn flashed before me. The anger on Herr Totz's face, the suspicious behaviour of his wife, the boy's terror of them both. I told Kant everything that Morik had revealed about the foreigners staying there, and added what I had seen from my bedroom the night before.

'It's just as Procurator Rhunken suspected,' I said. 'Insurrection. Foreign agitators. What better motive could explain these murders?'

'I could postulate a hundred,' Kant replied immediately. 'One certainly comes to mind.'

He gazed at the River Pregel, as if the dark waters were an aid to concentrated thought.

'I beg your pardon, sir?' I asked timidly.

'The sublime pleasure of killing, Stiffeniis,' he replied slowly, carefully separating his words.

I was amazed. Had I heard him right?

'Can you be serious, sir?' Sergeant Koch burst out. 'Excuse me, Herr Stiffeniis,' he apologised, 'I did not mean to interrupt.'

'I appreciate your frankness, Herr Koch,' Kant replied. 'Go on, Sergeant. Say what you feel compelled to say.'

'Could any sane person kill for such a reason?' Koch demanded. He did not seem to be the least intimidated by the mighty reputation of Immanuel Kant. 'For pleasure, and nothing more?'

Kant studied him quizzically for a moment. 'Have you ever been to war, Sergeant?'

Koch blinked and shook his head.

'But you do have friends or acquaintances in the army?'

'Yes, sir, but . . .'

Kant raised his hand. 'Bear with me, Koch. If you were to object that killing an enemy on the field of battle is a question of duty, I would not dispute it. But there is an ambiguity in doing the deed which may be worthy of our consideration. I have met few soldiers who are ashamed of their murderous capacities, or reticent in claiming to have perpetrated the most exquisite savagery in the sacred name of duty. And not on the field of battle alone. Duelling is common among the officers in our army.' He nodded down at the corpse. 'A man who possesses these lethal skills may find untold pleasure in using them.'

'A soldier, sir? Is that your theory?'

Kant directed his attention to me, as if Koch had never opened his mouth.

'Imagine the power of life and death in the hands of this person, Stiffeniis! He chooses the victim. He chooses the time, and the place of the execution.' He counted off these circumstances on his thin white fingers. 'Only God has such unbridled power on this Earth. The act of killing may be a source of immense power, of gratification in itself, but that is not the end of it. Look over there,' he said, pointing across the river at the crowds lining the opposite bank. 'Look at the soldiers manning the bridge. Consider our presence here, the terror that moved the authorities to summon us. Whoever he is, whatever his motives may be, this person has unleashed Chaos in Königsberg. *He* commands us all!'

'Power, sir?' Koch insisted with a frown. The hypothesis seemed to alarm him more than any other possibility.

'A power which accepts no human limits, Sergeant Koch. A Deity. Or a Demon, if you like.'

A cold wind swept over the waters of the River Pregel. When Doctor Vigilantius spoke, his voice sounded as sharply as the first crack of the polar ice-cap in Spring.

'Professor Kant,' he said. 'I can do no more for you, sir. I have urgent business to attend to. If you need me again, you know how to contact me.'

'Your assistance has been of incalculable value in this affair, sir,' Kant replied with all the respect he might have employed if David Hume or Descartes had been present. 'Stiffeniis will make good use of your findings.'

With a final, dismissive glance in my direction, Augustus Vigilantius, that glowing meteor of the Swedenborgian universe, turned and walked away along the river bank, never to appear again in Königsberg while I was there, except in the columns of *Hartmanns Zeitung*. His 'urgent business' turned out to involve a conversation with a billy-goat, the animal having been possessed by the soul of the farmer who had once been its master.

Kant smiled warmly at me. 'I hope we'll have no further need of him,' he said. 'Now, regarding your conspiracy theory, Stiffeniis. You should verify it.'

I was taken back. 'I thought you did not share my opinion, sir?'

'It is your theory, Stiffeniis,' he said warmly. 'You must put it to the test. That is the essence of modern scientific methodology. Go at once to the Fortress and interrogate those people from the inn. When you've finished, there is something I would like to show you.'

'Excuse me, Herr Stiffeniis,' Koch intervened. 'What about the fisherman who found the corpse? You'll need to speak to him, sir.'

Before I could reply, Kant turned sharply on Koch.

'Don't waste your master's time! That poor fellow knows nothing, I am sure. I'll pick you up at four of the clock,' he said to me as he turned away towards the bridge. After a few halting steps, he looked back with an enigmatic smile. 'Aren't you curious to know more about the Devil's claw, Hanno?'

He did not wait for my answer.

'I am at your disposition, sir,' I murmured, watching in silence until he had safely reached the stairway to the road. Then, I gave orders for the body of Morik to be removed, waiting while the soldiers went about the sad business. As they covered his face, I recalled the fawning smile of Frau Totz and her pretence of concern for the child that morning. A wave of anger swept over me.

'To the Fortress, Koch,' I snapped. 'It is time to loosen some tongues.'

Chapter 12

Koch glanced around the room with a show of concern. 'I had your personal belongings brought here from the inn,' he said. 'It was the best I could do at such short notice, sir.'

The accommodation on the first floor of the Fortress was tiny. There was just space enough for a narrow bed and a wooden chair on which my travelling-bag had been placed. The acid taint of stale urine from a cracked porcelain night-bowl peeping beneath the cot hung heavily in the air. A window high in the wall provided next to no illumination, and it was icy cold in there. No one had taken the trouble to light the stove. The screaming and shouting of the prisoners down below was muted, which was a relief, but had a turnkey come along and locked us in for the duration, I would hardly have been surprised.

'It will do well enough,' I said with less animation than I truly felt. I had taken possession of Procurator Rhunken's private chamber, the room he used for resting when the pressure of work denied him the comfort of returning to his own house. I glanced at the four walls as if to familiarise myself with their grey drabness. 'This is where I should have been lodged in the first place,' I added with the conviction of an anchorite examining the cave in which he was destined to spend the rest of his penitent life.

'You did make some important discoveries down at The Baltic Whaler, sir,' the sergeant reminded me.

'We should be thankful for small mercies, I suppose.'

'Professor Kant seemed pleased,' Koch continued, though his tight-lipped manner gave the lie to the compliment.

'Is something bothering you, Koch?'

He did not try to deny the suggestion, tugging at his shirt collar as if the room were ten degrees warmer than it was. 'A couple of things, sir,' he began with some hesitancy. 'I was wondering about Professor Kant, sir.'

'What of him?' I asked brusquely.

'I was most surprised to find the gentleman down by the river this morning, sir. At his age, it seems rather odd that he should take such a . . . morbid interest in murder. Don't you think so, sir?'

'He is not vulgarly interested in murder, Koch, if that is what you mean,' I replied quickly, for the sergeant had given voice to a perplexity which I shared. 'Herr Professor Kant cannot countenance the disorder that crime brings, that's all. He fears for Königsberg and would suffer any inconvenience for the city that he loves.'

'Nevertheless, he did not seem to share your theory about a revolutionary conspiracy being the cause of these crimes,' Koch went on.

'Professor Kant is neither a magistrate nor a policeman,' I explained. 'He did concede that it seems to be the most obvious explanation. He is the supreme theorist of Rationalism in Prussia. He wants a hypothesis that can be confirmed by solid evidence. When we meet him again this afternoon, I intend to provide the definitive proof that he seeks.'

'Indeed, sir,' said Koch. He did not sound entirely convinced.

'And the other matter?'

Koch placed a hand on his vest as if to calm the beating of his heart or apologise in advance for what he was about to say. 'It concerns your brother, sir,' he said. 'Herr Kant spoke of him in connection with that boy this morning. Was your brother murdered, sir?'

I half turned away, opening my bag, pretending to look for something.

'Not murdered,' I snapped. 'As I told him, Sergeant, it was an accident. A most unfortunate accident.'

I rifled through the contents of my bag to avoid his gaze. When I looked up again, I thought I caught an expression of bewilderment on Koch's plain face. Brushing past him, I strode through to the connecting room.

'Where are the prisoners?' I asked.

'Officer Stadtschen is waiting on your orders before he brings them up, sir,' Koch replied, straightening his jacket, his face a neutral mask once more.

'Ask him to step in on his own first, would you?'

As if I had called the Devil, the Devil came. There was a sharp rap on the door, and Stadtschen presented himself with a stack of papers in his hands. He was an enormous man with a bloated red face, resplendent in an immaculate dark blue uniform with white stripes on his sleeves and along the seam of his riding-breeches. 'Foreign visitors in Königsberg, sir,' he said with a bow, handing me a copy of the list of names that had been drawn up for General Katowice.

I took the paper from him and scanned the names.

'Twenty-seven persons? In the whole of Königsberg?'

'We don't get many outlanders these days, sir,' the Officer replied. 'There are sailing-ships, of course, but they come and go the same day, most of them, or the crews sleep aboard. Casual visitors avoid the city, sir. No sensible man wants to get himself murdered.'

'Are any of the names on the list known to the police?'

'No, sir. I checked them myself.'

I noted the names of the three gem-traders who had been at The Baltic Whaler the night before. 'You searched the inn, did you not?'

'Indeed, sir,' he said, placing a large bundle of papers on the desk before me. 'This is a sample of the material we discovered there.'

'Where was it hidden?'

'In a secret room, Herr Procurator. A trap-door beneath the carpet in one of the upstairs bedrooms.'

The image of Morik spying came back to me. Was that what he had been trying to communicate to me the night before? That a seditious meeting was going on in that room opposite my window?

'Papers and maps, sir,' Stadtschen went on.

'Maps?'

'Of Königsberg, sir, and other places, too. And pamphlets written in French. The name of Bonaparte figured large in the texts.'

'Did you find any weapons?'

'None, sir,' Stadtschen replied with a grin, 'except for an old pistol in the bedchamber of Totz. It's as rusty as a lost anchor and would blow up in the face of anyone rash enough to fire it.'

'How many persons did you arrest?'

'The landlord and his wife only. Those tradesmen that Sergeant Koch said you were interested in had left the city early this morning. They may have left by sea. The gendarmes are trying to trace them now.'

'Did Totz or his wife say anything at the moment of their arrest?'

'I didn't pay them much attention, sir,' Stadtschen replied. 'I had more important business to attend to.'

'What do you mean?'

'Well, sir,' Stadtschen wiped his hand across his mouth. 'The lads have been under a lot of pressure since these murders started up. I had a tough time keeping them in order. I didn't want them taking justice into their own hands, if you know what I mean.'

'Very good,' I said. 'We may as well begin.'

Stadtschen snapped to attention. 'First, sir, General Katowice wants the prisoners in Section D to be separated from the rest.'

'Section D?' I queried.

'The deportees, sir. The General wants them to be moved to Pillau port, sir. Ready for immediate embarkation. If there is a French plot, the prison will start to fill up with political agitators and terrorists. Königsberg Fortress could turn into the Prussian equivalent of the Bastille, sir. That was how the General put it. Sixty deportees left Swinemunde jail yesterday aboard the *Tsar Petr*. It should dock in Pillau some time tomorrow, sir. Procurator Rhunken had drawn up a provisional list' – Stadtschen took a deep breath, and dropped his eyes – 'but, well, he didn't have the chance to sign or seal it, sir.'

He handed me a document written in italic script on heavy parchment. I knew the Royal Edict referred to in the title. A copy of the original had been sent to my office in Lotingen some months before. Fear of a Jacobin revolution had taken hold in Prussia; all prison governors had been ordered to compile a list of 'men who pose a threat to the security of the commonwealth, using every violent expedient to free themselves from captivity, having frustrated the mission of the penal institutions to reform and chastise them.'

'Procurator Rhunken had selected six names for deportation, sir. General Katowice has added two more. He requests you to finalise the procedure.'

I took a rapid glance at the names inscribed on the parchment.

Geden Wrajewsky, 30, deserter
Matthias Ludwigssen, 46, forger of coin in base metals
Jakob Stegelmann, 31, evil disposition, 53 convictions for
    drunkenness and brawling
Helmut Schuppe, 38 . . .

'Good God!' I exclaimed with horror as I read the charges against him. 'The wolves of Siberia won't have much of a chance with men like these.'

'Aye, sir,' Stadtschen said with a grim smile. 'They're a bad lot, all right.'

Andreas Conrad Segendorf, murder and abduction
Franz Hubtissner, 43, cattle thief
Anton Lieberkowsky, strangled his mother . . .

My heart began to race. How many years of hard labour, flogging, ice and biting wind would be needed to punish such a Cain?

'If you want to add Totz and his wife to the list, sir,' Stadtschen added, 'I'll have them moved to Section D straight away.'

I dipped the pen in the inkwell and drew a line beneath the names. As I wrote my signature, I asked myself how many extra days of life this decision would grant to the murderer, Ulrich Totz, and his partner in crime. Prisoners condemned to hard labour in Russia were unlikely to last more than two or three months.

'I wish to complete my investigation before deciding what to do with them. Excellent work, Stadtschen. You have done well,' I said, handing him back the document. His face flushed with pride. Winning my favour, he could hope to accelerate his advancement. 'Now, we'll have Gerta Totz in first.'

I was eager to begin. Had the landlady known of Morik's fate that morning when she declared herself to be so concerned for the boy's safety? Would she be so keen to smile now that Morik was dead, and she found herself facing a charge of murder?

The prisoner was ushered into my office some minutes later.

'Come forward, Frau Totz,' I said, pointedly ignoring her, shuffling through the papers Stadtschen had left upon the table: red rags intended to foment political discontent, intermingling Bonaparte's name and catchphrases I had heard in France – Liberty, Equality and barbarous violence. 'Now, let us . . .'

I looked up. What I saw froze the words on my tongue. The woman had been more roughly handled than Stadtschen had admitted. Her face was swollen, bruised and puffy, the lower lip split and bloody. Nevertheless, she still managed a lopsided version of the sugary smile with which she had greeted me earlier that morning.

'Herr Procurator?' she said, clasping her hands together in a servile manner, as if waiting for me to order my food and drink.

'Sit down,' I said, avoiding her eyes.

Stadtschen placed a heavy hand on her shoulders and sat the woman down with such force that it made the chair creak. I was about to reprimand him, but the memory of the crushed skull of Morik, the eye dangling at the corner of his mouth, flashed through my mind.

'Well, Gerta Totz, what have you to say for yourself?'

She looked up with a pitiful grimace of hideous concern. 'Herr Stiffeniis, I humbly beg your pardon,' she mumbled, stifling tears with bunched fists. 'They closed the inn, sir. What will you do now? Where will you stay?'

'That is the least of your worries,' I replied. 'You told me this morning that you were looking for Morik. Did you know that he was dead?'

'Oh, Herr Stiffeniis! What are you saying, sir? I was fretted out of my mind. That boy's a blessed nuisance. I thought he might be bothering you . . .'

'Why should he bother me?' I interrupted.

'He knew you were a magistrate. He . . .'

'Is that why he was killed?'

'What an idea, sir!' she mumbled. 'I was right to worry, was I not, sir?'

'There have been some devious goings-on in your house,' I continued. 'Morik uncovered the plot. He knew that the murders in Königsberg had been planned and carried out by you, your husband, and other persons who frequented the inn.'

She did not contest what I said. Not directly.

'Is that what Morik told you, sir?' she replied. She joined her hands like a child at prayer and leaned towards my desk, struggling against the restraining hand of Officer Stadtschen, blood trickling freely from the split in her lower lip and running down her chin and throat. 'My Ulrich feared as much. He saw Morik hovering around your table last night. We both did, sir. I warned him off. And then I warned you too, sir, didn't I?'

I did not trouble myself to respond.

'I did, sir. Really, I did. But that boy had a wild imagination,' she went on. 'He was a danger. Who could tell where the truth started and the lies ended with him? When my husband was told of your coming, the first thing he said was this: "We'll have to send that lad away, Gerta." Ulrich was afraid no good would come of it if Morik got to know about your business in Königsberg. But we couldn't afford another lad.'

'The Baltic Whaler is a notorious haunt for foreign conspirators,' I pressed on. 'There were three of them present at dinner yester-night, two Frenchmen and a man of German origin, who claimed to be merchants in precious gems. What have you to say about them?'

'Those travellers, sir? It's not the first time they've stayed at the inn. Very righteous, hard-working gentlemen they are. Always paid their bills on time.'

'They are Jacobins,' I insisted. 'French spies.'

The woman blinked at the violence of my reaction. 'I don't know what's got into you, sir,' she protested. 'They're honest men, I'd swear!'

'You and your husband plotted with them, Frau Totz,' I persisted. 'That is why Morik was murdered.'

'It isn't true, sir,' she whined. 'It isn't. My Ulrich was glad about what happened in France, I won't deny it. Who wasn't? The Revolution was what the French went and done because they had that terrible king of theirs, not a gentleman with fair laws and respect for the people like our dear King Frederick. Them French ideas aren't so very terrible, sir. Liberty, Equality, Frat . . .'

'We are not talking about ideas,' I insisted. 'There was a plot against the government, Frau Totz.'

'A plot, sir?' she whimpered, raising her hands to heaven and shaking her head from side to side in denial. 'Is that what Morik told you?'

'I told you that I had seen Morik in a room across the courtyard from my own. You denied the fact this morning. Yet, in that room, the very *same* room, the gendarmes discovered this hoard of subversive material.'

'It's nothing but a storeroom, sir!' she cried. 'I denied its existence, 'cause I didn't want you worrying over the silly things in that boy's head.'

'The boy is dead!' I shouted. 'Murdered for those *silly things*!'

'We all use that cellar, sir,' she moaned desperately. 'All of us. Me, my husband, Morik. Yes, Morik, sir! It's crammed with broken furniture and all the summer linen for the inn, plus stuff that people leave behind without thinking. We never throw nothing away in case they come and ask for them back. Whatever was found, if it isn't used in the inn, it isn't ours, sir. I swear to you.'

'Stadtschen, where exactly was the subversive material found?'

'Well hidden in a trunk beneath some blankets, sir,' the officer confirmed.

'Those papers aren't ours, sir,' Gerta Totz protested. 'I've never seen them. And as for Morik, I only took him in to help my sister. He wasn't right in the head. And these murders didn't do him any good at all. It's quite possible that he believed the murderer was hiding in our house, but surely you don't think so? Not *you*, Herr Stiffeniis? Ulrich and me have been as scared to walk the streets as any innocent souls in all these months. It hasn't been easy, we've had a dropping-off in trade. Since that man was found dead out on the quay, we've been hard-pushed to keep the place going.'

All of this came out in such an impetuous rush that I had difficulty in writing it down. The brazen woman was lying, but I would need to break her resistance if I hoped to incriminate her and Totz.

'These lies are enough to condemn you,' I stated, staring at her coldly.

I saw a different Gerta Totz before me, a perverse, criminal version of the homely, comforting and all too inquisitive landlady I had met for the first time the night before. It was the fixed grin on her face that did it. Its mincing falsity gave me the shivers. She was accused of murder, yet she insisted on smiling, as if that smile were her most tried and proven resource. It haunts me still.

'You're going to torture me, aren't you, sir?'

I froze.

Had she read my thoughts, interpreted some malign expression on my face? Though King Frederick Wilhelm III had formally prohibited its use, the Royal Decree had not put an end to the practice. Karl Heinz Starbeinzig, a prominent Prussian jurist, had recently published an essay in favour of its reintroduction, which had been extremely well received at Court. 'Torture is fast and cheap,' he argued. 'It embodies those two essential principles of the modern state: economy and efficiency.' To obtain precise details of how and why Morik had been killed, torture might prove to be useful.

Frau Totz let out a whimper of fear. 'You have the power to kill me and Ulrich, sir. But what's happening in Königsberg won't end with us.'

'We'll see about that. Do you have anything more to add at this time?'

She wept aloud and tore her hair, but said not a word. I nodded to Stadtschen to take her out of the room. But as he tried to pull her to her feet, the woman threw herself forward onto my table. The bloody slobber from her lips dripped onto my notes. She stared up at me with defiance, the hideous smile still there, but twisted now with rage.

'Why did you come to The Baltic Whaler?' she snarled. 'What did you want from us?'

I pushed back from the spray of blood and bile.

'Somebody sent you. To catch us in a trap.'

Stadtschen had her by the neck and attempted to drag her from my desk.

'Somebody who holds the city dear,' I snapped.

'Someone who wants to destroy us,' she screeched back, hanging on by her nails to the desk. 'The Devil sent you! The Devil!'

'You'll never know how wrong you are.'

'*You* killed Morik!' she spat the words into my face. Blood splattered my hands and the linen cuffs of my shirt. 'You, and whoever sent you to the inn!'

'Stadtschen, take her out,' I shouted, but Frau Totz grasped the table like a fury, and pushed towards me.

'I knew you'd bring destruction on us. The instant I saw your face. You started Morik off! He told his stupid stories, and you believed them. There was nothing to discover in our inn. *You* came, and Morik died. *You* slaughtered him, Herr Stiffeniis. And now you're going to butcher us . . .'

It happened so quickly, I took myself by surprise. Before I knew it, my bunched fist shot out and hit the woman square on the nose. It was not a terrible blow, but sufficient to make the blood spurt from her nostrils. Her body jerked with pain as she slid to the floor.

'Take her down,' I ordered.

Both Koch and Stadtschen stared at me in silence.

'Stadtschen, take her down to the cells,' I repeated.

Officer Stadtschen blinked, then stepped forward and lifted the woman up from the floor. He cuffed her on the back of the head as he pushed her out of the door. 'They ought to string you up, you shameless whore!' he shouted. 'We'll give you a welcome here you won't forget!'

I sat down at my desk, took a long, deep breath, then carefully wiped away the spots of blood from my person and my papers with a bit of rag cloth I used to clean my pens.

'They'll hurt her, sir,' Koch warned in a low voice. 'The guards will do her serious harm.'

I did not look at him. Nor did I reply. What cruel thoughts passed through my mind in that instant? What punishment did I believe she merited for what she had done to Morik?

I picked up my quill, dipped it deep into the inkwell, then signed and dated the woman's deposition with great deliberation. I melted wax in the candlelight and carefully affixed my seal.

Then, and only then, I turned to Sergeant Koch.

'Tell Stadtschen to bring up the husband,' I said.

Chapter 13

Gerta Totz had told me the name of Morik's killer. Despite the absurdity of the accusation, I could not shake off the sense of responsibility and even guilt that it involved. Had I been the unwitting cause of the boy's death? Had the mere act of speaking to me been enough to provoke his killer?

I tried to displace these sombre thoughts with others of a more resolute kind. I would need to be more incisive if I hoped to confirm my suspicions of a political plot at The Baltic Whaler. I had learned little from Frau Totz. Unless her husband were more forthcoming, I would be obliged to resort to torture. Whether I felt happy with the idea or not, the worsening political situation would oblige me to use hot irons and crushing weights.

Officer Stadtschen entered the room a moment later, pushing Ulrich Totz before him. The innkeeper appeared to have been more liberally treated than his wife. He had suffered a dull, dark bruise high on his forehead, but nothing worse. There were no open wounds. No blood to spatter my papers and my clothing.

'Sit down, Totz,' I said, waving him to the chair.

'I'd rather stand,' he replied.

Stadtschen jabbed him in the back.

'Do as you are told,' he growled.

I observed Ulrich Totz from the corner of my eye while I organised fresh paper, and prepared myself to question him. A supercilious smile played about his surly lips.

'Does something amuse you, Herr Totz?' I enquired.

'With your permission, Herr Stiffeniis,' he began, 'that cell stinks. It's full of rats. You found comfort under my roof.'

'It is cosy compared to the unmarked grave of a murderer,' I snapped.

He answered this with a lazy shrug. 'Very well, Herr Procurator Stiffeniis,' he said, 'let's get down to business. It won't take long. I admit my crime. I killed our Morik with these here hands.'

He held them up to me for examination. They were large and meaty. I saw them picking up some heavy object, and smashing open the side of Morik's head. How many blows had it taken, I wondered with an inward shiver, before the boy's eye popped out from its socket and the skull poured forth its bloody pulp? Despite the feeling of revulsion, my heart leapt with excitement. The murderer was ready to confess.

'I want the facts, Totz,' I said calmly.

He nodded, then spoke for ten minutes without a pause, describing all that had taken place at The Baltic Whaler the night before. Such an ample confession should have pleased me, yet there was something mellifluous and practised in the telling that disconcerted me. Only the temptation to believe that these bare-faced admissions would soon release me from the investigation stilled the objections I might have raised. I let him go on unchecked, my hand racing over the page as I recorded his admissions.

'I've always supported what happened back in '89,' he declared proudly. 'Kings and nobles prancing around, while we slave day and night like dogs over the bones. I'm a Jacobin, all right, Monsieur Robespierre's my god. I don't give a hoot for religion. That's more bloodsuckers for you. Priests! Chop their stinking heads off, and good riddance, I say. Not just in France, but here in Prussia too. Damned Pietists! Just you wait 'til Napoleon gets here! He'll show 'em! I knew the inn was being watched by the police, but no one could prove a thing against me. Not 'til you arrived.'

Totz wiped his mouth on the back of his sleeve, and stared back at me with nonchalant indifference. 'The minute you turned up, I knew the danger we were facing,' he continued. 'Well, two can play at that little game, thinks I, and I played my part well enough. But then Morik had to go and stick his nose in the pie. I caught him spying again last night. He would have told you soon enough . . .'

'Is that why you killed him?'

Totz's eyes blazed with hatred. 'Revolutions have their victims! You might almost say you killed him yourself, Herr Procurator. If you hadn't come along when you did, no one here in Königsberg would have given Morik a second of his precious time.'

'Where was he killed?'

Ulrich Totz let out a long, weary sigh. 'I don't know why you're bothering to ask,' he sneered. 'You saw him from your window, Gerta told me. God knows how you didn't see me as well! I caught him lurking outside the store-room, so I just pushed him down the stairs.'

So, it was Totz's face that I had seen at Morik's back the night before. The admission should have banished any lingering doubts from my mind. So why did I have the feeling that he was telling me exactly what I wanted to hear?

'Pushed him down the stairs, Totz? You did much more than that!'

'When I found him snooping there, I knew for certain he'd tell you. I had to kill him, didn't I? He was courting you like a big, fat maggot on a tasty bit of red meat.'

'Let's be more precise about what happened, Totz,' I interrupted. 'You grabbed the lad and you pushed him down the stairs. Is that what you are saying?'

'I saw you blowing out your candle and closing the curtain to go to bed. That was when I decided to act.'

'Very well. You pushed him down the stairs, and then?'

'I ran down after him and struck him dead.'

'What did you hit him with?'

'The first thing I laid my hands on.'

'*What*?' I insisted.

He did not hesitate. 'A hammer we use for opening barrels. It was easy. He was that scared. But you knew that already, didn't you? He told you himself that his life was in danger.'

'You are not here to question me, Totz,' I warned.

'What do you want to know then, sir?' he replied with a shifty look.

'I want to know why you killed the boy there in the cellar. In your own house. Why not lure him out of the inn?'

Totz shrugged. 'He'd never have come with me. And sooner or later, you'd have paid attention. What else could I do? I had to silence him. And quick.'

'You could have sent him out of Königsberg. Home to his mother.'

'And you'd have been more suspicious than ever! No, better another victim of the Königsberg killer. Another dead body in the streets.'

'And your wife was a party to it?'

'Gerta don't know nothing,' he added quickly. 'She wouldn't hurt a fly.'

'You killed him by yourself, then? No one helped you?'

'That's right, sir. One proper blow and the boy was dead. There was blood all over the place.'

'If I may speak, sir,' Officer Stadtschen intervened, 'I can confirm that an attempt had been made to clean up the mess, but there were traces of blood everywhere.'

I turned back to Totz. 'Why did you take the body to the river?' I asked.

Ulrich Totz smiled that slow, dreamy smile once more.

'I wanted him to be found, sir. Like all the others. But not outside my own door again. Konnen brought trouble down hard on me. We lost a lot of business after that. The river's only a couple of hundred yards away from the inn through the back streets.'

'How did you carry the boy, Totz?'

'In a sack slung over the back of my old packhorse. He didn't weigh a mite. I threw the rags I'd used to clean the blood into the river. Ten, fifteen minutes, it didn't take no more. We come back unseen, and . . .'

'*We?*' I raised my head sharply from the words I had just transcribed. 'You, and who else, Totz? Your wife? One of the guests?'

'Me and *the packhorse*. Don't insist, Herr Procurator. Gerta knows less than nothing about all of this.'

'She knows that you killed Morik, does she not?' I countered, uncertain whether some vestige of humanity might be leading him

142

to shield his wife from her part of the blame in their nephew's death.

'She does not, sir. She'll ne'er forgive me. Morik was her sister's only son. She's always felt a duty to help that boy.'

'But who helped *you*, Totz? I can hardly believe that one man . . .'

'Herr Procurator, I've already told you,' Totz replied forcibly. 'I did it all on my own. By myself. No one helped me.'

'What about those foreigners who were staying at the inn last night?'

He shrugged. 'The Frenchmen? They were customers, paying guests. No more, no less,' he answered squarely, his eyes blazing fiercely into my own.

'I don't believe you,' I said.

He looked at me coolly for a moment, then an ugly smirk erupted on his face. 'Believe whatever you like, Herr Procurator. I'll not tell you any more about my private affairs.'

'We will see about that,' I replied, eyeing him coldly, letting the threat dangle. 'We have proven methods of making the recalcitrant talk.'

'Torture, sir? Is that your game? I bet you enjoy seeing 'em stretched out on the rack, screaming their guts out, don't you, sir?'

If Ulrich Totz was trying to taunt me, he succeeded. As a consequence, I felt less hesitation about the idea of subjecting him to pain. Indeed, I almost enjoyed the prospect. He would laugh from the other side of his insolent mouth.

'Give over with your threats, Herr Procurator,' he stared back at me with that look of open hatred I had seen before. 'I'm a dead man, you can't scare me with talk of torture. I don't mind dying for what I believe in.'

'They were harmless people, Totz,' I hissed. 'There is nothing noble in the murders that have embroiled Königsberg. Do you really believe that rebellion will automatically follow on because you have slaughtered a few innocents?'

'It serves the purpose!'

'Purpose?'

'Revolution, sir.'

I ignored this barb. 'Apart from Morik, how did you choose the other victims, Totz?'

He did not reply at once, but sat so long in silence that I thought the question had gone over his head. And all the while, he stared at me fixedly in what I took to be sullen reproach. Only later did I realise that there was crude calculation in his behaviour. He was trying to figure out how much I knew, while I was more than convinced that this was the devil who had unleashed mayhem in the city. The fact that he showed no remorse reinforced my belief.

'I will repeat the question, Totz,' I said more slowly. 'How did you choose the victims?'

'The time, the place,' he murmured. 'The fact that there were no witnesses hanging around. It was all a question of opportunity. That was the beauty of it. I'd seen Konnen in the inn the night I first got the idea . . .'

'There was no political reason behind your choice?'

Totz sat up straighter in his chair, his mouth drawn in a stiff-lipped smile, but he said nothing. I thought he seemed intent on outfacing me.

'You knew Herr Tifferch, didn't you? He was a prominent lawyer, a well-known hater of Napoleon . . .'

'All Prussians hate Napoleon!' he seethed, his face a mask of hatred. 'Any one of the buggers is a political target as far as I'm concerned. That lawyer was a parasite! Living off the *Junkers*! Helping to buy and sell for them, sending their tenants to jail for debts and unpaid rents. I'll get even with the lot of them!'

'You will hang from the gallows,' I stated coldly.

I added a note in my report to the effect that the anti-French sentiments of the penultimate victim had been the probable cause of his murder. Everything seemed to me to be suddenly sharp and clear, like a magic-lantern projection when the lamp is lit, the lens is turned and the first slide comes into focus. With one reservation only.

'Were you not afraid of being recognised?'

Ulrich Totz seemed to relax more comfortably in the chair. 'People here know me. That made things easier. I'm an innkeeper, see?

I know everyone. It was normal enough for me to walk up to some-one, stop them, chat for a bit, see that no one else was around, then strike. They didn't have time to take in what was happening.'

'Very good,' I said. 'Now, tell me about the weapon that you used.'

He stared at me. 'I've told you already,' he said.

'You used a hammer to kill Morik, you say. But what about the others?'

Despite his readiness to confess, I still had no idea how the other victims had died.

Ulrich Totz rubbed his knuckles and eyed me warily.

'I used whatever came to hand,' he said slowly. 'The hammer, stones, my own hands.'

'How did you kill Herr Tifferch, for instance? He had no visible wounds. What weapon did you use on him?'

For the first time, Totz was silent.

'What about this Devil's claw that all the town is talking of?' I insisted.

Ulrich Totz looked from me to Koch, then back again. He smiled, weakly at first, then with growing confidence. 'Oh, I can see your point, sir,' he said with a flash of cunning. 'I tell you all I know, you pack your things and go back home. Got a wife and bairns waiting for you, is that it? I've told you more than enough already, Herr Procurator. The rest you'll have to discover for yourself.'

Suddenly, he leaned forward and rested his forearm on my desk. I held up my hand to stay Stadtschen and Sergeant Koch. They had made to pounce on him to protect me.

'Well, Totz? What more have you to add?'

He eyed me without speaking for some moments.

'Listen, Herr Stiffeniis, and listen good,' he said in a low, surly voice. 'You can torture me if it pleases you. You can make me scream, but I'll tell you nowt. You can torture my wife, and she'll agree to any words you care to put into her mouth, knowing noth-ing for a fact. But that's the end of it. I don't intend to say another word to you, or to anyone else, 'til they lead me to the scaffold.'

'This is not the end of our conversation, Totz,' I returned, staring into his half-closed eyes. 'I will interrogate you again, and you will tell me everything. Every single thing! About the pamphlets and those foreign agents who helped in your conspiracy. Next time, there'll be no holds barred.'

'Do your worst, Herr Stiffeniis,' the innkeeper replied in a low murmur. 'That's your job. Mine is to resist.'

'We'll soon see which of us is the better at his task,' I said dismissively, pulling out my watch. It was almost four o'clock. Time for my appointment with Professor Kant. I had made enough progress for one day.

'Take him away, Stadtschen.'

The room seemed suddenly empty. Ulrich Totz had filled the space with his anger, his cruelty and his undisguised hatred for authority. Koch remained silent, and I was certain that he was waiting for me to make some comment. I stood up and walked across to the window. Outside, the daylight was fading. My throat was dry, and I felt light-headed. Ulrich Totz had confessed to killing Morik. My theory of a political plot aimed at creating terror had been confirmed, the murderer had a name. I should have felt proud of myself, and yet, for some niggling reason, I was not entirely convinced. Wasn't it all just a mite too easy? Could the mystery of Königsberg be such a simple thing? Surely, a magistrate of Procurator Rhunken's vast experience ought to have arrived at such a conclusion months before.

'If I may make a suggestion,' Koch spoke out, 'a public whipping in the square outside the Fortress would not go amiss, sir. I could request permission from General Katowice, if you wish. Procurator Rhunken was a great believer in the efficacy of the rod. Two years ago, a man was whipped for murdering his father. He was, of course, beheaded some months later. But the example made a lasting impression on the populace.'

Should I follow the lead of Rhunken? Corporal punishment and physical mutilation were still admitted within the *Constitutio Criminalis Carolina*, though it had been formulated in the sixteenth century by Charles V.

'Times are changing, Koch,' I replied. 'King Frederick Wilhelm is an enlightened monarch. He believes, quite rightly, that public cruelty may arouse the sympathy of the watching crowd, and thus frustrate the intended purpose of the punishment. If Totz and his wife are members of an active group of Jacobins, a public whipping may inflame the spirits of the other members. In attempting to douse the flames, we may succeed in fanning them. I will speak to the suspects first, and warn them of the danger. We have time a-plenty.'

I collected my papers together, and began to put them away in my bag.

'In any case,' I said, looking at my watch, 'we have an appointment to keep. Professor Kant and the mysterious Devil's claw await us.'

'Is there any point, sir?' Koch returned. 'I mean to say, you seem to be well on the way to concluding the case without his help.'

He was right, of course. I ought to have pressed on, there and then, with my interrogation of the Totzes. 'Beat the iron while it's red and hot,' the people say in Lotingen. But Professor Kant would never forgive me if I let him down.

'Since the case is so clear-cut,' I said with a smile, 'we can afford to indulge an old man's whims for an hour.'

As we left the room and hurried down the stairs together, I began to compose in my head the letter which would announce my success to Helena, and the prospect of my early homecoming.

I could not have imagined in that moment of heady euphoria the difficulty I would experience before the day was out in holding a pen, or in trying to form the letters with my shaking hand.

Chapter 14

A smart black coach was waiting for me outside the Fortress gate.

I could not avoid smiling as I made my approach. Professor Kant was busily consulting his pocket-watch behind the closed windows. His insistence on punctuality was maniacal, and all the world knew it. But as I raised my fist to tap on the glass and announce my arrival, a hand touched me fleetingly on the elbow, and a voice whispered, 'May I speak with you, sir?'

The servant who had been solicitous of Kant's safety that morning on the river bank was peeping from the rear corner of the coach. His large, strong face, which had appeared so expressionless then, now seemed tense and drawn.

'Johannes Odum, isn't it?'

With a pointed glance he indicated that I should join him behind the coach.

'Your master will not condone time-wasting,' I warned him.

'A word, sir, no more,' he insisted. He gestured towards the vehicle and its passenger with his thumb. 'Recent events have been a trial for him, sir. What we saw this morning down by the river is good for no man, sir, least of all a gentleman of his age and delicate nervous disposition.'

'You were there, you saw him yourself,' I whispered. 'Professor Kant may be frail, but he seems to be holding up.'

Perhaps I ought to have warned the servant that the danger was past, and that the case was closed, but I had no intention of wasting such momentous news on Kant's valet before I had told it to the man himself.

'He's been working night and day at this investigation, sir,' the servant replied. 'All night sometimes . . .'

'All night?' I interrupted. 'Doing what?'

'Writing, I believe, sir.'

I thought of the treatise that Herr Jachmann had mentioned, his incredulity regarding its existence. 'Do you know *what* he is writing?'

Johannes Odum shrugged his broad shoulders dismissively.

'He's in danger, sir,' he insisted. 'Real danger. He was seen with you this morning by the river. Now, you'll be seen travelling in his coach. And before we left the house this morning, I found something that you should see . . .'

'Johannes!' The fretful shout made both of us start. 'Where is Procurator Stiffeniis?'

I signalled to the servant to run around the other side of the vehicle, while I stepped out and attracted Professor Kant's attention.

'Here I am, sir,' I said brightly. 'I left some papers behind in the office, and had to go back for them. Do you mind if Sergeant Koch joins us?'

I nodded to Koch to stand forward.

'Of course not,' Kant replied with impatience. 'We must hurry. The way is long, and it is extremely cold.'

'Off to Siberia, are we, sir?' I joked. I knew I could not fail to hit the mark. Kant's hunger for information and gossip was as renowned as his clock-watching. The news of the ship that was about to moor in Pillau port could not have escaped him. It had featured prominently in all the recent Prussian papers.

'Not so far,' he replied with a smile, 'but just as cold.'

I laughed heartily. I was in an excellent humour. The case was over, except for the red tape. Even if they managed to escape the hangman, Ulrich and Gerta Totz would be deported to the frozen wastes. I had no idea where Professor Kant was taking us, nor what he intended to show us. Whatever it might be, I thought, humouring the old gentleman would add nothing material to the investigation. But nor would it detract.

As the coach sped forward, I expected him to ask me about the progress I had made that afternoon. Was he not curious to know what had happened? He had been so openly sceptical that morning, yet he had urged me to interrogate Ulrich and Gerta Totz. Surely he would wish to know what they had said?

'Do you like your new lodgings?' he asked suddenly. 'They hardly compare with the delights of The Baltic Whaler, I'd wager. Frau Totz is renowned for her roast pork.'

Was he teasing me? Was my ex-landlady's cooking all that interested him?

'The inn was certainly comfortable,' I conceded uncertainly.

'I knew you'd feel at home there,' Kant said with a warm smile. 'Of course, the Fortress of Königsberg is another matter altogether.'

Was this the behaviour that had so disturbed Herr Jachmann? Kant seemed to be absorbed in details which were of no importance, concerned about matters of which he could have no personal knowledge. He had dined in his own home and nowhere else for the last twenty years, as all the newspaper sketches of his doings habitually reported. Celebrity has no secrets from the intrusions of the press.

'What a depressing building the Fortress is!' he said next, his mood shifting suddenly. 'The sight of it used to put the wind up me when I was just a little child. Mother and I were obliged to pass each morning on our way to the Pietist Temple. The fear I felt, she said, was naught compared to the fear I'd feel the day I had to stand before my Maker and look into His eyes!'

Professor Kant looked out of the window like a lost child. The Fortress had fallen far behind, but it might still have been visible before his eyes. 'Will you be able to sleep in there tonight, Hanno? They say that the place is haunted by the victims of the Teutonic Knights who died in the dungeons.'

What could I reply? Koch and I exchanged glances, but neither dared say a word. As our coach clattered and rattled over an ancient wooden bridge, dense fog swirled in twirling clouds above the still waters of a dark moat. Only the towering keep of the Fortress on the hill above was visible in the fading afternoon light. The battlements seemed to peep over a solid wall of low clouds.

Kant glanced in my direction. 'Nearly there!' he exclaimed gaily as the coach turned sharply right and crossed another bridge. Clearly, he was excited by the prospect of what lay before us. 'I suppose that you have been counting the bridges?' he said.

'Bridges, sir?' I had no idea what he was talking about.

'Surely you know the problem?' he replied. 'Before he died, the great mathematician, Leonhard Euler, questioned whether it were possible to trace a route through Königsberg which crossed the nine bridges spanning the River Pregel without ever using the same bridge more than once. You ought to try it while you are here.'

I began to remind him of the reason which had brought me to Königsberg, but he had no mind for me. 'When I began to teach at the University,' he went on, 'I won a bet with a colleague who had been a great friend of the mathematician. He told me that, in fact, Euler himself didn't know the answer! Well, I provided two solutions to the problem . . .'

He did not finish. Turning to me instead, he laid his hand on my arm, and asked urgently: 'What have you to tell me about the Totzes?'

For some moments, I knew not how to reply. Should I tell him that the case was solved, the guilty closed in their cells, awaiting judgement? That the Devil's claw, whatever it might prove to be, was irrelevant?

'The husband confessed, sir. And quickly too,' I replied. With care, limiting myself to the sequence of events, suppressing the cry of victory which hovered on my lips, I related the facts to Kant as neutrally as possible.

'So, that's that,' he said. 'A political plot is at the root of all the evil which has poisoned Königsberg. Acts of terrorism aimed at . . .'

He halted abruptly, and looked at me.

'Aimed at *what*? Did the culprits reveal their final objective?'

'Not in so many words, sir,' I admitted. 'Ulrich Totz seems to believe that the fear generated by these murders will weaken the faith of the people in their rulers and provoke some sort of a revolution. I suspect that he targeted people who were known for their opposition to the French.'

Professor Kant sat back in his seat. He beamed with delight.

'Oh, I see! How clever of him! And he described the weapon that he used to kill Morik, I suppose?'

I shifted uneasily on the leather bench.

'A hammer, sir.'

My answer seemed to amuse Kant even more. 'A large hammer, Stiffeniis, or a small one?' he asked.

'It . . . it was only a preliminary interrogation,' I stammered. I had thought to win his praise. Instead, his penetrating mind had laid bare the limits of my method of proceeding. 'Totz did admit that he had used various weapons to kill the other victims.'

'Not one alone?' Kant frowned.

'Whatever came to hand, he said,' I added quickly. 'Of course, sir, I will question him until all the details emerge.'

'Details are of the utmost importance,' Kant confided. 'The King will want to know the exact strength and number of his enemies.'

Was he being sarcastic? I felt like a student who has just been handed back an essay by a tutor and told that the work was good, very good, though it should have been a great deal better. Suddenly, Kant laughed out loud. He did not say what amused him. This mercurial humour of his was new to me, and I was not reassured by it. Nor was Koch, as I could see quite clearly by the expression on his face.

'I am glad that you have found the high road to Truth,' said Kant. 'Did you, by any chance, ask Ulrich Totz about the Devil's claw, as the people call it?'

'Herr Procurator cannot be expected to complete his investigations in a single day, sir,' Sergeant Koch interrupted. His deference to my authority was as pronounced as his loyalty to Procurator Rhunken had been. The bureaucracy here in Prussia is famed for producing such men. They are obedient and subservient to a fault. And sometimes they are blunt, too.

'Whatever this Devil's claw may be,' Koch went on, 'whatever the common people say about it, it hardly seems relevant, Professor Kant. Procurator Stiffeniis has unmasked the plot.'

'Dear Sergeant Koch,' Kant returned mildly, 'do not presume too far. In my experience, there is more truth in the common voice than anywhere else on Earth.'

'Ulrich Totz admitted killing the boy,' Sergeant Koch replied staunchly. 'He admitted murdering the others. Herr Stiffeniis has caught his man, sir.'

To my surprise, Professor Kant showed no resentment at this rebuttal. He nodded thoughtfully. 'I can understand your reservations about the utility of what I intend to show you, Herr Koch,' he continued. 'And I appreciate your openness where my young friend shows only dutiful reticence. I am certain that Stiffeniis shares your opinion. I would ask you both to be patient for a short while longer. What you are about to see is the fruit of the most original research that I have ever undertaken in my life.'

My heart beat faster. Was Immanuel Kant going to show me what he had been hiding from his best and closest friends?

'A masterpiece, I am sure, sir,' I said with warmth. 'Any book from your pen . . .'

'A book?' Surprise was evident on his hollow face. 'Is that what you are expecting to see, Stiffeniis?'

'The world has waited too long for a new opus, sir,' I answered.

He made no immediate reply. When he did speak, he seemed even more animated than before. 'A book . . . A book! Why not?' he said, resting his chin on his bunched fist. 'And what could be the title? Why, given the circumstances, a *Critique of Criminal Reason*, I think.'

'I am eager to read it,' I enthused, as the coach laboured up the hill.

Kant was smiling gleefully, his lips drawn back tightly to reveal the few yellow, pointed teeth he still possessed. I must confess, it was not a pleasant sight.

'You have taken possession of Rhunken's office, I imagine. Have you read the reports that he cobbled together regarding these murders?'

'I did so yesterday,' I began eagerly. 'They have been most useful, sir. Indeed his theory seems to be confirmed by what Totz, the innkeeper, confessed this afternoon . . .'

'A political plot? Is that what you think lies behind these deaths?' Kant interrupted me with a dismissive wave of his hand. 'Vigilantius came closer to the truth!' He uttered these words with an energy which was very close to rage. 'You lost patience with him last night. You should have stayed until the end. Herr Rhunken is a magistrate of the old school. He is an information-gatherer, nothing more. He hopes to frighten the truth from people, and sometimes he succeeds. But not in this instance. His dull imagination is no match for the killer's. Vigilantius has discovered a great deal more, but you refused to take his insights into consideration.'

I glanced at Koch. His face was taut, the muscles clenched and stiff. Clearly it cost him a great deal not to speak out in defence of the dead man he had served so faithfully and for so long. But one thing was certain: Professor Kant had not been informed of the magistrate's death.

'Well?' Kant niggled. 'Why didn't you stay?'

'I considered it a pantomime, sir,' I protested uncertainly.

'Pantomimes sometimes represent a truth,' he replied. 'I expected you to be put off at the beginning, but I hoped that you would learn something useful from Vigilantius. I sent Rhunken's official reports to you for the same purpose.'

'I beg your pardon, sir?'

I could find no thread of coherence in his arguments. What could be the connection between Vigilantius and the police reports that I had been allowed to read on the journey to Königsberg?

He leaned close and spoke quietly. 'I knew that I could rely on your sense of duty. Who can refuse a commission from the King? Especially a magistrate who has chosen to hide himself away in a tiny village near the borders of West Prussia. What is the name of the place? Lotingen?'

For a moment I feared that he might be about to ask me why I had chosen never to return to Königsberg after our first meeting seven years before, why I had never made the effort to write to him. The possibility that he might know about Jachmann's interference in our affairs threw me into a panic. What could I tell him? In frenzied haste, I searched for excuses, ranging from my own bad health, to – God forgive me! – serious diseases that Helena or the children might have suffered.

But he did not bother to ask. He had other matters on his mind.

'I tried to whet your appetite for the obscure side of human behaviour with the help of those reports, Hanno,' he went on. 'I hoped that you would be intrigued by the strangeness of these deaths. I remember well at our first meeting, you showed a natural inclination for . . . how shall I call it, *mystery*?' He leaned back in his seat. 'I hoped that you would be puzzled. Not so much by what you'd read, but by what you did *not* read in those reports.' He started to number off the items on his fingers.

'Why was there no explanation of how the victims had died? Why was no mention made of the weapon used? Why was no hypothesis offered which might suggest a common motive behind all those murders? There was no question of theft or of passion, no apparent connection linking one victim to another. You cannot fail to have realised that what was happening in Königsberg had something peculiar about it. A magistrate of Herr Rhunken's fame was unable to resolve the enigma. Oh, I'd not deny that Rhunken did his job. He did what he was capable of doing. But his heavy feet never left the ground. His plodding intelligence was no match for the killer's. Sometimes such magistrates are fortunate, I have no doubt, but not in this instance.' He looked at me inquisitively.

'If you want to understand what is going on here, my young friend, you must learn to soar. You must pay attention, even to the most obscure and mysterious of sources available to you. Even to the likes of Vigilantius. If you continue to dig for reasons, to look for explanations, to chase proofs – as you began to do the minute you arrived in Königsberg – you'll get no closer to the truth than your predecessor did.'

His voice gradually faded away as he spoke. He was disappointed, I could tell. I had failed him in some way, though I was unable to say exactly how I had fallen short of his expectations. But suddenly, he shifted in his seat and changed his course, like a fish you think you have safely caught in your bare hands that darts away in another direction, leaving you with just an empty swirl in the water.

'By the way, how is your father?' he asked.

It was dark inside the carriage, and I was glad of that. I felt the blood drain instantly from my face. It was the second time that he had referred to the tragedy in my family. What strange association of ideas brought the question to his lips just then? And why was he so lacking in curiosity about the *new* family I had made? Were my wife and my children of no interest to him? I had baptised my only son in his honour. It was as if that part of my life did not exist. Instead, he harked back continually to the old life, the old me, the Hanno Stiffeniis that he had helped to exorcise seven years before.

'I have heard, sir, that he is somewhat better,' I replied, though Kant did not appear to be listening. He seemed to be following a delicate pattern that his mind had already traced out for him. He waved his forefinger in the air, following the movement with his eyes, as though his mental and his physical states were wholly separated, and equally fascinating, the one to the other.

Just then, fortunately, the coach began to slow down.

'At last! We have arrived!' he exclaimed, interrupting his private reflections with sudden animation. 'Let's waste no more time.'

Johannes pulled down the folding steps, and helped his master into the dark lane. I had no idea where we were, but then I caught a glimpse of the towering bulk of the Fortress again. We seemed to have circled around the defensive walls and come at the Fortress from another direction, standing beside a miserable hovel that flanked an approach road to the portcullis. The building might have been used centuries before as a customs post. It was in a remarkable state of dereliction and ought to have been pulled down. I was baffled, wondering what had driven Herr Professor Kant to choose such a forlorn place to work upon his final masterpiece?

With an eager nod from his master, Johannes Odum produced a large key from his pocket, and proceeded with some difficulty to unlock the ancient, worm-eaten door.

'Wait here,' Kant said to his man. 'Now, Stiffeniis, if you lend me your arm, perhaps Sergeant Koch could step inside and strike a light? There's a lantern hanging just inside the door.'

The cobbled road was slippery underfoot with packed ice and snow and a thin top-sprinkling of frost, as treacherous as a road could be. If I needed proof of Immanuel Kant's age and physical frailty, I had it then. He rested his feather-like weight on my arm as we stepped inside the door, where Koch was waiting with a storm-lantern raised high above his head.

'Do not touch anything,' Kant warned.

We were in an abandoned store-room of some sort. Broken armament boxes had been dumped in a large, careless heap on one side of the room. Cobwebs hung like shimmering shrouds from the ceiling. Dust lay in a thick blanket over everything else. In the centre of the room, a large rat caught by the neck in a trap had been stripped to a skeleton by its luckier fellows.

'Go ahead, Koch,' Kant ordered. 'We will follow you.'

He pointed towards a narrow, vaulted tunnel, whose once-white walls were stained and black with mould and smoke. Dropping my arm as if possessed of a demonic energy, he set off at a shuffling trot behind Sergeant Koch, and I was obliged to accelerate to keep pace with him. Our passage through this tunnel was made more difficult by the lowness of the brick vault, which grazed the top of Kant's three-cornered hat, whilst Koch and I were obliged to stoop. My nose tingled with the pungent odour of rot, and there was a sharp, acidic smell underlying it. If Doctor Faustus and his familiar, Mephistopheles, had leapt out to welcome us in the gloomy depths of the place, I would not have been in the least surprised.

As we entered a large room at the end of the corridor, and Koch held up his light, I caught my first glimpse of the voluminous alembic jars and the serpentine glass-tubes which gleamed upon the shelves, together with a neat pile of boxes set in an orderly stack on a workbench.

'Feel the cold,' Kant enthused. 'Siberia is closer than you think!'

He ordered Koch to take a spill from his lantern and light the lamps which were hung at intervals around the walls. As the sergeant added light to light, the objects assembled in that room began to stand out more clearly from the gloom.

Professor Kant turned towards the far wall.

'Now, Stiffeniis, let me introduce you to those who are obliged to dwell down here in this unwholesome twilight world,' he said.

From the darkest corner of the room, vacant, watery eyes stared fixedly back at us in the pale, flickering glow of the lamplight.

Chapter 15

'Can you guess who they are, Stiffeniis?'

Immanuel Kant's voice was hoarse with the cold. There was a strident, triumphant note in it which robbed me of the power of speech. I could not drag my eyes away from the large glass jars lined up on the shelf, where four human heads floated in a pale, straw-coloured liquid.

'Draw closer,' Kant invited, taking me by the arm. 'Now, let me introduce you to Jan Konnen, Paula-Anne Brunner, Johann Gottfried Haase and this one here, a newcomer that you probably recognise, having seen him last night in the cellar at the Court House. Would you bring down the exhibit on the far left, Sergeant Koch, and place it on this table?'

Stunned horror written on his face, Koch obeyed without a word.

I was incapable of forming any coherent thought as I stared at the gruesome contents of the glass jar that Koch set before us on a table, while Kant was the soul of affable sociability. He might have been arranging the chairs for a tea party.

'Bring another lamp, Sergeant Koch. That's it, yes. And place it there. Just there!' Kant's voice battered painfully on my inner ear. 'Now, tell me, Stiffeniis. What can you see inside this jar?'

The lights on either side threw the human lineaments into sharp relief.

I swallowed hard, my voice little more than a whisper: 'It is a . . . a head, sir.'

'This was Jan Konnen, the first victim of the murderer. Now, I would like you to describe precisely what you are able to observe, and with all the accuracy at your disposal. Come, come, Stiffeniis!' he encouraged. 'A head?'

'A human head,' I corrected myself, 'which belongs . . . that is, which *used* to belong to a man aged about fifty. Despite the distorting effects of the glass jar, the facial features are regular, and . . .'

I stopped short. I knew not what to say next.

'Describe what you can *see*,' Kant pressed. 'I ask no more. Start at the crown of the head, then slowly work your way down.'

I attempted to shake off the numbing sense of inadequacy which had taken possession of me. 'His hair is tinged with grey. It is thin on top, almost bald, and worn long around the ears.'

'Covering the ears,' Kant corrected me.

'Covering the ears, yes. The forehead is . . .'

I baulked again. What in the name of God was I supposed to say?

'Don't stop! Go on!' Kant prodded impatiently.

'The . . . forehead is broad and it is without wrinkles.'

'And that vertical split where the eyebrows meet? Was it there before the man died? Or did it appear at the moment of his death?'

I took a step forward and peered closely.

'I have no way of knowing, sir,' I mumbled.

'Use your intuition!'

'It looks like a puzzled frown,' I suggested, examining the furrow closely.

'Would you not expect such a frown to fade away after death?'

'But it has not,' I said at last.

'This was the final expression on his face. It appeared at the moment of his death. The victim's facial muscles were paralysed in that precise expression. This is a well-known phenomenon. Any soldier with experience on the field of battle has seen a similar expression a hundred times before. It is of some importance,' added Kant. 'Now, what have you to say about the eyes?'

I looked into the unseeing eyes inside the jar. If Man has a soul, the ancients say, its light is visible there. If the body has a vital spirit, the ghost manifests itself through those windows. What so disconcerted me about the detached head of Jan Konnen was the sensation that he was watching us as intently as we were studying him.

'The victim's eyes have rolled up in their sockets, exposing the whites,' I forced myself to say.

'Could there be an explanation?'

I was bewildered. 'There is no literature on such matters, sir. I . . . Anatomy texts exist, of course, but not in a case like this one. Not concerning murder.'

'Very good, Stiffeniis. You see the tricky ground we are on? We have no authority to guide us. We must use our eyes, trust our observations, and make the deductions that logical inference suggests. This will be our method.'

'Perhaps the blow came from above?' I suggested. 'He glanced up when he was struck?'

Kant made a sound of approval. 'Did the blow come from above, or from behind? We are uncertain as yet, but we will not allow ourselves to be distracted by the question. Now, look at that nose, Stiffeniis! What can you read in it?' he quizzed, though he did not wait for an answer. 'That it is long, thin, and utterly undistinguished? And so we come to the mouth. How would you describe that?'

'Open?' I offered.

'Wide open?'

'Not entirely,' I said, defending my choice of word.

'Would you say that he was screaming when he died?'

There was something in Professor Kant's hungry expression that caused me to quake. For a moment, my head began to spin and I thought I was about to faint.

'Screaming, sir?' I echoed.

'An open mouth suggests that he was screaming in the instant that he met his death, wouldn't you say?'

I forced myself to look more carefully. 'No, sir, I would not. I would say that he was not screaming.'

'What was he doing, then? What kind of sound could have come from his mouth?'

'A gasp of surprise? A sigh?'

'Would you say that something dramatic and violent happened to produce that expression?' Kant went on.

'No, sir.'

'And I would agree with you. Now, Stiffeniis, the cause of death. Can you suggest what might have been the death stroke?'

'There is no unsightly wound to the face itself,' I floundered. 'Was clear evidence found elsewhere on the body?'

'The body does not interest us. It is the head, the *head*, which has its story to tell. Would you turn the jar, Sergeant?'

The candlelight cast a jaundiced sickly glow as the head rolled lazily in the cloudy liquid. 'Observe, Stiffeniis. Here at the base of the cranium. There was no resistance. The instrument went in like a hot knife cutting lard. But it was not a knife . . .'

These were the words with which I originally began this narration. At that time, I intended to celebrate the incredible versatility of the genius of Immanuel Kant, and hoped to reflect my own small part in the resolution of a mystery which held the city of Königsberg in thrall. But those words marked the first clear signpost on my personal road into the maze of corruption, treachery and evil that had been so carefully mapped out for me.

'Can you see it?' Kant bent close and pointed. 'The mortal stroke was delivered here. Death came quickly and it was unexpected. It was not a violent blow, there is no unsightly penetration. Something sharp and pointed entered Konnen's neck just here, and he was dead on his knees before he even realised what was happening. This tiny spot is all the evidence that remains of the attack.'

He paused for an instant, as if to emphasise the vital importance of what he said next.

'If I have understood you well, among the variety of weapons that Ulrich Totz claims to have used, he made no mention of anything which would leave a mark such as this.' His eager eyes darted quickly at me, and I felt a drowning sense of nausea, as if I had just received a violent blow to my own head.

'Koch, bring down another. Any jar will do.' Professor Kant's voice was tremulous with excitement as he picked up the nearest lamp and moved it closer to the second severed head. 'The same mark is evident here,' he said, rapping his forefinger sharply on the glass. 'Do you see it now?'

The scalp of Paula-Anne Brunner had been shaved away at the back, long red hair remaining on the crown and at the sides only. To my young eyes, there was something foul in such a desecration, the bare nudity of the woman's skull somehow suggestive of the stealthy violence by which she had met her death.

'There is an identical mark on Tifferch's neck,' he concluded flatly. Then with a sigh he added, 'If you had stayed to watch Vigilantius at work last night, you would have known straight away that Morik was not killed by the person you are here to chase. Totz is not the killer we are looking for.'

'Is this the work of Vigilantius?' I asked in a whisper.

In the dim light I thought I saw an expression of satisfaction settle on Kant's hungry face. 'The doctor is the *crème de la crème* of European anatomists!' he confirmed with pride, as if he had done the disgusting work himself.

The ingratiating smile on the necromancer's lips flashed before my eyes, taking on a new and more sinister significance. 'You may have finished *your* business, sir,' he had said with scorn the night before. 'But I have something more to do.'

I imagined him, pulling out the instruments from beneath his large mantle. What could they have been? Sharp knives, a medical saw, pointed scalpels, as he bent over that anatomical table and assaulted the corpse, cutting mercilessly away at the vulnerable remains of Lawyer Tifferch.

My anger flashed at Kant's lavish praise of the man.

'This proves that he's a charlatan, sir. He had no need to ask the spirit of the dead man to tell him how he had been killed. He knew the answer already!'

Kant placed a pacifying hand on my sleeve. 'You are unjust, Stiffeniis. The doctor had not performed the first dissection when he suggested in that histrionic and slightly irritating manner of his that the cause of death was to be found at the base of the dead man's head. The corpse had already spoken to him. The cutting came later.'

The dead man spoke?

'Professor Kant . . .' I began to protest.

'How did you guess, sir?'

Koch's question took us both by surprise.

'Excuse me, Professor Kant,' the sergeant said, and flushed with embarrassment, 'I did not mean to interrupt your speculations, but I am puzzled. How did you understand so quickly the significance of the murder of Jan Konnen? At that time, there was no way of knowing that similar crimes would follow on.'

Kant half closed his eyes, a contented smile illuminating his face.

'I have been collating vital information regarding the incidence of death in Königsberg for many years, Sergeant,' he said. 'About a year ago, I received my weekly report from the local police. A corpse was mentioned for which no evident cause of death had been identified. Now, that was *most* irregular. The physician called to certify the death had failed to notice that tiny perforation in the neck of Konnen. Cause of death – unknown. How was I to include such a death in my statistics? Had the man died, or had he been killed? I asked for the body to be donated to the University, and, by a fortunate turn of events, Doctor Vigilantius was lecturing at the Collegium Albertinum that very week. Having learned in conversation that he was also an experienced anatomist, I took advantage of the circumstance in two ways. Firstly, I was curious to see how a Swedenborgian communicates with the spirits of the dead. Secondly, I wished to preserve the evidence that you have just seen. When a similar murder occurred some months later, I saw the link, asked for the corpse, and sent for Doctor Vigilantius to repeat the operation.'

'Did Procurator Rhunken know of this place, sir?' asked Koch, making a sweeping gesture with his hand to indicate the whole laboratory.

Kant dismissed the idea with a flash of annoyance.

'Your master was not prepared to consider the utility of the evidence I was assembling here. He ridiculed my findings as the ramblings of senility! By using standard police procedures, he would never have caught the killer. The murderer's taste for his work was gaining in momentum, terror was mounting in the city, the King was worried about a possible French invasion, and he wanted the case to be solved without delay. *I* suggested to His Majesty some weeks ago that Procurator Rhunken be removed from his post. Special talents were needed here. Talents such as those of Augustus Vigilantius . . .'

'And myself,' I added.

Kant placed his hand on my arm and smiled warmly. 'Now you know why I sent for you, Hanno,' he said. 'Only someone who has visited the land of shadows can cope with what is happening here in Königsberg. As you are well aware, the darkest impulses of the human heart go far beyond Reason and Logic.'

Impulses of the human heart which go beyond Reason . . .

I froze. I had used that very phrase myself, the first time that we had met.

'That's why I sent you to The Baltic Whaler,' he said, his eyes sparkling mischievously. 'It seemed to be the obvious place to start. That inn had been the scene of the first murder, and rumours were rife that the owner was a sympathiser of Bonaparte. Morik, the serving boy, aroused his master's suspicions, I'm afraid. Now, that I did *not* foresee,' he added thoughtfully. 'Still, Totz killed him, and he used a hammer to do the deed, as he confessed to you. In doing so, he eliminated himself from our investigation. That must be clear to you by now, I hope.'

'Why did you not tell me at once, sir? You let me go blundering on in the name of Logic.'

I had been too easily persuaded of a political cause. That is, I had too easily convinced myself of it. Everything had fallen into place: the lurid contents of Herr Tifferch's cupboard, Morik's idle gossip, all that I had seen and heard at the inn, Ulrich Totz's confession, his poor wife's smile! I had twisted the facts to suit my theory. And in doing so, I had proven myself to be a mindless fool in the eyes of the very person who had trusted so much in my good qualities.

'You believed that you had definitive proof,' Kant continued. 'You would not accept anything else to the contrary, even when it was as plain as the nose on your face. Remember what I told you, Hanno. Your investigation must aim to reconstruct *how* things happened. It will not tell you *why* they happened in that way. The motivation is still hidden in darkness. Logic and Rationality do not guide the human heart, though they may explain its passions.'

He extracted a document from one of the files, and laid it on the table.

'Look at this,' he said.

Koch and I bent close in the flickering light. It was nothing more than a sheet of paper, on which an image had been sketched. There was not a trace of art in the drawing, just a vague outline of a kneeling body propped against a wall. There was a ghoulish contrast between the technical imperfection of the picture, and the simple figure that it portrayed. As if a child, distracted from daubing flowers and fairies, had chanced upon a scene of the most irresistible horror and innocently tried to capture the image on paper.

'What is it, sir?' asked Koch uneasily.

'Two gendarmes were sent to the scene of the first murder by Rhunken. I had already begun to conduct a parallel investigation using my own methods, of which I had privately informed the King. I instructed the same two gendarmes to sketch what they remembered having seen at the scene of the crime. This became a standard procedure for each of the following murders. The other drawings are in those files over there if you need them,' Kant pointed. 'They portray the exact positions in which each of the bodies was found.'

'You sent soldiers to *draw* dead bodies, sir?'

Kant laughed shrilly before replying to Koch's question.

'Unusual, don't you agree? One of the soldiers proved his worth. Whenever a suspect corpse was found, I told Lublinsky to make a sketch of the scene for me. I paid him for his efforts, of course.'

'A cross on a pay chit's more than most of them can manage,' Koch returned with surprise. 'May I ask another question, Professor Kant?'

Koch's eyes darted anxiously around the room.

'All this, this . . .' he muttered nervously. 'Heads without bodies! Why, it's . . . it's a monstrosity, sir. What do you hope to achieve by it?'

Kant turned to me and smiled as if Koch had never opened his mouth.

'The dead *do* speak to us, you know, Hanno. Now, do not misunderstand me. I have not been converted to Swedenborg's way of thinking. In this room, in this instant, a murdered man is the object of our scrutiny. By examining the physical evidence and scrutinising the circumstances, we can draw reasonable conclusions about where and when his murder was committed. These factors may help us in their turn to understand how the crime was enacted, and what was used to do the deed. Finally, if our intuitions have not played us false, we may even be able to conclude who his killer is. Morik was killed by Totz, and no one else. Now, the body of *this* dead man can tell us a great deal about the person who killed *him*.'

'You aim to reconstruct conditions at the scene of the murder, do you not?' asked Koch before I could speak.

'That is my intention, Sergeant. You have witnessed the usefulness of this 'monstrosity', as you choose to call it. Without these glass jars and their contents, Procurator Stiffeniis would have proceeded blithely on in the wrong direction and accused Ulrich Totz of crimes that he had never committed. Now, he can correct that error,' Kant said with quiet satisfaction.

'I call this place my laboratory,' he continued, 'though I have not yet found a suitable name for the science that I have been exploring here. This material will be of use to a mind trained in investigative procedures. If Herr Stiffeniis can work out how these crimes were perpetrated, he may anticipate the murderer's modus operandi and apprehend him. Of one thing we may be absolutely certain. This person will kill again!'

'Totz had no idea how these people were murdered,' I admitted. 'But why should he have lied to me?'

Kant touched my sleeve lightly, as if to encourage me.

'Morik was killed for a political motive, Stiffeniis,' he said. 'Totz told you the truth in that respect, at least. He must have thought his conspiracy was about to be discovered. Hence, he murdered the one person who had direct knowledge of the facts, the one person he could not trust. Morik.'

'But why accuse himself of the other murders?'

Kant shrugged. 'Would you wish to appear in the pathetic guise of a ruthless murderer of defenceless children? Ulrich Totz may simply be trying to fashion a more attractive image for himself as a revolutionary, a pitiless local Robespierre. You'll have to force the truth from him.'

'I will!' I said, feeling a weight of anger building inside me.

Again, Professor Kant placed a restraining hand on my arm.

'Before you go,' he continued with great animation, 'there is something else for you to see. It was the pretext on which I invited you here. I am truly surprised that you have not asked about it already.'

Like a stage magician pulling a rabbit from a hat, he set a folded grey cloth down on the table. 'The Devil's claw! Its presumed existence inspires more fear in Königsberg than any tangible fact could do. Uncover it, Stiffeniis.'

I held back.

'It won't bite,' he said with a brittle laugh.

The wrapping was thin. My nervous fingers felt a tiny form cocooned within. Whatever it was, the object was small and weighed next to nothing. I unfolded the material on the table-top to reveal a tiny pointed fragment measuring less than an inch in length. It seemed to be made of ivory or bone.

'What is it, sir?' Koch whispered.

Kant shook his head before speaking. 'Part of the murder weapon. The tip, I presume. It was probably longer when the murderer jabbed it into the base of each victim's skull. Vigilantius found this fragment impaled in Jan Konnen's neck. We can assume that as the killer attempted to pull it out, the point snapped off.'

'In the night officers' report, the woman who found the body spoke of seeing the Devil's claw,' I noted. 'Obviously, she couldn't have seen this tiny piece. Does the discrepancy suggest that she actually *saw* the whole weapon sticking out of the dead man's neck?'

'It's a point worth investigating,' Kant suggested with a vigorous nod.

'I must speak to her. Lublinsky's reports are vague on this particular point.'

'Lublinsky might know where she is,' Koch added, picking up the fragment from the table and studying it with the sort of avid concentration a botanist might apply to an exotic fruit he had never seen before. 'If this one snapped and broke, the killer seems to have had no trouble obtaining a replacement, sir. I'd wager that they are easy to procure.'

'And to hide,' said Kant. 'No sensible man stands close to the butcher when he swings the cleaver in his hands.'

He turned to me, an amused glint in his eye.

'Do you see the way ahead now, Hanno?' he asked.

I looked at the glass jars, the files and the boxes stacked on their shelves.

'Everything here is new to me, sir,' I said with a shiver of excitement. 'But I promise to use these remarkable objects to the best of my ability.'

I might have been swearing a solemn oath.

'Here is the key,' said Kant with a kindly smile. 'The heads are there, the clothes the victims were wearing at the time are stored in those boxes. Each box is marked with the name. Sketches of the corpses are in those folders.' Kant pointed everything out with methodical calm. 'All you need, I believe, is in this room. The exhibits are yours, Stiffeniis. Use them as you think fit.'

Kant appeared to shrink before my eyes as he placed the key in my hand. I had the feeling that it had not been an entirely natural performance, though it had certainly been memorable. His nervous strength was utterly consumed.

'Take Professor Kant home in his coach, Koch,' I said. 'I will make my way on foot to the main gate. I want to speak to Lublinsky at once.'

'Oh no, sir. No!' Koch replied with force. '*You* take the Professor home. I will return on foot to the main building of the Fortress. You'll get lost, sir, while I know precisely where to find Officer Lublinsky.'

'It could be dangerous,' I replied, puzzled by the fierceness of Koch's opposition to my proposal.

'I'll keep my wits about me,' the sergeant replied, glancing in the direction of Professor Kant. In a flash I realised what was troubling him. He was not afraid of the dark, the fog, or the unknown criminal stalking the night. He was frightened of Immanuel Kant.

'Very well,' I conceded. 'Find Lublinsky and see what he has to say about the woman. I will join you shortly at the Fortress.'

Outside, night had fallen. The fog was even denser than before, and cut visibility on the dark stretch of road beneath the Fortress to nothing. Johannes Odum leapt forward to open the door while I assisted Professor Kant to mount the carriage-steps.

'Will you be coming home with Professor Kant, sir?' Johannes asked, a note of caution in his voice. I suddenly recalled that the valet wished to show me something at the house.

'Of course, I will,' I replied, handing Professor Kant into the coach, and again I was moved by his frailty and the effort of will that it cost him to match the incredible energy of his mind.

'Be careful, Sergeant,' I warned, as I climbed up behind Professor Kant, and Koch slammed the door. 'Take no risks.'

The coach pulled away and proceeded slowly. Neither I, nor Professor Kant spoke for some time. At last, he turned to me. 'I hope you'll join me in a warming glass of Bischoff's cordial? It has been a tiring day, and we both need something strong to fortify our spirits.'

'With the greatest of pleasure, sir.'

The promise seemed to content him. A few moments later, he was snoring lightly, his head reclining against the seat. I leaned back myself, thinking of the letter I had intended to write to Helena announcing my success in hunting down the killer. Thanks to Professor Kant, my days in Königsberg were not to be so quickly counted off.

Chapter 16

Professor Kant slept all the way home. The driving energy that had sustained him throughout that day seemed to have left him utterly spent. Only minutes before, eyes sparkling with excitement, his movements had been swift, unburdened by age, his mind quick, speech animated. But slumped there beside me on the carriage seat, that glistening cape of his looked like an empty cocoon left behind by some recently hatched creature which had taken wing to find its way in the cruel world.

But I was not in the least tired. By an inexplicable law of osmosis, the energy that had left my mentor now passed to me. That morning on the muddy banks of the River Pregel, I had seen the corpse of a boy, his head smashed beyond repair. I had just emerged from a sinister chamber of horrors which was barely conceivable in a howling nightmare. The streets of Königsberg were dark and dangerous. A killer was lurking there, a ruthless being who thought nothing of taking human life, leaving tragedy in his wake, promising worse violence to come. But my heart was singing. I might have been returning from a walk through the idyllic woods of Westphalia. As we left Professor Kant's laboratory far behind us, my mind was filled with sensations that any other man might have reserved for a refined and precious collection of *objets d'art*. Was I disgusted by what I had seen in that dark and gloomy place? Quite the opposite!

I held the key to Kant's laboratory tightly in my hands, which shook with awe and fascination. Those exhibits were remarkable, but more remarkable was the fact that Kant had entrusted the custody of his collection to *me*. To me, and to no one else! It did not surprise me to learn that Herr Procurator Rhunken had not been privy to the secrets of the place. Poor, loyal Koch had been shocked by the news, but I was elated by it. Now I knew why Kant had chosen me instead of any other magistrate. Other men might be more experienced in the traditional ways of criminal detection, but Kant believed that I alone would be able to comprehend the utility of the exhibits and appreciate the macabre *beauty* – there was no better word for it – which his incredible mind had conceived and created in that place. Seven years before, Kant had advised me to become a magistrate. And now he was offering me the opportunity I had purposely sought to avoid in Lotingen. He had placed the material in my hands and invited me to prove that I was the first of a new breed of investigative magistrates, that I was capable of employing a totally revolutionary technique involving methods that had never been used before in the fight against the worst of all crimes. Crimes that could endanger the very peace of the Nation.

This was the reason that had impelled him to call Vigilantius, and use both his anatomical knowledge and his arcane skills to assist the law. Was there a magistrate alive who would have dared to employ such a stratagem? That was why he had wanted me to watch the necromancer at work the night before. Suddenly, I saw the doctor's skills in a wholly different light. Kant's aged mind was drifting towards some dark and final shore, but the great philosopher had not lost his grip on reality, nor his ability to apply logic and sound reasoning to the resolution of a conundrum. He was teaching me to do what he was physically no longer able to do for himself. He was my Socrates, he was leading me towards a completely new way of looking and doing. Investigating a criminal act was not simply a matter of gathering circumstantial information and worming the truth out of a reluctant witness, as Rhunken thought. As I had thought myself, I reflected, with a flash of honesty.

Kant had been preparing me for what I had just seen, training me to use such knowledge for the good of Mankind, warning me not to discount any evidence in the light of its perversity or *monstrosity*, as Sergeant Koch had called it. Surely, that was how Rhunken must have viewed Kant's way of doing things. As recently as the night before, I would have agreed with Rhunken. In a trice, I realised what I must do. When the case was over, when the murderer was caught and condemned, I would write a learned treatise of my own to celebrate the incomparable genius of Immanuel Kant. He had ventured further in this field than any other man before him, and I was thrilled by the prospect of learning from the inventor of this new procedure. I turned to watch the Professor sleep, my soul crushed by waves of emotion and gratitude. I owed everything to him. He might have been my father. Indeed, I realised, I owed him more, far more, than I had ever owed my own father.

My head was spinning with the immensity of these considerations. I had to close my eyes to regain equilibrium, and did not open them again until the coach lurched suddenly and stopped. Outside, the fog was thicker than before. I glanced again to Professor Kant, but he slept blithely on. Beyond the window-glass, a face materialised in the milky darkness, and the ghostly apparition of Johannes Odum signalled me to step down into the road. I opened the carriage door with all haste and quiet.

'We can go no further, Herr Stiffeniis,' the valet announced as I stood beside him. The fog became an impenetrable wall at the point where a rippling stream ran beside the road. 'I'm very afraid of driving the coach into the ditch.'

'I'll walk ahead and lead the horse on,' I offered.

'Take one of the carriage-lamps, sir. Be careful, the way is treacherous here,' he advised.

I set off quickly in the direction of the house, but was forced to slow down. Beneath my feet the snow was tightly packed. Behind, the horse shied with fright. Johannes had him tightly reined in, fearing for the worst, but I was forced to plod on for an age before Professor Kant's residence finally loomed up out of the fog.

Johannes lifted Kant from the coach like a sleeping babe, while I held up the lamp and helped them by opening the door. Standing in the hall, I watched as the valet carried his master effortlessly up the stairs to his bedchamber, waiting there while Johannes made him good for the night. The operation took no more than ten minutes.

'He's truly worn out. Thank God for a moment's peace!' Odum

whispered, as he reached the bottom of the stairs. 'But now, if you follow me, sir, I'll show you what I found this morning.'

Taking up the carriage-lamp, he opened the front door and led me with difficulty to the rear of the house. The kitchen garden was enclosed all around by tall trees. Snow lay in knee-deep drifts and folds, and the going was difficult.

'This is Professor Kant's private study,' he said, stopping by a darkened window. He lowered the lamp closer to the ground. 'But look here, sir. This is what scared me this morning.'

I looked down. The snow gleamed like diamonds in the beam of light. Dark imprints etched like stepping stones in the frozen mantle led all the way from the window to a wicket gate at the far end of the enclosure. I examined these vague footprints in the snow for a moment, wondering to myself what Johannes was so concerned about. Had the responsibility of looking after Professor Kant begun to wear on his nerves?

'Is this what you wished to show me?'

He glanced at the ground, then back to me. 'After we returned from the river this morning, sir, I opened the curtains in the study. And there they were!'

'I do not follow, Johannes.'

'No one's been out here since summer.'

I felt the muscles tense in my jaw. 'Are you certain? A neighbour, perhaps? A beggar, or a tradesman?'

Johannes shook his head with energy.

'There's only one possibility, sir,' he said with great seriousness. 'Some person has been spying on him. Or trying to enter the house.'

There was something lumbering, heavy – almost stupid, I might say – about the man. The cold air seemed to have dropped an appreciable number of degrees, and I shivered violently despite the heavy woollen cloak that Lotte Havaars had providently seen fit to pack for me.

'Or worse, Johannes,' I said with far more calm than I felt.

'Worse, sir?'

'The killer may have followed him here.'

'Oh, God!' Johannes exclaimed with a groan. 'I told Professor Kant he was becoming too involved in those murders. I warned you, sir. Being seen down there by the river was dangerous. Now, you must . . .'

I held up my hand to stop this flow of recrimination, concentrating on the measures which would need to be taken straight away. 'We will protect him,' I said. 'Make sure to bar the doors and lock all windows, Johannes. I will call the gendarmes to guard the house and watch the road.'

As I spoke, I stared at those footprints in the snow. What would Kant do in such circumstances as these, I asked myself. The answer came in a flash. My mind turned in the direction that Professor Kant had so carefully plotted out for it.

'There's something we must do first,' I said with decision. 'Herr Professor himself would have done it. Hold up that lamp, Johannes.'

'You'll not bring Professor Kant out here, I hope, sir?' Johannes cried with fright.

'What are you saying, man?' I replied. 'I would not dream of disturbing him. What I mean to do is apply the analytical method that Professor Kant has just been showing me in his laboratory.'

'Sir?' Confusion glistened in the servant's eyes.

'We need to find a specimen which is whole and compact,' I said, looking around me.

'A specimen? Of what, sir?'

'Of a footprint, Johannes. Keep that lamp close to the ground.'

The wind had made the top surface of the snow as brittle as glass. As I bent closer and studied the surface of the snow, I could see that some attempt had been made to cancel the prints. Whoever had been lurking outside that window had let his feet drag as he walked, to avoid leaving the very evidence that I was seeking.

'Follow the tracks across the garden,' I said.

Johannes mumbled some complaint or protest to himself, then held up the lamp and led the way.

'Do not step on the imprints,' I warned him. 'There's confusion here enough already.'

The tracks led to the hedge and a wicket gate in the far corner of the garden. They seemed to have been left by a person who was in a hurry, and they had all been distorted. Not one was whole. We passed out into the lane at the rear of the house, but the footsteps of the passers-by combined to render the task impossible.

'This is a hopeless task, sir!' Johannes burst out nervously.

I led him back to the garden in silence, examining the trodden area beneath the window once again, then moving on to the three stone steps which led up to the back door of the house.

'He's been here, you see? And here . . .'

A cry of triumph erupted from my lips. On the top step, springing into sharp relief as Johannes raised the flickering lamp, was the reward for all my stubborn persistence: a footprint in its entirety.

'He tried to enter by this door,' I said, beginning to search for drawing paper in my bag.

'D'you think he got inside, sir?' Johannes asked, a note of fear in his voice.

I carefully examined the solid barrier of dark pine and the large metal keyhole. Everything was neat, intact, untouched. 'There is no sign of an attempt to force it open. The door seems to be locked from inside,' I said, trying the handle.

'I barred it myself, sir.'

'He must have abandoned his plan. At least, for the moment,' I said, my voice catching in my throat. What would happen, I thought, if he found the way to break in next time? 'Come, Johannes, we must determine if this is the murderer's footprint.'

'But how, sir? How can you do that?' he said, an expression of blank incomprehension on the servant's face.

'By comparing this print with the tracings of footprints made where the murders took place,' I replied, realising even as I spoke that I was using the new investigative language of Kant, which could mean nothing to the servant. 'This is what your master would have done,' I explained. I had found a sheet of paper in my bag, and was searching in vain for a pencil. 'But what am I to draw with?' I murmured, looking around as if I expected a quill and a pot of ink to materialise before my eyes.

'Draw, sir? I don't understand you.'

'Those prints. I want to copy them. Is there a pencil in the house?'

'In my master's room, sir. But I wouldn't want to wake him.' He glanced around the garden. 'One moment,' he said, breaking a brittle twig from a leafless rosemary bush beside the kitchen door. He opened the lantern, burned the wood in the flame, extinguished the lighted stick in the snow, then handed it to me.

'Charcoal, of course!' I exclaimed with a smile.

Daily contact with Kant's genius had evidently worked its magic on the uneducated valet. Never was such a simple instrument more useful. I laid the paper down on the snow next to the footprint to mark off the extension, then rested it on my knee and drew in the figure. There was a distinctive crosscut on the sole of the shoe – the left foot of the pair – which would be useful for the purpose of comparison. Warming to my task, I sketched out a plan of the garden and drew arrows to indicate the direction of the intruder's coming and going, while Johannes watched in silence.

'You heard nothing out of the ordinary last night, I suppose?' I asked him, as I was completing my sketch.

'No, sir, I . . . I did not,' he faltered.

I lifted my head and stared at him. His eyes shifted away from mine.

Had he let someone into the house, someone of whom his master might not have approved? But that was illogical. Would he have shown me the footprints if he knew for certain who had left them?

'Nothing at all, Johannes?' I insisted.

Might he have taken unfair advantage of the fact that his aged master was sleeping? Johannes was thirty years of age, no more. He might have a sweetheart or be married.

'Hold up that lantern,' I said, searching his face as he obeyed reluctantly. 'Believe me, Johannes, anything you choose to tell me, your master will know nothing of the matter. Did you invite someone into the house without asking the permission of Professor Kant?'

'Oh no, sir. No!' His denial was immediate. 'I would never dream of taking such a liberty. I give you my oath on it, sir.'

Despite this fervent plea of innocence, Johannes seemed to be on the verge of tears. I waited, watching in silence. It is a trick we magistrates favour.

'In truth, sir,' he added, 'I do have a . . . a minor confession to make. It means breaking faith, but . . . I . . . well, you ought to know of it.'

He set the lantern on the ground, rubbed his hands together, bunched them over the flaps of his pockets in tight fists, then stared unhappily into my face.

'Professor Kant could be in grave peril,' I reminded him.

'I . . . I was afraid to tell anyone, sir. Especially Herr Jachmann. I thought I'd lose my place if I told him. Herr Jachmann instructed me never to leave Professor Kant alone.'

'Quite right,' I said.

'And I have followed his instructions to the letter, sir. Except . . .'

'Except for what?'

'Except for Professor Kant himself.'

'What do you mean?'

'He asked me to leave him alone for an hour last night, sir. He gave me permission to visit my wife. You might say that he . . . insisted.'

'Alone, Johannes?' I was shocked. 'Why should he wish to send you away at night?'

'He's working on his book, sir. He said that he wanted no distractions. I tried to dissent, but he told me to make the most of the opportunity. Indeed,' he added, 'it has happened a number of times, sir.'

'When was the last time?'

'Why, yester-night . . .'

'Before *that*!' I hissed.

'A week, ten days ago, sir. He has released me from his service five or six times in the past month.'

I trembled to think of the mortal danger to which Professor Kant had exposed himself. I imagined the murderer spying on him alone in the house. Like a spider watching the fly that had fallen into its web.

'How could you?' I seethed. 'Alone in the house at night? At his age?'

Johannes was now in tears.

'What was I to do, sir?' he protested, wiping his eyes on his sleeve. 'Herr Professor was so kind to me. It would have been ungrateful to refuse him. I can't deny it, sir, living in this house I miss my wife and children.'

'You should have informed Herr Jachmann,' I said. 'It was your duty. He administers Professor Kant's domestic affairs.'

'I know it, sir. But Herr Jachmann comes no more.' He hesitated for a moment, then with peasant practicality he insisted, 'And Professor Kant *is* my master, sir. I had to obey *him*. It's put me in a very difficult position.'

He bowed his head and began to sob again like a child.

'You know what is happening in Königsberg,' I said, placing a hand on his shoulder to calm him. 'There is a murderer in the city. You must never forget it!'

Johannes bit his lip and choked back his emotion.

'I swear to you, sir! I'll never leave him alone again . . .'

'He is alone at this moment, is he not?' I said. 'Go back inside, Johannes. I will finish here. I'll send a squad of soldiers from the Fortress the instant that I arrive.'

He turned to go, then stopped. 'You won't tell Herr Jachmann, will you, sir?' he begged, looking back over his shoulder.

'I expect to hear from you at the first sign of danger,' I said, making no attempt to reassure him. 'Do not hesitate. Call the soldiers!'

I watched him return along the path to the front of the house. As I followed him some moments later, I heard the entrance door close behind him, the heavy bolts sliding into place. As I hurried away in the direction of the town, the urgency of danger prickled at my scalp. Servant and master were alone in the house, while a killer was stalking the streets of the city. He had set his sights on Professor Kant, and the soldiers had yet to be sent. Again, I felt the overwhelming burden on my shoulders. Before it had concerned the safety of the whole of Prussia. Now, the person that I loved and admired more than any other in the world. Except for my wife and my children.

I left Magisterstrasse, and turned down the dark lane which led towards the city centre and the Fortress. As I strode purposefully through the deserted, tree-lined streets, I was aware that the person who had dared to violate the *sancta sanctorum* of Immanuel Kant must have followed the same route that I was now treading. He could be hiding behind any one of those trees. I glanced around anxiously and increased my pace, the image of a large glass jar flashing before my eyes, my head floating inside it, while Doctor Vigilantius casually washed my sticky blood from his hands and put his knives away.

Slipping and falling on the icy surface more than once, my frantic progress matched the furious thundering of my heart. I did not pause to catch my breath until the flickering lanterns outside the Fortress appeared through the gloom on the far side of Ostmarktplatz. But as I began to advance again, more slowly now, a sudden movement in the shadows caught my eye.

A man was standing near the main gate in the freezing cold.

He looked up, saw me, and began to run in my direction, mindless of the ice and the snow which covered the cobblestones.

A sensation of helplessness possessed me then. I felt like a wooden puppet with a human brain. And an unknown, malignant hand had just jerked tightly on my strings.

Chapter 17

Sergeant Koch came slithering to a halt in front of me. His face was pale, drawn, his mouth gaping, puffing out clouds of milk-hued air as he fought to catch his breath.

'What's wrong?' I gasped, my heart racing like a cornered hare. My nerves were raw. The mysterious footprints in Kant's garden. The palpable sense of danger in the city which came with darkness. Each new fear was greater than the last.

'There's been a mishap, sir.'

'What's happened?' I shouted, catching at the lapels of Koch's pea-coat and shaking him.

He grasped my wrists with a strength that I did not expect and lifted my hands away. 'We could do nothing to save them, sir,' he said.

'To save *whom*?' I cried.

'Totz and his wife, sir. Half an hour ago. They killed themselves.'

The implications of this news flashed upon me. Two people whom I had accused of murder, conspiracy and sedition, two people whom I had thrown into prison, intending to torture the truth out of them, had taken the final decision into their own hands.

'I gave instructions to keep them apart,' I managed to say.

Koch took me by the arm and led me towards the gate. 'And so they were, sir. I spoke to Stadtschen. He vowed that your order had been obeyed to the letter. When Totz was taken down, he was obliged to pass the cell where his wife was being held. They must have exchanged some sign, a signal. It was all decided in an instant.'

Koch banged on the entrance, the gate swung open, and we stepped into the torch-lit inner court. 'I instructed the guards to bring the bodies up before the other prisoners catch on,' he said. 'They have six senses down there, they smell death like starving wolves. At all costs, we must avoid a riot. General Katowice won't stand for it. He'll hang the lot of them. Fortunately, the ship that's taking them to Siberia is on its way, Herr Procurator. It should arrive tomorrow, depending on the weather. Stadtschen is making arrangements for the Section D prisoners to be taken to the port in Pillau. They'll pass the night there. It'll be a darned sight safer than keeping them here in the Fortress, sir.'

I nodded, unable to find my voice.

'We have been lucky. Really, sir, if the word might be permitted,' he went on. 'Totz was in a cell by himself. His wife was with two women, and they were both asleep when she took her life. She didn't make a sound. A guard found the husband first, then went to check . . .' He stopped suddenly and looked beyond my shoulders. 'But here they come.'

Soldiers were crossing the courtyard with two heavily laden, grey blankets slung between them.

'They'll be buried in the morning,' Koch added.

The fixed expression on Gerta Totz's lips flashed through my mind. Had she smiled in that same ingratiating fashion while taking her own life? The urge to see was irresistible. I strode across the courtyard.

'Lay them on the ground!' I ordered. 'Throw those blankets off.'

The signs of violence were written clearly on the corpses. Gerta Totz's face was black, swollen to bursting, her eyes popping out, as if she had just been told something very rude. The strip of dress she had used to hang herself was tightly knotted round her throat, sliced above the knot when they had cut her down from the cell-grating. Her nostrils were still ringed with the blood that my punch had drawn. Otherwise, the distorting hand of death had wiped everything familiar from her features. That hideous grin was gone forever.

Ulrich Totz's face was a bloody mask.

'He smashed his head against the cell wall with extraordinary violence,' Koch explained.

'More than once to produce such devastation,' I added with a shiver.

A river of dried blood cascaded from his crushed nose to his white linen shirt-front. He had succeeded in smashing his pate or breaking his neck. I stared at the bodies for some moments, then turned away. How should I consider them? As the fifth and sixth victims of the monster of Königsberg, or, like Morik, were they the victims of my own bungling?

'Take them away,' I murmured. I watched the soldiers frog-march across the yard with their burden, and struggled to shake off my depression. 'Send a patrol at once to Magisterstrasse, Sergeant,' I ordered. 'Someone has been prowling in Professor Kant's garden. It could well be the murderer.'

Koch knit his brow. 'Kant's not been harmed, I hope?'

'He's well. But not safe. He won't be out of danger until this affair is over,' I muttered, grinding my teeth. 'It seems that the killer is growing bolder.'

'Do you really think he'd try to kill the Professor, sir? This monster has always chosen his victims at random. That was his strength. No one knew where or when he would strike next. So, why decide to attack a specific target all of a sudden?'

'Perhaps he has changed his strategy,' I replied helplessly. 'The killer is faceless, hidden by anonymity, yet he knows who we are. Clearly, he knows that Kant is involved, and also where he is to be found at any hour of the day or night. He rarely leaves the house.'

'I'll give orders to the duty officer, Herr Procurator,' said Koch. He ran away across the yard and an armed patrol left by the main gate at a half-trot a few minutes later. Relief swept over me like a massive wave, but I felt no better when that sea subsided. All that had happened that day in Königsberg, and all that might still happen, seemed to weigh on me like a granite tombstone. Darkness crowded in upon me. Darkness, and a terrible sense of responsibility. Three people were dead, and the fault was mine. I closed my eyes to block the awful vision out.

'You do look pale, sir.'

Koch was standing before me, an expression of concern on his face.

'You must keep your strength up. It's been a long day, sir, there's food in the regimental kitchen. You have not eaten a bite since breakfast.'

'Thank you, Koch,' I said, and attempted to smile. 'You are better than a wet-nurse.'

His imperturbable face relaxed a little. 'Follow me, sir.'

I was beginning to think that, if nothing else, I had made *one* wise decision in the past two days. Sergeant Koch had shown the better side of himself after the difficulties of our first few hours together. Throwing open a door, he led me into a large, vaulted room which was excessively heated by a ceramic stove of gargantuan proportions.

'The garrison refectory,' he explained.

Human sweat and the odour of boiled mutton hung ripe in the air, but I felt at home with the stench. After the pungent stink of methyl alcohol and human decay in Kant's laboratory, this smell was healthy. It came from living beings doing vital things: working, eating, drinking, protecting the city and its inhabitants.

Koch sat me down, then went out again, returning some minutes later with a young soldier in a white apron who laid a tray on the table before me. A bowl of mutton broth with knobs of fatty gristle, black bread, red wine. A soldier's repast. I fell on it with appetite, while Koch stood looking on like a proud restaurateur.

I felt brighter almost immediately.

'Not for a delicate stomach, Koch,' I said between mouthfuls, 'but the most invigorating dish I ever ate in my life. Now, what have you to report about this woman who found the first corpse and about the gendarme who spoke to her?'

I gulped another spoonful of broth. 'What's his name?'

'Lublinsky, sir.'

'Did you speak to him?'

He nodded. 'A most singular person, Herr Procurator,' Koch replied.

I stopped eating and looked up at him. 'What do you mean?'

'You'd better see for yourself, sir,' he smiled uncomfortably. 'It was a mistake to leave such delicate business in the hands of rough soldiers, in my opinion. Give them a battle, they know exactly what to do. Ask 'em to speak to a woman, you cannot guess what might come of it.'

'Is he quartered here?' I asked, sipping wine.

'He's in the infirmary, sir.'

'Is he ill?'

'Not *ill*, as such. One of the walking wounded.' Koch jabbed a finger at his cheek. 'Just about here, sir. He looks as if he's been stabbed.'

'Been duelling, has he?'

'Lublinsky would probably deny it. Soldiers deny everything as a rule.'

'I want to speak with him straight away.'

Koch indicated the tray. 'Don't you want to finish your meal first, sir?'

'He is one of the investigators, Koch. The sooner I see him, the better.'

'I'll go and get him from the Infirmary, sir.'

Koch went away, while I finished what was left on my plate. I felt like a new man by the time he returned in the company of Officer Lublinsky.

I did not pay the soldier any immediate attention as he entered the room, but poured myself more wine and drank it down, the warm liquid melting the cold of a dreadful morning and a worse afternoon from my frozen bones.

'Stand there,' I heard Koch saying. Then, he came around the table to stand at my shoulder like a guardian angel.

Lublinsky clicked his heels and stood to attention. Only then did I glance up, and my stomach churned on the food I had just consumed. A cry of revulsion rose to my lips, though I managed to stifle it. Never in all my life have I seen a man more horrible to behold. Every inch of his rough, red skin was pitted, potted with lumps, holes, every sort of excrescence that distemper could inflict. From his forehead to his chin, he had lost any resemblance to Nature. Among the peasants working on my father's land I had seen what smallpox could do to a human being. What it had done to Lublinsky was beyond description.

His uniform had a collar cut high to cover the livid pockmarks and festering boils which plagued his neck and his throat. A black, blood-ringed wound gaped in his left cheek. He deliberately wore a forage-cap two sizes larger than he required, in order to cover his face.

'Take off your cap in the presence of Herr Procurator,' Koch ordered brusquely. The man obeyed, and his baldness came to light with all the starkness of harsh deformity, the crown of his head as pocked and cratered with boils and scars as his face. Had it not been for his height and build, and his ability as a soldier of the King, he would have found employment in a travelling freak-show and nowhere else. He glanced beyond me, challenging Koch to meet his eye. Those eyes were large and black, and darted around with fiery energy. He would have been handsome if Fate had dealt him a better hand. With those high cheekbones, aquiline nose, square jaw and strong chin, he might have been an artist's model or the lover of a baroness in a better world.

'Shall I remove the plates, sir?' Koch enquired.

'Leave them be.' I had no wish to diminish Koch in the eyes of this man. 'You have been assisting in the investigation of the murders under the direct supervision of Professor Kant, have you not?' I said, addressing Lublinsky.

His eyes darted from me to Koch, then back again, and he opened his mouth to speak. If I had been shocked by his face, his voice horrified me. A spluttering wild baboon seemed to have been let loose in his oral cavity, a beast he had great trouble in taming. I must have shown my difficulty, for he suddenly stopped short, then started up again, pronouncing his words more slowly to avoid the nasal and guttural emissions that made his speech so difficult to comprehend.

'Professor who?' he whined, the words whistling from a severely cleft palate. 'I did what I was told. Reports, they wanted. Reports, they got.'

'But you were also paid to make drawings for Professor Kant.'

'Oh, *him*!' he exclaimed. 'Was he a professor?'

'Who did you think he was?' I asked.

Lublinsky shrugged. 'I wasn't paid to think, sir. I didn't care. I gave him what he asked for. The world is full of old men with strange tastes.'

I forced myself to look at him, and tried to imagine what was going though his mind. Everything in Königsberg seemed to be tainted, sick, removed from the normal light of day. In that instant I felt oppressed by the necessity that obliged me to be a part of it. What 'talent' had Professor Kant divined in this improbable man?

'Tell me about yourself,' I said, and soon I wished I had not asked.

A great deal of patience was needed to make sense of his babble. His name was Anton Theodor Lublinsky. He was a native of Danzig. He had enrolled in the light infantry ten years before, and seen fighting in Poland. For three years he had been stationed in Königsberg, where, he chose to specify, he'd been happy until quite recently.

'Are you not content here, Lublinsky? What changed your mind?' I asked, thinking that he had a perfect right to be unhappy wherever he might happen to find himself.

'I'd rather be fighting, sir.' He seemed to smoulder at the idea, then added gruffly, 'On the battlefield you see your enemy face to face.'

His coal-black eyes blazed defiantly, then looked away.

What had he seen to induce him to prefer military action and the risk of being killed? I leaned across the table, slammed my fist down hard, then stared into his eyes. The sharp odour of his person mingled with the stench that had impregnated the room. I had to force myself not to look away.

'I have read your official reports, Lublinsky,' I said. 'I found them less than complete. Tell me exactly what you observed at the scene of the murder near The Baltic Whaler. You were the first to see the body, were you not?'

He shook his head.

'That's not exact, sir. I was with another gendarme. Then, there was the woman . . .'

'One year ago,' I recapped, 'you were sent to the scene. You spoke with the woman who had found the body. Is that exact? I want to know precisely what was said on that occasion.'

Lublinsky began to speak in a gabble. Had I closed my eyes, I might been listening to some mysterious Greek oracle, or a voice conjured up from beyond the grave by Vigilantius. I studied the man's lips in the hope of understanding, while Koch prodded, corrected and interpreted.

That morning, he reported, a cold wind was sweeping in from the sea. He had risen at four to assume command of the guard. As he was relieving the night officer, word came in that a body had been found near the port. He and Kopka, his second-in-command, went off to examine the find, leaving the night-officer at his post. They both welcomed the opportunity to be out and about, instead of hanging around at the Fortress with nothing to do. At the scene, they found a corpse and a woman. There was no one else. The sun had not yet risen, the streets were still deserted.

'What did you see there, Lublinsky?'

He was silent for some time.

'I've stared Death in the face a thousand times, sir,' he said suddenly, glaring fiercely at me. 'Oceans of blood, fearsome wounds, the agony of grapeshot. There was none of that in Merrestrasse. But I felt no better on that count.'

He and Kopka had found no sign of violence, nothing to indicate how the murderer had dealt the *coup de grâce*. Even so, it was obvious that the victim had not died of natural causes.

'Obvious, Lublinsky?'

The body of Jan Konnen had pitched forward on his knees, the head resting against the bare stone. It was the same position Muslims adopted when they prayed to their God, he said. As nothing was to be learned from the corpse, they had turned their attention to the woman. A midwife on her way to deliver a baby. The woman refused to say a word. She was shaking with fright. Then, Kopka had a bright idea. He went to procure a pint of gin from a nearby inn.

Lublinsky paused, and seemed to think long and hard before he continued. 'She wasn't the killer, sir. That was clear enough.'

'Clear? What was clear about it?'

He sucked in a mighty gasp of air through his mouth like a suffocating animal. 'She was terrified.'

'What was this woman's name?'

He hesitated again.

'I want to know the midwife's name,' I repeated firmly. 'You failed to record that in your report.'

A cloud of emotions seemed to tear at his face and mouth.

'Withholding information is a criminal offence,' I warned him.

'Anna, sir,' he said, after some moments of brooding silence. 'Anna Rostova.'

'Did she tell you this while Kopka was away?' I asked.

Lublinsky's large hands began to trawl nervously over his uniform, adjusting his buttons, straightening his collar, rolling his cap up tightly into a tube. At last, he glanced at me and nodded.

'And why would she do that? How did you win her confidence?'

He flushed bright red. 'I don't know, sir,' he said. 'I . . . that is, I thought she might have taken a fancy to me.'

That a man so ugly might take advantage of the promise of sexual favours from a woman extravagant enough to offer them did not seem far-fetched. I could almost sympathise.

'For no other reason?'

An expression of pain took possession of Lublinsky's face. Of all the sordid details of this story that recur most frequently to my mind, Lublinsky's ruined face most disturbs my sleep and dreams. His eyes darted around the room, his mouth opened and closed like a carp beached on a fouled hook.

'It was pity, sir. Her only child had died of smallpox, she said. She knew what I had suffered. That was the reason she gave.'

I looked at Lublinsky long and hard. His laboured breathing was the only sound in the room.

'What *exactly* did this woman propose?' I asked, preparing myself to hear a squalid confession of sexual degeneracy.

Before he chose to answer, Lublinsky played with his fingernail at the hole in his cheek until the blood flowed. Then, resentment burst from him violently, as if some private dam of reserve had suddenly given way.

'She told me that the Devil had murdered him.'

'The Devil,' I repeated mechanically.

'She had seen his claws, sir.'

'Did you see them too?' I asked with all the ingenuity at my disposal.

'No, sir. There was nowt to see. I examined the corpse. There was nothing. No wound, no weapon. Only Satan could have done it, she said.'

'So, you saw nothing, but you believed her. Why did you not include these details in your written report?' I objected.

Lublinsky did not respond. Instead, a violent quivering shook his limbs. I did not comprehend the battle going on in his head, the invisible enemy that had him by the throat.

'She said . . . she'd . . . help me, sir,' he murmured at last.

'A midwife, Lublinsky? How could a midwife help you?'

He raised a hand to his scarred and blistered face. 'She promised to cure me. I caught the fever in Poland. I should have died, but didn't. I wish I had. I was engaged to a lass from Chelmo. She ditched me when she saw my face. And that was just the start of it. My mates in the regiment avoided me. Called me Son of Satan, they did. Five years this has been going on. Five years, sir! Anna said she'd save me. She swore I'd have skin like a baby's arse, and I believed her. She was the first female . . .' He gulped for air. '. . . to look at me in all that time. Before Kopka came back, I sent her on her way. I had her address . . .'

'One thing remains unsaid. Two things, to be precise,' I interrupted him. 'What had Anna Rostova seen that you did *not* see? And how did she intend to cure your ills? You risk prison for not having done your duty, remember.'

He needed no threatening. 'I'm as badly off as I was a year ago,' he said with anger, holding his face up to the light. He seemed almost to glory in the ruin Nature had made. 'Anna said the Devil would end my suffering. That was why he'd left his claw behind.'

I tried to keep calm. 'You've seen it, haven't you?'

Lublinsky shrank back in silence.

'Don't make things worse,' I warned. 'Describe this . . . claw.'

'A long thing like a pointed bone,' he declared at last. 'The claw of Lucifer. It has great powers. That's why she took it from the body.'

'Powers, Lublinsky? Which powers are you talking of?'

'To cure . . . To kill, sir. She said she'd cure my face with that object from Hell. It was charged with the life of the dead man. He'd been the sacrifice. His life was to be my healing.'

I sat back as Lublinsky leaned across the table, his misery turning to anger.

'Look at me, sir. Just look at my damned face!' he cried. 'Wouldn't you have done the same?'

I stared at the ravages of his illness, steeling myself against compassion.

'Your face is horridly disfigured,' I said, coldly. 'Am I to understand that you never saw this kind-hearted woman again?'

Lublinsky lowered his gaze.

'You know the answer, Herr Procurator.'

'What did she do to help you?'

'This, sir. She did this.' He touched the black hole in his left cheek, his voice tingling with rage. 'She pricked my face with the Devil's claw.'

'Were you not wounded in a duel?' I said, throwing a glance in Koch's direction.

'No blade could do this. Only a witch,' he replied in a whisper, slouching on the bench, wishing to appear less large a man than he actually was.

'How long has this been going on?'

'Since the first murder, sir.'

'The woman still has the claw in her possession, then?'

'Yes, sir.'

'When did you see her last?'

He turned his face away and stared at the wall.

'Yesterday, sir,' he whispered after some moments.

I understood at once what he meant. 'There was a murder the day before yesterday. You saw her whenever another innocent died. Correct?'

Lublinsky bunched his fists and turned to face me. 'Each murder made that thing more powerful. I'd be a step nearer healing. That was what she told me.'

I looked directly into his eyes, and made no effort to stifle the distaste I felt for him. The smallpox had deformed his mind as surely as it had ruined his once-handsome face.

'Why you are telling me this now?' I said.

He shifted uneasily. 'What do you mean, sir?'

'You *know* what I mean. You didn't write a word of this in your reports. You said nothing to Procurator Rhunken, nor Professor Kant. And yet, you have decided to tell me. Now! You know that she is lying, don't you? She cannot help you, no matter how many people die. You are handing her to me as a form of revenge. You want Anna Rostova to be caught and punished because she fooled you. Isn't that true?'

He did not answer.

'What happened to Kopka?' I pressed him. 'Where was he when the other bodies were found?'

Lublinsky wiped his nose on his sleeve.

'He deserted, sir.'

'Why would he have done such a thing?' I asked in surprise.

'I've no idea, sir. He ran away. That's all I know,' he said, staring fixedly ahead, his face as dark and vengeful as a demon's mask in a Lenten morality play.

'Very good,' I said, jumping to my feet. 'Now, you will take us to see this woman without any more delay. Come, Koch.'

Aboard the coach, travelling in silence, each locked in his own thoughts, towards the address that Lublinsky had given the driver, I found myself unable to look at the man sitting before me in the gloom without a sense of overwhelming physical revulsion. Of all the victims of the events that had taken place in Königsberg, and of those that had still to unfold, Anton Theodor Lublinsky aroused the most pity in me.

Now, that feeling is mingled with the taint of moral disgust.

Chapter 18

Königsberg . . .

The first time I heard the word, I was barely seven years old. General von Plutschow was returning to his country home when he called on us in Ruisling one day. My father's oldest comrade at the military academy was a national hero. He had been the guest-of-honour at a ceremony in Königsberg the previous day commemorating the twentieth anniversary of the glorious battle of Rossbach, which had taken place in 1757. General von Plutschow had led the charge of the Sixth cavalry that day, and secured the national victory. As a special treat, my younger brother, Stefan, and I were allowed to attend the guest in the visitors' salon. We listened open-mouthed to the colourful account that the general gave of the magnificent gala event at which the King himself had been present. And all the while the visitor was speaking, I could not drag my eyes from the place where his right arm ought to have been. General von Plutschow's empty sleeve was folded up and pinned to his silver epaulette with a gold medal.

'Königsberg is the essence of all that is most honourable, most truly noble, in our great nation,' my father enthused when the general had finished speaking, and my mother had dabbed the tears from her cheeks. Henceforth, the glorious name of Königsberg and the lost arm of General von Plutschow were inextricably linked in my mind long before I ever saw the city. To my way of thinking, Königsberg was a place where only glorious things could happen, and where the very best of people lived. Despite the murders that had brought me there, despite the killing of Morik, and the suicide of the Totzes, I still cherished the fond belief that Königsberg was a blessed place, and that it could be restored to its rightful peace with the help of Immanuel Kant.

But that evening, as the carriage followed the directions that Lublinsky gave the coachman and we left the centre of the city far behind, I began to see the other side of Königsberg, the dark underbelly of a wretched beast, a world of misery and poverty that I could never have imagined existing in the place where General von Plutschow had been honoured, where Professor Immanuel Kant had been born, a city that he praised as a sort of earthly paradise.

We were going to a district called The Pillau. It was a port of sorts, Koch explained, a shallow, shelving beach where whalers landed their catch, cutting up the meat and drying it on the windswept shore. Even with the windows closed, the stench that entered the coach was abominable. The rot of blubber and the decay of gutted carcasses fouled the air as the vehicle progressed along the eastern branch of the Pregel estuary towards the Baltic Sea. The way was dark, the dwellings few and miserable. An atmosphere of imminent danger seemed to lurk in every rut and pothole of the muddy track down which we jolted. The mingling of the cold salt water of the sea and the warmer waters of the river produced a dense fog, which seemed to thicken with every fateful turn of the carriage wheels.

'Are we going in the right direction, Sergeant?' I asked. I had no wish to lose our way in that forsaken place.

'I've only been out here a couple of times myself, sir,' Koch replied, peering intently out of the window. 'But I doubt that Lublinsky wishes to mislead us.'

Wrapped up in silence inside his dark military cloak, his disfigurement concealed by his oversized cap and high tunic collar, Officer Lublinsky stared fixedly out of the window as if to keep the sight of his unhappy face from our intrusive eyes.

I followed his gaze into the darkness, and thought of the fishermen hard at work out there on the boundless sea. If the fog were to swallow their boats and our coach, would anyone know where to start looking for us? Far off, a foghorn let out a mournful groan, but there was no comfort in the sound.

'This is it,' Lublinsky broke the gloomy silence, leaning even closer to the window and staring out, his nose pressed flat against the glass. The swinging carriage-lamp lit his deformed profile, and a strangely ambiguous feeling welled up inside me. Distaste for the part that he had played in helping the woman hide the murder weapon, embarrassment for the humiliation he was now undergoing on her account. But there was no time for idle sentiment that night. Everything happened at a rush. Koch tapped on the roof, the coachman stopped, and we jumped down. The fog was like a wet sponge, my face was damp in an instant, and Lublinsky set off briskly towards a row of lean-to hovels which loomed up out of the gloom. A feeble glow lit one of the dirty windows. At the porch of the cottage, he turned, looked at me for an instant, then began to hammer a military tattoo on the narrow door with his fist.

The door creaked open almost at once and the dark figure of a woman appeared in silhouette, her hair a fuzzy halo about her face, which was hidden in the shadow.

'You, Lublinsky? Here again?' a husky voice purred.

I stepped from behind the officer's bulk and the words froze on the woman's lips. Her eyes sparkled with fright, flashing from me to Lublinsky and back again.

'Who's this?' she hissed.

Koch appeared on the other side of Lublinsky and the woman let out a stifled scream.

'What do you want?' she snarled. 'I'm not working tonight.'

I pushed Lublinsky forward and we followed him into the cottage, the woman backing away in front of us, bumping into a low table before she stopped in the centre of the room. She picked up a candle and waved it in our faces like a shepherd trying to scare off wolves with a firebrand. She was tall, shapely, her dress a faded red, low-cut, revealing a deep, dark chasm between her breasts. By the quickness of her movements and the sharpness of her voice, I guessed her age to be around thirty. In the candlelight her glistening skin was so pale as to seem transparent, her eyes of the same ghoulish hue. Silvery-white hair cascaded over her shoulders in a bewildering mass of curls and ringlets. Meeting her in the street at night, one would have thought she had been sculpted from a solid block of ice. I had never seen an albino before. There was a riveting beauty about her doll-like face, her lips pursed in a distrustful bow of firm white flesh, cold eyes as wide and penetrating as an Oriental cat's above strongly defined cheekbones.

'I'm resting tonight,' she said, a coy smile on her lips. 'Unless you gentlemen want to make it worth my while, of course.'

'We are not your usual clients,' I said. 'I am investigating the murders in Königsberg.'

The smile faded. 'What do you want from me, then?'

'Bring a chair. You have much to tell me.'

With a resentful flash of white-lashed eyes, the woman went to drag a rickety stool with a frayed wickerwork seat out of a dark and dusty corner to the centre of the room. I looked around by the light of the candle. We might have been inside a pagan temple, or the tent of one of those indigenous medicine men described by travellers in the Americas. The walls were hung with animal skulls, whalebones, objects cast up on the shore, and stranger things whose nature and use were hard to comprehend. On one smoke-blackened wall, graffiti etched with a blade in the plaster showed matchstick men and women coupling in a variety of beastly postures. As I shifted the candle, the figures seemed to thrust and jerk together in wanton lust. I turned away quickly, my face burning with I know not what emotion, until the stool was brought.

The woman gestured to me to be seated.

'It is for you,' I replied. 'Sit down, Anna Rostova. That is your name, is it not?'

She sat herself down, though she did not bother to answer my question.

'A year ago, you discovered a body,' I pressed on. 'Jan Konnen, the blacksmith, was the first of four victims of a still unidentified murderer. Officer Lublinsky tells me that you found something at the scene of the crime, something important, and that you carried it away with you. You have shown him this object, I believe, on more than one occasion since.'

'You know what this means?' she spat like a venomous snake at Lublinsky, who looked away sheepishly.

'Address yourself to me,' I snapped, 'and to no one else.'

'No wench will ever look at you again, soldier,' she went on, heedless. 'They'll throw up in your filthy face!'

'What did you find on the body of Jan Konnen?'

'Mothers will scold their babes,' she intoned, her glistening, transparent eyes fixed on Lublinsky. 'That monster with the face of shit will kiss you if you don't go straight to sleep, they'll say. He'll come . . .'

I raised my hand and slapped her hard on the cheek.

'Shut your mouth!' I shouted. I don't know what provoked me, but there was something so barefaced, wild and intimidating about the creature.

Her eyes locked into mine, she touched her face, caressing the inflamed flesh as if she took great pleasure in the pain. 'Hmmm, that was *nice*,' she cooed with a smile. 'You like to hurt a girl, don't you, sir?' A wet, pink tongue snaked swiftly over her lips, then retreated to its lair again. 'Have me whipped, is that your plan? Enjoy yourself at my expense?' she sneered. 'They gave me thirty lashes last time. You should have seen the lumps in their trousers! Got all excited when my white flesh started bleeding, they did. Is that what you like to see, sir?' She laughed aloud. 'Prussia, home-land of the whip and the cane!'

The woman's glassy eyes never left my own for an instant. I had to look away, and I caught the glance of Koch as I did so. I saw puzzlement written on his face, too. By then, Lublinsky had retreated to the far wall and there he huddled, head bent low, shaking as if a violent fever had taken possession of him as the woman spoke.

'What did you steal from the body?' I insisted, struggling to master the tremor in my voice.

The woman stared defiantly up at me, a shaft of light gleaming triumphantly in her dilated grey pupils, as if the situation amused her. 'If that idiot already told you, what need have I to repeat it?'

'I have the power to make you talk, Anna Rostova.'

She giggled then. The sound started deep down in her throat and gurgled out in a crescendo of ridicule. 'Oooh, you are a *rough* young one, sir! I can see that. Does your missis like it?' The expression on her face was lustful, smiling, evil. 'Stroke your oar with the Devil's claw? Is that what you want? D'you fancy it, sir? Its touch killed that man on the dock, and other men too, but there are far pleasanter ways to die . . .'

Her cat-like eyes shone brightly, the pupils needle-sharp points of light. I had never been so intimately involved with a woman of that sort. She was so different from my wife. So distant from any woman who moved in Helena's sphere. Lechery seemed to crackle and spark from her pores like electricity. I ought to have been disgusted. But I was not.

'You have naught to fear if you tell the truth,' I lied, struggling to control my emotional confusion.

She laughed again shrilly. 'The truth, sir? Well, let me see now. That night, I was dossing down in Lobenicht.'

'What's that?'

'A hellhole,' Koch clarified. 'A slum down near the city port, Herr Procurator. It's ten minutes from The Baltic Whaler.'

Having seen The Pillau, I could only shudder at the thought of Lobenicht.

'A woman in Wassermanstrasse was going into labour, but her time had not yet come, so I went to see this friend of mine that lived close by. I stayed with her some hours, then I left to finish off the business.'

'What time did you leave your friend's house?'

'It was after three. I'd drunk to fortify myself. It was cold that night. Like a tipple of something strong yourself, do you, sir?' Before I could reply, she went on: 'I knew what was waiting for me. A screaming hag, a half-cut husband, a blood-soaked, wailing wean, if the Lord saw fit. I was praying for success as I hurried down the road.'

'Praying?'

The word sounded like an obscenity on her lips.

'I pray to God,' she smiled. 'And to the Devil too. There's a tussle 'twixt 'em two when a child is born. Sometimes one wins, sometimes t'other. But first, I pray to God. Things don't go well for me when He loses. If a baby dies, I have no work for a long while after. It wouldn't be the first time that I have suffered on the Devil's count. I've seen hard times. In this trade, reputation's everything.'

'What did you see as you walked through the streets?' I cut her short.

She held my gaze for some moments. 'There was no one, sir, not even a drunk, nor the gendarmes on their rounds. I saw no living soul 'til I came to the port. The lights along the quay were almost all blown out by the wind. There, I saw a man on his bended knees. At first, I thought he must be praying like I was doing. Still, it was a funny time and place to go down on your knees and say your prayers. First light was breaking, that's the coldest time of night. As I drew close, I saw that something wasn't right. Then, I smelt the evil.'

She wrinkled her nose and bared a perfect set of pearl-white teeth.

'What do you mean? What did you smell?'

'Brimstone, burning. The Devil's stink . . .'

She stopped abruptly, twitched her nose, and looked around the room, as if she had caught the first whiff of that infernal stench again. She was acting and she was good at it. The harlot was more than capable of entrapping a fool as desperate as Lublinsky.

'Don't waste my time,' I warned her. 'Just tell me what you saw.'

'The man was dead, sir.'

'You smelt evil. The man was dead, yet you approached the corpse. Why didn't you call for help first?'

She stared at me for some moments.

'The dead are special, sir,' she murmured at last, and she seemed in awe of them as she said it. At the same time, she seemed to be strangely intent on reading my own mind. 'But *you* know that, sir. Don't you? The dead . . . you've seen a corpse. Their bodies here in this world, their souls wandering in another place. You've got the knowledge, I can tell . . .'

'One minute, a dramatist; the next, a poet,' I said, cutting her short. More roughly, I added: 'Tell me what you stole from the body.'

She twisted in her seat to Lublinsky. 'Damn your soul!' she cursed.

I grabbed at her hair, and twisted her face around towards my own. 'I will shut you up in a cell if you persist,' I shouted.

'You'll do it anyway,' she replied with a shriek, 'but *he* will roast in hellfire. That *bastard*! I'll ask Satan . . .'

'Forget Satan!' I shouted, twisting her hair until she screamed. 'What did you *take* from the body of the corpse?'

She clenched her teeth, looked up at me and hissed. 'It was sticking out of the back of his head. A poniard quivering in the air. Or so I thought. Then I saw what it was.'

'Go on,' I urged.

'Let me be! Let go of me!' she screeched, her hands locked around my wrists as she tried to free her hair. 'I'll tell you all, sir. Honest . . .'

She looked at me directly as I released her, the fierce anger she had directed at Lublinsky gone. As if possessed of some unbridled terror, the woman seemed to physically shrink in size. 'The most powerful of charms,' she whispered. 'That man was dead, stone-cold, the weapon jutting out of him, but there wasn't a single drop of blood. Not one, sir. No blood was spilt. Who could have done that, if not the Devil? I'd been invoking God a minute before; the Evil One was answering. It was an omen. Satan wanted me to find that body, to show me His power over Life and Death. If a babe was to be born that night, a life had to be taken. The wheel comes round. It was a symbol of the Devil's power. A gift from Satan, so I took it.'

'You didn't inform the police?' I insisted.

The woman shrugged, then shifted the cascading mass of silvery curls from one shoulder to the other, flashing her sparkling eyes at me. 'The Devil's claw was meant for me,' she said. 'Others would find what was meant for *them*.'

'But the murders continued,' I countered. 'You knew that the police were searching for the weapon.'

She glanced at Lublinsky. 'I had other fish to fry.'

'You informed him,' I said. 'You used the power you claimed the

Devil's claw gave you to divert Lublinsky from his duty. You promised to cure his face. Am I correct?'

Anna Rostova returned my challenge with a derisive laugh. 'His own good looks were more important than Justice. I told him what I had found. He chose not to make it public. That's for him to square with his conscience.'

'Show me this object, Anna Rostova.'

She stared at me uncertainly. 'Believe me, sir . . .'

'Bring it here,' I said sharply.

As I stood over her, a strange transformation took place. The subdued expression gave way to one of seductive compliance. Her fingers lightly brushed the bare white flesh of her breasts, she flashed another dazzling glance into my face, and a cunning smile lit her lips.

She stood up, leaned towards me. 'With your permission,' she whispered in my ear. Her hair brushed my cheek and seemed to give off a sudden jolt of energy. Then, withdrawing to the darkest corner of the room, she disappeared behind a tawdry curtain. Koch and I exchanged glances. We could heard her rummaging about, cursing to herself. A few moments later, she came back into the pale circle of light, carrying something in her hands. Like a vestal priestess, she bowed and placed the bundle in my hands. If the material had ever had any distinct colour, it was now entirely washed out. Mould had penetrated and stained the fibre.

Fumbling to unwrap the strings, I was obliged to remove my gloves. The inner folds of the cloth were spotted with ugly-looking, rusty brown stains. As I unfurled the wrapping, a nerve pulsed frantically in my cheek. And then, I held it in my hands. Eight inches long, the colour of bone, straight and slender, like no weapon I had ever seen before. I passed it to Koch, who held it up to the light as if it were a specimen of some exotic beast.

'A needle, sir,' he said, down-to-earth and practical as always, before he handed it back to me. 'There is no eye. And the point has gone.'

I turned the thing in my fingers. Here was the weapon that had terrorised a city. The fragment in Professor Kant's possession was the broken tip of the same object, there could be little doubt of it. In a woman's workbox you would hardly have noticed it. Sticking from a dead man's neck, it possessed an awesome power.

'That night, my charge gave birth to a pretty little boy,' Anna Rostova murmured with satisfaction. 'While she was in her labour, I pricked her with it, three times on the face, three more on her belly. That babe survived, though he was choking on her cord when he came into the world. Satan saved him. That soul was worth the winning. I used the power of the claw to cure all sorts of ills that doctors wouldn't touch. Wenches came flocking to me when they had a baby coming . . .'

A moan escaped from Lublinsky.

'You knew it would do me no good,' he cried, his back to the wall like a cornered beast. Suddenly, he sprang at Anna Rostova.

'Beware, Lublinsky! You are an officer of His Majesty,' I warned, stepping forward to block him, laying my hands on his chest and pushing him away.

'She'd only help me if I kept my mouth shut,' he howled like a frenzied beast. 'She milked them dry. Pregnant women, old men that couldn't get it up, crippled babes. The White Witch, they call her. Look in that back room of hers, Herr Procurator. It'll turn your stomach. See for yourself what Anna Rostova does for money!'

I placed the needle on the table, grabbed up the candle, crossed the room, and threw back the curtain that served as a door. Dust flew into the air, and an abominable stench assailed me. Some reeking beast might have been closed in there since the dawn of Time. Covering my nose with my cloak, I raised the flickering flame above a kitchen table pressed against the wall. It was caked with dirt, spotted with the unmistakable dark, rusty stains of dried blood. Knives of different lengths were laid out in order of size on the table as if for a surgical experiment. Blood had dried on the blades in a dull, orange film. In the candlelight the metal gleamed and sparkled, despite the filth. On a narrow shelf above the table stood a row of filthy pots and pans. Brass glistened dully. A kitchen to all appearances, but not the sort of kitchen any decent housewife would keep.

I took down one of those pots and glanced inside. It contained something that looked like a large mangled radish, or some strange algae, and it gave off a dreadful smell of putrefying sweetness. I had never seen anything similar before. A large fat maggot, perhaps, congealed beneath a layer of gelatine, a worm with sprouting protuberances, a pale white worm. I swung the lantern close and almost dropped the pot. It was no algae, no radish decomposing in its fetid broth. It was a barely developed foetus, the tiny arms stretching out, the unformed head larger than all the rest, curving in towards the chest. I did not need to open the other dishes, nor ask myself what happened in that house.

I closed my eyes with disgust, and backed out of the place.

Lublinsky greeted me eagerly, the light playing on one side of his face, the rest in darkness. 'Abortion, sir! That's her trade. Got a pie in the pot, girls? The Devil's claw will solve your problem! That's what she says. That's how she lives. Ask the whores out on the Haaf! They come here snivelling when Nature plays them a foul hand . . .'

'You lying prick!' the woman screeched, leaping at Lublinsky, her clenched fist tracing a wide arc in the air. 'You'll carry the plague to Hell along with that rotten, stinking face of yours!'

Lublinsky screamed like a pig being butchered. Then the squeal choked in full pitch, and he fell back on the floor, his hands clasped tightly to his face, the Devil's claw protruding like a massive sting from between his clenched fingers. Blood flowed in rivulets over his hands, cheeks and neck.

Koch dropped to his knees beside Lublinsky, who lay flat on his back, crashing his heels hard on the floor against the pain. With a determined grunt, Sergeant Koch leaned over and jerked the needle out. A red fountain of blood spurted upwards, drenching his face and hands. Lublinsky spluttered and spasmed, then his body went limp. Koch called wildly for the coachman to come in, and between them, they carried the injured officer out of the house at a run. Like Lot's wife staring back at the ruins of Gomorrah, I watched them go, unable to move a muscle.

When I awoke from this trance, Anna Rostova was nowhere to be seen. Alone in the room, I seemed to breathe freely once more.

But outside in the street, Koch was calling frantically to me to run and open the carriage door.

'We need a surgeon, sir!' he urged. 'He'll bleed to death without help.'

We tumbled aboard the vehicle and galloped back along the dark road to town, lurching and bouncing over the ruts and the pot-holes. As the first lights of Königsberg began to appear, Lublinsky lay motionless on the bench seat, his face covered by his cloak.

'Is he still alive?' I shouted, as the coach thundered and clattered over the cobblestones, sparks flying from the horses' hooves.

Koch did not reply before we had entered the Fortress. As the gates closed behind us, he turned to me. 'We'll carry him to the Infirmary. Run across to the guard-house, sir. Call out the soldiers. That witch must be taken!'

Did I reply? Was I capable of forming a phrase to show that I was still the master of myself? Koch had taken command. He decided, he disposed, giving orders as the coach skidded to a halt and we manhandled Lublinsky down to the ground.

'That way, sir,' Koch pointed. 'Over there, Herr Procurator. Tell Stadtschen to send the troopers out.' He turned back to the coach-man, dismissing me. 'Help me, man!' he ordered.

I ran as I had been told to do, advancing blindly through the fog, praying that I was running in the right direction, stumbling for-ward in the cold, drenching void. And as the edifice loomed up above me out of the swirling mist, a phrase that Koch had used rang loud in my ears.

'You've found your killer, sir.'

I realised that I was clutching the needle tight in my fist. I did not recall picking it up, my fingers sticky with Lublinsky's blood. All the way from The Pillau to the town, I had held the Devil's claw clasped in my grip like a talisman of Truth.

Chapter 19

I sat in the guard room and sipped a fortifying glass of wine set a-sizzling with a red-hot poker while the officer-of-the-watch was sent for. I was still in a state of physical shock and emotional con-fusion when Officer Stadtschen came barging in through the door. I told him quickly what had happened, then ordered him to send out armed patrols.

'What does this woman look like, sir?'

I began to pace slowly up and down the room at his broad back, carefully measuring my words as I recalled what Koch had said earlier that evening about 'women and rough soldiers'.

'She is tall, Stadtschen. Thirtyish, as regards her age. And she is wearing a . . . red dress,' I began slowly, soon stuttering to a halt. Why had I begun with such tiny and secondary details? Why hold back information that would make her immediately recognisable? 'She . . . this woman's name is Rostova,' I added, reluctantly. 'She is an albino.'

'A *what*, sir?'

'She is white, Stadtschen. White all over,' I explained somewhat foolishly. 'Her skin, her lips, her hair. White as fresh-milled flour.'

'I know the freak you mean, sir,' he said with a sly grin. 'They call her Anna, that one.'

I did not bother to ask him where or when he had met her. I was able to imagine the circumstances all too easily, and an unwanted vision flashed before my eyes. As it faded, fear took its place. Fear for the chain of unpleasant events that I was about to unleash on the woman. The freak, as he had called her.

'Tell your men not to touch a hair on her head,' I said sternly. 'I hold you personally responsible, Stadtschen. Gerta Totz took her own life yesterday after the rough treatment she got from you and your troops. Bring Anna Rostova here unharmed. Without a single mark on her body. Do I make myself clear?'

Stadtschen stiffened. 'These things happen, sir. The lads give all the new prisoners a bit of a welcome, so to speak. To soften them up. There's nothing wrong with that, Herr Procurator. Guilty or innocent, they'll get another good thrashing before they're released.'

I winced at the thought of Anna Rostova falling into their hands. *'Prussia, homeland of the whip and cane!'* she had laughed in my face not two hours before. If the soldiers had been so hard on a creature as submissive and docile as Gerta Totz, how kindly would they react to exotic beauty, a sharp tongue and the certain knowledge that the woman was a common whore?

' . . . *thirty lashes last time. They got excited when my white flesh started bleeding, those animals did.'*

She would provoke them to the worst excesses, I had no doubt.

Had it been possible to call back the accurate description I had just given to Stadtschen, I would have done so. But it was too late for lies. He knew her. Could I tell him now that I had make a mistake? Would he believe me if I informed him that the woman I was chasing was, in fact, small, dark, fat and very ugly? All I could do to protect Anna Rostova was to lock her up within my own custody, and the sooner, the better.

'I know the barbarous things that go on in Prussian jails,' I said to him sharply. 'I do not want anything similar to happen in this case.'

A half-smile traced itself on Stadtschen's face. 'You gave that Gerta Totz a proper welcome yourself, sir. A right good punch, if I may say so.'

'I sincerely regret it,' I snapped.

'If she died, sir,' Stadtschen looked down, avoiding my gaze as he spoke, but accusing nonetheless, 'it was because you gave us no specific instructions.'

'I am giving them *now*!' I stressed. 'I mean to be obeyed. Anna Rostova must not be harmed.'

Stadtschen clicked his heels to signify that he had understood, though perplexity was written openly on his face. Anna Rostova was a criminal in his eyes. He knew how such people should be handled. I could only envy him for the clarity and the absoluteness of his judgement. The simple fact that she had put an officer's eye out was all the proof that he needed. In that respect, Stadtschen was transparently honest in his prejudices. I, by comparison, felt far less certain, more inclined to doubt. The fact that I had probably identified the assassin should have been grounds for rejoicing, but I was still without definitive proof.

'One more thing before you go,' I said, giving the fugitive a few extra seconds to make her escape, as I hoped she would do. 'A man named Kopka deserted from the regiment some months ago. I want to see his service records.'

Stadtschen frowned, then cleared his throat noisily. His face betrayed a look of concern that the prospect of hunting down Anna Rostova had not aroused in him. His eyes flashed away from mine, and when his voice came, it was hesistant, halting. He might have been walking barefoot on broken glass.

'I . . . I'll need to check the battalion files,' he said. 'It might not be easy, sir. You know what deserters are like. They leave few traces behind them. None at all, if they can get away with it. What exactly were you wishing to know about this fellow, Kopka, sir?'

I peered up into his face. It was large, chubby, as red as raw beef. His small black eyes crossed as he squinted down his nose at me. He appeared to be holding his breath, an effort that brought a flush of white to his rosy cheeks. Did his *esprit de corps* hold deserters in such contempt, or was he hiding something from me?

'I want to know who he was, and why he ran away,' I said. 'And just you remember one thing, Stadtschen. I will report any failure to cooperate here in the fortress of Königsberg to the authorities in Berlin. "Dumb insolence" is the military term for hindrance, I believe. I will report any such behaviour. Names, dates, all the details will be included in my report. I make no exceptions. Now, send your men out after that woman, tell them how they are to behave, and bring me any information which exists regarding

Kopka. I'll be waiting in my lodging. Send Koch up to me the instant he returns. If Anna Rostova is taken, I'm to be informed at once. Do you understand me?'

'Yes, sir,' Stadtschen barked. He spun on his heel and marched to the door.

'At the double!' I called after him.

Out in the corridor I heard him break into a trot.

I drained my glass of sweet, lukewarm wine, then retired upstairs to my quarters with an oil lamp. I could do no more. As I opened the door, I caught immediate sight of a letter. It was neatly folded, sealed and propped against a candlestick on the table. I recognised the hand that had written it at once. In other circumstances, I would have rushed to break the post-seal with joy in my heart. But that night, I hesitated, blinking like a convalescent who feels the heat of sunlight on his face for the first time after weeks in a sick-room with the shutters tightly closed. I sat down before opening the envelope.

Helena had taken it into her head to visit Ruisling. She had left the children with Lotte for the day and taken the morning coach alone. Ruisling was fifteen miles from Lotingen, a journey of a little more than an hour, though we had never made such an excursion together. Her purpose in going, she explained, 'was to lay an unhappy ghost to rest'. Helena has always been determinedly sentimental. She has a tender nature, as open and sincere as the day is long. Her sensibility to the needs of others, her passionate concern for all creatures, great or small, for myself and for her children, had always made her shine in my eyes. If something had to be said, she said it. If some other thing were to be done, she did not hesitate to do it. I had always loved and admired those sterling qualities. Her heart was her compass.

Suddenly, this goodness grated on my nerves. I would have preferred to read the vapid letter of a less enterprising wife. The idea of Helena standing before my brother's tombstone was unbearable. Had she not felt the abyss opening up at her feet? Had she not understood the mystery of the place? That grave was the dark pit in which my own soul was buried.

'I wished to say a prayer over Stefan's grave,' she wrote. 'I wanted to ask him to watch over you in Königsberg. What better way to close with the past, I thought, than to leave a sisterly kiss upon his grave!'

I knew what followed before I read the words. My father, hat in hand, dressed in black, had been meditating before the monument of a weeping angel which marked the family tomb. He kept a lonely vigil there, rain or shine, every morning from eleven 'til the clock struck noon.

'I guessed it was him the instant I saw him. I went to him directly, told him who I was and why I had come. I told him where you were, and that His Majesty had called you to His service. "You ought to be proud of Hanno," I said. "Your son has been given a most important commission. He is a feather in your cap, sir."'

I stopped reading. I could picture the scene. Sweet animation and simplicity of manner on the one side; on the other, the granite face of the man who had made me, the man who had rejected me for ever, the man who blamed me for the deaths of his dearest wife and his favourite son. My father had listened to Helena's plea for reconciliation in silence. Then, he had uttered one sentence before he turned and walked away from the graveside.

'"Leave Hanno while you can," he said.'

I stared at the words inscribed on the paper. My father's voice echoed hard, bitter and unforgiving in my ears.

'I cannot imagine the cause of such hatred in a father,' she continued. 'What does he think you have done, Hanno?'

I screwed the letter into a ball, and dropped it on the table. My heart might have been pickled in vinegar. I did not feel a thing, I am ashamed to say. I seemed unable to find the strength to react to the bitter news. Nor could I answer Helena's question.

What does he think you have done . . .

My father's attitude, my brother's early death, the demise of my mother, Helena herself, our children, all seemed to belong to another life. I knew that I was linked to them, but my memory of them was fading fast. Königsberg was like a rapid-turning kaleidoscope, the glittering images changed from one instant to the next, and it was difficult, nay, impossible, to hold fast to any single one of those coloured pictures.

I needed rest, restorative sleep, but the dark cell in which I found myself offered little comfort. The bare, stone walls were as cold as ice, the stove unlit in the corner. How I regretted the loss of the blazing fire in The Baltic Whaler, the hot water Morik had provided for my ablutions, the fine cooking of Gerta Totz, the well-stocked cellar that Ulrich Totz had kept. Unlatching my pantaloons, I took advantage of the one facility which was at my disposition, the chamber-pot peeping out from beneath the bed. After relieving myself, I took the Devil's claw from my pocket, unwrapped the filthy rag and laid it on the table next to the lamp. I must have sat there for quite some time, unable to remove my eyes from that object, questions rolling around my brain like echoing thunder in a fjord. What was it? Where had it come from? Why had the killer chosen such an unusual weapon? And all the time, like lightning breaching the dark clouds, the voice of Sergeant Koch rang in my ears: 'You've found the killer, sir.'

Was Anna Rostova that person? If she truly were the murderer, then Königsberg's troubles and my own would soon be over. I ached to discover the culprit, of course, but I did not ache half so much to catch Anna Rostova. Totz and his wife had died, and the fault was surely mine. Stadtschen had defended the actions of his men, as any officer must. It was true, too true, I had not protected the prisoners as I ought. I should have guessed the inevitable consequences of such slackness. Koch had warned me of the danger of indifference, but I had chosen to ignore his wisdom. The soldiers had pushed Ulrich Totz over the edge, and his wife had followed him faithfully off the cliff. And now I had set the same hounds loose on Anna Rostova. Wherever I turned – I thought of Morik, of Lublinsky, of my father, mother and brother – I had brought devastation.

Just like the murderer I was hunting . . .

I saw the albino woman in my mind's eye. Her wild silken tresses, her skin as white as frost, the lights in her eyes as she spoke, the sensuality of her full lips. The way she caressed herself so openly, running her fingers wantonly down into the deep, warm chasm between her ample breasts. Those same fingers had seized the Devil's claw and drawn Lublinsky's blood. I had struck her, I had touched her flesh. And with what pleasure of coy delight she had accepted my show of anger! There was perilous beauty in her. Anna Rostova . . . there was even something magical in the name. Evil and attraction, equally mixed. I sank down onto my bed, images of her coming thick and fast. And I was aroused by them. My pulse was quick, my breathing quicker. Struggling to wipe this alien invasion from my senses, I tried to conjure up the face of Helena – I was caressing her, she returned my love, my life, my darling wife . . . But the Devil's claw lay there on the table. What had Anna said? *Shall I stroke it for you, sir?* I turned on my face, willing myself to see Helena's hair, to smell my wife's skin and feel her mouth on mine. But other carnal images raged within my troubled mind and poisoned my soul.

I sat up suddenly and pressed my knuckles hard against my eyelids. Anna Rostova was evil. *Evil*! Lublinsky claimed that she was a witch. Was that it? Had she enchanted me? Why else would I wish to protect her?

'Proof,' I said the word out loud, over and over again. Proof was what was needed. Proof of her guilt. Until I had such proof, no harm should come to her.

I went across to the table, sat down, and began to pen a letter to Helena. I have no clear memory of what I wrote, nevertheless I wrote with a frenzy. As if by doing so, I could unburden my mind of the restlessness that troubled me. My hand shook as it moved over the page. That hand might have belonged to another man. I signed the letter, sealed it, then opened the door and called to the guard on duty at the end of the corridor. He came running and halted in front of me. The hands holding his gun were blue with cold, his green eyes watered with the wind which whistled out in the passageway.

'Orders, sir?'

I nodded and held out the letter. 'This message must be delivered to Lotingen. It is urgent.'

Was it, really? I wanted to reassure Helena, to tell her that the investigation was making progress, that I would soon be home with her and the children, that everything would be back to normal again, the slate wiped clean. That there would be no more murders, Königsberg a memory, Vigilantius and his jars of human heads, Lublinsky . . . all a dream, all left far behind. And what of Anna Rostova? If she truly *were* the murderer, I would sign her death sentence with a happy heart.

If, if, if . . .

'Sir?'

The soldier was staring at me. How long had I kept him waiting, the letter held out in my hand, his fingers gripping it, pulling gently against my reluctance to let it go?

'This message is very urgent,' I repeated, and relinquished the letter.

I watched him walk to the end of the corridor, then I closed the door and lay down on the bed again. But still sleep would not come. My mind was troubled and sore. Despite what Lublinsky had told me, despite what the woman had done to him, despite the weapon in her possession, I was less than certain that she was the killer. Anna Rostova was no fool. Lublinsky might believe that the Devil's claw would cure his ills, but did she? She was too worldly-wise and knowing. An abortionist, a harlot, a creature of the Underworld, Anna lived by manipulating the gullible. Why kill the hen that laid the golden egg? She made her living from the likes of Lublinsky, from child-getting, child murder. A murderer will often kill for gain, rarely at a loss. Would spreading terror on the streets of Königsberg serve *her* purpose?

And if it did, what might that purpose be?

Koch had suggested human sacrifice as a motive, trading lives with the Devil for power and wealth. But superstition, charms and magic were the tools of Anna's trade, she made money from them. Death would not profit her directly. If gold were not the cause, I concluded, only Evil remained to explain her behaviour, and I would just have to face up to the fact. I would be required to publicly accuse her of consorting with Satan. I would be cast in the odious role of a Sprenger, or an Institoris. I had read their *Malleus maleficarum*. In the Dark Ages, those two blinkered magistrates had condemned numberless women to the trials of the ducking-stool, and sent them to the flames in public squares in the hallowed name of Religion. I would be obliged to do the same in the name of the Prussian State. Would I be immortalised to future time as 'Stiffeniis, the witch-hunter of the Age of Enlightenment?'

A knock shook the door, and an immediate sensation of relief swept over me. At that moment, any distraction was better than the leaden weight of my own thoughts.

Chapter 20

The bulk of Officer Stadtschen blocked the doorway, his face an inscrutable mask in the gloom. As he stepped into the light, the expression on his face was no more reassuring.

'Have they caught her?' I asked quickly.

He shook his head, then drew a brown paper file from behind his back and held it out to me. 'Kopka, sir,' he said.

'You had no trouble finding the information, then?'

He looked away. 'I didn't need to look very far,' he murmured.

'So much the better,' I said.

He bowed his head as we stood facing each other in the cramped room. 'I knew where to look, sir,' he said quietly. 'I knew Rudolph Kopka. I would have known where to find those papers in any case, sir, once you said that the man was a deserter.'

The sombre expression fell away from his face. The muscles in his jaw seemed to pump and pulse with tension.

'Where might that be, Stadtschen?'

'"Dead Soldiers", sir. His file was there.'

'Dead? I thought that Kopka had deserted from the regiment?'

'He did, sir . . .'

'A court martial, I suppose?'

He shook his head and smiled wanly. 'It doesn't work that way, sir.'

I took the file from his hand, and sat down on the bed to read the notes he had given me. There were three sheets of paper in the folder, and I examined the first.

REPORT

On the morning of the 26th inst., Rudolph Aleph Kopka, absconder from the 3rd Gendarmerie, was captured by a search party in the forest to the south-west of Königsberg. He had been absent without leave for four days. No motive for his absence has been ascertained. Although questioned before incarceration in the holding-cell by the receiving officer, Lieut. T. Stauffelhn, Subalt. Kopka could offer no defence for his actions. After physical examination, the prison doctor, Colonel-Surgeon Franzich reports that the prisoner's larynx has been crushed by a violent blow to the throat. The capturing officer reports that during chase and arrest the prisoner fell from his horse after being struck about the head by a low tree-branch. Kopka will be remanded in the Fortress Infirmary until a statement can be taken, and a court martial convened.

Signed. Capt. Ertensmeyer, Company Commandant.

The second sheet confirmed the medical diagnosis: 'Crushed larynx caused by a severe blow to the throat.' It was signed by the regimental doctor.

The third, a death certificate, had been signed by the same doctor and witnessed by Captain Ertensmeyer: 'Prisoner died of wounds.'

Once again, I was struck by how incomplete these documents were. They were like a mosaic with important pieces missing. Who, in the first place, was the mysterious capturing officer, the man who had led the search for Rudolph Kopka and witnessed the accident that had muted him and eventually caused his death? Why was he not identified?

'Who led the hunt for him, Stadtschen?'

'I've no idea, sir.'

'Did Kopka die in prison?' I asked, setting the papers aside.

Officer Stadtschen leapt to attention, but his reply was slower coming. 'In a manner of speaking, sir,' he said.

'Well? Did he, or didn't he?' I burst out.

'Indeed, he did, sir.'

'That wound to the throat?' I asked. 'Or was it something else?'

Stadtschen looked first at the wall, then his eyes rose towards the ceiling.

'Something else, sir,' he said without expression.

I left him to simmer while I paced up and down the room in silence for some time. 'What actually happens when a man deserts, Stadtschen? When I mentioned a court martial before, you said yourself that it doesn't work that way. How *does* it work exactly?'

Stadtschen continued to stare at the ceiling as if his own larnyx had just been surgically removed.

'I will not warn you again,' I said sharply. 'Tell me everything you know. This is not an investigation into military comportment. I have nothing at all to say on that matter. Murder of innocent civilians is my only objective. What happens to a deserter who is caught?'

Stadtschen coughed uncomfortably. 'He is not disciplined by a military tribunal, sir. He has shamed his uniform, and he is punished by the members of his regimental company who are proud to wear the colours.'

'*How* is he punished? That's what I want to know!'

Stadtschen emitted a loud sigh. 'The company is assembled, two close lines facing one another. Then, on some pretext – like going to the jakes, or changing cells – the traitor is forced to pass between the rows.'

'It sounds harmless enough,' I prompted when he said no more.

'Each man has a large stick,' Stadtschen added slowly. 'And he doesn't hesitate to use it.'

I scrutinised him for some instants. 'In a word, Kopka was beaten to death. Is that it?'

Stadtschen said nothing. He now stared fixedly ahead, his eyes dull flints. Then, he slowly nodded his head.

'And is the capturing officer the one who oversees this final punishment?'

The answer to this question came quickly. 'It's likely, sir. In cases such as this one, names are rarely mentioned.'

'The authorities know about this unlawful practice, I presume,' I stated, picking up the papers again and glancing over them.

Stadtschen's mouth creased into a hollow smile. 'Not officially, sir. And in the army, if it ain't official, it never happened.'

I closed my eyes, and rubbed my eyelids. The death-roll in Königsberg seemed to be endless. Four people had been murdered in the streets for a reason that no one could divine. Morik's death made five. The Totzes, six and seven. Rhunken made eight. And now, I could add Rudolph Aleph Kopka to the list.

'Go away, Stadtschen. Get out,' I said, dismissing him with a wave of my hand.

As the door closed and his footsteps receded quickly along the corridor, I threw myself down on the bed, my head a whirlpool of conflicting thoughts. And that confusion is all I remember. Somehow, I must have drifted into sleep. A dark void opened up before me, a dreamless vacuum untroubled by the spirits of Morik or the Totzes. Lublinsky was nowhere to be seen. Kopka might still have been alive, attending to his duty in the rowdy company of his fellows. No intruder marred the snow in Professor Kant's garden. Helena's pretty face cancelled out that other face with its pale skin and silver hair.

When I awoke, the first glimmer of dawn illuminated the narrow window-slits, and the long, pale face of Sergeant Koch hovered above my bed like a ghostly impersonation of the early morning sun. He was sitting on the chair beside my cot. 'I'm glad you managed to get some rest, sir,' he said quietly.

The cold inside the room was less intense.

'Did you light the stove, Koch?' I asked. 'I didn't hear you enter.'

'I've been here a while, sir. Made myself useful while I was waiting. I did not wish to disturb you. It would have served no purpose.'

I sat up quickly. 'Is Lublinsky dead?'

Koch shook his head. 'He may lose his sight, according to the doctor. The wound's deep, and there's a danger of infection, but that can't be helped. He'll live.'

'Where is he now?'

'There's an isolation ward in the infirmary here in the barracks.'

'Anna Rostova?'

Koch shook his head.

I lay back on the pillow, breathing more easily. 'You think that she's the killer, don't you, Koch?'

The sergeant looked down at his hands. He might have been mixing a pack of playing-cards, looking at each figure, searching for a particular one before he spoke. 'Many things point that way, don't you think, sir?' he said. 'We know that she's done harm to more people than Lublinsky with that filthy Devil's claw of hers. Remember what she was doing in that back room, sir? That's prison, that is. A long spell, too.'

'But did she commit these murders, Koch?'

Anna Rostova was an abortionist, a prostitute, she had blinded Officer Lublinsky, harmed and tricked any number of people, but if no incontrovertible proof of her involvement in the murders came to light, I would be able to go more easily on those lesser crimes.

'Kopka's dead,' I said, my mind skipping to the latest horror. 'They made him run the gauntlet.'

Koch frowned. 'Who's Kopka, sir?'

'He and Lublinsky were the officers who were sent to guard Jan Konnen's body. They also wrote the reports and drew the sketches of the second murder. But some time later, Kopka decided to desert. What could have made him do it, Koch? He knew what his fate would be if they caught him. All the soldiers know, apparently. Lublinsky, too. That's probably why he never tried to run away . . .'

'Goodness!' Koch murmured. 'D'you think Lublinsky set him up?'

I shrugged. 'If Anna Rostova were the killer, and Lublinsky was her partner in crime, it would make some sense. Perhaps Kopka realised what was going on, and fled in fear of what Lublinsky and Rostova might do to him? It's just a possibility, of course. Until we catch her . . .'

My voice faded to a whisper, and we remained in silence for some time.

'I don't believe any clear-cut, rational motive will ever explain these crimes, Herr Stiffeniis,' Sergeant Koch said at last with great deliberation.

I studied his face. It was furrowed, wasted, mirroring my own confusion and frustration.

'I do not follow you, Koch.'

'I'm coming round to Professor Kant's point of view, sir,' he said with an attempt at a smile. 'Do you recall what he said about the pleasure of killing? He said that pure evil exists as a fact, and that it doesn't require any explanation. To be sure, a simple motive would make things crystal-clear and we'd all feel better for that, but what if no such justification exists?' He stared unhappily down at his hands, then glanced up again.

'Anna Rostova is evil. There can be no doubt of that, sir. And you don't need *any* proof to condemn her. The Prussian Law Code of 1794 has never been repealed, it is not subject to *habeas corpus*. Napoleon's army could come sweeping through the country at any time, Minister von Arnim was quite clear on the necessity for martial law. I remember reading the circular, sir.'

'But what would be the *charge*, Sergeant? Witchcraft?' I interrupted him angrily. 'Because the woman claims to invoke the Devil? Not so very long ago, an accusation such as yours would have lit a raging bonfire beneath her. If I am going to accuse Anna Rostova of anything at all – even trafficking with the Devil – I need to be quite certain in my own mind what it is.'

'Herr Professor Kant would not be so put out by the absence of a motive for murder as you appear to be, sir,' Koch replied at once.

'*What?*' I expostulated, shocked by the gravity of the accusation.

'Forgive me, sir,' the sergeant said with a shake of his head. 'But there seems to be no rational motivation for anything happening here in Königsberg. Kant's sudden interest in murder, for example. Would you call that rational?'

Koch knew of my respect for the philosopher, he had witnessed the special relationship which existed between us. Even so, I realised, his personal aversion to Professor Kant was stronger than his sense of duty in my own regard.

'Kant's interest in murder, as you call it, may well prevent a war, Koch. Surely, you have not forgotten our conversation with General Katowice? He was champing at the bit, and I almost gave him the excuse that he was looking for. I was convinced there was a terrorist plot behind all this. But it was Kant's help and the contents of his laboratory that corrected my mistake.'

'Nevertheless, sir,' Koch replied quickly, 'here in town there are many people better qualified to handle the situation than Professor Kant. Perhaps I ought to say, there *were* . . .'

'Procurator Rhunken, you mean?'

'Aye, sir,' he said, studying my reaction. 'Professor Kant had him removed because he wanted you to lead this investigation. But, if you'll permit me to speak freely, sir, that was altogether most irregular. You had no experience in cases such as this one. You told me as much when I first presented myself in your office in Lotingen.'

Only someone who has travelled in the land of shadows . . .

How could I make Koch understand the motive that had induced me to become a magistrate? Or explain the part that Immanuel Kant had played in the decision?

'I thought philosophy was at the root of it,' Koch went on thoughtfully. 'You share his interest in a rational method of analysis. Maybe *that's* what makes them different, I thought. But does philosophy drive a man to conserve human bits and pieces in glass jars? Does philosophy push a man to order soldiers to do things that would revolt them more than anything they've ever had to do on the battlefield? What sort of philosophy asks a common soldier to take up a pencil and draw the dead? Or store dead bodies under snow in a stinking cellar while they wait for the moon to rise? Lublinsky's mind has been affected by it, I'd wager. All this talk of the Devil! There's no clear cause or logical explanation that I can see in the whole affair.'

I stopped him there. 'All of this may appear odd, out of place, even motiveless to you, Koch. But what Professor Kant has created in that laboratory is a new method, a new science, I would say. It represents a revolution in our way of thinking. New ideas always surprise us. He is acting in pursuit of Clarity and Truth.'

Koch held up a finger, as if asking permission to speak. A deep frown creased his troubled forehead. 'May I finish what I was saying, sir?'

'Please, go on,' I said, suppressing my defence of Kant.

'Another idea came into my head at first light, sir, and I cannot shake it out. Professor Kant is unwholesomely interested in the mechanics of Evil. He's not in the least concerned about police business. That eel-fisherman down by the Pregel this morning, for instance. He should have been questioned. Instead of doing which, we sent him on his way. Professor Kant has more important things on *his* mind. He's trying to slip inside the skin of the killer, attempting to penetrate Evil, learn its secrets. That laboratory is just about the most diabolical place that I have ever been.'

The land of shadows . . .

'I was revolted by what we saw there,' Koch continued, 'while you two were in your natural element. You share a knowledge which goes far and away beyond my own comprehension, sir. If *that's* philosophy, I thought, I want none of it.'

If Sergeant Koch was horrified, I was dumbstruck at this description of what he believed Professor Kant and I were doing in the hallowed name of Philosophy.

'D'you really think that Kant believes in the powers of reasoning, sir?' Koch ploughed on, pulling a wry face of disbelief. 'After what we've seen in that room?'

'Clearly you do not, Koch,' I said bitterly.

He did not react to the jibe.

'I was shocked, to be honest,' he continued. 'He was hovering like a vulture over the body of that poor murdered boy on the river bank. He seemed to gather strength from what he saw there. Any decent man would shrink at the sight of such a thing, but *he* did not. His mind was charged with supernatural energy by the spectacle of that lad's corpse. I had the same impression in that room. Did you see the burning light in his eyes, sir? Wild with excitement, he was. His voice grew stronger, his whole expression changed. Why, he's eighty years old . . .'

Koch broke off for a moment, and rubbed his hands as if to purify them.

'His behaviour gave me quite a turn, sir. He seemed to revel in the fact of death. He's not diminished or humbled by it. No, I would say that he is fascinated by the subject in a manner that is not entirely . . . healthy.'

Koch paused before pronouncing the final word. Then, he waited for me to reply. But I had no reply to make. He had not specifically mentioned my own way of behaving, but he made no secret of the unwholesome fact that he thought that I shared Kant's unhealthy interest.

'Don't waste your time trying to explain what drove Anna Rostova to it, sir. Leave the explaining to Professor Kant. He'll come up with an answer.'

How could I defend the philosopher from such a perverse misreading of his intentions? Immanuel Kant had assembled the evidence in his laboratory in the interests of understanding and science. For the same reasons, he had made his way down to the River Pregel. He was not 'hovering like a vulture' over the corpse of Morik, sucking energy from the dead like a vampire. He was seeking Truth, regardless of the harm he might do to his own great mind and fragile body. And I was the only man alive who understood his working method to the extent that I could help him. Was this not patently clear to Koch?

Searching frantically for some winning argument to counter the sergeant's jaundiced view, my eyes darting hither and thither, I suddenly spotted a sheet of paper lying on the floor. It must have fallen from my pocket. The sketch that I had traced the evening before of the footstep enshrined in the snow behind Professor Kant's house. In that instant, profound peace descended on my troubled mind. I might have been walking through a vast and silent forest from which the chattering songbirds had taken wing with the first onset of winter cold.

'I will demonstrate to you that Professor Kant is not fascinated by Evil, Koch. I will prove it!' I said in a flash, wondering how in heaven's name I had forgotten such an important piece of evidence. 'Call the coach at once. Our own eyes will tell us whether Anna Rostova is the killer, or not. Thanks to Professor Immanuel Kant, I should add.'

Chapter 21

As I turned the key and pushed open the heavy door of Kant's dark *Wunderkammer*, my nerve-ends were tingling. At my side, Sergeant Koch appeared to be untroubled. Calm and detached, apparently in full control of his faculties, he might have been Professor Kant's most convinced advocate. We seemed almost to have exchanged roles. Koch looked steadily ahead, while I glanced anxiously here and there, examining the sandglass clock in its wooden frame, the lidded crucibles and the clay retorts that Professor Kant had used to conduct his scientific experiments with a good deal more attention than they deserved. I had reason enough to be uneasy; I was not entirely certain that I would find what I was searching for. Would I be able to confound Koch's doubts, and silence my own?

Neither one of us was so wholly unguarded in his motions, however, as to direct the lantern at the shelves lining the far wall. We seemed to have reached an unspoken pact on that score: those jars did not exist. Even so, we were aware of the glitter of light on the curved glass surfaces just beyond the edge of our vision. I could not shake off the notion that some unspecified 'thing' might take shape and step out of the dark shadows. Something evil and ominous. Had Kant really frequented that place alone? Or with Doctor Vigilantius, cutting and carving what the murderer had left in one piece? Koch's suggestion that Professor Kant found some morbid satisfaction in handling those distressing objects forced its way into my mind, but I shrugged it off.

'We must find the sketches that the Professor asked Lublinsky to draw,' I said, shifting an alembic jar from the worktop and taking my own drawing from my pocket. 'If any footprints were found beside the dead bodies, I intend to compare them with the print that I traced last night in Kant's garden.'

'Do you think that it belongs to the killer, sir?' Koch asked.

'That's what we are here to find out. If it does, we'll be able to match it against Anna Rostova's shoes.'

'The gendarmes will have to catch her first,' Koch objected.

'When they do, I want to be ready,' I stated guardedly. 'I must be sure in my own mind whether she is innocent or guilty before I proceed.'

Lifting down the fascicles from the shelf where Immanuel Kant had left them, I placed them on the table while Koch held up the lantern to assist me.

'Our job must begin in this room,' I said, splitting the bundle of papers into two roughly equal piles. 'Those are for you to check,' I said, moving the first pile towards Koch. 'These are mine.'

I did not need to encourage him. He shifted a large alidade measuring-instrument out of harm's way and bent over the table-top in silence, concentrating on the stack of documents I had placed in front of him. On the other side of the table, I began to sift through my own portion of the papers, and I was soon equally absorbed in the work. Not least for the meticulous order which Kant had brought to the task. My admiration for his methodology knew no limits. Each item in the first file I examined had been separated from what followed by a sheet of paper which noted the time and the date at which the report had been compiled, together with a short comment regarding the reporter and the weight to be attached to the evidence that he had supplied. The brilliant, organisational nature of Immanuel Kant's mind was precisely reflected in the physical disposition of his papers. The first file consisted of the finding-officers' reports. There was nothing new to me in any of them.

The next bundle was captioned 'Doctor Vigilantius' in Kant's distinctive handwriting. As I digested the first few lines that he had written, every distraction flew from me. It was the original transcript of the necromancer's communication with the departed soul of Jan Konnen:

I have been dead for two days now, the sights I've seen grow dim.
Be quick for I belong to light no more. Darkness consumes me,
my mortal spirit seeping from that perforation . . .

Clearly, Professor Kant had witnessed a séance like the one I had attended shortly after my arrival in Königsberg. *Were you not impressed by what you saw last night at the Fortress?* But what had the philosopher himself been thinking, as he watched Doctor Vigilantius at work? I sought some clue which might reveal his own most private sensations, but no hint was given away. Kant had transcribed the spoken words alone and had left no testimony regarding his intimate impression of their veracity.

I put the first file back on the table and took up a bulkier one. It was marked 'Spatial Characteristics of the Murders in Königsberg'. As I began to read, my heart tightened in my chest. Who but Immanuel Kant could conceive of a systematic enquiry into murder which might easily have been an additional chapter to the *Critique of Pure Reason*? Who but Professor Kant could maintain a semblance of calm enquiry when face to face with outrageous facts that would have driven any sane man to quaking terror?

I turned another page and let out a sigh of satisfaction. Drawings of the positions in which all the victims had been found were collected together and catalogued in a portfolio. A connoisseur of prints or a collector of anatomical drawings could have done no better. Professor Kant had inspired the hand of a rough, untaught soldier to replicate the sort of evidence that the untrained police ignored as a rule. The schematic reporting of such invaluable details opened up prospects regarding the nature and execution of crime which no man had ever contemplated before myself. I laid the drawings out on the table in the order in which the murders had taken place, and called for Koch.

'Just look at these,' I said, my voice echoing around the vault.

'What are they, sir?'

'The precise positions in which the bodies were discovered.'

The pencil lines were faint, uncertain. They had been gone over more than once as the amateur sketcher tried to get closer and closer to the horrid truth before his eyes. 'These doodles are Lublinsky's work. Now, let us see if the footprints left in Kant's garden match anything shown here.'

We began to study them together, Koch's intensity matched by my own, glued to those drawings, analysing every line and every mark until our poor eyes ached. But there was nothing to suggest that the sketch I had made the night before was similar to anything that Lublinsky had ever drawn.

'What about these smudges, sir?'

Koch's finger indicated some odd cross-hatchings traced near the body of Jan Konnen. We stared at them for some moments. They might have been marks in the form of a cross like those that I had found in the snow, but the scale was wholly different. I had drawn a shoe in its actual proportions, and nothing else, while Officer Lublinsky had attempted to sketch the entire scene of a murder.

'I don't know, Koch. It could be a cross. Indeed, I am inclined to believe that it is, but it might be something else,' I admitted reluctantly, picking up another sheet of paper. 'We must consider the possibility that the artist was not equal to his task. In trying to represent everything, he may have included too much. Still, this looks like a cross, don't you think?' I indicated the drawing with my finger. 'Officer Lublinsky may have excluded a great deal of vital information in pursuit of what he thought was clarity. Too much, too little? In either case, the drawings are not conclusive.'

'So, until we find Anna Rostova and compare her shoes with the drawing that you made,' Koch concluded, 'we'll never know for sure if it was she who entered Professor Kant's garden, will we, sir?'

The image of Anna Rostova flashed before my eyes. I saw the gendarmes chasing her, catching her, throwing her to the ground, doing her harm. It ought to have been my most fervent wish. Instead, it was my greatest fear. I had let the hounds loose before, and caused unnecessary suffering. Now, I wavered between extremes. If she were the killer, the case would be over, she would be condemned. But what if she were innocent of murder? She would escape execution, but not imprisonment for abortion, and the inevitable abuse of incarceration and forced labour. I hardly knew which I preferred.

'And yet,' I murmured, my eyes nailed to those sketches, 'they were all kneeling. Lublinsky is consistent in that respect. Each one fell down in more or less the same position.'

'Just like Tifferch, sir. He . . .'

'Herr Tifferch was lying on an anatomic table,' I interrupted. 'He was an isolated object without a context. Concentrate on the *drawings*, Koch. Here, you see, the victims are located in the real world. This is the world in which the killer moved. I . . . I had not fully understood the implications before. I had thought it a mere coincidence that they were kneeling . . .'

I paused, deep in thought.

'Perhaps, is it just a coincidence, sir? The violence of the attack may have knocked them off their feet.'

'Oh, no, Koch. No,' I insisted, shuffling quickly from one drawing to the next, then back again. 'You see? A man struck from *behind* would fall flat on his face if death were instantaneous, but that was not the case. These people are all *kneeling*. We have the entire sequence of murders here, as Lublinsky sketched them. It's as if we can see the crimes being committed one after the other. Each victim fell just so, and his or her forehead came to rest against something, a wall, or a bench in the case of Frau Brunner. So *why* did they not fall flat, Koch?'

'You seem to believe that there *is* a reason, sir.'

'There is, indeed. Because they were already kneeling when they were struck. That is, they knelt down in front of the killer, then they were despatched.'

Koch looked up and stared at me in wonder.

'But that's impossible, sir! Would any sane person do such a thing? I can't imagine . . . An execution, sir? As if they were being put to death.'

'Precisely, Koch. An execution. But how did he get them to kneel?'

Koch glanced from one drawing to the next. 'Why didn't Herr Professor Kant point this detail out to you, sir?' he asked. 'He cannot have failed to notice the fact.'

'He has done much more,' I replied vigorously. 'He has placed the evidence before my eyes. Kant made sure that Tifferch's body was preserved under ice and snow for me to see. Then, he made an issue of the fact that Morik's corpse had not been found in the kneeling position. It is not his way to point things out, Koch. He shows you the available data, then he invites you to explain the obvious. I ought to have understood all this before.'

'That's all very well, sir,' Koch objected, 'but Professor Kant had no way of verifying the *truth* of what Lublinsky had drawn.'

I was silenced for a moment. It was a reasonable objection, after all. But the answer came to me in a flash: 'Tifferch's trousers!' I exclaimed.

'Sir?'

'There we have the proof, Koch. In Tifferch's trousers. The knees of his breeches were caked with mud. Do you remember? If my theory is correct, all the victims' knees should be dirty, if Lublinsky has drawn precisely what he was told to draw.'

I glanced around the room.

'Over there, Koch!' I said, pointing to the upper shelf against the far wall. 'Shift that vacuum pump out of the way, and bring down a box. Any one will do. To verify Lublinsky's evidence, all we have to do is examine the clothing.'

Koch hauled down a long, flat, pressed-paper box, the sort used by tailors to deliver suits and gowns. With mounting excitement we removed the lid. A cloud of dust flew into the air and into our lungs.

'Paula-Anne Brunner,' Koch announced with a splutter. The woman's name was written on a slip of yellow paper listing all the items in the container. I could not fail to recognise Kant's neat handwriting.

'A thin, green cloak of braided cotton,' Koch began to read. 'A long-sleeved white blouse. A grey gown of thin, indeterminate fabric. One pair of heavy, grey woollen stockings. One pair of wooden clogs with worn heels . . .'

'The gown, Koch.' I interrupted the litany. 'Let's see the gown.'

Koch spread the garment out on the table-top, then stood back. I moved closer and bent over the woman's gown, flipping it over, then turning it back again, my anxiety mounting.

'There are no stains,' I spluttered, the words choking in my throat. 'Not a single spot of mud on the knees.'

Koch's voice was a low murmur close to my ear. 'What does it mean, Herr Stiffeniis?'

'I have no idea,' I admitted, my head spinning with confusion.

'Hold on a moment, sir,' Koch declared with energy.

Without a word of explanation, he picked up the list, read it again, then began to search through the items in the garment-box. I watched in silence, fighting the impulse to stop him, resentful of the rough way he was rummaging among the articles that Professor Kant had so carefully arranged there.

'Now, let me see,' he said quietly, pulling out a pair of woollen stockings. 'Frau Brunner possessed this gown, I presume, and no other. The stuff is thin for the season, which made it precious. If she had to kneel down on the ground, she'd have done what any other lady would. She lifted up her best gown and soiled her stockings. You see, sir?'

There was no hint of triumph in his voice.

Like Doubting Thomas, I stretched out my hand and touched the rough, grey worsted with my fingertips. There were holes in the toes and heels. The stockings had been darned and mended more than once. And on the knees were two large, dark stains.

'She put more trust in those heavy stockings to protect her from the winter,' Koch continued, 'than in the light gown she was wearing.'

'So simple, so logical,' I murmured. 'And quite conclusive. We may assume from this that all the victims knelt down voluntarily before the person who intended to butcher them. They seem to have helped the killer.'

The words I had read from Vigilantius's macabre colloquy with Jan Konnen flashed into my mind, and I felt a tingle of excitement. Could there be a grain of truth in what the necromancer called his 'art'?

Darkness surrounded me after I knelt . . .

'A ritual was being acted out, I'd say, sir. The victims were being sacrificed to some pagan deity, perhaps. This certainly strengthens your case against Anna Rostova,' said Koch excitedly.

I stopped him quickly. 'Put everything back in the folders. Replace those boxes. We still do not know if Anna Rostova really is the killer, but I am pleased to hear that you now appreciate the value of this room and its contents.'

Koch made no reply until he had packed everything away.

'What now, sir?' he asked as he turned to me.

'Let us feast our eyes on the stars!' I said.

'The stars, Herr Stiffeniis?' Koch stared hard at me. 'It isn't lunchtime yet!'

'I have not gone wholly mad,' I explained with a smile. 'An Italian poet used those very words to describe his escape from Hell and his safe return to the real world. You and I have been forced underground by this investigation, Koch. First, in the basement of the Fortress with Vigilantius, then in this laboratory. It is time for us to return to the "Realm of Light".'

Outside, sunbeam shafts filtered weakly through a web of gossamer clouds which extended in flimsy strands to the very rim of the earth. Occasional flakes of snow swirled in the air like autumn leaves on the wings of a piercing cold wind. Spread out below us lay the glistening slate roofs and the soaring church spires of Königsberg. Beyond, the sea stretched to the horizon in thousands of acres of rumpled grey silk. I stood gazing out on the scene for some moments, filling and refilling my lungs with the fresh morning air.

'I need to speak to Lublinsky again,' I said, as we boarded the coach and began to descend the hill in the direction of the centre of town. 'But there is something else that I must do first.'

'What's that, sir?'

'I must call on Professor Kant. We must pay our homage to him, Koch. He needs to know that his faith in me has not been entirely misplaced. I'm afraid that I have not been the best of students.'

Chapter 22

'*Now, let's see who'll be the first. Older does not always mean wiser. Remember that, Hanno! Don't let your brother beat you once again. He has a good head on his small shoulders . . .*'

The images of childhood that remain most clearly fixed in my memory are those associated with my father, Wilhelm Ignatius Stiffeniis. A martinet by natural inclination, religious to a fault, our father had no time for indolence or tantrums. But oftentimes, he would amuse himself at the expense of my younger brother and myself with a conundrum of his own devising. As with all the things my father did, there was a serious purpose in his games. He wished to impart a lesson which would serve Stefan and me in our adult lives.

The family house still lies in the drear hill country out beyond Ruisling. A large and rambling mansion, all the rooms were cluttered with knick-knacks. My father would delight in hiding a well-known trifle. Then, he would call us in, and invite us to speculate which object had been shifted from its usual place. Our memories became prodigious as we grew accustomed to cataloguing the entire contents of the house. Indeed, we knew the material and the substance of our inheritance by heart before we were out of the nursery.

'*Now, lad, what d'ye have to say for yourself? A curlicue paperweight of French glass? Bravo, my boy!*'

The winner was inevitably rewarded with a slice of brown bread coated thickly with the rich, dark honey from my father's hives. That was the prize. The chestnut-scented honey had brought renown and wealth to the house of Stiffeniis. To Stefan and myself, it represented a sort of condensation of all that our father stood for: the authority which he exercised with knowing severity, the promise that hard work would bear rich fruit, the notion that generosity would inevitably reward the effort required to overcome an arduous test. To taste my father's honey meant admission to his world. It signified his acceptance. And for no other reason than that he had decided that it should be so. The severe glance reserved for the loser was a sufficient punishment in itself. And that severe glance had left its mark on my less than perfect infancy.

Though younger by two years, Stefan was more competitive than I would ever be. Blessed with a quick intelligence and powers of intense concentration, he was the victor more often than not. And when our father was too occupied with the business of the estate, Stefan threw out challenges of his own, which became ever more physical and daring as we grew. Again – invariably, I should say – I was the loser. Stefan was taller, Stefan was stronger, Stefan was destined for a brilliant military career. Yet that military career would last less than six months. Father took me aside when his favourite son was brought home in a carriage and told me of the doctor's diagnosis. 'No more games,' he ordered. 'No physical trials of any sort, Hanno. I hold you responsible for your brother's life.'

In a word, he commanded me to treat my brother as an invalid. And so I did until the day that Stefan proposed a challenge that I was unable to refuse.

As the coach trundled slowly on towards Professor Kant's, I began to wonder whether my mentor had been playing his own sly variant of my father's game at my expense. I had the persistent feeling that Kant had been trying to test my abilities, perhaps to gauge how I might react to the provocation. On more than one occasion he had challenged me to reconsider something that I had failed to notice. But why did he wish to measure and probe my investigative capacities? Was he critical of my lack of attention to detail? Or was he more concerned about the superficiality with which I analysed the available evidence?

Just then, the carriage turned the corner at the end of the Castle Walk into Magisterstrasse. The cobbled street gave way to pebbles and the horse broke into a liberating trot. Glancing out of the window, I realised with a start that something was not as it ought to be at the house: black smoke was billowing in the wind from the tallest chimney at the gable-end. As I had read with interest in a colourful biographical sketch which had been published in one of the more popular literary magazines, Professor Kant forbade the lighting of fires before noon, both in summer and in winter. And the upstairs curtains were still drawn fast! As the writer had described the facts, Immanuel Kant insisted that they be thrown open with the first light of dawn. 'The slightest change in the mechanical regularity of the Philosopher's daily life', the writer concluded, 'means that something has occurred to prevent it from running its course in the manner which he has set for himself, and that it is a matter of some importance . . .'

I jumped down from the coach and ran swiftly up the garden path with Sergeant Koch hard on my heels. Before I had touched the knocker, Johannes opened the door. The expression on his face seemed to confirm my worst fears. His eyes flashed with what I took to be fright.

'What's wrong, Johannes?'

'You are very *early*, Herr Stiffeniis,' he said with a theatrical shake of the head, raising his forefinger to his lips. He nodded over his shoulder, and spoke out far louder than was necessary. 'Professor Kant has not yet donned his periwig.'

Could this simple fact distress the servant so much?

'My master is not yet ready to receive visitors,' Johannes explained, pointedly turning his head towards his master's study as he took my hat and gloves.

'But the fire is lit. I saw the smoke . . .'

'Professor Kant has a head-cold this morning, sir.'

Beyond Johannes's shoulder, the study-door was ajar. I could see only the writing-table set hard against the wall, an elbow resting on it, and a slippered foot extended beneath. I felt reassured to know that Kant was safe, out of bed and well enough to sit at his desk, though what he might be doing, I had not the faintest idea.

Following the direction of my glance, Johannes stepped quickly across the hall and gently closed the study door. 'I am attending to him just now, sir.'

'What's going on?' I whispered.

The servant glanced nervously over his shoulder again, then told me something that I would rather not have heard. 'Thank the Lord, he's safe, sir! He had a visitor this night.'

'Explain yourself,' I said sharply.

'I slept in the house, sir, as you ordered,' he continued. 'Professor Kant said he had some work to finish, and could do it all the better if he were left in peace. He asked me if I wished to have an evening free to visit my wife. Of course, I replied that I did not, sir. I informed him that I had much work to do about the house.'

'Thank the Lord, indeed!'

'I have learnt my lesson, sir. I told him that I'd be in the morning room if he needed me. He retired to his study, while I prepared a chair next door. I decided to stay on guard all night, but . . .' He swallowed a bitter sigh of mortification. 'I must have fallen asleep. Suddenly, something woke me. It was the French window to the garden, sir, I'd swear.'

'At the rear of the house?'

He nodded. 'It makes a creaking noise like no other.'

'What time was this?'

'Not long after midnight, I suppose.'

'Go on,' I urged him.

'Well, I thought at first it was Professor Kant, sir. He sometimes opens the window to change the air in the room. But then I heard, that is, I *thought* I heard something else.'

'Come to the point, Johannes!'

'Murmurs, sir. Voices. I jumped up and scraped my chair loudly on the flagstones. If some thief had broken in, I wanted him to know that Professor Kant was not defenceless and unguarded.'

'Had someone forced an entrance?'

'I knocked and ran into the study at once, but Professor Kant was alone. Then I heard a noise in the adjoining kitchen, and would have given chase, but . . .'

'But what, Johannes?'

His eyes opened wide and he stared at me for some moments. 'Professor Kant prevented me, sir.'

'He stopped you?'

'He was as pale as ash, holding his hand to his heart, clearly disturbed by whatever had happened. I couldn't leave him on his own, could I, sir? Not even to chase off the robbers. He was gasping for air as if about to suffocate. He was in a frightful tizzy!'

'He had seen the intruder, then?' Though shocked by the risk that Professor Kant had run, I was excited by the possibility that he might have seen the face of the murderer.

Johannes again shook his head. 'I don't think so, sir. I gave him a drop of brandy to calm him down, and the first thing he did was to thank me for waking him up.'

I looked at him with a frown. 'Forgive me, I don't follow you.'

'A nightmare, sir. He said he'd probably called out in his sleep. Well, I saw no point in alarming him further. If there had been any danger, it was past.'

'But you *did* hear a noise?' I asked.

He shook his head uncertainly. 'The kitchen door was open,' he blurted out. 'Either I had forgotten to lock it, or someone had let themselves out that way. But I'd swear I locked it from the inside, sir.'

'I am sure you did,' I reassured him. 'Did you call the soldiers?'

'First, I helped Professor Kant up to bed. I did not wish to frighten him even more. Then, I went to talk to the soldiers, but they had seen nothing, nobody. The fog last night was a real pea-souper.'

'How was your master this morning?' I asked.

Johannes looked down at his boots and mumbled, 'He seemed well enough, sir. I brought him tea in bed, and he smoked his usual pipe, but then he fell asleep again. I did not have the courage to open the curtains, sir. He's not himself this morning. He wanted the fire lit in his room, complaining of a chill which had risen to his head. And his bowels . . .'

'Tell him that I am here,' I said.

Johannes bowed and turned to go, but I placed my hand on his arm. What the servant had told me at the beginning came back in all of its importance.

'Wait a minute! He was working last night, you say?'

'So he told me, sir.'

'And what was he doing exactly?'

'He was writing, sir.'

'*What* was he writing?'

'I do not know.' The valet's eyes narrowed. 'And when I put away his implements this morning, there was no sign of the paper I'd set out for him last evening. Not a single page! His quills were worn, the inkpot dry, but whatever he'd been writing has disappeared . . .'

The study door opened with a creak and Professor Kant stepped out into the hallway. 'A *most* successful evacuation, Stiffeniis!' he exclaimed with a radiant smile. 'A finely formed stool, substantial in its density of faecal composition, and with a minimal liquid content. I hope that you have managed something of the sort yourself this morning?'

'Oh, decidedly, sir,' I managed to reply. The first time I had met him, he had spent a good half-hour discussing the workings of his bowels with his close friend, Reinhold Jachmann, over lunch. It was, apparently, a subject of which he never tired. 'Did you sleep well, Professor?'

'Never better, never better,' he replied dismissively.

And he did look to be in fine fettle. With the exception of two details. The first was his periwig. He must have donned it himself at the sound of visitors out in the hall. The mass of powdered curls sat uncomfortably far back on the crown of his head, his own silken hair, as fine and white as the gossamer threads of a spider's yarn, exposed beneath it. For the rest, as always, he was immaculately dressed in a padded three-quarter-length house-jacket, made of crushed satin the colour of Burgundy wine, brushed linen trousers reaching down to the knee, and pink silk stockings. The second anomaly, slightly ludicrous in the circumstances: he was still wearing his bedroom slippers. As a rule, Kant received guests as if, at any moment, he might be called to leave the house with them. He pointed down at his domestic footwear with an apologetic smile, and said, 'I was late in rising from my bed this morning.'

'I did not intend to disturb you, sir,' I apologised.

'Nor have you. I am sure you have much to tell me,' he replied, leading Koch and me into his study, where he took a seat in an upright wooden chair with wings. It was, I realised, a commode. Placing his elbow on the arm of the chair, he rested his head delicately on his upturned hand. There was a lingering smell of warm humanity in the room, and his nose twitched appreciatively. He looked like a silkworm wrapped up within a warm cocoon of his own making, though his ice-blue eyes were as sharp and wide awake as ever. Everything in his aspect seemed to deny the nocturnal drama that Johannes Odum had just narrated. For all his physical fragility, Kant appeared to be the very axis of a world that turned simply because he wished it to turn.

'Well?' he said.

'I have found the weapon used by the murderer, sir,' I began.

A lightning bolt of energy seemed to rocket around the room. Kant sat up straight in his chair. 'Have you really?' he said.

I drew the Devil's claw out of my pocket. Unfurling the filthy rag in which it had been kept by Anna Rostova, I held it up to his view.

'Goodness gracious me!' he exclaimed. I had hoped to impress him, and I was not disappointed. As he held out his hand to touch the object, I noticed that his fingers were trembling. 'What is it, Stiffeniis?'

'Sergeant Koch thinks it may be a knitting needle. It appears to be made of bone.'

'Would there not be an eye for the yarn in that case?' Kant asked, taking the needle in his hand and bending forward to study it more closely.

Koch had been silent, standing stiffly at my back all this while. 'It's been cut short, sir,' he said suddenly.

'Of course,' Kant nodded sagely. 'The murderer has fashioned a tool to meet his own precise requirements.'

'This needle was stolen from the body of Jan Konnen,' Koch went on, apparently warming to his tale. 'The piece that you found, sir, was the tip of this very item. It must have broken off as the murderer was trying to extract it from the corpse. We may deduce from this that the killer has a supply of them.'

'Equally, Herr Koch,' Kant responded sharply, as if he were

annoyed by something the sergeant had said. 'we may deduce that there is a precise reason why he chose this peculiar object, and no other, for the task. Where did you find it, Stiffeniis?'

'A person I have been interrogating gave it to me,' I began to say, spinning my triumph out, but Kant was impatient for details.

'A person involved in the killings?'

I nodded. 'I believe so, Herr Professor, though I wish to be certain before I make another arrest. She . . .'

'*She?*' He looked up quickly. 'A woman?'

'Indeed, sir.'

'Are you assuming that the owner is a woman because of the feminine nature of this object?' he asked, his eyes darting to the Devil's claw couched in the palm of his hand, as if it were a rare and precious butterfly he feared might fly away.

'That's why I came, sir. I needed to confirm my line of reasoning with you.'

Kant turned to me with a grimace of mad irritation on his face.

'Do you persist in believing that Logic can explain what is going on in Königsberg?' he snapped.

I blinked and swallowed hard. The oddity of the remark did not escape me. Professor Kant had spent his entire life defining the physical and moral worlds of Man by means of Logic alone. Did he now deny that vital principle?

'I see that I've disconcerted you,' he continued with a conciliatory smile. 'Very well, then, let us summarise the uncomfortable position in which we now find ourselves and see where *your* Logic leads us. The killer – a woman, if your suspicions are correct – has chosen a most unusual weapon. It is not a gun, or a sword, or a knife. Nothing that we would recognise as a weapon, but something banal and apparently innocuous. And with this domestic instrument, this woman has brought the city of Königsberg to its knees. Am I correct?'

He paused and looked at me. 'My first question, Stiffeniis. What can be her purpose?'

'There's reason to believe that witchcraft is the cause, Herr Professor.'

'Witchcraft?' Kant pronounced the word as if it were an insult addressed personally to him. He shook his head, and his face became a mask of malevolent sarcasm which, for a moment, shocked and entranced me. 'I thought you said just now that you had come here to be guided by Reason?' he went on with merciless irony.

I struggled to compose a reply. 'The woman describes *herself* as a familiar of the Devil, sir,' I said, attempting to justify my position. 'Witchcraft may well be a motivation for the murders, but I have no conclusive proof as yet that she is actually the killer.'

'So you still presume that there are rational motivations in this case,' he continued. 'My second question. Do you think that witchcraft will supply them for you? Not so very long ago, you believed that a terrorist plot was the cause.'

'That was my mistake,' I admitted. 'I don't deny it, sir. For that reason, I wish to make sure of her guilt before I arrest her. "We must bring light where the darkness reigns . . ."'

'How I detest being quoted!' he interrupted in a tone that was very near to rage. 'You have faced the turmoil which dwells within the human soul. You know it is a more powerful driving force than any other. Perhaps you ought to consider its role in this specific case.'

He leaned towards me, his musty breath invading my nostrils, throat and lungs, like a sour, suffocating wind. 'Once before, I seem to recall, you found yourself in similar uncharted territory, and what you saw there frightened you. You told me yourself, you had no idea that such passions could exist. Well, they do! You know your way through this labyrinth. *That* is why I sent for you. I thought that you would be able to put your own experience to good use.'

Against my will, I stiffened.

'Don't take it ill, my young friend,' he continued with a complicit smile. 'I assembled the evidence in that laboratory for someone with an open mind, a man who would be able to use it, and reach conclusions which are not so unthinkable as they appear. But come, tell me why you suspect a woman of the murders.'

I spoke of Anna Rostova with relief, describing the steps that had led me to her. I was careful not to mention the footprints that Johannes had found in the garden the day before. Nor did I tell him that although I had sent the soldiers out to search for Anna Rostova, I hoped never to see or hear of her again.

'So, this instrument has truly done the Devil's work,' said Kant with gravity when I had finished. 'The woman may, or may not, have committed the murders with this needle, but she has certainly put out Lublinsky's eye. I'm sorry to have been the cause of his involvement in this case. He's seen his share of ill fortune.' Kant shook his head. 'Lublinsky served me faithfully, or so I believed. But the money I paid him for those sketches came second to the desire to cure his good looks. And where did this lead him? He was an ugly brute before. He'll be uglier now. Goodness gracious!'

I listened in silence to this monologue, but I was not blind to what I could see, nor deaf to what I could hear. Kant showed no sense of pity for the man, no real sorrow for having involved Lublinsky in an affair that had pushed him into an abyss from which there was no coming back. There was no compassion in the Professor's voice. Nor in his eyes, which sparkled greedily over that instrument which lay exposed in the palm of his hand.

'It is about those drawings that I have come, sir,' I said, interrupting the silence that had fallen. 'Concerning the kneeling position in which the victims were found. You pointed out that missing detail when we examined Morik's body. I must apologise for my blind stupidity. Of course, I had seen the position of Herr Tifferch's corpse, but I only recognised its significance when I saw the sequence of drawings in your laboratory. As I understand it, the assassin induced the victims to kneel down before striking them. This is the mystery within the mystery. How do you think it was done, sir?'

'I hoped that you would find an explanation,' Kant said with a shrug. 'I have not been able to resolve this enigma. Nor could Doctor Vigilantius provide any clue, whether anatomical or paranormal,' he added thoughtfully, raising his hands to cover his eyes as if to isolate himself by excluding the sight of everything and everyone around him. He remained in silence for an unconscionable time. Then, suddenly, he looked up at me and a smile spread over his face like the sun coming up to illuminate the dark Earth. 'Do you recall the first thing I said to you about the weapon when we went to examine the jars in my laboratory?'

Could I ever forget those words? I inscribed them on the very first page of this testimonial. '"It went in like a hot knife cutting lard,"' I recited.

'Precisely,' Kant confirmed. He held the Devil's claw close to his right eye, which was less clouded by cataracts than the left, and peered at it. 'The ease with which this needle could be handled was the reason it was chosen. It requires no physical strength, no undue manipulative skill. The only thing needed is a little knowledge of anatomy. Knowing the most vulnerable point to enter the seat of the brain, the cerebellum. This is the key to its efficacy. And yet, it is not so easy to deliver the death-blow as it may seem.'

'What do you mean, sir?'

'The victim may not cooperate,' Kant replied with a mincing smile.

'They offered themselves up to be murdered?' I asked. 'Is that what you are suggesting, sir?'

Kant did not reply.

'It sounds like the Devil's own way of going about the business to me,' I heard Koch murmur dubiously, though I paid him no attention. Instead, I recalled a phrase that Doctor Vigilantius had spoken in the name of Jeronimous Tifferch: 'When asked, I felt no fear . . .'

What had Tifferch been asked to do? Had the necromancer sensed something vital concerning the modus operandi of the murderer?

'It was all done in a fraction of a second,' Kant said in a whisper. 'Before the victim realised what was happening, it was too late. The chosen one had to be immobilised. He, or she, had to acquiesce in some way. But how? If the needle struck an inch to the left or to the right, there was the risk of failure. The killer certainly foresaw this possibility. He – or *she* – must have thought long and hard about the danger before finding an answer.'

'An expedient that would prevent the victim from moving,' I murmured. 'Some stratagem that would convince the prey to pause long enough for the killer to strike. The murderer induced Paula-Anne Brunner to lift up her gown and kneel in the wet mud in her stockings.' Mounting excitement almost overwhelmed me. 'Why did she do so? Because . . . because the face we are convinced is hideous and evil was familiar to her. She did not feel threatened. "The Devil's is a face, no more," Tifferch said through Vigilantius.'

'A face like any other,' Kant added with conviction.

'She could have been obliged to kneel at pistol point,' Koch objected.

'Why not shoot her, then?' Kant's hand dismissed the suggestion with a quick flight through the air. 'No, no, Sergeant. The use of one weapon to compel obedience, and another to ensure death, defies common sense. There was no sign of a struggle, no testimony that cries for help were heard. The deed was done quickly. And there was compliance in it.'

'A weapon that excludes the need for strength, the use of a stratagem to distract and immobilise the victim, a face with nothing exceptional or frightening about it.' I listed the evidence. 'All this suggests that the psychological need to kill is greater than the killer's physical capacity to commit the crime. Cunning is used in the place of physical force. May we deduce that the murderer is unable to act in any other manner?'

Kant looked at me for a moment, and his thin lips drew back in a smile.

'A person who is weak? Is this what you are theorising, Stiffeniis?' I nodded.

'What sort of person has no alternative to strength?' Kant continued. 'A person who is frail by congenital nature. A person sick or infirm. A woman. An old man . . . Is that what you're suggesting, Stiffeniis?'

Was he trying to steer me towards Anna Rostova?

'Many elements point to this woman,' I said.

'You mentioned witchcraft,' Kant reminded me.

'I need to verify it, sir.'

'It is a start, Stiffeniis. At least we now know that the terrorism theory was a red herring.'

So, there it was. I had convinced him. Kant had sneered at the notion of witchcraft, but I had brought him round. I had his blessing for the new line of investigation that I was about to take. Just then, the doorbell tinkled loudly, and Johannes entered the room a moment later.

'Herr Stiffeniis, there is a man outside to speak with you,' he announced.

In the hall, a young gendarme was vigorously rubbing and blowing on his large hands, which were blue with cold. I knew what he was about to say before he opened his mouth, though I have always refused to believe in presentiments. Such coincidences are part of the general incoherence of Life, not emanations of the hidden design of God, or any other Supreme Being. Even so, it was a strange sensation.

'Anna Rostova?' I asked, the blood pumping quickly in my veins as he stepped forward and told me what I both wished and feared to hear.

'Yes, Herr Procurator. She's been found.'

Chapter 23

'Good news at last, Stiffeniis! They have found her. The efficiency of our police force offers you a second chance to question the woman and find the proof that you lack.'

'Indeed, sir,' I replied, though Kant's enthusiasm sounded strangely fulsome to my ears. I was troubled by a ringing note of irony in his voice.

But then his thoughts veered like a sailing boat in a squall. Looking out of the window, he said with equal passion: 'It must be *freezing* out there! Bring me my waterproof cape, Johannes.'

The valet threw a worried glance in my direction as he left the room.

'You are not thinking of going out, sir?' I asked, but Kant did not reply. He remained by the window, studying the formation of the dark clouds with boundless interest, while I stood waiting, awkward and embarrassed, fully aware that I ought to have been rushing away on more important business.

Johannes returned some moments later, bearing the large waterproof overgarment with its distinctive sheen of beeswax, which Professor Kant had worn on the banks of the River Pregel the day before.

'This is for you, Stiffeniis,' Kant announced. 'It was designed to my own specifications. That wrap of yours may do well enough in Lotingen, but here in Königsberg the climate is unforgiving.'

I did not dare to protest. Nor did I wish to waste another minute. I let the valet help me on with his master's cloak, then thanked Professor Kant profusely for his kindness. And with my own mantle bundled under my arm, I hastened out into the hall along with Koch.

'He's in a *very* odd mood today,' I muttered.

'It's age, sir,' the sergeant replied gruffly. 'Senility plays the strangest tricks. Even men of genius succumb to it eventually.'

I turned to the servant. 'Do not let him out of your sight, Johannes,' I warned. 'Call the soldiers if danger threatens.'

'I will not hesitate,' Johannes replied, and touched his hand to his heart.

I felt reassured by the solemnity of his promise. Then, calling to the waiting gendarme to follow us, I stepped outside with Koch to find that a howling Arctic gale had taken raging possession of the day. We hurried down the garden path to the coach, where the young soldier had to pit all his strength against the might of the wind to hold the carriage door open for Koch and myself.

I had just set my foot on the step, when something happened to prevent me from boarding the vehicle. At the time, I attached no importance to the incident. A tiny woman came trotting out of the villa next door, hurrying down the garden path, a black woollen shawl covering her head. This shawl whipped wildly about her shoulders, but provided little protection from the cold. She seemed to have grabbed the first thing that came to hand in rushing out of the house.

'Are you a friend of Professor Kant's?' she asked, stopping by the carriage door. Through the folds of the black shawl I could see that this woman was about the same age as her illustrious neighbour.

'I enjoy that privilege,' I replied.

'Is he well?' she asked bluntly.

'For his age, remarkably well,' I replied. 'May I ask the reason for your concern, Frau . . .?'

'Mendelssohn. I live next door,' she said, pointing to a large square villa which was almost identical to Kant's. 'I always exchange a word or two with Professor Kant when he passes on his daily walks in spring and autumn. He never refuses a sprig of fresh parsley from my kitchen garden.'

And I suppose you set your living-room clock by his comings and goings, I added silently. She gave me the impression of being one of those infernal busybodies who pay more careful attention to other people's business than they do to their own.

'I was worried about him,' she continued. 'I haven't seen him much of late. So, when I saw Herr Lampe, the gendarmes, and persons such as yourself, going in and out of the house at all hours of the day and night, well, I feared that some ill might have befallen him.'

'Herr Lampe?'

'His valet,' she explained. 'The man who tends to his needs.'

She has confused the new servant with the old one, I thought, and I made no attempt to correct her. 'Professor Kant has a slight cold,' I added. 'The inclement weather does not permit him to go out as often as he might like.'

The woman nodded her head. 'That's probably why he comes so often. He always did have a winning way with his master.'

The wind had risen to a fury, and it began to snow again in a flurry. I had no time for useless conversation with an old chatterbox.

'Frau Mendelssohn, I thank you on Professor Kant's behalf for your good intentions and wish you a good day.' I did not wait for a reply, but skipped up the steps and into the carriage, thinking to myself that Martin Lampe seemed to be a persistent ghost in the existence of Immanuel Kant.

Safe on board, shivering with the cold despite the weight of the borrowed cloak, I put that conversation out of my mind and let myself be hurried away in pursuit of Anna Rostova and the Truth.

'Has the prisoner been taken to the Fortress?' I asked the gendarme who was sitting stiffly opposite me in the coach. He was very young. His straggling blond moustache still bore traces of the scrambled eggs he had eaten for his breakfast.

'No, sir. She's still out by the Haaf, where she was found.'

'No one has laid a hand on the woman, I hope?'

'Oh no, sir,' the soldier replied. 'Your orders have been followed to the letter. Officer Stadtschen warned us very strictly not to touch her.'

'Very good,' I said with a genuine sense of relief. One glance at the soles of her shoes would be enough to condemn or redeem her.

Having spoken with Kant, I was mightily swayed to believe that Anna was guilty, though I still preferred to hope that she was not. As for motives – whether driven by witchcraft or some other mania – I would have the time and opportunity to discover everything. For the moment, I needed only to prepare myself for what lay ahead. I had already felt the power of the woman's attractions. Her mesmerising eyes and seductive mannerisms had entranced me then, and I would need to fortify myself against her charms. This time, I silently pledged, I would be more precise and insistent in my interrogation. Helena's face would not be so easily displaced in my mind and heart by that woman's white skin, piercing eyes and silver curls.

It took us almost thirty minutes to reach the Haaf, a sandy promontory not far from Anna Rostova's dwelling. But as we struggled across the windswept beach towards a group of soldiers huddling by the water's edge, I realised that there would be no questions, no interrogation, no temptation. Not unless I decided to avail myself of the services of Doctor Vigilantius. Anna Rostova was floating face down in the cold, grey waters of the Pregel estuary, her arms spread wide as if attempting to scoop up whatever the tide might bring within her reach. The driving sleet and the rippling waves bumped her corpse rhythmically against the whispering shingle. That distinctive red gown had ballooned above her white legs and ridden up her thighs. Her feet were caught up in a dense tangle of black seawort. Strands of tangled white hair were spread out on the water around her head like the rays of the moon. Five soldiers sat on the pebbles smoking pipes and swearing at one other and at the louring sky above, as they grumbled about who should fish the body out of the estuary.

Sergeant Koch spoke up sharply, and two of the men waded reluctantly into the icy flood and began to drag the body towards the shore, while I stood apart on the strand, watching in silence. Anna looked like one of those mythical creatures that Baltic fishermen sometimes report finding tangled in their nets, half human, half fish. Distracted thoughts rushed round wildly inside my head like a flight of disorientated swifts. Without the albino woman's testimony, would I be able to prove that she had killed those people? And if she were innocent, if she had been murdered like all the others, then the murderer was still free. In either case, I would be obliged to start my investigation from the beginning again.

At my back, Koch shouted angrily at the gendarme who had brought us out to the Haaf in the coach. 'Why was Herr Procurator not told that the woman was dead?' he thundered. 'You'll be punished! That thin white stripe of yours will be torn off, Lance-Corporal!'

I turned and laid a hand on his arm. 'It doesn't matter, Koch. Just tell them, at all costs, not to lose her shoes.'

Koch gave instructions to the soldiers.

'D'you think the killer got to her, sir?' he asked, standing by my side again, his eyes never shifting from the work-party.

I shook my head. 'I really don't know what to think,' I said.

'Suicide, perhaps?'

Anna Rostova's face flashed before me, and I had to force the image from my mind. 'Anything could have happened,' I replied. 'And yet, she did not strike me as the sort of woman who would take her own life.'

I followed the progress of the soldiers as they hauled the body onto the shore and laid her out on the cold shingle. 'God forgive me!' I murmured to Koch. 'She may be as useful to us dead as alive. One look at the base of her skull will clinch it. And her footwear will speak the truth more plainly than she ever did.'

I closed my eyes, gathering my strength for the physical examination I would soon have to undertake.

'Excuse me, sir.'

Looking up, I found a lean young soldier standing before me. His angular face might have been shaped with a blunt hatchet, his eyes pinched and raw. He was white with cold, his pointed nose red and runny. 'Officer Glinka, sir.'

'What is it?' I snapped.

'I spotted that woman's body while we were patrolling the shore, sir,' he said. 'Rolling in the shallows, I though it was a dead seal at first.'

'Did you see anyone else on the beach?'

'In winter, sir? The whalermen use this place in summer and autumn. Maybe smugglers land by night, but otherwise . . .' He stopped abruptly, staring out across the water to an isolated building on the far bank.

'Well?' I asked impatiently.

Glinka took off his forage-cap and flattened his lank hair. 'There's a sort of . . . well, there's a . . . a place over yonder, sir,' he said. 'On the other bank. A drinking den where tramps and suchlike seek shelter for the night. Oh, and felons are taken aboard there for the transportations.'

'Transportations?' I asked.

'To Siberia, sir. She might have been over there carousing, last night. A body could easily have floated across on the tide. Especially with this wind, sir.'

'Thank you for your suggestion, Glinka,' I said, dismissing him.

I walked down to the water's edge, looking across the estuary at the place that Glinka had mentioned. There was little to be seen at such a distance, just a breakwater, a small jetty, a building or two. The mountainous sky seemed to crush and flatten the scene like an immense lead weight.

'Sir!' Koch called.

I turned and found him standing beside the body. The seaweed had been removed from her corpse, and I was able to see Anna Rostova's feet at last. They were slender, fine-boned, as white as marble. And they were naked . . . Two of the gendarmes were busily throwing grappling irons into the turgid waters, hauling great swathes of black seawort onto the pebbly shore, while another group were sorting through the filthy mess then discarding the wrack further up the shelving beach, where it lay in stinking piles. If they were working with method it was only because Koch stood over them, barking orders from time to time, reminding them to look for the woman's shoes.

'Have the body taken to that hut over there, Koch,' I ordered, pointing up the beach a hundred yards. 'It looks deserted. Let's hope that no one thinks of going fishing.'

'Not today, sir,' he said, glancing around. 'Not with all these uniforms on the beach. Not in this weather.'

'So much the better,' I grunted, looking across the estuary again while Sergeant Koch gave the order for the body to be taken up.

Cold and wet as the gendarmes were, neither their shoulders nor their hearts were in the work. What did they care for Anna Rostova? She was dead, and she was heavy. That was more than enough for them. I walked behind the stumbling funeral procession as the soldiers staggered up the steeply shelving beach with the dripping corpse, the pebbles shifting and sliding beneath their boots, shuffling on towards the abandoned shack. Then the body had to be laid down, the door broken open, before Anna could be accommodated on the floor. It was dark in there, the atmosphere cloying, suffocating, impregnated with the smell of ancient, dead fish. Without waiting to be dismissed, muttering bitter complaints about the stench, the men began to drift outside.

'Bring a lamp,' I called after them.

Sergeant Koch went outside to repeat my order. No one had a lamp, of course. No one knew where to find one either.

'Run up to the carriage,' Koch shouted sharply. 'Tell the coachman to light his carriage-lamp for you, then bring it back here.'

I went outside to join him, and we waited in silence for the lantern to appear.

'I'll wait out here, Herr Stiffeniis, sir, if you don't mind. I . . . Well, I mean, first that body the other night. Yesterday, young Morik. Last night, the Totzes. It's more than enough for me, sir. I'll make sure that no one disturbs you,' he said. 'I need to keep an eye on this lot, sir. There's still work to be done on the shore, and . . .'

'Very good, Sergeant,' I said, cutting him short. I had forgotten all too quickly that he was an office worker, not a policeman or a soldier used to the rough-and-tumble life of the streets. 'Sights such as this are good for no man.'

Glinka returned at a run, panting as he held the carriage-lamp out to me.

'Thank you,' I said, turning away and stepping into the hut.

I placed the glimmering light on the carpet of pebbles, and knelt down beside the body. It was, I reflected, the first time that I had ever been alone with Anna Rostova. Closing my eyes, I instantly recalled her house in The Pillau. The darkness in that hut was heavy with nauseous unfamiliar smells, the space full of strange objects cast up on the shore, like those that she had draped upon the walls of her house. It was the sort of out-of-the-way place, I guessed, that she had often visited in pursuance of her trade.

I opened my eyes and looked down. A shudder of sadness and regret shook my body. Had it not been for Anna's silvery hair, I doubt that I would ever have recognised her. Her once-beautiful face was puffed and bloated. Jagged cuts and a thousand scratches scarred her fine features. The abrasive motion of the waves against the rocky, pebbled shore had removed the skin from her chin, nose and forehead. The whiteness of the skull-bone was a fraction paler than the natural pallor of her complexion. The crabs of the Pregel had done their scavenging well. Her eyes were gone, leaving two raw, black holes in their place. Those piercing lights would frighten Officer Lublinsky no more. Nor tempt myself, or any other vulnerable man, with their unspoken promises of lust and luxury. Seaweed draped her throat and her breasts, and other strands of the same rubbery stuff still clung to her legs and naked feet. I brushed away a sea-slug, then carefully unwound the straggling weeds that were matted around her bare throat. Dull, brown bruises stained the sides of her neck. I studied those marks for quite some time, aware only of the steady pounding of my heart as I turned my attention to her breasts and legs, and took her hands in mine to examine the nails, which were ragged, torn and ripped. Now that she could not reproach me, I held those cold hands for longer than I ought . . .

'She's been strangled, sir.'

Koch was at my shoulder. I had not heard him enter. Nor had I expected him to do so.

'So it would seem,' I said, gently setting down the dead woman's hand and standing up. I flexed my stiff knees, and gazed down at her. 'Turn her body over, Koch, would you?'

I was reluctant to touch her again in front of him. And yet, I had no other choice if I wished to examine the base of her skull. That important detail could not be avoided. The woman's body squelched, flopped, then lolled and settled, as Koch made himself useful.

'There you are, sir,' he said, shaking water from his hands.

Dropping down again on one knee, I removed the heavy wet hair from her alabaster neck, and felt the clammy coldness of her lifeless flesh. I ran my finger up along the knobbly vertebrae of her spine from the shoulder-blades to the start of the hairline. There was no sign of the Devil's claw. 'Whoever killed her,' I said, 'it is not the person we are looking for. We'll never know if she was the intruder in Professor Kant's garden unless her shoes . . .'

'Sir,' a voice called from the door.

Glinka entered, and in his outstretched hand he held a shoe.

A glass of iced water offered to a man who had just crossed a desert on foot would not have been more welcome. I sprang forward eagerly, and took hold of it with both hands.

'It was further down the shoreline,' he added. 'The other one must be somewhere near as well.'

'This is more than enough,' I replied, turning it over quickly, examining the shoe, the left one of a pair. My heart, which had soared not a moment before, now sank like a stone. The sole was as smooth and as worn as a pebble that had been washed and wearied by the tireless sea for a million years. There was no sign of the distinctive cross-cut that Officer Lublinsky had drawn at the scene of the first murder.

'It wasn't her,' I said, my feeling of disappointment and confusion growing.

'Do you think she may have had another pair, sir?' Koch suggested.

'I doubt it, Sergeant.'

We remained in silence, looking first at the shoe in my hand, then at the lifeless body on the ground, finally at one another.

'What now, Herr Procurator?' he asked, his voice subdued, distant, respectful. My investigation had come unstuck, and Koch knew it.

I thought for some moments before replying.

'I wish to go across to that tiny port on the far bank,' I said. 'She may have been seen over there last night.'

'But, sir!' Koch protested. 'This woman's death is not relevant to the case. It's a matter for the civil police . . .'

'Can you find a rowing boat to take us?' I insisted.

Koch's eyes widened at this suggestion.

'There's a footbridge down the way, sir. We can walk there and back in less than half an hour!'

I had to smile, despite the seriousness of our business. Suddenly, I realised just how much Koch's salt-of-the-earth common sense comforted me. I needed his presence, the dullness of his blinkered point-of-view provided a vital counterbalance to my own excitable nature. He never dared to ask me why, he only asked me how. For the same reason, I did not tell him truly why I wished to travel to the other side of the estuary. The fact was that I hoped to collar the person who had murdered her, and see him hang.

I stepped to the door and called in the gendarmes.

'Cover her up,' I said, though nothing better could be found after a great deal of raising dust than some dirty, stinking sacks and a tattered roll of netting.

I turned my head away as they carried her out, though I did not withdraw my hand when her damp curls brushed against my fingers. Koch and I followed them out, watching while the soldiers lifted her body onto a ramshackle cart they had found behind the hut.

Would Anna Rostova find peace beneath the earth? Or would she become one of those ghouls that country folk believe in, hovering between life and death, feeding on the blood of the living by the light of the Moon?

I dismissed these childish whimsies from my mind.

'Are you ready, Koch?'

Without another word, the sergeant clasped his hat more tightly to his head to keep it from blowing away in the roaring wind and the driving sprays of sleet, then he turned in the direction of a chain bridge which spanned the estuary, and marched away.

I had to run to catch up with him.

Chapter 24

'We're taking a bit of a risk going in here, sir,' Sergeant Koch warned, his hand on the door. The rough-hewn timber glistened black, stained here and there with salt, as if some miscreant had attempted to burn the place down, and someone else had put out the flames with sea-water. 'Do you want me to call up some of the squaddies?'

Hardly the Gates of Hell, I thought, as we stood before the low entrance.

'That won't be necessary, Sergeant,' I said boldly, but I began to catch his drift as soon as we entered the place. I had to halt for some moments while my eyes adjusted to the smoke and gloom, my lungs contracting at the rancid stench of unwashed humanity that fouled the air. Glinka had ennobled the place when he called it a tavern. We were in an abandoned warehouse where some enterprising soul was plying small ale and strong spirits to lost souls with no better refuge.

The lingering sweetness of malt suggested that the edifice had once been a grain store. Rough stone walls had been raised directly on the quay, the cobbled floor within impregnated with mud and mulch. An open fire in the centre of the room softened the bitter cold, the wood-smoke drifting up to a ragged hole in the raftered ceiling, where it fought a losing battle to get out, then settled in a suffocating cloud upon the occupants. Despite the bonfire, everything was slick with damp, which ran down the walls in rivulets. A solitary hanging lantern gave light enough to enter, hardly enough to leave, though no one gave the impression of wishing to go anywhere. There were forty men at a guess, lost to drink, sprawling on the floor or huddled together along the walls. A circle of them had gathered around the blazing bonfire. So many people, so close together, yet barely a word was said. The silence was sullen, oppressive, resentful. Eyes flashed nervously in our direction, as if they were expecting somebody. One quick glance supplied the answer to a question that no one had voiced aloud. They looked away, sank their faces in their ale, or turned back to their mute vigil beside the dancing flames. In a moment, we were forgotten.

'Over there, sir,' Koch murmured by my ear, nodding towards the wall on the left. Eight men were crowded shoulder to shoulder on a bench, like sparrows perching on a garden fence. I could not see the chain that tied them ankle to ankle, but a rattle and a clink as we moved in their direction gave the game away. Each prisoner wore a grey blanket around his shoulders. One man nursed a bandaged stump, his right hand had been amputated, probably for repeated thieving. Their heads were scraped bare to the scalp, with the exception of one felon, who wore a strange fur coat and cap of the same material that he appeared to have fashioned for himself, a mass of uncured pelts sewn roughly together. At either end of the bench sat a guard in a soiled white uniform and cap with a red-and-blue cockade, a musket erect between his knees. One of the soldiers appeared to be sleeping, his head low on his chest.

'They've been hanging about since yesterday, sir,' Koch murmured. 'The ship for Narva hasn't landed yet. There's some concern about its fate.'

The night before, in Rhunken's office, I had carelessly signed the order for this batch of deportees. The most dangerous men in Prussia were being herded together in Narva on the Baltic coast of Finland. A forced march across the frozen continent to the Mongolia–Manchuria border, six thousand miles distant, was planned to commence at the first sign of a thaw. Alexander Romanov had reduced the price of the grain he exported to Prussia in exchange for the men. 'Sold into Slavery', one Berlin paper had controversially reported the agreement, adding that their new owner was keen to make the most of his bargain. 'There is infinite labour for idle hands in the silver mines of Nerchinsk,' the new Tsar was reputed to have said with a smile, having inherited the agreement from the father he had murdered.

'We must find the landlord,' I said.

'I doubt there is one,' Koch replied. 'That's contraband they're selling. Strong liquor is the only cure for cold in The Pillau. God knows what those devils will do when they reach Siberia!'

'Indeed,' I said, calculating whether I might be able to purchase the confidence of one of the condemned men, or their guards. I had money enough in my purse to buy a barrel of gin to stave off the most violent ague.

But I had barely taken two steps towards the bench, when the soldier at the far end jumped up and swung his musket in my direction, clicking the flintlock into place. His companion followed suit, one eye wide with surprise, the other closed in a permanent palsied wink. His musket came to rest an inch from my heart.

'Hold fast!' he cried, his eyelid tremoring. 'One step, you're dead!'

I raised my hands in surrender.

'I am an Investigating Magistrate of the Crown,' I said loftily, attempting to maintain some semblance of dignity by means of my voice alone, for my posture was ridiculous. 'A woman has been found dead in the river. I wish to know if you or your prisoners saw her last night.'

The lazy-eyed soldier moved his musket down a trifle, no longer menacing my heart, now threatening to blow a large hole in my stomach. He was an ugly brute, his jaw a curving, monstrous thing, such as I had seen in the woods around Magdeburg, where the peasants are allowed to marry their cousins. The other one, a tall, thin man with a corporal's tab on his sleeve, raised his musket level with his shoulder and sighted along the muzzle into Koch's face.

'An' you?' he said with a snarl.

'The Procurator's assistant,' the sergeant replied. He slowly raised his forefinger like a pistol and pointed it at the guard. 'You are obstructing Herr Stiffeniis in the pursuance of his duties!'

Warily, they shifted the direction of their muskets.

'Did you see any women here last night?' Koch insisted.

'There were lots of folk,' the Magdeburger began uncertainly.

'The cold was bone-shaking . . .'

'Were there any *women*?' I snapped.

'This ain't no chapel, sir,' the man replied, resting the stock of his musket on the ground and stroking his jaw thoughtfully. 'We do what we can to keep the prisoners apart, but the night is long. The sooner they get on board the transport, the better. There'll be trouble if we have to hang around much longer . . .'

'I am interested in an albino woman,' I said, pointedly ignoring his laments. 'White hair, white skin, eyes as clear as . . .'

A startled look flashed between them.

'Was the woman alone?' I asked.

'It . . . well, a few hours after we got here, sir, that woman came in. Made her way to the fire. Shivering fit to crumble, she were. No coat, just a dress . . .'

Another glance passed between the guards. They were evidently gauging what to admit, what to deny.

'I am not interested in how you go about your duties,' I said energetically. 'I want to know who that woman was with, nothing more.'

'General Katowice will have your names within the hour,' Koch threatened. 'Speak out!'

'That'll serve ya!' one of the prisoners snarled at the guards.

'Well?' I said to the corporal.

'She were alone, sir,' he admitted. 'Stuck out like a parakeet, the colour of her. Soon as this lot saw her, the cat-calling started.'

'Did they know her?' I asked, my hopes rising.

The soldier shook his head. 'I doubt it. That red dress made them sit up smartish, though. They ain't seen a wench in months. Jailbirds all of 'em, sir. An' she weren't one to look the other way, know what I mean?'

It was not difficult to visualise the scene. Anna Rostova had been the only bright thing in the gloomy darkness of that den. The sight of her must have warmed the hearts and wakened the hopes of every man in the place, including the two guards.

'Did you speak with her?'

Both men shook their heads in violent denial.

'What about the prisoners?'

Furtively, they looked again from one to the other.

'You'll find yourself in irons aboard the ship carrying this lot to their fate,' I menaced, taking a step closer.

'She wanted to go a-ship herself,' the Magdeburger muttered. 'When no one was looking. To stow away, she said.'

He dropped his eyes to the ground.

'Did she offer to pay?' I asked. I had no need to guess what Anna Rostova would offer in exchange for help in getting away from Königsberg.

'I . . . I told you, sir. An' I told *her* too. There *was* no ship. We'd no idea how long we'd have to hang around. I couldn't, well, like, *promise* anything . . .'

'You used her, didn't you?' I tried to quell my mounting anger.

'No one forced her,' the Magdeburger objected. 'She was up for it, sir. Been a-ship before, she had. Worked her *passage*, was what she said. Passage. There was no mistaking what she . . .'

Wild shouts and bloodcurdling screams erupted behind us. Instinctively, the soldiers raised their firearms and pointed them into the ruck of people who had fallen to their knees in a tight circle gathered around two large grey rats, the bonfire forgotten at their backs. The rodents were light grey in colour, as large as cats, with curving front teeth, not unlike the massive *pantegane* I had seen creeping in their thousands along the alleys and the water's edge in the foul-smelling sewer that was Venice. These rats were battling for their lives, ripping and tearing at each other, raising wilder and louder cries from the spectators with each successful attack. No sooner had the fight begun than it was over. One man raised the loser by its tail, showing it off to the crowd. He whizzed it round and round his head in a wide circle splattering the crowd with blood, which brought more angry cries and protests, then suddenly he let the rodent go. It flew across the room, crashing against the stone wall with a sickening slap and a spray of blood.

The noise grew louder, with ear-splitting shouts of triumph as money changed hands; a brief scuffle broke out, then one man came hurrying over to the bench where the prisoners sat chained, and handed some coins to the felon I had noticed previously, the one who wore the strange fur garments.

'Who is that man?' I asked.

'Helmut Schuppe, sir,' the corporal ventured with a smirk. 'Bound for Siberia. If not for that, he'd be a lucky beggar. Been betting half the night, an' winning too. He spoke to her, though *spoke* is hardly the word I'd use for what 'e done . . .'

His voice trailed away.

'His crime?' I asked, studying the prisoner as he pulled out a fur pouch from inside his shirt, and put away his winnings. Though short in height, Helmut Schuppe was as heavy as a bear, and looked well able to defend himself if any man should think to rob him.

The corporal pulled a soiled sheet of paper from his pocket. 'Here we are,' he said, reading off what followed with great difficulty. 'Murdered his brother. In cold blood. Then ate his liver. Raw.'

So, I thought, this is the monster I had read about the night before.

'Free him of his chains,' I ordered, as the commotion started up again. More rats had been found, and another fierce argument was going on regarding their fighting qualities. I turned my back, unwilling to watch, though my ears were not deaf to the squealing and whistling of the rodents as their patrons held them up and taunted their opponents.

'Free him, sir?' the corporal answered insolently.

'You heard me,' I said.

He slouched to the bench, dropped on one knee, pulled a key from his pocket, and began to unlock the man's shackles. In a minute, Helmut Schuppe was free, but by no means liberated. The Magdeburger stood close behind him, his musket pushing into the prisoner's back, urging him in my direction.

Schuppe was not so tall as I, but his fur coat made him seem fatter than he was. With high cheekbones, narrow slits for eyes, a large nose and thin, sensual mouth, I took him to be a Laplander, despite his name. The leaping flames of the fire illuminated the livid brands he bore on his cheeks. A large letter 'M'.

'You've won a fair bit on those creatures,' I began in a friendly fashion. Koch stood close beside me, and though the soldiers had retreated a pace or two, they held their muskets ready.

'Want to know which one to bet on, do you?' the man replied with a lazy nasal hiss. There was no Arctic inflection in his voice, his German precise enough. 'I know them critters,' he said with a rumbling laugh which shook the loose skins of his furs.

'Indeed,' I agreed. 'Now, tell me about the woman.'

Schuppe narrowed his eyes and studied my face. 'What woman?'

'Anna Rostova,' I replied.

'Ah, *that* woman,' he smiled, and that laugh rumbled out of him again. 'When a man's condemned, he takes his pleasure where he can. He can't take nothing with him. Only money, sir. Money buys a dram, a warm blanket. There's not much else. A bite to eat. Women . . . I spent mine well enough last night. Grog, a bet, a warm body rubbing up to mine.'

'Tell me more about the warm body,' I said, as casually as I could, though it cost me a great deal. The image of Anna Rostova copulating like a beast in the darkest corner of that dark pit with a fiend who not only killed his brother, but ate him too, took my breath away.

'What did she tell you?' I insisted.

The rough laugh which erupted from his throat made all eyes turn in our direction. 'Between their thighs, they got warm lips that don't say much!'

'Before you part for the North, I may decide to have you whipped within an inch of your life, Helmut Schuppe,' I said coldly. 'Or worse, if I discover that you played any part in her death.'

The threat had had no effect on him, as I was soon to realise, but what he had heard from my tongue had worked its own small miracle. I had pitched a rock into a pool, and the ripples told me what I would never otherwise have believed. Helmut Schuppe, fratricide and cannibal, was moved by the news of the death of Anna Rostova.

'Dead, sir?' he whispered, his voice as tender as a child's.

'Strangled,' I replied.

'I saw her killer, sir,' he whispered, staring me in the eyes.

I caught my breath. 'Can you describe him?'

Schuppe shook his head and looked away. 'A shadow, sir. A shadow carried her off. I know evil when I see it. The rats went quiet when he entered here.'

'Beware!' I hissed angrily. 'Speak plainly, if you please.'

He stared at me intently for some moments. 'That man was hunting her like a hungry wolf. She knew where we were bound, sir. Wanted to come along, she did, so she tried it on with them two.'

He looked at the soldiers, his eyes flicking from one to the other.

'Over there,' Schuppe indicated the corner furthest from the fire and the lanterns, then he spat at the soldiers, staring hard at them. 'I'd give an arm an' a leg to get my teeth in those pigs' livers! But they got guns, and I must live. You can't get rid of *me* in Russia, bastards!' he shouted at them with hatred. 'I'll be back to feast on your warm guts!'

Six thousand miles on foot through a hostile country. The felons would be lucky to arrive, I thought, let alone come back.

'So, then she turned to the prisoners,' I said, my voice hoarse, low.

'One or two fancied their chance,' he said proudly, 'but I got money, I have. I gave her *Geld* to keep her close beside me. Promised this lot I'd make coats for 'em afore we got to Narva. Keep 'em quiet, like. There's rats a-ship. Fur's more warmin' in the ice and snow than the memory of a whore.'

I felt a wave of confused gratitude towards that rough man. Unlike the soldiers, his heart was not immune to the bewitching charm of beauty.

'You said that she was afraid. Of what? Of whom?'

Schuppe shook his head. 'People are dying in Königsberg, that was all she said.' He looked at me intently. 'What did she mean, sir? Is there a pestilence in the city?'

I ignored the question.' What passed between you?'

Schuppe blew out his cheeks and scratched his nose. 'Siberia, I told her. Forget it, women can't survive out there!'

He was right about that. The deportation agreement had been signed with Paulus Romanov in 1801, and two women had been shipped out with the first consignment. One was a prostitute, the other wretch had killed her husband and her children. I remembered the reports that had appeared in all the newspapers, the scandal that had emerged. The women had been raped repeatedly by the other prisoners, and the cold had killed them before they reached their destination. State Minister von Arnim had issued a Circular correcting the first, prohibiting any magistrate or prison commander from deporting a woman. Arnim insisted that only strong, healthy men should be sent, as the Tsar would not accept malingerers in his labour colonies. Ironically, the inflexibility of the Romanovs had worked more wonders on our penal system than any Enlightened discussion of the nature of crime and punishment would ever do.

'She'd been there,' he added. 'Siberia and back!'

'Deported?' I quizzed.

Schuppe nodded. '"Look at my hair, my skin," she said. "Where d'you think I turned to ice?"'

He was silent for a moment. 'I live by hunting animals, sir. I sells their skins and I chews their meat. Moles in the summer, rats in the winter. God knows how many towns in Prussia I've rid o'vermin! I'll make warm socks to see me through the snow. I'll be back!' he shouted, turning to the soldiers. 'White as ice like her, but I'll come back for you bastards!'

Come back from Nerchinsk? Only a ghost could return. A ghost or a tern, able to fly across the ice and the snow, flying high above the ravaging wolves of the tundra forest, the hungry polar bears, the frozen desert of the Steppe. No one would be coming back from Nerchinsk. A man who was deported there was dead before he set a foot outside Prussia. Again, that newspaper report flashed through my mind:

. . . the temperature of minus 55 degrees, 5250 miles from St Petersburg, 480 miles north of the Great Wall of China, 100 miles west of the Pacific Ocean, remote not only from Western Europe, but from the trade routes between Russia and China. Desolate steppe and bare mountain stretching for vast distances, inhabited only by a wandering horde of Tartar savages.

There was something gleefully punitive in the official gazette from Berlin.

Was this the final act of Anna Rostova? She had told a brazen lie and brought hope to this man. I prayed for her soul. For that falsehood, if for nothing else.

'She left you, Schuppe,' I said, flatly. 'Why was that?'

'I fell asleep after the ratting stopped. I'd had a skinful. Then I woke with a start, and I saw her near the door. Chained to this lot, I couldn't do nowt but yell at him. She glanced back, then they was gone. He dragged her out by the hair . . .'

'A man, you say?'

'In a big black coat, a hat pulled down low. They was gone in a flash.'

'Thank you, Schuppe,' I began to say, nodding to the guard to return him to the bench and his chains.

'You know what I done, don't you, sir?' he interrupted in an urgent whisper, moving his head close to mine.

I nodded in silence, drawing back from his person.

'I killed my brother,' he said, looking deep into my eyes.

'Why?'

He shrugged. 'I needed shelter, soldiers were searching for me. He told me to get lost, threatened me with an axe. I took it off him, an' I gave it back to him by the blade.'

He told this tale with stark simplicity. As if the sequence were inevitable. The brother. The need for sanctuary. The axe. As if there was nothing else to be done.

Could I have done the same? Could I have given a similar uncomplicated account of what had happened between Stefan and myself? This man was fated to die in Siberia, while I was hunting a killer in the company of Immanuel Kant . . .

'I have eaten human flesh,' he said, breaking in upon my thoughts. 'I'll do the same again, given the circumstances.'

'Which circumstances are you talking of?' I asked, curiously.

'War. Famine. A long march. Wait 'til Bonaparte gets here, sir, then see how many souls end up in the cooking-pot. When a man is desperate . . .'

I recalled the scene I had witnessed on my way to Königsberg with Koch, the gang of robbers at the bridge who had butchered the farmer's horse for meat.

'I'll eat my way across the Arctic waste unless you help me . . .'

'Help you, Schuppe?' I asked. 'How, in the name of Heaven, can I help you?'

He stepped so close that one of the soldiers shouted and dug his musket fiercely into the prisoner's spine.

'A man in furs can die of hunger,' he hissed, clacking his teeth together noisily, working his jaws as if he were chewing something tough but tasty. 'Save these poor creatures from my sharp fangs, sir.'

We stared at each other for a moment, then his hand rose up before my face clasping a stub of graphite.

'Extra rations,' he said with a disarming smile.

'Shackle this prisoner,' I ordered the soldiers, taking the pencil, turning towards the meagre light from the fire. 'And let me see your list.'

At my back I heard the clink of chains as Helmut Schuppe was returned to his place. Then I made a note next to the name of the last man who had shown any tenderness to Anna Rostova, a man who been condemned for murdering his brother and eating his liver, the man with 'Murderer' branded on his cheeks in large capital letters: 'Merits extra food'.

I turned to Koch. 'Take the names of the guards, Sergeant. I'll have them punished for negligence in the exercise of their duties. For taking advantage of the woman with false promises of a passage to Siberia.'

'They might end up in chains themselves, sir,' Koch advised. 'With a long, cold march in front of them.'

I turned away and strode towards the exit. I had no sympathy for animals who had slaked their lust on a vulnerable wench, then failed to protect her from the man who had murdered her. Outside, the smell of the estuary at low water was foul and damp.

'What now, Herr Procurator?' Koch asked, his voice subdued.

'Did you get their names?' I replied.

'Yes, sir.'

'Very well. Let's make our way back to town. To the Infirmary,' I said. 'Lublinsky had a motive to kill her. But did he have the opportunity?'

Koch was silent, and I thought that he might be sulking, that he dared to question my decision, though I could not have been more mistaken. He was a professional. Having closed the door on that hellhole, his mind was already moving forward.

'With your permission, sir,' he said, 'I'll not come with you.'

'Not come? What are you plotting, Koch?' I asked.

'I was thinking of my wife, Herr Stiffeniis,' he replied, and there was such abject melancholy in his voice that I was unable to meet his glittering eyes.

'Your wife?' I echoed, astounded. 'You told me that you lived alone.'

'Merete was taken during the last typhoid epidemic,' he continued in a low voice. The loss still caused him evident pain. 'She was an embroidress, sir. I was thinking of the needles that she used. I always knew what to buy on her nameday, or for the Saint Nicolaus feast. Last night, when you discovered the murder weapon, sir, I could not help but think of Merete. If I could find the man who sold those needles, I thought, perhaps he'd recall the people who had bought them in the past. It might provide a lead, don't you agree?'

'If such things are so commonly used by housewives, there may be a multitude of users in Königsberg,' I objected, but Sergeant Koch did not back down.

'Merete mentioned a man in the trade,' he went on with conviction. 'A gentleman who could supply anything that a person might need. If I could trace him, sir, he might be able to tell us something about the type of needle, and the people who buy them. It's not the common sort my wife used.'

The proverbial search in the haystack came to mind, but I had no wish to dampen Koch's enthusiasm.

'You don't need me at the Infirmary, sir,' he continued. 'Perhaps I can locate the man. There aren't many shops in Königsberg selling haberdashery.'

'That's a good idea,' I encouraged, though I had little hope of success.

Thus, it was decided. Koch would accompany me back to town, then our ways would part. As we stood there talking in the salty, windblown air, rivulets of damp formed on the waterproof surface of the cape Professor Kant had given me. I shook them off as we boarded the coach. At the same time, I could not help but notice that the sergeant's pea-jacket was soaking wet.

'You look like a drowned rat,' I said lightly. 'Take this cape. You'll be obliged to walk in town, while I will have the coach.'

'There's no need, really, sir,' he protested weakly.

I slipped the cape from my shoulders and handed it to him.

'Precisely, Koch. My lack of need is greater than yours,' I said, unfolding my woollen cloak once more and wrapping myself up in it.

Having crossed any number of wooden bridges to the centre of town, the carriage stopped; Sergeant Koch climbed down and strode off purposefully into the gathering gloom. Dressed in Kant's glistening waterproof cloak, I seemed to see myself in hot pursuit of the murderer. I had to smile, though it would be many a day before I managed to smile again.

Chapter 25

'Anton Theodor Lublinsky,' Colonel-Surgeon Franzich nodded vigorously. 'Lost his left eye, of course. No help for that, Herr Procurator. Putrefaction had set in. He'd have lost the other one, too. Do take a seat.'

As soon as I introduced myself, he had led me up three steps to his room, one wall of which appeared to have been recently constructed. Unlike any other room that I had observed inside the Fortress of Königsberg, this wall was entirely made of panes of glass.

'Far easier to keep a watch on the inmates,' Colonel Franzich said by way of explanation, waving his hand in the direction of the ward. 'All you have to do is stand up. Like a skipper on the bridge.'

'Ingenious,' I replied with an appreciative smile.

'They, of course, are forbidden to stand. We have "condemned" them to bed!' he joked with a tired smile. 'They cannot see us. All they can see is this wall at my back.'

'Indeed,' I replied.

'The Wailing Wall, I call it. Biblical reference, you know?' he replied with the same fixed, tired smile.

From where I sat, my back to the glass partition, I was obliged to look at the very wall he was talking of. And more than once, I asked myself whether the array of objects so carefully positioned on that Wailing Wall would convince any sick man to place his trust in Colonel-Surgeon Franzich. That wall was guaranteed to frighten all remaining hope out of any man at risk of dying, or losing a limb from the injuries he had suffered.

'Are those figures made of wax?' I asked.

'Most certainly,' he replied. 'Most of the victims are still alive and . . . relatively well, I suppose. Military surgery has come on by leaps and bounds in the past decade. Before these patients were allowed to leave the Infirmary, I had a wax cast made of their injuries. To an expert eye, the possibilities of reconstruction are . . . well, they are evident.'

His smile was meant to be reassuring, but it reminded me, disconcertingly, of Gerta Totz's. The exhibits arrayed on the wall were macabre in the extreme. Wax castings of hands, arms and legs which had been severed and torn by grapeshot, or lost forever to the chop and slash of bayonets and sabres. But worst of all were the faces. They hung in a row at the top like ghostly death masks. The faces of men unlucky enough to suffer the cruel and crushing deformation of cannonballs and the heavy machinery of war.

Surgeon Franzich sat calmly in his chair before these monstrous mementoes of his carving-block like the proud owner of a wax museum selling tickets to his tent of human horrors. The flame from the lighted oil lamp on his desk flickered and fluttered in the gloom, and I was reminded suddenly of a summer evening I had spent in a splendid hunting lodge with my father and his elder brother, Edgard Stiffeniis, in the hills near Spandau over a decade before. As moths and insects threw themselves wildly at the dancing candlelight, dying in an unending sequence of flashes of light and sharp crackles, Uncle Edgard recounted the hunting adventures which had resulted in the collection of stuffed, mounted heads of bears and boars which decorated the walls of his lodge. This was far, far worse. Those faces immortalised on the wailing wall of Surgeon Franzich seemed to live and breathe an agony of tortured nerves and stretched skin. The impression that the effigies made on my mind was not softened by the unmistakable stains of blood which had dried on the Company Surgeon's workmanlike grey apron.

One face in particular attracted my unwilling attention. It was hard to look away, more painful still to look. The man had lost his lower jaw. His upper teeth hung jagged, exposed and broken above the unthinkable gap, his tongue a naked, bulging purple snake with no place to hide, nowhere to rest, slopping forward where his lips had once been. The exposed parts of the poor man's throat and neck had been carefully painted in the colours of life, a brutal kaleidoscope of indigo, red and adipose yellow. As the light from the candle shifted and stirred, the tendons, muscles and membranes appeared to pulse with all the vitality of everlasting pain.

'You signed the death warrant for Rudolph Aleph Kopka, I believe?'

'Kopka?' the colonel replied guardedly, as if he had never heard the man's name before.

'A deserter. Six months ago, he died of a fractured larynx.'

Colonel Franzich drummed his fingers on the edge of the table for some moments. 'I'll need to check the files,' he said.

'You won't find much there,' I replied. 'I have already looked.'

'Well, then?' he shrugged. 'What more can I tell you?'

A great deal, I thought, but I did not say so.

'Let's speak about Lublinsky,' I said instead.

'What a face!' exclaimed the Surgeon with bounding enthusiasm. 'Once that eye of his has dried out, I'll have a cast made. Such wicked devastation! Smallpox, that lip, now the eye. My students at the University . . .'

'Is his life in danger?' I asked.

'Not in the least!' he replied energetically. 'No, no, that man's as strong as a lion. Refused to let me tie him down! Can you imagine? Refused to let me draw the pus from the socket with hiruda worms! "Get on with it," he said. "Just tell me when you've finished." You'd have thought he had some more important business in hand than saving his own life! Can you believe that?'

'May I see him?' I asked. I had a good idea what Lublinsky's more important business might have been.

'Certainly, sir,' Colonel Franzich returned. 'But let me warn you, that man has suffered a terrible injury, yet he seems to shrug it off. So far as I can gather, he doesn't care a damned fig about the loss of his eye. No, no,' he continued as he tapped his forefinger to his head, 'his problems are up here. He may turn on you. Shall we go?'

The Colonel-Surgeon led me down to the ward.

'There he is,' he said, pointing to the far end of the aisle.

There were fifty or sixty single beds lined up on either side of the room, but only one other patient shared the large hospital ward with Lublinsky. This patient had been allocated a bed next to the door, while Anton Lublinsky was placed on the opposite side, and at the farthest end, as if Colonel Franzich had decided that they were two very different species of wild animal and better kept apart.

'Is there any way a man can leave this room?' I asked.

Colonel Franzich looked at me in puzzlement. 'Not before he is fully recovered and fit for duty,' he replied.

'That's not what I meant,' I interrupted. 'Are they allowed free passage in and out of this ward while being treated?'

'This is not a prison, Herr Procurator. Just look at them! Do you believe that either man could have walked out of here without assistance? This man's leg has been amputated below the knee, while the fellow you wish to see has not eaten, or shifted from his chair since they brought him in last night.'

I nodded, though I was not convinced.

'Be careful how you speak to him,' Surgeon Franzich urged. 'I have rarely seen a man in such a dismal state of depression.'

'A few words, no more,' I murmured quickly, walking away towards the far end of the room.

Lublinsky sat facing a large window, though he did not seem to be gazing out at the world. He might have been looking at himself in a mirror. Wrapped up tightly in a large black great-cloak, his shaved head tucked into the high collar of his uniform, there was an air of such abject melancholy and shrunken manhood about him that I hesitated for a moment before addressing him.

'So, we meet again, Lublinsky,' I said.

He did not move. Nor did he turn or shy away, though he must surely have recognised my voice.

'I hardly thought to meet you,' he muttered after some moments. There was something flat and inexpressive in his manner that I took at first to be a doomed acceptance of his fate. 'I hardly thought to meet anyone ever again.'

I sat down on the bed and looked at him. A large padded dressing had been draped over the left side of his face. It was held in place with bandages. He shifted on his chair and fixed his good eye on me. He made a better impression than he had the first time we had met, the deformity of his face hidden by the medical dressings.

'I'm glad to find you better, Lublinsky.'

'Better than the last time, you mean?' His attempt at a smile appeared like a horrible distortion on his lips. 'You're right, though. I feel at home here. In a soldiers' hospice they've seen worse faces than mine. They don't baulk away from such revolting things, if you catch my drift.'

'We must talk, Lublinsky.'

He shifted in his seat again, showing only the bandaged side of his face. Clearly, he was not going to let me forget what he had been subjected to. Even so, I did not mean to harm him further. My only wish was to extract the truth and so conclude my investigation.

'I've told you all I know,' he said.

'Not all, Lublinsky,' I replied. 'Not everything. Anna Rostova is dead. But you know that for a fact already.'

He sat up stiffly. 'Do you believe that loss of sight has given me greater powers of vision? I have not learnt *that* trick yet.'

I noted this change of attitude. There was a sarcastic bitterness about him. A desperate vein of dark humour had ousted the timidity which marked him out at our first meeting. And yet, fear of what I could do to him was there. Resentment too. It seemed to charge his being, as if he lacked strength of character to master it. Well, I thought, I have played on his fear of my office once before, and I mean to do so again.

'You've told me but half the truth,' I began. 'I want to hear the rest. How did you manage to escape from this place last night?'

'I don't know what you're talking about,' he protested in that mewling nasal voice, raising the back of his hand to wipe the spittle from his lips.

'You know nothing of the murder of Anna Rostova?'

'Must I answer such a question?'

'I think you must, Lublinsky.'

'You know the answer, then.'

'Yesternight you swore to murder her,' I insisted.

Lublinsky turned full-face, and brought his good eye to bear on mine like a man-of-war coming around broadside and lining up its heavy cannons. There was something majestic in his manner of doing so which surprised me. I realised then that his life had changed. He had altered since our meeting the night before. I had expected a mutation, but I was not prepared for the nature of it. There was, as I have mentioned, majesty and dignity, but they were the majesty and the dignity of malevolence. Lucifer after the Fall. There was no evidence of self-disgust, no sign of repentance, nothing to denote the agony of a tortured Christian conscience. Had I been able to remove the bandages from his face, I doubt I would have found the features I had come to know. There was evil in him, and he made no attempt to suppress it. He appeared capable of any act, any offence, any degradation, and I felt myself defenceless before him.

As he stared at me in silence, his eye seemed to gleam and swell with evil pride. I could not tell what was going through his mind. I only knew that I would not like it. He did not flinch or look down as he had done the first time that Koch had called him into my presence.

'You killed her,' I said quietly. 'What have you to lose by admitting it?'

He held his silence for some moments.

'I was here in the Infirmary, Herr Procurator,' he said with a bitter-sweet smile. 'Anna saw to that.'

'She was seen with a man last night in a tavern out at Pillau,' I pressed on. 'They were coupling, Lublinsky. Rutting like wild animals. Is that her power of attraction over you, too?'

'Over *me*, Herr Procurator? Me? Over *you*, I would have thought!' he rattled off angrily. 'I've seen the way you ogled her. Me? With half a chance, you'd have given her a length! In spite of what she is. For that reason, maybe.'

I swallowed hard before I spoke.

'Do not accuse me of your own sins. I am a happily married man!'

'That's what they all say,' he replied with a dismissive shake of the head. 'Then they hand over the coin and unbutton their pants. A wife is only a wife. Anna was something really special.'

'It does not change the fact that you murdered her last night.'

Lublinsky did not reply immediately.

'Let's say, for just one moment, that you are right, Herr Procurator,' he said at last, and he was taunting me. 'What bloody difference does it make? Whoever killed her, God will forgive the deed. That man did the world a favour.'

'I am not interested in your opinions of Divine Justice,' I snapped. 'Nor am I interested particularly in the murder of Anna Rostova last night. The only thing I want from you is an admission of the truth.'

The pupil of his eye dilated, and I was faced with a dark, imponderable hole. 'What are you talking about, sir?' he said with a flash of exasperation. 'The truth about *what*?'

'I want to know what you really saw and did when you went to examine those murdered corpses in the streets with Kopka.'

Lublinsky swivelled towards the window and studied himself in the glass. A dense fog had swept in from the sea with the turn of the tide. It had suffocated the wind and banished the sleet, transforming the world into a silent milky void.

'I've told you *that* before,' he snarled. 'I saw what I drew.'

'I've seen your sketches, Lublinsky,' I said. 'They are incomplete.'

'What do you want from a soldier? I'm not an artist. I said that to the odd old gentleman, but he didn't seem to mind. He had money to throw away. I just did as he asked.'

'You didn't draw the footprints that the killer left on the ground beside the bodies,' I accused.

'Which footprints?'

'In the case of the first murder, you sketched in what you found around the body, including footprints bearing a knife-cut in the shape of a cross. But you did not trace out those marks in all the other cases.'

'Satan leaves no prints,' Lublinsky said with a bitter laugh. 'His cloven feet don't touch the ground.'

'Do not joke with me,' I flared with anger. Had he really omitted the footprints from his later drawings, or were there none to be seen? 'You believed that Anna Rostova was the culprit. And when the killings continued, you convinced yourself that she had committed them all. She was a witch sacrificing human lives to her demons. You chose to consort with her to cure your face. So, you covered the tracks that she had left behind her. That is why you drew no more prints. You thought that they would lead to her.'

A noise like shifting gravel rattled from Lublinsky's throat. He was laughing. 'That needle must have entered my brain,' he said. 'I don't follow you, sir. How could I have done such diabolical things? Kopka was with me.'

'Kopka is dead, and the dead cannot speak. You killed him, didn't you?' I hissed. 'He must have guessed what you were up to, that you were covering up for a criminal. Rather than denounce you, he tried to desert from the regiment. But you chased him, and you brought him back. *You* were the capturing officer the report talks about, Lublinsky, were you not? Kopka was made to run the gauntlet, while every man in the regiment, yourself included, tried to crack his skull open with a stick.'

'Deserters know the score,' he growled. 'It's no easy thing to leave the Prussian army. That bastard got what was coming to him.'

'How very convenient for you, Lublinsky.'

'You cannot frighten me, Herr Procurator,' he replied boldly. 'I've nothing left to lose. If you wish to believe that Anna Rostova was the murderer and that I was her accomplice, you're free to do so. If you think that I connived at Kopka's death, dream on. But you'll not put those words into my mouth. You won't get me to confess . . .'

I played my final card. God help me, I had no alternative.

'You are proud to be a soldier, are you not?'

'It was my life,' he grunted. 'I'll be cast off now, I suppose.'

'A dishonourable discharge,' I added, 'a barebacked whipping out of the regiment. Then civil charges to face. Complicity to murder, obstruction of Justice, theft from a corpse. You are going to pay in full for Anna Rostova's crimes, as well as for your own. You won't find much in the way of sympathy in any prison. An officer who's betrayed his trust? The lowest of the low. Sentence? Life. With forced labour and reduced rations. With a bit of luck, you may survive a year or two. I want you to suffer, Lublinsky. And to make quite sure of it, I will condemn you to serve out your time in a . . . military prison!'

'You can't do that!' he roared, the enormity of the threat opening up before him. He would be hated and brutalised by his guards, reviled and tormented by his fellow prisoners. Each moment of every day he would be hounded and harried by a heartless pack of wild dogs.

'Can I not, Lublinsky? You know the legal code by heart, I suppose? I can condemn any man to the sentence I think most fit. Article 137 of the Penal Code. You go where I decide to send you.'

There is no such article, but Lublinsky was not to know. I pronounced this threat like a pagan god who knows no pity for the creatures under his jurisdiction. And like a deity devoid of all Christian compassion, I obtained what I insisted on having. He blubbered for a moment, but then he found his voice. His mutilated tongue began to squawk in fractured measures.

'The first time, that morning, I went to see the corpse she'd found. I guessed she was hiding something. Some *secret* . . .' His voice was strained, low, and I had to struggle to understand. 'Then, Kopka went for gin. For her, for Anna. She put her spell on me while he was gone. "I'll cure your face," she said.'

'There is nothing new or interesting in this, Lublinsky,' I cut in. 'I want to hear the rest. I want to know about those footprints.'

'Kopka saw them . . .'

'And you assumed that the woman had left them?'

Lublinsky shook his head. 'Not the first time, sir.'

'You drew them on that occasion, did you not?'

'I drew what I could recall. It was months afterwards. I was no good at it, but Professor Kant was happy. There were footprints all around that body. On the ground. In the snow,' Lublinsky went on.

'There was a cross on the sole. When I told Anna, she said that cross was the sign of the Devil mocking the crucifixion. It was a sacrilege, she said. So when I saw that cross again, I did not draw it. Nor did I report everything that I found there . . .'

He paused, and peered into my face, looking for approval. He was offering me something, working to save his miserable hide, just as he had done when he surrendered Anna Rostova into my hands the day before.

'What did you find?' I asked, trying to sound detached.

'A chain,' he said. 'In the hand of Jan Konnen. A watch-chain with a broken link.'

'What did you do with it?'

'When Kopka wasn't looking, I slipped it in my pocket. It was silver.'

'That's theft,' I sneered.

He hesitated for a moment. 'I gave it to Anna. A gift from Satan, she said, and I'd be rewarded 'cause I'd done the right thing. She told me then what she had done. She'd pulled the Devil's claw from the dead man's neck before we arrived. Afterwards, she made me bring her any trifle that I found at the murder scenes. Those things were charged with the power of life and death . . .'

'If she was the murderer, why didn't she take them herself?' I objected.

'She wanted to tie me to her, sir,' Lublinsky mumbled. 'To make me her accomplice. She promised she'd heal me with the Devil's claw. I had to swear an oath. Tell anyone this secret, she said, and the spell won't work.'

'The second time, you found the same footprints by the body?'

Lublinsky nodded. 'There was that cross-cut again. It was hers, I'd swear, though I didn't see her that time. Her power was growing with each murder, she said. I thought she'd put a spell on Professor Kant 'cause he insisted that I should be sent out. Whenever there was another murder, I had to go and draw it. An' while I was there, I collected the Devil's gifts for Anna.'

I frowned. 'What are you talking about?'

'They all had something hidden in their hands, sir. All of them.

Those corpses . . . I took the objects and I gave them to Anna Rostova like an obedient dog.'

My heart beat fast. A new light shone on what I knew.

'What did you find?'

'A key in the fist of the dead lady.'

Professor Kant had surely been referring to something of the sort when he spoke of the murderer having used some stratagem to induce the victims to fall down on their knees. The list that Lublinsky gave me contained nothing of any import or value. The victims had died clasping banal objects of everyday use, sinister and mysterious by their association only with murder and witchcraft. The chain of Konnen, the key in Frau Brunner's hand, a brass button stamped with an anchor in the hand of the third, a groat from the fingers of Lawyer Tifferch.

'I cleaned the bones of the dead for her. I sorted through the muck for Anna Rostova,' Lublinsky went on. 'Like a carrion crow.'

'Did you take the weapon for her, too?'

'No, sir. She must have spirited it away. I never saw her there again. Not once after the first time.'

He stared at me in disbelief, as if awaking from a dream.

'She killed them, but I didn't give a damn. Not me. If people dying meant her power was growing, I was glad of it. God help me! I wanted her to kill again.'

He let out a strange cry, a strangled whimper, and I realised he was laughing.

'I carried a mirror in my pocket,' he said, his shoulders heaving, 'to see my face. Waiting for it to change after each murder. She promised much, but nothing changed. Still the same. Ugly brute . . .'

He was mad, lost in a world of vain hopes of his own creating.

'It's funny, is it not?' he said with sudden vehemence, his head jerking round at me. 'That woman terrified the city and commanded the King. No one would have given her a second glance if Nature hadn't marked her out. We're two of a kind, we are. Me, with a face disfigured by smallpox. That wild silver hair she had. Those blazing eyes. I wanted her. Even as she plunged that dart in my eye . . .' He fixed me with that mocking eye of his. 'Did you think to find the answer to your mystery in two such monsters, Herr Stiffeniis?'

There was a claim to omnipotence in his tone, I suddenly realised. He was proud of what he had done. He seemed to think that he and Anna Rostova had held Königsberg in their hands. And he was right. They had toyed with the authorities, with the police, the King. Professor Kant had been taken in by them. And so had I. Anger burst from me like hot water gushing from a Greenland geyser. All pity gone, I felt the urge to harm him, to repay him for his arrogance.

'You murdered Anna Rostova last night. You convinced yourself that she was the killer.' I struggled to control my voice, caught my breath, checked my anger before I continued. 'You were wrong, Lublinsky. *Wrong!* Now, how did you leave this room?'

He did not trouble himself to answer. Instead, like some hideous parody of Narcissus, he turned his head towards the winter scene outside the window and studied himself once more in the glass.

'By means of that window? Is that how you escaped? You're practically alone,' I nodded over my shoulder at the amputee. 'That fellow down there has pain enough. They give him something to help him sleep, I bet. But vengeance is the most powerful painkiller, and your legs are not hampered, soldier.'

'She'll be happy with the Devil she worshipped,' Lublinsky said with bitter intensity.

'She was *not* the killer,' I insisted coldly. 'Do you hear me? She did not *kill* those people.'

'I know what I know,' he growled angrily.

I shook my head. 'Those footprints that you saw beside the corpses were not left by Anna Rostova. She played with you, tricked you time and time again. She made you believe what she wanted. She took your money. You were her dupe . . .'

'Hang me, sir,' he moaned suddenly. 'Kill me. I was a good soldier before black wolves began to howl in my soul. Snap my neck in two. 'Twill all be over in a second.'

I looked at him in disgust. His face was deformed by anguish and fear, as well as ruined by uncaring Nature. Even so, I realised, the surgeon had been right. Lublinsky's soul was blacker still. I rose, grabbed for my hat, and strode from the room without a word or a backward glance.

I saw Anton Lublinsky no more. I had lied to him on that count. In the report I wrote that evening, unable once again to prove what I knew, I glossed over his part in the death of Anna Rostova, concluding that the midwife had been killed by a person, or by persons, unknown. I heard no immediate news of Lublinsky's fate, though when news did eventually come, it was not good. Demoted to assist in the regimental kitchen after losing his eye, he was subsequently condemned to a military prison for murdering a soldier who had mocked him once too often. There, Lublinsky swallowed broken glass and slowly haemorrhaged to death.

Outside the Infirmary, I stopped to try and collect my thoughts. I felt depressed, sick at heart, thoroughly dispirited. Perhaps desperate was the most apposite word to describe my state of mind. Where should I turn? What should I do now? If only I could find the courage to resign this thankless task and return to the monotony of my life in Lotingen with my wife and children, I would be taking a step in the right direction. I ought to write to the King, explain my incapacity, and ask to be released immediately from my burdensome duties.

But then, as always in times of doubt, my thoughts turned to Immanuel Kant. How would I justify the renunciation in his eyes? Would he dismiss me as a faint-hearted coward incapable of putting his suggestions to good use? If not for me, I could almost hear him say, Morik, the Totzes and Anna Rostova might still be alive, and Lublinsky might not have lost his eye and his soul.

'Herr Stiffeniis?' a voice sliced through my thoughts. A gendarme had appeared at my side. 'I've been looking all over the place for you, sir,' he said, rummaging in his shoulder-bag. 'I've got a dispatch here from Herr Sergeant Koch. And there's someone . . .'

'From Koch?' I interrupted.

I tore the letter open, and began to read.

Herr Stiffeniis,

I have found the man! His name is Arnold Lutbatz and he supplies various shops in Königsberg with wool, cotton, knitting implements, etc., for domestic use. Herr Lutbatz recognised the needle instantly from my description. The Devil's claw is used for carding tapestry wool!

I told him that I needed to know the names of persons here in town who use such instruments, and he informed me that he keeps a list of clients. He supplies private persons, as well as shops. I asked to see the list on your behalf and authority.

I am directed this instant to his lodging, and will inform you immediately of the outcome, sir, not wishing to delay the search a moment longer.

Obsequiously,

Amadeus Koch.

I had the sensation of joy one feels after a long, hard winter, opening a window one morning and finding the first frail butterfly of Spring quivering on the glass. All hope lost a minute before, my strength and determination returned with every word that I read. Each sentence sounded to my ears like a military fanfare calling me to battle once again.

'Herr Procurator?'

I had forgotten the presence of the soldier.

'An old gentleman is waiting for you downstairs, sir. He says his name's Professor Immanuel Kant.'

Chapter 26

If Immanuel Kant had come to the Fortress, I reasoned, something serious had happened, an event of such urgency that it had
obliged him to break with his usual routine. Something so simple
for other men, any unforeseen change of plan constituted a sort
of cataclysm for Professor Kant. Add to this the thick fog that
day, a phenomenon for which he declared an unmitigated hatred,
and the enormity of Kant's decision can be imagined. I ran down
the stairs without delay, and out into the courtyard, where a single
solid figure was barely discernible in the swirling fog. It was not
the person I had been expecting.

'I'm so sorry, sir!' Johannes Odum exclaimed at the sound of my
footstep. 'I *had* to bring him. I was left no choice.'

'Is he well?' I asked, recalling his master's agitated state of mind
earlier that morning, hoping that his indisposition had not deterio-
rated further.

The valet looked perplexed. 'He's not been right since you left
the house,' he said, his voice tense with concern. 'Then, he insisted
on speaking to you again, sir. At once, he said. He . . . he needs that
cloak he gave you.'

If I had been puzzled by the Professor's generosity that morning,
I was even more surprised by this sudden *volte face*. If that heavy
garment were so essential to his physical well-being, why had he
left the warmth of his fire for the freezing cold and the rheumatic
damp without waiting for me to bring it back?

'Whatever for?' I asked.

There seemed to be nothing logical or even rational in such
behaviour.

'I've no idea, sir,' Johannes replied. 'He has no clear idea what he wants himself. You saw the way he was this morning. So keen to give you that garment, insistent almost . . . Well, he wants it back! He was so overwrought that I hitched the horse to the landau, and drove him here to calm him down. I didn't know what else to do.'

'Where is he now?' I interrupted.

'In the guard-room. But let me tell you what happened this morning . . .'

I felt the hand of fright clasp at my heart.

'After you left the house with Sergeant Koch,' Johannes continued, 'he sat himself down in the front parlour for the best part of an hour and stared fretfully out of the window.'

'Was he expecting visitors?'

'Oh, no, sir,' Johannes said emphatically. 'No one comes to the house these days. You are the first visitor he's had in a month or more. I took him his morning coffee at eleven o'clock, as usual, but he didn't touch it. He jumped up suddenly, saying that he urgently needed a book from Herr Flaccovius, his editor, in town. It was for his treatise, he said. He could not go on without it.'

'That mysterious treatise again,' I said, hoping that Johannes might have discovered something in the mean time.

He did not rise to the bait. 'Professor Kant ordered me to run all the way to the bookshop,' he reported instead. 'He was a bundle of nerves until I had put on my overcoat and hat, and was preparing to leave the house.'

'You left him alone?' I burst out angrily. 'Unprotected again? Is that what you are trying to tell me?'

'What else could I do, sir?' Johannes whined. 'He was safe in his own home, it was daytime, and you had sent those soldiers to watch the house. There was no danger at all. How could I refuse to go?'

'The fog is so thick, I doubt that the gendarmes can see their own noses,' I seethed, truly vexed and frustrated by the news.

'I took my own precautions, Herr Procurator,' Johannes replied in an attempt to soothe me. 'I stopped at Frau Mendelssohn's and asked her to go across and sit with him while I was out. Frau Mendelssohn lives . . .'

'I know who the woman is,' I broke in, recalling my chance meeting with the inquisitive old lady as I left the house that very morning.

'She's a devoted admirer of Professor Kant's,' Johannes continued. 'I told her that I was obliged to run to town on an errand, and warned her not to let my master out of her sight. I made no mention of the real motive for doing so, saying that he wasn't feeling as well as he should. Then, I rushed off to the bookshop. But when I got there, Herr Flaccovius had no idea what I was talking about. He checked his ledger and found that my master had, indeed, ordered that particular book. But Herr Flaccovius himself had delivered it into Professor Kant's hands four months ago. I returned home rapidly, thinking I had made a mistake with the title of the volume. I expected Professor Kant to be angry, but when I told him of the mix-up, he didn't seem put out in the least.'

'We have witnessed many unpredictable and disconcerting changes of mood in him. He has a great deal on his mind with this investigation,' I said to mask my own perplexity, which was great enough. Could Herr Professor Kant be so wholly confused?

'The oddest thing comes last,' Johannes went on quickly, as if I had spoken my puzzlement aloud. 'When I saw her to the door, Frau Mendelssohn told me that my master had been in the most excellent high spirits. Not sick at all, she said. He had entertained her to a disquisition on the cause of her migraine headaches, which he attributes to an excess of magnetism in the damp air of the town. He had been so concerned about her health, he went to get some anatomical prints from his study to show her the nerves which react to humidity. Frau Mendelssohn offered to look for the illustrations, but he insisted on searching them out for himself.'

'So, he *was* left alone,' I concluded, angry with myself, above all. No matter how carefully I tried to guarantee his safety, Professor Kant still managed to slip outside my net.

'Could she prevent him from retiring to his private study?' Johannes protested with a show of helplessness. 'But then . . . then . . .'

'Then, *what*?' I prodded.

The valet ran his hand across his brow, as if to wipe away the troubled frown that etched itself there. 'She says that she heard voices.'

'Perhaps he was murmuring as he sorted through the prints? Old people often talk to themselves without being aware of it.'

My reassuring words did not sound convincing, not even to myself.

'It wasn't that, sir,' Johannes added with a sigh. 'She actually *saw* the visitor leaving by the garden path. The path where you and I examined those footprints in the snow last night, sir.'

I felt cold sweat break out on my brow.

Had the murderer somehow managed to set foot in the house despite the presence of the soldiers on guard? But no, Frau Mendelssohn reported that she had heard them speaking together. Would the killer have entered the house merely to speak with Kant? And even more to the point, what would Immanuel Kant have had to say to *him*?

'Was your master upset?'

'Not at all, sir,' Johannes replied promptly. 'As Frau Mendelssohn said herself, what possible harm could there be in Martin Lampe?'

'Martin Lampe?' I asked, recalling my brief conversation with Frau Mendelssohn that morning. 'What in heaven's name was he doing there?'

'I've no idea, sir. I could hardly ask Herr Professor.'

'Do you know Martin Lampe?' I asked.

'No, sir. I've never met him. Herr Jachmann forbade him ever to return to the house.'

'Where does he live, Johannes?'

Johannes shrugged his shoulders. 'Herr Jachmann might know, though I'd rather you didn't ask him, sir. Professor Kant certainly knows, but I have no idea myself.'

The cold was even sharper than before as night came on. The air nipped at my cold hands and at the surface of my face like an angry puppy, and I regretted my act of generosity to Sergeant Koch.

'Take me to your master,' I said. 'I have a confession to make, regarding the cloak that he so desperately wants.'

Professor Kant was seated comfortably before a huge, black,

cast-iron monster of a stove in the guard-room, staring fixedly at the little blue flames that darted playfully from its open maw, a brown felt hat resting on his bony knees. In the far corner, off-duty soldiers played pinochle and smoked their long clay pipes, blissfully ignorant of the hallowed company they were keeping. Seeing him there, so old and physically frail, I felt an overwhelming urge to protect him. Such bleak surroundings seemed so unnatural for a man of his immense talents.

'Procurator Stiffeniis has come, sir,' Johannes announced.

Professor Kant jumped to his feet, spilling his hat onto the floor. He was clearly surprised to see me. 'You are well, then?' he asked, as if I had just that minute returned from a long and dangerous journey. 'But where is my cloak?' he added with that sudden shift of focus that had become so characteristic of late, and so disconcerting.

I hesitated by the door, unable to reply. Such attention to inconsequential detail robbed me of the capability to form a thought. Was Kant offended by my appearing in his presence without the gift? Or had a more general concern for the state of my health provoked the first of his two questions?

'I loaned your cloak to Sergeant Koch, sir,' I said, not quite certain if it were the correct thing to say. It was, anyhow, the truth, and the confession was made. 'The poor man was soaked to the skin,' I added by way of explanation.

Kant looked at me in silence as if my words had enchanted him. He seemed put out by the news. I had done something unforgivable, it appeared. But what wrong had I done? Such an uncompromising reaction to a simple act of kindness amazed me. It was inexplicable in the light of his own selfless generosity to me. Desperately I searched for something to say that would placate his anger, but before I could speak, he turned and smiled at me. The brainstorm had passed. He was himself once more.

'Isn't it odd, Stiffeniis?' he said calmly.

'Sir?' I asked with circumspection.

'How circumstances alter cases. Unleash Chaos on the world and it has a boundless energy all its own.' His eyes looked straight ahead. He seemed to be staring at some solid figure, which he alone could see.

'What do you mean, sir?' I murmured, now doubly afraid of disturbing him in this perplexing state of distraction, wherever it might be leading him.

'I mean to say that the further I progress in this experiment, the more I understand that Reason operates on the surface alone. What happens *beneath* the surface shapes events. The Imponderable overrules us all. For the first time in my life, I can feel the invincible strength of blind Destiny.'

He turned to look at me. 'Don't you feel it, Hanno?'

He was deathly pale, and seemed more fragile than ever, his voice trailing away to a hollow whisper.

'Go home, Professor Kant,' I urged, my heart sinking within me. In that instant, I lost all hope of making my way forward. Immanuel Kant, my anchor, my compass in the storm, had gone adrift. He had left me alone on the angry, empty sea.

'I'll give you back your cloak,' I said soothingly, as if it were the answer to all his problems. 'The instant Koch returns . . . .'

'I do not want it,' he replied gruffly, turning to his valet. 'Leave us alone, Johannes. Be gone!'

Johannes darted a worried glance at me.

'Wait next door,' I said with a nod. 'I'll call you when it is time to leave.'

As the door closed, Immanuel Kant placed his hand lightly on my arm. Leaning forward, he peered straight into my eyes. 'That woman is *innocent*, Stiffeniis,' he whispered.

I was amazed. 'How did you reach this conclusion, sir?' I asked. These swings of the pendulum between confusion and lucidity were disconcerting. I could do no more than follow his lead.

'Am I not correct?'

I nodded slowly. 'You are, indeed, sir. But how did you discover it?'

Kant ignored my question. 'Never mind that now. What leads you to revise *your* opinion of the woman, Stiffeniis? You seemed so convinced of her guilt this morning when you spoke of witchcraft.'

'She is dead,' I replied. 'Murdered before I had the chance to question her.'

Kant hunched forward in his seat. 'The Devil's claw?'

'Strangled.'

'Go on,' he said.

'Those drawings that you instructed Lublinsky to make have been invaluable, sir,' I began. 'There were footprints left at the scene of the first murder, but Anna Rostova did not leave them. I have examined her shoes. The drawings rule her out. Your method of enquiry deserves to be publicised, sir,' I continued with enthusiasm. 'As soon as this affair is successfully concluded, I plan to write a memorandum which will, I hope, explain your methods to a wider public . . .'

'Your opinion is most gratifying,' Kant cut in with cold sarcasm. 'Perhaps I will find some new admirers now that the old ones have deserted me. Is that what you intend?'

I thought I knew what troubled his mind. 'Without your ground-breaking work in metaphysical speculation, sir,' I said with justified vehemence, 'there would be *no* new generation of philosophers.'

But he would not be halted. His temper exploded, his eyes flashed, his hands waved wildly about him. 'Nutcracker Kant, the scoundrels call me, claiming that I have imprisoned the mind and the soul in a world of rigid schemes and immutable laws. My last days at the University were unbearable. So humiliating. I have never been treated in such a way before. The *agony* I have suffered!'

Kant's eyes gleamed with passion. His voice was hoarse with malice. There was no suggestion of humour in the rancorous laughter which now escaped from his lips. 'They are such fools! Romantic dreamers . . . they cannot *imagine* what I alone have been able to conceive and carry out. They will never know the beauty of . . . of . . .'

He did not finish the sentence. His eyes slid away from mine and came to rest on an imprecise point on the barrack-room wall. He was silent for quite some time, and I knelt beside his chair, afraid to speak, uncertain how to quell the high tide of bitter resentment in his breast. Suddenly, his right hand falling to rest on my sleeve, he began to speak again, his voice all but inaudible above the hissing flames of the stove.

·'Can't you see the answer? Can you not, Hanno? I expected you to strike to the heart of the mystery. You're all I have left now that everyone else has deserted me. I cannot finish my work without your help . . .'

Clearly, I had let him down once again. But how exactly had I deluded him? What did he expect me to see that I still failed to see? Was it no more than an old man's dream of unattainable greatness? There is no quiet journey to the grave, I thought. What need had he of the good opinion of the new breed of philosophers? His genius was beyond the judgement of his peers.

'What made you decide that Anna Rostova was not the killer?' I asked, hoping to divert him from his morbid thoughts.

Kant seemed to shake himself from his torpor.

'A simple intuition, nothing more,' he said quietly. 'Would the murderer have chosen a weapon so decidedly feminine if she truly were a woman? This was a double bluff. You overlooked one important detail.' He raised his forefinger, bowed his head, and tapped the nape of his neck. 'A precise point of attack was chosen. This is the work of someone with a history of service in the Prussian army. A soldier, Stiffeniis. Such a mortal blow is used, so far as I can ascertain, only in two specific cases: for the immediate disabling of an enemy from behind, a sentry or guard who might give the alarm, or to dispatch a wounded comrade who is bound to suffer agony before dying on the battlefield.'

'A soldier, sir?' I was astonished by his perspicacity, and thought again of Lublinsky. Had I failed to see what was obvious to Kant? I let out a sigh, then all of my self-doubt came rushing out. 'Perhaps I am not the man for this task, Herr Professor. I have stumbled from one blind alley to the next. To be honest, sir, I am tempted to admit defeat and return to Lotingen.'

He stared at me as if trying to penetrate to the deepest recesses of my soul.

'You wish to resign?'

'I am not up to the challenge, sir,' I said, my voice breaking as I made the admission. 'I am lost in a maze. Every turn leads to another dead end. Something, or someone, confounds my every step. My blundering has produced more victims than the killer has claimed. I . . .'

I halted, unable to continue.

Kant's grip tightened on my sleeve. 'You ask yourself where you have failed. Is that it? You wonder what is the obvious fact that you have overlooked.'

'I do, sir. You have provided all the instruments necessary to comprehend what is happening here in Königsberg. Yet I have failed miserably. Can you still believe that I am capable of solving these murders?'

Kant did not reply immediately. He laid his hand on mine. His dry flesh settled gently on my own like dust. It was meant to be a comforting gesture, and I could not fail to respond to it. Then, he leaned closer, whispering into my ear.

'When you came to me this morning,' he said, 'with the murder weapon and a new theory about a witch, I admit it, I doubted whether I had done the right thing in naming you to run this investigation. I thought that it might be better to . . . free you from the tiresome burden I had placed upon you.'

'You did, sir?' I asked, the breath escaping from my body like the last wheeze of a punctured bellows. This judgement was the final blow to what was left of my pride and my faith in myself.

He sighed aloud. 'But I have changed my mind. That's why I came,' he said. 'My time on earth is short. In spite of your mistakes, you must continue what you have begun.'

'But I have failed you, sir! Ever since . . .'

He did not let me finish.

'You know something that the likes of Rhunken could never imagine,' he said with relish. 'I prepared the evidence in my laboratory for a rational man who would understand the logic of cause and effect. A leads to B, B to C, and nowhere else, of course. But this is only one side of the coin. There is another vital aspect to consider in these murders. The most important of all.'

'What is it, sir?' I asked, clasping my hands in a gesture of impotence. 'What can there be that you have not already indicated to me?'

'*The bent wood of the human soul*, Hanno. Logic has no place in human affairs. Have you forgotten what you came to tell me the first day that we met?' He did not wait for me to respond. 'I have never forgotten your words for one instant. I referred back to that first colloquy of ours when we were standing together over the body of that boy on the banks of the River Pregel the other day. Sergeant Koch – that perceptive man – expressed his surprise when I proposed the idea. He must have thought me quite a monster. But you ignored the suggestion, and now you persist in your obstinacy. You have known the answer for longer than you care to admit. "There is one human experience equal to the unbridled power of Nature," you said. "The most diabolical of them all. Cold-blooded murder. Murder without a motive." You remember saying that, don't you?'

His eyes searched mine. Then, he patted my arm again.

'You should take account of it, strange and horrible as it may sound. You are closer to the truth than you think,' he encouraged with a blinding smile. 'And this morning you told me about the mud stains on the victims' clothes.'

I frowned uncomfortably, while Kant sat back, his eyes narrowed. 'The killer induces his victims to kneel before he strikes them. We agreed on that, did we not?'

'And I assumed that a woman might be responsible.'

'But the killer was *not* a woman,' he said with a spurt of energy. 'This stratagem tells us much about the kind of person that the killer is.'

'You have formed an idea, Professor?' I asked eagerly, but Kant held up a finger to silence me, then laid it on his forehead as if to indicate the notion that was taking shape in his head.

'This person's desire to kill is greater than his ability to carry out the deed. He chose that weapon for its precision and the minimal effort its use required. Do you recall what I said when I showed you the severed heads and the incision at the base of the victim's skull?'

'"It went in like a hot knife cutting lard,"' I quoted.

'Precisely! But how did the killer induce the victims to stay still?'

'Lublinsky,' I murmured to myself.

Kant stared at me as if he thought I were mad. 'What about him?'

'I spoke with him an hour ago, sir. He told me something which would seem to support your argument. He said that each of the victims was holding an object clasped in their hand when they died. He did not mention the fact in his reports to his superiors. Nor to you, I imagine.'

'You see?' Kant exclaimed vigorously, his eyes shining brightly with excitement. 'Such purposeful cunning! Lublinsky is "bent wood" of the first order. But let us put the pieces of this mosaic together. First, the victims do not shy away from the person who approaches them. Second, they kneel down voluntarily before him. Third, they hold an object in their hands. Then they die. You prefer the path of Logic, Hanno,' he said with an ironic smile. 'Tell me, what do you deduce from these elements?'

Before I could reply, he continued in the same didactic tone: 'The killer asked for help. He appealed to human kindness, inviting the chosen one to pick up some small object that he had dropped on purpose as a bait. Of course, they all complied. That is human nature. And as they knelt, each one exposed the nape of his neck to the fatal dart. There, I've told you what I came to say. Now, I'll leave you to your task.'

In attempting to stand up, he succeeded only in scraping the bench on the stone floor as I jumped up to assist him.

'You must promise me one thing, sir,' I said.

'I never make promises,' he replied with a bewitching smile, 'until I know precisely what they involve.'

'Very well,' I laughed, my care and confusion set aside by his show of fresh confidence in me. 'In the future, if you have anything to tell me, send for me, and I will come to you.'

I did not finish the sentence. In that instant, the door flew open and a cold draught swept through the room as a soldier came bursting in. Johannes trailed behind, a worried look written on his pale round face.

'I hope you have good reason to enter in this rude manner?' I snapped.

The guardsman stepped forward and removed his black leather kepi.

'News, sir,' he said with a brisk salute, and my thoughts turned to Koch immediately. Had he sent another message?

'Body found in Sturtenstrasse fifteen minutes ago,' the soldier announced. He glanced hesitantly at Professor Kant, then back to me. 'I left the rest of the squad behind, and ran down here. Herr Stadtschen told me to run across an' tell you direct, Herr Procurator.'

'You were patrolling the area?'

'Marketplace to the town hall, sir. Up an' down. Every thirty minutes, sir, reg'lar as clockwork. Cathedral bell struck three. Daylight fading . . .'

Immanuel Kant's voice fractured the soldier's report.

'Behold, Darkness will cover the Earth!' he intoned with solemnity.

I turned to look at him in the half-light, and a smile seemed to flash across his face as he completed the citation like a clever child displaying his knowledge of the Holy Scriptures: 'Isaiah, Chapter 60, Verses 2 and 3'.

Chapter 27

Before my arrival in the city, the gendarmes had been instructed to report every instance of violent death to Procurator Rhunken. Having stepped into Herr Rhunken's shoes, so to speak, I was now directly responsible for the action to be taken in any such case. The fact that there was a cold-blooded murderer abroad in Königsberg did not simultaneously put an end to domestic squabbling or other crimes which might end in loss of life. I did not automatically attribute every new death to the chain of killings that I was investigating, therefore. Indeed, from what the messenger had told me, there were many reasons to induce me to think otherwise.

The timing of the murder was an important factor in my chain of reasoning. With the single exception of Paula-Anne Brunner, whose time of death had never been precisely ascertained, all the other victims had been killed at night, and I had no reason to expect such a dramatic change of modus operandi in my quarry. This latest corpse had been discovered as the clock was striking three, which suggested that the person had died during the hours of daylight. Next, there was the question of where the body had been found. Even I, who knew so little of the urban geography of Königsberg, realised that Sturtenstrasse was a busy street leading down to the fish market. The other murders had been committed in out-of-the-way places – again, with the exception of Paula-Anne Brunner, who had been killed in the deserted Public Gardens. Would the murderer I was chasing have taken the unwarranted risk of being seen and identified in Sturtenstrasse?

'Have you any idea who the victim is?' I asked, turning to the soldier. 'Or what may have caused the death?'

He shook his head. 'It's a man, sir, but we didn't go near the body. Our orders are to touch nothing if we chance upon a corpse.'

I turned away, satisfied.

'You pass near Sturtenstrasse on your way home, do you not, Johannes?'

'Indeed, sir,' he replied.

'With your permission,' I said to Professor Kant, 'I'll ride along with you in the coach. Johannes may set me down near my destination.'

Kant did not reply, though he did accept my supporting arm as we left the room. But outside in the courtyard, something very odd happened. As I was helping him into the coach, he grasped my sleeve and pulled me so close that the point of his hat struck me square in the centre of my forehead.

'Don't you understand?' he hissed in a sibilant whisper. 'I . . . I am losing control.'

'Control, sir?' I asked, disconcerted by his words. 'What do you mean?'

But he had lapsed into a graveyard silence. Johannes jumped aboard with a heavy woollen travelling-rug to cover his master's knees, while Kant seemed lost in deepest distraction, staring at me like a man who had seen a ghost. The fact that I had failed to understand yet again what, according to him, I ought to have understood seemed to have pitched him into a pit of depression.

'Something has frightened him, sir,' Johannes whispered.

'Let's take him home quickly, Johannes,' I said, as the valet prepared to leave the coach and take charge of the horse. 'I will walk back to Sturtenstrasse.'

I sat on the bench across from Professor Kant as the vehicle pulled away, uncertain whether to speak in an attempt to comfort him, or to remain silent. I might have been alone in the embalming room with the body of a dead Egyptian who was about to be mummified. His state was catatonic. He did not speak, or make a sound, as we drove the rest of the way to his house. Johannes jumped down at the gate, hitched the horse, and together we helped Kant to the ground, supporting him up the garden path as far as the front door.

'He has taken a fever,' Johannes whispered over his master's drooping head. Kant seemed to have lost the use of his legs, which trailed behind him, the toes of his boots dragging pigeon-toed on the paving-stones.

'Let's get him to bed,' I said.

Kant was ill. His face was pale, his breathing troubled; he seemed bereft of strength, his life force quite dissolved away.

We helped him across the hall, taking his arms on our shoulders, then we literally carried him up the stairs to his chamber. Johannes was a true tower of strength, somehow managing to do far more than I, and all the while carrying a lantern. In better circumstances, the fact that I was privileged to enter the *sancta sanctorum* of Professor Kant, by which I mean his private study and bedchamber, would have been a cause for elation. None of his friends or biographers had ever been allowed in there. Despite the fact that all my attention and concern were so concentrated on his well-being, I could not help but cast a quick glance around. The room was far smaller than I could have imagined. 'Monastic' was the word I would have chosen to describe it. A narrow cot stood hard up against one wall, a little chest of drawers by another, a tiny writing desk and a chair pressed close to the third wall. The fourth wall was taken up by a narrow slit of a window looking onto the rear garden of the house. Everything appeared to be sober, neat, functional, and I was moved by the thought that Immanuel Kant had written out sections of his monumental works at that very desk, including his latest, unseen treatise.

At the same time, my awe was stifled by the peculiar odour in that room. It simply could not be ignored. The narrow window I had noted to my left, looking onto the garden, had apparently never been opened. The air in the room was stale and mouldy, I would have said, as if the ceiling, floor and furniture were infected with woodworm, or dry rot. The atmosphere was impregnated with the smell of age and overused bedclothes which had never been adequately or frequently aired. I could not ignore the dry acridity of it. Without a doubt, Johannes took good care of his master, but I silently made a wish that he would attend more carefully to the laundry and house cleaning. What made it even more odd was the fact that all the other rooms in the house were immaculately clean and dusted. I jotted down a mental note to remind him of my critical observations before I left the house. But first, we had to get Kant into bed. As the light of the lantern fell on the pillowcase, a pale grey cloud seemed to shift and dissolve.

'What's that on the bed?' I whispered, breathing heavily after the effort of struggling up the narrow staircase with the inert body.

'Fleas, sir,' Johannes replied calmly.

My anger flared. 'The mattress needs disinfesting!'

'Oh, he won't have that, sir,' the servant responded blandly. 'Professor Kant has a method of his own to keep them off. It doesn't work, but he won't be moved.'

We had had similar problems at home two summers before. The fleas had invaded all the bedrooms and made our lives a misery until Lotte came up with a solution. She left a sheepskin out on the landing for two days and nights, then she rolled it up and burnt it out in the garden, far from the house. She and the children watched with glee as the poor fleas leapt up and down in the flames, crackling and popping, unable to escape their immolation.

'It's the only thing we've ever argued about,' Johannes continued. 'He says that lack of air and light will kill them off, and ordered me to stop up the window. Martin Lampe was a firm believer in the notion. That man's a constant presence here. Sometimes it seems as if he never left the house! Professor Kant has called me by his name on more occasions than I can count.'

Abruptly, he turned his attention to his master, preparing him for bed with a practised mixture of coaxing and firmness. 'Come, come, Herr Professor!' he called.

Sitting stiffly to attention on the edge of the bed while Johannes undressed him and put him into his nightgown, Professor Kant might have been a helpless infant waiting for his nurse to step up, turn the sheets, and hurry him to the Land of Nod. But unlike any child that I have ever known, he was struck dumb. He did not acknowledge my own presence by so much as a look. Johannes pulled back the covers and puffed up the pillows, ready to receive him.

Kant seemed lost in a deep trance as he settled back on the mattress and the eiderdown was pulled up to his chin. Though I felt better for seeing him safely to his own house, the fact that he was so completely passive did not augur well. The troubled frown on the face of Johannes reflected my own concern.

'My work . . . It must be finished . . .'

The low murmur came from the bed. Johannes was standing over Kant, staring down at his master. 'Herr Professor?' he called, his voice too loud in the muffled silence of the room.

'Professor Kant,' I urged, stepping up to the flea-ridden bed myself. 'Is all well with you, sir?'

Kant's left eye flashed open and he stared at me for a moment.

'A cold-blooded murderer,' he muttered. 'He bows to no one . . .'

He repeated the last two words over and over again.

'What is he saying, Herr Procurator?' Johannes whispered across the bed.

I shook my head, wanting silence, wanting Kant to stop this raving. My mind was in a whirl. Did he view my failure to catch the murderer as the defeat of Rationality and Analytical Science? Had the killer overstepped some mark that only Kant could see? Could this threat to the world as he conceived it account for his altered state of mind?

Suddenly, Professor Kant let out a shrill whimper.

'Oh, Lord!' Johannes exclaimed. 'He needs help, sir. Call a doctor!'

'Who takes care of him?' I asked.

'He treats himself, as a rule. His knowledge of physic is beyond the skills of most of the physicians in Königsberg . . .'

'In this state,' I insisted, 'he cannot help himself. He needs to be bled and poulticed. We need a professional.'

'There is a doctor living close by. He sometimes takes tea with my master. Perhaps he would be . . .' Johannes seemed to waver, as if crushed beneath the new responsibility that had been unexpectedly thrust upon him. 'But then again . . .'

A single glance at Professor Kant was enough to tell me that the time for hesitation was past. His eyes were closed, his face pale and expressionless, his respiration shallow and laboured.

'Where does this doctor live?' I asked.

'At the end of the street, sir. The first house on the left.'

I turned without another word and ran, the voice of Johannes following me down the stairs.

'But the man is *Italian*, sir, and he's very *young*!'

Five minutes later, short of breath, I reached the door of 'Dott. Danilo Gioacchini, Medico-Chirurgo', as the brass plaque described him. Beyond the door, I thought I heard the muffled sound of crying, and almost feared to break in on some domestic crisis. The house was made of weathered clapperboard that had once been painted blue, but now was a sadly faded grey. Crushed in between more substantial brick buildings on either side, I wondered whether its air of genteel poverty mirrored the cramped situation of the people living there. Was that the cause of the tears? It could not be easy for an Italian to make his way in Königsberg, despite the friendship of Immanuel Kant. Foreigners were held in low regard, Papists even more so, not only by the likes of Agneta Süsterich and Johannes Odum, but by every devout Pietist.

But what else could I do? I raised the iron knocker which was shaped like a closed fist, and let it drop. A moment later, the door opened a crack to reveal the face of a pretty, dark-haired woman. Standing by her knee, holding tightly to the young woman's skirts, a little girl of two or three years of age stared solemnly up at me.

'I am looking for the doctor,' I said, choosing my words with care for fear of not being understood. If this was the doctor's wife, she had probably come with him from Italy. 'It concerns Professor Kant . . .'

The name of Kant brought a fleeting smile to the housewife's lips.

'Danilo!' she called, turning towards the interior of the house, opening the door wide for me, and waving me to enter.

A moment later, the doctor himself appeared in the hall. He was, indeed, young, thirty-five at the most, though his long blond hair was thinning. Tall, slim, stylishly dressed in a high-collared jacket of black velvet, he welcomed me with a warm smile and sparkling brown eyes. Cradled one in each arm, he held up two identical infants which might have been born within the week. Both babies were screaming with all the strength in their tiny lungs.

'Twins!' he said. From the sudden creasing of his brow I could not have guessed whether he was proud of the fact, or apologising for the disturbance.

'I am sorry to bother you,' I said. 'Professor Kant needs help.'

He did not let me finish.

'I'll get my bag,' he said in flawless German. Then he spoke rapidly in Italian to his wife, who stepped forward immediately and took the wailing babies from him. A minute later, we left the house behind us.

Five minutes more, and we came to a stop in front of Professor Kant's. As we ran side by side along the snow-covered street, I had told him as well as I was able all that had happened, and tried to describe the patient's condition.

'Shall I come in with you?' I asked.

'It would serve no purpose,' the doctor replied, his foreign accent barely noticeable. 'His servant is with him, I presume?'

'Johannes is waiting for you. I am obliged to go to Sturtenstrasse,' I apologised, recalling my neglected duty. 'But I'll return the instant I can.'

I heard the front door open, then close, as I walked away quickly through the darkening, empty streets in the direction of the fish market, arriving out of breath and ruffled about ten minutes later. The fog was thicker near the harbour and the estuary. A solitary soldier was standing guard at the corner of the street. He might have been carved from ice, his leather cap and black waterproof cape glistening in the orange light of the flaming torch that he held in his hand. Until that instant, I had not given a thought to the identity of the person who was lying dead in that place. Kant's sudden collapse had been the only thing on my mind.

The guard stepped forward, his musket crooked beneath his arm, preventing me from advancing further.

'I am Hanno Stiffeniis,' I announced. 'The investigating magistrate. Where is the body?'

'Down that way, sir,' the man replied, glancing back over his shoulder. 'There's another squaddie standing over the corpse.'

'Nothing has been removed, I hope?'

'No, sir. We were told to wait for you.'

This phrase was uttered between gritted teeth, as if the harshness of the cold and the length of time he had been required to wait had turned to harsh resentment against my person.

'Let no one pass,' I said sharply. 'Except for Sergeant Koch, my assistant. He should be here soon.'

I had no idea where Koch's hunt for Herr Lutbatz, the haber-dasher, might have taken him, but I was certain that he would appear at the scene once he learnt what had happened. And I wished to have him there at my side. His experience, company and sound good sense would help me in the examination that I was about to undertake. My heart skipped a beat as I caught my first glimpse of the dark form huddled on the ground, and noticed at the same time the imprint of a man's shoe frozen in the ice. It bore a distinctive cross-cut . . .

Since that day, I have oftentimes asked myself whether Emanuel Swedenborg somehow touched upon a truth when he described the secret language of the dead. Now, I know for a fact that it exists. But then, I was incapable of translating the cold, silent mouthings into words. That night, I clearly heard the murmurings of the mysterious energy that Swedenborg tells us every departed soul transmits to the living.

Moving closer to the corpse, half-stumbling in a state of mounting anxiety which suddenly seized upon me, I was unable to swallow.

The young gendarme saluted and took a step backwards.

'Herr Procurator? I am glad you've come, sir,' he said with evident relief. The lantern in his left hand cast a sparkling aureola of dancing light on the packed blue ice of the pavement.

'Hold up your light,' I said. 'I wish to see the body.'

He closed the shutter with a sharp, metallic click, directing the narrow beam of yellow light against the high, brick wall which ran the length of the street. The dead man was kneeling on the ground, head bent forward on his chest, his right shoulder resting hard up against the wall. I stopped short, that question thudding in my head like a hammer beating heavily on an anvil.

'Draw close!' I cried sharply.

The soldier's teeth were chattering loudly. Little more than a lad, he was frightened. How long had he been standing there alone, waiting for me to come, not daring to look at the dark shape pressed against the wall in case the murderer emerged from the shadows and struck again?

As I drew near, a traveller's tale I had read flashed into my mind. It concerned the members of a mystic Asiatic sect, who believed that the souls of the dead lingered near the corpse until the moment of burial. I seemed to hover above the body kneeling there in the street wrapped in a glittering mantle, just like the one that . . .

Falling down on my knees on the frozen stones, I found myself staring hopelessly into the lifeless face of Amadeus Koch. His mouth gaped, as if he had attempted to shout for help, his eyes wide open in a startled flash of realisation. I knew there would be a tiny pinprick at the base of his skull. My thoughts began to rush in a maelstrom of guilt and regret, blood swooshing loudly in my ears and throbbing painfully at my temples.

Kant's cloak. My cloak. The cloak I had loaned to Koch . . .

Whom had the killer intended to strike: Professor Immanuel Kant? Me? Or had he chanced upon Koch by accident? I had to lean against the wall for fear of fainting, paralysed with horror, the muscles in my arms and legs as stiff and rigid as they were bereft of strength. Had the murderer mistaken his man?

As the cold penetrated my knees, the words Professor Kant had spoken earlier returned to plague me: 'Where is that cloak I gave you?' Had he somehow foreseen what would come to pass? Had he abandoned the high ground of Logic for the murky paths of Divination? Had Science led Kant to a conclusion that I myself could never have imagined? Was this the cause of his indisposition?

I remained some time in this bewildered state, kneeling beside the lifeless corpse of my assistant. Koch's eyes were twisted upwards and to the left, as if he had had an intuition an instant before the blow was struck. A film of ice had solidified the liquid surface of those sightless orbs. The lamplight flashed in a bewitching illusion of Life.

'Are you all right, sir?' a voice behind me asked.

The young soldier leaned forward with his torch, the light and shadows playing mercilessly across Koch's face. The sergeant seemed to live and breathe again.

'Herr Procurator,' he said. 'This man is holding something in his fist.'

With as much gentle care as I could summon, I introduced my forefinger inside Koch's clenched palm and prised his frozen fingers back. A bronze ring dropped to the ground with a clink and rolled away. The bait. Koch had exposed his neck to the murderer in Sturtenstrasse while picking up a bauble. Muttering a prayer, I asked his forgiveness as I rifled through his pockets and extracted all the objects that a cautious man carries around with him. A fine linen handkerchief, a house key, a couple of thaler notes, and a piece of paper that had been carefully folded and folded upon itself until it formed a square no larger than a snuff-box. Equally carefully, for fear of tearing it, I unfolded the sheet of paper and held it close to the lamp.

In all that I have written so far, I have endeavoured to lay bare the facts alone, to avoid weighing one detail more heavily than any other. It seemed to be the most objective method of describing the slow progress that my investigation made, and it provides the true sequence of events by which the affair in Königsberg clarified itself to the point at which I can give a true account of the matter. But now, I must allow my heart to speak for once. I must, for my head had no part in it.

As I read what was written on that paper, something died inside me. For an infinity of frozen time, I held my breath, my heart battering and flailing painfully within the confines of my breast while I examined that note and saw the asterisk that only Sergeant Koch could have made, the rest written out in a hand not his.

The note reported the complete list of shops and private persons who had purchased fabrics and needles for knitting and embroidery. It must have been supplied by the man from whom Koch's deceased wife had purchased such things. I write it out word for word as I read it there in the Sturtenstrasse:

6 reels of silk, colour ochre – Frau Jagger
10 skeins of undyed wool – ditto
6 pairs of knitting needles – Emporium Reutlingen
10 balls of wool, light blue – ditto
15 balls ditto, white – ditto
Four yards, Burano, embroidered – Fraulein Eggars

The list went on, but I had stopped at a large asterisk imprinted halfway down the page like a royal seal. The item reported was the following: '6 whalebone needles, size 8, for the beading of oiled tapestry wool'. Next to it was written the name of the purchaser. It was the only male name on the list.

I read the item again and again, spelling out the letters one by one like a child learning the alphabet on his first unhappy day at dame school. Like the puzzled boy, I had to conclude that the letter 'K' was truly a K, that the letter 'A' followed it, an 'N' came next, and that the 'T' which ended the name was the vilest letter in the whole alphabet. I chained the letters together to form the name of the person who had purchased those lethal ivory needles from Herr Roland Lutbatz.

Chapter 28

A biting easterly wind whistled up the hill from the nearby port and fish market, sweeping away the fog in rolling waves. High above my head, windowpanes rattled and shutters shook. Somewhere close by, a heavy metal gate groaned on its hinges, clanging shut, then opening again, with every fresh gust that came charging in from the Baltic Sea.

Alone in Sturtenstrasse with the lifeless body of Amadeus Koch, I started nervously at every sound. Frost formed crackling in my hair, my body seemed to be turning into stone, but only one thought possessed my mind: I would not desert him again. I had let Koch go his own way that afternoon, and his life had been stolen away. As I stared down with awe and nervous fright at the lifelorn body kneeling against the wall on the frozen pavement, I could only ask myself whether Sergeant Koch had understood what was happening as the needle bit home. Had he recognised the face of his killer?

'Herr Stiffeniis?'

I spun around. In the wailing wind I had heard no one approach.

A man in uniform towered above me. Another soldier even taller than the first, a dark scarf wrapped around his face, came slithering up the hill, dragging a long, wooden box over the ice and snow as if it were a sled. I recognised those men in a flash. I stretched to my full height, but I was still dwarfed by Corporal Mullen and his Magyar companion, Walter.

'What do you want?' I asked.

'That body's for the cellar, sir. Orders of Doctor Vigilantius . . .'

I did not wait to hear the rest. A tidal wave of resentment swept over me.

'He will not touch *this* body!' My voice bounded back off the stone wall and echoed down the empty street. My stiff limbs quivered with violent emotion. A sort of desperate hysteria, a cocktail of hopelessness and guilt, possessed me. 'There'll be no more dismembering here. Vigilantius has gone from Königsberg. He'll not be coming back! Koch must be buried whole. In Christian fashion. I want him taken to a church.'

The two giants exchanged glances.

'There's a chapel in the Fortress, sir,' Corporal Mullen suggested. 'Being as it's the only dry room in the place, they use it . . .'

'I don't care what they use it for,' I countered sharply. 'If it's been consecrated, I intend to see Koch's body laid out there. I'll pay for your trouble.'

Mullen's dark eyes glistened. His companion grunted.

'We'll see what we can do,' the Corporal replied. His tone suggested that my whim would cost God knew what effort to satisfy. 'Now, let's be getting the poor, unfortunate gentleman into the box, shall we, Walter?'

Rigor mortis and the freezing wind had fixed Koch's body in the kneeling position in which he had been found. Ice had formed on that waterproof cloak, and the soldiers struggled without success to find a hand-hold on the glistening material, their clumsy fingers slipping and fumbling.

'Strip that cloak from his back,' I ordered.

I must have sounded wild and heartless, for Mullen let out an excited hoot.

'Strip his cloak off? What for, sir? He's stiff as a board already. It won't come off that easy.'

The waxen fabric of Professor Kant's cape – the cause of Koch's murder, as I believed – encased the corpse like a gleaming winding-sheet. 'I'll not have Koch buried in that garment,' I insisted peevishly. 'Get – it – *off* – him!'

Mullen stared at me for a moment.

'Here, give us your knife, Walter,' he said with a groan. 'We'll need to lay him on his flank, sir. There's no other way to go about the business.'

'Do it!' I snapped, watching as they obeyed my instructions.

The blade was short but sharp, and Mullen made a slicing laceration from the collar down to the hem. Then, having freed one side, they rolled the body over onto the other flank, and exerted themselves to release the sergeant's arms from the sleeves. Kicking the ruined remnants of the cloak aside, the soldiers lifted up the heavy corpse with some difficulty by the stiff arms and bent legs.

'Go gently,' I urged, as they set him down on his back inside the box.

'We'll have to straighten him out,' Mullen stated flatly, 'or that lid won't go on.'

'What are you waiting for?'

They pressed down hard on his knees, first the left, then the right, and the joints gave way with a sharp crack. It was a heartrending sound, yet my spirits lifted a trifle, seeing Koch laid at rest, and in his own clothes. For one instant, I allowed myself to believe that life might return, that my faithful assistant would sit up, breathe and talk to me once more.

'Can I close it, sir?' Mullen asked.

I took one long last look, then nodded.

Walter put the lid on, covering Amadeus Koch for ever. Then Mullen slammed home half a dozen nails, and we prepared to march away through the dark, empty streets. News of the murder would keep the townspeople behind their doors more surely than any curfew. Mullen and Walter went first, pulling their heavy sled with vigour, swishing and bumping through the ice and the slush. I followed close behind them, the gendarmes who had discovered the body bringing up the rear.

Along the way, we were obliged to pass the entrance to the lane which ran alongside the rear of Professor Kant's house. A feeble light glimmered behind the curtains of the window of his bed-chamber on the first floor.

'Go faster, Mullen,' I urged, looking dead ahead, wishing to be far away from the sight of that window and that house as quickly as possible. The paper that I had found in the sergeant's pocket weighed on my conscience like a ton of lead: '6 whalebone needles, size 8, for the beading of oiled tapestry wool – Herr Kant'.

A show of bustle was made, but the procession advanced no faster than it had gone before, and we reached our destination no sooner. As we came in sight of the Fortress, I strode on ahead and ordered the gate to be swung open to receive the party.

'Corpse for Procurator Stiffeniis,' Mullen snarled at the watch as he and Walter passed inside. The sentinels crossed themselves and looked shyly away. One man half-turned and touched his crotch superstitiously, the way soldiers do when they see a coffin.

'Has he got a wife, sir?' Mullen asked, drawing up with the box in front of a low building on the far side of the courtyard. 'She'll surely want to watch over him this night.'

'I'll keep the wake,' I said. 'There's no one else.'

Mullen nodded to Walter, who muttered something back in that strange language of his, then they pushed open the chapel door, and began to haul the coffin inside. I followed them in. Then, a lamp was brought, and others hanging from the walls were lit from it. Inside the church, everything glistened. Pyramids of large silvery cannon-balls and chain-shot had been built in orderly piles as tall as a man down the central aisle. Along one wall, artillery pieces were stacked one on top of another like glossy black cheroots in a tobacco shop. The far wall was blocked by gun carriages stacked end to end. An odour of rats, of rat poison and decaying vermin stifled the air. Large canvas maps covered the vast walls. A plain wooden crucifix hung by a long chain from the roof. There was no other religious symbol in the place.

'This is the regimental chapel,' Mullen confided in a whisper. 'I tried to tell you before, sir. They keep the arms and explosives stored in here. The rest of the Fortress is as damp as a washer-woman's mop. We can set the coffin in that space over there, sir. They shifted the altar out to make more room, but the place is holy. Will it do you, Herr Procurator?'

I did not trouble to answer. Searching in my pouch, I found a ten-thaler note and handed it over. 'Drink something strong tonight in memory of the man who lies here, Mullen. Bring a pastor at dawn. We'll bury him then. Send Stadtschen to me on your way out.'

Corporal Mullen saluted, Walter clicked his heels, the door closed behind them, and I listened to the sound of their voices laughing and joking as they faded away in the distance. Alone in the chapel, I moved past the stacks of cannon and the heaps of munitions, and knelt down beside the coffin. I placed my hand on the cold wood, closed my eyes, and began to pray to God, imploring Him to welcome the soul of Amadeus Koch with open arms. Even more earnestly, I begged the Sergeant to forgive me. I had failed to understand the immediacy of the danger in which I had placed him. I have never forgiven myself for giving him that cloak. When my little ones kneel down beside their cots each night, join their tiny hands and say their simple prayers, they invoke the name of Amadeus Koch, as I have taught them to do in memory of the man who lost his life while innocently trying to help their father.

Behind me, the door-latch scraped and footsteps sounded sharply on the stone flags. I turned and composed myself as Stadtschen marched into the chapel. He glanced at the coffin for a moment, then looked at me, a puzzled expression on his broad red face.

'Herr Procurator?'

'It's Koch,' I said, and his name died on my tongue.

Stadtschen took off his cap and bowed his head towards the coffin.

'I want you to find a person for me,' I said, breaking in on his respectful silence. 'The man's name is Lutbatz. Roland Lutbatz. His testimony may be vital for the investigation.'

'Where do you want me to start, sir?'

'He must be staying somewhere. He's not a local man. A cheap hotel, or a lodging-house, perhaps.'

'I'll send the watch out.'

'Jump to it,' I said. 'He could leave town at any moment. Herr Lutbatz deals in haberdashery, supplying shops and emporia here in Königsberg.'

Stadtschen frowned. 'Haber-*what* did you say, sir?'

'Dashery, Stadtschen. Cotton, needles, thread, that sort of thing. People selling such items might know where he sleeps.'

'I've got an idea where to start,' the officer replied, to my surprise.

'Your wife?' I asked.

A light twinkled in Stadtschen's eyes. I took it to be a sign of amusement, though I would soon be obliged to revise my opinion. 'Not likely, sir! There's an old biddy that lives here inside the Fortress. She does . . . well, she offers various services for the soldiers of the regiment.'

'Services?' I returned, unable to suppress the note of sarcasm in my voice.

'Not what you are thinking, sir,' Stadtschen replied. 'She's long past that! She washes, mends and sews for bachelors who need a helping hand. She might well know the man you're looking for.'

'Inside the Fortress, you say? There can't be many women living here.'

'None at all, just her, sir,' Stadtschen confirmed.

I glanced towards the coffin. I had not intended to abandon my vigil so soon. But my most immediate duty was to the living. Who, better than Koch, could understand my motives? He would not feel abandoned in the Fortress chapel, surrounded by munitions, maps and firearms. He would hear the trumpet sounding as the guard was changed that night, the measured crash of heavy boots on the cobbled square-ground, the reassuring shout of orders, the rush to obey. His life had been lived among such things. I had brought him home, for he had no other home to go to.

Five minutes later, Stadtschen and I were walking quickly through a dingy honeycomb of towering stone walls and cluttered paved courtyards. We were in the medieval core of the Fortress, which seemed to accommodate all the trades and the services that make a barracks function. Each separate courtyard seemed to proclaim its trade by the odour it gave off: horses here, kitchens there, stinking of boiling meat; leather shops and bootmakers; bakers' furnaces; the foundry full of smoke and steam and coal-dust where shot and cannonballs were forged. It was a world within itself, it seemed to grow darker and become more odoriferous the further in we went, stinking of open latrines, vile excrement, and finally, total abandonment. In the darkest shadows, grey rats skipped squeaking from beneath our feet.

'Good work, Stadtschen,' I commented, as we stopped before a rotting door which had not seen paint since the coronation day of King Frederick the Great, or perhaps even before.

'This is the place, sir,' he confided, pounding at the flimsy wooden panels with force enough to smash them to matchwood.

A wizened old woman appeared almost immediately, peeping out, eyeing the white double-sash and the chevron stripes on Stadtschen's uniform. She might have been ninety years of age, or a hundred years older. There was so little light, it was impossible to tell, her complexion black with ingrained dirt, wrinkles engraved in her dewlapped cheeks and forehead like those of a stone gargoyle. Her ragged clothing seemed to cling to her like a skin. Ancient brown sacking for a dress, her bonnet of the same rough material, all stiff with grime. No doubt, she stank to high heaven, but the stench that issued from her dwelling was strong enough to overmatch the filthiest of ancient sluts.

'I was expecting His Excellency,' she said, peering up at Stadtschen.

'We've other business on our hands, mother,' he replied. The tone of his voice surprised me greatly. This giant had been entrusted with the watch, he was responsible for Section D of the prison with murderers, cannibals, thieves and forgers under his command. He ruled them all with an iron fist, yet his voice was soft, even deferential, when he addressed himself to this old hag.

'Three times I done it. Three! Allus comes out the same,' she muttered, her voice fading away to nothing. She looked up suddenly and said fiercely to no one: 'It will not be Königsberg, I'll tell ye that again. He'll not strike here, soldier, ye can rest assured of that!'

I glanced at the ancient, then back at Officer Stadtschen. Neither said a word, their eyes locked in silent communion, as if they understood each other perfectly well.

'What *is* she talking of, Stadtschen?' I asked.

I repeated the question more loudly when neither answered, and a terrific noise exploded in the farthest, deepest, darkest corner of the room. The flurried beating of wings, the cries of birds, many birds, a whole flock of them, chattering away excitedly like hungry starlings gathering in a wood as the winter comes on, before migrating in a swirling black mass. But what were these birds doing in the Fortress?

The woman pointed a gnarled and twisted finger into Stadtschen's face.

'Tell that booby not to scare my babes!' she screeched. 'His Excellency won't stand for it!'

Suddenly, she waddled away into the room, moving through the darkness like a fish through water, the door swinging open on its hinges.

'Come in,' she called over her shoulder. 'See for yourself, soldier. You can tell the General from me.'

Stadtschen stepped forward eagerly, like a hunting-dog that had spotted a falling grouse.

'What's going on?' I said, catching at him, holding him back by the sleeve. 'Let's waste no time. I intend to trace Roland Lutbatz tonight.'

Stadtschen snapped to attention, as if he had awakened from a trance.

'Her name is Margreta Lungrenek, sir,' he confided. 'She knows the man you're after, sir. I'd swear it . . .'

'Tell him what I do!' the woman shouted from the darkness of the room. Old she might have been, but her hearing was not impaired. 'I'll not invite ye in again!'

'Five minutes, no more,' I snapped, stepping into the room, holding up my lantern. 'Lutbatz, or we leave. I hold you responsible.'

In the receding gloom, I could just make out a pile of wicker cages stacked one above the other against the far wall. There were dozens of these cages, each one stuffed full of birds of all colours, shapes and sizes. I recognised sparrows, blue tits, pigeons, ravens, starlings, blackbirds, but there were more, far more, a hooded barn owl among them.

'Herr General loves 'em,' the woman clucked, waving her hand in a sweeping gesture towards the cages. 'He knows plain truth when it's laid out before his eyes.'

'She'd fallen on hard times, sir,' Stadtschen whispered. 'Her eyesight's failing. Can't hardly hold a needle no more. Then, the General heard about her talents. He gave her shelter in the Fort . . .'

'General Katowice?' I asked, astounded. What had he to do with this old woman and her winged menagerie? I had taken Mistress Lungrenek's references to the garrison commander as nothing more than the ragings of folly.

'She sees the future,' Stadtschen continued. 'His Excellency won't make a single move these days without consulting her. He's obsessed with the thought of Napoleon invading the city. Since these killings started, he's convinced himself that it's the work of French infiltrators. The General is a great admirer of Julius Caesar, sir. He swears them Romans never went to war without consulting people like her.'

'*Aruspices*,' I murmured. 'That was the name for them.'

Stadtschen stared at me wide-eyed. 'It's true, then?' he murmured.

The notion of Katowice trusting in omens and believing oracles was disconcerting in the extreme. If the commander of the Fortress and defender of the city placed his undivided trust in divination, all was lost. I recalled the energetic figure, the determination of speech, the directness of manner, which had seemed so reassuring on my own arrival at the Fortress. Was his ebullient state of mind induced by knowing that his forces were strong, his strategy secure? Or was it all bluster, based on the visions of a mad old woman?

'Look here!' she snapped, moving away from the cages, stooping over a small, round table in the darkest corner. A large, black bird, a dead carrion crow, had been laid out on the wooden surface. Its curving sabre of a beak hung loose, its plumage glistened red with blood, and the table had been strewn with its guts. The carcass had been arranged inside a circle of letters chalked apparently at random on the wooden surface. The innards had been ripped from the bird's breast, and arranged all around the body. The beak pointed one way, the rigid wings stretched out on either side. For all the world, it looked as if the bird had been crucified.

'Note the beak,' the ancient whispered, placing her hands on the table, leaning close and breathing in the stench. 'It points to this letter here. The wings indicate these two vowels. An' see the claws! That's the place, there, sirs! Jena! It's far from Königsberg. That's where General Katowice should be. Not here, messin' about!'

She peered short-sightedly at Stadtschen, a thin knowing smile on her lips.

I realised that I ought to have been chasing hot on the heels of Herr Lutbatz and the killer of Koch, but that woman's claim to read the future in the entrails of birds pricked my new-gained curiosity. If I had learnt anything from Immanuel Kant regarding my experience with Vigilantius, it was to pursue the light, even if it were nothing more than a pinpoint glimmer at the end of a long, dark tunnel.

'I'll tell him, mother,' Stadtschen said, his voice quick, nervous. 'I promise you, I'll tell him straight. But Procurator Stiffeniis has a question for you. Just answer him, then we'll be on our way.'

'Do you know a man named Roland Lutbatz?' I asked.

'Aye, sir, I do,' she replied quickly. 'I'd be lost without him. I know him like I know my birds. I saw him yesterday.'

'And where was that?'

'The Blue Unicorn, sir. That's where he stays when he's in Königsberg.'

'That tavern's near the Ferkel bridge,' Stadtschen explained. 'On foot, it's five minutes from here, sir.'

'I know far cheaper, if you want their names,' Margreta Lungrenek offered, as I thrust a thaler into her hand and made to leave.

'God curse you, sir!' the woman screeched, throwing the coin to the ground and rubbing her hand as if she had just been scorched. 'There's a presence hovering over you!'

'Now, mother,' Stadtschen warned her, his courage coming back as we prepared to leave. 'Watch that tongue of yours!'

'The Devil knows his own,' she hissed back, gathering her clenched fists close to her breasts, as if to fight the malignant presence off. 'I knows a troubled soul when I sees one. Don't I just!'

'A troubled soul?' I echoed, despite my wiser instincts.

My heart thrashed in my chest and rose up into my throat in a choaking, suffocating ball as the ageless one fixed me with her bright unseeing eyes.

'Your father's dead,' she said slowly. 'Dead and buried, but not at rest. He rises from the tomb by light o' moon, but he'll rest soon,' she chanted in a strange singsong voice.

I turned to Stadtschen quickly.

'This wise dame has told us all we need to know. Let's go.'

Outside in the courtyard, the cold, damp air was almost fresh enough to be invigorating after the suffocating pestilence inside that fetid hovel. We turned away and began to retrace our steps through the dark alleys of the Fortress in the general direction of the main gate.

'May I ask you something, sir?' Stadtschen enquired after he had walked in silence for some minutes at my side. 'General Katowice uses that old crone to see into the future, sir. And he believes her, too. One time, I asked her to read my own future life. She killed and gutted a bird, and told me lots of things that I would rather not believe, sir.'

'Such as?' I asked, glancing up at him. His face was dark, perplexed and puzzled.

'She strewed those guts on the table, like the one we just saw . . .'

He halted suddenly, and I was forced to stop.

'What did she see?' I asked him.

'She spoke just now of your father, sir. Is it true? Did she see the truth?'

Fear shone brightly in the soldier's eyes. He seemed to be affected by the sort of innocent fright that I had seen often enough in the eyes of my children when Lotte told them ghoulish bedtime tales of goblins and fairies, wolves and captured princesses lost in the woods. Lotte was a storyteller of awesome power, enough to frighten a child out of its wits if she chose. I had often taken her to task for the wildness of her imagination and the freeness of her tongue.

'What did you ask her, Stadtschen?'

'Oh, you know, sir!' he said, smiling with embarrassment. 'The things all soldiers want to know. I asked her what would be my fate if Napoleon ever came to Prussia . . .'

'My father is not dead,' I cut in, carefully measuring my words. 'Nor will he be for a long time yet, I hope most sincerely. Margreta Lungrenek was wrong about my father. Totally wrong. She has no idea at all what she's talking of. Curse her ignorance! I wonder that Herr General Katowice should take such nonsense seriously.'

His face lit up like the sun bursting forth from a dark cloud, though that same cloud still hung menacingly over me.

Shortly afterwards, we left the Fortress, turned left and dived into the town. And Stadtschen was correct in his estimates. Minutes later, we emerged from the maze of alleyways near an ancient stone bridge, one of the many that crossed the River Pregel as it wound back and forth upon itself within the confines of the city. We stopped by a quay lined with heavy barges, watching the sailors smoking their pipes and chatting quietly, taking a moment to catch our breaths, then we turned towards an inn sign fanning in the wind. A blue-painted mythical creature galloped across a field of silver clouds with golden sparks flying from its hooves.

'The Blue Unicorn, sir,' he announced.

Chapter 29

As Officer Stadtschen hauled on a bell-rope, all the church bells in the city of Königsberg seemed to clang and chime together. Before they fell silent again, a window creaked open high above the Unicorn sign, and a pale round face peered down at us in the street.

'D'you know what time o' night it is?'

'Police,' Stadtschen yelled. 'Open up, and quick about it!'

The same fat, frightened man unbolted his door some moments later and waved us into the bar. He seemed unduly concerned to be discovered in his nightgown and bedcap. All was dark in the low-ceilinged room except for a pale glow in the chimney-place from the dying embers in the grate.

'I was asleep, sir,' the innkeeper whined, wringing his hands and looking as thoroughly guilty as I have ever seen a man who might reasonably be supposed to have done nothing criminal.

Then, Stadtschen alarmed him all the more.

'Bring the register for Herr Procurator Stiffeniis to see,' he barked.

A large leather-bound ledger was quickly laid flat on the table in front of me. I sat down and began to turn the pages, all of which were blank.

'Is this some sort of joke?' I asked, looking up. 'Is no one staying here?'

Stadtschen leaned threateningly over the shoulder of the man and hissed into his ear. 'Withholding names from the police, land-lord?'

The fat man's fears became ever more visible. 'I would not

dare, sir! The beadles search the town so frequently in the present situation.' He bent over the book, saying, 'With your permission, sir?'

He licked the tip of his finger and fumbled his way through the pages. 'We've had so few guests, sir. Especially in the last month. Who'd come to town to be murdered? But here we are, sir.'

He pulled back and showed me what he had found. One name was written on the page, together with a date.

'Herr Lutbatz, sir. A merchant,' he murmured. 'There's no one else staying here tonight. He's a travelling gentleman, highly respected in his trade, I'm told. A touch eccentric in his way of er . . . doing, and . . . er, dressing, but I ain't got nothing against that, sir, 'ave I?'

There was something decidedly shifty about the landlord. He seemed to be dropping hints of some sort, and I believed I had a good idea of what he might be hinting at. 'Does anyone visit him?' I asked, leaning closer.

'Well, sir,' he began nervously, 'you know how it is, sir. When a man is travelling all alone, like he is, he . . . well, how can I put it? He sometimes falls into *company*, sir. That's what I would call it. Company . . . There's not a great deal I can do about it. His visitors come, then they go. We have so few guests to stay these days, I tends to close a blind eye. He is alone tonight, I do know that. Said he was feeling like junk for the knacker's yard when I gave him his dinner . . .'

He stuttered to a halt, looking at me with a sort of pleading grimace of helplessness.

I leaned back in my chair. Women! I thought. I had been hoping that the landlord might have something to say about the customers who had recently been to visit Lutbatz.

'Do any of his customers call on him here?'

'Not this trip, sir. Times is hard in Königsberg. For all of us.'

'I wish to have a word with this man,' I said.

'Shall I tell him to come down here, sir?'

'No,' I replied. 'I'd prefer to speak to him in the privacy of his chamber. Would you step up and tell him that I am here?'

The innkeeper wiped his damp brow with the back of his hand

and let out a sigh of evident relief. Another man's trouble was no trouble at all, so long as he himself was not involved in it, it appeared. He scuttled away up the stairs, returning a minute later to say that Herr Lutbatz was waiting for me in his room.

'Shall I come up with you, Herr Procurator?' Stadtschen asked.

'I do not need a nursemaid,' I replied sharply. The truth was that I did not intend to risk making public the name that Roland Lutbatz had inscribed on his list for Sergeant Koch. 'Return to the Fortress, if you will, Stadtschen. And remind Mullen to find a priest for the funeral.'

He saluted and left, while I began to climb the stairs to the second floor, where Roland Lutbatz was hovering by his bedroom door. I saw immediately what the innkeeper had meant when he used the word 'eccentric' to describe the man. Had I stumbled by accident into a house of ill repute, the whores would not have been half so extravagantly dressed for bed as Herr Lutbatz was. He emerged coyly into the corridor, and smiled anxiously in welcome. His peccadillo had little to do with women, I realised. The lemon-coloured turban on his head might have been bobbing on the surface of a tropical sea. His nightgown was a rich emerald-green damask with chevron patterns in a darker weave, the silky material shimmering and undulating in the candlelight.

'Herr Procurator?' he asked, stepping nimbly to one side and bowing me into his boudoir, the air of which was richly perfumed.

'What a fright I got when the landlord knocked!' he exclaimed, pushing a chair close to the fire for me. He threw a log onto the embers, which flared up in a bright explosion of sparks, and adjusted the lemon-coloured turban on his head. 'Now, what can I do for you, sir?'

'I need to ask you some questions, Herr Lutbatz.'

The man sat down on the opposite side of the fireplace, pursed his red lips in a most exaggerated and feminine expression of alarm and began to pat himself lightly on the chest, as if to calm the rapid palpitations of his troubled heart.

'Oh, do! Please *do*, sir,' he replied, spreading his hands on his knees as if to brace himself. His nails were carefully cut and buffed, except for those of the little finger on each hand which curled like an eagle's talons.

'There has been a spate of murders in Königsberg. You know that, don't you, Herr Lutbatz?'

He nodded gravely. Then, his dainty features grimaced into a mask of alarm. His eyes blazed. 'You do not think that *I* am involved, sir?'

I smiled to reassure him.

'I need some information connected with your trade, sir. Nothing more.'

His mouth formed a gaping 'O' of surprise.

'But I deal in fabrics,' he said. 'Are you sure that I'm the man for you?'

Without waiting for my answer, he leapt up from his seat with unexpected agility and ran to the far side of the room. 'Here, you see? This is my business, sir. Material of the finest quality.'

He threw open one of the boxes which covered a good part of the floor and drew out a sample weft of dark red velvet. 'I travel all over the continent, France and the Low Countries for the most part, to buy my wares, and I sell them here in Prussia. All the shops in Königsberg buy from me, and private customers too, of course. All the very best people . . .'

'Like Frau Koch?' I asked.

'Frau Koch, sir?' he repeated, his eyes wide with surprise. 'Frau Koch has been dead these past five years. The poor lady . . .'

He fell silent, evidently unsure where I was leading him.

'Sit down, Herr Lutbatz,' I said. 'I am not here to see your goods.'

He sank unhappily onto his chair and stared at me.

'Frau Koch was the wife of my assistant. Sergeant Koch came to see you today, did he not?'

He let out another sigh of relief. 'He did, sir. His wife was a seamstress. She traded with me for many years. I gave her material in exchange for samples of her best work. Frau Merete was a delightful woman.'

'I want to know what Herr Koch asked of you, and what you told him in reply.'

Lutbatz looked at me with a puzzled expression. 'I thought you said that he was your assistant, sir? Did he not tell you himself?'

'I wish to hear from you what the outcome of the meeting was,' I said drily.

'Well, he came to ask about some needles, sir,' Herr Lutbatz replied in a nervous flurry. 'The sort we use in tapestry work. I let him see my samples, and Herr Sergeant asked if I had sold any to persons living here in Königsberg.'

'And what was your reply?'

'I checked my books and found the information he was seeking, sir. I've sold no needles of that type so far this trip. But Sergeant Koch was interested in others I had sold in the past and I gave him the records.'

I took out the paper I had found on Koch's corpse and handed it to him.

'Do you recognise this as the list that you gave him earlier today?'

'I believe it is,' he said, jumping up and running to the other side of the room. He clipped a silver pince-nez on the bridge of his nose and peered intently at the note. 'Yes, yes, this is my handwriting. These are customers of mine. I had one or two more to see tomorrow, then I meant to leave for Potsdam.'

'Do you mean to say that you have not yet completed your business in town, Herr Lutbatz?'

'That is correct,' he replied.

'Have you spoken to Herr Kant yet?'

'Now, isn't that a coincidence!' he exclaimed. 'Sergeant Koch asked me the very same question. I can show you the needles Herr Kant ordered. Sergeant Koch was most interested in those.'

He stood up and crossed the room. 'Does Herr Kant come here, or do you attend on him at his home?' I asked.

'He comes to me, sir,' he answered, dropping to his knees, throwing open a large brown trunk. 'Here they are!' he cried, taking out a wooden box and showing it to me.

'Does Herr Kant buy only these?' I asked, as Lutbatz extracted a rolled bundle and placed it into my hands.

'Oh no, sir,' the merchant prattled on. 'He purchases other things as well, cotton, wool, sometimes a little strip of Flemish linen, or a bit of French silk. But these big needles! I don't know what he does with them all.'

'Have you ever asked him?'

'Oh no. No, sir. I supposed they were for his wife. It hardly seems delicate to ask, if he doesn't say for himself. I've often wondered what her work is like,' the merchant chattered on nervously. 'I'm on excellent terms with all my clients, they often show me the things they make. If their work is of a reasonably good standard, I sometimes buy it to add to my stock. In the case of poor Frau Koch, I would exchange finished work for fresh materials. There's an excellent trade hereabouts in local craft for a person such as myself that travels around, but . . .'

'But Herr Kant never offered to trade his wife's needlework for stock,' I concluded. 'And I don't suppose you've ever been invited to their house either?'

He arched his eyebrows in surprise. 'How did you guess, sir? She must be an invalid, I thought. If she sends her husband shopping for her, she can hardly be in the best of health, can she?'

I did not reply. As I unrolled the bundle, I was trying to imagine Koch's thoughts when he read the name of Kant on the list and saw the articles that the philosopher had purchased. I held the cloth in the palm of my hand, folded it back, and stared at the needles. There were six of them.

'Whalebone ivory,' Herr Lutbatz said proudly. 'Such a lovely colour! Creamy white with an undertone of yellow.'

They were a fraction longer than the one that Anna Rostova had hidden, a fraction brighter, as if whoever had made them had polished them lovingly. There was a large eye-hole at one end, a sharp point at the other. My head was spinning and I offered no resistance as Herr Lutbatz picked up one of the needles, and weighed it in his hand.

'These are perfect. Light, well-balanced,' he said. 'They need careful handling, but they're far more robust than they look. A skilled worker can do an excellent job with one of these. Can I give them to Herr Kant if he calls before I leave?'

'I doubt he'll have much use for them after today,' I replied.

'He won't find better anywhere else,' Herr Lutbatz insisted with an impatient shrug of his shoulders. 'That's what Sergeant Koch said. He'd never seen such fine tools before. His wife would have loved them.'

'I am sure she would, Herr Lutbatz. You can put them away now,' I said, and watched as he rolled the needles up, placed them in their box, and returned them to the trunk from which he had taken them. 'Thank you, sir. You have been a great help.'

'Think nothing of it, Herr Procurator. I've done my duty, I hope. But may I ask you something?' He looked at me for a moment. 'Why are you so interested in Herr Kant?'

'Do you know who he is?' I countered.

Roland Lutbatz did not hesitate. 'I told you, sir. He's one of my customers. Not the most regular, but in my business you must count the pennies as well as the pounds.'

'Herr Professor Immanuel Kant is a famous man,' I added. 'He used to teach philosophy at the university here in Königsberg.'

'Oh, that!' the haberdasher returned with a flutter of his eyebrows. 'He told me all about himself the first time he came to see me. It must be a year ago now. He was full of himself. A real peacock, I'd say! He was a famous *philosopher*, he taught at the *university*, he'd published any number of important *books*. I didn't take him seriously, I must admit.'

'Whyever not?' I asked.

He hesitated, searching for a word. 'He told me that he was on . . . intimate terms with the *King*. Well, I played along, of course, but I didn't believe the half of it.'

'Did Herr Kant tell you the sort of work his wife did?' I asked.

'What a question, sir!' Lutbatz cried, clapping his hands together excitedly. 'Naturally, when he returned to me the second time, I asked him if his wife had found the needles to her liking.'

'And how did he reply?'

'I found him most evasive. She was little more than an amateur, he told me, but she enjoyed herself, which was good enough for him.'

I glanced out of the window. Dawn comes early in the North and the sky was a rippled pearly pink.

'Forgive me, Herr Lutbatz,' I said. 'I have robbed you of your sleep. Thank you for all that you have told me. It will be most useful.'

I was still speaking when Roland Lutbatz went scurrying across to that table on the other side of the room again. 'Before you go, Herr Procurator, I hope that you will leave an inscription in my autograph album,' he said, carrying a volume across to me. 'I ask every visitor to sign his name and write a phrase to remember him by. It's a great comfort when you travel the world without a constant friend. I do hope you won't disappoint me? Sergeant Koch ran off without signing. But I won't be disappointed twice in one day!'

I took the book in my hands – it was a small thing to do by way of thanks – and examined the neat leather-bound volume. A large red velvet heart and the word 'Memories' had been embroidered diagonally across the cover in elegant white letters.

'I stitched it myself,' Herr Lutbatz said proudly. 'All my own work!'

'It's quite remarkable,' I admitted. Indeed, any housewife would have been proud of such handiwork.

'Now, here's a pen, sir,' he said, bringing over a pot of ink and a quill, while I wondered what on earth to write. 'If you turn back a way, you'll see the phrase that Herr Kant inscribed with his own hand.'

My hands trembled as I turned the pages and saw what the visitor had written the night that he came to Roland Lutbatz to collect the instruments with which he would inflict sudden death on so many unsuspecting souls:

Two things fill my mind with wonder – the starry sky above my head, the obscurity deep within my soul.

The epigram was signed 'Immanuel Kant'.

'Go on, sir,' Herr Lutbatz urged with a shrill laugh of excitement, 'let's see if you can do better!'

I took the quill and in a few seconds I had composed and written the following phrase of my own: 'Reason has vanquished the clouds of Obscurity, bringing Light.' Then, as Immanuel Kant had done before me, I signed my name beneath the inscription.

The first rays of the rising sun caressed the dark horizon in a golden fan as I left The Blue Unicorn and walked out into the new morning with a lighter step, and an even lighter heart.

Chapter 30

Did I truly believe that Immanuel Kant was the murderer? Even for a single instant? Had I been able to conjure up a mental picture of Roland Lutbatz chatting amiably away, while Professor Kant purchased six ivory needles for the purpose of massacring the innocent citizens of Königsberg in cold blood? At his age? In his frail physical condition?

If the idea had ever flitted across the ruffled surface of my troubled mind for the tiniest fraction of a second, that phrase written out so boldly in the merchant's autograph book saved me from taking a further plunge into unthinkable error. What I had read was a godless parody of the Immanuel Kant that all the world knew and respected. As I studied those ungainly letters written out so awkwardly, in such an immature and childlike hand, I suddenly realised that a familiar ghost had brushed my sleeve many times in the past few days, and that he had gained ground each time that I failed to recognise him.

The very first time I had *not* seen this ghostly presence was the day that I came to Königsberg seven years before and found myself so unexpectedly invited to lunch at Professor Kant's home. His ancient valet was absent that day, attending the funeral of his sister. In thirty years of constant domestic service, it was the only day when he had *not* been present at Professor Kant's table. And just a short while after I returned home to Lotingen, the sixty-year-old servant had been summarily dismissed from the house, forbidden ever to return. Yet, Frau Mendelssohn had seen him repeatedly entering and leaving at all hours of the day and the night. She had told me so. She had seen Martin Lampe!

Lampe had managed to worm his way in and out of Professor Kant's drawing room soon after I had left it, or shortly before I entered. Martin Lampe and I had been like twin satellites in parallel orbits around the same mighty planet, always circling, never meeting. But why had Kant allowed Martin Lampe to return from banishment?

I could only guess. Maybe the servant had played on the generosity of his former master. Perhaps he had answered some need, given comfort in the form of the regularity and continuity of his visits, or provided that sense of order and fixity which seemed to be so essential to the ageing philosopher's well-being. What must have sounded to Kant like harmless chatter with an old, familiar confidant was the key to Martin Lampe's power. Like an alien cuckoo in the nest, one by one, he had thrown out all the other chicks. Kant's dearest friends had thought to unsaddle the valet, but he had pitched them headlong from the intimacy of his master. Martin Lampe had never distanced himself from Immanuel Kant. Not for one single moment. He had known my every move. As I began to displace him in his master's confidence, he had sought to eliminate me. He had killed Sergeant Koch in the belief that he was murdering me. That waterproof cloak had been the signal. Kant must have mentioned in passing that he had given it to me; Martin Lampe could not have known that I had handed on the cloak to Sergeant Koch.

But why had Lampe killed the others? Had each one of them had some tenuous connection with Professor Kant that I had not yet been able to discover? That Professor Kant might consult a notary was certainly possible, but what about the others? Jan Konnen was a blacksmith, Paula-Anne Brunner sold eggs, Johann Gottfried Haase was a social derelict. And why had Kant himself said nothing about them if he knew these people?

I had identified the killer, but I could not fathom what had made him do it. I had to find him, and make him talk. But where should I start to look? Where did he live, where could he hide? I took out my fob-watch. It was half past five in the morning. Nevertheless, I walked away quickly down Königstrasse in the opposite direction from the Fortress, a nervous litany running through my head.

'Dear God, forgive the Totzes, husband and wife. Pardon Anna Rostova for her sins and her crimes. Excuse the weakness of Lublinsky,' I intoned. They had all been savaged by my blundering incapacity.

'And help me stop Martin Lampe!' He had found a modus operandi and a weapon ideally suited to his physical condition and his age. Like a watchful spider, he had woven a web of cunning to immobilise his prey. When the fly was caught and helpless, he had struck with all the venom at his disposal.

'O Lord,' I spoke out loud, 'preserve the soul of Amadeus Koch.'

Koch would never know how close he had come to the truth. I prayed most fervently for his honest soul as I pulled my cloak more tightly against the freezing cold of dawn.

'And Heaven help me!' I thought finally, though there was more irony than piety in the notion. I had been deceived, but I had not been forced to pay for the error with my life.

I reached my destination, pushed open the creaking garden gate once again, and knocked more furiously on the door than I had intended. The servant came at last. While straightening his wig, he announced brusquely that it was too early for his master to receive a social call. 'It's barely six o'clock!' he added. 'And in any case, my master has a head cold. He'll be seeing no one today.'

'He will make an exception,' I insisted stubbornly. 'Tell him that Procurator Stiffeniis must speak to him on a matter of the greatest urgency.'

The fellow closed the door in my face, only to open it again a few minutes later. Without a word of apology for his rudeness, he stepped back, waved me into the hall, and pointed to the top of the stairs.

Herr Jachmann was propped up in bed on a mountain of pillows, his head covered by a grey woollen cap which was pulled low on his brow. The air in the room hung heavy with the fumes of camphor.

'You again?' he greeted me without warmth. 'The last nightmare of a long night.'

I sat down on a chair near the bed without apologising or waiting for an invitation. 'I have come about Martin Lampe,' I said.

Jachmann sat up quickly.

'I want you to tell me all that you know about him.'

Falling back against the pillows with a loud sigh, he closed his red-ringed eyes. 'I thought your task was to find a murderer, Stiffeniis, not gossip about the servants.'

'I need your help if I am to protect Professor Kant,' I said stiffly, and waited for him to open his eyes and look at me, though he remained silent and still. 'Do you know Frau Mendelssohn?' I ploughed on.

He nodded without speaking.

'She told me that she thought she had seen Martin Lampe entering Professor Kant's house on more than one occasion.'

Had I told Jachmann that an Arctic tiger was roaming unchained on the streets of Königsberg, the effect could not have been more pronounced. His eyes flashed open, and he glared at me angrily. 'Keep that man away from Kant,' he cried with such force that he was afflicted by a fit of coughing. The violence of his disavowal of Lampe disconcerted me.

'Have you told me everything I should know about him, Herr Jachmann?'

The old man did not answer, but fussed instead with the woollen cap on his head, pulling his shawl more tightly about his shoulders, as if I had brought the winter cold into the room with me.

'Lampe was not simply a servant,' Jachmann replied slowly. 'He was more, much more. Without him, Professor Kant was lost. Like a child without a mother. Kant's intellectual accomplishments are due in very large part to the contribution of Martin Lampe.'

The incredulity on my face must have been clear.

'Do you think I am exaggerating?' Jachmann smiled a wan smile. 'Martin Lampe was discharged from the army, Kant was in need of a personal servant. At the time, it was a happy coincidence. Kant is incapable of the simplest household task; Lampe was taken on to remedy the omission. Why, he couldn't even put his own *stockings* on! Kant's daily life was arranged by this rough-and-ready soldier.

When the Professor gave instructions to be called at five o'clock each morning, Corporal Lampe obeyed that order to the letter. If the master attempted to snooze after the hour had struck, the servant pitched him mercilessly from his bed like a lazy child. And Kant thanked him for it. He needs the sort of inflexible discipline which only a mother, or a man like Martin Lampe, can provide.'

He stopped to wipe his nose.

'Why drive him off after a life of dedicated service?' I insisted.

'He represented the greatest danger to his master,' Herr Jachmann snuffled into his handkerchief. 'Martin Lampe had become . . . irreplaceable.'

I studied Jachmann's pale face. His lips trembled, his eyes were feverish. He seemed to be terrified of Martin Lampe himself. 'But *how* was he a danger, sir? I do not comprehend you.'

'Do you know Gottlieb Fichte?' he asked abruptly. He did not wait for me to answer. 'Fichte was one of Kant's most promising students. When his doctoral thesis was published, many people believed that Kant had written it. They thought he had used the name of Fichte as a convenient pseudonym, but there was no truth in the rumour. Fichte often went to visit him, and the professor had always greeted him with friendly warmth. But after that thesis was published, a degree of coldness and animosity crept into their intimacy. Philosophical thought had shifted direction. Sentiment, Irrationality and Pathos were the new keywords. Reason had had its day; Logic was long out of fashion, and Immanuel Kant was set aside. Then, Fichte published a stinging attack on Kant for no apparent motive, accusing him of intellectual idleness. And a short while after, as bold as brass, he appeared at the door, saying that he desired to speak to his former mentor.'

'Did Kant receive him?'

'Of course he did. You know what he's like. He declared himself keener than ever to talk to someone capable of formulating new concepts. But Martin Lampe saw the affair in a different light.'

I considered this for a moment. 'Lampe was only a servant. What could he do about it?'

Jachmann ignored my objection. 'Fichte wrote to tell me what had happened that day,' he went on. 'He'd been frightened for his life, he said.'

He sank back on the pillow as if he had no energy left.

'What did he tell you?' I pressed without allowing him a second's pause.

Jachmann placed a flannel to his mouth, breathed in deeply, and the cloying smell of camphor wafted through the room. 'Leaving Kant's house that evening, Fichte found himself alone in the lane. It was dark and foggy, and he thought that someone might be following him. He quickened his pace, but still those footsteps dogged his own. There was no one to whom he could turn for help. And so, at last, he turned to face the stalker.'

'Did he recognise the person?' I asked.

Jachmann nodded. 'He did. It was Immanuel Kant.'

For a moment I thought the fever had possessed his reason.

'Not the amiable Kant that Fichte had left at the house,' Jachmann went on. 'This was a demon, a terrifying parody who looked like Kant, dressed like Kant. He ran at Fichte with a kitchen knife, and would have slit his throat if the younger man had not been so nimble. Fichte recognised him then. He saw that it was *not* Professor Kant, but the aged domestic who had poured tea for them both in subservient silence half an hour before in Kant's own sitting room.'

'God help us!' I exclaimed, wondering whether Martin Lampe's madness had begun that night.

'Fichte described him as the evil personification of his master.'

'Why did you not tell me this before?' I asked.

Herr Jachmann stared at me in silence for some moments. 'What good would the knowledge have done you?' he replied coldly.

'Did Kant ever learn of the incident?' I corrected myself.

Jachmann jerked beneath the sheets as if an adder had nipped him. 'Do you take me for a complete fool, Stiffeniis? There was a catastrophic overlapping of personalities in that house. The servant had become the master.'

'So you dismissed him,' I concluded.

'I fobbed Kant off with the notion that he needed a younger

man. Then, I wrote to you, Stiffeniis, asking you to stay away from him. I wanted Kant to live out his mature years in peace. Professor Kant needs to be guarded from the world. He must avoid unsettling influences like yourself and Martin Lampe. Age has taken its toll on the stability and lucidity of his mind.'

The connection that Herr Jachmann had made between Lampe and myself distressed me. He still resented my short-lived intimacy with his former friend, and made no secret of his opinion. He viewed us both as a danger to Immanuel Kant.

'Soon after I dismissed him,' he went on, 'I made another discovery. It was most distressing. Lampe had a wife! He'd been married for six-and-twenty years, and no one knew of it.'

'But he'd been living in Kant's house . . .'

'Night and day. For all those years.' Jachmann shook his head. 'Marriage was strictly forbidden in the terms of Lampe's employment.'

He relapsed into a moody silence.

'Does Lampe know anything of philosophy?' I asked.

Jachmann shrugged. 'What does a footsoldier know of such things? He could read and write, I suppose, but a fixation had taken hold of his mind. Kant's work cannot proceed without my help, he told me one day. And on more than one occasion I found him sitting in the kitchen, leafing through his master's published works. God knows what he made of them! As he left the house for the last time, he warned me that Kant would never write another word without his assistance. The prophecy was all too true, I'm afraid.'

'Did you hear anything more of him afterwards?' I asked.

Jachmann seemed to swell with rage.

'I have little or no contact with Kant these days. Even so, I did everything in my power to make sure that Lampe was kept away from the house. I shudder to think that he has disobeyed my prohibition.' He looked at me with feverish eyes, rheumy tears trickling down his cheeks. 'Is Frau Mendelssohn quite certain of her facts?'

'She saw him leaving the house. Just yesterday. She told me so.'

'Find him, Stiffeniis,' Jachmann cried. 'Find that man before he does any more harm.'

'Do you have any idea where he is, sir?'

Jachmann stared at me like a hawk. 'The wife will know. She lives . . . *they* are living,' he corrected himself, 'somewhere near Königsberg. I do not know exactly where. I never felt the wish to learn anything more about him. And now, Stiffeniis' – he leaned forward stiffly and offered his cold, damp hand to me – 'you must excuse me. I am grateful for all that you have done to help Professor Kant.'

I noted the stinging sarcasm in his voice as he pronounced the last phrase.

'I will do everything that I can to prevent Martin Lampe . . .'

I halted, afraid that I might have said too much, but Jachmann was not listening. He had taken up his towel again from a small porcelain basin and had placed his head beneath the tent to inhale the fumes. Clearly, my visit was at an end.

I left the house, caught a two-wheeled cab at the end of the street, and told the sleepy driver to take me to the Fortress. I had not slept all the night, but that was the last thing on my mind as I rushed up to my bedroom. Where was Lampe? Where was his wife? I could not use the gendarmes to locate them. No one must ever know the connection between Lampe, those murders and Professor Kant. I closed the door behind me and felt like a house-fly trapped in a bottle. I buzzed up and down, hopelessly butting my nose against the glass, although the opening was there, if I cared to look for it. If I *dared* . . . The solution was all too obvious. There was one person I could ask about Martin Lampe: Professor Kant himself. He must know where the man was to be found. But could I ask him without revealing my reasons for seeking Lampe out?

A sharp double rap at my door sent this thought scuttling for the darkest corner like a fugitive sewer rat.

A bleary-eyed soldier stood before me when I opened up, his fist raised to knock again. 'An urgent message, sir.'

'What is it?'

'Downstairs, sir. A woman's asking for you.'

I was expecting no one. Had Helena, for some reason, taken it into her head to come to Königsberg? Just as she had gone on impulse to visit Ruisling and my brother's grave the week before?

'Says her name's Frau Lampe, sir,' the soldier added.

I hurried down the stairs, greatly relieved and thanking Providence. God works in mysterious ways, they say. And how truly impenetrable they are! Hope surged in my breast in that moment. But that noble sentiment was no more than the final step on my long slide to perdition and delusion. The messenger had brought me the key to a closed vault that I had been trying in vain to enter. I could never have foreseen the horror awaiting me once the key had turned.

Chapter 31

Frau Lampe was younger than I had expected. She could hardly have been forty-five years of age. Standing in the corridor outside the guard-room, her face was finely sculpted by the dark shadows. The flickering lamplight cast a waxen gloss on her pale skin. A thin shawl of grey worsted material covered her head and shoulders in meagre defiance of the rigours of the weather. Although she looked worn and tired, there was something timeless and beautiful about her appearance. She might have been a gypsy girl begging on a street corner for coins. Glancing up at me with a look of the most intense concern, her large black eyes glinted with unexpected directness into mine.

'Procurator Stiffeniis?'

'You must be Frau Lampe,' I said.

She bowed her head in reply.

'You'd better come out of the cold,' I said, and led her into a little room that was used as a rule by the officer of the night-watch.

'Thank you, sir,' she said with an eagerness which took me by surprise as I struck a flint to the wick of a candle. I imagined there could be only one reason for her coming: she had decided to confess all that she knew about her husband and his crimes.

'I should have come before, sir,' she began. 'It concerns my husband.'

I waved her to a chair and sat myself behind the desk.

'I know who your husband is,' I said.

Her eyes opened wide with surprise. 'Do you, sir?'

'I have heard his name mentioned many a time in connection with the affairs of Herr Professor Kant.'

Frau Lampe looked down, as if to hide her face. Her dignified bearing seemed to diminish like a sail when the wind suddenly drops. It was the work of an instant. At the mention of Kant's name, a change came over her.

'You know Professor Kant, then?' she murmured.

'Indeed,' I said, 'I have that pleasure . . .'

'Pleasure?' she interrupted sharply. 'I know him too, sir. Like a cripple knows his withered limb.'

Her words were like a blasphemy spoken aloud in a church. 'You had better tell me what you've come to say, Frau Lampe,' I said gruffly, managing with an effort to control my temper.

'You think me rude, I suppose?' she replied, looking me squarely in the face. 'Professor Kant may well be a friend to you, sir, but me and my husband know the darker side of his character. It's no lack of respect, but the fruit of bitter experience.'

Suddenly, I felt uncomfortable in the presence of that woman. There was a calm determination in her manner which I did not know how to handle or direct.

'I doubt that you've come merely to express your rancour towards Professor Kant,' I continued hastily. 'Very well, then. What brings you here?'

'Professor Kant is the cause of all my husband's troubles, sir,' she replied. 'That's why I've come.'

'If you have something to say to me as a magistrate,' I urged her, 'then say it at once. The fact is that I need to speak to your husband, Frau Lampe. Do you know where I might find him?'

She raised her coal-black eyes, a pitiful, tragic expression like a stain on her handsome face. 'That's just it, sir,' she said, and her voice broke into a sob. 'I've no idea where Martin is. He disappeared the night before last. I came to report him missing, and they told me to ask for you. But you are investigating murders, sir,' she said, mopping at her tears with her shawl. 'Why did they tell me to speak to you? Has something happened to him?'

Was there some further aspect of the case that escaped me? Sergeant Koch had been murdered the previous afternoon, so the killer was still at large. What the woman had just told me cast doubt on my suspicions regarding her husband's involvement in Koch's death. She had placed his disappearance almost twenty-four hours before the murder of my assistant. Might something tragic have happened to Lampe as well? Or had he come out of hiding solely to commit another crime? There was still a chance that Lampe was innocent. But then a more cynical idea took hold, and I studied the woman's face attentively. Did she possess the skill to act the role that she appeared to be playing? Might she be trying to provide an alibi for her husband?

I stood up with decision.

'I need to search your home, Frau Lampe.'

If he was hiding there with her connivance, I would catch him off his guard. If he were not, I would have the opportunity to scour the house for evidence that might be used against him.

To my surprise, Frau Lampe stood up and prepared to leave without a moment's hesitation. 'I'll do anything if it helps you to find Martin, sir,' she said, forcing a weak smile, following me in silence out of the gate to where a police coach was parked. I woke the driver with a shake, and we climbed aboard.

'Tell him where to go, Frau Lampe,' I ordered, and she gave the coachman an address in the Belefest village area.

'Will seeing the house help you to discover where he is?' she asked uncertainly as the vehicle gathered speed. 'I've searched it myself from top to bottom. He left no note, and nothing at all's been carried away, sir.'

'It is normal police procedure, Frau Lampe,' I replied in the vaguest terms. 'There may be some clue that you have missed.'

She nodded eagerly and seemed relieved to hand the business over to me.

A church bell tolled seven of the clock. At this hour, I reflected, looking out of the window of the coach, any other town in Prussia would be wide awake, the workrooms, shops and offices open for trade. But under the arches of the low porticos on either side of the narrow street, all was closed and tightly shuttered. There was not a soul to be seen in Königsberg, with the exception of the armed soldiers guarding every crossroads. Truly, the city was under siege.

And it was all the doing of Martin Lampe. Bonaparte's marauding army posed less of a threat than the enemy already within the city walls. I had to find him. Perhaps then, the city would begin to live again.

After one or two miles, the carriage began to slow down, then came to rest at last beside a sad row of dingy little country cottages with sagging roofs of ancient thatch the colour of ash. We were in the village of Belefest, the lady told me as I helped her to climb down into an unpaved muddy lane. There were tall leafless trees on either flank. In the spring and summer, when brilliant green and the brighter tints of hedgerow flowers salvage the world, the hamlet might have made a first impression which was less dreary, grey and depressing.

'You won't find much sign of Martin's presence in the house, sir. My husband and I have lived together so little. Professor Kant could not, *would* not, get along without him,' she said harshly. There was no mistaking her tone, or her meaning. She did not like Immanuel Kant. His name seemed to burn on her tongue like acid.

The house was tiny, standing at the lower end of the row. A small garden stood before the front door. Poor, I judged, but not destitute. Then, Frau Lampe explained that she and her husband occupied only two rooms of the place: they had been obliged to let the whole upper floor to lodgers. She opened the door with her key and an overwhelming odour of stale boiled cabbage drifted out. A lamp was brought, the tinder struck – in that room, it was never day – and soon the humble dwelling was crudely illuminated for me to see.

'May I look around?' I asked, glancing quickly about me, taking in the meagre furnishings. Frau Lampe watched me as I searched the place, opening cupboards and drawers, feeling under every cushion and coverlet, excusing myself as I stripped away the bed and examined the straw mattress for anything that might be hidden inside or underneath it. I found nothing more exceptional in the dwelling than a few cracked mugs and mismatched plates, the dirty old clothes they had used to work in the garden, odd remnants of Martin Lampe's past glories in the army, which consisted of a pair of corporal's epaulettes and a faded, moth-eaten uniform jacket.

Inside a chest, washed-out household linen, nondescript rags of clothing, an ancient horse-blanket Lampe had brought back from Belorussia, together with a pair of yellow spare sheets and some faded fineries Frau Lampe had worn when she was younger and had known better days.

'We had much, much more,' she murmured, 'but the pawnbroker got it all. My first husband, Albrecht Kolber, was the beadle. We were well-to-do, but he died of choleric dysentery.' The widow Kolber had married Martin Lampe nine years after his honourable discharge from the Prussian army, where he had served in Poland and in Western Russia under King Frederick the Great. Without any other trade to his name, Martin Lampe had entered into service as the valet to Immanuel Kant.

'Martin wanted to marry me, and I needed a husband,' she explained flatly. 'We had to wed in secret, of course. Professor Kant wanted only bachelors in his employ.'

I wiped the dust from my hands and turned to face her. My search had told me nothing more than Frau Lampe herself had told me while I was sifting through the material wreckage of her life. First, of her short but happy marriage to Beadle Kolber, then, her impoverished widowhood, and, finally, the new lease of married life she had found with Martin Lampe.

She watched as I turned away from what I had been doing and looked around helplessly. Had some detail escaped my notice? Were Martin Lampe's secrets locked up in his brain and nowhere else?

'I told you before, Herr Procurator,' she said gently. 'You won't find any sign of his presence here. There's nothing worth a brass half-farthing. Nothing worth a memory.'

'Do you have a hiding-place for money, papers, valuables?'

She shook her head ruefully. 'Everything I own, I wear on my back, sir. You're looking in the wrong place. If you want to know what Martin had on his mind, there's only one place to turn for help.'

'And where is that?'

An air of concern clouded the woman's face, but in an instant the look was gone. 'You say you are a particular friend of Professor

Kant's, sir. Why not ask him where Martin is? I'd ask him myself, but I cannot . . .'

I stiffened. 'What makes you think that Kant would know?'

'Martin often goes to his house,' she replied without hesitation. 'He's been helping Kant to write a book.'

'He's been doing . . . *what*?' I spluttered.

'Not that he makes a penny out of it,' she went on resentfully. 'I've no idea what he does precisely. He comes home so tired out, he's not fit for work in the garden.'

'After your husband was dismissed from service,' I interposed, 'he was prohibited from ever visiting the house again. Professor Kant's friends keep a close watch to make sure there's no communication between them.'

Frau Lampe laughed shrilly. 'Even his dearest friends have to sleep, sir. Martin goes there after dark. I warned him, but he would not listen to me. The forest is a dangerous place at night.' She frowned and her voice was suddenly tense. 'You've no idea what my Martin's life was like in that house, have you? For thirty years he waited hand and foot on the most famous man in Prussia. If you knew the truth, sir, you wouldn't envy him.'

'Your husband has been most fortunate,' I said stiffly, 'in having served the noblest mind that ever lived in Prussia.'

A veil seemed to fall over her face. 'I could tell you things that Kant's best friends don't know,' she replied in a low voice.

'Go on,' I said, steeling myself to hear the gossip that cast-off servants and their irate wives reserve for their former employers.

'Everyone in Königsberg – and elsewhere for all I know – has heard of Professor Kant. His precise way of thinking, the regularity of his habits, the stern morality of his temperament, the impeccable elegance of his dress. Not a hair out of place, not a word out of turn, not a spot on his reputation. A living clock, they call him in this town. A clockwork man, says I. Nothing happens in his life by chance. No accidents befall him. Have you ever stopped to think how that affects the people in his service? Martin had no freedom, no life. Every single instant of every day, from the moment Martin woke him in the morning to the second when he tucked the Professor up in bed and blew out his candle, my husband was at his side, and never a single thought in his head but what his master put there. Waiting hand and foot on that man like a slave.'

She halted, her facial expression changed. Some rebellious thought seemed to pass through her mind and ripple the furrows on her brow like wind over still water.

'My husband was obsessed with the need to assist Professor Kant. When Herr Jachmann dismissed him, I realised that something was wrong. He blamed Martin . . .'

'It was not a question of blame,' I interrupted. 'Herr Jachmann decided that a younger man was needed.'

'Perhaps,' she replied, shrugging her shoulders. A nervous motion of her hands and the glinting brightness of her eyes suggested a fear of something that I could not name. 'Martin had a special task in that house. Something only *he* could do,' she added, her voice sinking to a barely audible whisper.

'A special task?' I echoed. Distressed by her husband's disappearance, I wondered whether she had begun to imagine plots.

'"I am the water in Kant's well," Martin told me once.'

'And what do you think he meant by that?'

Frau Lampe's eyes flashed up at me.

'Why, the book Professor Kant was writing!' she exclaimed. 'Martin told me he was helping his master to put the finishing touches to his final work. Kant's hand was not so steady as it used to be, his sight was poor, he needed a secretary to write it out for him.'

'Kant was dictating the text to your husband?' I burst out incredulously. 'Is that what you are suggesting, ma'am?'

Frau Lampe closed her eyes and nodded. 'Night after night after night. Often dawn was breaking before he got home. Martin isn't young any more, but he always was so diligent. He was so proud of what they were doing together. Helping Professor Kant rewrite his philosophy. That was what he said.'

'When did all of this begin?'

Frau Lampe grimaced with the effort of recall. A chasm split her brow. 'More than a year ago, sir. Martin was torn from my bed once more by that ogre. He came home when he could, but some nights he didn't come at all. And when he did come, he was not the same man. He'd sit by that window there, looking out like a haunted soul. He didn't say a word to me.'

I gazed at the murky window and tried to imagine what Martin Lampe had been thinking about. Had the murdering demon in his soul risen to the surface while his wife looked helplessly on?

'Did he tell you what this work involved?' I asked.

'He said I wouldn't understand. He and his master were exploring a new dimension. That's what he said, sir. A new dimension.'

Martin and Professor Kant, I noted. *Not* Professor Kant and Martin. Was that how she had interpreted Lampe's words, or had the husband presented the case to his wife in that light?

'Has your husband ever studied philosophy?' I asked.

'Oh no, sir. But he learnt a great deal from his master. Martin was always going on about the new philosophers who'd been attacking Kant. He said they'd be obliged to eat their words when the book came out.'

There it was again. The final testament of Immanuel Kant. The book that no one had ever seen. Nobody, apart from Martin Lampe . . .

'That book turned Martin into a different man,' she continued. 'He frightened the life out of me sometimes, sir. He was obsessed, driven, and it was all Kant's doing.'

'Your husband was only executing his duty,' I suggested vaguely, 'unpleasant as it might have been.'

'Unpleasant?' she hissed. 'It was worse than that. Kant brought Martin to the verge of murder.'

'Indeed?' I said coldly, as if what she had just told me was a reasonable argument and not an obscene calumny.

'Martin told me so. One day a young gentleman came to visit Kant. When Martin served them tea, he said that they were pleasantly engaged in a discussion of philosophy . . .'

The relationship Jachmann had mentioned earlier flashed through my mind. 'Was the name of the visitor Gottlieb Fichte?'

Frau Lampe shook her head. 'I've no idea, sir. After they'd finished talking, Professor Kant accompanied his visitor to the door and saw him out.' She stared at me, a smile frozen on her face.

'What happened?' I asked.

'Kant told my husband to run after that young man and kill him with a knife.'

Here was the other side of Herr Jachmann's coin. Not a mad Martin Lampe, but a mad and murderous Immanuel Kant.

'Did your husband obey?'

'Of course, he did, sir. It was his duty. But that young philosopher ran away before Martin could catch up with him.'

'Would your husband have obeyed Kant up to that final point?'

She joined her hands as if she to pray. 'I begged him not to listen,' she whispered with a moan. 'Kant is senile, I said. He's demented. To tell you the truth, sir, I was glad when Herr Jachmann dismissed my husband. I thought he'd be out of harm's way. But nothing really changed. Professor Kant sent a secret message, calling him to the house under cover of night.'

'Frau Lampe,' I said, turning the argument aside, pointing to a piece of embroidered linen draped over the back of a chair. 'Are you interested in needlework?'

She glanced up in perplexity, then nodded.

'Where do you purchase your materials?'

She looked at me as if I were deranged.

'From a shop? A travelling draper, perhaps?' I suggested.

'There are two shops that I go to,' she said hesitantly.

'Do you know a man named Roland Lutbatz?'

'Yes, sir.'

'Have you bought anything from him recently?'

'I do not know him personally, sir,' she replied. 'He supplies goods to shopkeeper Reutlingen. I've seen him there on one or two occasions.' She stopped and frowned. 'What has Herr Lutbatz to do with my husband's disappearance?'

'He says that he spoke to your husband recently,' I answered. 'Martin was interested in buying needles for carding tapestry wool.'

'Carding wool?' she repeated, as if she did not understand.

'Did you instruct your husband to buy them for you?'

She did not reply. She was too frightened to answer, I could see that, calculating whether her husband would gain or lose by what she might have to say. I knew how I wished her to answer. I desired it with all the impelling force that Doctor Mesmer mentions when he speaks of the transference of thought. I wanted her to tell me that her husband had, indeed, bought those needles for her, and for no other purpose than that for which they were intended. I prayed with all my heart that the certainty I had felt in identifying the murderer would be dashed to smithereens. I wanted Lampe to be innocent. If Kant's unwitting influence had driven him to murder, there would be no end to the scandal.

'I did not ask my husband to purchase anything from Herr Lutbatz,' she said at last. 'He may have wished to surprise me with a gift. He sometimes does.' She studied my face carefully. 'Will this help you to understand what has happened to him, sir?'

'You have been a great help to me, Frau Lampe,' I said, standing up and preparing to leave, ever more convinced of the guilt of her husband. 'Please contact me if anything else occurs to you. With your assistance the police will find him soon, I'm certain.'

'There's something else, sir,' she said, stopping me on the doorstep. 'I should have mentioned it before, but I hoped it would not be necessary.'

'Of what are you speaking, Frau Lampe?'

'I'll show you, sir.'

She led the way quickly into the back garden, tramping through the deep, packed snow to the farthest corner of the enclosed land. It was a small plot in which Frau Lampe and her husband had managed to cultivate an apple tree and some rows of vegetables, the plants now frozen, black and withered with the frost. A dense, dark, untended wood stretched away up the hill behind the house. There was a vague, menacing quality about the place. Wisps of fog clung to the naked branches and the stark damp trunks. Dripping icicles hung from the trees like the stalactites in the gloomy caves of Bad Merrenheim.

'Can you see these marks?' she said, bending to the ground and indicating footprints in the frozen snow.

I knelt to examine them. They were little more than scuffs left by someone in a hurry wearing shoes unsuited to the weather and the terrain.

'It was snowing the night that Martin disappeared. I saw these tracks the morning after, when I went to the shed over there to get some dried herbs. It has not snowed since.'

'Why should he come this way?' I asked.

'It's a short cut to Professor . . . to the town,' she corrected herself.

Leaving her at the garden's edge, I ventured further into the wood, following the tracks until I reached a wild plum tree. Enshrined in the frozen snow was the first clearly delineated footprint. I stared at it for what seemed an eternity of time.

'Are you certain these traces were left by your husband?' I called back.

'I cut the soles of Martin's shoes myself. The leather was worn. I did not want him to fall and injure himself.'

I had seen the distinctive cross-cut that Frau Lampe had made three times before. In the drawing made by Officer Lublinsky at the scene of the first murder. The previous afternoon in Professor Kant's garden. And the night before, beside the lifeless body of Amadeus Koch in Sturtenstrasse.

Chapter 32

After leaving Belefest, I returned to my office in a troubled mood.

I knew exactly what I ought to do. The killer had a name. Martin Lampe should be hunted down and prevented from striking again. Yet, there was something else that I had to do, something no magistrate should *ever* do. I determined to hide the identity of the killer. Professor Kant must never learn who he was, or know how close he had been. If the murderer could be stopped, if I could cover his tracks, I would lead the investigation away from him until it fizzled out. If any man spoke the name of Martin Lampe again, it must only be to remember him as Professor Kant's valet. Anything else was a blasphemy.

I planted my elbows on the desk, pressed my head between my hands. I felt as though my brain might erupt from my throbbing skull. The first thing to do was to draw him into my net. He had murdered Sergeant Koch, but *I* had been the real target. Lampe had set his heart on slaughtering me, and he would not rest until he had eliminated the danger. Could I offer myself as a bait to entice him out of his hiding hole?

Suddenly, another course of action opened up before me, one which would set me for ever beyond the pale of the law.

Lampe had disappeared. His wife presumed that he was dead. She had come to the Fortress to report him missing. Could I turn the situation to my advantage? All I had to do was call Stadtschen, inform him that the man was nowhere to be found, provide a detailed description, and suggest that Lampe might have been murdered. A search would be set in motion. If he were found alive, he would be brought to me for questioning. Then, I would have him where I wanted him.

I poured myself a glass of wine, and drank it off in a single draught. As the liquid traced its acid path to my stomach, I realised with a shudder what would follow on once I had him in my custody. A terrible energy began to surge through my veins. My thoughts were swept up, invaded, conquered by the recollection of a cold grey morning ten years before. The intoxicating smell of blood as the blade scythed effortlessly through the neck of the French king. I clutched my fists to my eyes, trying to cancel that image from my memory.

I would kill Martin Lampe.

I sat still for quite some time, seeking to reclaim possession of myself, struggling to remember who I was, to understand what I had become – what I was *about* to become. I could not risk a public trial. The manipulation of justice is no simple matter. If Lampe were forced to stand before me in the dock, I would have to prove his guilt in full. A magistrate is charged not only to condemn guilt, he must also demonstrate what led the felon to his error. Too much might be said in a courtroom debate of Professor Kant's influence over his valet. But if I gave orders to take the man up for his own safety, who would question my motives? If something happened while he was in my care, would any man dare to accuse me?

A short time later, a knock came at the door, and a soldier entered carrying despatches. 'Begging your pardon, sir,' he apologised, setting them down on my desk. 'Officer Stadtschen sent these.'

I glanced at the two letters, waiting for the door to close. The larger one, a white envelope with an imposing red seal, brought a lump to my throat as I slit it open. It was one of those missives all Prussians in the civil administration dread to receive, an anonymous secretary informing me that I was to give a full account of myself. A report of my investigation to date was required for submission to His Majesty, King Frederick Wilhelm, the following morning.

I let the paper fall on the table.

What was I to do? Could I avoid the Royal Imperative? Postpone the task until I was in a better position to reveal to the King what I wished him to know of the situation in Königsberg? I picked the letter up, read it once more, let it drop back onto the table, turning my attention to the second despatch, which seemed less intimidating. This message bore no Hohenzollern seal. It was a single sheet of grey paper, folded in four, and closed with a loop of string. But as I read what Stadtschen had written, my heart began to race.

> . . . *a heap of bones. Tatters of clothing suggest the victim may have been a man. He had been chased through the woods, as streaks and stains of blood in the snow reveal, and was torn to pieces as he tried to escape. Pawprints indicate at least a dozen animals in the pack. The beasts were famished* . . .

Another body had been found. Why had I not been informed at once?

My conception of the murders that Martin Lampe had committed was well-defined, precise in every detail. Whoever he was, the victim had not been killed by Lampe. But that did not diminish my impatience with Stadtschen's interfering ways. With Koch dead, he had spotted an opportunity for his own advancement. He had taken upon himself the responsibility to have the soldiers collect the bones in a sack, and bring them to the Fortress. 'The remains will be held for a day in case someone comes to claim the body,' he noted officiously. 'If no one does, burial in a pauper's grave will follow on.'

A groan of angered exasperation escaped me.

Did he think I would tell General Katowice what a clever fellow he was? Did he hope that I would mention him by name in my report to the King? I read on, my annoyance flaring into white-hot anger as I neared the end.

'Though not within the city walls, the place where the body was found still falls within the jurisdiction of Herr Procurator,' Stadtschen continued, 'being the abandoned hunting ground of the ancient feudal manor of . . .'

I jumped up from my chair, threw open the door, and called out the name of Stadtschen with all the force of rage in my lungs.

The empty corridor boomed with the sound. Footsteps clattered further off, and the echo of my cry was taken up by other voices, all of them calling the name of Stadtschen.

The man arrived at a gallop a minute later, his wig set lopsidedly on his head, the top button of his uniform loose, as if my summons to duty had caught him unprepared. His sweaty face might have been wiped with a knob of lard, and I took some pleasure in his discomfiture.

'Sir?' he said, breathing heavily after the exertion.

'Where is it, Stadtschen? Where's the body?'

He stared at me, his face a theatre of alternating expressions: surprise, shock, fear, anxious submission to my authority.

'Body, sir?'

'The man in the woods near Belefest,' I snapped, waving his despatch in his face. 'Who gave you permission to tamper with it? Are you blind to what is going on in Königsberg, Stadtschen? Someone is killing people. The only way to catch him is to search each murder scene for clues. But *you* decided to move the corpse! I suppose your men have trampled all over the place like a herd of cows.'

'Procurator Stiffeniis,' he interrupted, his voice trembling, 'there was no reason to think that he had been killed by any man.' He pointed his finger at the despatch in my hand. 'I reported the fact there, sir. Near the end. "Ravaged by wild animals." Wolves, most probably. They'd torn . . .'

'What makes you think the wolves *killed* him?' I shouted. 'The murderer could have chased this man through the woods. The victim may have been dead before the animals got to him.'

The possibility had never entered the numbskull's mind.

'But, sir!' he protested again. 'The murderer always strikes *inside* the city walls. That's why I thought . . .'

'You *thought*?'

I mimicked him sarcastically, but his desperate reasoning struck a spark of hope in my heart. He was right. Martin Lampe had never killed outside the town. Yet Belefest was where he lived. Was he hiding somewhere near his house, or in the woods behind it? I had seen his footprints in the snow on the path that led from the

347

village to Königsberg less than an hour before. His wife had verified them for me. Had Lampe killed someone else on his way home from town? Or had he himself been torn to pieces after murdering Sergeant Koch?

'Is the body still in the Fortress?'

'Indeed it is, sir.' Officer Stadtschen seemed to grow before my eyes as he replied. Unlike the ones that had gone before, this question had not been prompted by anger, nor tainted by accusation. His massive chest swelled out, his back straightened, his puffy face relaxed once more, taking on its usual air of arrogant self-righteousness. 'We can go there now, sir. If you wish, that is, Herr Stiffeniis,' he added more cautiously.

'Lead on,' I said.

On the ground floor, not far from the main gate, Stadtschen lifted a flaming torch from the wall and handed it to me. He took another one for himself, opened a narrow arched door, and we went spiralling down the staircase that led to the dungeons and maze of passages lying beneath the Fortress. I had been there in the company of Sergeant Koch on the night of my arrival in Königsberg. On that occasion, we had met a necromancer, and heard his animated conversation with the lifeless shell of a murdered man.

This time, I intended the inspection of the body to be strictly factual.

At the bottom, we turned right and entered a narrow tunnel which had been hacked out of the solid rock at some time in the distant past. The rough walls were slick with damp, dark green with moss. Piles of broken chairs, tables, beds and stinking mattresses had been abandoned there to mould and decay. Stacks of ancient breastplates stamped with a double-headed eagle lay rusting and forgotten in a heap. Old-fashioned powder-muskets with blunderbuss barrels were ranged along the walls like fossilised flowers. Each object seemed malignly intent on tripping us up, blocking the way, or falling down and burying us alive. The flickering torchlight saved us from the dangers, but there was little the flames could do against the cold.

As Stadtschen said in utter seriousness: 'We are in the impenetrable bowels of the Earth, sir. Long before Königsberg existed, before men made houses, this is where they used to dwell.'

It was hard to imagine any human being surviving there for very long. The cold was penetrating, it seemed to filter through my skin and take possession of my bones. The heavy woollen garments that had kept me warm – despite the freezing fog and icy winds that had lashed Königsberg since my arrival – were useless in that dismal cave. I might have been naked for all the good they did me. I am not averse to cold weather. A crisp winter's morning, frost fresh on the grass, sparkling sun, clean air, is one of Nature's delights, but the desolate chill of the cold earth has an unpleasant effect on my spirits. I was terrified by the odour of damp and organic decay while still a child. Every year on the anniversary of my grandfather's death, Father would unlock the door and lead the family and servants down to the crypt to pray for the souls of our ancestors. I knew the smell of the tomb from a tender age. Indeed, I often asked myself in gaping terror whether the dead souls of my forebears would be condemned to breathe that musty stench for Eternity.

With a swoosh of his torch, Officer Stadtschen spun round to face me.

'Here we are, sir,' he said, indicating a heavy iron door. He seemed to have regained his mettle. Perhaps he hoped the visual evidence of his good work would convince me to revise my opinion of him. 'Cold it may be, Herr Procurator, but a corpse will not last long down here. It's the damp that does it. Rot sets in, then there's the rats . . .'

'I can imagine!' I cut in sharply. I did not need a catalogue of horrors to compound my discomfort.

'I only meant to say, sir, that bodies are kept in the charnel house as short a time as possible. Most of them have been exposed above ground to all sorts of horrible mis–'

'How long has *this* corpse been here?' I asked more forcefully, drowning out his evident delight in the mechanics of human decomposition.

'I'd hardly call it a corpse . . .'

'How long?' I insisted.

'Four hours, sir,' he said. 'Bills are being posted up around the town. I gave the word myself.' He stopped, uncertain of my reaction. 'Do you want me to stop them from being put up, sir?'

'Let them be,' I replied. 'Someone may come forward with news of the man.'

'I tried to tell you what I was about, sir,' he went on. 'But when I knocked at your door, you did not answer. They told me in the guard-room that you'd left the Fortress in the company of a lady. I wrote that note before I went to bed, and told them to deliver it the minute you came back. I'd been on duty all night, sir.'

I heard him, but I was not listening. I was doing my sums. If the body had been deposited in the charnel house four hours before, then it had probably been found two, three, or even four hours earlier. That is, the man had died at the very least eight, ten, or even more hours before. I glanced at my watch, and noted that it was twenty past ten. Midnight, then, was the likely hour of his demise, though it was possible he had died some hours before. Physical examination would give me a better idea of the state of preservation and the rigidity of the corpse, but the timing did suggest that this *might* be the body of Martin Lampe. If so, I calculated, some hours after killing Sergeant Koch, he had been ravaged by wolves while returning home along the forest path. Of course, he could have died at any time after three o'clock the day before (the hour at which Koch's body had been discovered in Sturtenstrasse), but if, as I believed, midnight proved to be the more likely hour, where had he been hiding? What had he been doing in the interval?

Then again, I reasoned, if the corpse were not Lampe's, but that of another of his victims – that is, having killed Sergeant Koch, he had chosen to attack someone else as he made his way to Belefest – then I was seriously in trouble. Had Lampe abandoned his chosen modus operandi and favourite weapon, and given himself up to casual slaughter? Two murders in one day. Was his homicidal fury growing? Was his lust for blood urging him to kill with greater frequency?

As Stadtschen pulled back the rusty bolt to the charnel house, the iron door grated noisily on the rough stone floor, covering the words of invocation that escaped from my lips. I prayed to God that the corpse of Martin Lampe would be waiting for me. Certain knowledge that he was dead would end the terror that had taken possession of Königsberg, and cancel the murderous obsession that had taken root in my own mind.

'Cover your mouth, sir,' Stadtschen advised, blocking the way, and holding me in check.

'One of our lads was carried off this morning with choleric fever. Spewing his guts up when he wasn't busy on the latrine. Day and night for almost a week. What a way to go!'

Stadtschen raised his hand to his mouth and nose, while I turned my head to the side and used my jacket collar for the same purpose. The stink as we entered the room was hideous and sweet. The walls had been washed with lime, and the flickering light from our torches rebounded off the walls in a blinding flash. The space was empty and bare, except for a large tin bath placed against the far wall. I stepped across, glanced into it, then looked away. The naked corpse of a man had been laid flat on its back, eyes popping, broad chest sunken, skin wrinkled and yellow, the stomach swollen almost to bursting. Though I struggled not to think of it, I realised it would not be long before the nauseous gases exploded out of him.

I struggled to concentrate my mind on the task at hand. I did not have Professor Kant to help or direct me, as he had done when he took me to visit his *Wunderkammer* for the first time, proudly showing me the severed heads of the victims suspended in distilled wine.

'Over there, sir,' Stadtschen replied, waving his torch towards the far corner.

The man found in the wood had been laid on a mat of rough hessian. Stadtschen was right, I admitted. 'Corpse' was not the correct word. I fought the rising tide of revulsion in my gullet, and heard Stadtschen clear his throat and spit behind my back.

'I hope he was dead when they stripped him clean,' he murmured, as I fixed my torch in a ring on the wall.

Resolving to do as Professor Kant had taught me, I knelt down to examine attentively what was left of the body. I noted ribs and bones, sections of vertebrae which had been broken in at least three places, skeletal remains of the arms and the legs, everything tinged pale orange or dark brown where the muscles and flesh had been torn away. Shreds of transparent tendon, scraps of gristle and elastic cartilage still clung to the joints, though hardly a trace of soft tissue remained. It was impossible to determine the state of rigor mortis. So, there was no way of guessing how long ago the man might have been dead.

'Jesus, they were hungry, sir!'

Stadtschen's words were blunt and crude, but I admitted to myself that his observation was apt enough. Searching through my pockets, I drew out the long key that opened the door to my office. With some difficulty, I used it to turn the glistening skull towards me. In that instant, the true significance of the *memento mori* with which we love to decorate our Prussian churches struck me with a force that I had never felt before. Indeed, it took me a moment to pluck up the courage to look more carefully at the skeletal face, and the detached lower jaw. The skin was gone entirely, the ears and flesh of the cheeks and chin having been devoured. On the crown of the head, a tuft of hair had escaped being pulled away from the scalp in the frenzy of feeding. Though the strands were soaked in blood, the tips were clean. And they were white. A man of a certain age, I decided, or one who had aged prematurely. Might his hair have blanched as the attack took place? I dismissed this fanciful notion, my thoughts turning instinctively to Martin Lampe, Kant's valet, the secretary who had transcribed his master's work at dead of night, the servant I had never ever seen. Lampe was almost seventy years old. His hair could well have been white.

'They started with the juicier bits, sir. Cheeks and lips, muscles and fat, the flesh on his arms and legs and whatever was attached to that *thing* there.'

Stadtschen was standing close behind me, leaning forward, peering eagerly over my shoulder. I would have preferred him to stand further off and let me get on with my work in peace, but his finger stretched forward and touched the skull, which lolled and rolled onto its side, then came to rest like a soup bowl, giving an extra twist to the gristly tubes of the trachea and oesophagus, which had somehow survived the onslaught.

'They ripped his head off, sir. It's plain to me, this case bears no relation to the corpse of that man of yours that was stabbed to death yesterday afternoon.'

I paused for a moment, remembering Amadeus Koch, whose body was safely housed in the Fortress chapel. At least, I reflected morosely, his death had been more sudden, and I had preserved him from the horror of the charnel house.

'Begging your pardon, sir. You an' him was close, I know.'

Once more, I tried to ignore this gushing babble as I sifted through the corporeal wreckage looking for some clue to the identity of the unknown man. The ribcage, pelvis, hips, and a mass of tangled bones lay in the centre of a horrid, bloody mash, which was all that remained of the internal organs. The larger bones bore marks of deep indentations made by pointed teeth, or fangs, as I suppose they ought more correctly to be called. Having caught up with their prey, the beasts had evidently dragged him to the ground by his arms and legs. Then, they had set to work. Blood-soaked scraps of clothing were tied up inextricably in the mess, and I made no effort to shift them. What purpose would it serve? Any colour they might have had was irremediably fouled and stained by the blood and the gore.

'No clothes to help us,' I said. 'No shoes.'

'I bet they ate 'em, sir,' Stadtschen answered, blandly unaware of the importance the discovery of those shoes with the distinctive cross-cut on the soles might have made. 'A hungry wolf'll dine on anything, sir. Got a digestion like a French grenadier. They eat their young, I've heard tell. The wolves, I mean.'

I bent even lower, as much to escape Stadtschen as to gain a better view of the skull. The upper teeth were unevenly ranged with broken points and tips, badly consumed with age and use, as if the dead man had chewed long and hard before he swallowed his meat. I peered more closely at the oral cavity, telling Stadtschen to lower his light. The tongue had been ripped out during the assault, blood had caked the gums and everything else, with the exception of a white strip of bone or naked cartilage which stood out like a jagged slit on the roof of his mouth. A fang had evidently penetrated the palate as the beasts tussled with the head of the man.

Could any death be more terrible?

I let out a sigh of helplessness, looking into the blood-rimmed cavities of the skull, the dark empty spaces where the eyes had once nestled. What did you see in the final instant of your life? I wondered. Who were you? Some drunken wretch wandering alone at night through the forest? Another hapless victim of the killer? The murderer himself?

There was nothing in that hideous mess of mute humanity to tell me what I wanted so desperately to know. If this were truly Martin Lampe, his identity had disappeared for ever.

'The medical officer will be coming to inspect them later this morning,' Stadtschen rambled on at my back. 'The innards of this one have begun to putrefy already. That other fellow doesn't look too good, either. The quicker they're in the ground, the better, sir, in my opinion. I should report this to the doctor.'

I could have ordered snow and ice to be carried down there, as Professor Kant had done in his effort to preserve Lawyer Tifferch for Doctor Vigilantius and myself to see, but the corpse was too far gone for physical recognition.

'Before you speak to the doctor,' I said, 'you can do yourself a favour.'

'Sir?'

'You acted out of order, you know that, don't you, Stadtschen?'

He held his breath, waiting for me to continue.

'I ought to mention your impulsive decision to move the remains in my report to the King,' I said, watching him. 'But I may yet be persuaded to change my mind. Find Frau Lampe quickly, and bring her here. The woman lives in Belefest village. She came to see me this morning, saying that her husband had disappeared. I doubt she'll be able to tell us anything, but duty requires it before these men are finally laid to rest. Make sure . . .'

Make sure she recognises him.

That is what I would have liked to say, but I didn't.

'You can count on me,' Stadschen replied with an ingratiating smile and a smart salute.

My torch had nearly burnt itself out. The prospect of remaining there without a light prompted me to remove myself quickly. With Stadtschen following hard on my heels, we soon arrived at the main gate. I dismissed him, and was gratified to see him running off in the direction of Belefest.

But the identity of the bones in the charnel house was not my only concern. Nor was the question of finding Martin Lampe, if he were still alive. The King and his report would have to wait until I returned.

'Take me to Magisterstrasse,' I shouted to the driver as I jumped aboard the waiting coach. 'As fast as you can go.'

Chapter 33

I had been so busily engaged the previous afternoon and night that I had hardly given a further thought to Professor Kant. Indeed, I did not realise just how long it had been since I had seen him, nor how tired I was, until I leaned my head back against the comfortable bench of the coach and gave myself up to the swaying rhythm of the vehicle, soon drifting into what must have been a sound sleep.

I sat up with a start as the vehicle drew up before the house in Magisterstrasse. And another alarm bell began to ring in my head when I glanced out of the window. The young Italian doctor that I had met the previous day was running up the garden path towards the door, and he was clutching a large brown medicine bottle in his hands.

I leapt down from the carriage, and hurried to reach the porch before Johannes Odum could close the door.

'What's the matter?' I panted.

'It's my master, sir,' the servant cried, the tears starting from his red-rimmed eyes. 'He's barely conscious. Doctor's been to fetch a cordial.'

I pushed past him, and flew up the stairs to Kant's bedchamber.

As soon as I entered the room, I saw that I had come too late. The tiny, shrivelled creature lying on the bed had already set one foot in the next world. Immanuel Kant's once-delicate face seemed to have turned in upon itself, his cheeks were two great, gaunt hollows, his closed and sunken eyes resting inside deep dark pits. His narrow shoulders protruded through the cotton sheet, like wings flanking his ears. His breathing was loud and regular, but he did not look like a man who was taking his rest. It was the beginning of a sleep from which he would never wake.

Herr Jachmann stood with bowed head on the far side of the room, while Doctor Gioacchini ministered to Professor Kant, gently prising his lips apart and spooning a dark green liquid into his mouth. I took a step closer to the foot of the narow bed. The doctor glanced over his shoulder and nodded quickly to me, then he turned back, concentrating all his attention once again on his patient.

Some minutes passed in silence, then a cry escaped from the physician's lips.

'Herr Professor!'

Kant had opened his eyes. He was staring fixedly at me.

The doctor dropped his head to the philosopher's breast, and listened to the feeble beating of the patient's heart. Moving his ear closer to Kant's gaping mouth, he suddenly looked up at me with a bewildered expression on his face.

'Professor Kant wishes to speak to you,' he whispered, raising his watch, counting off the seconds as he measured the dying man's pulse. 'Be quick, sir,' he urged. 'His strength is ebbing fast.'

I drew near and bent over the bed. Fright swept through me in an awful spasm. I had to struggle to control my emotions as the philosopher's eyes closed once again like shutters. He seemed to me to be drifting beyond the realm of physical communication.

'It is I, sir, Hanno Stiffeniis,' I breathed into his ear.

Kant's eyelids did not so much as flicker, his face was a mask of deathly anticipation, a film of perspiration glistening on his broad forehead.

'How long has he been in this state?' I whispered.

'Too long,' the doctor answered.

I turned to the bed once more. Kant's respiration was more regular, though his pale pinched face seemed to have retreated even more deeply into the hollow cavity between his shoulders.

'Professor Kant,' I called, more loudly than before.

Kant's blue eyes opened suddenly wide, and swivelled to look at me. The closeness of death made the orbs appear more pale and transparent than ever. His lips gaped open, then closed again.

'Call him back,' Doctor Gioacchini urged at my shoulder.

'Professor Kant, speak to me,' I implored, lowering my ear so close to his pursed lips that my being was filled with the sweet, rotting odour of approaching death. I did not draw back from it. I breathed it in as if it were the purest mountain air. A wild, mystical ecstasy stirred within my craving soul. Immanuel Kant was in his death throes, and his last desire on Earth was to confide in *me*.

My ear grazed his lips. I felt them quiver at my touch.

'Too late . . .' he said in a hushed, strangled expulsion of breath.

'Sir?' I whispered, swallowing hard, my mouth parched and dry.

He sank back on the pillow, the merest trace of a smile on his lips, like a wisp of cloud in a blue summer sky.

'The killer has not been caught yet,' I began to say, then instantly regretted it.

With a display of strength I could hardly believe possible in that weak state, Kant shook his head slowly from side to side, his eyes staring fixedly into my own.

'But he *will* be stopped,' I added.

The ghost of that body down in the charnel house rose up before me, as if I had called to it. I wanted to reassure Professor Kant that all was well, inform him that the murderer had been defeated, announce that the avenging hand of God had found the killer out, and struck him down as he deserved. But I did not. I could not. Perhaps I never would be allowed to tell him. Time was pressing hard, the sands were running out. Immanuel Kant was, I believed, beyond hearing, beyond hope, beyond pain or any sentient feeling.

'You were right,' he wheezed suddenly.

I held my breath as he continued.

'You saw the truth in Paris. Then, your brother . . .'

I was robbed of the power of sensible speech. I wanted to run away from that room, to escape from that dying man and the implications of what he was saying. But I was caught, unhinged, helpless.

'You watched him die,' he continued, each word a conquest, each pause a march to a mountain top. 'That's why I sent for you, Hanno . . . You have been inside the mind of a murde–'

He sank back exhausted. The air rushed out of his lungs in a long, whistling diminuendo, like a grace-note fading in an organ pipe.

'His mind is drifting,' Doctor Gioacchini murmured, placing his hand on my shoulder and squeezing it hard as an enigmatic smile began slowly to form itself on Kant's bloodless lips.

With a sudden yawning gasp, Immanuel Kant pronounced with crystal clarity the final phrase of his earthly existence. Everyone present heard the declaration. Herr Jachmann faithfully recorded it in his written memorial of the event which was published some months later.

'*Es . . . ist . . . gut.*'

He repeated the phrase again and again, his lips moving soundlessly now, as a heavy burden seemed to fall away from his body in a gentle ripple. Then, he moved no more.

I stood transfixed.

Immanuel Kant was dead.

Beyond the window, grey day surrendered slowly to the onset of dusk, heralding the coming of the night. There was something portentous and fitting in the rotation. My mind was a blank. Some moments later, when I came to myself, I was wailing aloud, clasping my spiritual master's ice-cold hand in mine. In that instant, the horrid nightmare of those frantic days dissolved away. It might all have been nothing worse than a bleak and terrifying dream. I had no thoughts for Martin Lampe, nor for any other creature on the face of the Earth. No space survived for anything, except the tiny corpse stretched out lifeless on the bed before me and the mystery of the words that Professor Kant had murmured as he died.

Es ist gut.

What was good?

What good had Kant discovered in the failure of my investigation?

You were right. You saw the truth . . .

In the name of God, what had I ever been right about?

What *truth* had I ever seen?

The image of Immanuel Kant on his deathbed ought to have swept away all other thoughts and considerations, and for a while it did so. I was consumed with sorrow as I drove away from the house, having taken my leave of Johannes Odum, Doctor Gioacchini and Herr Jachmann. But as I sat alone in the darkness of the coach, and the wheels turned, and the Fortress drew ever closer and closer, that perplexing, enigmatic smile on the dead man's lips began to trouble me. Indeed, it seemed to overlap and blend and meld with the characterless blank of that *other* enigmatic mask of death, the unknown face of the man whose skull and bones lay rotting in the charnel house.

Could any two deaths be more starkly different?

Professor Kant had died peacefully at home in his bed, surrounded by the love and respect that had accompanied him throughout the course of his long life; the man in the morgue had been torn to shreds by snapping fangs, alone and at night in a deserted wilderness. Infinite pain, infinite terror. No hope of salvation for him. It was as if a legion of demons had been released from Hell by a pitiless Creator for an hour, and on one condition: that they wiped out every single trace of that man's existence. I could imagine no more fitting punishment for a heartless killer.

But was he the killer? Was that man truly Martin Lampe?

I would never rest until I could put a name to that corpse. Resolution of that mystery would signal one of two things – that the desperate hunt for Martin Lampe must continue, or that peace had been restored to Königsberg. In the latter case, the troubled souls of those who had been annihilated by the fury of the killer would be laid to rest, along with their bones.

Then, and only then, I would find peace.

I entered the main gate of the Fortress briskly, intent on going down to the charnel house to take a second look. This time, I determined to go alone, without Stadtschen breathing down my neck. I crossed the courtyard and entered the North Tower without meeting anyone, and soon reached the ogive arch and narrow door which led down to the dungeons. Arming myself with a torch from the wall, I opened the door.

Before passing through, I hesitated on the threshold.

The smell of decay seemed to reach out from below like an effluvial tide to greet and drown me. It was a distillation of human and vegetal decomposition, and a million other age-old odours compounded together beneath the ancient mound of the Fortress. For an instant, I almost turned away. Only the desire to know led me onward, the desperate hope that some vital clue might still be found.

I entered, pulling the door closed behind me, and began to descend the dark staircase by torchlight. But as I went down, and down again, I became aware that another torch was coming up the stairwell towards me. Peering into the depths for some moments, I was at last able to discern two shadowy figures down there in the gloom. I recognised Officer Stadtschen at once. But who was the other person? My heart leapt into my throat. Had I come too late? Had the doctor already given the order for those putrid human remains to be taken out of the charnel house and buried?

I halted, anger and frustration mounting, waiting for Stadtschen to draw near, anxious to hear by his own admission what further damage had been inflicted on my investigation in my absence. But then, as they came within ten steps or so, my heart took a leap and a bound. Dressed in a trailing black shawl, which covered her head and her shoulders, was Frau Lampe, and she seemed to be leaning heavily on the arm of the soldier. For that, if for nothing else, I uttered a word of thanks to the Lord. She had seen the paltry remains, then.

They took a few more steps, then Stadtschen looked up, caught sight of me and stopped in his tracks. The woman raised her tear-filled eyes to mine a second later. Her skin was pale: it seemed to be as transparent as melted wax, paler even than the face of Professor Kant. Her cheeks and mouth were puffy and swollen. Her mournful appearance seemed to confirm what I desired to know above all other things. I almost rejoiced in her sorrow.

She had identified Martin Lampe!

'Frau Lampe?' I called, a chirping note in my voice that I hoped she would not perceive or understand.

The woman sobbed loudly, and looked away, shaking off the supporting arm of Officer Stadtschen, as if I had caught her in an unguarded moment of weakness that she did not wish me to see.

'The body was found on the woodland path that your husband

took,' I said as solemnly as I was able. 'Not much remains, I'm afraid. You must be upset, I am truly sorry . . .'

'Upset, sir?' Despite the expression of distress on her face, her voice was firm. Indeed, there was a stinging, acrimonious tone to it. 'Any soul would be *upset*, Herr Stiffeniis. I pray no other woman will be forced to see what I have had to see.'

I studied her face uncertainly.

'Nothing in that loathsome *thing*,' she hissed at me with barely controlled anger, 'can ever make me think it's Martin. Nothing! I hope the search for him is going on?'

I must have held my breath, for it exploded from me in an audible gasp.

It was not finished, then. Martin Lampe was still free to prey upon the innocent and the unsuspecting, like the beasts that had ripped the unknown man to pieces. Hungry for human life, he was hiding out there somewhere, poised to strike again at any moment.

'Frau Lampe was taken ill, sir,' Stadtschen explained quickly.

I heard the sound of his words, but did not absorb the substance of them. My thoughts were already racing wildly through the dark streets and dank alleyways of Königsberg in pursuit of the killer.

'Those bodies ought to be removed, Herr Procurator,' he added. 'Once I have seen the lady safe upstairs, I'll get the doctor to do something. They are no fit sight for any woman. No man, either. They ought to be interred at once, sir, or we'll have an epidemic on our hands.'

'Very well,' I said sharply. 'Inform the doctor. Take Frau Lampe home. But within the hour, Stadtschen, I want a signed affidavit on my desk to the effect that visual recognition was not possible, given the state of . . . alteration of the body. I will be in my office, waiting. I have a report to write, regarding my investigation. For the King.'

I stared at Stadtschen as I rapped out these final words. I had spared him once, I would not do so again. He had failed me, and I fully intended to tell His Majesty of the stupidity of the officer's actions. By removing that unknown corpse from the woods, he had struck a mortal blow against my investigation, leaving me no possibility of drawing any definite conclusion about the death or the identity of the man who would soon be laid to rest in an unmarked grave.

A look of alarm appeared on Stadtschen's face as he bowed his head, clicked his heels, and told me that he would do exactly as I had told him. Clearly, he had understood the meaning of my threat.

'Please accept my apologies,' I said, turning to the woman, 'for the ordeal which you have been subjected to. Had the bones been *left* where they were found, it might have made identification possible.' I glanced at Stadtschen, adding: 'Whoever is to *blame* will be punished.'

I studied the woman's face.

'I wonder if you know, Frau Lampe . . .'

I stopped. For an instant I had been tempted to inform her of the death of Professor Kant. But only for an instant. I contented myself, instead, by witholding the news. It was a small, meaningless act of spite, but she had just dashed my hopes of identifying Martin Lampe.

'What do you wonder, Herr Stiffeniis?' the woman asked.

'Oh, nothing very important,' I said, turning away and clattering up the stairs.

Given her opinion of the philosopher, she would hear the news and rejoice soon enough.

Chapter 34

I went upstairs to my office, calling for the sentry to come and light the candles as I set foot inside the dark room. The day was drawing on, it was high time for me to begin composing my report for the King. I had already put off the task far longer than I ought to have done, and I still had no real idea how much to tell. Nor how much to conceal. With Professor Kant dead, and the possibility that Martin Lampe was still loose on the streets of Königsberg, exactly *how* should I begin and end?

With deliberation, I picked up the feather quill, primed it full of ink, set the point to the smooth surface of the paper, then remained seated in that position like a statue carved from solid granite for fifteen minutes, or more. I felt the ire and the frustration of a shepherd building up inside me, a shepherd vainly trying to round up his unruly flock without the assistance of a trained dog, or a handy wicket gate in which to corner the skittish animals. Whenever I began to think that I had at last marshalled all my thoughts, some glaring inconsistency would jump up suddenly and slip out of the fold, preventing me from making a start.

The easiest way, I convinced myself at last, would be to report only those facts or events for which I had some corroborating written statement.

'On this, the 12th day in the month of February, 1804,' I began,

I, Hanno Stiffeniis of Lotingen, Assistant Procurator to the Second Circuit of the Judicial Magistrature of the High Court of Prussia, called to investigate the murders of four citizens in the Royal city of Königsberg, do solemnly swear and avow, having almost completed my enquiries, that the declaration which follows is true and incontestable. There is good reason to believe . . .

I paused, dipped my pen in the inkwell again, then let out a loud sigh. No good reason to believe *anything* came to my mind. Indeed, all the tiny pieces of the mosaic that I had managed to assemble led me to believe the very worst. I threw down my pen, pushed back my chair, walked across the room, and stared dismally out of the window. The sky was dark, low clouds driving in from the sea, bringing rain, sleet and probably more snow. I threw open the window for a breath of air, though it was already cold enough inside the room. Down below in the courtyard, soldiers were coming and going noisily. It was six o'clock, time for the changing of the guard. Men who had just come off duty ambled aimlessly up and down, laughing and joking, smoking their long clay pipes, exchanging insults and pleasantries, cat-calling and taunting their unfortunate fellows who were destined to pass the night marching round and round the icy ramparts.

Suddenly, I wished that I were one of them. I wanted to be free of this task, free of the responsibility and the care it had placed on my shoulders. More to the point, I wished that I could be at home in Lotingen, in the company of my wife and my children, idly roasting jacket potatoes before a roaring kitchen fire. Until the report was finished, I reminded myself sharply, there was little hope that I would be going anywhere. Unless I could produce a convincing account of every single thing that had happened in Königsberg, I would be left to rot there in the Fortress. With the unresolved question of Martin Lampe still hanging around my neck, I realised, I might be imprisoned there for a long, long . . .

The noise seemed to come from far away.

I had been so deeply lost in melancholy musing that a pitched battle might have been fought and lost for possession of the Fortress, and I would have known nothing of it.

Someone had been knocking at my door.

The sound was repeated a moment later, followed by a deep

voice that I recognised. 'Herr Stiffeniis, may I enter, sir?'

Officer Stadtschen was at my door. No doubt, he had come to plead for leniency. He could have few illusions about my intentions, little doubt of what I might write in his regard.

'Come back later,' I called out sharply. 'The King must have his report!'

But Stadtschen did not go away. He knocked again, louder this time.

'Herr Procurator, I beg you, sir. This cannot wait.'

I closed the window, strode to the door, my temper flaring into a blazing fire. What alternative did he leave me? I would tell Stadtschen *exactly* what I thought of him. By moving that corpse from the woods, he had ruined my investigation. If I had my way, he would be demoted. I would have liked to see him whipped into the bargain.

I threw the door open, saying: 'Well? What is it?'

He was standing to attention, stiff and straight as a flagpole. He glanced nervously into my face, then raised his hand and held out a sheet of paper.

'The affidavit, sir,' he announced. 'Recognition of the corpse by Frau Lampe, sir. That mark's the sign of the widow.'

'*Widow?*' I blurted out, snatching the paper, reading it greedily.

I hereby swear and affirm that the remains of the body found in the woods near Belefest, which I examined in the Fortress of Königsberg in the presence of an officer, belong to my legal husband, Martin Lampe.

The woman's name had been written out in the same bold letters as the text and the signature of Stadtschen. Frau Lampe had witnessed the contents of the affidavit by making a peculiar slanting cross at the bottom of the page.

'The woman cannot write,' Stadtschen clarified.

I studied his face. 'What holy miracle is this?' I quizzed. 'Frau Lampe was most adamant that it was *not* her husband's body.'

'Darn my breeches, sir!' he exclaimed, quickly begging my pardon for his language before he continued. 'It all came about while I was taking her home. The fact is, when I led her down to the charnel house, the smell was . . . well, sir, you know yourself, it was inde-scribable. Frau Lampe complained at once of feeling ill, and she asked to be taken out of there, insisting that those dreadful remains could not possibly be her husband's. I could hardly force her to examine the bones, could I, sir? When I met you, Herr Procurator, I was taking her up to the courtyard for a breath of fresh air. I'd have taken her down again immediately, but you ordered me to take the woman home instead, sir.'

'Go on,' I said, beginning to suspect that Stadtschen might have forced the woman to sign the affidavit in the hope of salvaging his own position. 'If she didn't even look at the corpse, what made her change her mind?'

'It happened while we were walking out to Belefest, sir,' he explained. 'I didn't speak again about that body. But I did ask her what distinguishing features to look for if we happened to come across him. Officially, he was missing. He might have lost his memo-ry, been wounded, or even killed. I was wondering whether he had a birthmark, or some other sign on his body to identify him by.'

Stadtschen paused, and a shadow of a smile appeared on his face.

'And he *did*, sir! She told me so herself.'

'What was this sign?' I asked. I might have been a man with a terrible illness who had just been told by an eminent physician that it was easily curable.

'We *saw* it, sir, but we took no notice at the time,' Stadtschen replied. A broader smile broke out on his face, as if he found the situation amusing. 'D'you recall that white strip of bone inside his mouth, Herr Stiffeniis? Remember when I turned the skull over? While serving in the Prussian army forty-odd years ago, Herr Lampe was lightly nicked by an enemy bayonet. It sliced through his bottom lip and ended up slitting the roof of his mouth!'

I remembered only too well. I had taken that jagged scar to be the exposed bone of the palate. I had even induced myself to believe that it had been caused by the fang of one of the wolves that had torn him apart. If Martin Lampe's blood-caked mouth had caused me to quake with revulsion then, it now began to seem like one of the most stupendous sights I had seen in my life.

'I hurried her back with me to town, and we arrived just in time. I searched for you, of course, sir,' he added quickly, scrutinising my face to gauge my reaction, 'but you had gone out. The medical officer had issued death certificates, the pastor had been called to adminster the last rites, the graves for him and the other man had already been dug. Another five minutes would have complicated matters. I explained the necessity to the doctor, and he made certain that she examined the skull and saw the scar, though wrapped up in a cloth. It was painless enough, and she identified him. I took her to the office, wrote out the affidavit, read it through to her, and she made her cross. As I said before, sir, Frau Lampe is now a widow.'

I looked away and closed my eyes for a moment.

Königsberg is safe, I marvelled. *My task is over.*

'This is excellent work, Officer Stadtschen,' I said warmly. 'I can now discount this corpse in writing my report. The part that you have played will appear in a more positive light.'

Though his face was stern and composed, I thought I saw a twinkle in his eyes. 'God bless you, sir,' he murmured.

God had already been extremely good to me that day, I realised. Better by far than I deserved. The killer not only had a name, but his corpse had been identified beyond a shadow of a doubt. I closed the door quietly, and sat down to work again. This time, I was brimming with confidence. Divine Providence was pushing me forward with both hands.

'The King shall have his report!' I announced to the empty room.

A triumphant proclamation of success was what I had always hoped to write. A triumphant proclamation of success was what the King would have. Picking up the quill again, I continued with all the artistry of an inspired poet.

There is good reason to believe that the authors of the crimes have been identified as Ulrich Totz, innkeeper of this city, and his wife, Gertrude Totz (née Sonner). By their own frank admission, the miscreants declared that their tavern and

lodging-house, named 'The Baltic Whaler', was a notorious
meeting-place for Bonapartist sympathisers and for sundry
other rebels. Their intention was to foment chaos in the city
and prepare the way for a military invasion by the French
armies under the command of Napoleon Bonaparte. These
heinous crimes of murder and terrorisation of the population
began, as Your Highness well knows, in January, 1803 . . .

I stroked my chin for some moments with the feathered quill,
then added more in the same colourful vein:

. . . and they were perpetrated with the assistance and the
material connivance of a woman of their acquaintance, Anna
Rostova, a known prostitute, dabbler in black magic, and
practitioner of illegal abortions, by her own admission under
unforced questioning. It was not possible fully to ascertain the
precise ideological scope of their rebellious intentions – there
may, indeed, be no formal connection with any foreign state,
nor any invasion planned as a direct consequence of their
actions.

Both Totz and his wife, having admitted their Jacobin
sentiments and their complicity in the murders, including the
slaughter of their own nephew, Morik Lüthe, committed suicide
despite strict surveillance while in prison. The lifeless body of
Anna Rostova was found three days afterwards in the River
Pregel. It remains unclear whether a suicide pact had been
agreed within the group, whether Anna Rostova had threatened
to betray her fellow conspirators and then been punished for
her treachery, or whether some other unknown person, possibly
unconnected with the group, was responsible for her drowning.
No arrest has been made with regard to this incident, though
enquiries are being made to clarify the question. Circumstances
suggest that the remaining members of the terrorist group, three
foreign infiltrators who were lodging at 'The Baltic Whaler', are
in flight. They are no longer to be found in Königsberg, but
warrants have been issued for their arrest. The names of the
three wanted persons, together with all pertinent documents,

*including transcripts of the interrogations, reports of the
searches, case notes, etc., etc., are contained in the official case
file, number 7–8/1804. With the diaspora of the terrorist cell,
we may safely conclude that the spate of murders in Königsberg, together with the consequent risk of internal disorders,
has been brought to a definitive conclusion.*

*I beg leave to take this opportunity to testify to the courage
and selfless devotion to his duty of the public official and clerk
of police, Amadeus Koch, my chosen assistant, who was the
final victim of these desperate conspirators. Without Sergeant
Koch's constant and devoted attendance on my person, and
his most valuable insights into the workings of the criminal
underworld in the city (and the deviancy of the criminal mind
in general), the onerous task of identifying the perpetrators
would have been one thousand times harder. The murderer of
Herr Koch is, in all probability, another member of the Jacobin
crew who frequented the inn run by Herr and Frau Totz. The
place was a hotbed of treason and conspiracy, as material evidence found there suggests. I contend that following the deaths
of the major protagonists, the Totzes and Anna Rostova, Koch
was struck down by an unknown hand with the precise intention of confusing the police enquiry into the earlier deaths and
lending weight to the misguided conviction expressed by my
esteemed predecessor, Procurator Rhunken, that the string of
murders was the work of one man alone, a man self-evidently
possessed of insane and murderous instincts.*

*I also wish to express my gratitude to the late Herr Professor
Immanuel Kant. The city of Königsberg owes him a debt
beyond estimate in terms of his absolute dedication to the
resolution of these crimes and the restitution of peace to the
city which he loved above all others on earth. The sagacity of
Your Royal Highness is known to one and all; I am certain that
You, Sire, will appreciate the importance of work undertaken
without any financial assistance or material encouragement
from the local authorities by this most noble Professor of
Philosophy in proposing and actuating a system of logical*

and analytical police investigation which will be inscribed in the annals of criminal history, not in this particular instance alone, but in every future attempt to counteract the social consequences of a violent crime and bring the culprits to fitting Retribution and Justice. I swear to advocate and disseminate the methods I have learned from Herr Professor Kant in my future career as a magistrate, certain of the fact that the inventor would have granted me permission to do so. I humbly suggest that Herr Professor Kant's revolutionary method be adopted immediately by the competent police authorities throughout Prussia and published at State expense for the benefit of Mankind. It would be a fitting memorial to a great Prussian.

Thus, swearing my allegiance to the Crown of Hohenzollern, and to Your Most Royal Person, I beg leave to return to Lotingen and my family, and take up once again the magisterial position that I was so suddenly called upon to vacate.

Your most humble and obedient servant,

Hanno Stiffeniis, Procurator

PS: Valuable assistance was provided by Officer Stadtschen of the Königsberg garrison. I recommend him for advancement.

I read through what I had written more than once, then made a copy of the document for the benefit of General Katowice without changing a single comma. By the time I set down my pen and sat back in my chair to ease the aching muscles in my spine and neck, the fiction had acquired the high polish of Truth. Indeed, it *was* the Truth. The Truth as I would tell it to my wife, my children, and my grandchildren after them. It was *The Truth* as all the World would know it.

I folded the report and the duplicate, sealing them with a lighted candle, red wax and my ring of office. As I did so, I told myself that I had been guided by the Lord, our God. *He* had brought me to Königsberg, *He* had led me to Immanuel Kant. *He* had induced me to insist that Sergeant Koch take my cloak. In His infinite wisdom, it seemed to me, *He* had declared that Koch should die for one cause, and that I should survive for another. The Lord had brought me to the conclusion of the affair, and *He* had suggested the epilogue that I should write. As I pressed my seal-ring into the hot red wax, I felt *His* heavy hand pressing down upon it. My own hand was the instrument, nothing more.

I set the seal down on the table-top to cool, blew out the flickering candle, and called for a gendarme. Having entrusted my despatches to his charge, I glanced at my watch, then retired to my bedroom. I just had time to wash and change my shirt, then I went down to attend to the burial of Amadeus Koch, which was scheduled to take place in the military cemetery at the rear of the chapel at nine o'clock.

No other mourner but myself was present as the plain wooden casket containing the body was lowered into the cold ground by four squaddies. I offered a silent prayer for the generous soul of Sergeant Koch. His sacrifice had led me directly to the killer. No other words were spoken. None was needed, except for those solemnly pronounced in prayer by the military chaplain.

As I replaced my hat and turned away, the sound of earth crashing down upon the bare wooden coffin, I halted for a moment. Had I done the right thing? After all, Merete Koch was buried somewhere in the city. Perhaps I should have made more careful enquiries before ordering Sergeant Koch's interment inside the walls of the Fortress? They had been partners in Life, they should comfort each other in Death.

But for that single detail, the affair in Königsberg was truly over.

Within two hours, I had packed my travelling-bag and boarded the same state coach that had brought me to the city in the company of Amadeus Koch. There was no 'starry sky' above my head to induce awe and wonder, as Immanuel Kant's most famous epigram declares. There had been a brief snowfall as Sergeant Koch was buried, but the louring sky overhead was now a leaden, pitch-black sheet. It weighed down mercilessly on the city of Königsberg and the irrefutable Truth that I had left behind me, as I thought, for ever.

Chapter 35

The weather went from bad to worse, and Immanuel Kant remained unburied for sixteen days. The earth had frozen so solid, no grave could be dug for him. Day after day, exposed to public view in the University Cathedral in Königsberg, the body withered and shrank. It had begun to look so fearfully like a skeleton, the local newspaper hinted, the city fathers were praying desperately for a break in the weather.

Back home in Lotingen, I threw myself into work. Hard labour should have been the best medicine for my ills, but I made little progress on those cases that had accumulated in my absence. I sat for hour after hour, staring at the repetitive flowery patterns on the walls of my office, or shuffling idly through the papers on my desk at home. The only solace that I could find was in my family. Helena revealed her loving care in a thousand looks and kind gestures. And her gentlest stratagem to ease my pain simply could not be ignored: I mean my beloved little ones. My wife saw to it that we were much together, far more than I had ever permitted before I went away. She was quick to curb the excitement the children showed after my absence, firm in tempering the unexpected freedom they now enjoyed before it got out of hand.

One morning, Helena came bustling into my study with a fresh copy of the *Königsbergische Monatsschrift* in her hand. 'It was as if the Earth refused to take him,' she said, as she lay the news-sheet down on the desk. There had been a heavy rainfall and a sudden thaw, the headlines announced: the burial service for Professor Kant would take place the following day at one o'clock. I read the article carefully, and turned to make some comment to my wife.

'Go to Königsberg, Hanno. See his soul laid to rest,' she said, her voice soft, yet so determined that I was left with little choice in the matter. She might have been comforting one of the children after a painful fall.

Though I had decided in my own mind never again to set foot in Königsberg, at dawn the following morning, dressed in a black suit and overcoat, a new black silk band pinned to the rim of my day-hat, I boarded the mail-coach. There were no other passengers, and I was glad that I would not be obliged to engage in conversation that I felt disinclined to sustain. I sat in splendid isolation, recalling with a heavy heart the last time that I had made the journey, in the company of Amadeus Koch.

The coach arrived at midday, and I made my way directly to the house in Magisterstrasse, where Professor Kant's mortal remains had been removed the previous day. The mass of common people jostling for a vantage point out in the narrow street, and the constant arrival of other persons more closely associated with the philosopher, made the lane seem more like a bustling cattle market than the haven of peace it had been in Kant's lifetime.

Passing in through the garden gate, I was swept up in a rushing sea of mourners, propelled along on the crest of a tidal wave by a large group of students in the academic robes of the Collegium Fridericianum who had come to pay their last respects. In the dining room a lavish oak coffin had been set up on a catafalque surrounded by ivy wreaths, and decorated with elaborate floral arrangements. The coffin lid stood propped against the wall, and I removed my hat in silent tribute to the remains of the philosopher lying there in state. A stark death's head stared up at me, the same enigmatic smile that I remembered written on the rose-painted lips. Neither Death nor the embalmer had been able to wipe it away.

'All is just as he would have wished,' a voice murmured close by my ear, and Herr Jachmann offered me his black-gloved hand. 'You left the town in such a fret, Stiffeniis,' he said. 'I was not certain that I would find you here today.'

'I had to come,' I said, the expression catching in my throat as the wooden lid was taken up, and the carpenter began to bolt it into place.

We watched in silence as six students hoisted the coffin aloft and carried it from the room to the street. Jachmann led me towards the front row of the endless column of mourners lining up behind a black carriage pulled by four black horses. The coffin was fixed securely in its place, the floral tributes and wreaths arranged all around it, then the cortège began to move slowly forward. The procession wound its way through the streets of Königsberg, which were lined on either side with silent crowds.

The University Cathedral was brightly lit by thousands of candles. A muted organ played solemn passages from Buxtehude while the invited mourners and city authorities took their places in the pews reserved for them. Johannes Odum was among them, Frau Mendelssohn and Doctor Gioacchini also. I sat myself down a few rows further back and sorrow swept over me in shuddering waves. I cannot say how long I remained in this distraught state, when my attention was distracted by a woman sitting in the pew in front of mine. As she removed her black scarf to settle it more comfortably on her head, I recognised her. She looked back over her shoulder and held my gaze for an instant.

It was Frau Lampe.

I had not thought for one instant to meet the widow at the funeral of the man she held responsible for all the woes of her husband. What was she doing there? I mulled the question over for some time without finding any answer, then turned my attention back to the memorial service, which was destined to last for another two hours. Herr Jachmann was one of many speakers sounding platitudes, which are as inevitable at a funeral as Death itself. When, at last, no more remained to be said, and no one remained to say it, the coffin-bearers came forward, the casket was taken up again on their young shoulders, and it was carried slowly from the church.

I stepped into the aisle to follow, but Frau Lampe stood blocking my exit, her dark eyes fixed in mine.

'I hoped to find you here, sir,' she said. 'I'd not have come otherwise. Would you have me pay my respects to the creature in that box?'

I made to move around her, but she refused to shift or give ground.

'I have something that you will want to see,' she whispered fiercely, drawing a slim leather document-case from under her cloak.

'Whatever it is,' I said coldly, 'give it to the local police. My jurisdiction here is ended.'

She turned her head, glanced towards the altar, then back to me.

'You were a friend of his,' she said and pursed her lips. 'I think that you should have it, sir.'

I looked down at what she was handing to me.

'I found it some days ago. The book they were working on.'

I studied the woman's face for a moment. She was not stupid by any means. Did she truly not know what her husband had done? Had she never suspected?

'I've taken up too much of your time,' she said quickly.

Thrusting the package into my hand, she turned and ran from the church.

I grasped the unexpected gift to my chest with the same surge of burning excitement that I experienced when the wet-nurse handed me my first-born child. Immanuel Kant's philosophical testament . . . He himself had hinted that it would change the entire course of Moral Philosophy. Falling down on my knees, I uttered my thanks to Almighty God for His immense generosity. I had been chosen as His instrument to exalt the incomparable greatness of the late Immanuel Kant.

I rushed from the cathedral and pushed through the milling throng in the churchyard, not caring about the people I elbowed roughly out of my way. The air was cold, but I was hot with agitation. Herr Jachmann's voice called out my name, but I looked the other way and fought against the high tide of people flooding into the burial ground from the street. And all the while I clutched that precious packet to my heart like Moses carrying the sacred tablets down from the Heights of Sinai.

In the relative quiet of the avenue, I stopped to catch my breath. Where could I read without fear of being disturbed? For a single, guilty moment, my blood froze at the immensity of the greed which consumed me. My only desire was to be alone with Kant's papers.

Why, in the name of all that was sacred, did I not go directly to Herr Jachmann and the other intimates of Professor Kant and tell them the wondrous news? Why did I avoid them all as if they threatened to carry off the priceless treasure that Frau Lampe had placed in my hands? The truth was that I had no intention of sharing the philosopher's last unpublished thoughts with any other living person. Somehow, I felt that Kant intended the words he had dictated to Martin Lampe for me, and no one else. The valet and I were blood brothers in our arrogance.

Further down the street there was a coffee house. It was crowded with university students as a rule, but they would all be at the funeral. Glancing in at the window, I saw that the place was deserted. I went in, sat down at a table in the far corner, and asked for a glass of hot chocolate to justify my presence there. As soon as the beverage arrived and the waiter turned away, I pulled that manuscript from under my cloak like a thief bent on examining his booty.

The leaves were held together with a soiled red ribbon. Sifting through, I noticed that the ink in places was caked with sand which should have dried it. There was no title. No author's name appeared on the cover. Opening the text at the first page, I recognised the writing immediately. The words were strung out in wavering, uneven lines, the letters ugly, childlike both in size and shape. I had seen that script in the autograph book of Roland Lutbatz. The same perplexing thought returned to my mind: what dire necessity had driven Professor Kant to entrust his final thoughts to such an unlikely amanuensis?

As I began to read the opening paragraphs, I began to realise just how jealous I was of Martin Lampe. Kant reiterated his fundamental thesis that the moral nature of duty makes human behaviour subject to universal laws which are based on the precepts of Rationality. All action should strive, he averred, towards a Common Good which represents true Freedom. Despite the valet's dreadful handwriting, I could not fail to recognise the inimitable voice of Immanuel Kant, the purposeful exposition of the rigorous concepts of moral philosophy that he had first expressed in the *Foundations of the Metaphysics of Behaviour*, before expanding them into the monolithic moral code of the *Critique of Practical Reason*.

I cannot say at which point uneasiness began to creep up on me. The fact was that I began to feel increasingly uncomfortable as I read on. The author seemed, somehow, to have veered off the old, familiar path. Suddenly, I found myself lost in a terrain which I did not recognise. Scanning the lines ahead, looking for solid ground on which to rest, I searched for an idea or a concept that I could safely identify as Kant's. Had Frau Lampe made a mistake? Was the document not what she had presumed it to be? There was something so rough and ready about the writing, far removed from the refinement of thought and elegance of expression that one habitually associated with Immanuel Kant. Even so, what I was reading was, somehow, very familiar . . .

I sat back and sipped hot chocolate, trying to gather my thoughts and concentrate my attention. Naturally, I had been upset by the funeral. I glanced around the coffee house and noticed that the empty tables were beginning to fill up. People were coming in from the cold, the service must have ended. Fortunately, I recognised no one, and no one appeared to know me. I drank the remains of my beverage, and called for another cup. The landlord brought a long-necked pot of piping hot chocolate across to my table, and we exchanged a few words about the weather and the magnificent funeral. No other topics were worthy of interest in Königsberg that day. But then, as soon as I decently could, I returned to my reading, struggling with difficulty through another page. And another, until I reached page four. Halfway down.

Oh, God!

My heart throbbed painfully.

I closed my eyes, hoping that everything would be different when I opened them again. Was this the true substance of Hell? Not burning flames, the eternal agony of unbearable pain, but a shadow world where holy angels suddenly threw off their cherubic masks and glistening diaphanous wings to reveal the hideous reality hidden beneath? Heavenly choirs chanting blasphemous rhymes in unified harmony, and making obscene gestures while they sang?

The philosophical testament of Professor Immanuel Kant, written out in the clumsy hand of Martin Lampe, expressed my own words.

The words that I had spoken in private to Kant, seven years before . . .

Chapter 36

The memory of that day seven years before came flooding back, tormenting in its clarity.

'Walk me around the Fortress, Stiffeniis,' Immanuel Kant suggested, as soon as the plates were cleared away after lunch.

'In such dreadful weather?' Herr Jachmann objected, a worried expression plainly written on his face.

Professor Kant chose pointedly to ignore the warning of his friend as we donned our coats and scarves. Out in the lane, the fog was as thick and heavy as a damp towel, and Kant caught hold of my arm immediately.

'You lead, Stiffeniis. I will follow,' he said.

He seemed to suggest that something more than youth and strength were expected of me. As I closed the gate, I spotted Herr Jachmann peeping anxiously from behind the curtains, but the fog was like a living thing. Kant and I walked straight into its gaping maw, and were swallowed up in one gulp.

As we pressed forward, I began to prattle nervously about the previous summer which I had spent in Italy. I told him of the relentless sun, the welcome cool as the autumn came on, the cold dampness of winter as I began my journey homeward through France, my preference for the dry cold of our own mountains.

Kant suddenly halted.

'Enough of the weather!' he snapped. I could barely see him in the faltering light. His deathly pale face seemed to blur in and out of focus, like an ectoplasm struggling to materialise. 'One human experience is equal to the power of Nature, you said during lunch. The most diabolical of them all. Murder without a motive. *Cold-*

blooded murder. What did you mean, Stiffeniis?'

I hesitated before replying. But I had come to Königsberg for that purpose, and for no other. I told him quickly what I had witnessed on a cold, grey morning not two months before. Intoxicated by Enlightened ideals, curious to see how the revolutionaries would deal with the monarch that they now disowned, I broke off my homeward journey in Paris. On 2 January 1793, I was standing in Place de la Révolution when Louis XVI mounted the steps to the guillotine. I had never seen a person put to death before, and I watched in thrall as the King knelt down before that fatal instrument. As the gleaming metal triangle was drawn up, drums rolled thunderously. Their thumping matched the clamour of my heart.

'I stared into the Devil's eyes,' I told Kant, melodramatically, perhaps, 'and the Devil stared back. The blade fell with a loud screech, stopped with a sickening crunch, and the whole of my being was invaded by the smell of blood.

'I inhaled the salty tang as if it were frankincense. I drank in each spasm of that body as the severed head bounced into a waiting basket. The simplicity of the action: a lever shifted, a life was gone. It was the essence of Cause and Effect. So quick, so devastating, so final. I wanted to see it happen again, and again . . .'

A monster had risen up from the depths of the rational person that I had always thought myself to be. This *Doppelgänger* had a taste for death and the wild euphoria it brought. I tried to evoke the sensation for Kant in a word I thought that he would relish. 'The experience was *Sublime*,' I confided. 'I was ravished by it, sir. My mind was petrified, my soul was thrilled.'

There! Finally, I had said it.

Professor Kant was silent for some moments.

'There's more, isn't there?' he said suddenly. 'Why speak of murder *without* a motive? The people of Paris had reason enough to kill the King. You have something more to tell me.'

He seemed to be looking through me.

'Indeed, there is,' I admitted. 'I brought the madness home with me. A month ago my brother died . . .'

What Kant said next was pronounced in the same polite tone

with which, not an hour before, he had asked me whether I preferred my bread with butter, or without.

'Did you murder him?'

Even in my shocked state, I was aware of the lack of emotion in his voice. He had made the connection that I had feared to make for myself, yet he showed no horror, no revulsion at the thought. It was simply a question that needed to be asked.

'Stefan was discharged from the army a year ago,' I hastened to explain. 'He was voted the best cadet at the Academy, the son my father craved. The very opposite of my own moody character. But Stefan was sick. He had begun to fall down in a death-faint for no apparent reason. The sweetness of his urine was the cause. Only honey could revive him. If naught were done to help, the doctors warned, his life was in danger. Everyone in the house knew of it. The servants had all been instructed what to do if a fit came on. A pot of honey and a spoon had been positioned in every room. If Stefan were pale, sweating, confused in speech or behaviour, we must give him honey. He was prohibited from leaving the house unless he took a corked vial in his pocket.'

I paused, expecting some reaction from Professor Kant, but he remained silent, watchful, a pale shadow in the swirling fog.

'When I returned,' I went on, 'the turbulence I had felt in Paris was still inside me, like a poisonous, invisible dart. I dared tell no one. Only Stefan, my brother. He listened to me in silence. He did not judge or criticise, but stared unflinching into my eyes. Then, some days later, out of the blue, he challenged me to do what Father had warned us never to do again.'

'And what was that?' asked Kant, tiring, perhaps, of my narration.

'There is a rocky outcrop near the house called the Richtergade. When we were little children, sir, a race to the top was our favourite sport. I ought, nay, I *should* have refused the dare, but I did not. He egged me on, he provoked me. Stefan had proposed a distraction, a *divertissement*, a game, which I enthusiastically embraced. Physical, exhausting activity would take my mind off the problems which bore down on me. I did not think of him, except to remind him to take a glass of honey in his pocket. He answered with a quick nod, then off we went. It was cold, a good day for a climb, and I was the first to stand on the summit of the rocky mound. I had never ever won the race before. Standing on the brink, facing into the wind, the rush of elements subdued the storm within me. I yearned to tell Stefan of my exhilaration. I wished to thank him. But then I heard him panting as he struggled to grasp the rocky ledge below me. Looking down, I . . . I froze once more in the face of Death. Froth bubbled from his lips, his eyes rolled back, his muscles quivered as he tried to speak. His tongue was a balled fist. His nails scraped and slithered on the damp stone. A battle was being fought before my eyes, but it might have been a . . . a scientific experiment. Stefan slipped, fell back into the void. And what did I do? I did nothing. Nothing at all. I watched him fall to his death. Stumbling down from the heights at last, my mind in a turmoil, I found his lifeless body stretched out on the grass. A sharp rock, like an angry beast, had bitten a chunk out of his head as he fell. Blood and tissue spattered that mossy bank.

'That evening, my father stormed into my room. In his hand he held a golden vial of honey. "I found this in *your* pocket," he accused. The expression on his face is engraved in my memory. "Why did you not save your brother?" it seemed to say. Perhaps he had found the honey in a different jacket from the one I wore that day. I cannot say. I swear to you, I had taken no honey along with me. At least, I do not remember doing so.

'He did not call me a murderer. That was the last word my mother spoke before she died. She lay in bed like a statue for weeks after Stefan's death, her glassy eyes staring at nothing. She turned to me at the instant of her death and made an accusation that no faithful son should have to bear. I was allowed to attend her burial, then Father ordered me to leave the house, never to return.'

I paused to catch my breath.

'At the funeral, a friend of my father's spoke of you, Professor Kant. He told me that the moral dictates of Reason are far stronger than the sentimental impulses of Man. I *had* to speak with you, sir. I felt that you might understand. I hoped that Philosophy would rescue me. That's why I came today,' I explained. 'And so, at the end of the lesson, I made my way to your desk, saying . . .'

'"I have been bewitched by Death."' Kant finished the sentence for me. He leaned close and peered into my face, a craving curiosity burning in his eyes.

'Am I a murderer, sir?' I asked.

I might have been standing before God, waiting for supreme judgement, but Kant was silent for some time.

'It was your brother who issued the challenge,' he said quietly at last. 'He knew the risks better than you. Let us say that you picked up the honey mechanically, without thinking. In that case, you really did not know it was in your pocket. Your brother, on the other hand, took for granted that he had done as he always did, whenever he left the house. But he had not done so. The mind plays strange tricks,' he observed with a smile, tapping his forehead with his finger. 'Have you never noticed? Sometimes there is a forgetful blank where habits are concerned. We forget to do the most obvious things, vital as those things may be.'

'A blank, sir? But I stood watching. Why didn't I try to save him?'

'I would guess, Stiffeniis, that you were so unnerved by what was happening that you failed to react. Immobilised by fright, there was no one else to help. You take the burden of his death upon yourself, but this is only half the picture. The same thing might have happened, there or in some other place, whether you were present or not. He was ill, as you said.'

'I was *there*,' I repeated obstinately.

'Unfortunately, yes,' Kant replied soothingly. 'And in a very odd state of mind after what you had seen in Paris, I imagine. You were still haunted by the decapitation of the King when your brother's death occurred. Death commands us all. Horror does possess us. Sublime terror calls forth,' he hesitated, searching for an expression, 'a most *peculiar* state of mind, a mental condition for which I can find no better term . . .'

He paused and stared distractedly at the ground, as if he were searching for a word or concept that stubbornly refused to unbend and make itself known even to his penetrating mind.

'What must I do?' I pleaded, waiting for his verdict.

What Professor Kant said was destined to change my life.

'You've been inside the mind of a murderer, Hanno. You have harboured thoughts that few men would dare to admit. You are *not* alone! And the knowledge makes you special. Now, you must turn it to good account,' he replied warmly.

'But how, sir? How?'

As he spoke, his words settled on my troubled spirit like a healing balm.

'Bring order where crime brings chaos. Right wrongs. Study the law.'

Two weeks later, I enrolled at the University of Halle as a student of Jurisprudence. Five years afterwards, my bachelor's degree confirmed, I began my working career as a magistrate. Accompanied by Helena Jordaenssen, my wife of seven months, I started out in the country town of Lotingen. It was a quiet, regular sort of life, but I enjoyed the drab anonymity of it. I was not called upon to judge and punish, so much as to officiate. But I had only partly followed Kant's advice. Violent crimes being unknown in the town, I had never been truly called upon to test myself.

Until the day that Sergeant Koch entered my office.

I looked down at the page and read what Kant had dictated to Lampe.

The laws of Nature are turned upside down in the exercise of God-like power over another human being. Cold-blooded murder opens the doorway to the Sublime. It is an apotheosis without equal . . .

The question presented itself to my mind with the force of a hammer blow. Had Professor Kant been infected by the insanity that he had meant to cure in me? Had I opened a barred path and handed him the Golden Apple of forbidden knowledge which lay at the end? Kant's philosophy had been foundering on a reef, and I had unwittingly thrown him a lifeline. Had he found, in his declining years, the pathway to Absolute Freedom which the exercise of rational discipline and logical disputation had denied him? Just before the body of Sergeant Koch was found, Kant had been feverish, his voice hoarse with passion.

'They cannot imagine what *I* have been able to conceive,' he had raged. He had been talking of his detractors, the Romantic philosophers, the high priests of *Sturm und Drang*. 'They cannot begin to know what *I* . . .'

I completed the sentence for him.

They cannot begin to know what I have done with your help, Stiffeniis.

This thought erupted in my mind like red-hot magma exploding from an uncapped volcano. Had Immanuel Kant sown the evil seed in the mind of his valet with that book, dictating night after night, knowing that Lampe would take him at his word? Had Kant knowingly created a murderous Golem in his valet, then set him loose on Königsberg?

If Kant knew . . .

Jan Konnen, Paula-Anne Brunner, Johann Gottfried Haase, and Jeronimus Tifferch were his victims. He had provoked the humiliation that led to the death of Procurator Rhunken, he had precipitated the murder of the serving-boy, Morik, driven the Totzes to suicide, pushed Anna Rostova beyond the pale, and made Lublinsky's soul as monstrous as his face. The lives of Frau Tifferch and her embittered maid would be forever blighted by his meddling. Like those of everyone who had known or loved the murdered ones. The city and the people of Königsberg had been entangled in the web of terror that Kant had woven so artfully.

And he had killed Koch. My faithful, stolid adjutant. Humble servant of the State and of myself. Sergeant Koch had found nothing safe in Kantian philosophy, nothing reassuring in Professor Kant himself. Koch had sensed the sinister nature of Kant's involvement in the case, detected evil in that laboratory, while I had been overwhelmed with admiration.

If Kant knew . . .

He had chosen me for one reason alone. I had been inside the mind of a murderer. He had said it himself. He had chosen *me* – not Herr Procurator Rhunken, or any more expert magistrate – to admire the infernal beauty of his final philosophical thesis. The sublime expression of will, the act that went beyond Logic or Reason, Good or Evil:

murder without a motive. The moment when a man is free, unchained from the claims of morality. Like Nature. Or like God. When I insisted on the need for logical proof, credible explanation, when I *failed* to understand what he intended me to see, Kant had opened the door and sent me out to be murdered with his own cloak on my shoulders. But Koch had stepped in the way. He had taken the fatal blow that was meant for me.

If Kant knew . . .

He had not been interested in the man I had become, a diligent magistrate with a wife and two babes from tranquil Lotingen, when he summoned me to him. He had appealed, instead, to a confused and troubled creature he had met only once before, spattered with blood as a king was butchered before his eyes in Paris, a morose individual who had watched his own brother die, a fool who had unwittingly revealed to him the darkest secret of the human soul as they walked together through the fog one cold afternoon beneath the Fortress of Königsberg. By entrusting that case into my hands, Professor Kant had intended to exhume the demon that he had met seven years before.

And during those days in Königsberg, I thought with a violent shudder, had he not almost succeeded in calling up that ghost?

Those heads in jars had thrilled me more than I had dared to admit. Was it science alone that fascinated me? Had I felt no shiver of excitement as I examined the frozen corpse of Lawyer Tifferch? The split skull of Morik? As I smashed my fist into the bloated face of Gerta Totz and gazed on the bloody mask of her husband's self-destruction? I had embraced the idea of torture too warmly when the occasion presented itself, despite Koch's warning. Augustus Vigilantius had poked a gaping hole in my shallow veneer of normality at our first meeting. Then Anna Rostova had bowed before my dark *animus*, recognising a fellow traveller, a nature perverse and damned like her own. I cannot deny that I had been aroused by her murderous carnality . . .

I closed my eyes in shame.

But a protest bubbled up from the depths of my heart.

No! I had done it all to catch a murderer. I had used Kant's laboratory in the interests of science and methodology. *That* was what I admired, not the macabre exhibits for themselves alone. Tifferch's rigid body had told me how the victims had been killed. I had lifted my hand against Gerta Totz to spare her a far greater punishment. I could not have foreseen the desperate determination that had tied the husband and the wife together. Then, Anna Rostova had appeared. She was different from Helena, the woman that I had chosen as my companion. There had been moments when I hoped to protect the albino from the consequences of her crimes. Not to possess her body, but to save that beautiful flesh from the violence of the troopers.

In Kant's eyes, I had failed to appreciate the beauty of those murders. But I was no longer the creature he had thought me to be. That ghost had fled for ever. My heart had been warmed, redeemed, *saved*, by love. Love of my wife. Love of my little ones. Love of the Law. Love of Moral Truth. Nothing that Immanuel Kant had thrown in my way had brought out that dark and secret side of myself again. Seven years before, walking around the Fortress in the freezing fog with Professor Kant, I had been truly cured. I had been reborn. And it was all *his* doing . . .

Sweeping up the papers, I dropped a coin on the table and rushed from the cafe. Outside, the cold night air was a benediction of sorts. It cleared my mind of doubt about what I was going to do. For what I knew I *must* do. As Professor Kant himself would have said, it was a Categorical Imperative. The irony was not lost on me. I had no choice. Reason obliged me. In the circumstances, there was no other way to achieve the Supreme Good.

I dashed along the cobbled lane in the gathering gloom. Rushing out across the stone bridge at the end of the street, I stopped at the middle span. The swollen grey-brown waters of the River Pregel bubbled below me like hot treacle. Leaning out over the flood, I began to shred the leaves of the document that Frau Lampe had entrusted to my care. The white scraps fell like a flurry of fresh snow and were gobbled up by the hungry waters.

Thus, the final work of Immanuel Kant, Professor of Logic at the University of Königsberg, was launched upon an unsuspecting world.

Chapter 37

Back home in Lotingen, I returned to work more convinced than ever that the daily round of a country magistrate was sufficient for my happiness. Disputes about common land and small legacies occupied my days, controversies between rival shopkeepers, farmers stealing fodder from their neighbours' barns by the light of the moon, occasional bad manners, frequent drunkenness, minor breaches of the peace. These were my daily concerns. Nothing more violent troubled my days or disturbed my rest than the accidental crushing of a mature rooster as a horse-drawn cart went trundling home in the dwindling light of dusk.

The events in Königsberg did not fade from my mind, but the experience seemed to retract and diminish with time and distance. That memory was like a raw scar that aches on a cold day, reminding us that the danger and pain are over, that the worst is past, that we are getting better day by day. Indeed, life was all but back to normal when early in April, I received a letter from Olmuth Hanfstaengel, who had been the family lawyer for as long as I could remember. Without any preamble, the writer informed me that my father had expired ten days before of a sudden fit, that he had been buried, according to his last wish, beside my mother and brother in the family plot in Ruisling cemetery, and that Hanfstaengel himself had been appointed to execute my father's will. In this terse communication, the lawyer noted that the estate, the land, the house, and all that it contained had been sold off, with one exception, as my father had specified, and that the proceeds had been donated after death duties to the Junior Military Academy in Druzbha where Stefan had served his country for a few brief months. In a short codicil, Lawyer Hanfstaengel informed me that I had been directly mentioned once in my father's will, and that I would have news from him again within a very short while. And with that scant announcement, the communication ended.

Helena stood mute at my side as I was reading. Hands clasped tightly across her breasts, she seemed to be struggling to quell the mounting anxiety which the arrival of that letter had provoked. Without a word, I handed it her. Her eyes raced over the page, and when she lifted her gaze to mine some moments later, there was a sort of mirthful glee, a welling up of joy in her expression which, try as she might, she could not suppress.

'I do believe that Stefan prayed for us, as I begged him to do when I went to Ruisling to lay fresh flowers on his grave,' she said with a vehemence that I did not expect.

Evidently, she was still inclined to believe that her chance meeting with my father that day in the cemetery had worked a miracle. She seemed to think that a reconciliation had been brought about, a change of heart which had led my father to remember me in his will, posthumously embracing me as his only surviving son. For an instant, I persuaded myself that she was right. But there was something perplexing in that letter, some unspoken impediment which would not permit my own optimism to flourish as hers had done. Whenever he mentioned my brother, my father spoke of 'Stefan, my beloved son,' but when he referred to me, it was by my name alone.

Still, in a state of heightened expectation – if that is the correct word – we waited for further news from Lawyer Hanfstaengel. It arrived two weeks later. A few words, no more: 'Herein lies your inheritance, as prescribed in the last Will and Testament of the late Wilhelm Ignatius Stiffeniis.'

We watched in a state of nervous agitation as the baggage was taken down from the wagon by the carrier and his boy and manhandled into the entrance hall. I recognised that trunk immediately. It was of steel-bound oak. The largest trunk in the house in Ruisling, it had always been kept in my mother's dressing room. I did not need to open it to know what it contained. A creeping paralysis seemed to overpower my limbs. My heart froze within my chest, thudding painfully as it struggled to fight against the horror that consumed my mind.

I knelt down on the cold stone floor and raised the lid.

All the worldly possessions that had belonged to Stefan were stuffed haphazardly into the trunk: the clothes he most loved to wear, the trinkets he had kept in memory of happy days, the favourite books that he had read, and read again. And on the top of the pile, five glass vials of golden honey. For the latter, tormented part of his life, those tubes of sugary sweetness had guaranteed his well-being. A sixth vial had shattered during the journey. Fragments of broken glass and syrupy stickiness lay everywhere.

That was my inheritance.

My father did not intend to let me forget. He would not bequeath me peace of mind. The curse that he had laid on my head while living would not be laid to rest with his mortal remains. The relics of my brother's shattered life had been transported into my own home.

Turning to Helena, I saw that the joy and hope had faded from her eyes. She stared at me accusingly, wonderingly, and in her pro-longed silence, I thought I heard again the questions that I had never answered. The questions in that letter she had written to me in Königsberg after her one and only meeting with my father. *What can cause such hatred in a parent, Hanno? What does he think you have done?*

The trunk was consigned without another word to the attic, where it lay collecting dust for some months. An unusually wet summer had passed and a cold and gloomy autumn was upon us when I was obliged one evening to repair to the attic in search of candles. Having found what I was looking for, I was just about to return down-stairs when a sudden impulse took hold of me. Morbid curiosity, set aflame by a spark of resentment for my father, prompted me to open the trunk and examine the contents with more care than my first state of shock had allowed. As the lid fell back on its rusty hinges, a dusty cloud of pain and sorrow seemed to rise into the air. The sham-bles of my brother's brief existence on this earth had been tumbled into that box with violent energy and total disregard. Honey had congealed like amber on a bundle of love letters tied up with a faded pink ribbon, and stained the covers of Stefan's favourite book, *The Sorrows of Young Werther*.

I sat down on the wooden floor, that book as heavy as lead in my hands, recalling how much he had loved the tale. He must have read it a hundred times with a passion which seemed never to diminish, but, rather, to increase with every reading. How often had he recited passages aloud in the study that we shared? And how frequently had I dozed with Goethe's noble phrases ringing unheard in my ears? In a moment of distraction, as I relived this lost Arcadia of youth, the volume slipped from my hands and fell on the floor. Looking down, I saw that the novel had fallen open at the pages that describe the untimely death of the young protagonist. Stefan had scribbled critical notes in the margin with a pencil, as he was wont to do. But then, I espied my own name written there. 'Dearest Hanno,' I read,

You may have asked yourself why I was silent when you spoke of Paris, and the murder of King Louis. All my life I had plagued you with my questions. But I said nothing. You could not know the emotion that your words provoked in my soul. And how was I to tell you? If there is no life after death, no place where we may meet again, I thank you now for sharing your secrets with me. I thank you for showing me the path to follow. Can suicide be defined as cold-blooded murder? It is the most momentous decision that any man can make. Is any freedom more absolute?

If we must wait to be annihilated, to 'suffer the slings and arrows of outrageous fortune', as the English Poet tells us, why defer the crisis another day? To die is the sublimation of every life that was ever lived.

I have decided to end my suffering.

And with your help, dear Hanno, though you will never know it. I doubt that you will ever read this book of mine! Tomorrow we will climb the Richtergade. You will not fail me.

Our minds and our hearts are troubled, dearest friend. You have your reasons, I have mine. A race to the top will do us both the world of good. But I will ne'er return, for I am sick of honey! Perhaps you will discover the trick . . .

He had slipped his own life-saving vial of nectar into my empty pocket as we left the house that morning. Tears came to my eyes as I read the final line of what he had written:

As you have given me a glimpse of Freedom, I bequeath you the vision of my death.
  Ruisling, 17 March 1793.

Thus I came into my true inheritance.

Could I have received a more bountiful legacy? In his unloving wish to damn me beyond his death, to taunt me with a crime that I had never committed, my unforgiving father had restored to me the peace of mind that I had all but lost seven years before.

The following morning, strolling in the countryside around the house, enjoying the first bright day in weeks and the uncertain trials that little Immanuel made to get about on his own two legs, I finally answered Helena's questions: I spoke out plainly about Stefan's death, and told her what my father thought I had done. She listened in silence. Her eyes gazed calmly into mine. Like my brother when I had told him what I had seen in Paris. Like Kant when I confessed to him the fear of the obscure creature that had taken possession of my mind. I told her of the troubled youth that I had been before we met, and of the man that I had since become. At that point, she laid her hand tenderly upon mine and raised a finger to her lips, directing my attention towards our infant son with a curious gesture of her head. Immanuel had broken free from her guiding hand and was stumping solemnly but steadily ahead of us on his own two chubby little legs.

'He is a good, brave lad, Hanno. A trifle independent, perhaps. Exactly like his father,' Helena observed. 'I do believe the time has come for us to pay a visit to Ruisling. Don't you?'

That evening, I overheard Lotte and Helena chatting in the kitchen. Our maid sounded both puzzled and concerned, saying that she was glad to find me so serene after the news of my father's death and the financial disappointment it had brought upon us.

'I've never known him so carefree as he was today,' Lotte exclaimed. 'The master seems to have recovered from a long and terrible illness.'

The answer my wife returned was coined in that animated, joyful tone of voice she normally employed with the children.

'He has, Lotte. He most certainly has.'

Two days after, we made our pilgrimage to the family plot in Ruisling. The thanks I addressed to Stefan, the prayers I uttered for the souls of my mother and father rang all the louder for the profound silence of the place, which seemed to wrap itself around me like a warm and comforting cloak.

In the month of May, a bright and sunny morning after a dismal week of lingering, dreamlike fog and early morning frosts which had set the untilled fields a-shimmering, Lotte Havaars entered the kitchen with a theatrical air of secrecy about her.

She held out her clasped hands to the children, then opened her fingers with a sudden gesture, revealing two bright orange ladybirds nestling together in her palm.

'The whole of the country is infested with them, sir,' she announced with a happy smile. 'This summer will be a good 'un. Ladybirds this early in the season! It's an omen of plenty. Napoleon will ne'er prevail against a nation that's so rich an' good an' strong.'

Mindful of how we had laughed at her sour predictions the previous year, and of all that had come to pass in the mean time, Helena and I exchanged a wan smile. We were more than well disposed to believe that Lotte was right.

And so she was.

The summer of 1805 was a season of great bounty and fruitfulness. Peace reigned in Eastern Prussia. Like Königsberg and all the other towns great and small in the kingdom, Lotingen returned to the steady industriousness of former times. Napoleon Bonaparte turned his armies south to face the combined forces of the Austrians and the Russians at the Battle of Austerlitz. To all effects, the French Emperor appeared to have turned his back on us. But how long would the undeclared truce persist? He had marched into Hanover and occupied the city in 1802, and everyone knew that he could do exactly the same again, whenever he chose. Margreta Lungrenek, the *aruspice* to General Katowice, had foreseen the possibility, cunningly divining the name of the nation's graveyard in the tangled, bloody entrails of the dead crow that lay crucified on her table.

History was to prove her right.

The Prussian seed had been planted in Napoleon Bonaparte's indomitable mind, and it would flower within a year, carried south, perhaps, on the innocent wings of a migrant ladybird from a cornfield on the outskirts of Jena . . .

Acknowledgements

Many wonderful books have influenced the development of this novel, but one of the most enlightening explorations of life and thought in Prussia in the early nineteenth century must be *Tales from the German Underworld* by Richard J. Evans (New Haven and London: Yale University Press, 1998). Regarding the life and opinions of Immanuel Kant, the recent *Kant – A Biography* by Manfred Kuehn (Cambridge: Cambridge University Press, 2001) debunks a thousand myths, and adds enormously to our knowledge of the philosopher. Both books are highly recommended.

Special thanks go to our agent, Leslie Gardner, for her critical insights and endless encouragement, and to everybody at Faber and Faber, particularly our editor, Walter Donohue.

Hanno Stiffeniis's adventures continue in Michael Gregorio's new novel, *Days of Atonement*, published in Summer 2007. Here is an exclusive extract.

Chapter 3

I sat bolt upright in bed.

Wide awake, I turned to Helena, unable to see her in the darkness. Her breathing was deep and regular. Beyond her, the sleeping child let out a whimpering sigh.

Was that the noise which had disturbed my rest?

I listened attentively. Outside, not even the hoot of an owl breached the peace. But I felt no easier. War robs a man of his tranquillity. With exaggerated care, I pulled back the coverlet and slipped down off the high bed. Stepping to the window, the rough-hewn floorboards cold beneath my feet, I lifted back the curtain and looked out over the rear of the house. The garden was a formless black pit. The hazel trees marking the edge of our domain were a solid wall, the starless sky tinged an impalpable shade of violet. At the break of dawn, farmers' carts would clatter past our gate on their way to market, men driving cattle to the slaughter with their dogs . . .

A low moan sounded somewhere in the house.

I moved towards the door, grabbing the first garment which came to hand, throwing it around my shoulders against the icy cold, as I stepped out onto the landing. I looked down the stairwell, where a figure in a white shawl was hovering in the hall, holding up a candle, as if transformed into a pillar of salt. Nothing moved, except the the flame. Then, that strangled sound escaped once more from lips that I could not see.

A hand brushed by my ear, and came to rest upon my shoulder.

'What is it, Lotte?' my wife called in a whisper.

Like an imp, her bare feet and slender ankles stretching forth from beneath the hem of her nightgown, Helena skipped down the stairs. The wild thicket of her untied hair bobbed before me as I followed in her wake.

Lotte turned, her eyebrows arched, eyes wide.

'Soldiers,' she hissed, causing the flame to flicker.

Edging Lotte aside with my shoulder, I raised the brass thaler and exposed the hole that I had drilled in the oak the day the news of the defeat at Jena reached Lotingen. At the time, I had convinced myself that this spy-hole would provide an advantage against any unwelcome caller armed with evil intentions. But hard as I tried, all that I could see outside was as black as pitch, and the cold air streaming in caused my eye to water.

As I peered out from my fragile fortress, I prayed that Lotte had been mistaken.

Just then, the garden-gate swung open with a creak, pushed back too hard on its ancient hinges. There was a click, and a lantern was raised. Three men huddled on the path in a tight group. I recognised the uniforms: two privates in trench-coats, an officer wearing a black leather kepi with a tall white plume, their faces etched in stark *chiaroscuro* by the lamplight. They were consulting a piece of paper.

This is the moment, I realised with a start.

If Lotte took the baby in her arms, and Helena led Süzi and Manni out by the back window, I might be able to hold them off for a minute or two.

'Don't think of it!' Helena had read my intentions as surely as if I had shouted them out at the top of my voice.

'They seem uncertain,' I said, my eye glued to the spy-hole. 'Perhaps they are seeking a fugitive . . .'

The officer swung around and took a pace forward, his face filling the spy-hole. The shock of recognition flashed upon me. I had seen the man at Dittersdorf's feast. I had argued with him. Was that why he had come? There was a determined set to his face, the number 7 writ large in gold lettering on his kepi above the peak.

Helena's voice was amazingly calm.

'Open the door,' she said. 'We have no choice.'

Her face was close to mine, our noses almost touching. She seemed so cool and calculating, as if some scheme had formed in her mind. Pulling the mantle from off her shoulders, she twirled it around and held it out to me.

'You wouldn't wish to be seen like that,' she said.

I was wearing her lemon-coloured dressing-gown. The first thing that had come to hand in the dark. Whatever was about to happen, Helena had decided that I must face it with the dignity befitting a true Prussian. She thrust the mantle into my hands, stretching out to remove the feminine garment from my shoulders.

'Lotte, run upstairs. Anders will sleep, but the other two will wake. I will hold the candle, Hanno. You remove the bar and open the door.'

I shifted the wooden bar, slid the well-oiled bolt, and pulled back the door with such rapidity that it seemed to stop the soldiers in their tracks. All three took a step backwards, eyes wide, mouths open. The squaddies pointed their muskets, but did not shoot.

Cold air rushed into the hallway.

'Are you looking for me?' I asked, surprised by the firmness of my voice.

The officer's eyes flashed. Now, he had recognised me.

'I know you,' Helena said. 'We met last week at dinner.'

'Lieutenant Mutiez, *madame*. Seventh dragoons,' the officer said in heavily accented German, touching the peak of his cap.

I took a deep breath, and held his gaze. Nothing induced me to relax my guard. These foreigners were dangerous. More dangerous, now that the door was open wide.

'*Le papier, vite!*' he urged, turning to one of the privates. His eyes dropped to the paper in his hand: 'Procurator Stiffeniis . . .'

Helena gasped out loud.

This was how the military behaved when instructed to take up a man who was destined to disappear. The time was right, the hour before dawn, when human resistance is at its lowest ebb point. The physical and mental capacities of the condemned man were reduced to a minimum by terror, and the unexpected interruption of sleep.

'Yes?' I prompted him.

'You must come with me, sir,' Lieutenant Mutiez responded.

'God save us!' Lotte cried from the top of the stairs, her shrill voice echoing in the hallway.

'What do you want with my husband?' Helena demanded, stepping in front of me, facing them with a ridiculous show of bravery. 'Has the victorious French army nothing better to do?'

I placed one hand on my wife's shoulder, and told her roughly to be quiet. My other hand reached down and grabbed her wrist, holding her back. Fear or frustration seemed to have taken possession of her senses. If Helena insisted on spitting venom in their faces, those men might slit every throat in the house. No-one would punish them for it.

'Lieutenant Mutiez,' I said quickly, 'what brings you here? If some false charge has been brought against me, knowing what it is, I'll be better able to defend my name.'

'Herr Stiffeniis,' Mutiez replied, his voice softer than before, 'it is cold out here, very cold. For the sake of these ladies and yourself, sir, allow us to step inside.'

I stepped back two paces.

The Frenchmen advanced to the same degree. To my surprise, he removed his hat, an expression of relief, or something similar, stamped clearly on his face.

'This is for you, sir,' he said, holding up the paper. 'See for yourself, it is an order.'

I took it from him, glanced at the contents. There was very little written there. My name, my address, and another address which I did not recognise. No mention was made of an arrest.

'You must come with me,' he repeated. 'I have my instructions, sir.'

'For what reason?'

Helena snatched the note from my hand.

'I'm going with him!' she cried as she tried to make sense of it.

Lieutenant Mutiez turned on her quickly. 'Do you have children?' he asked, his mouth moving energetically as he forced his tongue around the foreign words.

Helena stared at him, then nodded.

'It would not be wise,' he added, glancing at Lotte, who was halfway down the stair, 'to leave them alone in the house with just this person to protect them.'

'Why not?' Helena demanded.

He did not reply, but turned to me. 'Be quick, sir. Get dressed to face the cold. It's a night for wolves . . .'

'The only wolves in Lotingen wear uniforms like yours!' Helena hissed.

I held my breath. This insult must be the final straw.

Instead, a smile began to form itself on the lips of Lieutenant Mutiez.

'Believe me, *madame*,' he said with a polite, ironic bow, 'I would rather be in my own warm bed. And in my own home town. We have no wolves, and the winter is warmer in Arles. The sooner we leave,' he added more gently, 'the quicker the business will be done.'

'Helena, would you help me find my clothes?' I said to break this deadlock.

Then, I turned to Lotte. 'Please, show these gentlemen into the day-room.'

As the intruders made their way into the parlour, Helena and I returned upstairs. Tight-lipped and nervous, my wife made haste to lay out my clothes. I rinsed my hands and my face with cold water from the ewer. One thought was racing through my mind. I ought to hold her, kiss her, assure her of my love. The sight of little Anders sleeping in his cot on the far side of the bed, the knowledge that Manni and Süzi were safe in the next room, brought a lump to my throat. I longed to hold them all. But even that small comfort was denied me.

Helena would interpret such a gesture as a final farewell.

She handed me my shirt, my heaviest trousers, a thick woollen over-vest, knee-length boots, seal-skin jacket, and woollen cape.

And not a single word was said.

I left the house, believing that I would never see her and the children again.

*****